THE DEAD MARCH

The Dead March

A History of the Mexican-American War

PETER GUARDINO

 Harvard University Press

CAMBRIDGE, MASSACHUSETTS · LONDON, ENGLAND · 2017

First printing

Library of Congress Cataloging-in-Publication Data
Names: Guardino, Peter F., 1963– author.
Title: The dead march : a history of the Mexican-American War / Peter Guardino.
Description: Cambridge, Massachusetts : Harvard University Press, 2017. |
  Includes bibliographical references and index.
Identifiers: LCCN 2017006231 | ISBN 9780674972346 (alk. paper)
Subjects: LCSH: Mexican War, 1846–1848. | United States—Economic conditions—To 1865. |
  United States—Social conditions—To 1865. | Mexico—Economic conditions—19th century. |
  Mexico—Social conditions—19th century. | North America—Economic conditions—19th
  century—Regional disparities.
Classification: LCC E404 .G83 2017 | DDC 973.6/2—dc23
  LC record available at https://lccn.loc.gov/2017006231

For Jane Walter, Rose Guardino, and Walter Guardino

Contents

THE DEAD MARCH

Introduction

ISAAC SMITH, reflecting on his experiences as an American soldier in Mexico, wrote that "the dead march was heard nearly every day."[1] The "dead march" was the music that accompanied funerals, and Smith was referring to the many comrades who died of illness while in camps in northern Mexico. Yet his words resonate far beyond that specific reference. The war that took place between the United States and Mexico between 1846 and 1848 was, more than anything else, tragic. During this war thousands died from disease, hunger, and thirst, as well as the more direct forms of violence people inflict on each other during wars. More than thirteen thousand American soldiers died. Mexican casualties are difficult to count. In official reports on battles, casualties tended to vary more; many Mexican soldiers were buried in mass, unmarked graves; and the Mexican versions of the careful records of military units that form the basis for the American numbers remain mostly inaccessible in uncatalogued and disorganized sections of Mexican archives. Moreover, many Mexican civilians died. Together these problems make estimating the number of Mexican deaths an uncertain business, but probably at least twice as many Mexicans as Americans died in this war, giving a number upwards of twenty-five thousand.[2] Death was one of the things that united the experiences of Americans and Mexicans in conflict: death in many forms is also central to the thousands of documents created by this war.

The American government, led by President James K. Polk, indisputably "won" this war. It forced its Mexican counterpart to renounce its claims to Texas and also cede the territory that later became the states of California, Nevada, Arizona, New Mexico, and Utah, as well as pieces of Colorado and Wyoming. For this reason the dominant narratives about this war in the histories of both countries center on American success and Mexican failure. The transfer of resources had a stark impact on the future of both.

I

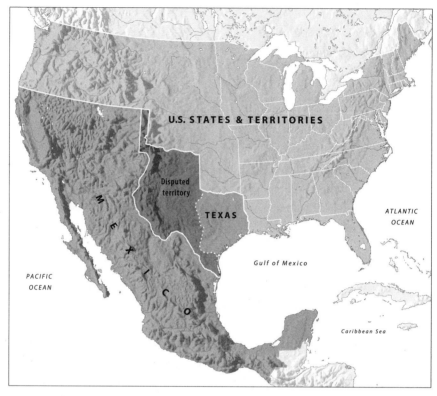

MAP I North America in 1846

For the United States the war opened up the immense resources of the Far West. In 1846–1848 people saw the most important resource there as land, especially the relatively well-watered land that gave California obvious agricultural potential. Another asset some Americans prized was access to Asia through Pacific ports. For Mexico the territorial loss foreclosed agricultural expansion into these lands, but such expansion would probably not have happened soon anyway. Mexicans saw most of this territory as too dry for agriculture, and all of it as too far from potential markets. Most Mexicans were in no great hurry to move north. What neither Americans nor Mexicans knew even in 1848 was that the region's agricultural potential was only part of the wealth transferred. The later history of the region also contains a long litany of mineral strikes, beginning with the famous California Gold Rush of

1849 but continuing with many other finds of gold, silver, copper, lead, and other minerals. The pickaxe and explosives were as central to the nineteenth-century history of the area as the horse and the plow, and the same can be said for their more modern replacements.

However, success and failure can be funny things. The new territory brought the United States not only opportunity but also pain. The question of who might be allowed to take advantage of it led Americans directly into the Civil War, a cataclysmic conflict that brought death on a scale that even the veterans of 1846–1848 could not have imagined. The Civil War killed between six hundred thousand and eight hundred thousand people.[3] Before 1848 American politicians had been able to cobble together a series of compromises that allowed an economy centered on free labor in the northern half of the country to coexist with one centered on slavery in the southern half, along with the regional social and cultural differences that accompanied those economies. This balancing act could not survive the acquisition of so much territory at once.[4] The United States split apart, and it was only reunited after the North delivered a crushing defeat in a long, bitter war of attrition. The country that emerged after the Civil War was very different from the one that had invaded Mexico two decades earlier, with a more powerful government and also a more powerful capitalist economy that soon made the United States one of the leading powers on the planet.

The Mexican-American War also led to civil war in Mexico, although the path was less direct. Losing the war with the United States sparked serious debates among Mexican politicians and intellectuals about how to make the country more unified and prosperous. Some powerful and wealthy Mexicans pushed for a Mexico that embraced what they believed were Hispanic values of religiosity and hierarchy, moving Mexico toward a form of modernity that would be more consistent with its colonial past and more like certain European countries they admired. Voting rights would be limited to the wealthy and social peace would be ensured by a strong Catholic Church and professional military. Their opponents believed that the United States had defeated Mexico because Mexico's postindependence changes had not gone far enough. They wanted to make Mexico more democratic and free the Mexican economy from the limits placed by poorly functioning markets. These liberals also came to see the power of the Catholic Church as a hindrance for Mexico.

Political conflicts between conservatives and liberals gained momentum as increasingly violent coups, revolutions, and civil wars directly involved more and more Mexicans, culminating when the conservatives tried and failed to implant a monarchy in Mexico with the aid of European troops. Ironically, the Mexico that emerged from these conflicts tightly embraced free markets but drifted away from the more democratic aspects of liberalism. Mexico became a society that paid a great deal of rhetorical attention to democracy and individual rights but ensured social peace through a pragmatic authoritarianism that allowed social mobility for ambitious politicians but oriented social and economic policy toward making Mexico one of the best places in the world for wealthy entrepreneurs to earn profits.

Neither the high human costs of the Mexican-American War nor its important consequences have brought it much attention in either country. There is no memorial to the fallen of this war in the American capital, and its place in American textbooks is minimal. Americans have generally wanted to see their country as one in which democracy and prosperity have both increased over time. Wars of conquest, unfortunately, are associated with tyranny and immorality, not the advance of democracy. There is a certain guilty ambivalence that follows from being successful thieves. Moreover, the Civil War's momentous consequences and massive casualties overshadowed the 1846–1848 war. Even historians and novelists who write about the war with Mexico often are drawn to it because many Civil War generals were young officers during the Mexican conflict.[5] Mexican historical consciousness also often slides over the war. Who wants to remember defeat, especially a defeat that many saw as resulting from weakness? Mexican schoolbooks instead emphasize conflicts that can be spun more positively, such as Mexico's successful fight against French intervention in the 1860s or the Mexican Revolution of the 1910s.[6]

Wars force people to explicitly discuss fundamental questions about their lives and societies that remain in the background in happier times, and wars generate enormous quantities of the documents historians need to access the distant past. This book is a social and cultural history of the 1846–1848 war that focuses on the experiences and attitudes of ordinary Mexicans and Americans, both soldiers and civilians. Writing about those experiences and attitudes requires attention to the causes of the war and the views of politicians, as well as the battles and campaigns people often imagine when they think of wars. However, here the emphasis is on what some people call the "new military history," which is centered on who soldiers and civilians were and how wars were shaped by the societies that waged them. The war's events, on both the grand scale of the conflict between nations and the more intimate scale of campaigns and battles, cannot really be understood without considering this social and cultural history. Armies did not spring into being at the whim of politicians, and generals could not manipulate troops as if they were chess pieces devoid of ideas or attitudes.[7] This approach actually helps us understand why the battles turned out as they did, and why military leaders made particular choices. It also helps us understand the war's outcome.

Explaining the War's Outcome

The most common explanations offered for the Mexican-American War's outcome, both immediately afterward and subsequently, have focused on the political differences between Mexico and the United States, projecting the powerful argument that Mexicans were divided and lacked commitment to their newly formed country, while Americans were united and more nationalistic. Yet when we delve deeply into the cultural and social history of the war, this argument simply does not fit the evidence. Mexicans from a variety of social groups made great sacrifices to oppose American aggression, and they often understood their efforts as representing a commitment to Mexico. Certainly political conflicts within Mexico hampered the war effort, sometimes very seriously. Yet these conflicts were always about what Mexico was to be, not whether it should exist, and every important political group opposed the Americans. There was nothing automatic about this identification with Mexico, and nationalism was always intertwined with other forms of identity, but it was quite strong. National identity was likewise complicated in the United States. Social and political groups put forward different ideas about what the United States should be, and those arguments continued even during the conflict with Mexico. Moreover, political conflict in the United States prevented expansionists from achieving all that they hoped for. President Polk did not lead a united nation bent on military conquest. Instead he was able to start the war by adroitly exploiting the very serious political conflicts that existed in the United States. There was a significant burst of popular enthusiasm for the war in some regions at the beginning of the conflict, but it began to erode quickly, and the war became increasingly controversial as time went on.

If American unity did not defeat Mexico, what did? The greatest advantage the United States had was its prosperity. Examining the social and cultural history of the war makes it very clear that the economic differences between the two countries contributed much more to the American victory than did the political differences. Mexico's politicians were able to fill the ranks of its armies, but those armies were always poorly equipped and supplied. Mexican soldiers often lacked adequate clothing and nearly always faced the Americans with worn-out and fragile weapons. The lack of food shaped their experience even more dramatically. Soldiers and the women who accompanied them commonly marched hungry and fought hungry, and when they left their units without permission it was usually to find enough calories to ensure their survival. Armies that could not be fed melted away. Mexico's economy was much smaller than that of the United States, and even before the war its government struggled to generate enough revenue to support routine operations. In the decades preceding the war, the lack of revenue repeatedly cornered governments into covering shortfalls with foreign and domestic loans at high rates of interest, and an increasing percentage of the revenue the government did collect was dedicated to paying the interest on these loans.[8] War pushed the Mexican government's rickety finances into catastrophic collapse. American aggression forced the government to ramp up military expenditures, worsening the problem. Soon, an American naval blockade of Mexican ports drastically exacerbated this fiscal crisis by preventing the Mexican government from collecting the import taxes that were the most important source of its revenue. The war also slowed the Mexican economy, further squeezing government revenues and worsening living conditions for Mexican civilians. In contrast, the U.S. economy was so productive that even modest taxes generated enough revenue to support an expensive foreign war. American soldiers had better clothing, much better weapons, and enough money to buy most of the food they needed from Mexican civilians who, ironically, lacked other economic options in part because of the economic disruption caused by the war.

Mexico and the United States in 1846–1848

Focusing on the social and cultural history of the Mexican-American War helps explain its outcome, but this approach also offers an unusual opportunity to compare the two nations.[9] Our ideas about the societies we live in are shaped by implicit comparisons. We see some societies as wealthy and others as poor. We see some governments as democratic and others as authoritarian. We see some governments as effective and others as weak. We tell ourselves stories not only about the relative success and failure of political, social, and economic systems but also about the reasons for success and failure. Yet, to a remarkable degree, the comparisons that fuel our analysis of the world are implicit and not explicit. Implicit comparisons are typically sloppy. As Americans contemplate Mexico, we tend to compare an ideal vision of the United States to an exaggeratedly disappointing reality farther south. Mexicans often do the same thing, idealizing the United States and emphasizing their own society's problems. Examining the social and cultural history of the war of 1846–1848 has the potential to drag these comparisons out into the light of day, where they can be made not only more explicit but also more precise. This book seeks to view both Mexico and the United States as they were in the middle of the nineteenth century, not as their most optimistic boosters or pessimistic critics saw them. Even more, it aims to avoid the common mistake of comparing the Mexico of 1846 not with the United States at the same moment but instead with the stronger United States that emerged after the Civil War.

Any attempt to compare the United States and Mexico by examining the war must begin with some sense of what the two countries were like in 1846. Most contemporary observers would probably have agreed that they were very different places. The American economy was much more prosperous than the Mexican economy, and it was growing more rapidly. At the time of the war, the United States had at least three times the per capita income of Mexico.[10] It also had a more stable political system, in the sense that political conflict was generally confined to institutional channels specified in laws and constitutions. Coups were not common, and no civil war had occurred since the American Revolution. Certainly the United States was not quite a democracy, at least for most people, and it was hardly devoid of social and political violence. However, it had been governed under the same constitution for more than half a century, and officeholders almost always managed to complete their terms and hand their posts over to successors who were chosen through the ballot box.[11] The same could certainly not be said for Mexico. Mexican leaders were sometimes chosen through elections, but they rarely completed their terms before being removed by coups, revolutions, or civil wars. Many of these conflicts were not especially violent, but they contributed to a reputation for political instability. The economic and political differences were intertwined. Undoubtedly American prosperity helped maintain political stability by providing economic opportunities for many people, while political stability helped the economy by making investments more secure. On the other side, the economic frustrations of many Mexicans probably contributed to their willingness to participate in coups, revolutions, and civil wars, and Mexican political instability definitely hurt its economy.

Geography explains much of the economic disparity between the two countries. The United States had much more cultivable land. Although in 1846 it had its share of mountains, there was almost no land with too little rain to sustain agriculture, and much of the land was level enough to farm. Moreover, much American farmland was close to the Atlantic Ocean, the Gulf of Mexico, the Great Lakes, or the hundreds of rivers that moved slowly enough to allow them to be used for transportation. In the early nineteenth century a spurt of canal building even further lowered the cost of transportation for American products. None of this could be said of Mexico. Much of Mexico's land was either too dry or too mountainous to farm, and those very same mountains and the highly seasonal nature of Mexico's rains meant that Mexican rivers were almost never navigable. Moreover, the best farmland in Mexico was generally located far from the coasts. The lands that could be farmed based on the seasonal rains were clustered in the center and south of the country, along with most of the population, and markets for the goods produced there were typically regional at best because land transport was so expensive. In contrast, the availability of farmland and the options for water transport in the United States spurred both early industrialization and early agricultural specialization by particular regions, which made the economy more efficient by allowing landowners to profit from the specific crops best suited to local ecologies.[12]

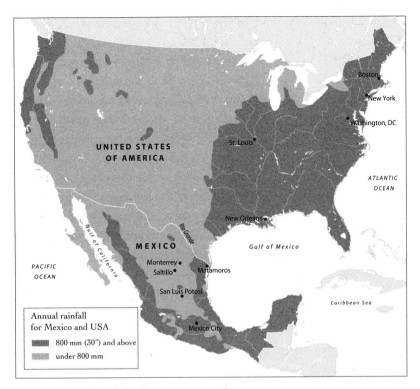

MAP 2 Areas with rainfall sufficient to grow staple crops

Political differences between the two countries also contributed to the economic disparities. British rule had not greatly hampered the economies of the colonies that later became the United States, partially because the British government never saw those colonies as significant sources of revenue but mostly because the laws and legal system the colonies inherited from Britain provided relatively secure property rights and relatively predictable dispute resolution. Mexico did not have either of these advantages. The Spanish colonial system subsidized the efforts of Spanish kings to project power in Europe. Partially as a result, the economic rules of the game in its colonies were designed to funnel economic activities into areas that the government saw as particularly lucrative for itself, like mining, or sometimes activities that were lucrative for well-connected groups, such as particular forms of commerce.[13] Another political root of Mexican economic weakness was its long and bloody war of independence. The war exposed stark social divisions in Mexican society, years of guerrilla warfare disrupted agriculture and made transporting goods even more difficult, and no European power came to the aid of the rebels and cut short the war.[14] Ironically, the opposite was true of the United States. France had intervened very decisively, helping to defeat Britain a mere six years after the war began. Moreover, the agricultural entrepreneurs of the newly independent United States found to their delight that Europe's rapidly industrializing economy had a voracious appetite for their cotton, while the slaves of Europe's Caribbean colonies had an equally voracious appetite for the food they could grow.[15] American agricultural entrepreneurs had level and well-watered land, they had access to transportation, and now they had markets. This moment in American economic history gave the country an impetus that still reverberates today.

The United States became independent forty years before Mexico did, and this provided an advantage in 1846. American political elites had had more time to build the ties that bind nations together.[16] An additional forty years of Independence Day celebrations, school history lessons, and politicians publicly debating what the nation was or should be undoubtedly strengthened American nationalism. Mexican political elites worked along similar lines after independence was achieved in 1821, but their efforts were hampered by the nation's relative poverty. Mexico also did not enjoy many of the political advantages that the colonists of North America had received. The British government had been less interested in its colonies because they did not seem to offer revenue, and thus the British Crown had tended to allow the leaders of the colonies considerable self-government. Moreover, in British political tradition, self-government was representative government. Property owners selected representatives to help make laws, and in America, unlike Great Britain, men of relatively modest means could afford property. Mexico had none of these advantages. Although certainly the wealthiest residents of Mexico benefited greatly from colonial government, their only formal roles in it tended to be on the municipal level, and few Mexicans had any experience exercising broad political power before independence.[17]

The religious diversity of the North American colonies also had a significant political impact after independence. Although Great Britain had its share of religious conflicts even as it was colonizing North America,

MAP 3 Transportation in the United States and Mexico

colonial leaders came to grudgingly tolerate more religious diversity, partially because it was difficult for any sect to maintain its dominance and partially because religious dissidents from the Old World often were desirable economic contributors.[18] Religious pluralism tended to facilitate political pluralism. In Mexico Catholic evangelization had been the most important ideological justification for conquest and colonization, and the dominance of Catholicism did not allow any transfer of religious tolerance to political pluralism. Generally the political culture inherited from Spain valued unanimity, and there was a tendency to see political opponents as threats to cherished values. The introduction of representative government in the 1810s actually reinforced this tendency, as the Enlightenment ideal of the government representing the will of the people implied that there was only one true will. Any political actor who believed his views represented that will tended to believe that his political opponents must be consciously opposing it.[19] One of the colonial advantages that most facilitated American political stability after independence was the degree to which British colonialism marginalized racial others from politics. In British America neither the colonists nor the Native Americans had very centralized governments, and as a result the colonists tended to displace Native Americans rather than try to conquer and assimilate them. The African Americans imported as slaves were also not considered political subjects, and thus representative government in the colonies, and later the United States, was by and for a relatively homogenous group. In contrast, the Spanish conquest of Mexico had been justified by the need to bring Catholicism to Native Americans, and they had always been considered part of colonial society. The Spanish had imported slaves from Africa, but the vast majority of their descendants were free before Mexico became independent. Although certainly economically exploited and subject to racial prejudice, both Native Americans and Afro-Mexicans were clearly within rather than outside society when Mexico became independent. Finally, due to racial mixing, most Mexicans were culturally Hispanic but biologically the heirs of Spanish, African, and Native American ancestors. For these reasons many Mexican politicians were from the start committed to building a government that would both govern and represent people of all races. The difficulty of this task contributed to political instability.[20]

Mexico had great difficulty achieving political stability after independence. Although some political struggles took place through institutional means, and even elections, many of them did not. It was quite common in the colonial period for rural people to express their points of view through riots. After independence rural people still rioted, but they also sometimes participated in larger rebellions in alliance with politicians. Urban riots in Mexico were never as common as they were in the United States in the same period, but there seem to have been more after independence than there had been before. In Mexico both urban riots and rural rebellions tended to involve relatively poor people. Wealthier Mexicans, however, were also willing to step outside institutional channels to promote their political ideals and interests. Coups by alliances of military and civilian politicians were common. Some relied mostly on the professional military but others involved units of part-time soldiers with particular political views or even sometimes crowds drawn from the urban poor or middle classes. The most successful coups were virtually bloodless because successful plotters did not act until they had sufficient support. However, before 1846 Mexico also experienced some civil wars. These became more common as political groups began trying to draw rural people, in other words the vast majority of Mexicans, into the great political conflicts of the day. Still, these civil wars were usually confined to specific regions, holding down the casualties. None of this means, however, that Mexicans ignored the procedures and institutions laid out in constitutions. Elections were often important and widely attended, especially in urban areas, and political groups of various kinds worked hard to win them. Those who lost elections did not always resign themselves to the results. Yet elections continued to be symbolically important as an expression of the idea that in independent, republican Mexico the government was supposed to represent the will of the people.

Mexico, like the United States, was divided by regional interests, which in Mexico tended to involve clashes between the center and periphery. In colonial Mexico the economy and political system had been mostly organized in ways that benefited wealthy families in the center of the country, especially Mexico City, and after independence these families wanted to centralize power in the hands of the national government to replicate or revive their colonial advantages. Their desire for a strong central government was shared with some people who lived far from Mexico City, mostly those who saw such a government as a bulwark of social order. This conflict between center and periphery partially overlapped with another conflict, which was sometimes more violent. Mexicans argued about what it meant to be a republic based on the will of the people in a society of extreme economic inequality and significant ethnic diversity and ethnic prejudice. Some believed that economic and social hierarchies could only be defended by a partially authoritarian government. These Mexicans believed in government based on the will of the people, but only of the right sort of people. They often worked to restrict political participation to relatively wealthy Mexicans, and they tended to be prejudiced against Mexicans with indigenous or African ancestry, which is to say most Mexicans. For other Mexicans, a truly republican Mexico had to be more egalitarian than colonial Mexico. In fact, they believed that nominal egalitarianism and the end of official ethnic distinctions were the most important results of the War of Independence and were consistent with the spirit of the age in the Western world. These people usually sought to increase political participation, building political movements with mass participation characterized by a rhetorical emphasis on liberty and equality. They mostly mobilized the urban poor, which limited their success because the vast majority of people lived in the countryside. Still, in parts of Mexico even some rural people adopted this egalitarian stance.

There were very real issues at stake in the unruly Mexican politics of the years leading up to the war with the United States. There certainly was no scarcity of ambitious politicians, Mexico did not yet have enough experience with representative government, and the weak Mexican economy contributed vastly to its political instability. However, the importance of the issues at stake for many Mexicans is what kept politics so fractious. The idea that Mexico was politically very different from the United States because its politicians were unusually unscrupulous simply does not stand up to scrutiny, especially when we look carefully at American politicians like Andrew Jackson and Polk, men who were much more interested in ends they believed were noble than means that fell within the parameters of institutional politics. Moreover, the United States was simply not as politically stable and peaceful as many Americans would like to think. The differences have been overemphasized.[21]

Although the United States developed a multiparty political system soon after independence, there was significantly less tolerance for opposing political opinions than we might assume. Historian Harry Watson points out that early nineteenth-century Americans were inclined to see politics as a struggle between good and evil. In Watson's words, "When republicans of that era quarreled with one another, they tended to regard their opponents as enemies of liberty itself, not as rival interests having equal claims to public favor."[22] Political vitriol was very common in the United States, and the political victories and very existence of one's opponents were grudgingly accepted rather than embraced as evidence of democracy. In fact, democracy itself was watered down by the party system, as party leaders rather than voters selected candidates. Democracy in the United States, as in Mexico, was also limited by indirect elections in which voters typically chose not the people who would fill government posts but instead electors who were in theory free to cast their own ballots as they saw fit. The secret ballot was a thing of the future, so in the United States, as in Mexico, voters were required to state their preferences publicly at polling places, which were typically surrounded by raucous, partisan crowds who lobbied for their favorite candidates with their fists or even more lethal weapons. Candidates plied these crowds with alcohol, increasing their volatility, and Election Day riots were common.[23]

Envisioning these riots leads us to the problem of violence. The United States did not experience the coups and civil wars Mexico was famous for, but it was far from devoid of political violence. Americans did not calmly vote for political leaders and abide by their decisions or the laws that they enacted. Instead they often used individual or collective violence to achieve their goals and express their identities. The United States experienced more than 1,200 riots in the period between 1828 and 1861. Americans came together in groups not only to fight at the polls but also to attack immigrants, free blacks, abolitionists, Catholics, Mormons, rival gangs, rival volunteer firefighting companies, and accused criminals.[24] Historians David Grimsted and Michael Feldberg point out that this violence was not separate from politics. Grimsted sees the riots as part of the "ongoing process of democratic accommodation, compromise, and uncompromisable tension between groups with different interests."[25] Feldberg specifically connects the rioting to popular democracy and points out that it was justified by references to majority rule and the will of the people. Feldberg lists as the sources of violence "the racial and ethnic tensions of the period; the era's ideological climate; the inability of political systems and legal institutions to resolve group conflict by peaceable means; rapid urbanization and population changes; and economic and technological innovation."[26] Notably, when we consider the first three sources, Feldberg might just as easily have been writing about Mexico.

Some of the worst violence was inflicted on those accused of committing crimes. In 1838 the young lawyer Abraham Lincoln criticized

> the increasing disregard for law which pervades the country; the growing disposition to substitute the wild and furious passions in lieu of the sober judgment of courts and the worse than savage mobs, for the executive ministers of justice. This disposition is awfully fearful in any community; and that it now exists in ours, though grating to our feelings to admit, it would be a violation of truth, and an insult to our intelligence, to deny.

> Accounts of outrages committed pervade the country, from New England to Louisiana—they are neither peculiar to the eternal snows of the former, nor the burning suns of the latter—they are not the creature of climate— neither are they confined to the slaveholding, or the nonslaveholding states.[27]

Vigilantism was common, and it was connected to some of the trends we see as contributing to the American democratic tradition. Vigilantes justified their actions by claiming that if laws expressed the will of the people, the people could enforce the laws.[28] The evidence against many of the people vigilantes tortured and killed was very weak at best, and, like much mob violence, vigilantism tended to target scapegoats from undesirable racial or religious minorities.

This brings us to another point of comparison with Mexico. In reality, some kinds of social conflict that in Mexico tended to find expression in explicitly political violence like rebellions, civil wars, and coups were expressed in the United States through the use of violence to exclude certain kinds of people from having any legally recognized role in politics. Vast numbers of African Americans were held as chattel slaves without legal rights, a system enforced through the violent punishment of slaves who disobeyed or tried to leave slavery but also upheld through riots directed at free blacks in both the North and the South. Nineteenth-century Americans did not see this violence as political, but from our perspective it is hard not to. Whites also became victims of the violence used to maintain slavery, as even in the North mobs frequently attacked abolitionists and tried to prevent the expression of abolitionist viewpoints.[29] Native Americans were also violently excluded through social violence. Most readers no doubt have some familiarity with the long history of conflict, beginning early in the colonial period and lasting until the end of the nineteenth century, in which American whites steadily pushed Native Americans out of territory. What might be less well known to many is how much of this violence, sanitized by references to it as "Indian wars," lacked both direction and explicit approval from governments. Typically settlers moved illegally onto lands that the government recognized as belonging to natives but was unable or unwilling to help them defend. When some natives turned to violence, informal groups of settlers attacked any they could find, killing noncombatants and destroying their homes and crops. This effectively kept forcing native groups to accept displacement from the lands they held.[30] Nineteenth-century Americans did not see this continuing process as political violence, but again it is hard not to.

Politicians in Jacksonian America also used individual political and social violence. Jackson himself killed a rival in a duel, and many politicians and other relatively wealthy and well-educated Americans engaged in similar behavior. Duels were extremely common in much of the United States, although the word "duel" exaggerates the degree to which protocols of formality and fairness were followed. Incidents that were later portrayed as duels often involved sneak attacks, attacks on unarmed men, and ganging up on victims, even if the motives were cloaked in a language of honor.[31] Much of this violence was sparked by political rivalries, and sometimes political motives were quite explicit. In the early 1840s the United States Congress itself was the scene of threats, beatings, and at least one pistol shot, and members increasingly took to carrying weapons into the chambers.[32]

Historians of nineteenth-century Latin America sometimes emphasize the role of so-called caudillos, military leaders who built groups of supporters using political patronage and were not inclined to "feel strictly bound to observe all legal technicalities."[33] Although these men were ambitious and sometimes unscrupulous, they also had strong ideological visions about the form their new nations should take.[34] Nineteenth-century Mexicans and Americans saw Antonio López de Santa Anna as the quintessential Mexican caudillo, yet Alan Knight points out that in fact Jackson was very similar to a typical caudillo as well.[35] During the War of 1812 Jackson gained fame and supporters by leading part-time soldiers against Native Americans and the British in the southern United States. He was a defender of the right of frontier whites to govern not only their own affairs but also their racial inferiors. What these whites saw as "governing their own affairs" was predicated above all on their unfettered domination of blacks and Native Americans. Jackson was, according to Feldberg, "no great respecter of the due process of law."[36] This was displayed most openly in his illegal and unauthorized invasion of Florida in 1818. The Florida adventure was aimed at not only expanding the United States but also attacking Native Americans and escaped slaves who had taken refuge in the Spanish possession, and it was highlighted by the illegal trial and execution of two British merchants. Although it earned Jackson fierce criticism, it did not derail his career, and he later served two terms as one of America's more controversial presidents.[37] In general, when we consider the violence of the early nineteenth-century United States and the willingness of even prominent political leaders to ignore the rule of law, the country begins to more closely resemble Mexico in the same period. The massive explosion of American political violence in 1861 also becomes all the more comprehensible.

In 1846 the two countries shared some key characteristics. They were young republics led by political elites that were united in a commitment to the idea of forming national states. Yet political conflicts were very notable in both countries, and those political conflicts were driven in part by the contradictions between ideals of egalitarianism and freedom on the one hand and social realities organized by hierarchies of class, gender, and race on the other.

American Expansionism

The war was more than anything a direct consequence of American expansionism, driven not only by the rapid economic growth of the United States but also by central aspects of America's political culture and changing social identity. Americans wanted to add territory to the republic for a variety of reasons. For many, the drive to expand the United States was an expression of their confidence in the superiority of their civilization, culture, and mode of government. They saw the United States as continuing a forward movement that had begun in Europe and was associated with a religious mission and representative government.[38] This aggressive confidence is summed up by the phrase "Manifest Destiny." However, the desire to expand American territory was also paradoxically fueled by American anxieties. Some saw expansion as a way to protect the United States or at least what expansionists believed the country stood for. The United States was rapidly urbanizing and industrializing, and many people thought that the chaotic cities in which many white men worked for others rather than farming their own land were un-American. They believed that expanding the land available for cultivation could help ward off this trend and forestall the possibility of class conflict. Yet much American land was cultivated not by independent white farmers but instead by slaves. The specter of racial conflict hovered behind expansionism. Some expansionists believed that acquiring more land from Mexico would forestall race warfare either by preventing that land's domination by blacks or by allowing blacks to migrate to Mexico.[39] Even personal participation in expansionism was as likely to be motivated by anxiety and failure as it was by confidence. Individuals often migrated after failed farming ventures or other economic hardships prevented them from realizing their ambitions in more settled parts of the country. Yet migration to new lands did not guarantee success. Many migrants failed repeatedly and found themselves moving even farther each time. Thus American economic prosperity spurred expansion, but hard times and individual economic failures often increased the number of people on the move.[40]

Not all expansionists had a personal desire to move west. Expansionism was intimately related to debates about who could claim the prestige of being an American citizen. Support for expansion and the necessary aggressive domination of Native Americans and later Mexicans was tied to the elevation of all white males to citizenship and the consequent relegation of racial others, and to a certain extent females, to secondary status.[41] The racial aspects of this are fairly obvious, but the gender aspects are also fascinating. During this period gender norms that pushed women away from public life and political participation were extolled, and those few women with local voting rights lost them.[42] Yet the term "Manifest Destiny" actually may have been coined by a female journalist, Jane McManus Storms, although some scholars attribute it to her colleague John L. Sullivan.[43] More generally, expansion through military action was advocated by proponents of a particular kind of masculinity that historian Amy Greenberg calls martial masculinity. This model of proper masculine behavior emphasized action, dominance, and shrugging off societal restraints. It jousted with another model of masculine behavior that she calls restrained manhood, adherents of which believed that men should support their families, practice evangelical Protestantism, and seek sober success in business. They also believed that America was destined for greatness, but they thought American ideals could best be spread through example and the development of commercial ties across the continent and indeed the world.[44] Gender also figures into expansionism in another way: the idea that Mexicans were racial inferiors was justified in part by claims that Mexican men were less masculine than their American counterparts.[45]

Destiny is at root a religious concept, and the notion that God willed American expansion was encoded in the very phrase "Manifest Destiny." Although some scholars argue that by the 1840s the religious character of the idea had been superseded by a more secular version driven by an exaltation of republicanism, that does not seem to be the case. Americans connected the prosperity and political system of the United States to its Protestantism, and American images of the country's positive economic and political aspects were not separate from its religiosity.[46] That religiosity was increasing in the 1830s as evangelical revivals and utopian mobilization rocked much of the United States. Expansionists often expressed the idea that God willed the acquisition of new territory, and more specifically the U.S. aggression against Mexico.[47]

Not all Americans were expansionists, and certainly not all Americans supported the American invasion of Mexico. The Whig Party, one of the two major political parties, certainly believed that the United States had a religious destiny to spread its influence across the continent and indeed the globe, but it wanted to spread that influence through example, not conquest. The Whig dissent against the ultimately successful expansion at the cost of Mexico was quite bitter.[48] They favored a more compact United States, one focused on prosperity through commerce and industry. They believed that the federal government should promote this economic development through internal improvements like canals and railroads. Their image of proper male behavior aligned more with Greenberg's restrained manhood, and they worried about all of the disorder described previously. Expansion, in their view, threatened to dilute American identity and even eventually dissolve the United States. Moreover, expansion through conquest would undermine the shining example of the United States by diminishing its claim to represent a new and more moral kind of political system. Imperialism was incompatible with a commitment to liberty.[49] In the early 1840s a few Whigs were beginning to worry that acquiring new territory would lead to the expansion of slavery, but they did not yet express those concerns overtly. Many Whigs also believed that adding more territory to the United States would undermine their party's electoral chances, because new territory was likely to favor the agricultural rather than industrial economy and new states would likely be populated, and represented, by their political rivals. The Whig Party's real stronghold was in the Northeast, and the party seemed unlikely to expand with an expanding nation. Yet the popular base of the Whigs was somewhat weak even in the Northeast, partially because, although they welcomed the labor provided by new immigrants, they felt that these immigrants were slow to embrace what they saw as America's core values of hard work, self-improvement, and Protestant piety.[50]

If the Whig Party's base of support mostly consisted of respectable middle- and upper-class people in the Northeast, the Democratic Party united those who felt excluded from this group and disdained its merchants and financiers. Southern planters, farmers of modest means in the West and the western parts of the South, and working-class immigrants in eastern cities tended to be Democrats. Generally the party combined the agricultural interests of the West and South with the urban workers of the East. It was almost evangelically avid about expanding the boundaries of the United States. Democrats wanted the United States to remain an agricultural nation in which white males could achieve social mobility by acquiring, developing, and farming land. These white males would have local autonomy with minimal interference from the national government. Expansion would also aid planters, who could find new land to replace fields exhausted by the cotton monoculture and also higher prices for the slaves they owned. Democrats feared the urbanization and industrialization that Whigs saw as the country's future, and they saw Whigs as pretentious and un-American imitators of British culture. The disparate groups in the Democratic Party were united by a commitment to white supremacy, which would support the institution of slavery in the South and the acquisition of new lands from Native Americans and Mexicans. White supremacy also offered even poor whites, both urban and rural, status and potential social mobility. Here the key word is "potential": poor men had difficulty saving or borrowing the money that would be needed to migrate to western lands and farm. One needed funds not only for land but also for transportation, food to live on until the first harvest, tools, draft animals, and, for Southerners, slaves. Migrants often began their new farms with deep debts and never came out ahead. The profits of expansion tended to go to those who were already wealthy enough to set up new farms or those who speculated in land, and it is therefore not surprising that men like this were often among the most important supporters of both the Democrats and expansion.[51] It is not at all an accident that when the United States went to war with Mexico, it was under the leadership of a Democratic president, Polk. Although he was able to manipulate the Whigs in Congress into supporting the war's official authorization, he could only do so by starting the war first and clouding the situation with a number of false statements about Mexican actions.

Gender, Race, and Religion

Most of this book tells the story of the war in roughly chronological order, juggling characters, events, and their causes. Nevertheless, it differs from many books written about wars. Although it describes and explains battles and campaigns, it focuses as much as possible on the experiences and motivations of Mexicans and Americans of relatively modest social status, the men and women who did the hardest work and faced the greatest risks not only in Mexican and American armies but also in Mexican and American societies. Although their vast numbers and the scarcity of documents in which they appear as individuals push us to think about them in groups, they are the most important characters in this story. This approach has become more common among historians who share a sense that wars are best understood using social and cultural history. The commitment to telling the social history of the war means that at times the book does not narrate the war in a strictly chronological way. It delves into specific social groups when they became important to military and political events, but understanding a group's experiences often requires attention to earlier and later events. Some departures from a strict chronology are also necessary because the war took place across a huge expanse of space. Moreover, the book does not cover every battle and campaign but rather concentrates on those most emblematic of people's varied experiences and most central to the war's outcome. This book also differs from many books about wars in that it is about Mexico and the United States in equal measure, a balancing act that makes the war more understandable and helps compare the two countries. Both the focus on common people and the comparative aspirations of the book are facilitated by frequent and sustained attention to three themes—gender, race, and religion—that together help us understand the complicated motivations of many different people, as well as how people interpreted their experiences. These three elements were central to the ways in which both societies were organized and the ways in which people in both societies thought about their lives.

"Gender" is a shorthand term for ideas about masculinity, femininity, and how men and women should relate to each other. Most people in both countries thought about what behavior was appropriate or proper in gendered ways, and people thus understood and experienced the war in gendered ways. Much of the political language that people used to debate what they had in common and organize collective efforts is full of gender references. Different kinds of Mexicans and Americans often thought about gender norms and behavior in quite similar ways. During the war observers sometimes commented on foreign masculine or feminine behaviors that seemed somehow different from what they were used to, and they used these ideas to reinforce their beliefs in fundamental racial differences between Americans and Mexicans. Yet usually what they were actually observing was the expression of similar gender values in slightly different circumstances. Moreover, observers also exaggerated differences in behavior to emphasize their own superiority. The same can be generally said about differences across class and racial lines within the United States and Mexico. A wealthy observer often saw a poor or racially different person as dishonorable or even promiscuous even though the person observed was more than likely actually trying to follow gender norms that were shared across social lines.

In both countries there were two basic forms of masculinity that people often thought of as being exercised by different kinds of men, although in fact the same man might lean toward one or the other depending on circumstances. In one of these forms, men had a duty to be hardworking, sober, responsible providers for their families. This behavior entitled one to honor and respect, and it was central to the vitality of the families that actually kept society going by giving birth to and raising subsequent generations. Men who behaved this way were responsible citizens. Yet in both countries there was another pattern of behavior considered to be equally masculine if not always equally appropriate. It was centered less on providing for families and more on competition, dominance, and diversion. Men following this pattern used violence to intimidate and dominate others, including their wives and children. They also caroused, gambled, and drank. Although many people in both countries tended to think of these two models as representative of two different kinds of men, the evidence actually suggests that at least sometimes behavior varied more with their changing circumstances. Even respectable men in both countries sometimes slipped into rowdy behavior in spaces like taverns and Election Day polling places. Both countries also tolerated a certain amount of violence against spouses or even other men as long as it stayed within limits.

The situation for women was a bit less complicated. In both Mexico and the United States, they did almost all the cooking and cleaning, and they also had the most constant daily contact with children. Like men, they were also supposed to contribute to the economic well-being of families with their labor, often by performing tasks similar to those they performed in the home, preparing and selling food on the streets of cities, serving as laundresses for construction camps, or working as domestic servants in the houses of wealthier families. Yet women were considered safest and most proper when at home. It was easier for wealthier women to adhere very closely to these ideals; poor women who were working to keep themselves and their families alive often were assumed to be dishonorable or promiscuous because they had to leave their homes.

The second theme running through the book is race. The fact that race was central to a war of conquest will probably not surprise many readers, but they might be a bit surprised by some of the ways in which it was important. This period in U.S. history is known as the era of Jacksonian democracy, and race was critically important to the changes implied by the term. Ideas about race permeated both intellectual publications and the more popular media.[52] Different American states removed the provisions that restricted suffrage to people with higher incomes, effectively allowing even poor white men to vote. This development expanded the electorate and made society seem more egalitarian, and in this sense the Jacksonian period had liberating aspects. Moreover, these newly enfranchised voters participated quite exuberantly: in the 1840 national election, around 80 percent of adult white men voted.[53] Jacksonian democracy deliberately included all white males, but it also deliberately *excluded* nearly everyone else. Egalitarianism stopped at the gender line, and it stopped at the increasingly sharp line dividing whites from nonwhites. Racial others actually lost rights during the period because the Jacksonian ethos was all about raising all white males to equal status and enhancing their ability to dominate others. In historian Harry Watson's words, "All white men would be equal, at least in theory, but no one else would be the equal of a white man."[54] Free blacks lost voting rights in the few states where they had them, and in some states they were newly denied even the right to own property.[55] Native Americans also lost ground in the Jacksonian period, as more people claimed they were racial inferiors who could neither be assimilated into American civilization nor treated as members of equal nations separate from it. This left natives with no legitimate claim to land. Their decreasing status was most visibly manifested in the forced removal of even tribes that had adopted European institutions and ideas, and the confiscation of their valuable lands.[56]

It was just before and during this war that American whites decided "Mexican" was not only a nationality but also a race. Expansionist Americans had to construe Mexicans as constituting an inferior race to justify taking their land, and racism was central to American nationalism during the war. The idea that Mexicans constituted a separate and inferior race had roots in the biological ancestry of most Mexicans. White Americans already saw blacks, Native Americans, and people of mixed race as inferior, and many Mexicans had mixtures of white, black, and Native American ancestry.[57] In this period, though, culture was seen as an important component of race, and Mexicans' Catholicism was also seen as proof of their racial inferiority.[58] The racialization of Mexicans began to gain momentum in the 1830s as American colonists in the Mexican province of Texas justified their revolution against Mexican rule. American Texans and their supporters argued that the atrocities Mexican officers had committed against the rebels were proof of racial inferiority. As historian Brian DeLay points out, they also claimed incorrectly that the Mexicans had invited Americans into the province because the Mexicans were too weak and cowardly to defeat the region's Indians.[59] Expansionists hailed the superiority of the American, Anglo-Saxon race, and American soldiers arrived in Mexico primed to see inferiority. Their reports back home further fueled anti-Mexican racism.[60] Americans, crucially, came to believe that Mexicans had no more right to territory than Native Americans did.

Why should the United States not expand at their expense?[61] Ironically, even opposition to the acquisition of Mexican territory and the war was sometimes driven by racism. After all, there were people on those lands, and who would want to add racially inferior people to the population of the United States?[62]

The American belief that Mexicans were a race, and an inferior one at that, shocked many Mexicans. Mexicans believed that their society contained several different races, and although racial prejudice was important socially in Mexico, racial categories had been written out of political respectability. Race had been important in Mexico from the beginning. The Spanish adventurers who conquered it in the sixteenth century had been attracted as much by its sedentary, agricultural native population as by the precious metals natives had accumulated during centuries of civilization. Early in the colonial period Spaniards exploited some members of this population through various forms of forced labor, including chattel slavery, but over the centuries most Native Americans had become Hispanicized free laborers or indigenous peasants who farmed their own land. The Spanish colonists had also imported a significant number of African slaves to work in particularly difficult situations such as mines or lowland plantations. Yet in the 1700s the native population was growing rapidly, and chattel slavery became more expensive than free labor, leading to the emancipation of most slaves. Over the colonial period Mexico also came to have a very large population of mixed-race individuals in cities and those rural areas that had been too dry to support large sedentary native populations. The late colonial economic system relied on free labor, but race remained important in Mexican society. Native Americans had limited legal rights, people with African blood were denied social prestige and access to religious or political posts, and mixed-race people faced severe social prejudice from an elite that claimed its pure Spanish blood gave it special honor and social prestige.

In the 1810s Mexico underwent overlapping upheavals. A long and bloody civil war resulted in political independence. Simultaneously, the official use of racial categories was abolished, and equal rights were granted to all Mexicans regardless of racial or ethnic identity. These political and social revolutions were intertwined. The most famous leaders of the War of Independence, Miguel Hidalgo and José Maria Morelos, had made the abolition of racial categories and the official abolition of slavery a key part of their programs even before they openly advocated independence itself. Their followers were mostly Native Americans and people of mixed race. Racial discrimination received another blow during the war when Spanish liberals abolished discrimination against Native Americans in a constitution that was temporarily implemented in Mexico. Independence was finally achieved under a compromise between royalists and insurgents brokered by the relatively conservative general Agustín de Iturbide, but he was forced to accept the end of racial discrimination against not only people with indigenous blood but also people of African descent. Official documents simply no longer referred to people using racial categories. All could serve in political office, all could vote, and thus all could aspire to social respectability. For many people of mixed race, in other words most of the people who populated cities and some rural regions in Mexico, the principal result of this revolution was the chance for more political power and social mobility. Although very few slaves existed in Mexico, the abolition of slavery was an important symbol of the end of prejudice, and it tended to be extolled when politicians who drew support from urban and rural mixed-race people were in power. In fact, many slaves escaped from the American South to Mexico. The weakness of racial prejudice among lower-class Mexicans of mixed race allowed them to assimilate into Mexican society through work and marriage. Americans in Mexico often remarked on this. One anonymous American, for instance, remarked of one of them that he, "though black as a polished boot, had succeeded in marrying a Mexican woman."[63] However, the abolition of official racial categories did not by any means wipe out social discrimination rooted in centuries of history. The members of Mexico's wealthiest families believed themselves to be of Spanish descent, and they believed this made them more honorable and rational than their social inferiors. They particularly disdained people believed to have African blood, and they accused politicians espousing a more egalitarian political system of having African ancestors.[64] Moreover, many relatively wealthy Mexicans believed that Native American peasants were eager to conduct race warfare to recover land lost to large estates. They explicitly feared that Mexico would suffer the fate of Haiti, where whites had been violently expelled from the country by the vengeful, darker masses.[65] These social prejudices, however, were not encoded in laws, and politicians were quite circumspect about race in their explicit political debates.

The third theme that helps us understand how people from many different social backgrounds understood and experienced the war is religion. Religion is often important in the construction of national identity and the justification of warfare, and that was certainly true for this war. People in both countries made much of the religious differences between them and used those differences to justify violence.[66] The United States was more religiously diverse and boasted of religious tolerance, but its diversity did not diminish the intense attachment of most Americans to religion, and tolerance was not extended equally to all religions. Some new sects like Mormonism faced notably violent repression, as did the much older religion of Catholicism. Religious fervor was clearly increasing in the United States. A wave of Protestant revivals called the Second Great Awakening swept over many American regions, and increasing numbers of Americans embraced evangelical versions of Protestantism. Religion became more important to many Americans in political and social life, sparking reform movements like temperance, abolitionism, and feminism. These movements remained largely on the margins in the 1840s, but the belief that the United States had a special religious destiny as a Protestant beacon of liberty took on more and more momentum.[67] Most Americans believed that Protestantism was one of the roots of liberty, republicanism, and democracy, and they had the opposite view of Catholicism. They believed that Catholics owed allegiance to the pope and that the Catholic Church was too hierarchical to be compatible with democracy.[68] They saw Catholicism as positively threatening. More and more Catholic immigrants were arriving on American shores, and the often violent backlash against them was as much anti-Catholic as it was antiforeign.

This fear of Catholicism was linked to American expansionism. Some Americans believed that the Catholic Church was encouraging this migration to undermine the United States and populate the lands to the west with Catholics, inhibiting the growth of liberty. One of the most violent anti-Catholic riots took place in Boston immediately after the famous preacher Lyman Beecher had sermonized about the threat posed by the extension of Catholicism into the lands of what became the western United States.[69] Even worse, the lands to the west were controlled by Mexico, where Catholicism was the only religion legally allowed.[70] For many Americans, the Manifest Destiny of the United States was to spread liberty and democracy by taking these lands from Mexico, a country whose religion was incompatible with such values.[71] Most Americans believed Mexicans' Catholicism was one of the roots of their racial inferiority. Race was not strictly biological, and cultural characteristics were seen as intertwined with physical ones. Catholicism made Mexicans, like Catholic immigrants to the United States, ignorant, backward, weak, slothful, and unsuited for democracy.[72]

Mexicans were convinced that Catholicism offered the only route to eternal life, and they were proud of their religion. The Spanish conquest of Mexico had been justified by the need to bring Catholicism to the heathens, and the Mexican War of Independence had been started by priests who argued that violence was required to protect a pure Catholicism threatened by European trends and events. After independence some Mexican intellectuals wrote that Mexico's mission was to redeem men in the New World, providing a beacon of hope to a decadent Europe. Politicians and intellectuals insisted that Catholicism was central to Mexican identity. Catholic prayers and services marked Mexican civic ceremonies, and public officials promoted collective religious rituals. To be Mexican was to be Catholic: immigrants seeking citizenship were required to join the Catholic Church. Catholicism was not only a force for national unity; because it was the only path to eternal salvation, one purpose of government was to facilitate the religious work of the church. Americans might see their religious toleration and religious diversity as good things, but for Mexicans religious toleration and the plethora of denominations would only mean that fewer people would reach heaven.[73]

AMERICAN EXPANSIONISM did not necessarily have to result in a bloody war. Mexico could have responded to the desires of the Polk administration by agreeing to give up its claims to Texas and sell New Mexico and California to the United States. Polk was certainly not interested in a war as long and bloody as the one he sparked. The war played out the way it did because Mexicans did not at first understand the depth of the American expansionist impulse and Americans understood neither the depth of Mexican national identity nor how thoroughly Mexicans of many social groups rejected the idea that they were inferior to Americans. Many Mexicans saw the desire of Americans to take territory from their neighbor as a criminal impulse, one they did not expect from a sister republic with so many admirable qualities. The American republic founded by immortals like George Washington must be in the process of becoming degraded.[74] Other Mexicans were not so surprised. In the early 1820s the first Mexican ambassador to the United States, José Manuel Zozaya, reported that Americans saw Mexicans as inferiors and might expand at their expense.[75] He also remarked on their greed. Other Mexican visitors to the United States echoed this view, linking that greed to the incessant impulse to farm new land.[76] Some Mexicans came to believe that Americans or American residents of independent Texas were encouraging the Native American raiding that caused northern Mexicans so much economic loss and death.[77] If Mexicans were surprised at the depravity of Americans, Americans were surprised that Mexicans resisted their aggression as much as they did. The racist vision of a Mexico whose weak, inferior population had little stake in a national identity made many Americans believe the war would be short and glorious.[78] Americans did not understand the degree to which Mexican politicians of several different parties had come to believe that the survival of the very idea of a Mexican nation required them to defend all its territory, a formulation that historians Marcela Terrazas y Basante and Gerardo Gurza Lavalle call the national fetish of territory.[79] Mexicans knew that the territories the Polk administration wanted had few Mexican inhabitants, but they were unwilling to abandon those few people to the domination of an American people of proven racism and brutality. At the beginning of the war the Americans also did not realize that the obnoxious behavior of American soldiers, fueled by those very notions of Mexican inferiority, would stiffen resistance. The war showed that Mexican national identity was stronger than Americans believed to be the case, and it also strengthened the attachment of many inhabitants to Mexico. Ironically, though, these facts were not widely recognized by Americans or Mexicans during or after the war. Americans interpreted Mexican resistance as a sign of their violent character, further proof of their inferiority. Later both Mexicans and Americans often argued that the fact that Mexico lost the war was evidence that Mexicans had lacked the unity and commitment needed to win.

CHAPTER 1

The Men Most Damaging
to the Population

In the summer of 1845 almost four thousand soldiers of the U.S. Army traveled from the coastal fortifications and isolated frontier posts where they had previously worked in small groups to the coastal Texas settlement of Corpus Christi. Under General Zachary Taylor they began training to fight in the formal battle order most of their officers only knew from manuals or from reading historical accounts of European wars. Corpus Christi would be their home for the next several months, and it was not a comfortable place. Their tents were inadequate protection from the extremes of heat and cold, and the water available was brackish. Moreover, the behavior of their officers must have been disquieting. More than a few did not understand the large-scale, formal maneuvers they were practicing, and soon officers began quarrelling over rank and privileges. Both officers and men felt an undercurrent of tension about what clearly seemed to be preparations for battles whose outcome was uncertain.[1]

Officially these men were there to protect the recently annexed state of Texas. Mexico had lost effective control of Texas due to a series of miscalculations by first Spanish and then Mexican leaders. The geographical barriers that made Texas so distant in practical terms from the most populated areas of Mexico, the lack of mineral resources that might have regardless encouraged substantial settlement, and the strength of Native American groups there had combined to leave Texas with a very small Spanish-speaking and culturally Mexican population. This lack of people was a relatively minor problem until the 1810s, when the rising population of the United States and growing demand for cotton motivated Southerners to aggressively force

Spain to cede Florida and the southern parts of Alabama and Mississippi. Texas, too, was vulnerable, and the authorities decided to encourage its settlement by foreigners. Authorities in both Spain and later Mexico believed foreigners could be effectively assimilated into Mexican society, and they were granted land on the condition that they do so, especially by becoming Catholic. The new immigrants from the United States simply ignored the conditions, and they were quickly reinforced by others attracted by the possibility of cashing in on the opportunity to grow cotton on virgin land.[2] From the new settlers' point of view, such cultivation required slavery, which created further tensions. Both Mexico and Coahuila, the state to which Texas belonged, had passed laws prohibiting the sale or introduction of slaves, and eventually slavery itself.[3] The question of slavery created a significant wedge between English-speaking colonists and Mexican authorities. Yet the impetus that drove many Texans, both Anglos and Mexicans, to rebel in the middle of the 1830s was the introduction of a centralist constitution in Mexico. By limiting the autonomy of regional governments, it eliminated the possibility that Anglo and Mexican Texans could build a regional policy and economy that drew them together to prosper from their proximity to the United States.[4]

At first the rebels espoused federalism, but once the national government sent troops to bring them to heel, many of the Mexican and Anglo Texans began to advocate for independence from Mexico. The shift was partially driven by a flood of new Anglos from the American South who saw fighting for an independent Texas as a relatively quick and cheap way to acquire new cotton lands. The new arrivals were crucial to the eventual defeat of the Mexican army in Texas.[5] Texas independence was a catastrophe for Mexico, and not simply because it lost a geographic area that would eventually become extremely wealthy. Mexico's bloody efforts to suppress the Texas rebellion and the ways American politicians and writers publicized both those efforts and the rich land available in Texas set in motion a dramatic transition in American views of Mexicans. Mexicans, no longer the freedom-loving denizens of a sister republic, came to be firmly placed among the racial inferiors white Americans defined themselves against, a group that included African Americans, locked ever more tightly into slavery, and Native Americans, increasingly pushed aside as both unproductive and unassimilable.[6]

FIG. 1.1 U.S. president James K. Polk.

Texas remained independent for a decade, and its eventual annexation roiled American politics. In 1844 the U.S. Senate refused to approve a treaty of annexation. After the little-known James K. Polk won the 1844 presidential election, the supporters of Texas's annexation cleverly bypassed the Senate's authority to approve treaties, which required a two-thirds majority, instead arguing that Congress could admit new states through joint resolutions passed by a simple majority of all members.[7] Annexation created an international crisis because Mexico considered Texas a rebel province, while the U.S. government now saw it as American territory. While Texas was independent, Mexican troops had occasionally raided the province and Mexican politicians had talked often of the need to reconquer it, so it surprised no one when Polk sent troops to the new territory.

Polk undoubtedly wanted to protect Texas, but he was also playing a much grander game. One clue was the size of the army, which was larger than any force the United States had gathered in one place since the end of the War of 1812. Another clue was its location, which was far from any area where Mexicans and Texans had clashed but convenient to the Mexican town of Matamoros, and even more convenient for resupply by sea. Polk sought to take advantage of a neighboring country whose political and economic weakness he despised and whose possessions he coveted. His goals were daring. Polk wanted Mexico to sell the United States vast portions of its northern territories, especially California, and he wanted Mexico to officially recognize Texas as American territory. He also wanted Mexico to recognize the river Mexicans call the Rio Bravo and Americans call the Rio Grande as the border rather than the Nueces River, which had marked the limit of the Mexican province of Texas. Although the places where the two rivers reach the Gulf of Mexico are only a few miles apart, their inland courses diverge greatly. There were no Texan officials in the land between the two rivers, and the inhabitants were Mexicans. Many observers in both countries believed that Polk's claim that the land between the Nueces and the Rio Grande was part of Texas was a deliberate fiction. Lieutenant Colonel Ethan Allen Hitchcock, an officer in Taylor's force, stated this repeatedly in his diary. When the army received a new map from Washington, Hitchcock wrote, "It has *added to it* [original emphasis] a distinct boundary mark to the Rio Grande. Our people ought

to be damned for their impudent arrogance and domineering presumption!"
Writing later, Mexican José María Roa Bárcena derisively suggested that the
historical basis for claiming the Rio Grande as the boundary was so ridiculous that the United States might as well have claimed Texas extended to the
Straits of Magellan.[8]

The trouble with believing the country had a manifest destiny to expand
was that the space to be expanded into was inhabited. How could Polk believe
Mexico could be intimidated into giving up so much without fighting a major
war? Polk held Mexico in contempt. He believed it had a bankrupt, undemocratic, corrupt, and unstable political system that would not or could not
rally its population to a major war to defend remote territories where few
Mexicans lived. Polk, a Southern slaveholder, also viewed Mexicans as racial
inferiors.[9] If Mexico did not fold without fighting, it would undoubtedly do
so after a very short frontier war. Even as Polk negotiated a relatively meek
compromise with Great Britain over the boundary between the United States
and Canada in the Pacific Northwest, he deliberately provoked the Mexican government by supporting the exaggerated claims of U.S. citizens who
wanted compensation for property destroyed during Mexican political strife.
Polk then further exacerbated tensions by sending emissary John Slidell on
a diplomatic mission designed to fail. Mexico had severed diplomatic relations when the United States had annexed Texas, but Mexican president José
Joaquín Herrera, who believed the province unrecoverable, signaled a willingness to negotiate with a special envoy over Texas. Polk instead sent Slidell as a
general diplomatic representative with orders to purchase further territories
from Mexico, a move that implied that the Texas question was settled and
diplomatic relations had already been reestablished. Herrera was unable and
unwilling to accept this, and Slidell returned to the United States. The Slidell
mission was designed to simultaneously assure the American public that Polk
was seeking a peaceful resolution and signal to the Mexican government that
a conflict was inevitable.[10] The ultimate provocation, however, came when
Polk ordered a decidedly unenthusiastic General Taylor to move the American army at Corpus Christi past the Nueces River to the mouth of the Rio
Grande, where it would be a stone's throw away from the Mexican town of
Matamoros and its substantial garrison.[11]

Unlikely Agents of American Prosperity and Freedom

The men of Taylor's army were the leading edge of a government buoyed by many Americans' confidence that they were destined to bring prosperity and freedom, or at least versions of prosperity and freedom that included chattel slavery, to an entire continent. Ironically, the vast majority of the men in this army had experienced little of that prosperity or freedom, and most American citizens despised them. In the 1840s, military service in the U.S. regular army was only attractive to men who were very poor. Army recruiters stressed the economic benefits of joining, which included a modest wage, food, shelter, and clothing. Men who explained why they joined the army invariably stressed their dire poverty and the pressing need for food. Frederick Zeh, for instance, remarks that in the weeks before he joined, he "often passed out from hunger"; George Ballentine enlisted after a fruitless search for work in New York; Charles Stratford joined after a robbery left him destitute and he could not find work; and William McLaughlin, John Davis, John O'Donnell, and Charles Isdepski explained that they chose the army over starving to death.[12] One indication of the low social status of regular army recruits is the fact that, in a U.S. population where 90 percent of whites were literate, 35 percent of recruits could not even sign their names to recruitment documents.[13]

The army mostly recruited among the urban poor of eastern cities, men who, like other members of the international working class, struggled to make a living in a rapidly changing economy characterized by employment insecurity and increasing reliance on wage labor.[14] When they could find work, it was in occupations that were brutally physical, temporary, and poorly paid, such as cleaning streets, digging canals, unloading ships, and serving as deckhands on whaling ships or the steamboats that plied the continent's rivers. Some were immigrants who had previously served in European armies.[15] The very precariousness of their existence made them mobile and rootless, as they needed to pursue work or rumors of work wherever they heard of it. Their poverty, insecurity, and mobility made it extremely difficult for them to form and support stable families, one of the hallmarks of respectability and citizenship in the United States. These workers often lived in boarding-houses and construction barracks.[16] Settled respectability was beyond their grasp, and their transience generally kept them from being considered local residents and citizens.[17] One would think that such rootless and mobile men would be likely to take advantage of opportunities on the expanding agricultural frontiers of the West, but these men were so poor that they could not scrape up the money needed for transportation, tools, land, and the provisions needed to survive until the first harvest. They were thus trapped in cities already oversupplied with labor.[18] Worse yet, poverty itself was increasingly stigmatized, as the poor came to be seen more and more as victims of their own laziness, lack of thrift, and dependence on others.[19]

Economic opportunities in the United States were limited, but they still seemed better than the possibilities poor people faced in several parts of Europe. Thus immigration continued, and immigrants fazed by the limited opportunities in eastern cities often found their way to recruiting sergeants. Around 40 percent of the men in the regular army were recent immigrants from Europe, especially Ireland, Germany, and Great Britain.[20] Immigrants were held in even more contempt than other poor people due to intense nativism. They faced discrimination in employment and satirical depictions in the newspapers hawked on the streets of U.S. cities.[21] The army did not offer a safe haven from such nativism, but at least its constant need for more men meant that recruiters could not turn up their noses at immigrants. The steady pay, food, and clothing that recruiters offered made army service the best available option for many an immigrant.[22]

American nativism was very tightly bound up with anti-Catholicism. Anti-Catholic attitudes had been originally inherited from England's Protestant Reformation and its struggles in European politics, but these attitudes were relatively muted in the newly independent American republic before large numbers of Catholic Irish and German immigrants began to cross the Atlantic in the 1820s and 1830s. Critics argued that Catholicism's hierarchical organization and emphasis on emotion rather than reason were incompatible with American culture and democracy. Anti-Catholic tracts by ministers like Lyman Beecher and cultural figures like Samuel F. B. Morse espousing these arguments sold well in U.S. cities, and they were supplemented by even more sensationalist tracts that luridly described sexual crimes supposedly committed in monasteries and convents. It is not surprising that anti-Catholic, nativist riots were among the deadliest forms of urban political violence. Riots in Boston in 1834 and Philadelphia in 1844 showed Catholic immigrants how precarious their foothold in American life was.[23]

To many Americans, Catholic working-class immigrant males seemed to live the wrong kind of masculinity. These men demonstrated their worth with feats of alcohol-fueled physical prowess both on the job and in the streets but bowed to a hierarchical church that tried to bring men closer to God through their senses rather than their brains. Nativists doubted that this kind of masculinity made good citizens, and they increasingly doubted that these immigrants were truly white. Many came to see the Irish in particular as belonging to a separate and inferior racial category.[24] Enlistment in the regular army did not shield immigrants from nativism and anti-Catholicism. The officer corps was mostly native and Protestant, and many officers embraced nativist criticisms of immigrants and Catholicism. They often forced Catholic soldiers to attend Protestant services in which anti-Catholic ministers railed against Catholicism. Faced with this kind of coercion, one Irish Catholic soldier exclaimed it would be a sin to attend a service "to hear a swaddling preacher mocking the holy religion."[25]

Many Americans believed theirs was a land of freedom and economic opportunity, and they found it hard to understand the barriers that limited the economic and social possibilities of poor urban males. Who would give up their opportunities and freedom for five years in exchange for a low wage, clothing, and food? Army soldiers were often seen as lazy men without the work ethic and habits that would allow them to succeed in civilian society. It is not surprising to see this view reflected in the accounts of European travelers like Frenchman Achilles Murat or Englishman James Alexander, who after all could be expected to absorb views on just about anything from the relatively wealthy Americans who served as their hosts.[26] What is interesting is how much this view seems to have pervaded America's middle class and even parts of its working class. The recently recruited Ballentine found that his fellow passengers on a New England steamboat saw him and his comrades "in the light of a degraded caste, and seemed to think that there was contamination in the touch of a soldier." One remarked that the men were "a fine set of candidates for the State's prison." When recruit C. M. Reeves and his comrades marched through Pittsburgh, they were followed by a crowd of jeering street urchins, who chanted, "Hey, see the dirty soldiers will you work," answering, "No, I'll sell my shirt first." When recent West Point graduate Ulysses S. Grant was mistaken for a common soldier in Cincinnati, a street urchin subjected him to almost exactly the same chant.[27]

Regular army soldiers were also despised because they had voluntarily given up their autonomy. In a country that extolled white male freedom, these men had agreed to follow orders for five years. On his first night in the army, Reeves agonized over the fact that he had "forfeitted in a great measure, that inestimatable boon to all Americans, 'Liberty,' and placed myself in a position where I would be subject to the orders of those in authority above, whom to obey would be degradation." Many Americans believed soldiers had become servile, forfeiting at least part of their masculinity because masculinity was incompatible with dependence.[28] The greatest sign of that dependence was the prevalence of corporal punishment in the regular army. The methods used were often inventive and always painful. In the words of Ballentine, they included

> placing the culprit standing on a barrel in the open street, exposed to the heat of the sun all day, and the derisive admiration of the street passerby. Of course, a sentry was always in attendance to short him or run him through with a bayonet if he tried to escape from his uncomfortable position. Another mode consisted of placing the victim on a high, wooden horse and compelling him to sit for a series of days and nights in that same position. One night while asleep, the soldier being punished fell from the back of his inanimate steed, which was about eight feet high, onto the hard pavement and was so severely hurt that he died a short time later. But the favorite punishment was that called the "buck and gag," which is administered after the following manner. The culprit is first seated on the ground; his feet are drawn up to his hams and his wrists tied firmly in front of his legs; a long stick or broom handle is then inserted between his legs and arms, going over his arms and under his bent knees; a gag is then placed in his mouth and tied firmly behind his head. In this helpless condition, unable to move hand, foot or tongue, he is left for a series of hours or even days according to the feelings of his tormentor.[29]

Other punishments included flogging, being forced to march incessantly with weighted knapsacks, confinement in an iron collar with inward-facing prongs that made it impossible to lay down and sleep, and branding with the letter *M* for "mutineer" or *D* for "deserter."[30]

In Jacksonian America, men were supposed to be autonomous citizens, not subject to arbitrary authority. Corporal punishment implied a certain degree of feminization and above all a lack of autonomy. It was something to which men subjected domestic animals and, even worse, slaves. Officer Abner Doubleday later wrote that his experience taught him corporal punishment "destroys the manhood of the soldiers and makes the service little better than the old fashioned slave pens," while after witnessing a military flogging Thomas Tennery wrote that "it chills one's blood to see free born Americans tied up and whipped like dogs." The association with slavery could be explicit, as Reeves describes how men were restrained in degrading positions and had their faces blacked.[31] Regular army soldiers chafed at corporal punishments, which they saw as evidence not only that officers despised them but that officers wanted them to blindly obey like machines or animals. Enlisted men tried to surreptitiously alleviate the punishments of fellow soldiers, and they sometimes tried to murder particularly brutal officers. A few literate regular soldiers used their memoirs to expose the army's brutality and hypocrisy to the American public.[32] Soldiers also sang satirical songs such as the following:

> Come all Yankee soldier, give ear to my song;
> It is a short ditty, 'twill not keep you long;
> It's of no use to fret on account of our luck,
> We can laugh, drink, and sing yet in spite of the buck
>
> Derry down &c.

> "Sergeant, buck him and gag him," our officers cry
> For each trifling offence which they happen to spy;
> Till with bucking and gagging of Dick, Tom and Bill,
> Faith, the Mexican ranks they have helped fill.
>
> Derry down &c.

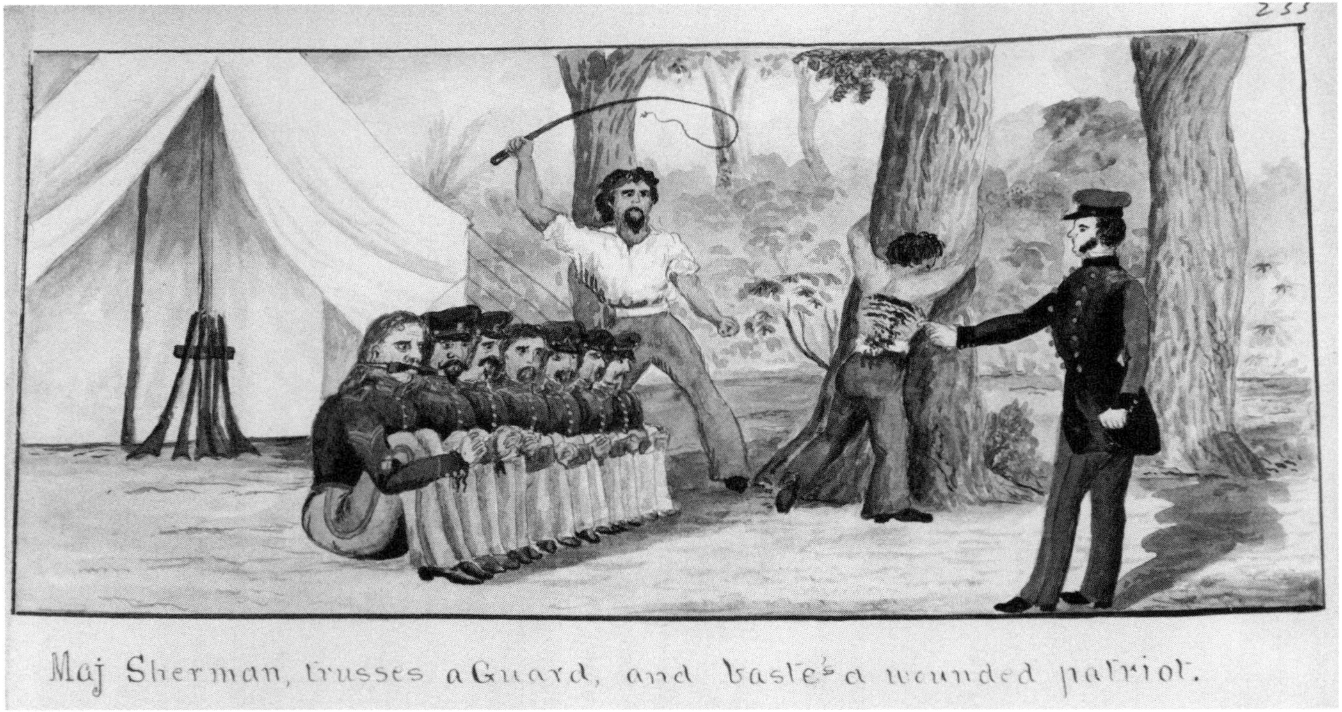

Maj Sherman, trusses a Guard, and bastes a wounded patriot.

FIG. 1.2   Bucked and gagged soldiers witness a flogging. Drawing by Samuel Chamberlain.

The treatment they give us, as all of us know,
Is bucking and gagging for whipping the foe;
They buck us and gag us for malice or spite,
But they're glad to release us when going to fight.

Derry down &c.

A poor soldier's tied up in the sun or the rain,
With a gag in his mouth till he's tortured in pain;
Why I'm bless'd, if the eagle we wear on our flag,
In its claws shouldn't carry a buck and a gag.

Derry down &c.[33]

In an extreme case Private John Kennedy shot himself in the hand to force the army to release him because he could no longer take the constant physical abuse.[34]

Officers often saw their men as brutes and inferiors who had to be motivated by fear of punishment, but there is a great deal of evidence that the men saw themselves differently. For them, the army was first and foremost a difficult and sometimes dangerous job they had contracted to do. It is not at all surprising they associated the army more with work than fighting, as in peacetime regular army men were certainly put to work. Training itself could be a form of work, as soldiers practiced in the hot sun with heavy packs and muskets and bayonets. At the western posts from which most of Taylor's force was gathered, soldiers also cut trees, grew crops, and built roads, bridges, barracks, and forts. As a young officer on the frontier, Taylor wrote that soldiers used axes, picks, saws, and trowels more than they did their weapons.[35] As contract laborers, soldiers felt that they could and should protest if the army did not uphold the promises made when they were recruited. Frederick Zeh describes the case of a comrade who refused to perform guard duty because the men had not been issued food for three days and had not been paid for four months.[36] Others protested with their feet. Ballentine believed that most desertion happened when soldiers felt like their contracts were being violated, and this is confirmed by the testimony of deserters.[37]

The army had a nearly insatiable appetite for new recruits because it had a very difficult time keeping men. Constant desertion kept the army habitually understrength. Between 1820 and 1860 around 14 percent of regular army soldiers deserted every year. In many ways this desertion reflected the men's position as laborers in a changing national economy. Laborers were accustomed to constantly leaving jobs to take advantage of new opportunities and remove themselves from situations where wages were low or they were mistreated.[38] Here the army's penchant for corporal punishment did not help its retention efforts. This mobility was so pronounced that it was not uncommon for a soldier to desert one unit and later join another if he did not fare well in the civilian economy.[39] The army, however, was in a particularly unfavorable geographic situation. As previously mentioned, most urban laborers were trapped in eastern cities because they lacked the money needed to migrate to the frontier. Potential recruits knew that army postings were often on the frontier, so many accepted their enlistment bonuses and let the army transport them to western posts, where they promptly deserted and disappeared into the civilian economy.[40] Regular army soldiers continued to desert during the 1846–1848 war at roughly the same rate as before the war.[41] Soldiers who absented themselves from their units during the war fell into two distinct categories. Some basically took vacations from military service, leaving their units for binges of drinking and partying that they called "sprees." It seems that their emotional release outweighed their later punishment, as many of these men returned voluntarily after a few days, perhaps when they ran out of liquor money and sobered up.[42] Others left the army in the hopes of bettering their economic circumstances in the Mexican economy, something that we will return to later.

Urban laborers who entered the regular army brought with them ideas about masculinity. They lived a masculine sociability that stressed their independence and centered on drinking, demonstrations of physical strength during the workday, brawling, and raucous amusements.[43] Recruits gave up large measures of one masculine value, their independence, but they were able to reproduce many other aspects of their masculinity in the new setting. Life for enlisted men in the U.S. regular army had a definite rough-and-tumble quality.[44] It seems that in the army, as in civilian life, alcohol made difficult conditions seem more tolerable, but it also contributed to the violence. In court-martial cases, one gets the sense that men believed that they needed to project toughness to earn their comrades' respect. Men argued or "jawed" with each other, they got into fistfights with other enlisted men or even corporals or sergeants, and in all of this they employed much rough language.[45]

Army camps and barracks were a very male environment, but the authorities recognized that cleanliness was important to soldiers' health. Each company was allowed four laundresses. These women were almost invariably soldiers' wives, and they were allowed to draw army rations. They were also paid for washing the clothes of the men. In this way living in the army was like living in a laborer's camp on a canal project: some of the work that women would have done as domestic partners was done for multiple men in exchange for money. Not surprisingly, soldiers report that some laundresses, though married, sold sexual favors. We know that some of the laundresses for Taylor's units accompanied the army as far as the Rio Grande, but after that they were left behind as the army proceeded farther into Mexico.[46] Men report that without the laundresses, the washing was done much less often, although sometimes they were able to pay Mexican women to wash their clothes.

The army was very hierarchical. There was a yawning social gulf between officers and enlisted men. Officers were from middle- or upper-class families. Although many of the older officers had been appointed directly to the officer corps, a substantial portion of the younger officers were graduates of West Point, which made them some of the most educated men in the young republic. Both direct appointment to the officer corps and admission to West Point were only available to relatively educated young men with access to political influence. Thus service as an officer was beyond the reach of talented but impoverished men. In the U.S. regular army literate enlisted men were only able to become officers through very rare promotions for exemplary courage and skill on the battlefield.[47] Officers enforced their authority with brutal punishments and kept great social distance from enlisted men, something that many enlisted men deeply resented.[48] Soldiers also chafed when officers received plaudits for the battlefield exploits, and sacrifices, of the men under their command. Reeves, for instance, bitterly wrote that any officer lauded for capturing enemy cannon usually "had to walk over the dead bodies of his own men before he could get in to claim the great feat."[49] Enlisted men tended to interpret the power of officers and the social gulf that separated them from the ranks using one of two social models for hierarchy that were common in nineteenth-century American society. Officers whose exercise of power was arbitrary and who lorded it over their men were said to treat their men like slaves, while officers who were fair and tried to look after the needs of their men were seen as acting like fathers.[50]

Bridging the huge gap between the officers and the enlisted men well enough for the army to work and fight was the function of sergeants and corporals. These men were called noncommissioned officers because they led other men but did not hold official commissions. In the U.S. Army of the 1840s, the officers commanding companies decided who would serve as sergeants and corporals. A soldier became a sergeant or corporal through unusually effective service in the enlisted ranks, practical intelligence, literacy, and a degree of moral or physical authority that suggested to the officers that the other men would take orders from him. They were crucial intermediaries who needed to be literate enough to handle most routine paperwork about personnel and equipment but who also needed to excel in the rough-and-tumble social world of the enlisted men. Sergeants and corporals sorted out many problems and meted out much discipline informally with their fists, without the noxious paperwork of a court-martial or, perhaps more importantly for the men, bringing down the extremely harsh corporal punishment that officers could mete out. Sergeants and corporals who could not train men effectively and keep order rapidly found themselves back in the ranks. Service in these roles provided a small increase in pay and probably more informal benefits but was onerous enough that many men were uninterested.[51]

Infantry training stressed the commands and movements that were needed to maneuver large groups of men in a coherent fashion, as well as the use of the infantryman's principal weapon, the muzzle-loading smoothbore musket. Muskets were both inaccurate and slow to load, and for more than a century officers had understood that they were most effective in battle when fired in coordinated volleys at close range. Thus soldiers were forced to memorize the complicated loading process under the watchful eyes of officers and noncommissioned officers and move together under their orders. Rapid loading, cohesion, and discipline were the keys to success on the battlefield, and units that could continue their routine amid the clouds of smoke and terrific noise of battle as their men were killed or maimed were prized. Extreme methods of corporal punishment were considered necessary to achieve this result. Fredrick the Great, one of the most widely read and admired military leaders of the age, believed that the dangers of the battlefield were so great that soldiers would only face them effectively if they feared punishment by their own officers more than those dangers. In his words, "Good will can never induce the common soldier to stand up to such dangers: he will only do so through fear."[52] Cavalrymen and artillerymen were taught to use different weapons, but they faced similar levels of danger and the psychology of their training was similar: it was aimed at conditioning them to manage their weapons and work together under orders despite the chaos and violence of battle.

Comradeship was at least as important as fear in making effective soldiers. Officers encouraged group pride. Each regiment had a battle flag that symbolized its identity, and men took extraordinary risks to protect regimental flags from capture.[53] Men fought with the men with whom they had eaten, slept, marched, caroused, and trained for months if not years. This closeness made such groups of men like families—they might harbor internal conflicts, but they faced external threats together. Love could be a powerful motivator in battle. Soldiers not only fought with these men, they fought for them and, perhaps more importantly, under their gazes. In the words of Ballentine, "Soldiers are keenly sensitive to the ridicule of their companions, whose good opinion they usually esteem more highly than that of their officers. To stand well in the estimation of his special comrades, and of the company to which he belongs is the most powerful incentive to a soldier's good conduct in the field of action; and in the absence of a bold officer to lead them to the attack, the love of Bill, Tom, or Harry's approbation or the dread of being called a coward has often been the means of gaining a battle."[54] These fraternal bonds, so often described in soldiers' own words in the literature of war, are staples of the soldier's existence, and they would be crucial to the experience of the men who marched with Taylor from Corpus Christi toward Matamoros.

The Mexican Regular Army

When Taylor's army reached the Rio Grande opposite Matamoros, it was already several hundred miles past the Nueces River, which the Mexican government and even many Americans believed was the boundary of Texas. In other words, a foreign army had not only occupied a region that Mexico saw as a rebel province, it had advanced beyond the borders of that province farther into Mexico. This advance did not surprise Mexican politicians and officers. Polk was not fooling anyone. Mexican officials in New Orleans had reported the plan to station troops at Corpus Christi before the first American soldier arrived there, and they had reported the plan to eventually move them to the Rio Grande in September 1845, months before Taylor marched.[55] During the years since Texas's independence, Mexican politicians had repeatedly tried to concentrate troops nearby for a campaign of reconquest. During the long American discussion of Texas's annexation, these expensive and difficult troop movements had gradually become more oriented toward the task of maintaining Mexican sovereignty along the Texas border. This evolution was quite gradual, and months after the war with the United States began, some Mexican politicians, journalists, and officers continued to refer to the war as the Texas war and to American soldiers as Texans.[56]

The Mexican force that existed at Matamoros represented an enormous effort on the part of its members, the Mexican government, and many Mexican civilians. The Mexican economy was much less productive than that of the United States, and thus collecting the resources needed to build military forces represented a comparatively greater financial burden on Mexicans. However, that was only the tip of the iceberg. The Mexican government faced a stark geographic problem. The Texas border was separated from most of Mexico's population and the bulk of its economy by wide spaces with scarce rainfall. Growing corn, Mexico's staple crop, with the moisture from rainfall alone was a reasonable proposition in central Mexico, stretching continuously almost as far north as the mining city of San Luis Potosí, several hundred miles south of the Rio Grande. However, from there it was at least a two-week journey through harsh deserts to the region of Saltillo and Monterrey, where some agriculture was again possible. From Monterrey a further two-week journey through harsh terrain brought one to the Rio Grande valley. The desert, where food and water for soldiers and grazing for their animals were very scarce, formed a formidable barrier between the parts of Mexico where troops could be recruited and supplied and the region where Mexican troops confronted Taylor in 1846. Moreover, any troops and supplies transported by sea would have to move hundreds of miles over rough terrain to ports and then cross a Gulf of Mexico controlled by the United States Navy.

For this reason San Luis Potosí, though never invaded by the United States, was an absolutely crucial location in this war. Capital city of the state of the same name, it was the organizing and jumping-off point for just about every military force Mexico sent north, first to garrison Texas before independence, then to try to subdue the Texas rebels or reconquer the rebel province, and finally to defend against the United States.[57] Evidence of this importance is seen in the attitudes of Mexican soldiers. They knew that marching north from San Luis Potosí meant facing serious risk of death through hunger and thirst because for long stretches they would have to rely on the food and water they could carry, never a particularly attractive option for armies before the advent of powered transport. Mexican soldiers were generally believed to be brave and were also considered to be among the hardiest marchers in the world. Yet on three occasions, in August 1845, March 1846, and August 1846, the enlisted men of different Mexican units publicly protested orders to march north from San Luis Potosí, specifically citing the hardships and risks involved in crossing the deserts. In the first episode, there are indications that officers encouraged the men's resistance for political reasons, but the second two episodes seem to have only involved enlisted men. These were episodes of passive resistance, although passive resistance by heavily armed men was in each case a tense affair. Each time the men were eventually persuaded to follow orders and undergo the hardships of the dreaded northern deserts, but their reluctance is telling.[58]

The roughly five thousand troops that awaited Taylor in Matamoros in April 1846 included many of the men who had initially balked at crossing the deserts. It did not, however, include other men whose movement north had been short-circuited by one of the most damaging miscalculations that any Mexican politician made in the nineteenth century. In 1845 President José Joaquín de Herrera had tried to steer a moderate course between radical federalists who wanted more decentralization of power and more equality of opportunity and centralists who wanted stronger guarantees for property and social hierarchy. Herrera also understood that the recovery of Texas was very unlikely and that preventing further U.S. aggression was imperative. He thus devoted a large proportion of the limited fiscal and organizational capacity of Mexico's national state to preparing troops to send to northern Mexico. Most of those troops were put under the command of General Mariano Paredes y Arrillaga in San Luis Potosí.[59] Paredes had orders to organize his twelve thousand men and then take them to Monterrey, where they could be held as a reasonably well-fed and well-supplied reserve ready to reinforce the troops along the Rio Grande if it became necessary. Strategically, this was not a terrible idea. Maintaining a respectable force at the Rio Grande and a larger force within striking distance at Monterrey, where it would be easier to feed them, might have been enough to deter the United States.

Unfortunately, Paredes believed that property and hierarchy were at significant risk in Mexico and that a strong leader like himself was needed to save them. He also simply did not believe that the United States would actually invade Mexico. In his view the gathering of a U.S. army in Texas was only a show of force to deter Mexican attempts to reannex the rebel province.[60] Given this, why should he not use the strongest military force in the country, the troops gathered under his command at San Luis Potosí, to take his rightful turn as president? He was encouraged in his beliefs by a highly placed group of Mexicans and foreigners who believed that Mexico's internal peace, prosperity, and property could be best safeguarded by the abandonment of republicanism and the introduction of a monarchy.

Thus, Paredes decided to use the troops gathering at San Luis Potosí to save Mexico from an internal threat, not a foreign one. This new plan required him to covertly prepare the ground and wait for the right moment to declare his intentions. So, rather than march to Monterrey, he repeatedly stated that he had not yet been given enough money to properly equip and supply his troops.[61] These arguments allowed him to claim that Herrera was lukewarm about fighting the United States. Meanwhile, Paredes negotiated with the monarchists, who were his wealthiest and most influential potential supporters.[62] Simultaneously, centralists spread rumors that Herrera was favoring radical federalists or even that the radical federalists would arm the poor of Mexico City to back his administration. Paredes also lined up support among various officers for his impending coup.[63] In December 1845 he was finally ready. He claimed that Herrera's administration was opening the door to anarchy and assaults on property, and that it had starved the army of the resources needed to confront the United States.[64] Paredes took his force south to Mexico City, forcing Herrera out of office. He kept some men there to safeguard his rule, and dispersed the rest in small groups in various parts of Mexico to keep opponents in line.[65] Opponents emerged almost immediately, as many politicians saw through Paredes's declarations of patriotism to the mostly naked ambition that lay underneath, and some spread news of his heretofore clandestine connections with the monarchists.[66]

Paredes's decision to use the army under his orders to make himself president rather than reinforce the troops who ended up toe to toe with an expansionist United States had a profound impact on the events of the next two years. If he had understood how aggressive the Polk administration was prepared to be, he might have acted differently. If his troops had been in Monterrey as planned, they could have marched quickly from Monterrey to Matamoros once the government understood that Taylor was crossing the generally accepted boundary of Texas. Instead they were simply too far away and too scattered to be a factor. Thus there were only about five thousand Mexican troops in Matamoros when Taylor arrived at the opposite bank of the Rio Grande, rather than what could have easily been ten thousand or more. A larger force would probably have been enough to deny Taylor the early victories that encouraged Polk to pursue his ambitions, though it is also possible that American defeats in those first battles might have only spurred Polk on.

The vast majority of the Mexican soldiers at Matamoros belonged to regular army or "active militia" units. Active militia units were only theoretically militia: their rank-and-file soldiers were recruited in the same way that regular soldiers were, their officers were professionals, and the units had been mobilized more or less permanently years before. Their principal difference from regular army units was that the units had geographic names that indicated their original headquarters and the origins of most of their troops.[67] Our brief discussion of Mexican politics has undoubtedly given a pretty unflattering picture of the officer corps. The oldest officers had fought in the 1810s as insurgents or royalists during the Mexican War of Independence. Some of the former royalist officers were Spaniards who had decided in the end that allegiance to an independent Mexico was preferable to continued affiliation with a weak and factious Spanish state.[68] Like their American counterparts, these officers were educated in the tactics of Napoleonic-era conventional warfare, in which battles were won by the proper placement and maneuvering of disciplined infantry, artillery, and cavalry, all wielding muzzle-loading gunpowder weapons. Many had military experience in Mexico's myriad internal armed conflicts, in which tactics ranged from small-scale versions of formal battles to guerrilla warfare.

Mexican officers had political beliefs, and political connections were important to military careers. Ideologically, former insurgents tended to favor more egalitarian versions of what Mexico should be, and former royalists tended toward commitment to more hierarchical forms, although there were exceptions. The independence war was more than twenty years in the past, and the officer corps had welcomed many new men since then. Some were graduates of Mexico's military academy, which had a curriculum not unlike West Point's, but many more had obtained commissions through family and political connections.[69] Some were first commissioned as militia officers but then moved into the regular army when they showed military or political aptitude.[70] Political connections were needed to advance, which made Mexico's army like most armies of its day.[71] The effect of Mexico's continual parade of armed political conflicts on the officer corps was paradoxical. It probably did not improve the average quality of officers, since backing the winning side was at least as important as military effectiveness in gaining promotion.[72] It did, however, allow for more social mobility both within the officer corps and, interestingly enough, *into* the officer corps. Unlike their American counterparts, many Mexican officers had begun their careers as enlisted men. Mexican enlisted men who became effective soldiers, decided that they liked military life, and pleased their superiors could become corporals and sergeants and then climb from there into the lower and even middling ranks of the officer corps.[73]

Most corporals and sergeants did not reach such lofty heights, yet, as in all armies, they were the sinews that held the army together. Noncommissioned officers were usually promoted from within the ranks. As in the U.S. Army, literacy was necessary, since sergeants did quite a lot of routine paperwork.[74] Accepting promotion meant accepting responsibility for not only leading but also training other men, and this could be a rough-and-tumble business. Musket drills were taught by corporals wielding sticks to provide quick physical correction for errors, and soldiers who resented the disciplinary role of sergeants sometimes sought opportunities to retaliate physically. For instance, one night in 1845 Private Felipe Delgado and First

Sergeant Damasio Guzmán both tried to pass at the same time on a narrow city sidewalk. Delgado shoved Guzmán off the sidewalk. When Guzmán reprimanded Delgado for not respecting his rank, Delgado responded with obscene words, adding that in the light Guzmán was a first sergeant but in the dark he was just like everyone else.[75]

The vast majority of Mexican soldiers came from very poor families because the vast majority of Mexicans were very poor.[76] Only a few Mexican soldiers actually volunteered for service in the regular army. In the United States, joining the army could be the best option available in a rickety working-class economy. Opportunities for Mexico's poor were even sparser than they were for the poor in the United States, but the army still was not attractive because the Mexican government was also poor. Although soldiers were supposed to receive both a small wage and money for food, payment of these amounts was extremely irregular. Few volunteered to be constantly hungry, so instead the Mexican government drafted men, enlisting them for six-year terms.[77]

Actually, it is somewhat misleading to say that the *Mexican* government drafted men. Like other early modern central governments, it had neither the bureaucracy nor the technology to identify individuals. Instead Mexico's national government assessed its needs for military manpower and then assigned each state a quota of men based on its estimated population.[78] Each state then assigned part of the quota to every locality, again based on population estimates. States would also instruct local officials about the general qualities they expected to see in recruits.[79] These quotas presented local officials with a difficult problem even in the best of times, but the number of men needed became even larger as tensions with the United States increased.[80] Sometimes a local official successfully asked to have his locality's quota reduced because its people faced unusual burdens or because the locality included many indigenous people. Army officers did not consider Indians desirable recruits because it was easier to train soldiers who already spoke Spanish. This preference became weaker once the war started and the army's need for men increased dramatically.[81]

Local officials did not like providing men for the army. These officials were typically elected or appointed from among their locality's literate professionals or businessmen, including agricultural entrepreneurs. Men like this had a vested interest in protecting the local supply of labor, and they felt that the draft made labor scarce.[82] Some were particularly concerned by the fact that many potential recruits owed money to their employers, as it was common for employers to attract workers by advancing them cash or goods against their wages.[83] Local officials also worried about the consequences of removing breadwinners from the families that relied on them. This empathy did not conflict with their class interests, as securing a region's long-term labor supply required creating conditions under which families could survive and reproduce.[84] Officials in northern regions struggling to maintain enough population to fend off Indian attacks were particularly vexed by the demands of the draft.[85] Thus local officials sometimes responded to recruitment quotas by alleging that they could not find the required men, or could not do so without causing excessive damage to the local economy.[86] Other times they simply claimed that no men were available.[87]

Local officials usually still had to come up with men for the army. They first turned to men who had already been enlisted but who had deserted. Thus, every new recruitment drive initiated a hunt for deserters. In fact, the family of a new conscript could get him exempted by turning in a deserter.[88] Still, there were never enough deserters to fill the quotas. Sometimes officials forcibly recruited men who were passing through their localities, but there were never enough such men.[89] Since state and local officials effectively decided both the general categories of men targeted and the specific men selected, they used that power to try to protect local economies and local society as well as they could. In recruitment they found they had a powerful tool to get rid of the men they most wanted to get rid of, men who behaved badly and were not productive. State governments often issued explicit rules about what categories of men should be drafted, but whether or not they did, local officials universally drafted those whom they considered, in the words of the town council of San Pedro, San Luis Potosí, "the men most damaging to the population."[90] Sometimes officials used recruitment to rid themselves of their political opponents, especially those who organized lawsuits or complaints.[91] More often officials sent the military men who had been convicted of serious crimes. Crimes that might result in a sentence of military service included assault, rape, robbery, and unlawful possession of weapons.[92] Yet, since Mexico was far less crime-ridden than is sometimes assumed, there were still not enough men to fill the ranks.

Caught between orders to send men to the army, on the one hand, and the imperative to protect the labor supply and the survival of families, on the other, local officials tried to target those men who were least useful to the economy and least useful to their families. Fortunately for them, these two sets of men were actually the same—men who did not work were useless to both employers and their families. The rules different states gave local officials to guide their efforts were very consistent. They specified that those drafted should include *vagos* (bums), the argumentative, those who did not work very much, unmarried sons who did not support their aged parents or younger siblings, those who did not support their wives, and those who engaged in excessive domestic violence. As one official put it in 1846, a man could be conscripted if he was "totally useless to society," and sending such men would "purge the villages of vicious people."[93] Thus it is not surprising that, when selecting recruits, officials first looked in "the billiards parlors, bars, parties and other places of amusement."[94] Often they chose men less for specific acts for which they had been convicted than on the basis of their public reputations.[95]

What kind of reputation could make local officials decide that a man should be removed from the population and sent to the regular army? Many of these men were seen as prone to boasting, loud arguments, and fighting.[96] Some were viewed as disrespectful of official authority, men who were inclined to resist officials who scolded or attempted to arrest them.[97] Others were drafted because they had reputations as thieves.[98] It is easy to see how local officials who were required to round up a certain number of men for the army would be eager to rid their jurisdictions of men with these kinds of reputations.

Gender and Conscription

The vast majority of the reasons given for the forced recruitment of these men were explicitly gendered, as they were closely related to how they behaved *as men*. Officials believed that peace and prosperity depended on the existence of stable nuclear families, in which a married couple successfully raised children to adulthood, and these children in turn supported their parents in their old age. Men who damaged this pattern were seen as pernicious to society, and recruitment drives offered opportunities to get rid of them. There were many ways in which men could damage this pattern, and some were explicitly sexual. Men who slept with the wives of other men were damaging family harmony, as were married men who slept with anyone other than their own wives. In the words of officials, Antonio Ysaguirre was drafted because he had "unsettled marriages," and Pedro Escobedo because he caused "the disunion of marriages." The use of the plural is worth noticing here: officials were particularly vexed by men who repeatedly engaged in such womanizing.[99] Some men were drafted simply for engaging in sexual relationships without marrying their partners, although here officials moved into a gray area. Poor people did not always have the economic resources needed to marry as soon as they might want to, and sometimes couples were functionally married long before any ceremony. Moreover, customs allowed premarital sex if it was preceded by the promise of marriage. Some of the men were drafted precisely for violating this promise, using it to seduce women and then not following through.[100] These customs were complicated further by the fact that parents were supposed to consent to their daughters' marriages. In many rural areas it was common for couples to elope, forcing parents to give ex post facto consent in order to restore the family's honor. Elopement cases could shade into sexual violence, partially because mores suggested that young women should feign reluctance to yield their honor, making it possible for men to rape women and argue that they were really only eloping.[101] Sometimes local officials used conscription to exile reputed rapists.[102]

A married man could be drafted even if he was not suspected of sexual infidelities. For example, men who abandoned their wives were often conscripted.[103] Additionally, a man's simply living with his wife did not fulfill gender norms. Surviving and reproducing required the work of both halves of the couple. Women contributed crucial domestic labor, cooking, cleaning, and minding children, and also often augmented the family income through handicrafts or selling agricultural surpluses at village markets. Men did the bulk of agricultural work, whether it was done on family land, communal land, rented land, or someone else's land in exchange for wages. Men who did not uphold their end of this crucial economic relationship were being irresponsible to their wives and children, and local officials often conscripted them.[104] This certainly served to enforce gender norms, but since local officials wanted to limit conscription's damage to families, it was perfectly logical to draft men who were not supporting their families anyway. Many officials also drafted men who assaulted their wives. Cultural norms clearly placed men at the heads of families, and it was believed that men could correct wives' misbehavior with physical punishment. However, such punishment was supposed to be limited in both frequency and degree, and when those limits were passed, a husband was seen as "giving his wife a bad life." Communities policed the boundary between acceptable and unacceptable domestic violence through gossip, intervention by the couples' parents or religious leaders, and the involvement of local officials who imposed fines, counseling, or short jail sentences to try to restore marital harmony. When these measures failed to end chronic abuse, officials sometimes consigned the men to the draft allotment.[105] This was another way the draft was used to enforce gender norms.

Men's gendered responsibilities were also intergenerational. Adults owed their parents obedience and respect, and as those parents became too old to provide for themselves, their children were supposed to support them.[106] Single men who did not have wives or children to support received a measure of protection from conscription if they provided economic support for elderly parents. Those who did not fulfill their cultural obligation to support their parents were drafted. Recruit Obispo Rodríguez, for example, was described as a man "very estranged from his elderly father, who he does not support or help at all," and Martin Castillo as "not helping his parents with what is needed for their subsistence."[107] Concern about the economic relationship between adult sons and their parents was difficult to separate mentally from concern about the other things sons owed their parents. Conscription documents often record comments about sons disrespecting or disobeying their parents. One official wrote of Sixto Ordaz that "his bad conduct has reached the extreme of failing to respect his father," and another wrote of Antonio Bracamontes that not only had he failed to support his parents, but his disrespectful behavior had reached the level of "once putting his hands on his father."[108] By the 1840s, more than twenty years after the beginning of forced recruitment for the Mexican army, the notion that it was associated with filial piety was so strong that some fathers turned in their own sons for army service, saying that the sons had developed bad habits and refused correction from their fathers.[109]

Even bad habits that do not on the face of it seem to be connected to the gendered obligations of family life were seen that way by nineteenth-century Mexicans. Gambling was a common entertainment in nineteenth-century Mexico, and in fact Antonio López de Santa Anna, Mexico's most famous general and politician, was known to love gambling.[110] However, recruitment documents often mention gambling, because excessive gambling could lead a man to neglect his financial responsibilities to his family. It both took a man away from work and wasted money the family needed.[111] Drunkenness was another bad habit that interfered with a man's gendered obligations. Depending on region and social class, Mexicans imbibed a number of alcoholic beverages, from the mildly alcoholic pulque to various forms of distilled liquor. No one begrudged Mexican males, or, for that matter, females, a convivial drink. However, some men drank to excess and did so repeatedly. Such a man had lost control of himself. A habitual drunk was likely to miss work, diminishing the family income, and a man who drank up all of his earnings would give little to his wife for necessary expenses. Officials were very explicit about these connections. One said of Sisto Ramirez that he "never supported his family as was his duty but instead occupied himself in wine shops and bars drinking without dedicating himself to honest work."[112] Excessive drinking and excessive gambling were linked to argumentativeness, thievery, and laziness in a complex of behaviors that together led public opinion and authorities to label some men as *vagos*. Some wandered from place to place looking for ways to steal or perhaps earn a little money that they could quickly spend on their pleasures. Whether wanderers or rooted in local communities, such men damaged the social fabric by not supporting wives and children, and the draft offered officials a way to get rid of them.[113] In many cases officials stated that they only sent men to the army after repeated warnings and minor punishments. They saw these behaviors as bad habits that men could and should control. When youths began to develop such habits, officials sometimes warned their fathers to correct them to prevent future conscription, although in one case an official eagerly shipped off Julián Silva, a badly behaved fourteen-year-old, pointing out that, despite his youth, he could be useful as a fifer or bugler, roles that early modern armies typically assigned to underage recruits.[114]

The system under which local officials directly chose the men used to fill their manpower quotas was called the *leva* (levy). Local officials, often in consultation with the leading men of their area and parish priests, were able to select pretty much whomever they thought could be best spared by society. As we have seen, they mostly selected men who did not behave as responsible workers and providers, or men who violated gender norms through sexual behavior. Earlier, in the absence of the army's need for men, local officials had sought to reduce these kinds of problems through reprimands and mild punishments. They might sentence misbehaving men to a couple of weeks in jail, make them pay the costs of childbirth for their illegitimate children, insist that lovers formalize their relationship with marriage, warn serial domestic abusers to moderate their behavior, or insist that the seducers of young women compensate them with a dowry to make them more attractive to other potential marriage partners. In all of these situations officials sought to restore harmony and protect the institution of nuclear families.[115] With the pressure to provide men, officials often used the same conflicts to fill their quotas. The draft was actually a double-edged sword in the fight to preserve nuclear families. It gave local officials a very powerful threat to correct the behavior of men, as few wanted to be taken from the life they knew to face the discipline, risks, and hunger characteristic of army service. However, the act of conscription in itself removed the possibility that men could be made to responsibly provide for their families.

Army officers believed that the *leva* yielded recruits that were less healthy and less honest than average Mexicans. They also preferred to avoid drafting rootless men, because if they deserted they were more difficult to find than men who felt affinities to their communities and families. Some officers also claimed that the *leva* was unjust because it gave too much arbitrary power to local officials. In the late 1830s the army tried to replace the *leva* with a draft lottery. Yet even this law shows how gender categories were used to limit the impact of forced recruitment on families. Those whose names were placed in the lottery included single men or widowers without children, married men who did not "make life with their wives," and married men without children. Men within these three groups were excepted if they lived with and supported aged parents, or supported sisters or brothers too young to fend for themselves.[116] More importantly, regional and local governments consistently thwarted this law, either by openly writing conscription regulations that borrowed the lottery's categories but did not actually refer to the operation of a lottery, or by informally continuing the *leva*.[117]

Local officials preferred to have the power to choose who would be removed from society. They were also aware that having regular army service decided by chance would conflict with ideas that had become ingrained not only in their minds but also in the minds of most Mexicans of every social class. Decades of conscripting dishonest troublemakers who did not properly fulfill their roles as masculine providers had made army service disreputable. Honor was extremely important not only to upper-class Mexicans who mostly associated it with lofty birth but also to lower-class Mexicans who believed that maintaining a family through honest work and behaving respectably gave them honor. This reputation could be very important for poor families, not only because it afforded them a measure of self-worth but also because they engaged in many economic transactions that depended on trust.[118] By the 1840s being chosen for regular army service had become a mark of dishonor. Local official Luis Alvarez insisted in 1844 that "no honest man with an active and honest job can be destined for military service."[119] Not surprisingly, those who protested their conscription or that of their relatives often referred to the honor and honesty of the unfortunate recruits.[120]

The idea that Mexican recruits were dishonest quasi-criminals was reinforced by their treatment after selection. From the dispersed localities where they were chosen, recruits were funneled toward larger and larger towns until they were handed over to the army in the capitals of their states. This sad journey took place on foot, and to prevent recruits from fleeing during transit, they were roped together, with their hands tied behind their backs. Through all of this they were guarded by armed and often mounted men. When they stopped for the night, they were housed in local jails, and if a jail was not handy, they were placed in the most secure building available. Although they were fed, little care was taken for their comfort. In general the recruits' pilgrimages, if we can call them that, followed the routes taken by prisoners accused of serious crimes, who were also sent along this way to state capitals for sentencing. In fact, recruits were often moved with such prisoners.[121]

Recruits and their families did not passively accept their fates. They could appeal to state governors for their release, and thousands did, but it was far from easy. Appeals were accepted in written form, so at the very least the recruit or, more often, his family had to pay a scribe to write up their petition. Sometimes they could do this in a nearby town, but if that was not possible the petitioner had to walk to the state capital, which could take days. In her appeal Maria Bonifacia Gutierrez from Tancanhuitz, San Luis Potosí, tells of "having to travel following the fate of my husband to see where he ended up. After a passing through many sufferings, labors, and discomforts resulting from this long road, leaving without support three young minor children, such that one died, because they, like I, have no other means of support than the personal labor of their absent father."[122] Why would anyone go to such trouble? Bonifacia's complaint itself provides half of the answer. Losing a man to the army impoverished many poor families to the point that it placed them on the brink of starvation. Mexican society lacked any social safety net beyond the little help that extended families that were also poor could provide.[123] The appeals have a heartrending quality to them, as wives and aged parents vividly explain the fate that awaits them if they cannot rely on the support of the men who were drafted. As distressing as this is, the other half of the answer is that in fact state governors often granted these appeals. It is impossible to calculate the percentages because, although many petitions in archives are marked to indicate that they were granted or denied, most have no notation at all. State governors balanced their own humanity against the army's need for men, and they often sent appeals back to local authorities for investigation, understanding that the information in them could be faked.[124] Family members mobilized respectable local officials, priests, and employers to attest the honesty of the men and their dutiful fulfillment of family obligations, just as the conscription process itself relied on local officials who could investigate the reputations of potential recruits. Often there was clearly an aspect of patronage at work, as those who supported appeals included employers, but many of the letters written in support of appeals suggest a degree of compassion.[125]

Sometimes petitions and the letters that supported them criticized the process. Families claimed that local enemies had spread rumors about recruits, officials targeted political enemies for recruitment, or local officials were simply prejudiced against the recruits.[126] Generally, even in these cases the core of the argument was about the kind of man the recruit was. Petitioners and their supporters argued that the recruits were not guilty of the behavior attributed to them, whether it consisted of sexual escapades, drunkenness, laziness, or failure to support their families. They insisted on the honor or honesty of recruits. Martin de Ortar, for instance, wrote that he had known recruit Pedro Arriaga "since his infancy, he has been an honorable man, attentive to his work, obedient to his mother," while Felito Benitez wrote of Eulalio Ortiz that he was "an orderly man of honorable conduct and good deeds who has never been stained by disagreeable notes, obedient to the law and to all authorities." Many referred to recruits as *hombres de bien,* or honorable men.[127] Petitions also stressed that these men supported their wives, children, elderly parents, or younger siblings, waxing eloquent about the economic devastation their absence would wreak on their families.[128] The army took men away, it fed and paid them irregularly, and there were no mechanisms that would allow a soldier to send part of his pay to support his family. Soldiers' widows and orphans did not receive pensions, although sometimes state governments collected donations for the relatives of especially heroic soldiers.[129]

The extreme poverty faced by lower-class Mexican women who lost their husbands to recruitment was the root cause of one of the most striking differences between American regular army units and their Mexican counterparts. As previously mentioned, American regular units were allowed a few laundresses, typically the wives of enlisted men, but these women were left behind once the invasion of Mexico started. American observers thus almost always remarked on the very large numbers of *soldaderas,* women who attached themselves to Mexican regular army units. Mexican units, in the words of Doubleday, were usually accompanied by "a perfect army of females."[130] These women were objects of curiosity, pity, and sometimes contempt. The curiosity stemmed from difference, the pity from the hard life of these women, and the contempt from Americans' belief that these were women of loose sexual morals, something Americans also believed of their own laundresses. Sometimes Americans even stated that the principal motive of camp followers was the chance to steal from the dead.[131] Although these women sometimes fought, the other services they provided were just as valuable. They acquired and prepared food, carried possessions, and often actually marched ahead of the men so that they could have food ready when the men reached camp. They also nursed wounded soldiers and provided sexual companionship.[132] The presence of these women is very easy to explain. The Mexican regular army could not attract volunteers because the impoverished Mexican government was not able to feed and clothe its soldiers well enough to make military service an attractive option even to the many Mexicans who were very poor. Yet, the equation was different for women. Their economic prospects were even worse than those of lower-class men, and those prospects depended almost entirely on partnerships with such men. A woman alone was unlikely to be able to earn enough for a secure supply of food and clothing. Thus, if a woman's husband was conscripted, following him and even bringing children along was often the best option available. Soldiers might be hungry, but hunger was better than literal starvation. Moreover, when units were stationed in cities, especially Mexico City, they were paid and clothed more regularly. This made it feasible for soldiers to have their wives with them, and it seems to have even made forming partnerships with soldiers attractive to some poor urban women.[133] As these units left relatively comfortable garrison life to march to different regions to face American forces, the best alternative for these women was to march with them, sharing their pay and rations, however scarce they became. Looking at the issue in these rather stark economic terms does not mean that there were not often genuine bonds of romance and affection between soldaderas and soldiers.

Given the devastation that military service meant for families, it is not surprising that recruits, their families, and their communities resisted the draft. News of draft drives caused some men to flee their villages and hide in the wilder parts of the countryside, or to migrate to neighboring regions with smaller recruitment quotas. Others rushed to marry to reduce their odds of being chosen.[134] Military service was particularly unpopular with indigenous peasants because life in indigenous villages relied on an orderly progression of service to one's father and community as a young man, marriage, and eventual

FIG. 1.3 American soldiers witness the passage of soldaderas. Drawing by Samuel Chamberlain.

status as a head of family and, later, a respected elder. Removing a young man from this situation meant that even if he later returned, he could never catch up with his peer group. During periods in which the military was turning away recruits who did not speak Spanish, bilingual Indians often feigned monolingualism.[135] Recruits often tried to flee, even attacking their guards to facilitate their escape.[136] The local officials charged with filling draft quotas were troubled by rumors of riots and rebellions. These rumors sometimes panned out. In the village of Santa Anna in San Luis Potosí, a local official reported that the friends and family of a recruit gathered to use their fists, stones, and knives in an effort to free him.[137]

The most accepted interpretation of the war argues that Mexicans lacked national consciousness, and it might be tempting to see the unpopularity of army service as evidence of this. However, as we have seen, even voluntary enlistment in the U.S. regular army was not seen by soldiers or the people who observed them as evidence of national consciousness. Moreover, even in Mexicans' appeals to free themselves or their relatives from military service, many acknowledged the importance of their duty to their nation. José Albino Hernandez, for instance, wrote in his appeal that "we were born for the patria and not for ourselves, and it is a sacred duty to loan it our services." Mexicans simply believed that that duty should not come before their duty to support their wives, children, aged parents, and younger siblings. In their minds, duty to family trumped duty to nation.[138] When you add that cultural imperative to the widespread notion that regular army service was the fate of disreputable men, it is not surprising that Mexicans avoided and resisted recruitment into the regular army.

Service in the Mexican Regular Army

One would think that an army composed mostly of impoverished conscripts who were either troublemakers or constantly worried about the fate of family members left behind would be an ineffective army, one that would simply melt away at the first sign of danger or hardship. However, that turns out not to be true. Certainly Mexican regular army soldiers could be a handful for civilian officials. Some carried the rough-and-tumble masculinity that landed them in the army not only into their relationships with their comrades but also into their relations with civilians. The hunger that came from military service to an impoverished government led them to steal food. Civilian officials occasionally complained of gambling and drunkenness in the streets near barracks. Like the soldiers of other armies, including the U.S. Army, Mexican soldiers commonly helped themselves to the possessions of enemies killed in battle. In extreme cases where discipline broke down and units disbanded after military defeats, fleeing troops looted openly.[139] Soldiers who victimized Mexican civilians posed a particular set of problems. They were often better armed than the officials who sought to arrest them, they could call on comrades to help them violently resist arrest, and, legally, they were entitled to be tried before military rather than civilian courts.[140] Sometimes Mexican civilians feared Mexican regular soldiers, while at other times tensions between local civilians and troops escalated to the point of open brawling between groups.[141]

Nevertheless, both Mexicans and Americans judged the military effectiveness of Mexican regular troops to be very high. Americans praised them for their training, their discipline, and above all their courage, which was notable in many of the battles that we will discuss later in this book.[142] Biases may have influenced these accounts, since American soldiers denigrating the courage of their vanquished enemies would minimize their own achievements, but given the propaganda about Mexican racial inferiority, one would not expect American soldiers to respect their opponents. A few American observers criticized Mexican soldiers as cowards, but they were the exceptions.[143] In memoirs written after a long and bloody military career, Ulysses Grant, a young officer in the war, criticized the organization of the Mexican army, with its forced recruits and lack of food, pay, and clothing, but he added that "with all of this I have seen as brave stands made by some of these men as I have ever seen made by soldiers."[144] Mexican soldiers were particularly known for their mobility and endurance. Their ability to quickly march long distances with little food and water astonished observers, especially when they went directly into battle afterward.[145]

How did reluctant soldiers who had often been ne'er-do-wells in civilian life become an effective army? As with their American counterparts, training and discipline were extremely important. Most training was done by sergeants and corporals, and it was backed with corporal punishment. In the first years of Mexico's existence as a republic, corporal punishment was seen as beneath the dignity of citizens, even those in the army. The prohibition of corporal punishment in the military was never effectively enforced, however, and an 1842 law restored its legality. Corporal punishment was common in the Mexican army. Soldiers were beaten with sticks or with the sheathed swords of officers. Twenty-five blows were often given for serious crimes like desertion, but there are accounts of soldiers being given far more.[146] More commonly corporal punishment was administered informally in smaller quantities to reinforce points being made in training or punish minor infractions. Generally one gets the impression that corporal punishment was neither as widespread nor as brutal as that seen in the American regular army, and leaders who used it excessively sometimes found themselves facing courts-martial.[147]

Most observers believed that discipline was less important than comradeship. Just as in the U.S. Army, soldiers came to feel deep bonds with the men with whom they lived, marched, and suffered. Circles of comradeship reached out to one's platoon, company, and regiment, in that order. The regimental flag embodied a regiment's identity and honor, and regiments whose flags were captured by the enemy considered it a mark of shame. Knowing that comradeship could be the difference between success and failure on the battlefield, how did the army foster it? The process is not very well documented, but some records are suggestive. Training deliberately stressed the importance of pride in one's unit, but the true keys seem to have been keeping men together throughout their service and using more experienced soldiers to mentor new recruits. Within regiments elite companies grouped the most experienced soldiers, and sergeants and corporals needed to supervise the new recruits in other companies were chosen from their ranks.[148] In the middle of the war, when every man was needed, the government not only offered amnesty to deserters, it gave deserters who returned to the army the right to serve with their old units.[149] These bonds of comradeship could be extremely strong. When José Saldivar was arrested for brawling twelve days after he was discharged from army service, he was accompanying a comrade from his unit to a bullfight, and they fought against men from another regiment. In another instance, two jailed sergeants asked to be transferred to their unit to serve the rest of their sentences, claiming the other military prisoners did not treat them well.[150] Mexican regular army soldiers may have been eloquent in their daily lives, but they did not write memoirs like some of their American counterparts. Their feelings about their comrades are generally undocumented. This lack of documents makes the judicial file about the death of soldier José Maria López extremely valuable. In 1844 López was with his good friend Manuel de la Cruz. Cruz took a nap, and while he was sleeping López took some coins from his pocket. When Cruz found out, he argued with López, and in the heat of the argument he stabbed López in the abdomen, producing a wound that both knew would lead to a lingering and painful death. Officers immediately interviewed the dying man, and he pointed out that he took the money as a joke, something he would not do if he were not Cruz's good friend. Cruz confirmed that López was his friend, saying that in three years of service in their unit, he had never argued with

López but that they instead had been intimate friends. López, the dying man, insisted that the crime had been an accident. He forgave Cruz and asked that Cruz not be punished because Cruz was his true friend. The love between these two friends was stronger than the lethal act of violence one committed against the other.[151]

The bonds of discipline and comradeship that held Mexican regular army units together were under constant stress even in peacetime, and the greatest cause of that stress was hunger. Mexican soldiers often only received part of the pay due to them, they often received inadequate clothing, and they were only fed part of the time. American lieutenant Theodore Laidley quite aptly referred to them as "half fed, half clothed, half paid."[152] However, pay, clothing, and food were more readily available to favored units stationed in the major cities. Revenues collected by the national government in these places were often enough to support troops, and even when they faltered it was possible to pressure wealthy individuals into loaning the necessary funds. If even that failed, officers might send troops out to earn money with their labor.[153] The situation for troops on the march was much worse. As previously mentioned, logistics plans relied on officers pulling together enough money to buy food from the people of the countryside their units marched through. Mexican troops knew that traversing areas with little rainfall and population meant deprivation that could be severe enough to kill some of them. While marching in the north, even officers went hungry.[154] These problems were severe before the war, and they became worse as the war simultaneously demanded the organization of larger military forces and destroyed government revenues. Throughout the period military service was seen as condemning the unfortunate recruits to hunger and inadequate clothing, a fact readily admitted by both generals and state governors.[155]

Mexican soldiers, like their U.S. counterparts, often left their units without permission. Frequently, these absences were temporary. Soldiers would essentially give themselves vacations to enjoy alcohol or other amusements, and then return to the ranks when their pockets were empty and their heads were sore. The situation became more serious when soldiers had committed acts for which they expected punishment.[156] Some soldiers left their units during battle. Officers and civil officials tended to call these men "dispersed" rather than deserters, perhaps to avoid having to deal out the kind of severe punishment that armies often imposed on those who fled in the face of the enemy. Other men deserted their units when they were retreating from the enemy, moments when both morale and resources were probably low. Yet, when we look at the numbers from different battles, they are often quite small even when we know that units essentially disbanded. That suggests that most men quickly returned to their units and few used the temporary dissolution of discipline as an opportunity to actually leave the army.[157]

The striking thing about desertion from the Mexican army, though, is how it was associated with hunger. Even when desertion happened in temporal proximity to battle, it happened most often on the hungry march toward the enemy or the even hungrier retreat.[158] Officers were convinced that the enemy was less a problem than hunger, and that soldiers most often left the ranks when they were not fed. Soldiers themselves corroborated this. Sergeant Rafael Quiñonez, for example, pointed out that various men from his unit deserted during one lean period when they were progressively given less and less pay and food.[159] The hunger of the soldiers themselves was duplicated by the hunger their families faced without them, and the latter could be a powerful factor motivating desertion. In 1845 Pomposo Hernández admitted to authorities that he had deserted, but added that he did so to support his family.[160] The hunger of both soldiers and their families was a factor in one of the most common comments officers made about desertion. Officers pointed out that men were most likely to desert in the first days, weeks, or months of their army experience. After that men became more accustomed to the irregular pay and rations and more attached to their companions. Francisco de Garay, for instance, complained to his superiors in 1847 that he had no money to pay and feed his troops, and that it was particularly difficult to get by without it when he did not have "men used to discipline and suffering, but instead men without military training, who have been forced to leave their homes, leaving their families in grief and misery." It seems as if during men's first weeks and months in the army, their families joined them in their new life, found new sources of support, or perished. After this period men were unlikely to desert to return to their families. The association between length of service and desertion seems to be borne out by personnel records.[161]

As we have seen, many of the men conscripted into the Mexican regular army already had dubious reputations, and officials felt that this was also a factor in desertion. Some men made a habit of deserting, selling their uniforms and weapons, and then repeating the process after they were caught.[162] The steady need for manpower made locating deserters and returning them to the army a constant preoccupation of the authorities. The gentlest method was the periodic declaration of amnesties for deserters, during which they were given a certain amount of time to turn themselves in and promised that they would be returned to the army and even their old units without punishment. Officials also offered bounties to civilians who turned in deserters, or ordered authorities in their hometowns to look for them. They allowed newly conscripted men to go free if their families denounced a deserter, and sometimes they discouraged civilians from hiding deserters by saying that any recruit who deserted would be replaced by a new recruit from the same village.[163] Generally one gets the impression that deserters were condemned to always look over their shoulders. Some people blamed the cycle of forced recruitment and desertion for making Mexico more lawless by ripping men out of their home environments and creating a floating population forced to live at the margin of the laws.[164] Despite all of these pressures, some people did hide deserters, moved by the plight of those forced into army service, or perhaps interested in the labor that deserters could provide, especially in the labor-starved north. Military authorities often suspected that their civilian counterparts were not doing everything possible to find deserters.[165]

The constant risk of desertion could have tactical consequences. Manuel Balbontín, author of the best memoir of the war by a Mexican officer, pointed out that the risk of desertion meant that Mexican officers were compelled to concentrate their soldiers in the field, not spreading them out in pickets or outposts that could serve to guard against surprise attacks.[166] This pattern might even have been a factor in two important battles, Cerro Gordo and Padierna or Contreras (which each military gave a different name to), when American units were able to flank Mexican units and get very close before surprising their counterparts.

The two armies that faced each other uneasily in the spring of 1846 were similar in important ways. Both were composed of men whom civilians despised as the dregs of society. Patriotism did not motivate their enlistment, as recruits for the American army were driven by economic hardship and their Mexican counterparts did not join voluntarily. Their units were made effective by strict and often violent discipline and the bonds of comradeship, both literally embodied in the sergeants and corporals who were the sinews of the army. Soldiers were known for a rough-and-tumble masculinity that was often lubricated by alcohol. Although both Mexico and the United States were in the throes of building new nation-states, regular soldiers were not seen as patriots or even, in many cases, as citizens.

The Mexican and American regular armies were far from unique. They were part of the long history of what we might think of as noncitizen armies, the most common type of army in the period in which muzzle-loading, smooth-bore muskets and cannon ruled the battlefields of the Western world. Armies emphasized discipline and rote training. It was not necessary that soldiers be motivated by patriotism, only that they act as ordered, and men who were forced into the ranks by hunger or conscripted by local authorities could be trained to do so.[167] These soldiers of the Mexican and American regular armies were very similar to counterparts who fought on battlefields from the steppes of Russia to the plains of Germany to the pampas of Argentina. Armies were commonly made of the dregs of society, disciplined with corporal punishment and held together by comradeship.[168] Although by the early nineteenth century some of these armies served governments that justified themselves as the representatives of nations, the armies themselves were not really national armies, and this was as true of the Russian army or the British army as it was of the Mexican and American armies.[169]

CHAPTER 2

We're the Boys for Mexico

In the spring of 1846 President James K. Polk ordered General Zachary Taylor to move his men from Corpus Christi to the banks of the river that Mexicans called the Rio Bravo and Americans called the Rio Grande. This was a deliberate provocation, as the boundary of Texas when it was still part of Mexico had been the Nueces River, much farther north. Yet, as Taylor's army marched past the Nueces, they found themselves in curiously empty territory. A few decades earlier this area had been inhabited by a substantial number of Mexicans who supported themselves by raising cattle, but in recent years it had become the target of raid after raid by Comanche warriors. The Comanche used the region as a reservoir of livestock and laborers that they drew on periodically for the needs of their empire on the southern Great Plains. The livestock was sold into the expanding economy of the United States, while the laborers helped tend livestock and process animal products for sale. The voracious market the American economy provided for horses, mules, hides, and even labor encouraged the Comanche to raid Mexican territory. The Mexicans had plenty of cattle but often could not defend the animals or even themselves. Forced to spread out by the same ecological conditions that supported ranching, the Mexican inhabitants of any given ranch or town could not gather together enough manpower to counter the Comanche's large war parties, and the fiscally weak and geographically distant Mexican government was in no position to provide substantial help.[1]

Comanche were funneling their loot into the expanding American economy, and this actually hampered the efforts of Mexican settlers to take advantage of the same market opportunities. Mexican inhabitants of the lower Rio Grande valley also had products that the American economy needed, and they had been drawn increasingly into that economy, especially through the port of Matamoros. These people were distant from the center of Mexico's notoriously unstable national state, which could do little for them. The northerners felt a significant attraction to American opportunities, which was only further fueled by the largely ineffectual efforts the Mexican state made to raise funds by taxing the trade through Matamoros. The military commanders that Mexico sent north suspected that local people were more attracted to the commercial possibilities offered by the growing U.S. economy than they were to the cultural bonds that tied them to Mexico.[2]

When Taylor's army arrived at the Rio Grande and set up camp opposite Matamoros, the largest city of the frontier, Polk was deliberately putting his own wealthy, populous nation toe to toe with a neighbor he saw as economically and politically weak, one he believed to be populated by the sort of racial inferior that American whites had centuries of experience dominating. Polk wanted territory, and he believed that he could force Mexico to cede rights to Texas and sell the United States large swaths of its northern territory, particularly California and New Mexico. Polk would certainly have been pleased if the mere presence of Taylor's army was enough to intimidate Mexican politicians into these concessions, but he believed that a war would be necessary. He was willing to fight a short war, and it surely seemed that any war between two such unequal foes would be short.[3]

Why did Polk not get his wish? Why did Mexico's politicians and people not readily give up a Texas that was already lost and a strip of territory between the Nueces and the Rio Grande that had already been depopulated by Comanche raids? Why did a chronically insolvent Mexican government not seize the opportunity to sell California and New Mexico, places that were far from Mexico's heartland and added to its fiscal problems, places in which some inhabitants, even those of Mexican descent, were strongly attracted to the tidal wave of economic opportunity set in motion by America's incessant expansion? Why did Mexicans not only fight a war, but fight one whose length and severity dramatically exceeded anything Polk had envisioned?

The answer lies in Mexico's domestic politics. Domestic political considerations often drive states to commit acts in the international arena that seem irrational in hindsight. Yet in this case such politics were shaped by how states were changing in this period of world history. Polk's notion that Mexico would cede territory after a short war was oddly illogical. His desire

FIG. 2.1 General Zachary Taylor became famous as the U.S. Army commander during the war. Elected president in 1848, he died in office in 1850.

for the territory was driven by a vision of the United States *as a nation*. Polk wanted the territory for the American people as he saw them, which for him basically meant white males who could make the land productive by dominating racial others, especially through slavery. This might not be a vision of the American nation we find attractive, but it definitely was a vision of the American nation. Nation-states, in which governments were supposed to embody the desires of a subset of the inhabitants, the people, were still relatively new. Even though Polk was motivated by an idea of the American nation-state, he believed that Mexico would act not like a nation-state but instead like one of the dynastic monarchies whose conflicts had shaped the territorial histories of both Europe and the Americas for centuries. In that gradually dying era, conflicts were between monarchs, not peoples. These monarchies fought limited wars because they could mobilize few resources and because in the end wars were fought to enrich only the monarchs and their wealthiest subjects. When one of these monarchs lost control of a territory and judged its recovery too costly, he or she quickly ceded it at the bargaining table. Mexico did not and in fact could not act this way because its politicians, like their American counterparts, had long been involved in an effort to build a national state whose legitimacy rested on its role as the instrument of its people. In both countries this effort had so far been only partially successful, but it had advanced far enough to preclude the easy cessation of territory, especially territory over which conflict had already occurred and blood had already been spilled. Territory belonged in theory to the people rather than the ruler, and once they fought over it, land became more than a little sacralized.[4] How could any politician cede such territory without a prolonged struggle?

There was more than a little irony in the situation. Before Texas became independent, the northern territories that Polk coveted had been quite marginal to Mexican political debates, and probably also to Mexican ideas about what Mexico was. The loss of Texas made Texas and the looming danger the United States posed to other northern territories symbols of national sovereignty and self-respect. It became impossible for politicians to simultaneously project the idea that Mexico had a bright future as a nation and concede that the far North was marginal. Thus, Texas's independence, itself partially the product of domestic political conflicts in Mexico, was instantly unpopular with all Mexican political groups, and it changed the way Mexican politicians and intellectuals saw the United States. Before 1835 the United States had been most often viewed as a sister republic that shared political values with Mexico, and its prosperity and apparent political stability led some politicians to wish to emulate it. The refusal of American settlers in Texas to accept membership in the Mexican nation underlined the danger of American expansionism and the differences between American and Mexican society. The result was an avalanche of both calls of alarm about American expansionism and criticisms of American society.[5]

Opposition to the United States and to Texas's independence became a crucial test of any politician's nationalism and faith in Mexico's future. Mexico's politicians continued to argue about what Mexico should be and how its government should be organized, in other words, about hierarchy and egalitarianism, about centralization and decentralization, about how the government might foster prosperity, and about how closely church and state should be connected. Yet every significant group, right, left, and center, opposed the recognition of Texas's independence and, eventually, the cessation of territory to the United States. Even the slightest evidence of a politician deviating from this stance became a cudgel that opponents could use against him.[6] The result was a decade of efforts to overcome the fiscal and geographic obstacles that prevented the concentration of a sufficient force to reconquer Texas or to block further U.S. expansion. Finally, in 1845, President José Joaquín de Herrera tried moving toward a more realistic policy on Texas. He believed that Texas was irrecoverable, and that an independent Texas tied commercially to Great Britain was preferable to having the United States on Mexico's doorstep.[7] Yet the arguments Herrera and his allies made to this effect came to naught when the United States annexed Texas, and Mariano Paredes y Arrillaga used Herrera's supposed softness on the United States to justify a coup.

Mexico fought a bloody war rather than make concessions to the geographical problems hindering the integration of its north into Mexican society and to the balance of power that heavily favored the United States. One could see this as evidence of weakness.[8] However, one could also see the commitment of all factions to opposing the United States as evidence that, despite its poverty and political instability, Mexico was well on its way to becoming a national state in which loyalty to the nation was the paramount political identity. Moreover, many Mexican politicians and generals believed they could defeat the United States. Some thought that the fierce rhetoric American politicians, including Polk, deployed against Great Britain on the Oregon question and the efforts of Great Britain to keep Texas independent meant Great Britain, the most important commercial and naval power in the world, would help Mexico against the United States.[9] They could not know that secretly Polk was offering a compromise on Oregon that was very favorable to Britain and that the British government would decide that conflict with the United States over Mexico was not worthwhile. Other Mexicans believed American society suffered from fundamental divisions that would hamper its fight with Mexico. Foremost among these was sectionalism, but Mexicans also did not see the effervescent religious pluralism of the United States as a positive and were acutely aware of both nativist and racial tensions in American society.[10] American news reports and political opinion pieces, readily available in Mexican newspapers, could be read as evidence that the United States was a country about to fall apart, and optimistic readings of American opposition to the war further encouraged this idea. Arguably these assessments were not totally unrealistic; in 1861, the United States did explode, even if this explosion came fifteen years too late for Mexico. Mexicans also had confidence in their army, which they considered to be superior to its American counterpart. Indeed, the U.S. military had performed miserably in its last major conflict, the War of 1812. Thus, although some Mexicans understood that they were at an extreme disadvantage in a potential military conflict with the United States, others were more optimistic.

Taylor's army and the Mexican army that awaited it on the other side of the Rio Grande were poised at the beginning of a war that would be more difficult and damaging than most imagined. When Taylor's army arrived opposite Matamoros, General Pedro de Ampudia, who was in command there, demanded Taylor leave Mexican territory. In response Taylor asked the American naval squadron poised at the mouth of the river to initiate a blockade, preventing supplies from reaching the Mexican army. This was without doubt an act of war. It also gave the Mexican army a time limit for action, as without the ability to bring food in via the sea, the Mexican troops would be forced to either fight or retreat within a matter of weeks.[11] Taylor's army also began building a large fort on its side of the river. It rapidly became clear that dislodging the Americans from this fort would require larger cannon than the Mexicans had in Matamoros, and such cannon could only be transported overland with great difficulty. Ampudia was placed under the command of another general, Mariano Arista, and Arista began sending Mexican cavalry across to patrol around the American army. On April 25, a Mexican unit trapped and defeated an American cavalry patrol, starting the bloodshed. News of the skirmish would give Polk his excuse for declaring war, but during the weeks it took the news to reach Washington, operations continued.

Ampudia, now Arista's second in command, was confident the Mexicans could defeat the Americans. He knew that the Mexicans faced a demoralized and heterogeneous army. As the two armies met, dozens of American regulars deserted and swam across to Matamoros, causing Taylor to order sentries to shoot soldiers attempting to desert. The deserters described to the Mexicans an army full of men who had joined out of hunger. Many were immigrants with little attachment to the United States and great resentment of the harsh punishments meted out by officers who were often nativists. Deserters also explained that many soldiers were recent recruits who had only begun their training in Corpus Christi. It seemed to Ampudia that in the kind of battle that both armies had trained for, Mexican troops would win because they were more disciplined and cohesive. The odds would be increased if some of the immigrants could be induced to desert in the moment of battle, something the Mexicans tried to arrange.[12]

Arista was less confident, but he came up with a plan designed to take advantage of the situation. Taylor depended on supplies landed from ships and stored at Point Isabel, more than a day's march away from his fortification opposite Matamoros. Arista planned to take four thousand men across the river and block the road between the two places. This would force the Americans to attack his disciplined troops in a location of his choosing. But Taylor realized the danger and took most of his troops to Point Isabel. His object was to prepare its defenses and then bring back a large load of supplies to his fort. Taylor spent several days at Point Isabel, and in the meantime Arista and his troops crossed the river. Tired of waiting, Arista ordered Mexican artillery in Matamoros to begin bombarding the American fort, hoping to force Taylor to hurry to its rescue. Taylor, having completed his work at Point

Isabel, marched with his army and many wagonloads of supplies back toward Matamoros. The first major battle of the war was about to begin.

Arista had chosen a location called Palo Alto for the battle. It was an open prairie broken up in spots by patches of woods and marsh. He arrayed his infantry in a long double line blocking Taylor's path to the beleaguered American fort and carefully placed his few small cannon to stiffen the line. Arista also positioned cavalry units to extend his line, preventing Taylor from flanking him, and readied them to attack if Taylor's army showed signs of wavering. Given the tactics of the age, Arista had prepared well. An enemy he believed was demoralized would have to attack his disciplined troops, and when their attack failed, his cavalry would break the retreating Americans. Taylor seems to have planned to clear the road with an infantry attack. However, first he halted his army out of range of the Mexican cannon and deployed his own artillery. Here, even at the very beginning of the fighting, the American economic might that would win the war began to show. Although both the Mexican and the American cannon were muzzle-loading gunpowder weapons, the similarity ended there. The American guns were more powerful, and even their gunpowder was of higher quality. Despite their larger size, they were more mobile, as the Americans had reequipped recently with more modern weapons with lighter carriages. The horses moving the American guns and ammunition were integral to artillery units, and they were trained to ignore the enormous sound the cannon made. This training was an extremely expensive proposition, as horses were very costly to feed and few armies could afford to keep many draft horses around in peacetime. In contrast, throughout the war, the Mexicans had to hire animals and their drivers whenever they went on campaign, and neither the animals nor the drivers were trained to maneuver the heavy guns quickly. Moreover, at Palo Alto the Mexicans had only a few small cannon and limited ammunition, partially because they had had to cross the river to even be in a position to take the fight to the Americans.[13]

The American guns began to bombard the Mexican line, killing infantry who could not reply. The Mexican cannon shot back, but between their smaller size and inferior gunpowder, they were less of a threat. Their cannonballs barely were able to reach the American troops, and by the time they did so, their energy was sometimes so spent that they rolled through

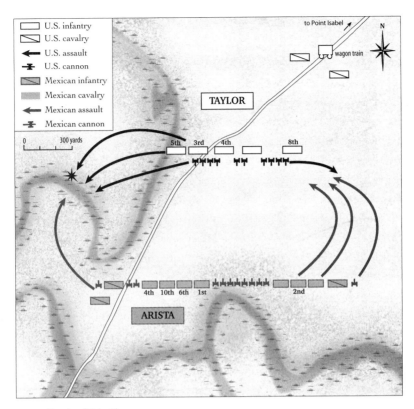

MAP 4 Battle of Palo Alto

the stiff prairie grass slowly enough that soldiers could actually dodge them. Although few Americans were hit, when a Mexican cannonball struck, the results were horrendous. American soldier C. M. Reeves describes how the force of a shot that destroyed one man was so great that it drove one of the unfortunate soldier's teeth into the back of a nearby officer. The tooth penetrated the officer's thick woolen coat and shirt, breaking his skin and causing enough pain to convince him that he had been shot.[14] Meanwhile, the Mexican troops were being mown down by American artillerymen, who, in the words of Reeves, worked "more like butchers than military men, each man stripped off his coat and rolled his sleeves above the elbow."[15] This image emphasizes the particularly methodical routine of artillerymen, but it also underlines something distinct to this occasion: many Mexican soldiers were being killed by men they could not fight back against. As long as the two armies were too far apart to use muskets, the Americans had a terrific advantage. Taylor soon realized this and decided not to attack with his infantry.

Arista's plan relied on blocking the Americans' march, preventing them from bringing supplies to their fortification opposite Matamoros. He could not have known the potency of the American artillery, and even after it began its bloody work, he did not know how much ammunition the Americans had. So, for minutes that stretched into hours, he stuck to the plan, probably hoping the cannonade was only a short preparation for the kind of frontal attack he wanted the Americans to make. At one point the prairie grass was inadvertently set on fire, and the resulting smoke prevented the armies from seeing each other. Meanwhile, the Mexican troops stood and died. In the words of Reeves, the American artillery "tore complete lanes through the enemy's lines but they stood it most manfully."[16] These troops, including some of the same units that had months earlier protested orders to brave the desert march to Matamoros, stood their ground, occasionally shouting, "Viva México" or "Viva la Independencia."[17] As Arista began to realize how seemingly inexhaustible the American ammunition supply was, he improvised. He sent Mexican cavalry to attack the flank of the Americans, but their movements were so hampered by the marshy terrain that the American infantry and cannon were easily able to redeploy to foil the attack. Meanwhile, hundreds of yards beyond the range of the weapons they carried, the Mexican infantry continued to suffer from the American artillery. Eventually it was the apparent futility of that suffering that told on them. In two elite units, the Engineer Regiment and the First Light Infantry, men began to murmur and then to shout, asking that their officers allow them to advance or retreat rather than die for nothing. Some shouted that they did not have officers worthy of leading them. Men from the two units broke ranks, not to retreat but to move forward. Arista ordered the units to attack in order to regain control of his own men. When the men were finally told to attach their bayonets to their muskets, a move that typically preceded an attack, they cheered with joy. However, they were already in disorder, and the Americans were distant. The men only advanced partway to the American lines before they retreated.[18] Arista also again sent cavalry to try to flank the Americans and reach the supply wagons, but again American redeployments successfully checked these efforts. The maneuvering meant that soldiers on both sides had to march under fire and the positions of the armies changed somewhat, but throughout Arista kept his line between Taylor and his destination, and the American artillery continued to kill Mexican soldiers, who refused to break. Ampudia, the Mexican second in command, later wrote proudly that Mexican troops had proven themselves to be as courageous as Napoleon's legendary Old Guard. They had stood and maneuvered serenely for five hours under cannon fire without being able to reply. When the fighting ended at dusk, only twenty-six of the more than four thousand Mexican soldiers engaged had deserted, while over a hundred had been killed and more than a hundred had been wounded.[19] Both armies camped on the battlefield, but by then Arista knew that the effectiveness of the American artillery made his original plan untenable. The Americans could kill his men with relative impunity without ever approaching closely enough for the Mexican infantry to be effective.[20]

Arista decided to redeploy to a new location that would negate the American advantage, which had become even more pronounced because the Mexicans had used most of their cannon ammunition. The next day he placed his troops at Resaca de Palma, about halfway between the battlefield of Palo Alto and Taylor's fortification opposite Matamoros. This shallow, muddy ravine was fronted by dense woods and its depth of three or four feet would provide natural protection from the American artillery. Arista deployed some cannon to cover the road and spread most of his men out along the ravine.[21] Taylor resumed his march and eventually reengaged the Mexicans. He pushed his army into this resistance without any particular effort to get around it, and soon American artillerymen were firing on their Mexican counterparts along the road and sending shots into the trees above Mexican troops while American and Mexican infantry confronted each other at extremely close range.

At first most of the Mexican troops fought well, but as small units of American troops worked their way around the Mexicans' flank, their morale faltered. Most had not eaten or slept in more than twenty-four hours and some had interpreted Arista's relative passivity the day before as evidence that he was a traitor.[22] The American artillery could not actually kill many Mexicans here, but the noise it made as it bombarded the woods reminded the Mexicans of the previous day's slaughter. Mostly, though, the very terrain Arista had chosen to protect his troops from the American cannon hampered their solidarity. Mexican soldiers who the day before had been able to see thousands of comrades along almost a mile of front now could only see the handful closest to them. When a few Americans worked their way around the flank and the Mexican soldiers heard firing from the side rather than the front, many feared their ability to retreat toward the river was compromised. Although many Mexicans fought hard, fear spread, and eventually most units retreated.[23] Their dismay increased when they reached the river and realized there were only a few boats available to ferry them over it. Some even tried to swim across, convinced the American army would soon arrive at the bank. Even so, officers were able to calm the initial panic, set up a rear guard, and arrange to transport the vast majority of the troops across with boats. Palo Alto had been a disappointment for the Mexicans, but Resaca de Palma was a disaster. There, 160 men were killed, compared to the roughly 100 killed at Palo Alto, but the number of troops who deserted was more telling: 157 compared to only 26 at Palo Alto.[24]

Although men who had struck out on their own in the confusion of the rout continued to return to their units, those who now tried to regroup in Matamoros were thoroughly demoralized and had lost confidence in their commanding general. Worse yet, the American naval blockade meant that a defensive posture that might have given them some breathing space was not an option. There was little ammunition left, and the army had at most food for two weeks. The Mexican generals decided to abandon Matamoros because it was more important to keep an intact army in northern Mexico than it was to defend the city. Their retreat required the men to move through harsh terrain with little water, carrying what food they could on their backs because there were not even enough draft animals to drag the cannon and the remaining ammunition. Soon their rations were cut to the bare bones, and at times the men marched for more than two days straight without water. Cavalry horses began to die from lack of food and water, and soon men began to die, too. Under these conditions some of the very same soldiers who had stood their ground under American bombardment at Palo Alto and fought well in the confusion of Resaca de Palma came to believe that their best chance of surviving the desert lay in separating themselves from the army and striking out on their own. After ten days of this grueling travel, the survivors arrived at the town of Linares, where food, water, and rest awaited them.[25]

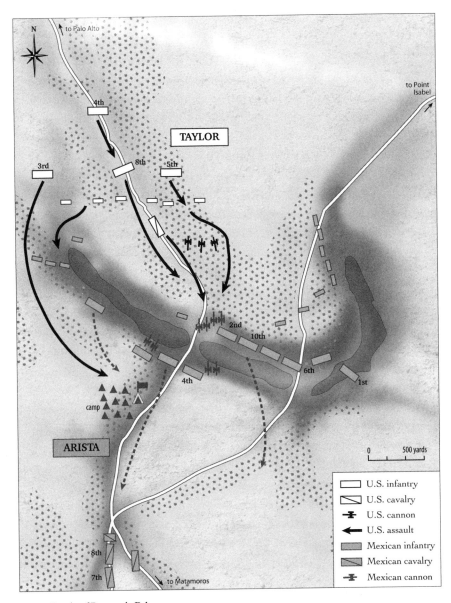

MAP 5 Battle of Resaca de Palma

The army that confronted Taylor in northern Mexico was only a fraction of the force that President Herrera had hoped to have in place, because Paredes had taken many of the men destined for the north down to Mexico City to force Herrera out of office. Although probably not all of these men would have ended up in Matamoros, it seems reasonable to suppose that three thousand or so would have. Would Arista have attacked rather than stood on the defensive at Palo Alto if he had had these additional men? Would Taylor's much smaller force have withstood this attack? Would Taylor have been able to rout this larger force at Resaca de Palma? We will never know.

It is possible that a Mexican victory against Taylor would have made it harder for Polk to continue an offensive war against Mexico. However, it is equally possible that the determined American president would have pushed Congress to authorize war anyway. When Polk sought this authorization in May 1846, he did so with no knowledge of Taylor's victories, and he justified the request using the skirmish on April 25 in which an American cavalry patrol was destroyed. Moreover, he had been planning to ask for a mobilization even before hearing about that event. Once he knew that blood had been shed, Polk worked rapidly, preparing a request that Congress authorize the mobilization of volunteer troops to rush to the aid of Taylor's army. The message gave a litany of Mexican provocations, from refusing to pay the claims of U.S. citizens for property damaged during Mexican domestic conflicts, to refusing to negotiate with American envoy John Slidell, to menacing the Texas frontier. It argued that Taylor's army had been sent to defend Texas against a threatened Mexican invasion, and that it had moved to the Rio Grande to defend the land between the Nueces and that river, which Polk claimed was part of Texas. Polk stated baldly that by attacking an American cavalry patrol in this area, Mexico had "invaded our territory and shed American blood upon the American soil."[26] The argument that war had already started suggests that even if Taylor had been defeated later at Palo Alto or Resaca de Palma, Polk would have been able to achieve his goal by playing on American fears and desire for revenge. In that sense, perhaps the first American victories of the war were not that essential to Polk's political strategy. Still, reports of the heroic victories undoubtedly helped build enthusiasm for the war in the next few months.[27]

Polk's allies in Congress worked to get the bill passed with a minimum of debate. They allotted only two hours to discussion in the House of Representatives, and then spent an hour and a half of that time reading the bill out loud. Opponents in both the House and the Senate were caught in a quandary. They did not want to be responsible for the destruction of Taylor's army or a Mexican invasion of Texas, and they thought they had to give Polk the authority to spend money and to call up volunteer troops. Yet they did not believe Polk's justification for the war, and they strongly suspected he wanted a war to take territory from Mexico. In both the House and the Senate, opponents tried to separate the preamble authorizing the war with Polk's pretexts from the bill calling up new troops. These attempts failed because Polk used the seductiveness of Manifest Destiny and the Democratic Party patronage machine to keep most Democrats in line. Once efforts to amend the bill failed, every representative and senator was faced with the stark choice of either voting yes or abandoning U.S. troops to potential defeat. Under these circumstances, almost all voted yes. Polk had gotten his war bill, in the words of historian David Pletcher, using "tactics that exploited partisan loyalty and Whig patriotism."[28]

Polk had deliberately avoided any explicit discussion of aggressive war or territorial expansion at Mexico's expense even as he had publicly taken a hard line toward British claims to Oregon. By claiming that Mexico was the aggressor and American troops were in danger, he successfully tapped the anti-Mexican racism sparked by the War of Texas Independence and further strengthened by American anti-Catholicism. Mexico had become oddly both contemptible and dangerous. More importantly, even many who opposed territorial aggression soon came to see the conflict as a test of the mettle of the young American republic. When the call for troops was sent to American localities, many of Polk's political enemies collaborated with him, fostering enthusiasm for the war as a symbol of American nationalism. America's local leaders competed with each other to raise troops quickly, trying to outdo neighboring states and even neighboring counties.[29] We have seen how in 1845–1846 various Mexican political groups agreed that belief in Mexico's future as a strong, sovereign nation required them to refuse to satisfy the territorial ambitions of the United States. Here we see the reverse side of the coin: even most American politicians who opposed those territorial ambitions agreed at this moment that prosecuting the war with Mexico was important to the future of the United States as a strong, sovereign nation. Without these dreams, the cataclysm of 1846–1848 would have been stillborn.

Santa Anna Returns

While the first victims of the war were dying in the Rio Grande valley, the regime of Paredes was tottering hundreds of miles to the south in Mexico City. Paredes had used a large military force destined for the frontier to instead overthrow his predecessor, Herrera. His pretext had been Herrera's reluctance to fight a war with the United States, but all along Paredes's real preoccupations were with domestic politics. He and his supporters felt that federalism and excessive democracy had weakened Mexico by encouraging the political participation of many Mexicans who lacked the wealth needed to make judicious choices. They believed this excessive democracy would, if unchecked, threaten private property itself. Paredes and his supporters evidenced nostalgia for the cultural values and social norms of colonial Mexico, and some believed Mexican political stability and the country's independence could best be ensured by installing a limited monarch from one of Europe's royal families. Paredes himself blew hot and cold on the idea of a monarchy, but monarchist support for his regime evolved from an open secret into a well-publicized reality, and it further reduced his already restricted base of support by alienating both moderate federalists and many centralists. These men feared the urban masses the radical federalists increasingly sought to mobilize, but they were not ready to give up on republicanism.[30]

In the late spring and early summer of 1846 a grand alliance coalesced against Paredes. Some members were moderate federalists who believed a decentralized, republican constitution that allowed the wealthy men of Mexico a strong hand in governing their localities was best for a sprawling and diverse country, even if it might sometimes lead to an excessive dose of democracy.[31] Others were radical federalists from both rural and urban areas. Rural radical federalists often were led by professionals and small merchants of market towns, but they included agriculturalists of modest means and, in some regions, Indian peasants. They believed the principle of decentralization should be extended not only from the national to the state governments but from the states to the municipal governments. Enhanced local autonomy would facilitate the participation of rural people in making a strong republic, and it would help counteract the excesses of wealthy landowners and merchants whom they believed limited rural economic development and sometimes forced the poor off lands rightfully theirs. These rural federalists also advocated reduced taxes on the poor.[32] Urban radical federalists had similar beliefs about the economy and the importance of bringing humble people into the republic. They resented the ways in which centralists had stripped the citizenship of many, and they wanted to reclaim that citizenship to assert their self-worth.[33] Rural and urban radical federalists shared a suspicion of wealthy merchants who often used their Spanish roots to assert social prestige, and this suspicion tended to make radical federalists among the most nationalist of politically active Mexicans.[34]

Federalists of various kinds were joined in the anti-Paredes coalition by supporters of Antonio López de Santa Anna, Mexico's most mercurial and enigmatic leader. Santa Anna had been an active military politician since the early 1820s, helping to make and break various governments, as well as holding the presidency several times. Over time his own politics had evolved from a rather hopeful popular republicanism that aligned him with the radical federalists toward more centralist and even authoritarian positions as he became disillusioned by the chaos that seemed to follow from radical ideals.[35] He had alternately courted and turned against every political faction in Mexico. As the war with the United States started, Santa Anna offered two advantages: he was supported by important sectors of the officer corps, and he had repeatedly proven he had the connections and knowledge needed to raise, equip, and fund troops. He also knew how to move them across Mexico's vast and difficult landscape. He had managed to get a force into the field to check Spain's 1829 attempt to reconquer Mexico and had later taken a significant Mexican force all the way to Texas to fight the rebels, an extraordinarily impressive political and logistical feat later marred by the poor tactical choices that eventually led to defeat. Santa Anna's proven ability to organize armies in Mexico's chaotic political and fiscal circumstances made him an attractive ally to those who wanted to overthrow Paredes and oppose the United States.[36]

Santa Anna's motivations were always under suspicion. Some federalists felt his ambition would lead him to betray them again, and their hesitation was one reason it took several months for the coalition to become a practical reality. Eventually the leading federalists, especially Valentín Gómez Farías, became convinced Santa Anna was a Mexican nationalist who wanted more than anything to fight the United States.[37] However, Santa Anna was in exile in Cuba, separated from Mexico by a sea controlled by the U.S. Navy. Fortunately for the anti-Paredes coalition, American intelligence operations regarding Mexican politics were conducted by a haphazard set of shady intermediaries managed by President Polk. In this arena of skullduggery Santa Anna was in his element, and he convinced Polk that if the United States let him return to Mexico and remove Paredes, he would work quickly toward a settlement that would allow Polk to achieve his war aims without prolonged Mexican resistance.[38] Nothing could have been further from the truth. Despite his many faults as a tactician and his overbearing political ambition, Santa Anna was committed to fighting to the bitter end. His actions would prolong the war for at least a year, and more than any other single person it was Santa Anna who denied Polk's dream of a short war. Thus it is particularly ironic that Polk ordered the U.S. Navy to let Santa Anna return to Mexico.

The coalition against Paredes did not wait for the arrival of Santa Anna. In April 1846, Juan Alvarez, leader of the rural radical federalists in what is now the state of Guerrero, began a rebellion demanding that Mexico remain a republic and that Santa Anna become president. Over the next several months, pockets of regional unrest grew, weakening the Paredes government. Momentum toward a change of government accelerated, and on August 4, 1846, troops in Mexico City occupied the National Palace and arrested Paredes. On August 16, Santa Anna landed on Mexican soil, and on August 24 it was decreed that Mexico would again be governed under the 1824 federalist constitution, which remained the law of the land throughout the remainder of the war.[39]

FIG. 2.2 Mexican military politician Antonio López de Santa Anna denied the United States the short war it expected.

What difference could a change in constitution make in the course of a foreign war? The answer is quite a bit. Scholars have pointed out that this decentralization of power sometimes hampered the national government's military efforts. State governments now had a greater share of fiscal resources and they controlled part-time military units. Regional elites who had chafed under centralist rule zealously defended their autonomy and were sometimes reluctant to follow the strategic dictates of the central government. Thus they were often accused of not providing all the money and men they could have for the war.[40] Politicians in coastal states who feared American landings and those in northern states who faced both Native American raids and incursions by U.S. troops felt that they had first call on the part-time troops and painfully expensive weapons. After all, their regions were also part of the nation, and why should the defense of some other part have priority?[41] State politicians also knew that the long-distance deployment of part-time troops would prevent these men from earning the income needed to support their families, a cruel hardship in a rickety economy without any social safety nets.[42]

However, the effect of federalism on the war effort was not entirely negative. State governments were sometimes uncooperative, but until very late in the war they still remitted money to the national government and recruited troops for the regular army. They even sent part-time troops at moments of crisis. More importantly, the 1846 turn toward federalism dramatically increased popular mobilization for the war. Centralism had been from the beginning dedicated to tamping down the surprisingly enthusiastic embrace that Mexico's middle classes, urban poor, and sometimes peasants had extended to the new national state, deliberately demobilizing them by both imposing income restrictions for suffrage and reducing the number of elections. This effort to restore colonial-style hierarchies had never been completely accepted by many Mexicans who wanted not only a role in choosing leaders but also the validation that came from being considered honorable Mexican citizens as worthy as anyone. In fact, the state constitutions first written in the 1820s and put into use again in 1846 tied citizenship to honor by suspending the citizenship of those who engaged in dishonorable behavior such as crime.[43] For many Mexicans, federalism was less about decentralization than it was about egalitarianism, broader definitions of citizenship, and the corresponding acknowledgment that one did not have to be white and wealthy to be honorable. A more inclusive Mexico was a Mexico for which more Mexicans were willing to sacrifice, and the restoration of the federalist constitution was accompanied by popular expressions of support for the war that often rivaled those seen in the most bellicose regions of the United States. One anonymous Mexican author admitted that in normal times he would say that too much democracy would be a disaster for Mexico, but in times of war democracy was needed to "make the people enthusiastic and nationalize the war."[44] Federalism aided Mexico's war effort this way, and frankly it is impossible to imagine Mexico resisting its wealthier neighbor as well as it did without having rejected centralism. Thus, the turn toward federalism both hampered and aided Mexico during the war.[45]

American Volunteers and Jacksonian Democracy

We left Taylor and his army at Matamoros, and we left Polk using hook and crook to get a bill through Congress combining a declaration of war with the authorization to raise more troops. These troops were needed because the U.S. regular army was not nearly large enough to fight an offensive war against Mexico. The bill that passed Congress allowed the president to raise fifty thousand men organized in volunteer regiments, although in the end about fifty-nine thousand volunteers and thirty-one thousand regulars served in the war.[46] The distinction between volunteer regiments and regular regiments is crucial for understanding the experience of both types of soldiers and the experience of Mexican civilians. The volunteer regiments were not an expansion of the regular army. They were a different animal entirely, composed of citizen-soldiers, recruited specifically for this war, who would return to civilian society afterward.

Citizen-soldiers were a relative novelty in the Western world. Like many of the ideals put forward by the Enlightenment, the citizen-soldier had classical roots in Greek antiquity. Before this ideal was revived and reworked, rank-and-file soldiers were employees of the state whose military role was unrelated to any political identity. The citizen-soldier model was very different, as the state represented the will of the citizenry, and the service of citizen-soldiers was considered a patriotic duty.[47] This model had various implications for the character of armies and the nature of citizenship. It made armies national in ways they had not been before, and this made foreign mercenaries, one of the West's oldest military traditions, less welcome. Armies could be seen as the embodiment of nations, even to the degree that military service might take people from diverse regions with little national sentiment and teach them to see themselves as national citizens.[48] The ideal of the citizen-soldier firmly tied citizenship not just to military service but also to masculinity. Military service as a citizen-soldier entitled one to citizenship, and women were implicitly excluded.[49]

We associate the rise of the citizen-soldier with the American Revolution and the French Revolution. However, this model was also attractive to many politicians working to construct nation-states, including those in Latin America.[50] Still, national armies made of citizen-soldiers did not replace the early modern military pattern of what we might call armies of non-citizen-soldiers like the men of the American and Mexican regular armies. The citizen-soldier ideal took root in institutions and popular culture alongside rather than in place of the earlier model. Citizen-soldiering was for units of part-time soldiers or for full-time units mobilized for specific wars, but most peacetime soldiering and in fact most wars not considered to be national wars were handled by the earlier type of soldier, even in France and the United States, the originators of the citizen-soldier concept. Thus, for instance, the expansion of European colonial empires was not accomplished by citizen-soldiers. Military service in peacetime or in these kinds of wars was neither attractive enough nor politically compelling enough to justify participation by respectable men as part of their civic duty. The fact that both the United States and Mexico mobilized thousands of citizen-soldiers for the 1846–1848 war provides compelling evidence that it was seen as a war between nation-states, vital to both their futures. The mobilization of thousands of citizen-soldiers also increased the tragedy of the war. David Bell has pointed out that citizen-soldiering intensified warfare, partly because the increased identification of soldiers with the nation blurred the lines between soldiers and civilians but also because, when all citizens were potential soldiers, states could mobilize much larger armies and tacticians did not need to avoid heavy losses. As Hoffman Nickerson memorably put it, "Democracy had made men cheap."[51]

The ideal of the citizen-soldier found a particularly congenial home in the newly independent United States. It resonated with republicanism's emphasis on citizenship, and much fighting conducted in the American Revolution had involved militia units of citizen-soldiers, associating the very existence of the United States with citizen-soldiering.[52] However, the strength of the ideal in the United States was also tied to race. In Europe and Latin America the idea of the citizen-soldier helped keep women at arm's length from citizenship, and it could also be used to differentiate between respectable men entitled to citizenship and disreputable lower-class men who were not. In the United States it played those roles, but it also played an even more important role in racial differentiation. Citizen-soldiering in militia units yielded military forces that provided some security against the possibility of slave uprisings, as well as most of the Indian fighting used to gradually free more and more land for white settlement. Perhaps more importantly, it also was another place where sharp lines could be drawn between nonwhite and white groups, providing an expression of a racialized masculinity and reaffirming that the United States was a nation of white men.[53] It was perhaps the quintessential ideal of Jacksonian democracy, which was about raising white men to equality while subordinating women and racial others.[54] Andrew Jackson himself was most famous for leading citizen-soldier militias during the War of 1812, and the men who saw themselves as his political heirs were deeply committed to the ideal. The most prominent of those heirs was President Polk himself. Polk not only planned to use mostly citizen-soldiers to defeat Mexico, he constantly praised them and insisted they were as effective as regulars and more compatible with American ideals.[55]

Before Polk's 1846 call for volunteers, the citizen-soldier ideal was manifested in the United States by the existence of militia units. However, they were mostly just political and social clubs that allowed men to assert their status as citizens and advance in local politics. Although militia units drilled and had uniforms, their military utility was close to nil. Some militia companies volunteered en masse for the war with Mexico, but they were incorporated into new volunteer regiments where men with militia experience were a distinct minority.[56] Moreover, the new regiments could not be militia regiments because militia regiments would be under the control of the states and would include many men with family responsibilities. This problem had been one of the principal military headaches of the War of 1812 because militia units were not enthusiastic about long campaigns or campaigns far from home. To fight a war of conquest, a different kind of citizen-soldier unit was needed, and hence Polk asked for the recruitment of volunteer regiments rather than the mobilization of state militias.[57]

Polk forwarded the initial call for volunteers to states that seem to have been selected both for the ease with which their men could be transported to the war zone and their affinity for citizen-soldiering and Manifest Destiny. These two factors intersected in the southern and western states tied together by the vast watershed of the Mississippi River. These states, including Ohio,

Indiana, Illinois, and Missouri in the Midwest, and Kentucky, Tennessee, Alabama, Mississippi, Louisiana, and Arkansas in the South, together formed an economic and social system that revolved around the expansion of agriculture and the export of cotton farmed by slaves.[58] Notably, the southern sections of Ohio, Indiana, and Illinois had been settled by migrants from the South. Slavery even existed under other names in southern Illinois, and both that region and the southern portions of Indiana and Ohio relied on the production of corn and pork sold to Southern planters or exported through New Orleans. These southern parts of the Midwest were significantly more enthusiastic about the Mexican War than the northern parts of their states, which had been populated by New Englanders and New Yorkers who had moved west along the Great Lakes.[59] All these states, from Alabama to Missouri, had been settled by whites only a few decades before, and the young men coming of age on farms and in small river towns were caught between adventurous stories of their parents and the limits the relative scarcity of land put on their own economic prospects.[60] These men found the expansionist and racial aspects of Manifest Destiny easy to swallow. They provided twenty-six of the twenty-nine volunteer regiments or battalions organized in June and July 1846.[61]

The news of the first fighting on the Rio Grande and Polk's call for the organization of volunteer regiments hit these regions more or less simultaneously, and they initiated a war fever. In Washington many congressmen had been skeptical about Polk's claims that Mexican troops had invaded American territory, but such skepticism was scarce in the Mississippi watershed. Instead there were calls to defend U.S. territory and the country's national honor, anxiety about the possible fate of Taylor's small army, and considerations of the possibility that more land could be secured in the West at Mexico's expense. The Texas Revolution had let loose a flood of arguments that classified Mexicans with Indians and blacks as racial others, and particularly treacherous ones at that, and in 1846 some Texas veterans spoke at many meetings and rallies as ambitious local politicians sprinted to organize volunteer companies. Patriotic songs and adulation for recruits filled the air. Even Whigs, whose first instincts were to doubt Polk and whose principles steered away from expansionism, were pulled onto the bandwagon by the emotional tug of nationalist glory and their desire for political self-preservation. It was hard not to go along. Witnessing this scene, Paul Anderson wrote from Hannibal, Missouri, that "the fact is a considerable degree of moral courage is requisite to be a composed and silent spectator."[62] Each state was allotted a specific number of regiments, and so many men wanted to volunteer that some were unable to serve because the units filled too quickly.[63]

Some volunteers no doubt found the economic terms of service attractive. However, volunteer soldiers were very different from the recruits who had joined the regular army in peacetime. The men who volunteered in June and July 1846 were the sons of respectable families and they usually already had employment. They almost all knew how to read and write, and they had solid roots in their communities. They sent thousands of letters home, kept diaries, and often published memoirs after they returned from the greatest adventure of their lives. It is difficult to imagine the daily life and preoccupations of soldiers ever being better documented than they were in this case. In many ways these men had more in common with the officers of regular army units than they did with the enlisted men.[64]

The recruitment and organization of volunteer regiments was extraordinarily local. As war fever swept these regions, community leaders issued calls to sign up. Young, unmarried men faced significant peer pressure to join up, and they did so with their friends. Companies typically recruited in specific towns, counties, or neighborhoods, and when they were accepted into service, they became parts of regiments named for their states. In states that organized more than one regiment, often the regiments hailed from different sections of the state. Although young men were mobile enough that some found themselves away from home and enlisted in companies organized in other towns or cities, this was considered exceptional.[65] Volunteers were from the beginning serving with their friends, a fact that shaped their experience and the experience Mexicans had with them to a remarkable degree.

Not surprisingly, these volunteer units had strong identities that aided them in battle.[66] In this they were no different from other military units, even those of the U.S. regular army. What is particularly striking about the volunteer units, however, is that such unit identities were centered on their places of origin. Volunteers saw themselves as representatives of their states, and people back home saw them that way, too.[67] Officers used this as a motivational tool. On the way to battle, volunteers were told to "never disgrace yourselves or your state in any way."[68] As his Kentucky unit drew closer to its first combat, Levi White of Louisville wrote to his wife, Sara, that "we will have a chance of showing Kentucky spunk and if I am not mistaken the boys of Louisville will not disappoint the expectation of their friends."[69] After one battle William H. Daniel wrote in his diary that "Old Kentucky done her duty on that day, both regiments fought most gallantly."[70]

Men often criticized the patriotism, training, courage, behavior, and appearance of units from other states.[71] A. C. Pickett of Alabama wrote that regiments from Kentucky, Ohio, and Indiana were not "as well trained as the Alabamians." A few pages later he wrote that the Maryland volunteers "committed depredations disgraceful to volunteer soldiery."[72] The rivalries between the units of different states were not confined to the written pages volunteers produced in such abundance. Verbal altercations and physical brawls between units were remarkably common. Ohioans fought Marylanders, Kentuckians fought Louisianans, and Hoosiers also fought Louisianans, although of course not side by side with the Kentuckians. Sometimes these began as fights between individual soldiers, but they often escalated into sprawling brawls. Violence could be triggered by something as momentous as boasting about the relative courage of different units or as trivial as possession of a freshly caught catfish, and it sometimes escalated to the point where firearms were nearly used.[73] Soldiers of the U.S. regular army also lived a very rough-and-tumble existence, but their fights were typically between individuals or perhaps groups of close friends. In contrast, the fights of volunteers often escalated into border warfare. In some ways the mobilization of these volunteer units to invade a neighboring country was evidence of national identity. However, the attachment of these men to their towns, counties, and states was much more real, and states commanded a kind of patriotism. Historian Paul Foos points out that "if the Mexican war was a step forward for U.S. 'nationalism,' it was in the achievement of state-sponsored murder through a loose confederation of communities."[74] The behavior of these volunteer units toward each other makes the later outbreak, and extreme violence, of the U.S. Civil War more understandable.

Comradeship was very important to the volunteers. As in other military units, the need to maintain one's reputation and not let comrades down was an important motivator on the battlefield.[75] However, it was also crucial to making daily life bearable. Men formed social bonds through music, dancing, and drunken horseplay, and they held outsiders at arm's length, so much so that they resented any effort to introduce new men into their units. As with other kinds of soldiers, their relationships were fostered by hardships shared, from boredom to bad food and from illness to the terror of battle, but the volunteers' comrades had often been friends since boyhood. Jacob Oswandel, writing of his friend Simon Schaffer, underlined this closeness when he wrote that the two often talked of home and "were chums, in camp we slept together, and on the march we marched together, and slept under one blanket, divided our crackers, and often drank out of one canteen and our coffee out of one cup."[76] One's closest friends usually were the five or six men who pooled their rations and cooked them together, taking turns cooking and cleaning. This was called the mess system, and although volunteers joked about the poor quality of their cooking, fellowship over meals was one thing that made the boredom and discomfort of camp life bearable. Occasionally officers tried to replace the mess system with more organized, mass cooking, but the men usually resisted bitterly because their messmates were their military families.[77] Comrades also replaced families in nursing the ill. Volunteers were vulnerable to a host of often fatal illnesses, and the task of providing food, water, and personal care to those immobilized fell on their friends. Daniel Runyon of Maysick, Kentucky, wrote to his sister Molly that she should "have no fears of my needing any comforts or assistance in case I should be sick knowing I am surrounded by friends." Tender acts of nursing tied men more closely together.[78]

Tales of men cooking for each other or caring for ill friends underline one of the ways in which their temporary life in the army was different from the civilian life men expected to return to after the war. Volunteer units lacked the soldaderas who accompanied Mexican regular units or even the laundresses who served with American regular units during peacetime. They were entirely male environments, and men made much of this in the letters they sent home, referring not only to cooking and nursing but also to the more onerous task of laundering clothes, one they avoided as much as possible, at least judging from the comments Mexicans and U.S. Army regulars made about the cleanliness of the volunteers.[79] Adventure fiction written during and after the war includes one purported memoir by a woman who claims to have served clandestinely in a volunteer unit, and more reliable documents indicate that at least one woman tried, but in reality serving in a volunteer regiment meant spending one's time among one's fellow men.[80] This was disconcerting in many ways for both the people at home and the men in the field, but for the latter it had its benefits. It released them from the behavioral constraints placed by the scrutiny of their mothers, sisters, spouses, or potential spouses, putting them in the type of social space that they otherwise experienced only temporarily in taverns, on hunting expeditions, or perhaps on Election Day.[81]

Before they were fully integrated into the male environment of the invading army, these men were given quite a sendoff by their communities, with music, speeches, and food. Even the voyage down the rivers toward the war was marked by people rushing to the banks to cheer on the passing soldiers. Not surprisingly, women were crucial to the sendoff. Volunteer memoirs vividly portray not only the food cooked for them but how the women clustered around to speak to the brave warriors. Oswandel writes of the young women swelling "around the soldiers as if they were in love with them."[82] This formed quite a contrast with the negative interactions regular army recruits had with American civilians. Women sent the volunteers away not only with pleasant memories but also with more tangible tokens of their esteem. Volunteer units designed their own uniforms, and women of their communities often created the actual clothing. They also sometimes sewed tents for the volunteers.[83] Perhaps the most symbolic talismans women made were flags. A unit's flag served as a crucial rallying point in the confusion of battle and a sign of its identity and honor. These flags were embellished with units' names and sometimes their mottos, and women not only made the flags, they also presented them to units in elaborate ceremonies. The flag the women of Louisville gave to one unit, for instance, was embroidered with the words "Kentucky Trusts You," while the women of Columbus, Indiana, gave the company raised there a flag embroidered with the more pointed words "None but the Brave Deserve the Fair."[84]

Although a few of the volunteers who rushed to answer Polk's first call for troops were married, most were young men of courting age. They were often still living with parents or at least contributing economically to their parents' household, but they were also actively considering potential romantic interests that would lead to the founding of new nuclear families. They could contemplate this step because they had decent economic prospects, but they were also obligated to do so by the fact that, according to historian Malcolm Rohrbough, "families were the basic unit of labor; their presence ensured the development of social and cultural institutions."[85] Thus, the correspondence between the men and their families not only documents their lives as soldiers, their adventures, and the foreign places they invaded, it also focuses on the gender anxieties created by their absence from the normal pattern their lives would have taken had they not left. The soldiers wrote in a jocular tone about having asked friends to keep an eye on their girlfriends or potential girlfriends while they were gone, or, as Oswandel did, asking them to "give my love to all the pretty girls, the ugly ones need not apply." They also wrote more plaintively about missing specific young women or missing out on the whole activity of courting. On Valentine's Day 1847, Thomas Tennery of Kentucky wrote in his diary, "This being Valentine's day no doubt the young folks at home are employing it in making love, or visiting, or receiving company, and making merry."[86] Letters the folks back home sent to soldiers are more difficult to find, because the soldiers would have had to preserve them through their long deployment, but they are even more suggestive on the topic. Families and friends wrote to the soldiers about exactly who was marrying whom.[87] They also wrote of having seen soldiers' girlfriends, of how those girlfriends missed the men, and, more pointedly, of the possibility that soldiers were missing out on opportunities. William H. Massey of Kentucky wrote to soldier John Cox that "there are plenty of pretty girls that will wait for you till you get home all that are married are all ugly." More alarmingly, R. Marshall wrote to Cox's comrade John Minton that "we have lots of marrying going on unless you get back pretty soon I am afraid all the girls will be married I think the boys are acting very wrong when you are all out fighting the battles of your country they are here sleeping with all the girls that is to say nearly all but you and John Cox need not be uneasy for I will save one a place."[88]

Both soldiers and the people they left behind displayed a palpable anxiety about this delay in forming families, and it was not helped by a national flood of newspaper editorials and even novels that extolled the possibility that conquering American soldiers would use their superior masculinity to annex Mexico by marrying Mexican women, perhaps the creepiest expression of the mania of Manifest Destiny.[89] This act would make the absence of these men from their families permanent, much as migration to the Far West would separate men from their parents and siblings. The young women of the United States would not be the only people to lose out if this were to take place. Many parents relied on these men to help with family businesses. Cox's father wrote to him in March 1847, "I am hardly able to attend to my business myself and need you at home very much & think you can make $5 here to one in the army." Families thus wrote to soldiers insisting they not reenlist, and parents found themselves torn between pride in their sons and fear about the impact of their enlistment on families.[90] Some even tried to prevent their boys from joining up.[91]

Some men who joined volunteer regiments were already married and even had children. How would these families fare in the absence of their bread-winners? One Kentuckian wrote that some married men decided not to join because they feared that "their wives would freeze this winter."[92] The U.S. government, unlike its Mexican counterpart, could pay its soldiers. However, there seems to have been no provision for pay to go directly to families rather than to men thousands of miles away. Many of the men with wives and children were relatively prosperous, politically ambitious, and older men who stimulated the organization of volunteer units and often later became their officers. Their wives and children were probably able to get by, especially with the help of extended families. Even when married men who volunteered were not well off, the relative prosperity of the United States, popular enthusiasm for the war, and the community-based nature of the units created the possibility that the communities would pitch in to support families. In at least some cases communities promised such support, although little evidence exists that such promises were fulfilled.[93] Eventually the war became less popular, new volunteer regiments became more difficult to fill, and the recruits who did sign up were often less wealthy. In several cases new recruits tried to get some of their wages paid before embarking for Mexico precisely so that they could leave cash in the hands of their families.[94] Some men were allowed to leave their units before they departed for Mexico when they explained that their families would be left destitute. Others who left their families exposed to economic hardship soon came to regret it, filling letters and journals with their laments.[95]

Reeves, one of the few U.S. Army regular soldiers to write a memoir, pointed out that the differences between regular army and volunteer soldiers owed much to the fact that "to us it was our business to be soldiers, with them it was only for a short time."[96] Volunteers' relationships with their communities of origin drove that home. Their symbolic reintegration into these communities, which usually took place after a year of service for the first volunteer regiments and after the war was over for the others, was in many ways quite similar to their sendoff. Volunteer units were met by parades, speeches, barbecues, balls, and banquets in which their deeds were praised and their service acknowledged. Again women prepared the food, such as the 1,500 pies baked for a single barbecue in Indianapolis. They also lined up to greet the men. One gets the impression that some part of this ritual was designed to show the men off to potential marriage partners. Oswandel, whose description of his unit's sendoff also noted the romantic tension in the air, wrote in his journal that when his unit had made its way back to Pennsylvania, women boarded the steamboat with baskets of food, and "I think that some of the ladies are falling in love with some of our men, and one of our men told me that he fell in love with one of the girls."[97] Regular army units were not greeted with any fanfare. Their men had not yet completed their contracts and were simply on their way to other posts, the family members of units were not concentrated in any particular location, and civilians continued to view them as disreputable men. As regular Alonzo Sampson pointed out, "There were plenty of us who had no home, strictly speaking, and I was one of them."[98] The end of the war was not a return to respectable, community- and family-based life for them.

Volunteer Misbehavior

Historian Amy Greenberg argues for a contrast between the notion that a proper man was restrained, moral, and a good provider and the notion that men should be strong, aggressive, and dominant. Both models were patriarchal, and both supported expansionism, but restrained men were likely to see trade and the spread of American social and religious institutions as the proper means, while martial men were fascinated by violent conquest.[99] In both the towns and farms of the Mississippi watershed and the eastern cities that later provided a second wave of volunteer regiments, it seems that these two models coexisted in the same spaces and even the same persons. In civilian life many men could be restrained providers much of the time, but they valued opportunities to act out more martial forms of masculinity in taverns, on hunting expeditions, and on Election Day. These settings were all known for drinking, boasting, demonstrations of physical prowess, brawling, and even mortal duels. Men defended their honor and asserted their ability to dominate others, including not only women but racial others, and they did so in an extraordinarily social way that was particularly notable for the absence of women.[100] The actions of volunteer soldiers, from the moment they were mustered into camps in the United States, through their experiences in Mexico, and up until their return to their home communities, indicate that in many ways being in a volunteer unit during the Mexican War was like having an unusually long interlude on a hunting trip, in a tavern, or at an election.[101]

Generally the volunteers elected their officers. In many cases men who already either filled or aspired to positions of political leadership in their communities actually drummed up the first volunteers, and they expected that leadership in volunteer units would help their future political prospects. Rumors indicated, for example, that the formation of Arkansas's volunteer regiment was designed to further the career of its colonel, Archibald Yell. Elections for officers were part and parcel of a highly partisan political system in which Whigs and Democrats vied for supremacy, and in more than one unit electoral results were disputed. Both electoral intrigue and partisan feelings ran very deep.[102] Not surprisingly, elections for officers were much like other American elections, in which stump speeches were accompanied by lavish promises and even more lavish distribution of alcoholic beverages, usually whiskey. Elections were also accompanied by boasting and plenty of brawling. As Oswandel describes, "Generally, like at all other elections, fighting, and knocking one another down was the order of the day. Some of our company fought like bulldogs if anyone said aught against Capt. Small. The row was kept up by the different parties nearly the whole day."[103] Although the men sometimes elected officers who proved to be effective military leaders, the qualities that led to electoral success did not necessarily overlap with those needed for military leadership, and volunteers often complained that their officers were incompetent. Regular army officers were particularly bemused to see that some of the men elected had flunked out of West Point.[104]

Volunteers were citizen-soldiers, and from their point of view the citizen part of their identity trumped the soldier part. They saw themselves as every bit the equals of their officers, and they insisted on being treated that way. Lieutenant Daniel Harvey Hill of the regular army observed of one Ohio regiment that "the men are on terms of the most perfect equality with their officers."[105] Volunteers often explicitly stated that they should not be treated like slaves. Oswandel, chafing at how hard one general pushed his unit, wrote, "Remember, these men are not slaves on your plantation. Nay, they are your equals and peers in all and every society in the whole United States of America."[106] Some even insisted on the right to hold meetings to express their opinions about orders, or even to vote officers out of office.[107] Open confrontations with officers were common. Kentucky volunteer William Glass bristled when Lieutenant W. C. Jones ordered him to return to camp. He told Jones off emphatically, saying, "God damn you! You are no better than I am no how. . . . Because you have got some straps on your shoulders, you think you can order me about like a dog."[108] Free men were ready to defend their rights violently, as Corporal Harvey of Indiana insisted when Lieutenant James Epperance tried to confiscate a keg of stolen whiskey. Harvey defied Epperance, saying, "You are an officer, I wish I had my way with you a few minutes. You will not always be an officer."[109] Volunteers were in theory subject to the same forms of corporal punishment as regular soldiers, but they insisted that corporal punishment not be applied to them because they were free American citizens. They even took direct action to prevent it on the rare occasions that officers dared to sentence volunteers to it.[110] Army practice was to regularly read the Articles of War that specified rules and punishments aloud to groups of soldiers, and Richard Coulter writes that when an officer read the articles to his volunteer regiment, his audience was much amused because it considered them "entirely unapplicable to their case." Later Coulter extended this difference to include training when he wrote that "the policy of frequent roll calling and drilling is good when applied to regulars but the volunteers should be exempt from all duties except such as are absolutely necessary." The notion that their service was unlike that of the regulars was so strong that after volunteers had worn out their distinctive uniforms, they balked at being issued uniforms the same color as those of the regulars.[111]

The fact that volunteer officers had been elected by their men and generally hoped to continue successful political careers after returning home dramatically reduced any incentive for officers to exert themselves to keep their troops in line, and everyone knew it.[112] Officers were generally a few years older than the men they led, and successful officers often exerted a kind of genial, paternal authority. Captain John Lowe wrote that he had "80 wild, thoughtless, careless boys to look after with as much care as you would look after the members of your family."[113] One Indiana officer insisted to his peers that volunteers would behave well if treated as citizens to whom one could make reasonable requests, but later he found that this, also, did not give results.[114] The problems officers had controlling their men were dramatically worsened by the local origins of the units. Officers feared that punishing their men would hurt their political careers, and, even more ominously, soldiers were reluctant to testify about the crimes of comrades who would be their neighbors again. Military authorities were unsuccessful in getting volunteers to admit crimes or admit to witnessing them. Comradeship for volunteers was strong enough to allow them to defy their officers because their social bonds extended beyond their army service, both into a shared past in their boyhoods and into a shared future as neighbors. As a result, military authorities despaired of controlling their behavior.[115]

The undisciplined behavior of Mexican War volunteers was notorious, and it is documented not only by the writings of many regular officers but also by the memoirs and letters of many volunteers themselves.[116] The consequences of this indiscipline were myriad. It was difficult to teach volunteers the complicated maneuvers and steadiness under fire that were central to tactics in the age of unrifled muskets. Volunteers also were extraordinarily accident prone, and many were killed and wounded in firearms accidents or in friendly fire incidents in which men mistook comrades for the enemy.[117] More seriously, volunteers were notorious for directly refusing to obey orders that displeased them, such as orders to stay in camps or columns on the march, orders to stand guard, orders to drill, and orders to work.[118]

When armed men of what might be most charitably called an independent disposition refused to obey orders, the situation sometimes became very dangerous. Very often officers faced verbal abuse or threats.[119] These words could escalate to assault, either by individual soldiers or by groups.[120] Soldiers unhappy about orders often were emboldened by the support of their peers to the point where units engaged in open verbal or physical defiance. Riots and mob action were very common in Jacksonian America, and these volunteer units were more than anything extensions of Jacksonian America. Disgruntled men pelted officers with rotten eggs or went even further.[121] Often, officers faced with mutinous soldiers backed down or sought compromise, but more than once open violence broke out.[122] The most famous case occurred when Colonel Robert Paine of the North Carolina Volunteers, irritated by the rowdy behavior of his men, threatened to inflict the corporal punishments common in the regular army. Outraged men surrounded his tent and began stoning it. The men assigned to guard it refused to help him, and Paine fired on the mob with his pistols, killing a man.[123] Soldiers also inflicted more surreptitious violence, using the confusion of battle as an opportunity to kill officers who had offended them.[124] Officers were inclined to appease their men not only in order to further their future political careers but also to avoid the possibility of mutiny and violence directed at their own persons.[125] The volunteer officers themselves were the product of this proud Jacksonian culture in which men felt compelled to violently defend their honor, and there were many instances in which disputes between officers led to the very edge of violence. One of the most telling broke out between Joseph Lane and his cousin James Lane. The dispute between these two Indiana officers escalated until they pointed loaded weapons at one another in front of an entire regiment.[126]

The volunteers saw themselves as free men, and some took that idea far enough to desert before their term of service was up. Regular army soldiers also deserted, but desertion for volunteers was in many ways quite different. Around 13 percent of regulars deserted in the war, and around 6 percent of volunteers. Regulars deserted both while on U.S. soil and in Mexico, and in many cases even in Mexico they sought permanent separation from the army. Once volunteer regiments were actually deployed to Mexico, volunteers tended to stay attached to their units except for brief unauthorized absences, typically to drink or attack Mexican civilians. The volunteers who truly left the army usually did so before their units reached Mexico. These were men swept up in the enlistment fever who later realized that war service could only bring them glory and plunder through risk and long-term separation from their families. They often deserted within days of enlistment, sometimes even with the permission of their commanders. It seems that authorities made little or no effort to compel them to continue their service unwillingly, although at least one unit publicly humiliated those unwilling to go Mexico.[127]

The vast majority of volunteers stayed in their units. They entered them swept up not only in war fever, with its invocations of patriotism and, more ominously, plunder, but also in the activities usually associated with holidays and elections—drinking, boasting, and other forms of revelry. These activities continued in the temporary camps as regiments were formed at strategic towns along the river systems, and then again on steamboats to New Orleans and in camp there. By then the volunteers were being introduced to the reality that soldiers spent surprisingly little time in battle, and endless amounts of time waiting in typically uncomfortable conditions as generals and politicians planned campaigns and worked out logistical details. While they waited, the volunteers continued drinking and gambling in camp and on visits to the local populace. American society was noted for its high alcohol consumption, and the gathering of men away from women—as on hunting trips, in taverns, or for elections—was an occasion for extra drinking. The boredom of weeks of waiting also contributed. Certainly regular army soldiers also drank, but they could not do so without restraint because excessive drinking and misbehavior while drunk led directly to fierce corporal punishment. The volunteers did not face this problem, and they and pretty much everyone who observed them remarked on the prevalence of drinking, and the fighting, gambling, and so on that went along with it.[128] A few stalwart souls, inspired by the growing temperance movement, started temperance clubs in their units, but these were definitely minority efforts, small islands in a sea of alcohol.[129]

These undisciplined, often drunken, volunteers, removed from the restraints imposed by the gentler half of local society and simultaneously emboldened by their solidarity with their male friends, were prone to crime, even against other Americans. As a Kentucky cavalry regiment made its way on horseback through Arkansas, its soldiers stole "pigs, turkey, geese, melons and milkpans," in the words of one volunteer. Indiana volunteers engaged in a drunken riot and stole food from vendors in their first camp by the banks of the Ohio River. Their first casualty, incurred before they even started down the river toward Mexico, is reported to have died from alcohol poisoning. Many volunteers spent some time in New Orleans awaiting transport to Mexico, and there they not only caroused but also committed theft, assault, and vandalism against civilians.[130] Some repeated this behavior by stealing from American civilians even as they made their way up the rivers on the way home after their service.[131] In the war zone volunteers stole government property and the personal property of other soldiers.[132]

The volunteers were removed from society's restraints and simultaneously wrapped in the approving embrace of their friends under the theoretical control of officers who needed the soldiers' favor or were cowed by their violence. This perfect recipe for military indiscipline was not an accident of history. These men were not gathered for a hunting expedition or an election; they were gathered to fight a war against Mexicans they had been taught were racially inferior, on par with the slaves held in thrall in the South or the Native Americans who had been systematically overrun through decades of bloody warfare.[133] We should not be shocked that these volunteers victimized Mexican civilians systematically and horrifically. For an overview, we can turn to General Winfield Scott, the army's highest-ranking officer, who wrote to Secretary of War William Marcy that the volunteers,

> if a tenth of what is said is true, have committed atrocities—horrors—in Mexico, sufficient to make Heaven weep, & every American, of Christian morals *blush* for his country. Murder, robbery, & rape on mothers & daughters, in the presence of the tied up males of the families, have been common all along the Rio Grande. I was agonized with what I heard—not from Mexicans, and regulars alone, but from respectable individual volunteers—from the masters & hands of our steamers. Truly it would seem unchristian & cruel to let loose upon any people—even savages—such unbridled persons—freebooters, &c., &c.[134]

Sadly, it appears that much more than a tenth of what Scott heard was true.

Volunteers stole from Americans, but they stole much more thoroughly from Mexicans, almost everywhere their campaigns took them. In their memoirs and letters home, volunteers themselves described these thefts, although the man actually writing rarely admitted personal involvement but instead reported the activities of others. During their recruitment volunteers had been tempted with the possibility of plunder, and, even though quite unofficial, it was an offer they accepted wholeheartedly. Certainly, in the military culture of Europe and the Americas, it was considered normal for soldiers to steal from enemy dead on the battlefield, or to plunder cities taken through bloody attacks. U.S. regular army soldiers and indeed their Mexican counterparts engaged in these behaviors. The volunteers, however, went much further. They stripped Mexican individuals and houses of their valuables. They also systematically plundered the economic resources Mexicans relied on, everything from the food that market women offered for sale to the livestock that formed so much of the capital of poor settlers in the north and their fence posts and houses, so handy for the volunteers' campfires. Nothing that could be consumed in Mexico or that was valuable and small enough to be carried back to the United States was safe, and they seem to have considered themselves entitled to it all. The men chafed at any efforts to restrain their larceny. Volunteer Oswandel criticized a general who scolded his unit for stealing, insisting that volunteers' marching and fighting earned them what they stole, and added that "soldiers who have to fight their enemy in an enemy's country will never go hungry as long as there are any chickens about."[135] One of the striking things about these thefts is how well documented they are in memoirs and letters, and how little they show up in the records generated by military trials. The discrepancy almost certainly results from the fact that volunteers would not testify against other volunteers, and without such testimony the military justice system was impotent.[136]

The promise that volunteering would provide a chance to steal from Mexicans was unofficial, but the promise that volunteering would give soldiers a chance to fight Mexicans was not. Certainly President Polk meant that the volunteers would get to fight Mexican soldiers, but the volunteers found that encounters with Mexican soldiers were relatively rare and brief. How, then, could they act out their manhood and connect it to Manifest Destiny? For many the answer was close at hand in the bodies of Mexican civilians. The two groups sometimes got along fairly well due to mutually beneficial commerce, as well as more gentle impulses like kindness and curiosity.

More often, drunken, bored, or just plain angry, volunteers, accustomed as they were to violent interactions even with their American peers, turned their attentions to Mexican civilians. In a lighthearted mood, they might engage in violent pranks, such as forcing a Mexican to run through the streets in his nightclothes. Brawls were common. Hoosier Henry Smith Lane wrote of how a brawl in which some Mexican civilians bested some of his comrades led to revenge in the form of arson.[137] Assaults on Mexicans were often carried out when Americans were drunk, but, as we have seen, that stipulation seems to have covered a remarkable portion of the hours the volunteers spent in the army.[138]

The crimes volunteers committed against Mexican civilians extended far beyond larceny and battery, often to murder and rape. Sometimes Americans reported these crimes under blanket terms that also covered less heinous crimes, using words like "excesses," "outrages," and "depredations."[139] These general terms might have sometimes been efforts to mask the most brutal crimes, but since the same sources sometimes refer to specific crimes, it is more likely that the general terms were a shorthand, a way of saving paper while communicating a known fact.[140] The murder of Mexican civilians was very common from the time volunteer soldiers first arrived on the banks of the Rio Grande in the early summer of 1846 to the time the last volunteers left Mexican territory almost exactly two years later. Volunteers often murdered Mexicans who protested the theft of their possessions: a Mexican not willing to let volunteers walk away with a blanket or drive away his livestock without protest could quickly become a dead Mexican.[141] Often, though, the murders do not seem to have had such a well-defined motive. Mexicans were killed in a variety of contexts: on the streets of Mexican towns and cities, on the highways, and even right on the outskirts of American camps, and the reasons are more often than not unvoiced. The American volunteer and regular soldiers who wrote of these murders were more likely to state that volunteers thought nothing of Mexican lives or were simply bad people than they were to describe specific motives, and Mexican sources have a similar attitude.[142] American commanders did not approve of the casual murders of Mexican civilians, but it was difficult for them to prosecute volunteer criminals. Hill reports poignantly how the parents of a murdered boy carried his corpse to General Taylor's tent.

Taylor was told that the murderer was from the Kentucky regiment, but none of the criminal's comrades would give authorities his name, even though forty of them witnessed the crime.[143]

Volunteers admitted freely that other volunteers committed murder, but they never admitted the same of rape. However, both Mexican sources and American regular officers indicate that volunteers often raped Mexican women. Sometimes rapes are reported in veiled language: American regular lieutenant Theodore Laidley explained that volunteers "rob houses, sack churches, ruin families," and Mexican civilian José Maria Aldrete reported that the volunteers had "done horrors with some families."[144] The use of veiled language suggests how terrible this crime was to people, and the specific language used in both the American and the Mexican sources suggests that rape was terrible in both cultures precisely because attacks on the honor and bodies of women were attacks on the families that both cultures saw as the foundation of moral society. These attacks also damaged the honor of the women's fathers and brothers, something volunteers sometimes deliberately drove home by forcing them to witness the attacks.[145] These nineteenth-century American men used sexual violence against Mexicans as a way of emphasizing racial domination, much as they commonly did against African Americans and Native Americans.[146] Many Americans, especially regular officers and enlisted men, deplored these rapes, and their testimony is the best corroboration that Mexican outcry against the volunteers' sexual violence was not exaggerated.[147]

What seem to us to be senseless acts of violence were not anomalies or even senseless, at least if we take "senseless" to mean "inexplicable." They were the logical result of the identities of the volunteers before they joined the army, their reasons for the momentous decision to travel far from home and run great risks, and their beliefs about Mexicans. These crimes did not generally serve the military goals of the U.S. Army, and they did not directly further the political goals of expansionists. They were, however, a product of the expansionist, racist aspects of Jacksonian culture that drove the United States into this war. Thus it seems appropriate to examine why the volunteers joined and what they believed about their relationship to the United States and about Mexicans.

Most volunteers were young, unmarried men, and one motive for heeding the call for recruits was obviously adventure. In the parlance of the day, they wanted to "see the elephant," a phrase that signified the unusual and the stirring.[148] Certainly military glory was seen as adventure, but just the chance to travel to foreign lands was also important. The first volunteers were convinced that they were headed to either the fascinating new land of Texas or the Far West; both were associated with individual opportunity. Some volunteers may have seen a chance to join the western migration at the government's expense. Yet Congress did not pass an act granting western land to recruits until February 1847, after recruiting new troops had become difficult. Still, Congress had previously given land to those who served in the Revolutionary War and the War of 1812, and it is possible that even some first-wave volunteers believed similar grants were likely for this war.[149] The most tangible benefit offered to volunteers in the first wave was the pay, probably more cash than these young men were likely to earn soon. It was a particularly strong incentive for the volunteers raised later in eastern cities, for all of the same reasons that some men served in the regular army.[150]

For volunteer recruits, unlike their regular army counterparts, patriotism was an important motive. American leaders had worked for almost fifty years to instill a sense of national identity through education and commemorations of independence with speeches, music, and festival atmospheres. The volunteers were consciously patriotic, and they were fond of singing patriotic songs and celebrating patriotic holidays, even when far from U.S. soil.[151] They believed they were following the example of America's past military patriots, and they spoke often of their Revolutionary War forebears but even more often of their predecessors in the War of 1812. The latter was particularly true of the first wave of volunteers from the Mississippi watershed. In New Orleans before shipping out to Mexico, they camped on the battleground where Andrew Jackson had defeated the British in the Battle of New Orleans. This battle was a particular touchstone for them, partly because they were eminently Jacksonian, and partly because they grew up believing Jackson's victory had been achieved with citizen-soldiers like themselves. Many volunteer memoirs and letters describe their emotional connection to this battlefield.[152] For them Jackson, even more than George Washington, was the quintessential war hero, the man who from a modest background rose to lead citizen-soldiers at the Battle of Horseshoe Bend and humble the haughty British at New Orleans.

Robert Johannsen has pointed out how romanticism, probably the strongest strain in American popular culture at the time, shaped these soldiers' views of war. Many volunteers had read William H. Prescott's *History of the Conquest of Mexico,* whose romantic descriptions whetted their appetites for a glimpse of "the Halls of the Montezumas." Walter Scott was a beloved author, and patriotic literature on America's past wars also painted them in a chivalric, romantic tone. In Johanssen's words, "An idealization of the past found analogies to the Mexican victories in the world's military annals; a tendency to view the war as a moral drama; the quest for honor and glory on the battlefield; and the reverence for heroes, heroism, and the heroic ideal."[153] This vision had important consequences for how the volunteers behaved, for example, by delegitimizing Mexican guerrilla tactics as dishonorable. More prosaically, though, the romantic image volunteers had of war meant that they in no way associated war with labor, unlike their peers in the regular army. Volunteers sometimes were reluctant to drill, the work officers considered most important for soldiers because it prepared them for the battlefield. Volunteers sometimes more or less willingly performed other tasks typical of soldiers, such as keeping camps and other quarters clean, helping move supplies, and preparing siege fortifications.[154] However, the volunteers generally had a strong aversion to work.[155] Oswandel reports that when the men of his unit were ordered to sweep their quarters, "this made the men rave and curse, telling Col. Wynkoop plainly that they would not sweep up the streets, as they did not enlist to sweep, and if the United States could not afford to hire its sweepers, they would pay it themselves out of their scanty means, sooner than to be slaves."[156] One Arkansas volunteer remarked, "I came here to fight them Mexicans, and not to make a mule of myself to haul wagons, and I say again, if this is war I ain't in no more."[157] Dramatically, in February 1847, as the Americans retreated before an advancing Mexican army, Arkansas volunteers refused orders to load wagons, and tons of supplies had to be burned to keep them out of the Mexicans' hands.[158]

Volunteers' View of Mexicans

Our anonymous Arkansas volunteer and his brethren in the volunteer units believed they were there to fight the Mexicans, and their ideas about Mexicans were central to the experience of the war for both the volunteers and the Mexicans they encountered. These ideas had been shaped by the ways in which Americans had come to understand Mexicans as members of a different and inferior race. The key moment in this racialization of the Mexicans was the War of Texas Independence. The war had not begun as a conscious extension of American expansionism, but it rapidly became one as thousands of Americans flooded into Texas to aid the rebels. This massive illegal immigration was egged on by a terrific propaganda campaign in American newspapers and public meetings. Supporters of the rebels argued that Mexicans were not martial enough to defeat Native Americans, that they were too lazy to make the wonderful lands of Texas productive, and that they were treacherous and cruel to the Anglo Texans.[159] Continued warfare between Texans and Mexicans stoked these beliefs in the decade before 1846. In reporting on the war, any Texan defeat was portrayed as a massacre by cruel Mexicans, and any Texan victory was portrayed as proof of Mexicans' cowardice or weakness. These negative images of Mexicans were probably strongest in the vast Mississippi watershed because many of the Anglos who had migrated to Texas during and after its independence hailed from there.

One of the most important ideas the propagandists of the Texas Revolution spread was that Mexicans were too lazy to make effective use of the natural resources found in their territory, and writings by Americans who had lived in Mexico parroted this idea.[160] When the volunteers reached Mexican territory, they attributed the persistent poverty and sometimes visible lack of activity on the part of Mexican men to laziness. In hindsight it becomes clear that the poverty and inactivity had everything to do with a scarcity of capital, a lack of water for agriculture, and above all the transportation difficulties that prevented the cost-effective transport of most goods to markets more than a few miles away. Moreover, some of the supposed indolence that volunteers saw no doubt stemmed from the fact that in Mexico even the hardest-working people typically divided their long workdays into two halves, resting in the middle of the day when the temperature was highest.

The volunteers were not culturally equipped to observe these details because they expected to see lazy Mexicans and such laziness was important to their ideas about their own racial superiority.[161] Volunteers observing what they believed to be rich soil and a warm, benign climate convinced themselves that many Mexicans were content to work only enough to support a minimum level of subsistence. Thomas Barclay wrote that Mexicans "only work enough to keep themselves from starving," while William Carpenter wrote that Mexican land was underutilized because "all its occupants wished for in this world was enough to eat from day to day, never thinking of providing for the future."[162] Mexican laziness was one of the principal justifications for taking their land. Henry Smith Lane wrote in November 1846 that the land

> along the Rio Grande is very fertile but miserably cultivated; the people are lazy, ignorant & perfidious with no patriotism, no public spirit, no enterprise and it would be a great mercy for them to take their country. . . . We have a singular climate here at least it seems so to a Northern man, there is now in the market here green corn, peas, beans, water melons, musk melons, onions, radishes & every variety of vegetables which we have in the Spring at the North, besides a great many more which are peculiar to this climate. In a word God has done as much to bless & man to curse this country as any region on earth.[163]

A. C. Pickett added that he "saw many sites which with American industry & enterprise would bloom like a garden."[164]

The Texas Revolution and the resulting propaganda campaigns also spread the idea that Mexicans were not trustworthy, which likewise shaped what the volunteers believed they were observing in Mexico. The volunteers believed Mexican males to be cowards and thieves likely to steal or commit violence surreptitiously.[165] Franklin Smith wrote that "the Mexicans as a people are capable of any treachery bribery corruption fraud and robbery," and "everything Mexican is perfidious and deceptious and false."[166] Many Americans believed that the Mexicans in occupied territory were outwardly willing to accept their presence and even sell goods to them but only awaited opportunities to strike without retaliation. Robert Milroy reported to his sister that "the Mexicans seem to be perfectly subdued in this part of the country and mix with us and trade with us as sociably as if they never thought of war, but they are all treacherous devils and there are a great many robbers among them who are skulking through the country every place."[167] This idea that Mexicans would not fight openly and honestly due to flaws in their character greatly influenced Americans' reactions when some Mexicans began to use guerrilla tactics against them.

Views of Mexicans had much to do with gender. Latin American men were seen as effeminate, perhaps the root cause of their laziness and untrustworthiness. Volunteers sometimes commented on this. Amy Greenberg points out that this negative image of Mexican men is tied to a positive image of Mexican women, and both served to justify expansionism: "Images of attractive Mexican women and effeminate Mexican men in the popular literature of the war helped to justify aggression against Mexico."[168] Greenberg shows that in the writings of expansionists the attractiveness of Mexican women was not simply an abstract idea. Many of them wrote that Mexico could be best absorbed into the United States through the marriage of American men and Mexican women, and this idea was taken up even more vigorously by novels and stories written during the war. Generally, in these stories the women are relatively wealthy and more Spanish than Indian, the tone is highly romantic, and the ultimate idea is that the conflict could be resolved through reconciliation.[169]

Many volunteers participated in their Mexican adventure at the moment in their lives when they were expected to be looking for potential wives. When you combine this fact with expansionist propaganda that urged them to consider annexation on a more personal scale, if we can call it that, we should not be surprised that many volunteers evaluated Mexican women as potential marriage partners. They often commented on the looks of Mexican women, particularly valuing wealthier and lighter-skinned women.[170] However, they also commented on the women's kindness, work ethic, and sexual morality.[171] This last question was crucial, because for the volunteers to see Mexican women as marriageable, they had to be much more trustworthy than the volunteers believed Mexican men to be. Many volunteers concluded that they were not, claiming that they were unfaithful to their husbands. A few disagreed. It seems very possible that the idea that Mexican women were not chaste drew some of its force from the fact that many Mexican women dressed in ways Americans considered immodest.[172] The volunteers were clearly aware of the propaganda suggesting they marry Mexican women, and in letters exchanged with home, both sides made teasing references to this possibility.[173] Yet few volunteers actually married Mexican women, although some had sexual relations with them. These relationships, however, seem to have stemmed more from the ways in which being removed from their hometowns offered the possibility of sexual adventures without long-term repercussions than from an embrace of the expansionist idea of personal annexation.[174]

People often convince themselves that other people belong to a different and inferior race by disparaging their hygiene, and Mexican women were not spared this insult.[175] Mexican men also were accused of lacking hygiene. Volunteers often referred to Mexicans as "greasers," and one even referred to Mexican women as "greaseritas."[176] The idea was that Mexicans had a dirty appearance, and this seems often to have melded into more general ideas of the physical differences between Mexicans and white Americans. Whites in Jacksonian America were increasingly obsessed with racial differences and the hierarchy of races, and they brought this obsession with them to Mexico. American volunteers looked to the complexions of Mexicans for reassurance that they themselves were white and that, because the Mexicans were not white, they could be justifiably and safely dominated. Mexicans were criticized for being the descendants of Indians or Africans. The mixed-race heritage of many Mexicans unsettled volunteers. Thus Kentuckian Levi White wrote to his wife of the women he observed at a dance that "I do not like the complexion of the prettiest of them there is even in the fairest a sort of dirty-mottled appearance that looks like a mixture of Negro, or Indian and the dance looked more like a Maryland negro dance than anything I can compare it to."[177] If Mexicans were not white, how could a single volunteer contemplate marrying one? The answer for many was to see Mexican women as white and their men as dark. Adolphus Engelman thus wrote that "the only difference between Mexican men and mulattoes lies in the straight coarse hair of the Mexican. That being the case we wonder at the white complexion of their women, who look just like ours."[178] The racial diversity of Mexico and Mexican racial attitudes baffled the volunteers. Albert Brackett was surprised to see that in religious art Jesus was not always depicted as white, with his complexion varying "from the white skin of the European, to the darkest African tinge. Why they have them white and black I cannot tell unless it is to suit all classes."[179] Racial superiority served to justify the war with Mexico, but in some sense Mexico also represented a threat precisely because Mexicans were not willing to accept the rigid separation between races that was becoming so crucial to the identity of American whites.[180]

Even though some aspects of American racial views were physiological, others were more cultural, and of these nothing was more important than Mexicans' Catholicism. As previously mentioned, in the 1840s many Americans harbored anti-Catholic sentiments.[181] The volunteers arrived primed to despise Mexicans for their Catholicism, but most had never seen a Catholic church or ceremony. Used to a relatively austere and very literate Protestantism, they were particularly struck by how much Catholic buildings and ceremonies relied on visual and symbolic means to communicate the intellectual subtleties and emotional depth of religion to a population in which many could not read. Ceremonies conducted by priests in full regalia seemed more theatrical than religious to the volunteers, and efforts to use art to reach Mexican souls through their senses seemed extravagant at best and irreligious at worst.[182] Volunteers were also puzzled by some Mexican religious attitudes, such as the fact that Mexicans often enacted the funerals of children as happy farewells to souls destined to proceed directly to heaven.[183] Generally, the volunteers interpreted what they saw as confirmation that Catholicism was a religion of ignorance and superstition, one some even saw as idolatrous. They often called Catholic ritual "mummery," implying not only that it was ridiculous but also that the worshipers themselves were faking.[184]

Volunteers blamed Catholicism for Mexico's poverty and lack of democracy. They constantly referred to the money Mexicans invested in churches and religious art, so different from what the Americans were accustomed to. However, to them this was not just a theological or cultural difference. They believed that this spending, along with the properties church institutions used to provide income for worship and education, impoverished Mexico's people to benefit a priestly class. Thomas Barclay wrote, "The holy fathers who like locusts of Egypt darken the land are content with vast possessions in real estate, with treasures amassed by a system of robberies and with palaces both as residences and places of worship which in gorgeous magnificence recalls the fairly palaces of Arabian tales."[185] American critics of Catholicism in the United States saw it as undemocratic, and, not surprisingly, the volunteers saw Mexico's Catholicism as one of the principal obstacles to democracy there.[186]

Catholicism was also important to the ways in which American volunteers understood Mexican priests as immoral and Mexico as feminine. Americans found the vows of chastity taken by Catholic nuns and priests difficult to fathom. American anti-Catholicism was fed by extraordinarily popular, sensationalist tracts that implied that nuns were the sexual slaves of priests. If priests did not violate their vows, this was evidence that they were not masculine, while if they did, it was evidence that they were fakes.[187] All of these attitudes about Catholicism worked together to make Mexican men seem feminine to most volunteers, and gender, religion, and physical characteristics blended to convince volunteers that Mexicans were an inferior race.[188]

Neither Polk nor American generals wanted to arouse Mexican ire because they wanted to fight the war against the weak Mexican government rather than its large population. Democratic political machines in eastern cities were also eager to attract the votes of Catholic immigrants. Thus, even as Democrats in the Mississippi watershed embraced anti-Catholicism, Polk worked to take religion out of the war, not criticizing Mexican Catholicism and endorsing efforts to prevent volunteers from attacking the Catholic Church. Unfortunately, neither the generals nor the leaders of the Democratic Party were able to control what had become a powerful ideological force. Volunteers often disobeyed orders to leave Catholicism alone.[189] Some committed deliberate sacrilege, for instance, by stabling their horses in churches. Others took care to openly defy customs that underlined the social prestige of Catholic priests or treated the Holy Eucharist with great respect. A few deliberately disrupted Catholic ceremonies, especially Mass.[190] However, most sacrilege committed by volunteers involved theft. We have seen how the volunteers remarked on the rich adornment of Mexican churches, designed to impress the majesty of God on the senses of worshipers. Catholic worship often uses vessels made with precious metals or adorned with jewels. The volunteers knew this, mostly through best-selling works on Mexico. Among the volunteers was open talk of the "Golden Jesuses" of Mexico and the possibility of them becoming loot. The sweetheart of one volunteer supposedly told him that "one bed should hold them both if according to promise he brought her a little Gold God and silver Jesus." Volunteers even sang the following song to the tune of "Yankee Doodle":

> We're the boys for Mexico
> Sing Yankee Doodle Dandy
> Gold and silver images,
> Plentiful and handy.
> Churches grand, with altars rich
> Saints with diamond collars
> (That's the talk to understand,)
> With lots of new bright dollars.[191]

Once in Mexico, volunteers acted on these desires. They stole many religious objects from churches, outraging Mexicans in the process.[192]

The anti-Catholicism of many volunteers was tightly connected to a growing backlash against Catholic immigrants back home. Many volunteers also expressed strong nativist feelings in their writings. They believed immigrants were coarse and stupid, and they criticized the immigrants they encountered in the army.[193] Many volunteer companies excluded immigrants from their ranks. However, leaders among urban immigrants, the American Catholic Church, and the urban, eastern parts of the Democratic Party realized that the war presented both a threat and an opportunity. The association between Mexico and Catholicism might provide further fuel for the idea that Catholic immigrants could not be loyal citizens of a democratic United States. Yet if immigrants could show that they, too, were willing to sacrifice for their new country, their assimilation would accelerate, strengthening the Democratic Party and helping protect the church. Thus these leaders worked to organize companies of German or Irish immigrants.[194] These companies were inserted into regiments in which many volunteer soldiers viewed immigrants with suspicion and contempt, and the results were not always comfortable. Nativists did not hide their feelings, and one of the most violent riots seen in the volunteer ranks was a prolonged and bitter brawl between an Irish company and its fellow companies in the Georgia volunteer regiment.[195]

As the war wore on, American civilians became more and more aware of their sons' behavior in the volunteer regiments, and many did not approve. The peacetime regular army and its soldiers were despised, but American civilians had treated the volunteers differently, as exemplary citizens off to fulfill their duty to defend their nation through an exotic adventure far from home. Soon, however, disquieting reports began to make their way home, mostly from the volunteers themselves, who began to see that their disorderly behavior and the constant presence of death by disease were coarsening them. Observing a Sunday in Matamoros, Henry Smith Lane wrote, "Instead of the sound of the church bells & the hum of prayers & thronging of thousands of Christian votaries, we have here the sounds of mirth, of rioting, of blasphemy, & all manner of irreverence & ungodliness. It is strange that men become more & more hardened & obdurate as the chances for sudden death are increased. A camp life is demoralizing in all its tendencies."[196] Some men who constantly saw comrades die of disease became callous, hardly paying attention to the funerals.[197] Some soldiers were troubled by the crimes Americans committed against Mexican civilians and reported them in American newspapers. Laidley wrote to his father that "most of those who come out here seem to have left all conscience of right and wrong at home and commit actions without shame that they would blush to do when under the restraints of society at home. A long, long time will it be before we get over the ill consequences of this war."[198] Civilians at home began to express their disapproval, sometimes directly to the soldiers. The mother of Indiana volunteer Benjamin Franklin Scribner wrote to him that she was "sorry to see in the publick prints that the Ohio volunteers and the 2nd regiment of the Indiana vol had conducted in unbecoming and dishonorable manner toward the unhappy Mexicans, in taking liberties and undue advantage with poor females, and also robbing them of their property and causing them to flee from their homes."[199] The behaviors common in taverns and at elections, which might have been tolerable for short periods in the United States, threatened to damage American society when they dominated men's existence month after month.

Military service was not only corrupting young men, it was killing them. The death rate for men serving in Mexico was ten times that of the U.S.

population. That fact probably would not have surprised the young men who gathered to listen to recruiting speeches: there could be no glory without the risk of death. What they did not know when they signed up was that most casualties would not happen on the potentially glorious field of battle but instead in camps and hospitals. Seven times as many men died of illness as died on the battlefield.[200] Fatal illnesses like malaria, smallpox, cholera, yellow fever, and, especially, various forms of diarrhea and dysentery began to affect units as soon as they were organized. Disease stalked these men on the riverboats as they made their way to New Orleans, on the muddy campground at New Orleans where many awaited ships to Mexico, and in every camp and city where they were quartered. Many ill men died even on the way home, after they were mustered out. The toll taken by disease was one of the defining experiences of these volunteers, and they wrote about it incessantly in their letters, diaries, and memoirs.[201]

The deadliest locations, however, were the camps near the Rio Grande. Many of the first-wave volunteers spent much of their terms of service there because Zachary Taylor only had enough supplies and transport to take part of his troops on his campaign into Mexico, and also because he doubted that these regiments were ready for battle when he began the campaign. The camps were charnel houses for the volunteers. Intestinal illnesses spread like wildfire among men crowded together on marshy ground with inadequate tents and a water supply of dubious quality. So many men died there that the volunteers ran out of wood to make coffins and the mockingbirds learned to sing the funeral march. Henry Smith Lane of Indiana described his camp as "a graveyard, a very hell on earth." Three months after the arrival of his regiment, Lane reported to his brother that it had lost sixty dead, with another two hundred or so discharged from the army for ill health. Lane, an ambitious politician, had been one of the most vociferous boosters of the war in Indiana, and in June 1846 he personally raised a company of the First Indiana. By September, however, after witnessing yet another funeral, he wrote, "I thought of the gallant young men whom I had induced to leave their home & all its comforts for the pestilential vapours & poisonous breath of a southern clime until every note of the funeral sunk like a leaden weight upon my heart & almost stilled its pulsations. I could not help thinking that

I in some sort was responsible for their death, & the thought planted daggers in my soul."[202] Morale sank as soldiers constantly witnessed funerals. Isaac Smith wrote that "the dead march was heard nearly every day."[203]

Military doctors could do very little for the sick, and soldiers saw that ill men who entered military hospitals were largely neglected, with inadequate shelter and nursing.[204] Soldiers and officers criticized the decision to keep their units in the unhealthy camps far from the prospect of battle, and they soon began to tire of the war that had seemed so exciting when they mustered in.[205] These deaths clashed with the volunteers' romantic view of war, but arguably that same view greatly contributed to the toll of disease. Fifteen percent of the volunteers who served in the war were killed by illness, while only 8 percent of regular soldiers died that way. Some of this difference can be explained by the fact that many first-wave volunteers came from small towns and farms, where they had not developed immunities to many pathogens, while regular army recruits were usually from large cities, where they had already been exposed to more microbes.[206] However, the higher death rates for volunteers also had another cause. Soldiers and politicians had long known that in wars illness was usually more deadly than violence. Although they did not yet subscribe to the germ theory of disease, military doctors and other officers had developed a practical respect for the importance of cleanliness and drainage. Both were the result of work, which was something regular army soldiers expected to be part of military life and regular army discipline could make happen. The volunteers, however, associated soldiering with glorious battle, not the tedious and difficult work that would have limited the toll of disease. Even when officers understood the problem, they could not compel the volunteers to work, and many observers realized that this contributed greatly to the illnesses that ravaged the volunteers.[207]

CHAPTER 3

Like Civilized Nations

THE SOCIAL COMPOSITION and beliefs of American volunteer units led directly to guerrilla warfare between Americans and Mexicans in northern Mexico. Guerrilla warfare was not a new concept in Mexico: Mexican politicians and military leaders were very conscious of its importance during the Mexican War of Independence and the Spanish war against Napoleon's invading armies. Eventually various Mexican leaders began to promote guerrilla warfare, and guerrilla tactics were sometimes very successful. By the end of the war, some Mexican politicians came to believe that Mexico would have benefited from even more use of such tactics.[1] However, in the summer of 1846 all of this was in the future. Mexican politicians and military leaders did not make a significant effort to encourage guerrilla warfare before December 1846, and by then American soldiers in the north were already being ambushed by guerrillas.[2] Thus we need to look elsewhere to understand why guerrillas began to oppose the U.S. invasion in the north.

The lands that Taylor's army invaded in the spring of 1846 had been partially depopulated by Comanche raids. The Comanche were using Mexico's north to acquire livestock both for their own use and for U.S. markets, as well as to acquire labor for their own economy. Comanche raids were difficult for northern Mexicans to counter because the region was too dry to allow dense concentrations of population. Even a large hacienda housed at most a few dozen people, and their work required them to tend scattered herds. Comanche raiding parties with sometimes hundreds of warriors could simply overwhelm any possible defense. However, Mexicans were not passive in the face of this onslaught. There was a long tradition of gathering forces of informal soldiers who pursued raiders to recover livestock or captives and make raids costly to natives. Northern Mexicans saw themselves as warriors who sought to protect their own in a harsh environment, and they were adept at transmitting news of attacks, gathering reaction forces, and either pursuing raiding parties or preparing ambushes on the trails used by natives. This warfare was extremely violent. In Comanche culture the ritual torture and killing of captives was used to avenge and grieve slain kin, and mutilated bodies seem to have served to demonstrate their military superiority and instill fear in Mexicans. The Mexicans responded in kind, creating a certain grotesque cultural grammar in which both the Comanche and the Mexicans used exemplary violence to communicate with each other.[3]

The first hint that this pattern of warfare might expand to encompass conflict between Mexicans and Americans came at the battles of Palo Alto and Resaca de Palma, where apparently some of the informal militia cavalry of Mariano Arista's army killed and mutilated wounded Americans.[4] However, immediately after those battles there was a period of calm as the Mexican people of the Rio Grande valley tried to make sense of what life under American occupation would be like. Many local people had lost faith in a Mexican government that had not protected them from Comanche attacks but still insisted on taxing them, and some had been tempted by the idea of separating from Mexico. The American army bought goods, and it was now easier to export cattle to the United States than it had been before the war. Moreover, American leaders were very aware that the people in northern Mexico were suffering from Native American raids, and their proclamations made the most of this fact, offering protection the Mexican government had not been able to provide.[5] The arrival of large numbers of volunteer soldiers, first temporary units from Texas and Louisiana and then regiments from the Mississippi watershed, dramatically changed the situation. Taylor's regulars, victors at Palo Alto and Resaca de Palma, had not harassed Mexican civilians much. In contrast, the volunteers were for many intents and purposes a more numerous and well-armed version of the Comanche raiders.

The volunteers were removed from the restraints imposed in their normal lives by the presence of their mothers, sisters, and wives or potential wives. They were officered by men who could gain little and lose everything if they punished infractions. They were also inflamed by months of rhetoric about Mexican inferiority and perfidy. Now they found themselves in conquered territory, bored, drunk, eating monotonous preserved foods, and surrounded by Mexican civilians. Within weeks and sometimes days of their arrival, the volunteers began to prey on the property and bodies of Mexican civilians. As we have seen in previous chapters, they shot and ate their cattle, stole their corn, used their fences and houses for firewood, and took just about anything else that was not nailed down. They raped women and killed Mexicans who protested all of these crimes.[6] Lieutenant George Meade wrote to a friend in July 1846, barely two weeks after the arrival of the first volunteers, that the volunteers "in fact act more like a body of hostile Indians than of civilized whites. Their own officers have no command or control over them, and the General has given up in despair any hope of keeping them in order. The consequence is they are exciting a feeling among the people which will induce them to rise up en masse." Other regulars called the volunteers "Mohawks" or "Goths."[7]

When American regulars compared the volunteers to Native Americans, they were drawing on sensationalized and racist stories of Indian wars in American popular culture. Northern Mexicans who had been struggling to resist Comanche attacks also saw the volunteers as acting like Indians. They quickly began referring to the American volunteers as white Comanche, or the "Comanches of the North."[8] As they had with the Comanche, they tracked the volunteer units that committed crimes and waited for opportunities to exact revenge. Within weeks the volunteers found themselves embroiled in guerrilla warfare. Mexicans ambushed volunteers who left their units alone or in small groups to visit towns, to hunt, or to commit crimes. Sometimes they were dragged to their death by mounted cowboys, sometimes they were tortured, and often their bodies were mutilated and left in prominent locations as a macabre way of communicating outrage to their comrades.[9] The violence appalled Mexican regular army officers. However, they were no more able to control the behavior of the guerrillas than Taylor was able to control the volunteers. Mexican civilians in occupied territory reported to their government that Taylor had admitted to them that he could not control the volunteers and gave the Mexicans tacit approval to retaliate against them. Although the latter seems unlikely, it suggests the mind-set that prevailed among Mexican men in occupied territory.[10] Many people in Mexico's far north were dissatisfied by a Mexican government that could not protect them from Native American raiders, and some were attracted by the economic possibilities offered by the rapid expansion of the population, economy, and even territory of the United States. However, the behavior of the volunteers soon made these people fierce enemies, initiating a desperate, dirty, and extremely violent conflict that bled both the American army and Mexican civilians for more than a year.[11]

When the volunteers began to lose comrades to Mexican retaliation, they ratcheted up their attacks on Mexican civilians they already saw as treacherous racial inferiors. Volunteers murdered Mexican men, burned villages, and, like the Mexicans, displayed the corpses of their victims as a macabre message.[12] Soldiers in other wars faced with guerrilla tactics have responded with violence against civilians as well. David Bell, in his work on the Napoleonic Wars, traces this to the identification between the people and the state that characterizes wars between nation-states, an identification that turns civilians into a legitimate enemy. American historians like Reginald Horsman, Wayne Lee, and Mark Grimsley have argued that American soldiers were more likely to kill noncombatants from despised racial groups, and James McCaffrey and Eliud Santiago Aparicio point to how the Americans' anger about atrocities committed earlier during the War of Texas Independence fueled violence against Mexican civilians.[13]

Although undoubtedly all of these factors contributed to the violence, even together they are not quite satisfying. The extremes seen in northern Mexico were driven by the volunteers' cultural attitudes about Mexicans and about warfare itself. The volunteers had a romantic view of war. They expected conventional battles in which their bravery, honor, and marksmanship would win the day. Battles could be terrifying, but they were mercifully brief. No battle of this war lasted more than two days, and most were over in a few hours. Guerrilla warfare presented a different challenge to the volunteers' psyches. They were an occupying force, surrounded by Mexicans who sometimes visited their camps to sell things. Yet soon it became clear that volunteers who strayed even a short distance from their units might find themselves dead, left as a message on the road or in a back alley in some town. Moreover, they believed that the same Mexicans they bought goods from or passed on the street were implicated. William H. Daniel of Kentucky wrote in his diary that the Mexicans "are very treacherous, they pretend great friendship for any American and if then three or four of them could ketch him out with arms they would make nothing of killing him."[14] The American volunteers did not see guerrilla tactics as legitimate warfare. Again and again they referred to guerrillas as robbers and murderers, and they even went so far as to claim that many guerrillas had been robbers before the war.[15]

The idea that guerrilla warfare was criminal made the Mexicans seem even more like another disdained racial group, Native Americans. The volunteers arrived in Mexico already inclined to classify Mexicans with Native Americans, but surreptitious violence and the mutilation of cadavers tilted their perceptions even more dramatically in that direction. Daniel wrote in his diary that the "Mexicans call the Comanches cruel they say they are like wolves. So they are cruel but I think that in cruelty and treachery that the Mexicans are full brothers to them, as for my part I hate them worse than I do the Comanches."[16] Most volunteers hailed from regions that had been on the frontier of white settlement only a generation before. As military historian John Grenier describes, for a long time warfare against Indians had often been conducted in a particular way. Settlers had responded to any violence from Native Americans defending their lands by forming informal, ad hoc armed groups. These groups, usually lacking the ability to identify and locate the specific Indians who had attacked settlers, had instead conducted revenge attacks against whatever native settlements were closest at hand, targeting the Indians' crops, livestock, and homes. They also had killed and often mutilated Indian noncombatants. Volunteer units reacted to Mexican guerrilla attacks in precisely this way, forming informal groups to take revenge against whatever Mexican noncombatants were unlucky enough to be nearby.[17]

Another cultural pattern shaped the way the volunteers reacted to guerrilla warfare. In the mid-nineteenth-century United States, especially in the regions that most volunteers came from, there was a very strong tradition of vigilantism. A community's men often informally organized themselves to decide who had committed crimes and violently punish them. Vigilantes did not use rigorous rules of evidence, and many people punished were innocent.[18] This system of "justice" was most often applied to the marginalized—the poor, certainly, but above all those marginalized by their race: African Americans, Indians, and, after Texas's independence, Mexicans. In Jacksonian America many people believed that courts left many crimes unpunished, and that the community should act in their stead. The democratization of the period actually reinforced this tendency, because it emphasized the legacy of the American

Revolution, one of popular violence.[19] Once "justice" was done this way, citizens protected themselves by not testifying to the authorities. The volunteers who left American camps to avenge guerrilla attacks, which they believed were criminal acts, were not acting under orders but instead organized themselves as vigilante posses. When they wrote about their actions, they often cited dubious evidence that the men they killed were implicated in guerrilla attacks.[20]

The high command in northern Mexico consisted mostly of regular army officers. Although Taylor and his commanders vociferously criticized atrocities against civilians, they were stymied by their inability to identify specific perpetrators, a result of the volunteers' refusal to testify against their comrades. As Taylor put it, it was "next to impossible to detect the individuals who thus disgrace their colors and their country."[21] Moreover, Taylor and his generals were perturbed by the continuing losses their soldiers faced, the killing and mutilation of some soldiers after capture, and the threat that guerrilla activity posed to their supply lines. They ordered American troops to kill any guerrillas found with arms in their hands, and threatened to make Mexican civilians pay economically for supplies lost in guerrilla attacks. These measures convinced some volunteers that American commanders actually approved of revenge attacks on Mexican civilians.[22]

An incident that took place in February 1847 near Agua Nueva, Coahuila, exemplifies the tangle of reprisals and justification that northern Mexico experienced during much of the war. Six different volunteers, other American writers, and at least one Mexican reported on this incident. All agree on the basic outline of events, but they differ on various details. Mexican guerrillas killed an Arkansas cavalryman named Samuel Colquit while he was out alone. When the Americans found his body, they saw that he had been dragged by the neck over rough ground and through cactus patches. A group of his comrades set out to exact revenge, followed by some Illinois volunteers, who lagged behind because they were not mounted. The Americans proceeded to a remote and rugged location where they knew that the inhabitants of Agua Nueva had camped to avoid volunteer depredations. In this place, variously described as a cave or a ravine, the Arkansas volunteers conducted a search and brief interrogation before beginning to systematically murder the males. They killed between five and thirty men; most accounts estimated the dead at twenty-five. One of the first Illinois men to catch up tried to stop the killing,

Massacre of the Cave.

FIG. 3.1 Arkansas troops massacre civilians near Agua Nueva. Drawing by Samuel Chamberlain.

but the Arkansas volunteers ignored him until he asked that they leave some Mexicans for his comrades to kill. When the rest of the Illinois men arrived, they instead protected the survivors and brought them back to the American camp. Some Arkansas men, disappointed that the Illinois men were only imprisoning the survivors, tried to continue the massacre, even firing their weapons in the direction of the guards.

This account relies largely on the diary of an Illinois volunteer and the memoir of an Arkansas volunteer, but it is clear that the incident was much discussed among American soldiers, and during the discussions details were added or embellished. Several aspects of these accounts illustrate the cycle of violence and justification. One memoir states that the Mexicans who killed Colquit were themselves avenging rapes that Arkansas soldiers had committed in Agua Nueva. In every version the Arkansas men who sought to avenge him were not under orders but were instead an informally organized posse. Most Americans state that the Arkansas men found physical evidence that the Mexicans had participated in Colquit's killing. The Arkansas writer claims that they found the sling of Colquit's carbine, and as the story made the rounds, others added items like the carbine itself and Colquit's clothing. Clearly those who participated in the massacre or approved of it felt it important to tag its victims as criminals, much as vigilantes did in the United States. As the tale traveled, the tellers also added details about Colquit's corpse, saying that he had been tortured and his body deliberately mutilated. When we consider the versions together, the incident appears to be more akin to vigilantism than counterinsurgency warfare. While some versions written by Americans thoroughly condemn the Arkansas men, most consider their actions to be to some degree justifiable.[23]

The massacre appalled both General John Wool, commander of the immediate area, and Taylor. Some versions say that Wool heard the firing and sent the Illinois volunteers to investigate, although in most versions the Illinois men had planned to help find Colquit's killers. In any event, Wool and Taylor decided to take action. They may have been partially motivated by the fact that the Arkansas troops were among the least disciplined of the volunteer units, which is saying a lot. Arkansas was a rough, frontier state, noted for its violence and lack of order, and vigilantism was very common there. The Arkansas men had already been implicated in a number of crimes against the Mexicans and other discipline problems.[24] Wool ordered the rescued Mexicans released, indicating openly that he did not believe that any evidence tied them to Colquit's death. Wool and Taylor pressured the leaders of both the Arkansas and the Illinois troops to identify the killers, but they all feigned ignorance. Taylor decided on a collective punishment. He ordered the Arkansas troops involved in the massacre to return to the camps on the Rio Grande that had proven a disease-ridden hell for several volunteer units. He also condemned the perpetrators in a letter read aloud before his entire army, saying that they "cast indelible disgrace upon our arms, and the reputation of our country," and implying that men who killed unarmed and innocent Mexicans were cowards who would not perform well in battle.[25] The men did not leave due to rumors that a large Mexican army was approaching, and Taylor's words about these men's battlefield performance proved prophetic.

The cycle of volunteer depredations, guerrilla reprisals, and volunteer attacks on Mexican civilians, which had begun in the summer of 1846, became fiercer in January and February 1847 when the Mexican army began sending forces of regular cavalry to help the guerrillas cut American supply lines. Successful Mexican attacks on wagon trains included the execution and sometimes mutilation of American teamsters, and the volunteers inflicted more violence on Mexican civilians in response, turning many towns into wastelands. In May 1847 there was a remarkable exchange of letters between General Ignacio de Mora y Villamil, the Mexican commanding the northern front, and Taylor. Mora y Villamil explained that Pedro María Anaya, who served as substitute president while Antonio López de Santa Anna led armies in the field, had ordered Mora y Villamil to protest American atrocities against civilians and ask Taylor whether he wanted to prosecute the war in accordance with "the law of nations, and as it is prosecuted by civilized countries, or instead as it is waged between savage tribes," adding that Mexico would follow America's lead. Mora y Villamil described and condemned various atrocities, but he also tried to soften the blow to Taylor's honor by saying that he hoped that Taylor had not yet heard of the atrocities and would now work to stop them. Even so, Taylor was not pleased to have the responsibility placed so boldly on his shoulders. In response he wrote that the letter implied a deliberate "insult to me and the government which have the honor to represent." Taylor went on to say that the atrocities mentioned became known to me soon after their occurrence, and I can assure you that neither yourself nor the president of the republic could have felt deeper regret than myself on those occasions. Every means within my power, within the operation of our laws, were employed, but in most cases in vain, to identify and punish the delinquents. I cannot suppose you so badly informed as to believe that such atrocities were committed with my connivance or consent, or that they furnish a fair example of the mode in which the war has been conducted in this part of Mexico. They were in truth unfortunate exceptions, caused by circumstances beyond my control.

Taylor argued that individual Americans had been "murdered" by Mexicans, implying that guerrilla warfare was criminal. He added that Mexicans had killed wounded Americans on the field of battle, as well as murdered and mutilated unarmed American wagon drivers. Neither Anaya nor Mora y Villamil actually compared the Americans to Native American tribes in their letters, and Anaya instead explicitly referred to the savage tribes that had invaded the Roman Empire. However, after news of this exchange leaked out, Jonathan Buhoup, the Arkansas volunteer who described the Agua Nueva massacre in his memoir, wrote that the Mexican commander had asked "whether Gen. Taylor was resolved to wage a war similar to that of the Camanches, or a war like civilized nations."[26]

American volunteers who had signed up in search of glory, adventure, the chance to defend their country, and plunder found themselves locked in a sordid and bloody cycle of ambush, revenge, and atrocity. American cultural views of how to make war against racial others like Native Americans and how to address crime drove the volunteers into this mess, but it certainly was not the war they had hoped to fight. Several volunteers remarked on how the cycle of vengeance brought both Mexicans and Americans to commit acts that would have been repugnant to them before the war. Extreme violence and cruelty begot more extreme violence and cruelty.[27] This kind of war eventually tarnished the reputation of the volunteers. Most reporting in American newspapers consisted of dispatches penned by the volunteers themselves, sent to hometown newspapers and then sometimes reprinted multiple times in papers across the nation. At first these men overlooked the

FIG. 3.2 Mexican guerrillas capture a wagon train. Drawing by Samuel Chamberlain.

atrocities committed by the volunteers, and the few that were reported were in newspapers already inclined to oppose the war. After the Agua Nueva massacre, though, correspondents could no longer ignore what was happening, and they both reported and condemned the atrocities.[28]

The war between the volunteers and Mexican guerrillas continued until American troops finally withdrew from what is now northern Mexico at the end of the war. Although at times it threatened American supply lines, Mexican guerrilla activity could not drive the Americans from these regions. Some Mexican men who might have joined the fight were too busy trying to defend their families and property from Comanche raids, which actually accelerated even as the American invasion was taking place. Those same raids drove many Mexicans from the region, reducing support for the guerrillas.[29] The civilian population of northern Mexico, already thin because of the region's ecology, suffered greatly in this period, as America's expanding economy sparked Comanche raids before the war, James K. Polk's territorial ambitions led to an American invasion and the need to provide economic support to Mexican regular units trying to stop it, American volunteers preyed on Mexican civilians, and the Comanche continued their own violent activities throughout.

The Monterrey Campaign

The war against the guerrillas was not the only fighting the volunteers experienced. When we left the more conventional narrative of battles and campaigns, the Mexican army defeated at Palo Alto and Resaca de Palma had retreated across the desert, experiencing more deaths and considerable desertion as men struck out on their own to find water and food. This force moved on to Monterrey, and eventually many of the men who had separated themselves rejoined it. Monterrey, the largest city in northern Mexico, was the most obvious goal for the American army, but first it stayed near the Rio Grande for months awaiting more supplies and men. Ordered to invade Mexico, Taylor faced a difficult strategic problem. How could he move a large army successfully through the same dry terrain that had tortured the Mexican soldiers? The Americans decided that a more practical route to Monterrey was possible. They moved supplies and troops up the river to Camargo and from there followed a road with more water sources. They could only do this because, by lucky circumstance, the seasonal rains had been unusually strong that year, putting enough water in the river to make steamboat travel possible. They also were benefiting from the economic might of the United States and the geography that had made it possible. The government simply rented steamboats that had been built for the profitable trade on the American river system, the same system that had allowed them to move massive quantities of men and supplies to Texas in the first place. Even so, the march from Camargo to Monterrey was difficult due to high temperatures. The troops rose in the middle of the night and completed their daily marches before the heat became unbearable, and both the quantity and the quality of the water made them suffer. The army also needed to overcome other logistical difficulties. Without enough wagons and animals to pull them, Taylor had to contract with dozens of Mexican muleteers to transport food and ammunition. He also took only about a third of the volunteer regiments available because he was not sure he could move enough food and ammunition to sustain more. Taylor was unwilling to use scarce draft animals to drag the very heavy artillery pieces that armies typically used to destroy the defenses of fortified places, a decision that puzzled some of his young officers. Mexican authorities tried to make this march even more difficult by evacuating Mexican civilians and

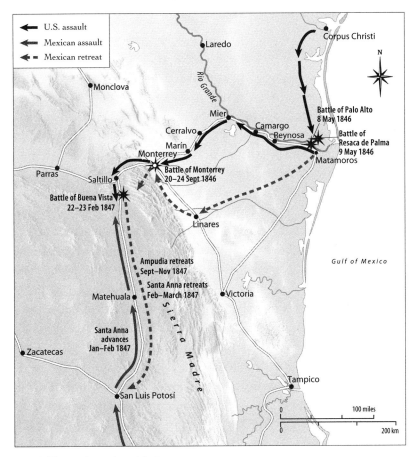

MAP 6 The war in northern Mexico

livestock along the route, and American observers remarked on the emptiness of the landscape through which they passed. This contributed to their feelings of foreboding as they neared Monterrey, feelings that deepened as they noticed the increasing nervousness of the Mexican muleteers and the few other civilians they encountered.[30] The Americans, from Taylor down to the privates, knew that Monterrey would be defended.

In hindsight the decision to defend Monterrey seems obvious. Monterrey was definitely not the frontier: it was a major city surrounded by a vibrant regional economy. Thousands of Mexicans lived in and around the city, and it was the capital of the state of Nuevo León. Moreover, this region was one of the few places in northern Mexico with enough economic activity to support a large army. How could Mexico not defend Monterrey? Yet Santa Anna, who had recently arrived in Mexico to assume the presidency, advised against making a stand there because he was not sure that there were enough troops available. Santa Anna, who knew firsthand the difficulties faced by troop movements in northern Mexico from his experience mobilizing against the Texas rebels, may also have believed that the desert barrier farther south would prove too formidable for the Americans to cross.[31] However, he lost the argument with his fellow officers, and the Mexicans prepared to defend Monterrey.

The Mexican military could not defend the city without men. The first men available were the survivors of the battles near the Rio Grande and the retreat south through the desert. General Francisco Mejía worked to restore their morale and convince the soldiers who had separated themselves during the retreat to report to their units. By July 1846 he reported that their morale was better and soldiers were no longer deserting, and he moved these troops from Linares to Monterrey. However, he feared that he could not hold the city without more troops and money to feed the troops he had. Mejía pleaded with his superiors, but the decline and overthrow of the Mariano Paredes y Arrillaga administration slowed the accumulation of money and men to defend northern Mexico.[32] Fortunately, Taylor had also been delayed while waiting for troops, steamboats, draft animals, and wagons. This bought the Mexicans the time they needed, and Pedro de Ampudia arrived on September 1, 1846, with fresh forces to take command of the defense.[33] Ampudia was eager to defend the city, and he approved of the basics of Mejía's plan to do so. The Mexicans had been defeated at Palo Alto by the effective American light artillery. Fortifying strategic locations around Monterrey and converting the stone buildings of the city into de facto forts would negate that advantage, forcing the American soldiers to advance in the open under the fire of Mexican cannon and muskets. However, there were not enough troops to garrison all the heights above the city and the city itself, and this caused indecision about exactly what to defend. Soldiers and civilians worked to construct fortifications, acutely aware that they might not be able to complete them before the Americans arrived.

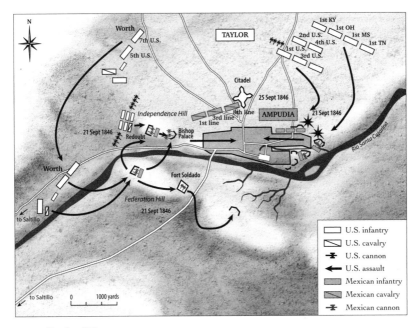

MAP 7 Battle of Monterrey

Some soldiers were still demoralized by their defeats on the Rio Grande, while those recently arrived from the center were inexperienced. Moreover, the Mexican officers, always political animals, were divided between those who favored Mejía and those who favored Ampudia. They were also divided socially between the veterans of the north, used to doing without resources, and the men recently arrived from the center, who believed that their skill and valor would prevail against the Americans.[34]

Taylor's six thousand men, roughly half of whom were regulars who had fought at Palo Alto and Resaca de Palma and the other half volunteers from Texas, Mississippi, Ohio, Kentucky, and Maryland, arrived near Monterrey on September 19. He camped his army at a pleasant spot and sent engineers to scout its defenses. After considering his options, he sent a large force under General William Worth to swing to the north and west around the main Mexican defenses and attack the city from the other side. Taylor planned to distract the Mexicans from this threat by staging a diversionary attack straight at the Mexican defenses. As they prepared for battle, the regulars, combat veterans already, noticed how the volunteers bantered nervously about their chances.[35]

Things did not go well for the Americans under Taylor's direct command. Last-minute decisions to tear down and then rebuild various strong points had exhausted many of the Mexican soldiers, but when Taylor's diversionary attack got started, it quickly stalled. The Mexicans were defending a series of small forts and fortified buildings that were close enough to each other that American attacks faced cannon and musket fire from multiple directions. When they reached the defenses, the Americans were trapped in narrow streets, still under fire from Mexicans who were mostly under cover. Officers and soldiers alike were killed or wounded, and the only volunteer unit in the initial attack broke and went to ground. Taylor sent more regiments forward, but they faced similar problems. Initially begun as a diversion, Taylor's attack had become a full-scale assault. Hours of bloody effort allowed the Americans to take one important fort, but the cost was enormous. Almost four hundred of Taylor's men were killed or wounded. Both regular and volunteer regiments suffered grievously, and it is difficult to see this effort as anything other than a defeat for the Americans. However, the Mexican perspective was not exactly sanguine. They also had suffered losses and had used up vast quantities of ammunition, and they knew that the Americans were not done yet.[36]

Meanwhile, Worth's division was very successful. After defeating an attempt by Mexican cavalry to disrupt its march, it captured various Mexican fortifications on the heights west of the city. The Mexican soldiers who garrisoned the forts resisted fiercely, but in several cases the very steepness of the slopes the Americans had to climb protected them from Mexican firearms. Here the American losses were very light, not even a tenth of what Taylor's force experienced on the other side. Now Worth's force had cut off Ampudia from any possible reinforcement and also occupied commanding heights. Ampudia had to pull back from the westernmost part of town because Worth had cannon overlooking it. On September 23, Worth attacked the city itself. On this side, Worth and his men employed tactics more appropriate for urban warfare, tactics the Texas volunteers with him had learned in earlier fights with the Mexicans. Rather than try to advance down the streets, exposed to fire from the stone houses that lined them, they would break into a house with axes and crowbars and then break through the side walls into neighboring houses, preventing the Mexicans in nearby houses from being able to fire in support. Although the Americans suffered casualties, they made steady progress.

On the same day, Taylor renewed his efforts to attack the city from the north, and now his troops employed tactics similar to those of Worth's men in the west. They cut into houses and then took to their flat roofs. These tactics allowed the Americans to negate the advantages the Mexicans had used to repulse them two days earlier. The Mexicans resisted, but they were forced to give ground. Attacked from both sides, Ampudia's force was being steadily compressed toward the very center of town, the central square that housed its cathedral and main government buildings. This was also where most of the civilian inhabitants had taken refuge. Ampudia's situation worsened further when the Americans took advantage of their proximity to place a mortar where its high-arcing, explosive shells could fire on the main plaza. Ampudia had very few cannonballs left for his artillery, but there were still tons of gunpowder in the cathedral, which was being used as an arsenal. There was a real danger that an American shell might touch off a massive explosion, much as had happened at Almeida in Spain in 1810.[37] Such an explosion would have killed hundreds of civilians, and many were also likely to die if the Americans broke into the Mexican defenses. In the customs that governed early modern warfare, soldiers forced to assault a fortified city would inevitably attack its civilian population, looting, raping, and killing, either as a reward for the extreme risks they had taken or from sheer loss of control. Up to this point the American troops had treated the civilians in outlying neighborhoods relatively well, but Ampudia had no way of knowing that.

Faced with this dilemma, Ampudia decided to negotiate a withdrawal because he judged civilian lives and the continued existence of his army to be more important than holding Monterrey.[38] This decision was exactly what one could have expected from a military leader educated in the ways of early modern professional armies, which were so difficult and expensive to raise, train, and feed that they almost never fought any battle to the bitter end. By preserving his army, Ampudia kept a significant military force between Taylor and his next possible major objective, San Luis Potosí. Many people, including some of his own officers, criticized his decision to negotiate, but it is difficult to see how he could have defeated Taylor, and the destruction of his army would have severely hampered Mexico's ability to continue the war. Negotiation, like the tango, requires two partners, and it is interesting to note that Taylor thought that a negotiated withdrawal was also in the Americans' interests. Taylor's men were definitely winning the battle, but they continued to lose many men. He believed that storming the center of the city would cause heavy casualties among both his own men and civilians, and he did not have enough troops to prevent the Mexicans from retreating in any case. He also believed that Polk desired a negotiated end to the war, and an armistice in Monterrey would facilitate that possibility.[39] Taylor and many of his men were clearly impressed with how tenaciously the Mexicans had defended their positions, and they were no doubt a bit shocked by their own casualties, so much heavier than they had suffered at Palo Alto or Resaca de Palma. After considerable negotiation, it was decided that Ampudia would be allowed to leave with his men; their muskets, swords, and lances; and even some of their cannon. Two months of armistice would follow, allowing time for their governments to negotiate. Taylor faced considerable criticism for his decision to negotiate. He may have wanted to emulate Ampudia, who publicly responded to his critics that it was easy for men far from the scene of action to explain what should have been done.[40]

Ampudia and his men marched out of the city and headed south, observed by a largely respectful American army. The attention of many of the Americans was drawn by two sights. One was the presence of so many women marching with the men. These were the soldaderas, who were simultaneously the source of much logistical support for Mexican soldiers and evidence of how difficult it was for women to survive economically in Mexico without the partnership of men. The other sight was a group of soldiers who were definitely not Mexicans: a number of men who had deserted from the U.S. Army fought on the Mexican side at Monterrey, primarily as artillerists.[41] We will learn more about these men later, but for now I will say that their presence in the Mexican ranks is yet more evidence that both the U.S. regular army and its Mexican counterpart were typical early modern professional armies rather than the armies of citizen-soldiers that we often associate with struggles between nation-states.

Leaving more than two hundred wounded men behind under the care of Mexican and American doctors, Ampudia's army marched to Saltillo and then undertook the much longer march to San Luis Potosí. It struggled mightily on its retreat. Ampudia and his men had to travel through extremely dry and sparsely populated terrain. They could not take much food with them, partially for lack of transport but also because Ampudia had no money to buy it. Authorities in San Luis Potosí sent word that anyone who gave food to the army on its march would be reimbursed from state revenues, but there simply was not much food to be had in this sparsely settled region. The men suffered hunger and thirst, and by the time they straggled into San Luis Potosí under the eyes of the recently arrived Santa Anna, they were, in his words, in a lamentable state of "nudity, hunger, and misery." Many soldiers became ill, and without enough carts and draft animals, they had to be left behind to be cared for in settlements along the way.[42] No official numbers were reported, but it is possible that Ampudia's army lost as many men on the march south as it had in the heavy fighting in Monterrey.

Santa Anna's Northern Campaign

In October 1846, when Santa Anna arrived in San Luis Potosí, the situation was complicated. The Americans had allowed him to enter the country and take charge because he had tricked them into believing that he would negotiate a quick end to the war. The Americans moved to occupy Saltillo, the next large town on the road south, but Santa Anna understood that the desert between it and San Luis Potosí was extraordinarily difficult to cross with an army. The question was, what would the Americans do next? Santa Anna had deliberately suggested to Polk that the Americans would have to take San Luis Potosí to force a settlement favorable to the United States. Now Santa Anna hoped the Americans would try, allowing him to defend a fortified city against a weakened U.S. Army with the desert at its back. However, Taylor was starting to understand how difficult it was to campaign in northern Mexico. Even the relatively short march from Camargo to Monterrey had been trying. Taylor had not been able to bring all his troops or weapons, and it was fortunate that he was even able to rest the troops in a shaded and well-watered place before assaulting Monterrey. Moreover, Monterrey had proven that Mexican soldiers, despite their lack of resources and largely worn-out weaponry, could fight tenaciously when given some protection from the light artillery that had mowed them down at Palo Alto. Taylor sent scouts to see if the terrain south of Saltillo had enough water and food to support an advance on San Luis Potosí. Their reports and his experience at Monterrey convinced him that such an advance would be very unwise, so he decided to occupy Saltillo and hold tight, using the barrier of the desert to help protect him from any Mexican counterattack.[43]

For several months Santa Anna did not know that he would not get his wish. He worked from October to January to build a formidable army in San Luis Potosí, asking for mounted auxiliary units from Guanajuato and Celaya in Mexico's richest agricultural area, the Bajío. These men were probably intended to harry the defeated American army as it retreated across the desert from San Luis Potosí. Most of Santa Anna's units, though, were from Mexico's regular army. It included units that Paredes had kept in Mexico City to support his government, and the troops who had retreated from Monterrey. Santa Anna also called in regular army units from other parts of Mexico, concentrating most of Mexico's military strength in one place. He did not just bring the regiments to San Luis Potosí, he demanded that their numbers be built up to full strength. Mexican units usually did not have all the men they were authorized to have due to desertion, illness, and other losses. The Mexicans now sought to fill out the ranks of the units in San Luis Potosí, asking nearby states to send in thousands of recruits. These recruits were acquired the usual way by local officials who, despite the military crisis, tried to protect the families of the laboring population as best they could. Officials filled their quotas with the men whose absence local society could best bear— men who did not have the reputation of hard workers who supported their families. Thousands of reluctant men were soon on their way to the city of San Luis Potosí, roped together and overseen by armed guards.[44]

The gathering, arming, and clothing of an army approaching twenty thousand men in San Luis Potosí between October 1846 and January 1847 was a prodigious feat, probably one of the great accomplishments of the nineteenth-century nation-state in Mexico. That it was an accomplishment of the nation-state, however, does not mean that that state was highly centralized. Mexico had, after all, just adopted federalism again. The men were recruited by local authorities, mostly in San Luis Potosí and nearby states like Michoacán, Jalisco, Querétaro, and Guanajuato. Moreover, San Luis

Potosí provided most of the economic resources to clothe and arm the men. This required the cooperation of the state's government, its wealthiest residents, its religious institutions, and many common people. Almost all the churches became barracks to house soldiers or magazines to store ammunition. Blacksmiths and carpenters made or repaired weapons. Church bells were melted down and made into ammunition. An office was set up to collect donations of corn, beans, firewood, lead, copper, and money for the army, and donations were celebrated with music as they were brought in. The role of the women of the city was notable. They set up committees to solicit money and material. A committee of the city's most prominent women also oversaw the hospital where so many of Ampudia's troops were recovering from illness.[45]

Expressions of nationalism abounded in San Luis Potosí, and many people there made an enormous effort to construct and supply this army. However, here, as in the United States, the nation was not an abstraction. It was bound up with other values and identities, including religion, family, the local community, and people's sense of social status or self-worth. In this particular situation more people could easily believe that those values and identities were threatened, and that rallying for the nation might protect them. Many people thought that the American army would soon advance south from Saltillo, and by now many reports had described how American volunteers treated Mexican civilians and Mexican religion. Santa Anna, local officials, the state government, and local priests stressed the need to pull together as Mexicans to face the threat.[46] The fact that Santa Anna continued to believe that the Americans would march against San Luis Potosí probably helped to build enthusiasm for the tremendous task of assembling and then feeding this army. In fact, Santa Anna urged the construction of fortifications to protect the city. These fortifications required a great deal of labor, from both imprisoned criminals and people who worked voluntarily. Observers were particularly impressed to see the inhabitants of some outlying neighborhoods destroy their own houses and orchards to create the forts.[47]

The economic effort required to gather and equip an army in San Luis Potosí was enormous, but these men also had to be fed. Ideally the national government would have been frequently remitting sums to San Luis Potosí, but that was not happening. The fiscal situation of Mexico's national government had been rickety since the 1820s. It struggled to make payments on its foreign debt and pay its employees, including soldiers, from revenue derived from the markedly unproductive economy. The war made this fiscal situation disastrous. It increased demands on government revenue just as the American blockade choked off the customs revenues the government typically relied on. Valentín Gómez Farías, the vice president who led the government in Mexico City while Santa Anna built his army, had very little to send north. The national government eventually took extreme measures to obtain funds for this war, but they were too late for the army at San Luis Potosí. As November became December and then January, the situation became direr, and Santa Anna repeatedly asked San Luis Potosí's state government for help. The state gave what it could from its revenues and mortgaged its properties to leverage loans from merchants. Calls to other states for funds, though, went largely unanswered because they were all in dire fiscal straits and some feared American landings. By late January Santa Anna was desperate, as Mexican troops were more likely to desert if they could not get sustenance in the army. He began spending his own money to feed the troops, and then he took the extreme measure of confiscating almost a hundred bars of silver that belonged to foreign merchants, promising to repay them with his personal wealth if necessary. He argued that he had to take this step because "without food men cannot march, nor fight."[48]

During this economic struggle, Santa Anna came into possession of intelligence that must have terribly disappointed him: on January 11 guerrillas had ambushed and killed an American courier carrying orders for Taylor to send many of his regiments to the coast so they could invade Veracruz under Winfield Scott. The U.S. government had decided that only an invasion of central Mexico would make Mexico sue for peace. Taylor would not advance to San Luis Potosí, and Santa Anna's plan of trapping his army between the fortified city and the harsh desert would not come to fruition.[49] Santa Anna now had two choices. He could try to march his force south and east to Veracruz, with the hopes of either defending the port itself or keeping Scott's army in the coastal lowlands, where yellow fever would weaken it. However, this would mean a very long and costly march over Mexico's typically bad roads, and there was no guarantee that the Mexicans would get there on time. The other option was very daring. Taylor's army had just been reduced in size, and it was near Saltillo, much closer to San Luis Potosí. The terrain in between was terrible, but if Santa Anna could get his army to Saltillo, he might be able to utterly crush Taylor's force, delivering a blow that would encourage the American opponents of the war and also encourage Mexicans in occupied territory to rise up. Harried by the populace and Mexican cavalry, the Americans might be driven all the way back to Texas. This plan was probably more feasible than trying to get the Mexican army to Veracruz. It also was more in keeping with the ambitions of a man who styled himself after Napoleon. As one American lieutenant put it, the "plan was bold and masterly." Of course it was the option that Santa Anna chose.[50]

The force that marched out of San Luis Potosí was impressive in size, but it had significant weaknesses. Most of its men had only been in the army a few months, and although officers made serious efforts to train them and instill unit cohesion, the government's poverty seems to have dissuaded the army from having many of the men actually fire their weapons in training. The muskets themselves were mostly veterans of the Napoleonic-era British army and thus were older than their users. Their worn-out barrels made them inaccurate, and their age made them prone to breakdowns.[51] The Mexicans' biggest disadvantage, however, was that they had to survive a long march through a sparsely populated and dry region just to reach the enemy. This march would be made even harder by the lack of food. For the first few days the population of the northern part of San Luis Potosí state could provide some food, but after that things would get really hard. Santa Anna knew the terrain, and he thought he understood the difficulties. He arranged for his troops to march in large groups separated by about a day's travel, hoping not to overwhelm the water sources along the way, as well as the little food the inhabitants could provide. Altogether he had around twenty thousand soldiers and at least five thousand soldaderas. The route was well known, as Mexican troops had often used it, and it was expected that there would be significant casualties on the three-week march through the desert. Before setting out, he told his troops that the march would be a hungry and thirsty one but that enduring it was a form of valor that would prove their strength. He also appealed to their pride, pointing out that "the Mexican soldier is well known for his frugality and ability to bear suffering, he has never needed warehouses in order to cross deserts, and he has always relied on taking advantage of the resources of the enemy. Today we start a march through uninhabited lands, without help or provisions, but you can be sure that soon we will be the owners of the enemy's provisions, and his funds."[52]

What Santa Anna could not have known was that his army was setting off into the worst winter weather northern Mexico had seen for several decades. Night and day they faced cold, rain, and snow, and both men and women began to die of exposure. The precipitation was enough to chill the soldiers but not enough to fully fill the reservoirs and water holes the army relied on, so thirst remained a problem. Moreover, the marching men burned many more calories than they took in from the little food available. Some men deserted, but for the most part discipline held, fortified by exhortations that food and water lay ahead, not behind. The cold only worsened as they drew nearer Saltillo. On one of the last nights of the march, Santa Anna prohibited campfires because he was afraid they would alert the Americans to the presence of his army. It was one of the coldest nights yet, though, and some soldaderas, believing it impossible to survive it with the scanty blankets the men had carried so far, set fire to the trees around the camp. Other women and even troops soon followed their example, and, in the words of the young Mexican officer Manuel Balbontín, "the camp was lighted in all directions, making a lively contrast with the black background of the sky." Santa Anna held his tongue, unwilling to confront the soldaderas. By the time his army approached the Americans, it had lost thousands of men and undoubtedly many women to exposure, illness, and desertion, leaving perhaps fourteen thousand for battle.[53]

Although the Mexicans tried to keep their movement a secret, Taylor understood the danger. Sending almost all of his regulars and most of his volunteers to Scott had put Taylor's army at risk, and, having seen the Mexicans fight well, Taylor undoubtedly understood this risk better than Polk or even Scott. Taylor also understood that the desert was a formidable barrier to an army, which explains both why he did not march against San Luis Potosí and why he moved his main force to the edge of the desert south of Saltillo. There are various stories about how Taylor found out about the specific danger that his forces faced in late February 1847. Santa Anna blamed a deserter the Americans had captured as he was trying to reach his family in Saltillo. Others reported that rumors had reached Mexican civilians in Saltillo, and when some of them hid sacred images, the Americans realized that something was happening. In any event Taylor sent cavalry south to confirm the rumors, and when they encountered large numbers of Mexican cavalrymen, they retreated to Agua Nueva, where Taylor had a supply depot. The Americans decided to pull back to a more defensible position. Volunteer infantrymen set off immediately on foot, but the Arkansas cavalrymen were left to load as many supplies as they could on wagons. They refused to do so, and regular cavalrymen were sent to do the work while the Arkansas men watched. Suddenly Mexican cavalry arrived and the Arkansas men fled in a panic, joined by the regular cavalry, who first set fire to the remaining supplies, lighting up the skies for miles. Ironically, the sight of panicked Americans burning the supplies at Agua Nueva helped the American cause, because it fooled Santa Anna into believing that he had totally surprised the Americans and that their whole army was fleeing in panic. Rather than rest, feed, and water his exhausted men at Agua Nueva, he sent them in pursuit and ordered his cavalry to try to get between the Americans and Saltillo while the infantry quickened their pace. Exhausted by a long and rapid march without having eaten for more than a day, the Mexican army arrived at the site the Americans knew by the name of the hacienda situated there, Buena Vista, but which the Mexicans knew by its local geographic nickname, La Angostura.[54]

Death in a Narrow Place

The Mexican name, which translates as "the narrow place," accurately described the geography. There, the road to Saltillo passes between steep bluffs to the west and a tangle of ravines that flow mostly west from high hills to the east. General Wool had decided earlier that this location gave the Americans the best chance to survive a Mexican attack. The position was not impossible to outflank, and it was quite wide to defend with the five thousand Americans present, but the terrain restricted the movements of an attacking army. Wool arrayed the available regiments and cannon and awaited the return of Taylor with a few more units. On February 22 the Americans witnessed the arrival of a Mexican army that outnumbered them approximately three to one. More than a few American soldiers were intimidated by the sight.

The resulting battle, which Mexicans call La Angostura and Americans call Buena Vista, stretched over almost two days, and like most battles it actually consisted of many smaller but very violent confrontations. As usual, even the generals in charge had a hard time visualizing all that was happening, and the action was even more confusing because no one on either side had a clear geographic picture of the twisting ravines to the east of the road that both were forced to use to move troops through. Whenever an officer sent a group of troops into a ravine, he did not know where they would emerge. Generally, though, the action can be summarized as a series of efforts by Santa Anna to send forces through this terrain east of the road to outflank the Americans, cutting them off from Saltillo and, not coincidentally, getting at the Americans' stored supplies.

On February 22 Santa Anna asked Taylor to surrender his heavily outnumbered force, and Taylor quickly declined. That afternoon the Mexican general feigned a frontal attack down the road toward the bulk of Taylor's forces, simultaneously sending his light infantry, which, like the light infantry of other armies, were selected from among the best marksmen and most motivated soldiers, to try to take the hills that stood just to the east of the ravines. These men approached the nearly vertical hills through a ravine that hid them from the Americans until they began to climb. General Andrés Terrés recalled seeing "our light battalions climbing like cats . . . the sharpshooters were vertically one above the other forming a line like a lamp cord; it seemed incredible that men after having walked 25 leagues without stopping and without eating could climb those unpassable heights." Taylor sent some of his light artillery to fire at these men, and ordered men from some Kentucky and Indiana units to try to get above the Mexicans. They failed, and the Mexicans found themselves on the higher ground as the light faded away. During the cold night that followed, men from both armies grabbed what sleep they could and ate what food they had, which for most Mexican units was little or even none. Many of the Mexicans also got little sleep as Santa Anna moved more regiments and artillery into position for renewed flanking attacks the next day. Meanwhile Taylor went back to Saltillo to make sure the supplies there were protected from Mexican cavalry, leaving Wool in charge.[55]

On the morning of February 23 Santa Anna sent a divisionary attack down the road toward the center of the American army but also sent a series of

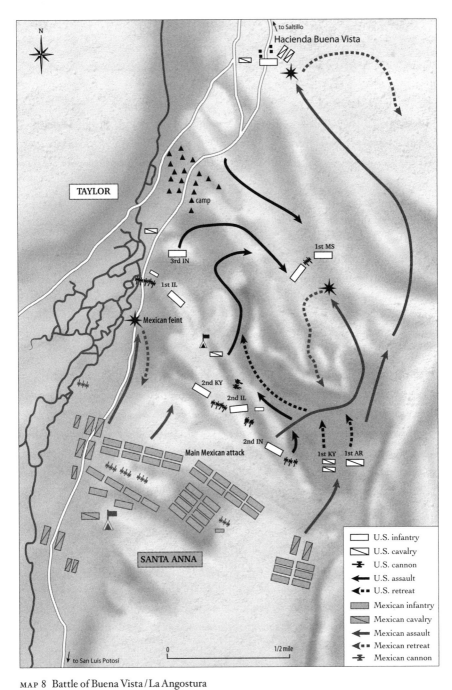

N

to Saltillo

Hacienda Buena Vista

TAYLOR

camp

3rd IN

1st MS

1st IL

Mexican feint

2nd KY

2nd IL

Main Mexican attack

2nd IN

1st KY   1st AR

SANTA ANNA

	U.S. infantry
	U.S. cavalry
	U.S. cannon
	U.S. assault
	U.S. retreat
	Mexican infantry
	Mexican cavalry
	Mexican assault
	Mexican retreat
	Mexican cannon

to San Luis Potosí

0   1/2 mile

MAP 8 Battle of Buena Vista / La Angostura

stronger attacks to the east side of the battlefield, trying to use the jumbled ravine system to get behind the Americans. The control of the heights mattered less than it would have in more modern times because unrifled muskets had very limited range and thus could reach only a small part of the battlefield. At first the principal force opposing the flanking attack was the Second Indiana Regiment, supported by three of the American light cannon. Once Wool realized an attack there had begun, he sent reinforcements from Illinois and Kentucky units. Now the social composition of the American army really came into play. Taylor's only regular troops were his artillerymen and a few cavalrymen. Scott had taken the vast bulk of the regulars for the Veracruz campaign. Moreover, very few of the volunteer soldiers present had been in battle, because Scott had also taken almost all the volunteer regiments that fought at Monterrey. The troops Taylor had with him on the day of crisis were regiments who had been left in the camps on the Rio Grande during the Monterrey campaign precisely because Taylor did not consider them to be disciplined and effective. Their military experience had mostly consisted of brushes with Mexican guerrillas and, as we have seen, retaliatory attacks on Mexican civilians. They were unprepared to fight a battle with thousands of Mexican troops.

Probably no unit was less prepared than the Second Indiana. Its first commander, the relatively competent Joseph Lane, had been promoted out of the slot and replaced by William Bowles, a physician and hotel owner with political connections to the state's Democratic governor but no military aptitude. Bowles had neglected the training of his men and did not inspire confidence. Partially because of this, Wool sent Lane to take command of the eastern sector of the battlefield once he realized it was vulnerable. At a crucial moment early on February 23, the Second Indiana regiment found itself at the center of the action. A Mexican force far outnumbering them was scrambling out of a ravine to their front, and the Hoosiers were simultaneously being bombarded by Mexican cannon. Supported by a battery of light cannon, the regiment stood its ground for several minutes, firing volley after volley from their muskets as almost a quarter of the Hoosiers were killed or wounded. Lane ordered an advance, hoping to move to ground that the Mexican cannon could not reach and to get closer to the ravine to bottle up the attack before the Hoosiers were surrounded. Bowles instead hysterically ordered the regiment to retreat. He had to repeat the order twice more before it was obeyed, but what in better circumstances might have been an orderly retreat became headlong flight. The Hoosiers ran as fast as they could, joined quickly by the men who had been fighting the Mexican light troops on the nearby heights. Although fresh regiments from Illinois and Kentucky formed a new line to confront the Mexicans, at this point close to a thousand Americans, nearly a quarter of Taylor's force, were running away, and Mexican cavalry were using the space gained to loop around the American army, headed for the American provisions piled at the farm buildings of the Buena Vista hacienda.

Taylor arrived from Saltillo, bringing with him his son-in-law Colonel Jefferson Davis and the latter's Mississippi Regiment, the only volunteer unit present that had fought at Monterrey. Taylor had been withholding this experienced regiment as a reserve, and now he needed them. Together with the Third Indiana, which had been guarding a sector not attacked by the Mexicans, they prepared to face the massive Mexican force headed for the hacienda. The two American units were soon augmented by many of the men who had fled, as their officers worked to find them in the ravines where they had taken shelter and lead them back to the battle. Among this group was Bowles, who picked up a musket and fought as a private in the Mississippi ranks, ignoring the survivors of the Second Indiana who had formed a few yards away, a sight many of them never forgave him for. Together these units halted another flanking attack. More or less around the same time, a large force of Mexican cavalry routed the mounted men of the Kentucky and Arkansas volunteers, killing Arkansas colonel Archibald Yell and soon reaching the hacienda. Here, however, they received an unpleasant surprise. Many Americans who had fled the earlier fighting had taken refuge in the buildings and walled courtyard, and once they were there, officers convinced them to defend it. Many had heard that any effort to flee to Saltillo was useless because Santa Anna had sent a large cavalry force under General José Miñon to cut the road, ironically helping the American army by preventing its refugees from being able to get clear of the battlefield. Thus, when the Mexican cavalry at Buena Vista came pelting up to the buildings full of supplies that they thought they had already won, they were met with deadly gunfire. The surprise was too much for these exhausted men, and they retreated, harried by some of the very same American cavalry that had only moments before been fleeing from them. Later in the day Santa Anna organized another major attack, this time sending troops straight north near the road to try to break the American center. Again, outnumbered Americans, this time from Illinois and Kentucky, broke and fled before the Mexican attack was finally halted by American light artillery and other infantry regiments. Among the men killed in this episode was Colonel Henry Clay Jr. of Kentucky, son of the famous Whig politician.

In the ebb and flow of the day's slaughter, various American units broke in terror and then re-formed. The famished and thirsty Mexicans pressed home many of their attacks, but some of the recent recruits took cover or fled when faced with the weight of American firepower. More often than not, Mexican attacks were blunted less by the efforts of the shrinking (and sometimes fleeing) American infantry regiments than they were by the ability of a handful of regular army artillerymen to rapidly shift their cannon from crisis point to crisis point, inflicting heavy casualties on attacking Mexican units that the terrain forced to bunch up. Many American and Mexican soldiers were killed by cannon fire, and, ironically, some of the most effective artillerymen in the Mexican army were men who had previously deserted from the American army. Mexicans and Americans were often close enough that bayonets and lances became the most important weapons, and both sides killed enemies who were fleeing, wounded, or trying to surrender. It was a day of desperate attacks and counterattacks, pitting famished, thirsty, and exhausted Mexican conscripts with worn-out muskets against better-armed but heavily outnumbered Americans who were finding more adventure in Mexico than they had bargained for. Bloodlust mingled with terror on both sides. Hours into the battle, a passing thunderstorm sent torrents of water down the sides of the hills and into the ravines. Terrés reports that this water was tinged red with blood but that many soldiers were so thirsty they drank it anyway. After the storm passed, the cycle of attack and counterattack continued until nightfall made further fighting impractical.[56]

Many Americans understood that they had skirted disaster several times, and they were deeply impressed by the courage and numbers of the Mexican troops. They believed that the American army would soon collapse when the fighting began the next day. What they did not know was that Santa Anna believed that his army was also trembling on the brink of collapse, not due to

The Capture of O'Brien's Guns

FIG. 3.3 Mexican troops capture American cannon at Buena Vista. Drawing by Samuel Chamberlain.

the heavy casualties it had sustained but because most of the men had gone days with little or no food. One Mexican officer even reported that during the fighting some men were so hungry and thirsty that they conducted unauthorized attacks just so that they could take food from the Americans. Up until nightfall the possibility of breaking through to the American supplies had kept most men with their units, but Santa Anna knew very well that hunger was always the most important factor driving Mexican desertion, and his sergeants and officers were not likely to be able to forcibly contain desertion among soldiers dispersed in small groups across the battlefield. There were some cattle and other provisions available a few miles farther back at Agua Nueva, but Santa Anna had no way to transport them to the battlefield. He decided to pull his forces back to Agua Nueva so that they could eat at least a little. Some Mexican soldiers and officers disagreed with this decision, believing that the cattle could be driven to the Mexican troops on the battlefield and that one more day of fighting would destroy the American army and capture its supplies.[57]

During the night the Mexicans retreated to Agua Nueva, leaving lit campfires to confuse the Americans. When the Americans realized what had happened, most were overcome with relief. Before them was a sight most would never forget, acres of jumbled terrain dotted with dead and wounded men of both sides. Kentuckian John Halsey wrote to his family, "The Mexican wounded were crawling from hiding places and begging for water in the most touching supplicating manner. Yonder we saw on the mountain side the poor wretched waving shirts for white flags, crying 'amigo, amigo' with a feeble voice, here we saw where a bomb exploded and many gallant lancers with his fine horse strewed the ground, some with headless trunks, some with legs and arms torn off some completely disemboweled. *awful, awful, awful sight!* [original emphasis]." Even as some Mexicans begged the Americans to help them, others hid, sure that the only thing they could expect from the Americans would be a quick death and the theft of their possessions. Dogs and coyotes ate dead and wounded alike. The Americans sent out to search for the wounded encountered soldaderas and their children engaged in the same task. Many of the wounded from both sides were transported to the cathedral of Saltillo, whose floor was soon stained with blood as doctors amputated limbs and bandaged wounds. The butcher's bill had been shocking for both sides. Almost three hundred Americans were dead and almost four hundred were wounded, while almost six hundred Mexicans were dead and over a thousand were wounded. Nearly two thousand Mexican soldiers also left the ranks during the battle, although, as we will see, many of these men were later reunited with their units. The bones of many of the dead still lie exposed today, either because they were never found and buried or because erosion later exposed them. It is, of course, impossible to tell the nationality of their owners.[58]

At Agua Nueva, Santa Anna and his officers had a new dilemma. He had intended to soon renew his attack on the Americans. Taylor sent a subordinate to offer a truce and an exchange of prisoners. Santa Anna accepted the exchange but rejected the truce, and he made sure to show the officer that his army was still large and disciplined. Even as he did so, soldaderas approached the American cavalrymen who escorted the officer. Seeing these Americans surrounded by thousands of Mexicans, the women assumed they were prisoners and offered them some food. Understanding that the Mexicans themselves were starving, the Americans instead gave all their food to the women. This touching incident underlines the crux of Santa Anna's problem. There was not enough food at Agua Nueva to sustain his army even for a few days, hungry men continued to desert, and an epidemic of dysentery further undermined his men's strength. As the soldaderas struggled to clean wounds with rags dipped in the only water available, water already darkened by blood and mud, Santa Anna and his senior officers discussed their options. They realized that a starving army could not renew its attack and, worse yet, a starving army would soon be a nonexistent army. They decided to retreat to San Luis Potosí. Later, Santa Anna would write that at Agua Nueva he learned of the civil war roiling Mexico City and decided that he needed to hurry back there, but his first reports of the decision do not mention this.[59]

The Mexican army marched south, carrying its wounded as best it could on the shoulders of the soldiers or on improvised stretchers made from muskets. One Mexican witness described the force as less a marching army than a walking hospital. Many wounded were left at Encarnación after only a short journey. A few days later the American army heard that there were hundreds of Mexican wounded there without food or medical help, so it sent some cavalry with wagonloads of food and medicine. Some of these men reported that the scene there was worse than that on the battlefield itself. Chamberlain called it a "den of horrors, death was on all sides, while miserable wrecks of humanity with fearful wounds lay in the square, on the bare ground, while in the houses and the little chapel, nearly three hundred wounded wretches lay without bedding or blankets on the hard cement floors, wallowing in a mass of filth, while maggots and vermin crawled in and out of the horrid undressed wounds."[60] As the men still able to walk continued south, their rations were limited to some brown sugar and rotten meat. The water holes were scarce, and the water in them was almost too salty to drink. The intestinal illnesses that already plagued the army worsened, and more and more men simply became too weak to continue walking. Terrés, marching with the rear guard, wrote of the army leaving a trail of ill men behind it, and he added that the retreat was worse than Napoleon's retreat from Moscow, because the Mexican soldiers faced not only the winter weather but also the lack of water.[61]

Struggling to survive, many men struck off on their own, looking for food and water. For weeks small groups of men labored to reach the towns and haciendas of northern San Luis Potosí, where they approached local officials, seeking food, water, and help returning to their units. Even those who did not report were quickly picked up, as these walking skeletons did not exactly blend in with the local population, no matter how poor the locals were. More ominously, a few men robbed or even killed their officers to obtain cash that might help them make their way to their home regions or other places far away from the army.[62] The army lost more men to death or desertion on its retreat than it did on the bloody ground of battle. As the men began to reach settled territory in northern San Luis Potosí, the same authorities and inhabitants who had struggled to feed them on their march north swung into action again. They gathered sick men, fed them, and kept passing them from town to town to the city of San Luis Potosí, where the governor was collecting further donations of food and money from rich and poor alike. The prominent women of the city had worked hard to help feed and equip Santa Anna's army as it prepared for its offensive, and now they quickly organized a hospital for the many ill and wounded. Many men who made it back hurried to churches, where they were observed praying for a long time, no doubt giving thanks for survival or seeking a balm for the scenes that the bloody battle and the awful retreat had burned into their memories.[63]

News of the battle traveled much more quickly than the retreating army, and the first Mexican reports described it as a Mexican victory. These reports were sometimes the first news of the battle received even by Americans in Mexico. As different American units dissolved in confusion, the Mexicans had captured two of the flags regiments used to rally themselves and three cannon abandoned by fleeing gunners. These were the kinds of talismans that signaled victory in military culture. Yet the American army had been left in possession of the battlefield itself, which, by another military convention, indicated that it had won. American reports claiming victory made their way to central Mexico through the New Orleans newspapers, to the relief of Americans who had been worried by the Mexican accounts. Eventually the losses the Mexican army suffered on its retreat became known, and these depressed Mexicans. In hindsight, it is clear that the survival of the American army prevented the Mexicans from ejecting the Americans from northern Mexico, which was after all Santa Anna's aim. In this sense the campaign was a Mexican defeat, and that defeat seems even more damaging when we contemplate the losses suffered on the return march through the desert. Yet the battle itself was a near-run thing, and most Mexican and American witnesses were sure that if the Mexicans had been able to continue for a third day, the Americans would have been crushed. Their inability to continue the fight had little to do with losses suffered during the battle and everything to do with the challenge of the desert, a challenge that had been dramatically intensified by the unusually severe winter weather that had tortured the soldiers. Whomever one believes won the battle itself, clearly it was the desert that defeated the Mexican campaign.[64]

After May 1846 the war in northern Mexico was dominated by the massive infusion of manpower that American volunteer units provided. As discussed in Chapter 2, these citizen-soldiers were very different from the American and Mexican regulars who had clashed at Palo Alto and Resaca de Palma. They came from more comfortable social backgrounds, and they were largely motivated by ideology rather than economics. They were the kind of soldier that the champions of nation-states imagined as their standard-bearers. Not surprisingly, they looked down on the regulars as lower-class men who had chosen to give up their liberty for the fierce discipline of regular units. Volunteers often insisted that they were braver and more effective than the regulars.[65] Regular officers felt an almost visceral dislike for the volunteers' disheveled appearance and lack of discipline, and they were appalled by the volunteers' crimes against Mexican civilians. They also pointed out that during battles, volunteer units had sometimes dissolved, fled, or taken cover when they were supposed to be fighting. Abner Doubleday probably summed up his fellow officers' opinions of the volunteer units pretty well when he described them as "more like organized mobs than military forces."[66]

Probably no volunteer regiment became better known for breaking under the stress of battle than the Second Indiana, which made one of the most spectacular and untimely retreats at Buena Vista / La Angostura. In Taylor's army, men from other units soon began calling the unit "the flying infantry," an insult that stung deeply. Worse yet, news of their behavior made its way home quickly, along the way also attaching to the other two Indiana regiments in northern Mexico, the Third, which actually stood its ground in the battle, and the First, which was miles away on garrison duty. On April 5 Mary Gibson wrote to Thomas Gibson, who was in the Third Indiana, expressing relief that she had not seen his name on the lists of men wounded and killed but then adding that "it is reported here that the Indiana troops showed themselves great cowards it is said they all run when the battle came on . . . we all would rather you had stood like good soldiers since you have gone there."[67] The damage was even greater because Taylor mentioned their disorderly retreat in his official report and minimized the large number of Hoosiers who returned to fight. These men stood their ground in situations that were arguably as dire as the one that had earlier caused them to break, helping the American army survive two of the later crises it faced that day. The Indiana troops took steps to repair their reputation, writing explanatory letters to Indiana newspapers that also publicized their more heroic actions later in the day. They pushed for a court of inquiry, which placed the blame for their first retreat on the shoulders of their incompetent colonel. Two of the very first memoirs published by American volunteers in this war were written by Hoosiers who devoted significant space to defending the actions of Indiana troops at this battle.[68] Nevertheless, the Hoosiers who had been feted so much on their way to the war never quite recovered their reputations.

CHAPTER 4

Even the Fathers of Families

As discussed in Chapter 2, the American government, lacking enough professional soldiers to fight an offensive war against Mexico, recruited numerous citizen-soldiers whose service would be both temporary and explicitly linked with nationalism. This effort had mixed results from the point of view of both American commanders and Mexican civilians. Still, these men were essential to the hard-won American victories of Monterrey and La Angostura / Buena Vista, and in general it would have been impossible for the United States to win the war without these troops. Mexico also mobilized many citizen-soldiers for the war, but, due to Mexican politics and geography, they did not fight in those northern battles. Their moments of terror and glory came instead when the Americans invaded central Mexico. As we will see, the record of Mexican citizen-soldiers in this war is, like that of their American counterparts, mixed. Although they were poorly trained and, like other Mexican soldiers, poorly fed and supplied, they sometimes displayed notable courage and cohesion in battle, inflicting heavy casualties on the American army. However, the organization and arming of these citizen-soldiers also disastrously exacerbated tensions in Mexican politics.

Mexico's Citizen-Soldiers

With the fall of the conservative, centralist government of Mariano Paredes y Arrillaga, federalism was restored in August 1846. Mexican federalism, especially in its more radical varieties, emphasized not only the decentralization of power but also the extension of citizenship to even poor Mexicans. It stressed citizenship as the basis of the nation-state, and, not surprisingly, it extolled the ideal of the citizen-soldier, expressed beginning in the fall of 1846 through the recruitment of new regiments of the National Guard. However, the National Guardsmen organized that fall were far from the first iteration of citizen-soldiering in Mexico. Mexico had a strong militia tradition going back to the colonial period, and the National Guard had a postindependence predecessor called the civic militia. In the early national period most men were required to either serve or pay a special tax. The civic militia generally did not go out on campaign but instead served locally to keep order.[1] In the fractious politics of Mexico, the political sympathies of civic militia units varied regionally, and they often took part in civil wars or coups. After the centralists came to power in 1835, they deemphasized these units and diverted resources to Mexico's regular army. Regional elites still found it a practical necessity to maintain part-time forces to police rural areas, but the civic militia was essentially dead. As tensions over Texas grew in 1845, there was an anemic attempt to create a new part-time force composed of respectable citizens to keep order as regular military units were shifted north. However, at that point only relatively wealthy men could be citizens, and very few joined.[2]

When the federalists returned to power, practically their first priority was reviving citizen-soldiering, and in September 1846 they decreed the establishment of a National Guard. In many ways the National Guard units were similar to American volunteer units. Like them, they were organized on an intimately local level. Units were recruited from the men of different villages, neighborhoods, workplaces, schools, or occupational groups. These units were organized into regiments named for their city or state. Thus, in the Federal District, which contained both the city of Mexico and outlying rural villages, one battalion was composed of employees of the cigar factory, and various companies were recruited in different rural villages or smaller workplaces like the mint or the theater. Another whole battalion was composed of men working in commerce. In Xalapa, Veracruz, each company included members of a distinct occupation or set of occupations. In San Luis Potosí, Ponciano Arriaga, a leading lawyer and politician, organized a company that he explained was to consist mostly of commercial employees but was open to other members of the urban middle class. He addressed his call for volunteers with an interesting intimacy to "all of his comrades, to his friends and co-citizens."[3] Local pride was fierce in rural Mexico, and the organizers of

National Guard units sometimes explicitly asked that their companies not be grouped with companies from other districts or even villages. Similar rivalries existed among the companies organized around neighborhoods or occupations in urban areas.[4] Yet, as with American volunteer units, the most explicit references to geographic pride and unit solidarity were to the states of the National Guard units. Unit pride was symbolized by the same kinds of unit flags used by the Americans, often likewise made by the women of a locality and presented to units in elaborate ceremonies.[5]

The National Guardsmen were emphatically citizen-soldiers, men who took up arms because they were respectable citizens. Since the nation represented their will, they must defend it. The decree establishing the units stated that the institution was "inherent to democratic institutions" and insisted that National Guard officers conduct themselves "as citizens who commanded other citizens." Calls for recruits were full of rhetoric extolling citizenship. Arriaga, for instance, wrote that National Guardsmen should never forget that they were citizens with equal rights. The National Guard was established just as Mexico's federalists returned to power and citizenship officially recovered the egalitarian dimensions that the centralists had denied it, and in many locations the National Guard took on this egalitarian mantle. Observers noted that men of all social classes participated in the units, while federalist politicians like Prefect Juan Maria Balbontín of San Luis Potosí pointed out that the National Guard allowed "the countryman and the soldier, the rich and the poor, the artisan, farmer, merchant, in a word everyone who can honor themselves with the title of citizen" to become a "republican soldier." Balbontín emphasized that these units were unlike the regular army units conscripted from the dregs of society, and he wrote ecstatically, "A thousand times blessed the day that has illuminated true equality among all classes. A thousand times blessed, because by imposing on all the sweet duty of defending the fatherland, it has relieved the impoverished class of the burden of covering by itself this sacred obligation."[6] The National Guard was clearly not only a military institution, it was also an expression of the federalists' extravagant embrace of egalitarian citizenship and the ideal of Mexico as a nation of citizens.

Like the American volunteers, National Guardsmen elected their own officers. The men directly elected lower-ranking officers and sergeants, who then elected regimental officers. Often in Mexico these elections were held at the very first organizational meetings of units, and the records of these meetings are very similar to the documents produced during civilian elections. As with the American volunteers, this culture of meetings sometimes extended into areas unauthorized by regulations. The members of one National Guard unit organized to force out a commander they believed was not willing to prepare them for combat, and those of another voted to dissolve after a political controversy.[7]

Since each National Guard unit was organized around a specific local group, each typically had distinct political leanings. In this they were like their American counterparts, but in the United States between 1783 and 1860, citizen-soldiers did not employ force in internal politics. In Mexico they did, beginning with militia units during the War of Independence and continuing with the civic militia afterward. The National Guard units, in theory established to keep order and help repel the American invasion, also became crucial in internal politics. The radical federalists had shaped the National Guard law and the rhetoric surrounding it, giving both an egalitarian tone, but individual National Guard units did not necessarily back the radicals. The political leanings of specific units flowed from their geographic origins, local political conflicts, economic interests, and ideology, with strong hints of patron-clientelism, in which people lent support to leaders and received material benefits in exchange. The result was a fascinating mosaic of sometimes dizzying complexity. In Oaxaca's Sierra Mixteca, Antonio de León organized units that leaned toward conservatism, while in most of the regions that later became the states of Guerrero and Morelos, as well as parts of Veracruz, units had a distinct affinity with radical federalism. In all of these places the rank-and-file soldiers were peasants who were building visions of what the nation-state should be based on their cultural preoccupations and material interests, using processes mediated by political leaders. Yet if we increase the magnification of whatever imaginary instrument we are using to view the mosaic, the complexity similarly increases. Thus, even within the area that became Guerrero, one of Mexico's smallest states today, different National Guard units grouped Afro-Mexican sharecroppers who were longtime supporters of radical federalism, indigenous peasants who had adopted radical federalism after initially autonomous peasant revolts, mestizo townspeople who had fought against those revolts, and even Afro-Mexican sharecroppers from another area who had opposed both the indigenous peasants and radical federalists for decades.[8] All of these groups were legitimized, armed, and mobilized to fight alongside each other against the American invaders. The whole situation seems like it was ripe for disastrous political strife. Yet the only National Guard units that actually fought each other were radical and moderate Mexico City units that clashed in February and March 1847.

As has been discussed, the vast majority of men who filled the ranks of Mexico's regular army had been conscripted because they were not considered to be respectable, hard-working, responsible family men. The National Guard, however, inherited some of the positive cultural connotations of the earlier colonial militia, in which service was considered a mark of honor. The National Guard went even beyond that because now Mexico was a republic of citizens. Citizenship, respectability, and responsible patriarchy went hand in hand, and the National Guard was designed to be a force of citizen-soldiers. Citizens who did not sign up and were not exempted lost their right to vote. Oddly, foreign residents of Mexico were supposed to serve unless their countries were at war with Mexico, something that flies in the face of the citizen-soldier rhetoric that permeates so many documents associated with the National Guard but probably stems from the typical militia role of keeping public order. This moment of radical federalist euphoria deliberately extended citizenship, and respectability, to most of Mexico's lower classes. However, the rules also recognized that it would be cruel to compel the very poorest men to serve in the National Guard, as only their daily earnings allowed their families to survive. Thus the very poorest, identified as rural day laborers, were excused from service, along with some men considered too necessary to daily social functioning: priests, government employees, doctors, teachers, members of the regular military, domestic servants, sailors, and mine workers. Yet all men who were not priests or the citizens of nations at war with Mexico were allowed to serve voluntarily, and many relatively poor men served in National Guard units.[9]

One of the most striking things about the National Guard is how often contemporaries linked it with families. Guillermo Prieto extravagantly described the sight of National Guard units marching out to face the Americans as "the family fighting in defense of the great home that is called the fatherland." When these men fought close to home, their families publicly saw them off to battle, with pride and also tears. In the heat of battle, the men were sometimes urged to fight in the name of their families. All of this was possible because, unlike the soldiers of the Mexican regular army, National Guardsmen were seen as family men, respectable fathers and sons.[10] Forming a military force composed of respectable citizens and family men was ideologically important because it underlined the duty of Mexicans to their nation and created a military force whose image was inherently positive. Unfortunately, military units composed of family men also were of inherently limited military utility. How could the government actually put these units to use without causing severe and perhaps fatal hardships for Mexican families?

The problem first surfaced as the units were formed. Mexicans were already familiar with the recruitment rules for the regular army, rules that were designed to shield the precarious economy of families from the devastating poverty caused by men's absence. In these rules the government itself was endorsing the idea that the survival of families was more important than service to the nation. Some responses to efforts to get family men into the National Guard were clearly influenced by this idea.[11] However, we have to keep in mind the practical reality behind the idea: given the limited productivity of Mexico's economy and the absence of any government safety net, dire, possibly fatal, poverty stalked most Mexican families. It was held at bay only by the labor of almost all members, including husbands, wives, and most children. Even families we might consider middle class, headed by urban professionals or the owners of some small farms, had little or nothing in the way of savings, living instead on their regular income. Without that income, poverty was close at hand. Thus, as the first National Guard units were being organized, officials were often faced with requests to exempt men from service so that they could support their families, and they sent in queries about exactly who could fall under the exemption for rural day laborers.[12] It would not be correct to interpret the qualms of men about plunging their families into poverty as an unwillingness to fight to defend those same families: many manifested a willingness to fight if the Americans actually attacked their vicinities. What they could not do was stop working for months, weeks, or even days to go on campaign.[13] Substantial numbers of men joined, organized themselves into units, and trained, but they were only able to do this because their duty was part time. Except for during the training, often conducted on Sundays, or periodic guard duty at unit headquarters, most could continue to support their families. Even these temporary duties could be a hardship, a problem magnified for those who were elected as officers and therefore had to devote time to organizational tasks.[14] In theory National Guardsmen on duty received pay, but, as with regular soldiers, the penury of the government meant that pay was disbursed infrequently at best. When National Guardsmen who had been mobilized deserted, it was often because they needed to work to support their families.[15]

State governors had effective control over National Guard units, and several times during the war governors refused to send units to campaigns far from their homes. This has typically been interpreted as evidence of excessive federalism, putting local needs ahead of the nation. Some governors argued that local defense needs came first, especially in northern Mexico, where Native American raids accelerated during the war, often posing as much of a threat as American soldiers.[16] Yet even governors in states that did not face direct threats from Native American raiders or American soldiers were sometimes reluctant to send National Guard troops on campaign. This reluctance has to be understood as stemming from the damage National Guard deployment would do to families, a point that the governors of Michoacán and Guanajuato both made explicitly.[17] The problem makes it even more remarkable that some National Guard units left their families for weeks at a time to fight in the most crucial campaigns of the war. Units from the Federal District, Puebla, and Veracruz fought at the Battle of Cerro Gordo, which we will consider in this chapter, and units from Michoacán, Oaxaca, and present-day Guerrero fought in the Mexico City campaign, as we will see in Chapter 6. In all cases these men put the economic well-being of their families aside, and they knew it. Juan de Dios Ovando, prefect of Tlapa, Guerrero, in describing the scene as a local battalion left for the Mexico City area, explained that he had to close his ears to the cries of the women left behind, but that the soldiers' enthusiasm had not been diminished by "the misery in which they left the families of which they are the only support, nor leaving their fields abandoned in the most critical period for farming."[18] Despite the thorny problem presented by their duties to their families, National Guardsmen sometimes expressed great enthusiasm for the war, which in its own way mirrored the initial enthusiasm of American volunteers. During the first recruiting drives in the fall of 1846, very large numbers of men enlisted voluntarily in cities like San Luis Potosí and Mexico City. Austrian naturalist Karl Heller, an intellectual from a place where professional armies of non-citizen-soldiers were the norm, reported bemusedly in September 1846 from Mexico City that "all the large cities have witnessed assemblies and speeches in the plazas for the purpose of forming voluntary troops, who lack not only arms but all munition. In many places—and this is especially the case here—demagogues already have the population so whipped up that even the fathers of families are inclined to take the field."[19] Many National Guard units were filled mostly with volunteers rather than conscripts throughout the war. In recruitment meetings men exclaimed their willingness to fight. A Mexico City unit deposed its commander when it judged him not eager to take the unit out on campaign, and in some locations enthusiasm for National Guard service actually increased when people heard about battles lost to the Americans. This willingness to fight was even greater when Americans directly threatened a locality. In May 1847 the commander of an American warship ordered the town of Papantla, Veracruz, to submit to American authority. The townspeople immediately met to organize a new National Guard unit, and district administrator Hilarion Perez y Olaso wrote that he "had never seen in the town square a more numerous meeting of all classes in which were mixed even many old men and others asking to be armed in order to prevent the infamous usurper from entering this place."[20]

As citizen-soldiers, National Guardsmen saw themselves as being very different from the kind of men who were conscripted into the regular army. As we have seen, regular army conscripts were often chosen because they did not follow cultural rules that required them to work hard, support their families, and treat their parents with respect. The citizen-soldiers of the National Guard resented efforts to put such men in their units, saying that doing so made National Guard service dishonorable.[21] National Guardsmen, as free citizens, also did not want to be subject to the harsh corporal punishment used to discipline regular soldiers. The National Guard law specified jail sentences for various offenses, not mentioning corporal punishment. When the government of San Luis Potosí issued more specific regulations for its

National Guard, it prohibited corporal punishment. National Guardsmen complained bitterly when superiors beat them with their staffs.[22] National Guardsmen saw regular army service very negatively, and at times authorities threatened to transfer National Guardsmen who committed crimes to the regular army.[23]

National Guardsmen, like regular soldiers, were militarily useless until they had been trained in the use of muzzle-loading firearms, edged and pointed weapons, and the tactics employed with them. They had to learn to move in coordinated units, stay together in the confusion of battle, and repeat the meticulous steps needed to load and discharge muzzle-loading firearms amid the smoke, noise, and screams of human agony that characterized the battlefield. The best instructors were officers and sergeants with regular army experience. Fortunately, in many cases such men were available either because they were retired or because they were temporarily without units. National Guard commanders sometimes paid these men, although in this national crisis many instructors agreed to work without pay. Yet there was another problem. When would National Guardsmen who continued to work to feed their families find the time to train? They gave up Sundays and other bits of free time, but in general the time available was not enough to train them to the standards most regular army recruits reached before they were thrown into battle.[24]

How effective were the National Guardsmen during the war? National Guard units of diverse social origins took part in some of the direst fighting in central Mexico. At Cerro Gordo they defeated an American attack and only surrendered after they were surrounded, at Churubusco they fought until they were out of ammunition, at Molino del Rey they turned back an American attack and even counterattacked before being overwhelmed by fresh American troops, and at Chapultepec they held their position until the heights above them had been taken. In each case they inflicted heavy casualties on the Americans despite their deficiencies in training and weaponry.[25] Moreover, many men served far from their families, although, like other Mexican troops, they faced the problem of serving a government that often could not come up with the fiscal resources necessary to feed them. Leaders struggled to keep men in the ranks not because these men were unwilling to fight but because army life was one of hunger, hunger that undoubtedly reminded them of what their families were simultaneously experiencing back home.[26]

Mexico's Fiscal Disaster

For many years the government had struggled to derive enough income from an unproductive economy to support basic services. The difficulty was exacerbated by the unwillingness of wealthy Mexicans to pay direct taxes, which led to a fiscal system that relied too heavily on taxes on foreign trade that never met overoptimistic expectations. Governments repeatedly covered budget deficits with loans from domestic and foreign merchants, taken at increasingly unfavorable rates of interest. The fiscal problem had an enormous impact on Mexico's ability to defend itself. Even before the war, officers whose men had not been paid or fed sometimes resorted to forcibly seizing government revenues that had not been allocated to their units.[27] As the government tried to mobilize more troops, its financial problems only increased, because every man had to be fed, clothed, and equipped. The army that Antonio López de Santa Anna took to La Angostura, as hungry as it was, had been equipped with thousands of items of clothing, saddles, cooking gear, and axes, as well as its weapons. Experts estimated that food, pay, and equipment for each soldier consumed about one peso every day he was in the army, whether he was directly engaged in battle or not. The cost of the war, once it started, dragged Mexico's government further and further into the red, and the American government knew this.[28]

The American government was able to make the situation worse. Not only was the United States wealthier than Mexico, its citizens owned many merchant ships that traded all over the world. The desire to protect this trade had led the United States to invest in a navy of substantial size, far larger than its Mexican counterpart. Its warships and seamen blockaded Mexico. Goods could no longer be imported into major Mexican ports, where customhouses collected the tariffs that were the largest source of revenue for the national government. This disruption in the normal flow of commerce hurt the interests of some Mexicans, especially merchants who had been heavily involved in legitimate foreign trade. However, it never entirely choked off commerce. Mexico had a very long coastline, and goods could be imported or exported through a host of small ports. Moreover, after the United States captured some ports, it allowed imports and exports. However, contraband trade by definition did not yield revenue for the national government, and trade through U.S.-controlled ports was actually taxed by the United States, not Mexico. The blockade's most important effect was on the resources of Mexico's national government. It seems to have eliminated about half of the regular income of the government, and it did so just as the government needed to increase revenues.[29]

More than anything else it was the lack of fiscal resources that prevented the Mexican national state from mounting a successful defense against American aggression, and this lack of resources also defined the experiences of most Mexican soldiers and civilians during the war. Mexican forces always had fewer and worse weapons, fewer animals to move weapons or supplies, worse clothing, and, above all, less food than the American forces they faced. Although both Zachary Taylor in the north and Winfield Scott in the center of the country believed that the American government should have delivered more resources to their armies, they were still much better off than their Mexican counterparts. Mexican observers often marveled at how wealthy American forces were. American soldiers were paid fairly regularly, they had better weapons, they could hire civilian laborers to transport supplies or build fortifications, they could buy and feed the horses and mules they needed to transport supplies and artillery, and, above all, they could pay for their food. In the faltering Mexican economy many Mexicans, from wealthy landowners down to poor peasant women, were willing to sell them this food for cash, especially when it was clear that a refusal to sell would likely lead to confiscation without compensation or even to physical violence against those who held out.[30]

Mexican forces lacked all of these advantages. We have already seen how the lack of resources shaped the strategic situation faced by Santa Anna and his army in late 1846 and early 1847. It drove him to make the desperate gamble of crossing the desert to confront Taylor, leading to the bloody ravines of La Angostura and the even greater tragedy of the withdrawal across the desert, one of the war's defining moments. Yet this was far from the first or last time that the Mexican government's lack of money affected the military situation. Throughout the war Mexican officers complained to their superiors about the lack of resources. The most fundamental problem they faced was feeding their troops. In the north this problem was exacerbated by the arid climate, but even where the climate allowed Mexican civilians to produce more food, commanders were hamstrung by the lack of money. This was true for commanders in Monterrey, an agriculturally viable region; for Santa Anna's army in San Luis Potosí before the Angostura campaign; and, very strikingly, for the Mexican commanders who prepared to defend the relatively well-watered and agriculturally productive lands of the Gulf coast. As American troops advanced from the Gulf toward the Valley of Mexico and the climactic battles that awaited them there, Mexican commanders operating in the most populous and prosperous region in the country still had trouble coming up with the cash needed to feed their men.[31] The military impact of this problem was immense. As we have seen, hunger was the most important reason why Mexican troops sometimes deserted. Discipline and loyalty to their friends could keep Mexican regular army troops effective on the march or in battle, and political ideology and loyalty to friends could do the same for National Guard units, but these forces for cohesion paled beside the simple imperative of hunger. Hungry people go looking for food, and that drive is incompatible with maintaining organized military forces.

The scarcity of fiscal resources had other military impacts. Professional officers relied on their pay to feed not only themselves but also their families. Now they often did not receive any pay for months, and their morale was damaged.[32] Weapons were another huge problem. Mexican cannon were often antiquated, Mexican gunpowder was not as potent as that used by the Americans, and the muskets used by the Mexicans were worn-out leftovers from European wars that had ended thirty years before, bought used from the British. These muskets broke easily and their worn barrels made them more inaccurate than the much newer smoothbore muskets used by the Americans. The war matériel Mexicans were forced to use was so substandard that when American troops captured it, they could find no use for it. They instead disposed of the gunpowder by blowing it up and burned piles of captured Mexican muskets.[33]

Aside from its strictly military impact, Mexico's fiscal crisis had contradictory effects on Mexican politics during the war. Surprisingly, it built both unity and dissension. The unity stemmed from the way it kept the cost of the war squarely in front of all inhabitants of Mexico, even those who lived far from any battle and did not know any soldiers. All were constantly reminded of the fact that the war was a Mexican one, and that therefore all Mexicans should help pay for it. Yet the fiscal crisis also drove dissension. Mexico was already politically divided before the war, and the constant pressure to come up with enough money to fund the war dramatically increased political tensions, leading to what for many Mexicans was the worst moment of its brief political history: the spectacle of armed Mexicans confronting each other in the capital city even as Americans were invading the country.

The fiscal crisis shaped the experience of Mexican civilians by dramatically increasing the urgency and frequency of politicians' efforts to communicate with them. The financial needs imposed by the fighting and the simultaneous undermining of the usual sources of funds forced the government to turn to extraordinary means. All over Mexico government leaders and concerned citizens organized what were essentially fund drives. These efforts to collect donations had all the trappings we associate with charitable giving today, including committees of prominent citizens, pledges, benefit events, emotional speeches, and the publication of lists of donors. None of this was totally unprecedented: Similar campaigns had taken place in Europe during the late eighteenth- and early nineteenth-century wars that gradually transformed polities governed by monarchies into entities more akin to nation-states. The territory that later became Mexico also saw intense campaigns to raise funds for wars during that time.[34] Yet those campaigns pale compared to the intensity of the 1846–1848 campaigns in Mexico.

Campaigns collected cash or pledges, including pledges to donate small amounts every month, often identified as the living expenses of a single soldier. Earmarking donations as support for a soldier may have been a way to personalize the war and give it more emotional content, and the same might have been true of donations specifically directed to the care of wounded soldiers. Some government employees even donated portions of the back salary that the perennially impoverished government already owed them, a decision that is not as cynical as it sounds, as it removed an obligation from government accounts and simultaneously sacrificed an asset the employee might have used to secure a loan for living expenses. The wealthy obviously donated more cash, but what is striking is how many people of much lower incomes donated, including artisans, cowboys, shepherds, and peasants.[35] Blacksmiths offered to repair or make weapons, and after the Americans captured Tampico, authorities desperate to preserve heavy cannon from capture found hundreds of peasants eager to throw themselves at the arduous work of dragging them along the rural roads they had just repaired for the task. Estate owners contributed horses or cattle, and many less wealthy rural people similarly donated livestock. Others gave food, especially corn, the staple grain central to Mexican diets. The villagers of the district of Villa Alta, Oaxaca, far from the fighting, donated bushels of dried tortillas, products not only of the indigenous men who worked the fields but also of the women who laboriously ground the corn and cooked the tortillas. Shoemakers gave sandals or shoes, and seamstresses and tailors donated clothing or bandages.[36]

Efforts to collect voluntary donations drew many people into the war effort. Thousands of people served on committees or attended meetings. Women were extremely prominent in these efforts. They sponsored theatrical events to raise money, collected donations, and used their time to sew bandages, clothing, sheets, and unit flags for National Guard regiments. Their activities in support of the war were heavily publicized. Along with the long lists of donors of all social classes that were printed in newspapers, the writings about women's efforts clearly aimed to make a very salient point: all Mexicans should contribute their wealth, their labor, and if necessary, their blood.[37] In some ways the actions of Mexican women were similar to those of some American women who had created clothing or tents for volunteer units from their communities. However, in the United States these intense, tangible connections between women and the war were confined to a few communities and to a short span of time. In Mexico the efforts of women were more widespread, and they continued throughout the war. The drives to raise funds allowed the war to become real not only for those who actually faced American soldiers but also for those far from the fighting. They could all participate vicariously and practically by donating, and in doing so they could all feel Mexican. The residents of Mazatlán, Sinaloa, collected money to help the men wounded at La Angostura, expressing the hope that, in their words, "the Mexican soldier will see in this small aid that his service and blood spilled bravely in defense of Independence and the honor of the Nation, are justly appreciated by those of his fellow citizens who, although distant from the theater of war pray for the triumph of the arms of the Republic in the most just of causes." Donations flowed in from the primarily indigenous regions bordering Central America to the south, from the Pacific coast, from major cities, and from peasant villages or haciendas.[38] Ironically, the very penury of the Mexican state was helping many of the country's residents express their desire to be Mexicans.

Not all the funds collected for the war were given up voluntarily. Mexican authorities also sought to collect more taxes. In an early sign of fiscal desperation, the Paredes government reestablished the national head tax in May 1846. This deeply unpopular tax had been suspended in February 1845 after peasant resistance to it had contributed to the fall of the previous national government, and now Paredes reinstated it despite the growing opposition to his administration.[39] The head tax was soon removed again, but throughout the war both the federal government and the states sought to raise funds by more rigorously collecting existing taxes or imposing extraordinary taxes for the war effort. However, the Mexican economy was struggling, and the weakness of the federal government hampered tax collection. Thus taxation involved much more persuasion and negotiation than one would expect. Authorities sought to persuade taxpayers of the urgency imposed by the war, but taxpayers were often able to negotiate postponements or partial payments.[40]

Several times during the war the national government or state governments resorted to what were called forced loans. In forced loans individuals were obligated to give the government money, but they were also promised repayment, sometimes in the form of exemption from future taxes. The amount the government hoped to raise through a forced loan was apportioned to different individuals, supposedly in proportion to their assets. For wealthy people a forced loan was no doubt better than an extraordinary tax, but it presented its own problems. Was the amount they were asked to loan the government reasonable? Not surprisingly, those subject to forced loans often sought to negotiate lower quotas by explaining their financial difficulties or enumerating the contributions they had already made. Moreover, these negotiations were unfair in their own right: some wealthy people had more political connections than others. Foreigners sometimes claimed unsuccessfully that foreign citizenship made them exempt. People who made forced loans also faced another problem. Their assets were not necessarily liquid, and liquidating them might require one to sell them in an unfavorable market. Wartime was a terrible time to sell land, and the urgency of a forced loan might also cause a landowner to immediately sell produce that would have fetched higher prices later. In Mexico's rickety economy, forced loans were a real hardship for even some relatively well-off people, and some spiraled into bankruptcy as a result.[41]

The recurring campaigns for donations, enactments of extraordinary taxes, and demands for forced loans all kept the war in the forefront of public discussion throughout the country, making it a national experience and helping to reinforce Mexican identity. However, even as it built unity, the fiscal crisis created dissension. Like the demand for manpower for the regular army and National Guard, it brought many Mexicans to the brink of familial ruin, which might mean starvation for a poor family or bankruptcy for a wealthier one. Faced with demands for sacrifice, Mexicans looked around them to see if others were sacrificing as much. They also wondered if it was worth it. Nazario López of Matehuala, San Luis Potosí, wrote in January 1847 that he was a "good Mexican" and detailed more than a thousand pesos he had given the government as loans or donations in the previous three months, asking to be exempted from future sacrifices. He also listed a number of peers that he believed could give more. Balthazar Cuebas, administrator of the hacienda of Saucedo, likewise detailed the contributions it had made, and named a nearby hacienda that in his view had not done enough. As the war wore on, more and more complaints of this ilk arrived in the hands of politicians. In April 1847 the district administrator of Rio Verde, fearing that American forces in Tampico might advance and attack the district, called its principal citizens together to discuss how to organize a defense. A third of those invited did not attend, and those who were present met his request for suggestions with an uncomfortable silence. Twice more without success he urged those present to speak. After adjourning the meeting, he individually questioned many of the attendees. Several individuals said they had already given a lot, and during the meeting they had been waiting for those they considered to be wealthier to take the lead.[42]

The effect of the fiscal problem on Mexican national politics was similar. Through most of the war, none of Mexico's political factions ever openly favored peace or agreement to the territorial concessions the United States was after. Despite this remarkable consensus, the scarcity of resources raised domestic politics to the boiling point and kept it there. The penury of the government was a constant theme in political discussion. Dramatic debates in Congress were paralleled by sarcastic political cartoons on the theme, lampooning both the organizational ineptitude of the government and the unwillingness of people to actually pay for the war they seemed so enthusiastic about. The pressure roiled politics not only in the national capital but also in many states. In some cases it led poor rural people to mobilize, and more generally it undermined the legitimacy of authorities.[43]

The Polkos Rebellion

Mexican desperation about how to pay for the war sparked the so-called *polkos* rebellion, in which National Guard units of differing political sympathies confronted each other in Mexico City beginning in late February 1847. Many Mexicans understood this as the worst moment of the war, one in which Mexico's fractious politics undercut its defense just as the Americans threatened the center of the country. The conflict made it much easier for the Americans to launch the invasion of central Mexico that eventually defeated the country. The polkos rebellion turned back an effort to use the wealth of the Catholic Church to solve the most urgent funding problems, and in Mexican history it is mostly understood as a stark example of struggle between church and state that eventually led to the violent civil wars of the late 1850s and early 1860s. The winners of those civil wars wrote the polkos rebellion into the history books studied by Mexican children as an example of the Catholic Church putting its interests ahead of the national interest in the middle of a foreign war.[44] The story is more complicated than that. The church could only act to protect its financial interests because the organization of the National Guard had created units of part-time soldiers representing different political factions. The existence of these units allowed the church to acquire armed allies. The group that took up arms on the side of the church also had motives rooted in fears of class violence. Moreover, church leaders had already devoted thousands and thousands of pesos, as well as other resources, to the war because they believed that it was religiously important. Finally, even though some supporters of the controversial law saw it as a way to curb the power of the church, their opportunity only came about due to the profound fiscal crisis of the war.

The large army Santa Anna organized in San Luis Potosí was built and fed largely with resources from that state. As this army grew, Santa Anna sent appeal after appeal to the national government, stressing the urgent need for funds for equipment, arms, and, above all, food.[45] As pressure to act grew, the national government, led by Vice President Valentín Gómez Farías, turned to Congress. After heated discussion, on January 11, 1847, Congress authorized the government to raise fifteen million pesos by mortgaging or selling property belonging to various Catholic Church organizations.[46] Many radical federalists supported this law, and many moderate federalists opposed it. Santa Anna approved the idea after Gómez Farías explained that there were no other funds available. However, the government knew from the beginning that the law would be controversial. Even some radical federalists felt that it would make the radicals' hold on power very tenuous without raising much money for the war effort.[47]

The law assumed, as many radicals did, that church entities held a very large amount of wealth as investments to fund their activities, and that this wealth could be quickly converted into cash. The first assumption was certainly correct: many monasteries, convents, schools, and other religious organizations had accumulated real estate that they rented out or funds that they lent out to provide steady incomes to fund their activities, much the way that many institutions use income from their endowments today. The second assumption was more difficult to sustain: Who would buy these assets in Mexico's current situation, with its weak economy and the threat of foreign invasion? Some of the radicals also believed that church organizations had not done their fair share to pay the costs of the war. They believed that although church leaders overtly supported the war, they had dragged their feet in delivering funds in order to protect their assets.[48]

Assessing the attitude of the Catholic Church toward the war before, during, and after the polkos rebellion is complicated. The church was not really a single entity. Individual clergymen had different views about the relative importance of winning the war and financing continuing religious activities, and some church assets were controlled by laymen who managed the finances of various religious organizations. Many Catholic leaders authorized copious payments to the government both before and after the polkos rebellion, even more preached the importance of resisting the Americans, and many contributed portions of their personal wealth to the war effort. It is only possible to understand the moment of rupture, when some of them openly defied the government, if we consider why they supported the war in the first place.

Many believed that an American victory might seriously hamper their mission of offering religious salvation to Mexicans. James K. Polk and his commanders repeatedly insisted that the United States would respect the rights of the Catholic Church, and that their war was against the Mexican government, not the church. However, this insistence was drowned out by the anti-Catholic rhetoric in American politics and discussions of the war in American media. As we have seen, many American supporters of the war saw Catholicism as antidemocratic, corrupt, and even unchristian. They believed Catholicism held Mexico back, causing ignorance, authoritarianism, and poverty even as the church amassed wealth. Mexicans were very aware of this rhetoric. It made them fear that at the very least the Americans would insist that Protestant denominations be allowed to operate in Mexico, a development that Mexican priests believed would tempt some Mexicans away from the only faith that could lead them to eternal salvation. Some also believed the Americans might confiscate the very financial assets that they were being asked to dip into to support the war. This anti-Catholicism, moreover, was not abstract and distant: church leaders and other Catholics were horrified by accounts of the physical and symbolic attacks on sacred objects, places of worship, and ceremonies that many American volunteer soldiers were committing in occupied territory. It was very logical for most church leaders to work against the Americans. Most likely, only a few priests bought into official American assurances that the American government would protect the church and Catholicism.[49]

There is overwhelming evidence that many church leaders and other priests worked hard to support the war against the Americans. They organized many public religious ceremonies to pray for victory, taking religious images out in procession. These were appeals for divine intervention, but they also contributed to increasing popular support for the war effort, building on the already well-established idea that Mexico had a religious destiny as a Catholic nation.[50] On countless occasions priests used sermons to exhort Mexicans to put their money and their bodies on the line to defend the country, and their religion, against the Americans. Father Luis García, for instance, explained in November 1846 that he was making all possible efforts to instruct his parishioners about "the need to unite now more than ever to defend our beloved country against an enemy who we can see not only wants to usurp part of our territory, but also seems to want to attack the rights of our religion."[51] From the arrival of the first news of fighting along the Rio Grande until after the fall of Mexico City, priests continued to urge their parishioners to oppose the Americans.

Religious leaders also transferred church financial resources to the government. From the mid-1830s on, the government had insistently pressured the Catholic Church to loan it more and more money, and that pressure only increased with the dark events of 1845, 1846, and 1847. Church wealth was mostly invested in real estate so that regular rents would provide a steady income to support the activities of its various organizations. As the government repeatedly turned to the church for cash, its needs overwhelmed that income, leading to deferred maintenance on many buildings. By the late spring of 1846, the church was also selling properties in an unfavorable market so that it could loan the proceeds to the government, with no hope of prompt repayment. As the effects of the blockade further weakened its fiscal position, the national government pressured the church more and more. The church continued to deliver loans, and religious leaders and church institutions also donated money for the war effort. The financial position of the church grew weaker and weaker. Many churches and convents also donated their bells, which were melted down and made into cannon or ammunition.[52]

In hindsight, the anticlerical radicals' view that the church was not doing its share seems to have stemmed more from an exaggerated view of church resources and a predilection to blame the church for Mexico's problems than it did from a sober consideration of the financial situation of the church. It was also based on the assumption that the church, as a Mexican institution, should have subordinated its goals completely to the nation-state's need to defend Mexico against the Americans. Many church officials did not believe this: they cooperated with the war effort as part of their own mission to try to lead as many Mexicans as possible to eternal salvation. In other words, the church supported the war effort because it saw its mission as congruent with the nation-state's war, not because it subordinated the church's mission to the state. The church's mission had existed for centuries before there was a nation-state, and it would continue literally until the end of time. In January 1847 church leaders did not feel that their long-term mission was compatible with the radical notion that the government could simply decree the disposal of church property. The government was no longer asking, or even pressuring; it was taking and assuming the right to do so.

Church leaders thus vociferously opposed the January 11, 1847, law. They pointed out that the church had already contributed greatly to support the war. They argued that under church law, its wealth was to be devoted solely to its religious mission, and they could not carry out their religious duties without the wealth the government was confiscating. They threatened to excommunicate government officials who enforced the law and individuals who bought property that should remain dedicated to the Catholic Church's mission.[53] The threat underlined the seriousness of the church's stance, and undoubtedly stoked the conflict that followed. However, it is telling that religious leaders also reached out to Mexico's wealthy. Some pamphlets pointed out that the law would necessarily reduce the role that church institutions had played as de facto banks, lending money to entrepreneurs. Who would be able to find the cash to repay these loans in this weak economy? Others, more ominously, argued that if the government could confiscate the church's property, then no one's property was safe. Notably, those who eventually resorted to force in opposition to the law repeated this argument.[54]

The men who later rebelled against the Gómez Farías government certainly supported the church's position on the importance of its mission of salvation. The possibility of eternal life had enormous emotional power in a nineteenth-century world in which life on Earth was all too short, and this was as true in the United States as it was in Mexico.[55] It also resonated with the fears of many well-off and even middle-class Mexicans about their more immediate fate on Earth. They feared not only hell but also the possibility that the extremely democratic politics that had returned to Mexico in August 1846 threatened the wealth they counted on to provide a decent life for their families and their descendants. The financial emergency might lead the government to confiscate not only from the church but also from the rich. The perception of risk was only heightened by the exalted egalitarianism that many radical federalists in Mexico's cities espoused. These men, the very men who had passed the January 11 law, seemed to be taking democracy and republicanism to a dangerous extreme. This fear, more than anything else, allowed the church to find allies willing to take up arms against the government.

Although there were dramatic incidents of opposition to the January 11 law in some other locations, the one that made a difference was the polkos rebellion in Mexico City itself. This rebellion certainly targeted the January 11 law, and had the backing of important church leaders, at least in its initial stages, but it also was the product of political conflicts in the city itself that stretched back for decades, conflicts that were shaped more by questions of class than they were by church-state relations.[56] The word "polkos" itself was a reference to urban class differences. The polka, at that point recently arrived from Europe, was the fashionable dance that dominated the amusements of the wealthier young men of the city. Their political opponents called these young men polkos in satire, a genre that they also used to make light of the way the wealthy young men dressed and showed piety. One poem insisted that they attended Mass at the cathedral mostly to meet young women of their class.[57] The political conflicts that eventually spurred the rebellion sometimes included explicit references to economic policy. However, much more often they centered on arguments about the social meaning of republicanism. What did the establishment of an independent, republican nation-state mean for social relationships? Did an identity as Mexican citizens offer even poor urban men the possibility of being considered honorable, contributing members of society, regardless of their racial background? Did independence invalidate colonial social, as opposed to political, hierarchies? Radical urban federalists believed that it did, and they were acutely aware that their enemies, identified with wealth, privilege, and a sense of themselves as whiter than other urban people, still believed that they were more honorable than most Mexicans. Notably, earlier manifestations of this conflict had been characterized by extreme expressions of nationalism, especially in violent and nonviolent attempts to expel the large numbers of Spaniards from Mexico. The urban supporters of the radicals saw themselves as being the most stalwart defenders of the Mexican nation.[58]

These conflicts over the social implications of republicanism and independence had heated up with the August 1846 overthrow of centralism. The turn to federalism brought with it not only a conscious decentralization of power from the national government to the states but also the return of broad suffrage and an openly exuberant egalitarianism. For the urban poor and the lower middle class, this egalitarianism was an expression of self-worth and honor, but for the upper middle class and the wealthy, it threatened anarchy and possibly attacks on private property. They feared that urban poor people empowered through the ballot or through arms would attack their betters and steal their wealth. Meetings that seemed highly democratic to the radicals looked like borderline riots to the wealthy, especially since many speeches criticized not only the Americans but also the elite. Carlos Maria de Bustamante described the participants in one such meeting as "the vilest rabble of the mob." Even before the centralists took power in 1835, relatively wealthy people who saw themselves as the guardians of order and sober republicanism had worked to limit electoral participation, and the raucous elections Mexico City experienced in the fall of 1846 frightened them. Rumors circulated that the government would use the backing of the poor to confiscate private property, supposedly for the war effort. Bustamante disparaged radical federalist politicians for not understanding that "the rich and poor have always been in conflict because the rich have the money that the poor lack and want to make their own in any way possible. At any time democracy can get out of hand."[59] Soon the National Guard law, which encouraged groups of affiliated men to form their own units of part-time soldiers, raised the political temperature of Mexico City's neighborhoods even further. Over the next few weeks several National Guard units were organized, each with a distinct political identity associated with a profession or neighborhood and represented by the men elected to be officers. Some units were composed of men of relatively humble origins, poor enough to sometimes be mistakenly conscripted into the regular army. Bustamante called these National Guardsmen "naked sans-culottes . . .

full of fleas and poverty." As the wealthy grew more fearful, they organized units specifically to protect their political interests and property against this "rabble."[60] These different National Guard units almost came to blows in the fall of 1846, and their existence gave Catholic leaders the hope that armed protest against the January 11, 1847, law might succeed. When the polkos rebellion finally did break out, its critics focused as much on the rebels' hatred of equality as they did on the problem of church property, and one of the rebellion's principal leaders later admitted that the leaders were more interested in overthrowing the radical government than they were in what happened to church property.[61]

The rebellion was an alliance of convenience between church leaders who believed that their long-term mission would be imperiled if the government established the principle that church property was national property and wealthy residents of Mexico City who feared that the war was allowing the impoverished urban supporters of radical federalism to threaten social hierarchies and even private property itself. It also had support from property owners who feared that suddenly throwing millions of pesos worth of church property onto the market would affect their interests. The first group provided crucial funds for the rebels, the second group provided the armed men, and the third group provided a sympathetic audience outside Mexico City. However, historians of the polkos rebellion have sometimes overlooked one of the most crucial factors. The polkos were relatively few, around three thousand men. How could this group hope to overthrow the national government? The answer is simple: the vast bulk of the regular army, including units that normally provided security for the government, were hundreds of miles north with Santa Anna, campaigning against the Americans. The polkos therefore were only opposed by roughly two thousand soldiers, most of whom were radical National Guardsmen.[62] The war itself had given a mere handful of men the chance to overthrow the government.

Though the law authorizing the government to appropriate church property was passed on January 11, 1847, the polkos did not openly rebel until February 27. The intervening weeks were filled with rising tensions in the Federal District and various states. Church officials published pamphlets criticizing the law and some went further. On January 13, church officials locked the doors of the cathedral, perhaps to provoke a popular revolt against the law. The national government asked the city council to help it arrest any-one who threatened order, including priests. The city council in turn asked the priests to open the cathedral, and approved the publication of a letter pointing out that the government needed the church's wealth to defend not only the nation but also Catholicism itself. Soldiers guarding the National Palace had to use their firearms to turn back an armed crowd on January 19.[63] Meanwhile, protests against the law continued to mount, including one from a group of merchants. Opposition to the law was very open in the states of Puebla, Guanajuato, Mexico, Querétaro, Oaxaca, and Durango. In some places crowds rioted, and state legislatures and city councils criticized the law openly. The governor of Durango resigned rather than enforce the law.[64]

The national government, led by Vice President Gómez Farías, was well aware that the law was extremely controversial. It faced not only provincial unrest and the public ire of the church but also fierce criticism from its enemies in the newspapers. It countered by stressing the crisis of the war and Santa Anna's own support for using church wealth. Yet the government seems to have understood that the polkos National Guard battalions in Mexico City represented an immediate threat. Intelligence that these units were plotting against Gómez Farías led the minister of war to prohibit unauthorized National Guard meetings and also to order one of the units to transfer its headquarters out of a very central location in the city. The battalion obeyed the order, but it marched very publicly, accompanied by a crowd chanting antigovernment slogans.[65] The final straw came when Gómez Farías, hearing of the imminent American invasion of Veracruz, decided to use his authority to send several polkos units to Veracruz. The reasoning seems clear: The U.S. invasion of the coast was imminent, the vast bulk of the regular army was up north with Santa Anna, and if National Guard units were the only ones available to reinforce Veracruz, why not simultaneously short-circuit a possible coup by removing disloyal units from the capital?

The move backfired. On February 25, the government ordered the Independencia, Hidalgo, Bravo, Victoria, and Mina battalions to march to Vera-cruz, and two days later they instead declared themselves in rebellion. Thus the armed resistance began more than six weeks after the passage of the law affecting church property, and the immediate trigger was a move in the complicated politics of class in Mexico City. Transfer to Veracruz would have separated the middle-class and wealthy men of these units from their families, exposed them to the dangerous disease environment of the coast, and left the security of their property and families in the hands of radical National Guard units they considered to be little better than avaricious rabble. For the rebels, armed defiance of the government was preferable, even in wartime.[66] That the rebellion was a continuation of the fractious, class-based politics of the capital, however, does not mean that church leaders and opposition to the January 11 law were not also crucial. The rebels followed the established Mexican tradition of laying out their political aims in a formal document. This plan argued that the rebels were true federalists but that Congress had acted unconstitutionally. It called for the overthrow of Congress and Gómez Farías but the continuation of federalism under the constitution. All of this was aimed at removing the radicals from office. The preamble, however, also criticized Congress for passing the January 11 law, saying it had violated "the principles that regulate the property of individuals and corporations" and had not taken into account "the connection between Church wealth and the other kinds." The plan called for the law's immediate abolition.[67] Some members of the clergy involved in managing church wealth were directly involved. The men of the polkos units needed, like all troops, food, because part-time soldiers who were mobilized were not making a living at their civilian jobs. At the beginning of the revolt, that money was provided by the administrators of several convents and monasteries, and it was reported that they had a hand in writing the plan.[68] The soldiers of the rebel battalions openly wore religious medals, signaling that theirs was a religious cause. Given this, and the severe church-state conflict that characterized Mexico in the 1850s and 1860s, it is not surprising that the rebellion was later widely understood as the result of the church placing its own interests ahead of those of the nation.[69]

The backers of the rebellion were hoping for a quick and bloodless coup, but neither Gómez Farías nor his allies were easily intimidated. For more than a month, radical and moderate National Guard units confronted each other in Mexico City, while the few regular army troops in town remained loyal to the government. The result was a military stalemate, with some street fighting but surprisingly few casualties. Most state governments either backed the Gómez Farías government or maintained a de facto neutrality. The political impasse dragged on as the Americans prepared to invade Veracruz and Santa

Anna's army conducted its epic campaign in the north. The rebels insisted that arming the poor and confiscating church property threatened Mexican society with anarchy and would not help win the war. Government supporters pointed out that the rebellion was undermining the Mexican war effort, and that if the Americans won the war, Mexican Catholicism would be at risk. They also accused the polkos units of being too cowardly to go to Veracruz and fight the Americans. Trying to broaden their base of support, the rebels deemphasized the question of church property while continuing to insist that Gómez Farías must leave office. This move was unpopular with their financial backers and gained them little in the end.[70]

While the stalemate dragged on, the national government was unable to send troops or money to Veracruz. It became clear that only Santa Anna could bring a solution, and as he made his way south, envoys from both sides sought his support. At first he seemed inclined to back Gómez Farías, since in the beginning the rebellion appeared to be also aimed at Santa Anna. The moderate envoys, however, insisted that it was class unrest and the danger to private property that had caused them to act. They also may have promised Santa Anna an immediate infusion of church funds for the war effort if he was willing to give up the offensive law. Santa Anna chose the moderates. Gómez Farías was removed from power by the simple expedient of overturning the decree that had originally created the vice presidency. The church anteed up with millions of pesos, the polkos regiments paraded before their supporters in Mexico City, and, ironically, the radical National Guard units were sent toward Veracruz. Some of their leaders resigned, alleging family duties. Vicente Carbajal, commander of one of the units, did not go so quietly. His resignation letter to Santa Anna insisted that the radicals had been defending Mexican independence and Santa Anna's presidency, while their opponents had undermined Mexico's defense. He ended by writing that he refused to be the equal of "traitors that were bought with gold from the clergy and the foreign enemy."[71]

Carbajal's words bring us to one of the most enduring charges against the polkos, that they were traitors encouraged or even financed by the American government. The American government did have an agent on the scene in the form of Moses Beach, an American journalist and prominent Catholic. Beach had been sent to work toward a negotiated solution to the war, and he was able to gain access to many Mexican Catholic leaders. Later he claimed to be the mastermind behind the polkos rebellion. He certainly did what he could to encourage resistance to the January 11 law, and he met many of the key players. He may even have transferred some money to the polkos. However, his self-serving report is not very good evidence of the efficacy of his efforts. As we have seen with Santa Anna's previous dealings with the Polk administration, Americans were often quite naïve about their discussions with prominent Mexicans. Some Mexican leaders were definitely willing to accept money or other support, but they then put it to their own uses.[72] The polkos rebellion was firmly rooted in Mexican politics, and it almost certainly would have come about without the efforts of Beach. Most Mexican Catholic leaders still opposed the U.S. invasion. They were appalled by the aggression of American volunteer soldiers toward Catholicism and worried about the long-term impact an American victory would have on their mission. Mexican Catholic leaders contributed millions of pesos to the war effort as soon as the government gave up the idea that it could dispose of church wealth against their will. They also reinvigorated their efforts to convince Mexicans to fight against the Americans.[73]

Scott's Invasion Campaign

The U.S. government won the war by launching a new invasion of central Mexico through Mexico's Gulf coast. The shift in American emphasis was partially a response to the stark geographic realities that prevented the Americans from advancing south from Saltillo. It was a long way to Mexico City, and on the first part of the campaign an invading American army would face a difficult desert. It was also a response to the surprising amount of resistance that the Mexicans had put up in the north. The decision to launch a central Mexico campaign was a tacit admission that, despite Taylor's repeated tactical successes, his northern campaign was actually a strategic defeat because it had not forced Mexico to seek negotiations. The only way to win the war was to go to the heart of Mexico's most populated areas. This would be a difficult task: the state was stronger there, and it was risky to send what would have to be a relatively small army into a situation in which it would be surrounded by enemies. Moreover, this army would have to first land on a hostile shore

FIG. 4.1 Lieutenant General Winfield Scott.

and secure a base. Polk also understood that the war posed political risks for his Democratic Party. Taylor, who had been victorious at Palo Alto, Resaca de Palma, and Monterrey, was a Whig, one with evident presidential ambitions. Polk needed a new general for the decisive campaign, and with some trepidation he settled on Scott, also an ambitious Whig, but one who was more militarily competent and less politically competent. Ironically, both Taylor and Scott had suggested the Veracruz plan, apparently independently, although Scott would reap the awards. Scott, a very professional soldier and an avid student of military history, was a great advocate of flanking maneuvers, in which an attacking force endeavors to go around the center of enemy resistance and attack a weakly defended side. The whole invasion plan was, aptly, a massive flanking maneuver, one that would sidestep both the Mexican forces gathered at great cost in the north and the geographic obstacles that separated the north from Mexico City.[74]

A flanking maneuver aims at a weak point of the enemy's defense, and it is hard to imagine any weaker point than Veracruz in the spring of 1847. Although the harbor was guarded by a massive fortress, San Juan de Ulúa, many of its cannon were ancient, and there were not enough men to fully garrison its walls. The same was true of the city itself. There a mixed bag of regular and National Guard units from Veracruz and neighboring states struggled against the most typical enemy faced by Mexican troops: poverty. They did not have enough food, ammunition, and clothing, and in January and February 1847 none was coming from Mexico City for all the reasons we have seen. It was reported that soldiers had to go begging from door to door to get enough money to eat. The women of the town organized a benefit concert to repair the cannon of San Juan de Ulúa, but when the massive American fleet bearing Scott's army arrived in early March, the city's commander, Juan Morales, wrote to his superiors that, faced with this challenge, he could only count on "a handful of brave men, shoeless, badly paid, and badly dressed."[75] The threat of Fort San Juan de Ulúa prevented the Americans from sailing directly into the harbor, but Morales did not have enough troops to defend the surrounding coastline, and the Americans simply landed on the beach a few miles away. Although this was the first large amphibious operation in the history of the U.S. Army and Navy, the two services cooperated well, and soon an overwhelming American force began to prepare for a siege of the city. Morales could only sit and hope for reinforcements.

Although Scott could land troops and supplies on the beaches when the weather was good, sustaining a campaign into the interior would require a port where ships would have shelter as they unloaded. Veracruz could not be bypassed. Moreover, Scott was in a race against time. He had to take the city and get the bulk of his army out of the coastal lowlands before the yellow fever season arrived. This mosquito-borne disease would otherwise decimate the invading army. Thus, he not only needed to take Veracruz, he needed to take it quickly. The weapons and tactics of the day left Scott with three options. He could besiege the city, cutting off supplies until hunger and disease forced it to surrender. A siege was a lengthy process, though, and he did not have the time. Scott might also send his troops on a frontal assault. Given the American advantage in numbers, the Americans would likely succeed, but such an assault would be very costly for the attackers, as the Americans had seen at Monterrey. The losses might weaken his army enough to doom his later invasion of central Mexico. The third option was bombardment. Firing exploding shells over the walls would bring death and destruction to all the city's inhabitants, soldiers and civilians alike. This could prepare the ground for a frontal assault, and it also might force surrender without such an assault. With any luck a successful bombardment would also cause enough civilian casualties to make other cities likely to surrender quickly.[76] Scott chose this third option.

Scott's forces cut the city off from the interior, landed cannon, and prepared fortified emplacements for them. The American army artillery was reinforced by heavy naval cannon manned by sailors. On March 22, 1847, the Americans opened fire. The Mexican defenders replied with their own cannon, but the American guns and gunners, entrenched in the sand dunes around the city, were almost completely immune to return fire. The stone walls and houses of the city offered no effective protection. Stone fortifications had been made obsolete by the advancement of artillery technology: American cannon firing directly at the city walls or buildings simply delivered enough kinetic energy to break stone. Moreover, many of the American artillery pieces lofted explosive shells on ballistic trajectories so that they cleared the walls and dropped down onto the city beyond, smashing through fragile clay, wooden, or thatched roofs and exploding in the very buildings where civilians were forced to take refuge. For three and a half days the bombardment continued. During this time the Mexican troops began to run out of food and ammunition, and hundreds of them were killed. However, their morale was undermined much more by the seeming uselessness of their sacrifice: their return fire, although accurate, was ineffective because the sand Americans sheltered behind simply absorbed the kinetic energy of Mexican cannonballs and smothered exploding shells. The Americans, understandably, seemed unwilling to leave their trenches and attack openly. Worse yet, Mexican officers and soldiers were acutely aware of the toll the bombardment took on civilians, in many cases their own family members. Shocked and wounded, Mexican women and children wandered the streets, mourning their dead and trying to find someplace safe. The ports' foreign consuls asked Scott for an interview so that they could ask him to allow the evacuation of foreigners and noncombatants, but Scott refused to even see them because he understood that the plight of civilians gave him much greater leverage over the Mexican soldiers. Scott had very consciously chosen the lives of his soldiers and the preservation of his ability to complete his long-term mission over the lives of Mexican civilians. In his memoirs Scott stated openly that "tenderness for the women and children—in the form of delay—might, in its consequences, have led to the loss of the campaign, and indeed the loss of the army—two thirds by pestilence, and the remainder by surrender."[77]

The Mexican commanders faced tremendous pressures. Soldiers and officers lobbied to be allowed to break out of the city and join other Mexican troops to continue resistance elsewhere. Some women and children considered leaving the city and advancing toward the American lines, hoping that American troops would not continue to slaughter them if they had to see the results of their actions. Others implored Mexican officers to surrender to save the civilian population. Morales resisted as long as he could. Honor demanded that the city not surrender until the situation was hopeless, and rumors indicated that a Mexican army was advancing from the interior to relieve the city. Eventually, though, he heard that some women were claiming that he did not value the lives of the city's civilians because he was not from the region. Morales resigned his command and his successor, Juan Landero, agreed to the capitulation of the garrison. The men would be allowed to march out and leave freely under their word of honor that they would take no further part in the war. The Americans had feared that the harbor fortress of San Juan de Ulúa would hold out, preventing American ships from entering the harbor. However, Landero also surrendered it because it was considered part of the Veracruz defenses, although likely he did not believe that it had sufficient supplies to hold out for a significant amount of time. The Mexican troops marched out and gave up their weapons under the respectful gaze of their American counterparts. In the words of Pennsylvania volunteer Jacob Oswandel, "Everything passed off quietly; no insulting remarks or fun were made towards the Mexicans as they passed out, we looked upon them as a conquered foe, who have fought for their firesides and property, the same that we would have done if attacked by a foreign foe."[78]

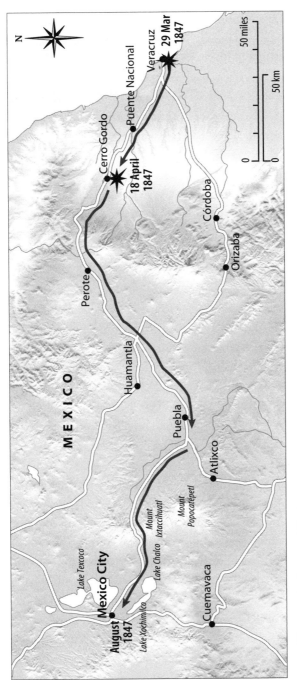

MAP 9 The campaign for central Mexico

The rapid capitulation of Veracruz was widely commented on in Mexico, the United States, and Europe. Partially this was the result of an exaggerated sense of how defensible the city was: most people did not yet understand how improvements in artillery had made older stone fortifications vulnerable, and in Europe and the United States, many still did not understand that the poverty of the Mexican government meant that every Mexican soldier was always underequipped and underfed. However, most of the sound and fury resulted from the way in which Scott had taken the port. The bombardment had killed around 350 Mexican soldiers and between 300 and 600 civilians, and wounded hundreds more. Astute Mexican observers understood that it was the civilian deaths that had forced the capitulation. The Americans had proven that they were willing to use civilian casualties to achieve their aims, and this tactic might be used in the future in other cities. Guillermo Rode, for instance, suggested garrisoning the high ground outside cities to keep American artillery pieces from being in a position to bombard civilians, while Juan Alvarez advised commanders to evacuate the women and children from any city prior to its defense, because, in his words, "the men most hardened and most accustomed to calmly seeing the destruction and horrors of war, often lack resistance when it comes to the death of children, the elderly, and women."[79] However, most commentary on the bombardment was about its morality. American war correspondents like George Wilkins Kendall and Jane McManus Storms reported on the civilian deaths but portrayed them as a military necessity. The same was not true outside the United States. Mexican observers roundly condemned the morality of Scott's choice and deployed it as yet more evidence of the injustice of the American invasion and the need for Mexicans to sacrifice to defend their nation. Some foreigners reacted similarly to Scott's bombardment. The editors of the *Times of London* wrote that "we have seldom had occasion to record an operation of war more revolting to every feeling of humanity and justice than the bombardment and capture of the city and castle of Vera Cruz" and called the bombardment "one of the most atrocious and barbarous acts committed in modern times by the forces of a civilized nation."[80]

Even as the Americans triumphed at Veracruz, Santa Anna was gathering new forces to oppose them. Their core was, remarkably, regular army infantrymen who had fought at La Angostura. These men had then marched more than six hundred miles in seven weeks, with the first third of that march taking place in the terrible desert between La Angostura and San Luis Potosí. They had rested very briefly there before racing to get between Scott's army and the Mexican highlands. Mexican troops were well known for their speed and endurance on the march, but this movement was frankly spectacular.[81] These long-suffering veterans were experienced and tough, but no doubt they suffered physically from the hardships of the journey. Santa Anna also had two regular army regiments from the Mexico City garrison, two radical federalist National Guard battalions from Mexico City, and National Guard units from the states of Puebla and Veracruz. These National Guard units, like their counterparts elsewhere in Mexico, had received little training.[82]

The Battle of Cerro Gordo

Santa Anna's choice of where to fight was the result of the Mexican environment. In the Angostura campaign the environment had worked in the Americans' favor, killing Mexican soldiers in the desert. In this instance it might work to the advantage of the Mexicans. Santa Anna understood that he had to get this force into position to stop the Americans before they could climb out of the coastal lowlands, where yellow fever and other tropical diseases could be expected to cause them heavy casualties. These diseases were very dangerous for men who had not previously been exposed to them. Yellow fever, which had first been brought to the New World by African slaves, was so dangerous that it contributed to widespread depopulation in lowland Mexico after 1500. Militarily, it had crippled the Spanish attempt to reconquer Mexico in 1829 and the French effort to reconquer Haiti in the first decade of the 1800s. It was a serious threat even for Mexican soldiers who were transferred to the lowlands. Mexican intelligence reports about American activities along the coast carefully tracked the progress of yellow fever and other tropical illnesses among the soldiers and sailors even while they were still aboard ship because all understood that disease could be a decisive factor in the war.[83]

Santa Anna's decision about where to put up the next fight was also influenced by another factor. Above the port of Veracruz, in the foothills between the port and the temperate highlands, Santa Anna was on home ground. He had grown up in the region, he had fought there during the Mexican War of Independence, and he had built his political and economic fortune there as a powerbroker and the owner of large estates. Here he could call in favors to acquire intelligence and feed his troops. The latter was particularly important because, although church officials had provided a new infusion of cash, this money soon began to run short, and by the time the Mexican soldiers were in position, they were again hungry. Moreover, Santa Anna believed that he knew the ground. From reports of Palo Alto and his personal experience at La Angostura, Santa Anna understood that the greatest American advantage was their ability to quickly deploy artillery against concentrations of Mexican troops caught in the open. He now sought a battlefield whose terrain would negate that advantage. He chose a place called Cerro Gordo. Here the road between Veracruz and the highlands wound its way between ridges to the south and high hills to the north. American movements would be further hampered by a steep canyon farther south and very rugged terrain covered by dense brush farther north. Santa Anna believed that the Americans would have to come straight up the road, and placing Mexican troops and cannon not only across their path but on the ridges and hills to the north and south would make that a deadly mistake. Santa Anna's chief of engineers, Lieutenant Colonel Manuel Robles Pezuela, disagreed. He feared that the terrain north of the road was not too difficult for the Americans, and thus he favored a position a few hundred yards farther on, where the road came out from between the hills and Mexican cavalry might be more effective. Robles Pezuela, however, had not seen the American light artillery at work, and Santa Anna overruled him. Robles Pezuela then tried to convince Santa Anna to station more troops north of the road to protect against an American flanking attack, but Santa Anna demurred, probably because his army simply was not large enough to cover all possible avenues of approach. He could only cover the most likely contingencies, and a significant American attack through that difficult terrain seemed unlikely. At the very least he believed that such an attack could not be supported by artillery.[84]

As Santa Anna gathered troops and rushed them into position, Scott worked to organize his army to push inland and reach the highlands before the onset of yellow fever season. Taking Veracruz had given him a port, greatly facilitating the arrival of more supplies. Scott's advantages in transportation,

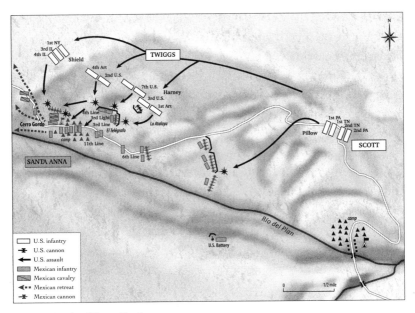

MAP 10 Battle of Cerro Gordo

however, ended at the water's edge. The American navy and the country's vast array of civilian ships could guarantee relatively quick and very cheap transport from American ports like New Orleans, but on land Scott was limited to Mexican roads. Moving troops and supplies on them required careful planning, wagons, animals, and food for the animals. Scott could not begin marching up from Veracruz until he had these things, and that took time. The Americans waited at the port for more than a week after its fall, and even then only a portion of their army, led by General David Twiggs, could leave. They found the deep sand of the road near Veracruz to be tortuous marching in the tropical heat, and soon many began discarding items of clothing or even their complete packs. On April 11 scouts from this group exchanged fire with Mexican scouts a few miles from Cerro Gordo. Twiggs pushed his troops forward and called the next division, led by General Robert Patterson, to accelerate its march. Twiggs wanted to attack immediately, but a reconnaissance party sent ahead came back with the first inklings of the size and strong position of the Mexican army. Twiggs waited a day for Patterson's troops, and they were so exhausted from their rapid march that he waited another day. He used the delay to collect more information, and a young officer named Pierre Beauregard was assigned to examine the area north of the Mexican position. Hours of arduous travel up and down ravines and hills covered in thick scrub brought Beauregard to a place near the rear of the Mexican army. There a few dozen soldiers with a handful of cannon occupied the highest hill, called El Telégrafo because it had once been the site of a semaphore station used to communicate news from the coast to the highlands. These soldiers were the extreme left flank of the Mexican army, and there were not enough of them to hold the hill against a major attack. Beauregard had struck the military equivalent of gold. Now all he had to do was convince Twiggs, who was still in command because Patterson, who outranked him, was ill.

Beauregard communicated what he had found to Twiggs, and Twiggs amended his previous idea of a frontal attack to also include a flanking attack on El Telégrafo on the early morning of April 14. This plan worried both Beauregard and Patterson, and Patterson rose from his sickbed in the middle of the night to take command and cancel the plan. Many observers believed that this decision prevented a disastrous frontal attack. Scott arrived at noon that day. On April 15 and 16 he sent more engineers out. One of these young men, Robert E. Lee, worked to the north of the Mexican position. He confirmed what Beauregard had found and explored further, finding a route all the way to the road behind the Mexican position. Scott settled on what seems in the abstract to be a classically elegant plan. A division under General Gideon Pillow would assault the Mexican front, holding their attention, while another under Twiggs would use the northern route pioneered by Beauregard and Lee to launch a surprise attack on the enemy flank. Yet plans are not actually carried out in the abstract: flanking the enemy required the Americans to move large numbers of troops through ground that Santa Anna believed to be practically impassible. Moreover, being Americans, they took cannon with them. This was an extremely difficult task, as they had to clear a path through the brush. The terrain was so broken that the soldiers repeatedly had to lower cannon down into ravines with ropes and then haul them up the other side. On the plus side, the brush and broken terrain hid the Americans' slow progress from Mexican observers for several hours.

After the Americans were discovered, Mexican officers sent more troops to El Telégrafo and a neighboring hill called Atalaya. Meanwhile Twiggs became uncertain of just where his troops were in the dense woods, and he sent a scouting party to climb Atalaya. There the fighting began, as relatively small groups of Mexican and American soldiers disputed possession of an unpretentious hill. The Mexicans, however, had too few men in position to hold Atalaya, and after fierce fighting they retreated to El Telégrafo. There they rallied and held against an American attempt to dislodge them. The Americans retreated to Atalaya, followed by a barrage of insulting banter.[85] During the afternoon and night, both armies reinforced this side of the battlefield. The Americans brought in a brigade of volunteers, and the Mexicans deployed regiments of regulars, dragged more cannon to the top of El Telégrafo, and emplaced more artillery on the left side of their main camp. Tellingly, though, the Americans spent a great deal of effort bringing three of their heaviest cannon over the rough path through the woods and dragging them up to the top of Atalaya, placing them in a position to fire on the Mexican-held El Telégrafo at almost point-blank range. Moreover, Santa Anna still incorrectly believed that the main American effort would be against the Mexican right flank, and this meant that, given the limited number of troops available, the men of the Mexican left flank facing the Americans' actual main attack would be heavily outnumbered. Ironically, the very woods and hills that Santa Anna had counted on to protect his left flank instead served to conceal the size of the American forces sent to attack there.

On the morning of April 18 Scott's forces launched three attacks that were supposed to happen more or less simultaneously. Pillow's brigade, which consisted mostly of volunteers, launched a frontal attack on the Mexican right flank to the south of the road. This had originally been planned as a diversion, but in his final orders Scott commanded this group to actually pierce the Mexican line. American artillery and regular infantry under William Harney attacked the Mexican forces on El Telégrafo. A third American force, under James Shields, worked its way farther north past El Telégrafo to cut the road behind the Mexican army. These three attacks had widely different degrees of success, but the end result was one of the American army's most complete victories of the war.

Pillow's attack south of the road was a complete failure. His four regiments of volunteers moved through the hundreds of yards of brush that separated them from the Mexicans very slowly, as units had to cut through the vegetation and some lost their way. Neither army could see the other because of the vegetation, but each heard the other army clearly. The Mexican troops, mostly National Guardsmen from Mexico City and Puebla, were completely ready when the disorganized Americans, running more than an hour late, finally worked their way free of the tangled bushes into the area that the Mexicans had cleared precisely to give them a field of fire. The disorganized volunteers had pushed forward into a killing ground, swept by Mexican fire. The brunt of the fighting fell on the Second Tennessee, which had fought at Monterrey but found the going here much tougher. Unable to keep moving forward, those not wounded or killed sought cover or retreated. The other units never arrived in position, and the attack ended. In this first clash between citizen-soldiers of the two countries, the Americans had failed. Fortunately for them, word soon arrived that the rest of the Mexican army was retreating. Eventually the Mexican units that had stood their ground realized they were cut off without food or water and had to surrender. They had stopped the Americans, inflicted heavy casualties, and suffered, according to one source, only one of their own, but their situation had been made hopeless by developments on other parts of the battlefield.

The second major American effort was against El Telégrafo. The Americans of Harney's force slid or climbed down the steep slope of Atalaya and then pulled themselves up the other hill. Here, too, the Americans took heavy casualties, but the affair was not as one-sided. They were greatly aided by covering fire from the American cannon, and after a time they reached an area a few yards from the summit where the curve of the hill protected them from Mexican fire. Santa Anna was beginning to realize that the real threat was to the north and sent some reinforcements, but the attackers had an overwhelming advantage in numbers. Their advantage grew after Twiggs detached more troops from Shields's force and sent them to assault a Mexican unit that had just been posted to protect the western flank of El Telégrafo. Harney's men organized themselves in their sheltered location and then charged the last few yards up the hill, suffering a few more casualties from firearms before reaching the first Mexican line. Sharp hand-to-hand fighting cleared it, and after a brief exchange of musketry with a second line of defense, the Americans successfully charged that one, too. In vicious close combat, men inflicted wounds with swords, bayonets, and musket butts.

The outnumbered Mexicans, losing heart, began to retreat. The Americans now held the steep hill overlooking the camp where Santa Anna's reserves waited. They continued to attack the Mexicans retreating from the hill, and in the heat of the pursuit they killed some of the Mexican wounded. At this point the Americans had essentially won the battle: having been flanked, the Mexican army clearly could not hold the road, and it would have to retreat.

The third attack turned defeat into disaster for the Mexicans. Even as the Mexicans lost the struggle for El Telégrafo, Shields's brigade completed its long, difficult slog through the rugged forest north of the road and attacked the rear of the Mexican army, cutting off its retreat. Its appearance was a nasty surprise for the Mexican soldiers who waited there, and although some rallied quickly and confronted the Americans, there were not enough Mexicans nearby to protect the army's escape route. Realizing the danger, whole Mexican units began to disband, and individual soldiers or small groups looked for a way out of the trap. A surprising number succeeded in either fleeing up the road toward Xalapa or making their way out via narrow paths, but many left behind their equipment. Others were victims of one of the paradoxes of nineteenth-century warfare: infantrymen were often most vulnerable when they were retreating in disorder because only teamwork could protect them from pursuing enemies. Santa Anna and his staff got off the road quickly and survived, but the Americans captured his carriage and its contents, including a spare wooden leg and thousands of dollars in cash.[86]

The Americans were also in possession of dozens of acres covered in the wounded and dead of both armies, around three thousand Mexican prisoners, forty-three cannon, and several thousand of the Mexicans' worn-out and rickety English muskets, which the Americans promptly burned because even an army operating in enemy territory at the end of a long and precarious supply line could find no use for them. More than four hundred Americans lay dead or wounded, along with two or three times that many Mexicans. Around six thousand Mexicans escaped, but they were scattered and their morale was damaged. Rumors began to circulate about the physical prowess of American soldiers and about the possibility that Santa Anna had fled even before the fighting became bad.[87] Eventually most of the dispersed soldiers would rejoin their units for more battles, but for now there was almost nothing between Scott and Mexico City.

Santa Anna's decisions, especially those against occupying more hills on the north side of his position and against posting detachments in the woods to give timely information about the strength of the American flanking movement, certainly led to this defeat. Yet he was hampered by the small size of his army: although the Americans believed they faced twelve thousand Mexicans at Cerro Gordo, they only faced about nine thousand, a force roughly the size of their own. Santa Anna could not simultaneously keep his forces concentrated enough to stop the enemy and garrison every possible approach. The social character of the Mexican army also came into play. Although the conscripts of the Mexican regular army usually fought well in large units, men sent out in small groups or singly as sentries tended to simply desert, so scattering pickets in the woods north of the road would likely have been useless. If Santa Anna wanted to keep the Americans in yellow fever country, he had to block their advance with a strong force, and Cerro Gordo was a decent choice of location. The Americans actually came close to disaster. If Twiggs had really launched his attack before Scott arrived, it probably would have been a costly failure, much as Pillow's was, and the Americans might not have had enough men left to later carry out the more elegant plan Scott put into effect.

Ironically, at Cerro Gordo Scott's troops succeeded in doing what Santa Anna's troops had nearly accomplished at La Angostura: they had moved in force through difficult terrain to successfully outflank the enemy. American military historians like to cite the efforts of Beauregard and Lee, West Point–educated professionals who found a way around the Mexican position. However, it was the rank-and-file troops who actually made this information useful: the physical labor involved in making their way through the rugged, tangled woods and building a path that allowed them to haul heavy artillery through such terrain was amazing.[88] American troops could only do this because they were well rested and well fed: the days spent in camp waiting for the battle and the wealth of the Americans contrast vividly with the experiences of their Mexican counterparts at La Angostura, who arrived at the scene desperate to strike quickly because their best hope of ending their starvation was capturing the American supplies. Much of the American work at Cerro Gordo was done at night, and even during the day the vegetation mostly screened their efforts from Mexican observation, allowing the

Americans to deliver the kind of nasty surprise that could panic even the most disciplined troops. And that is precisely what happened: although the Mexican regulars put up quite a fight against the American flanking maneuver, once their retreat was in danger of being cut off, they knew that their only salvation lay in flight.

Victory at Cerro Gordo dispersed the Mexican army, and it let Scott and the Americans out of the deadly yellow fever country. They moved quickly a few miles up the road to lovely and temperate Xalapa. However, they were still at the start of a very long campaign. Scott and the Americans took advantage of the Mexicans' disarray as best as they could, pushing past Xalapa up toward Puebla, one of Mexico's largest cities. There Santa Anna had surprisingly been able to again gather together a few thousand troops, including regulars who had escaped from Cerro Gordo and National Guardsmen from Oaxaca, Puebla, and Veracruz. As the Americans approached, Santa Anna tried to launch a lightning cavalry attack to take advantage of the fact that the Americans were spread out as they marched, but the Americans quickly deployed their signature light artillery to scatter his cavalry. Without enough troops to hold the city, Santa Anna retreated. Puebla fell without a significant fight; in fact it is the only major Mexican city that did so during the war, a distinction that led some Mexicans during and after the war to question the patriotism of its inhabitants. Santa Anna contributed to this reputation by publicly criticizing Pueblans' martial spirit, saying they had been reluctant to support his force.[89]

However, attitudes in Puebla were complicated. The city's civil and religious leaders were demoralized by the defeat of Cerro Gordo, which had used up both money they had raised and men from the state's National Guard battalions. They were also concerned that a fruitless attempt to resist would lead the American troops to loot, kill, and rape. In the Western military culture of the day, it was accepted that troops that took casualties assaulting a defended city would be impossible to control once they were in its streets, and this was a psychological weapon attacking armies often used when bargaining with enemy leaders. Scott was very interested in preventing his troops from committing the kinds of excesses that had been seen in the north, and his officers were willing to offer the city's civilian and religious leaders guarantees if they agreed not to urge resistance. This offer was too tempting to pass up, even though some witnesses wrote that the city's poor very much wanted Puebla to be defended. Thus the Americans marched into the city unmolested, surrounded by crowds of curious and grieving Mexicans.[90] However, once in Puebla the Americans found themselves in an unusual and often awkward position. Many of the city's wealthy families, as well as its civil and religious leaders, wanted to keep the peace in order to protect their property and the lives of all civilians. They even deployed the municipal police against Mexican guerrillas.[91] However, many of the poor were upset about the American presence, and Americans who wandered from their quarters at night were assaulted and murdered. Beginning early in the occupation there were rumors of planned uprisings, and people aided Mexican guerrillas who daringly penetrated the city limits.[92] In yet another twist, some American soldiers report that poor Mexican women who sold them produce eventually came to appreciate the American soldiers, or at least their business, so much that they passed information to them or even intervened to protect wounded Americans.[93] The story of Puebla's occupation belies simple answers to the question whether Mexicans lost the war because they were not invested enough in the idea of the nation to fight for it.

CHAPTER 5

Each Chapter We Write
in Mexican Blood

W INFIELD SCOTT'S army stalled for two months at Puebla for reasons
that had as much to do with American politics and the social composition
of the army as they did with Mexican resistance. The steady expansion of
U.S. territory in the decades between 1776 and the Civil War has partially
obscured the reality that not all Americans desired expansion or approved
of the methods used to achieve it. In the spring and early summer of 1846,
as news from Zachary Taylor's army on the Rio Grande reached Americans,
many were enthusiastic about the idea of fighting Mexico and acquiring
territory, but even at the height of this war fever, support for the war was
hardly unanimous. More than a few Americans were uncomfortable about the
morality of aggression and the possibly negative impact of acquiring territory
on American democracy and unity. From the beginning there was significant
opposition to the war.[1] Some of the most vociferous opposition came from
what then were considered fringe groups, especially abolitionists and advocates of women's rights. Yet these groups were dedicated, highly literate,
and well funded enough to publish many newspapers and pamphlets. They
kept the questions of the morality of the war and the possibility that a victory might actually hurt the United States alive in American political debate
even as news first of the vulnerability of Taylor's army and then his repeated
victories in the north washed over the populated areas of the United States.
Abolitionists believed that the Democrats were waging war on behalf of
Southern slaveholders who constantly needed new land because their obsession with cotton quickly exhausted soil.[2] Advocates of women's rights, who
overlapped with abolitionists but were considered even further from the

mainstream, saw the war as promoting a version of aggressive masculinity that further marginalized women from politics.[3]

In 1846 and 1847 supporters of the war had little to fear from abolitionists and supporters of women's rights, who had the support of a tiny fraction of the electorate. Whigs, however, could not be so easily dismissed. As we have seen, they believed that American influence in the world should grow through commerce, not conquest. Even successful conquest would weaken the United States by undermining its morality. They also feared that a United States that sprawled across a vast territory would be less unified and less democratic, especially if it contained large numbers of racial inferiors.[4] From the very beginning, the war with Mexico made them feel queasy. However, James K. Polk adroitly trapped the vast majority of congressional Whigs into voting for the war by tying its authorization to the precarious position of the American forces on the Rio Grande. Most Whigs were unwilling to set themselves up as scapegoats if the army failed disastrously. Moreover, Whigs in the states where the recruitment of volunteers deepened war fever found it politically impractical and perhaps psychologically impossible to stay on the margins. They, too, joined the new volunteer regiments. Yet even news of Taylor's successes did not make them approve of the war. They continued to authorize supplies for the army but simultaneously criticized Polk. Some antiwar Whigs were officers in the regular U.S. army who kept their beliefs to themselves even as they served as the instruments of American aggression. Most were more public in their opposition. The most impassioned not only denounced the fundamental immorality of American aggression, they stated that if they were Mexican, they would resist the American aggression, or even encouraged American soldiers to desert rather than take part.[5]

Counterintuitively, opposition to the war steadily grew despite the seemingly unending stream of American victories that had the war's supporters crowing. Even efforts to taint opponents by calling them traitors, including Polk's public statement that they were giving aid and comfort to the enemy, did not stem the tide.[6] The possibility that the United States would come to include vast swatches of Mexico that were densely populated with racial inferiors turned even some Southern Democrats against the war, as their racism overpowered their avarice.[7] Some Northern Democrats became skeptical of Polk because he had not ultimately supported their demand for serious territorial concessions from Great Britain in Oregon but now seemed eager for Mexican territory. Northern Democrat David Wilmot signaled this discontent by forcing a congressional vote attaching a rider forbidding slavery in any territory acquired from Mexico to one of Polk's requests for funds. This Wilmot Proviso was passed by the House with the support of northerners from both parties but never approved by the Senate.[8]

American domestic politics drove opposition to the war, but it is hard to imagine it growing without the increasing consciousness of its costs, costs driven mostly by Mexican resistance. Polk certainly hoped that the Mexican state would be willing to make territorial concessions after losing battles along the Texas border, but that did not happen. Instead of a short war, Polk had brought a long one, one that was expensive even for the United States. Taylor's campaign could not force Mexico to the bargaining table even after the infusion of thousands of volunteer troops, and this failure had led to Scott's campaign. Even many volunteers who had joined during the war fever found the actual war itself disheartening. They watched friends die violent deaths or waste away with disease in boring camps, and they wondered if it was all worth it. As the vicious conflict with civilians and its endless series of crimes, reprisals, and counterreprisals raged in northern Mexico, volunteers began to wonder about how the war had changed their friends and neighbors. Reports of the crimes committed by volunteers seeped into the U.S. press, making civilians back home fear the damage war was doing to the men's morality.[9]

Opposition to the war against Mexico brought forward eloquent statements from men whose ideas would have lasting impact on American political life. Writer Henry David Thoreau was inspired to deliberately break the law and then explain his action in the famous essay "On Civil Disobedience." By the fall of 1846 the war was so unpopular that the Whigs won a majority in the House of Representatives. A young congressman named Abraham Lincoln called Polk out in December 1847, challenging his claim that the war had begun with the loss of American lives on American soil. Lincoln insisted that the land between the Nueces and the Rio Grande was Mexican, and that therefore the United States was already invading Mexico when the first skirmish took place. Calling Polk a liar did not go over well in some quarters: Lincoln was accused of treason.[10] The fame of other, equally important and eloquent opponents did not last into our era. Whig Thomas Corwin of Ohio was not a marginal politician. He had served in that state's legislature, as a U.S congressman, and then as the governor of the state before becoming a U.S. senator. Later he would be secretary of the treasury and serve as U.S. ambassador to Mexico, appointed by none other than Lincoln. On February 11, 1847, Senator Corwin delivered a lengthy speech to his colleagues in which he called the war with Mexico a grave threat to American democracy, stating that "each chapter we write in Mexican blood, may close the volume of our history as a free people." Corwin insisted that Polk had unconstitutionally wrested the power to declare war from Congress. He pointed out how the American annexation of Texas had been a provocation and boldly stated—several months before Lincoln's similar assertion—that the strip between the Nueces and the Rio Grande was part of Mexico, not Texas, openly calling Polk a liar, guilty of a "bold falsification of history." Corwin emphasized the fact that the Mexicans living there fled from Taylor's army, and that the Mexican government had enforced its laws and collected taxes there undisturbed in the seven years between Texas's independence and the state's annexation to the United States. Throughout this speech Corwin cleverly cited American army officers and Democratic politicians to support the facts behind his argument. Corwin also insisted that the Mexicans had the right to defend their territory with violence, a statement that was taken by many to be an incitement to further Mexican resistance. Corwin ridiculed the arguments of expansionists by saying that coveting territory did not make stealing it just. To the argument that the United States must have San Francisco because it was the best harbor on the Pacific, Corwin replied that he was an experienced criminal lawyer, but that he had "never yet heard a thief, arraigned for stealing a horse, plead that it was the best horse he could find." Corwin cited various examples from human history to show that those who fought wars of conquest were later humbled, and he finished by predicting correctly that prosecuting the war with Mexico would lead to civil war in the United States.[11]

Yet for all Corwin's fire, the most influential speech against the war might have been that of Henry Clay on November 13, 1847. Clay was already known as one of the country's most eloquent speakers and one of the most powerful politicians of the Jacksonian era. He had represented Kentucky in the House and Senate and served as Speaker of the House and U.S. secretary of state.

He had run for president against Andrew Jackson in 1832, and was the Whig candidate against Polk in 1844, when his focus on internal improvement and opposition to the annexation of Texas contrasted with Polk's open advocacy of expansionism. Clay barely lost this election, which in the end probably was determined by a few thousand New York votes that went to a third party that directly attacked slavery.[12] In 1846 Clay was near the end of a long and eventful political life, and he opposed the decision of his namesake and son, Henry Clay Jr., to join the Kentucky volunteers. The politician was devastated when he learned of his son's death on the battlefield of La Angostura.[13] Privately Clay had continued to oppose the war, but except for one widely misinterpreted joke, he did not make a public statement about it until his eagerly anticipated speech in November 1847. He openly called the war an unnecessary act of aggression and said he would never have voted for it. He lamented the loss of life and said that the war had made some volunteers so violent and unruly that it would be difficult for them to return to civilian life. He argued that the war had sullied America's reputation abroad, and he worried that adding so many racially different people to the United States was a mistake. Clay's speech was reported and debated throughout the country, and it gave impetus to meetings in which Northern Whigs and other opponents of the war condemned it.[14]

In the United States, opposition to the war probably limited its duration and forced Polk to settle for less territory than he believed American soldiers had won. In Mexico, many soldiers chafed at the news of opposition, believing that it criticized their morality, undermined their own achievements, and encouraged Mexican resistance.[15] Americans who argued this last point were not totally off the mark. Mexicans closely followed political news from the United States, especially news that seemed pertinent to their own problems. Mexicans were often hopeful that the opinions of such obviously powerful politicians as Clay would influence the policy of the American government. Once war was under way, Mexicans eagerly reported news of American war critics, but they had difficulty interpreting that opposition. In particular, they did not understand how effective American political institutions were in channeling dissent into nonviolent pathways. When they heard that some Americans grumbled about the cost of the war, they predicted rebellions against new taxes. Tellingly, when Corwin's speech reached Morelia, Michoacán, the Mexicans not only reprinted it, they asked Americans there whether Corwin might raise a military force and rebel against Polk's government.[16] This idea seemed absurd to the Americans, but if we compare Corwin's heated rhetoric to that used in the formal calls to rebellion so often seen in Mexican politics, or even the U.S. Declaration of Independence, the Mexicans' error is quite understandable. Corwin had called Polk a liar who violated the Constitution. In Mexico a powerful politician who used those words was preparing to revolt. What the Mexicans did not understand was that American institutions were still strong and elastic enough to contain such strong dissent, although that would change by 1860.

Some news from the United States was a bit easier to interpret. In November 1846 the Polk administration, realizing that the first wave of volunteers was insufficient, issued a call for new regiments. News soon began to circulate, first in the United States and then in Mexico, that these new regiments were not filling out with the speed seen in the summer of 1846. War fever had subsided, and by the winter of 1846–1847 news from Mexico was discouraging new volunteers. Potential recruits now were aware of the fatal illnesses that stalked volunteer units, and Mexican resistance had convinced many that the war would drag on indefinitely. The latter point was of particular concern for the new volunteers because, although the first group had only signed on for one year, these new men were asked to commit for the duration of the war. No new regiment filled with anything like the kind of enthusiasm seen during the first blush of war fever. Mexicans correctly saw the difficulty of recruiting new volunteers as evidence that American enthusiasm for the war was flagging.[17]

New regiments recruited in the vast Mississippi watershed, which had been such a fertile ground for recruiting in the summer of 1846, filled slowly, perhaps because there the negative experiences of the first set of volunteers were well known. In Kentucky, Henrietta Blackburn wrote to her husband that a local man trying to raise a company spoke to a "great crowd" in town for circuit court, but he was able to recruit only fifteen men, all "inexperienced—self-willed—half-grown boys—If they go it will be a dear bought lesson to them." Other regiments recruited in new areas like New York and Boston. Here, too, recruitment went slowly: it was so slow in Massachusetts that the regiment was allowed to recruit two companies in New Hampshire, where, not surprisingly, a recruiting poster criticized the reluctance of Massachusetts men to sign up. This poster included some of the ideological bombast one would expect to see in a call for citizen-soldiers. It called New Hampshire the "strawberry-bed of patriotism," criticized Antonio López de Santa Anna for treachery, and called Mexicans "half civilized." It also struck a different note, emphasizing that volunteers would be paid ten dollars per month, with thirty dollars in advance, and would also receive 160 acres of land. This emphasis on compensation brings out one of the key characteristics of this second round of volunteer regiments: many more of the volunteers were actually poor and urban, more like the typical recruits of regular army units than the men of respectable families who had joined in the summer of 1846. The economic incentives were more important to them, and in both New York and Boston new recruits agitated to receive pay in advance, apparently so they could leave some money for their families.[18] The American authorities also responded to their need for cannon fodder by authorizing the addition of new regiments to the regular army, but they did so with a catch. These regiments, first the U.S. Mounted Rifles authorized in May 1846 and then ten more regiments authorized in February 1847, would only exist as long as the war with Mexico persisted. Recruits were promised land grants at the end of their service. Polk appointed officers from civilians he considered apt for service, ignoring the many able officers who had passed through West Point. In many ways these new units were like volunteer units, but of the variety seen in the second wave, with men from more modest means who were attracted by material benefits.[19]

Scott's invasion of central Mexico made the need for new manpower acute. Scott was stuck in Puebla for months because he did not have enough men to advance toward Mexico City. He had been given most of the regular army, as well as the best of the volunteers who had signed up for twelve months in the summer of 1846. The problem was that the twelve months would expire before Scott had any hope of taking Mexico's capital. The best solution for the American force in Mexico would have been the reenlistment of these men for the duration of the war, but the overwhelming majority of these volunteers refused to do so.[20] This actually continued a pattern: the Louisiana volunteers who had signed up for three months at the beginning of the war had gone home rather than continue to serve, and the same had been true of the

Texas volunteers who had signed up for six months.[21] However, it was striking that as May and June 1847 approached only a handful of the thousands of men whose enlistments were expiring were willing to continue. For some in the north, the decision was shaped by the fact that it had become an inactive front, where volunteers lived in boring camps when they were not engaged in the dirty and desperate counterinsurgency struggle, with its sudden ambushes and reprisals against civilians. This was not the kind of fight they had signed on for.[22] For the men with Scott's army, there was still plenty of possible glory to be earned, but as they neared the end of a year in the army, they were also well aware of the costs. Death on the battlefield would be bad enough, but there were more deaths from disease than anything. A new guerrilla campaign was starting in this theater, and fighting guerrillas was more terrifying than glamorous. The men did not believe that Scott was receiving enough support from the American government to take Mexico City quickly, and they were also not at all sure that even capturing Mexico City would end the war: as veterans of actions from Monterrey to Cerro Gordo, they were impressed by the ability of the Mexicans to put new armies into the field after every defeat. These men felt that they had fulfilled their bargain and now it was someone else's turn. Disillusioned by the war, they were ready to go home.[23] Mexican observers were cheered by these sentiments, which undermined American strength and suggested that determined resistance might yet win the day for Mexico. Some Americans criticized the patriotism of the men who left after twelve months.[24] This brings up an interesting point: the result of this war is widely interpreted as evidence that the United States was a nation and Mexico still was not because Mexicans often placed their personal interests ahead of the national good. However, is that not exactly what these volunteers did? In reality, for both Mexicans and Americans, patriotism had its limits.

War and Identity in Mexico

The question of patriotism invites us to consider how the war itself may have changed Mexicans' relationship with their nation, determining who felt that they were Mexicans, how deeply they felt so, and what other parts of their identity might have become entangled with their nationality. As Scott waited impatiently in Puebla, the fighting had been going on for more than a year, and now Americans were in the most populated part of Mexico. For months Mexico's political elite had worked to convince people that they were Mexicans, and that this required them to make sacrifices for their country. What means of communication did they employ in this country whose population was much less literate than its American counterpart? What arguments did Mexican intellectuals and politicians use to inspire patriotism, and how successful were they? Would Scott succeed in his desire to make war on the Mexican government and keep the Mexican people on the sidelines?

Although the majority of Mexicans could not read and write, archives and libraries are stuffed with evidence that Mexican intellectuals and politicians employed the written word widely in their efforts to inspire resistance to the Americans. Mexico's dozens of newspapers focused most of their energy on the war, calling Mexicans to action. Presses also published many political pamphlets and broadsides with the same themes. Some had official origins: government proclamations and decrees were usually published both in newspapers and in broadside form. Other broadsides emanated from different political groups. Certainly literate Mexicans were well informed about events and deluged with propaganda. Yet it is important to understand that there was a long tradition of reading aloud and discussing newspapers, pamphlets, and broadsides in the streets, plazas, and drinking establishments. Even in indigenous communities where only a few people spoke or read Spanish, there were literate specialists who interpreted written materials for village elders and other leaders, undoubtedly again leading to discussions involving larger groups.[25] Still, Mexican intellectuals and politicians did make concessions to widespread illiteracy. Politicians and generals made public speeches, and many priests preached sermons about the war. Mexicans also made the war the central theme in many religious and civic ceremonies, where again the idea was to make information and ideas accessible to large groups of mostly illiterate people.[26]

How did these leaders try to inspire resistance? On a fundamental level they saw the war as a contest about sovereignty, that is, about Mexico's independence, the notion that the people of Mexico should govern their own affairs. Hundreds of speeches and documents included this idea. Independence is, like the nation itself, an idea that is quite abstract when viewed in isolation. Propagandists therefore had to make it seem more tangible. One of the most common ways to signal that the nation was worth fighting for was to remind people that Mexico had been fought for in the past. Mexican leaders invoked the long and bloody Mexican War of Independence, pointing out that the forefathers of the current generation had sacrificed greatly to achieve independence from Spain.[27] Propagandists, eulogizing the sacrifices and achievements of previous generations, insisted that the current generation prove itself worthy of its parents by defending the family legacy. Leaders of the 1840s also tried to make the notion of nation real by connecting the common people of their own era to those who had fought for independence. The fact that fighting had been widespread during the independence war was helpful. Eugenio Vázquez, giving a public speech in an isolated valley in southern Mexico, pointed out that people there had been among the first to take up the cause of Mexican independence and had fought on for years even after most of the rest of Mexico had been pacified.[28] References to the sacrifices made during the independence war were particularly evocative when made by people who had actually fought in that war. Many veterans still lived. Santa Anna himself had participated in the final campaign for independence, along with quite a few other Mexican regular army officers who had begun their careers fighting for the Spanish crown. Other army officers, like Juan Alvarez, had both begun and ended the independence war on the insurgent side. Now, in 1846–1847, even independence fighters who had long been civilians returned to the fray.[29]

Religion was extraordinarily important in the propaganda used to encourage Mexicans to oppose the Americans. The belief that Mexico was Catholic was very firmly tied to ideas of nationhood: the Mexican War of Independence had been launched by the priest Miguel Hidalgo and sustained by many priests for years, and the idea that Mexico had a particular role to play in the religious destiny of the planet was a prominent part of political discourse.[30] By the mid-nineteenth century, devotion to the Virgin of Guadalupe had become a symbol of this national religious destiny, and Mexicans voiced both pleas for her protection and calls to protect her image during the war.[31] Yet the role of religion in inspiring resistance also had more intimate roots. In an era in which life expectancy was low, infant mortality was high, and death was more likely to happen in the home or a public space than out of sight in a hospital, faith in an afterlife where loved ones might be reunited was of great emotional importance. The vast majority of Mexicans believed that only Catholicism and Catholic sacraments could open the door to that afterlife. Although we might see religious diversity as desirable, in the 1840s most Mexicans saw it as evidence that many people were making mistakes that were both terrible and terribly permanent. They saw U.S. religious diversity and religious tolerance not as evidence of greater freedom but as evidence that Americans were mistaken. A citizen's committee in San Luis Potosí called the Americans "a people without religion, one that allows all beliefs, and mocks the most sacred." As has been discussed, many Mexicans were afraid that the Americans would impose religious tolerance and build Protestant churches, luring Mexicans away from the one path to eternal life. Juan Martín de la Garza y Flores, governor of the state of Tamaulipas, believed that an American victory would give Mexicans up to "the foolish superstitions of a thousand ridiculous and extravagant sects and the most complete immorality."[32] Many Mexicans believed that losing the war might lead to them losing their religion. It is worth noting that even figures who would later come to be known as anticlerical liberals, like Governors Ramón Adame of San Luis Potosí and Francisco Modesto de Olaguibel of the state of Mexico, expressed this fear.[33]

The Polk administration and the commanders it sent to Mexico made strenuous efforts to convince Mexicans that they were not making war on Catholicism. Those efforts, however, were offset by the prevalence of anti-Catholic opinions and specific criticisms of Mexican Catholicism seen in the American press, and they were even more amply outweighed by the behavior of American volunteer soldiers in Mexico. As we have seen, those soldiers often showed their disdain for Catholic beliefs, stealing from Mexican churches and committing sacrilege. This behavior horrified Mexicans. Mexican propagandists publicized it as proof that American conquest threatened Catholicism and pointed out that the best way to prevent more such sacrilege was to stop the invaders. Alejandro Ihary motivated the men of Catorce's National Guard unit by citing the "depraved, immoral and irreligious conduct" of Americans "profaning churches and using in a savage way the sacred vessels," while a newspaper editorial in San Luis Potosí warned that if Mexicans did not fight, they would see "our temples profaned by the dirty sole of the murderers, our images destroyed and robbed of the jewels that

Christian piety has given them; the very tabernacle of the divinity destroyed to convert into coins the reliquaries and pure vessels that keep the Supreme Majesty."[34] The latter comment demonstrates the importance of the Catholic belief that the consecrated Eucharist is the actual body of Christ. When the Eucharist was carried to the dying or taken out into the streets for other processions, passersby kneeled, removed their hats, and bowed their heads. Mexican leaders pointed out that American soldiers did not pay due respect and sometimes even mocked these processions. They suggested that in an occupied Mexico it would be difficult to administer the sacraments essential to eternal life.[35]

The behavior of American volunteer soldiers in Mexico was also crucial to another of the central themes of Mexican propaganda. Invading armies have often been accused of having designs on the bodies and virtue of conquered women, and this idea has been used to urge men to defend their own masculine honor by force of arms.[36] Writers in the aggressive country have rarely been quite so open about their interest in sexual conquest as they were in the Mexican-American War.[37] These writers were referring to the romantic conquest of Mexican hearts and bodies, and sometimes that did take place. Sadly, though, there is much more evidence from both Mexican and American sources that American soldiers, especially the volunteers, brutally raped many Mexican women.[38] These crimes were assaults on the bodies of Mexican women, but they were also attacks on the honor of Mexican families and the patriarchs who headed them. Honor was a crucial social value: in lamenting rapes by the Americans, the town council of Zacatecas called honor "the most precious belonging of society . . . in all its relations with the world and morality." Honor was a possession of Mexican society, but even more it was a possession of particular families, one that patriarchs should defend with their lives.[39]

Dozens of newspaper editorials, poems, broadsides, speeches, and sermons criticized American soldiers for raping Mexican women and called on Mexicans to avenge these crimes and fight to protect their daughters, wives, and even nuns. These arguments appeared with the beginning of the U.S. aggression along the Rio Grande and they continued through the end of the fighting almost two years later. They were made by politicians and military leaders of all ranks and types, from Santa Anna himself down to

National Guard commanders in isolated villages, and from bishops and state governors to priests and common citizens.[40] Rapes allowed Mexican leaders to portray American soldiers in the worst possible light, as Benito Juárez, governor of Oaxaca and future president of the country, did in 1847 when he called them "vile mercenaries coming to loot your houses, to rape our wives and daughters."[41] References to the rape of virgins emphasized the loss of honor even more deeply, as did references to men being forced to watch helplessly as Americans raped their daughters and wives. Maximo Albarran of Guanajuato explicitly said that he would rather die fighting than endure "the disgrace of witnessing the rape of my dear wife."[42] These graphic and emotionally powerful images were intended to spur Mexicans to action. One editorial proclaimed in October 1846, "How could it be conceivable that a Mexican tolerate that this eruption from the North unleash itself on the virginal honor of our chaste daughters, of our innocent and faithful wives without preferring to die a thousand deaths?" while another proclaimed in July 1847 that peace could not be made "with the murderers of our fathers, with the rapists of young women, with those who dishonor our wives, with the vile men, those whose hands are soaked in the blood of our children!"[43]

The themes of independence, religion, and the need to defend or avenge Mexican women were each very powerful, and in each case some of that emotional power stemmed from connections to the family. This connection is least obvious in the case of independence, which at first glance seems an abstract political ideal. However, as we have seen, when Mexican leaders brought up independence, they usually pointed out that the parents of the current generation had sacrificed to achieve it, and the current generation could only prove itself worthy by fighting to preserve it. Religion was connected to national identity, but calls to defend Catholicism focused on the much less abstract idea that Catholicism was the only path to eternal life, an idea whose emotional power was at least partially drawn from the possibility of eternal union with beloved family members. Defending Mexican women from rape was defending both the bodies and the honor of the family. These three elements were powerful individually, but propagandists usually invoked more than one, and often all three, in any given document or speech. Repeatedly, Mexicans were told it was their duty to fight, in the words of one newspaper, "for independence, for religion, and for the honor of our families."[44]

These were without a doubt the three most powerful cannon in the rhetorical artillery battery available to Mexican propagandists, but writers also employed a number of other effective weapons. They argued that justice was on the Mexican side, and that world opinion did not approve of the Americans' naked land grab.[45] Mexican intellectuals and other leaders often criticized Americans for being exceptionally greedy. Manuel Zavala, commanding Mexican forces in the state of Aguascalientes, stated that "their God is gold." According to one editorial, for Americans "there is no other religion, no other patria, no other virtue, than the dollar." American greed became the object of Mexican satire and ire: one newspaper published a joke, saying that in the United States someone had patented a means to revive the dead: "To revive a Yankee, even one buried for three days, all you need to do is talk to him about money, or search his pockets." Mexicans were particularly incensed that Americans viewed Mexicans as violent and dishonest even as they invaded Mexico and committed crimes there. A parish priest in northern Mexico, hearing that Taylor had decreed that Mexican guerrillas would be treated as bandits, told a guerrilla unit that "this is the worst infamy: they are the starving bandits, and they call us that just for defending our rights."[46] Mexicans were very aware that Americans saw them as less than civilized, and they pointed to American behavior as evidence that it was the Americans who were not civilized. A committee of priests from San Luis Potosí described the crimes committed by American troops and compared them to the barbarian hordes that had invaded the Roman Empire, calling the Americans "those Vandals vomited from Hell."[47] References to Old World barbarians were matched by those to New World tribes. The city council of Mexico City referred to the Americans as Caribs, a Caribbean group that Spanish conquerors believed were cannibals, and, as we saw in Chapter 3, rampaging volunteers were often likened to Comanche raiders.[48]

These last references bring us closer to the question of race. Both Mexican and American intellectuals saw race as partly biological and partly a set of cultural characteristics that were also usually inherited, the most prominent of which may have been religion. We have seen how Americans came to view Mexicans as constituting an inferior race.[49] How did Mexicans react to this? Mexican intellectuals were well aware that many Americans believed that, as an Anglo-Saxon race, they were superior to a Mexican race described as mongrel due to its mixture of Indian, African, and Spanish races, and even the Spaniards were considered inferior to the Anglo-Saxons.[50] Some writers accepted the idea that this was a racial war and used it to sharpen Mexican attitudes about the war. Many pieces of Mexican propaganda referred to the need to struggle against the "Anglo-Saxon race" and its desire for dominance. Racializing the conflict increased its seriousness: as Carlos Maria de Bustamante put it, Mexicans who understood American views came to see the war as "an interminable and profound race war."[51] Race war, or, as it was often called, caste war, was not a new idea in Mexico. Images of war between races originating in descriptions of the Haitian Revolution had been a staple of conservative politics in Mexico for decades, and armed political activity by indigenous Mexicans was often seen as evidence of their desire to dominate or even exterminate other races. Now these ideas were applied in the war with the United States. Soon after the first battle of the war, Pedro de Ampudia declared that "the war that has broken out is a caste war." Mexican propaganda often stated that the Americans wanted to destroy or exterminate the Mexican race.[52]

Accepting the American racialization of the war did not require accepting that their race was superior. Some Mexicans argued that the Anglo-Saxon race had degenerated from an earlier, nobler version. More commonly, Mexican commentators cleverly focused on the prevalent notion that mongrel races were inferior, and they portrayed Americans as a heterogeneous group that incorporated the castoffs of other nations.[53] Undermining the myth of Americans as a superior race was not enough, though. If it was a war between races, what race did Mexicans belong to? For conservative Mexican intellectuals, the answer was the Spanish or Hispanic race. This choice was related to their position in Mexican politics. They were not at all comfortable with the egalitarian interpretation of republicanism and citizenship that equated all honest and hardworking Mexicans, regardless of their ancestry and income. Emphasizing Mexico's Spanish roots suggested that the lighter-skinned Mexicans at the top of the socioeconomic structure were the best Mexicans. Moreover, it also supported another argument conservatives were beginning to lean toward, the notion that those who believed in a more egalitarian and democratic Mexico were contributing to Mexico's political instability by ignoring the best features of Mexico's more orderly colonial past.[54] It is possible that their prior interest in race as a social category made conservative intellectuals and politicians among the first to understand that Americans considered all Mexicans as racially inferior.[55] However, even commentators from the political center and left sometimes mentioned Mexico's Spanish racial roots. Unlike conservatives, however, they often also referred to Mexico's indigenous heritage. For instance, one editorialist spoke of Mexicans as "the last of the Spanish race, the last of the children of Moctezuma."[56] Although they did not use the word "mestizo," it was this mixture of Spanish and Indian they were gesturing toward in their efforts to portray the war as a race war. Here they found it helpful, ironically, to invoke the desperate resistance of the Aztecs against the Spanish conquest of Mexico.[57]

Astute Mexican observers of the Jacksonian political and cultural scene came to understand that many Americans saw them as similar to the Native Americans whom whites stole land from and the blacks they enslaved.[58] They were appalled at how quickly the general hardening of racial domination in the Jacksonian period and the propaganda campaign for Texas's independence lowered Mexicans' status from that of citizens of an honored sister republic to racially inferior prey. Since the object of expansionism was land, it is not surprising that references to Mexicans being treated like Indians quickly surfaced.[59] Yet these were not as common as references to the possible enslavement of Mexicans, a possibility that writers both before and during the war often warned about. One explanation for the frequency of these arguments is that in both the United States and Mexico, slavery was already prominent in political rhetoric as a symbol of tyranny. It was the antithesis of freedom, and the idea that some political action or social development might reduce individual autonomy often led critics to see it as imposing a form of slavery on people who should be free. In Mexico, moreover, slavery also symbolized racial inequality.[60] It seems likely that Mexicans also understood that any land acquired through conquest would be useless without laborers to work it, and, at least in Texas, those laborers were mostly slaves. In other words, the question of slavery in newly acquired territories that was so important in American politics during and after the war had a different inflection in Mexico. Mexicans repeatedly argued that American racism would lead them to enslave Mexicans, especially those with indigenous or African roots. General Zavala of Aguascalientes warned that if Mexicans did not stop them, the Americans would "stamp on their faces the infamous seal of a shameful slavery like that suffered by that unlucky race they call people of color." Bustamante reported rumors that Mexicans in occupied lands were being branded and sold in the slave market of New Orleans.[61] Propagandists based these dire predictions on what they saw happening in the Jacksonian United States. Why would the Americans not remake Mexico in their own image, oppressing those with African or Indian heritage, reestablishing slavery, stealing land from Mexico's Indians, and even exterminating the Indians?[62]

Mexicans' observation of the Jacksonian scene also allowed them to see the contradiction between the American ideals that proponents of Manifest Destiny claimed to be spreading and the realities of life in the United States. The United States was not the land of equality and freedom. As one editorialist put it, it was a country that "worships equality and protects and promotes slavery, for which equality is a joke, because it distinguishes men by their colors." Bustamante pointed out ironically that "by a strange anomaly slaves are sold in the freest country in the world."[63] Mexicans repeatedly stressed American hypocrisy. For all its boasting of freedom and civilization, the United States was a country that exterminated Indians, oppressed racial minorities, bought and sold people, and tortured them to make them work, while Mexico was a place where all races enjoyed the same legal rights, there was no slavery, and Indians were allowed to keep their lands.[64] The contrast was so strong that some Mexicans believed that slaves and Indians in the United States might take advantage of the war by rebelling against their oppressors there.[65]

These Mexican optimists did not get their wish. Slaves and Native Americans in the United States did not help the Mexican cause by joining in a grand war of resistance. Fortunately Mexican propagandists did not have to look north of the border to find examples of wars of resistance that they could use to inspire Mexicans. Some argued that Mexico's efforts would be more successful than China's failed efforts to defeat the British or Algeria's to defeat the French. Generally, though, propagandists preferred to cite successful resistance. Governor Adame of San Luis Potosí, for instance, compared Mexico's situation to the conflict between Greek independence fighters and their Ottoman overlords, a conflict that not only had inspired Romantic poets but also had drawn decisive intervention from the most important European powers. Another example cited several times was the resistance to the 1807 British invasion of Buenos Aires, one of the many sideshows that marked the Napoleonic Wars.[66] However, the example most often cited was Spanish resistance to Napoleon's armies, which included many of the elements Mexicans eventually saw play out in Mexico: sieges, heroic resistance by urban civilians, clashes between armies, and the most famous guerrilla war in European history. This war was well known in Mexico, partially because it was linked to Mexico's own war of independence and partially because the lengthy and titanic struggles of the Napoleonic Wars were so central to nineteenth-century ideas about both war and history throughout the Western world. As we will see, the Spanish example was one feared by American planners and embraced by many Mexicans.[67]

Taylor's forces had experienced several military successes in the north, and now Scott's army had won victories at Veracruz and Cerro Gordo and reached Puebla, one of the largest cities in the country. Mexico's leaders could not point to military success even as they desperately tried to mobilize the civilian population of the center of the country threatened by Scott. Did the arguments laid out in the previous few pages have any positive effect? This question is of extreme importance because Mexico's eventual defeat in this war has often been interpreted as evidence of a lack of national identity. To approach it we have to understand that the history of efforts to convince Mexicans to adopt a national identity did not begin when the first American soldier crossed the Nueces River in 1846. The same is true of the related history in which Mexicans of many social strata and walks of life tried to fit their different dreams into the larger political and social project of making Mexico. In uneven and halting ways, Mexico had been becoming a nation, and many Mexicans had been becoming national since at least the Napoleonic Wars, when Spain's role led to arguments that all subjects of the Spanish empire had something at stake. These efforts had paradoxically fed into Mexico's own long war of independence, and independence leaders had tried to draw distinctions between Spaniards and Mexicans that would have meaning for even poor Mexicans, with often effective if bloody results.[68] These processes continued after independence as the struggle between more egalitarian and more hierarchical visions for Mexico became interlaced with the role of Spaniards in Mexico's society and economy, as well as arguments about loyalty to the nation. These conflicts involved lofty rhetoric but sometimes produced bloody acts of xenophobia against Spaniards and other foreigners in Mexico.[69] This connection between egalitarian politics and xenophobia carried to the war with the United States. President Mariano Paredes y Arrillaga had been backed by monarchists who included the Spanish ambassador to Mexico, and in one San Luis Potosí town the revolution against Paredes sparked the murder of Spanish merchants accused of exploiting Mexicans. The nationalist egalitarianism of the radical federalists, usually directed at foreign merchants, began to merge into the fight against the Americans.[70]

San Luis Potosí is one state where the war inspired popular ire against the Americans. The Americans never invaded it, but it had long had an important role in organizing, provisioning, and recruiting armies headed north. Moreover, early in the war the Americans occupied territories just to the north and east of the state, making many people in San Luis Potosí see themselves as on the front line. The state government kept firm track of foreigners, and it singled out Americans for expulsion. Foreigners found their every action under popular scrutiny, with people reporting to authorities any inkling of enthusiasm for the American cause or any surreptitious acts. William Ward Duck, a British merchant living in Guadalcazar, San Luis Potosí, complained that his rivals in the town elite had aroused so much ire against him among the poor by claiming that he was really an American and even a spy that he fled for fear of his life.[71]

Popular suspicion and hatred of Americans became important in other parts of the country, including places the U.S. Army occupied. We have seen the ambiguous situation in Puebla, where religious and civilian leaders tried to prevent costly violence while many plebeians seethed under American occupation. In Saltillo, foreigners reported great anti-American sentiment both before and after the arrival of the American army.[72] Such sentiment seems to have been common among the poor in many parts of the country. William Carpenter, an American soldier who traveled through large parts of northern and western Mexico first as a prisoner and then as a fugitive, reported that sometimes he was treated well, especially by women and educated Mexicans, but that often he was in fear of his life from groups of impoverished Mexicans. In one town he was surrounded several times by mobs that "abused me with all sorts of vile languages, and even threw clods of dirt and stones at me." Other American prisoners reported similar experiences. This sort of popular violence against Americans continued throughout the war. Even the Americans who in May 1848 delivered the final treaty to the Mexican Congress in Querétaro were stoned by a mob.[73]

Scott's army was tasked with subduing the center of the country. He faced not only Mexican armies but a dense population, many literate Mexicans, and many printing presses. Moreover, he was also in regions that, unlike the north, had experienced significant and prolonged mobilization during the Mexican War of Independence. Not surprisingly, antiforeign sentiment was common, especially among relatively impoverished people. Austrian naturalist Karl Heller wrote from Mexico City in September 1846, a year before Scott's army reached it, that "animosity against foreigners, which until now was still slumbering, grows more virulent with each passing day, and yesterday evening in the vicinity of the Plaza de Voladores a cry rang out, 'Mueren los extranjeros e invasores!' ('Death to foreigners and invaders!'), so that a person cannot reveal the slightest sympathy for North America if one wants his life to be safe. In the most recent days several have fallen victim in this way." The better part of a year later, in the nearby village of San Angel, British subject Alexander Marshall was stoned by a crowd yelling "Death to the Yankees!"[74] Men who seemed to be foreigners, especially if they spoke English or could otherwise be identified with the invading army, continued to be attacked by mobs in Mexico City right up until it fell to the American army.

Scott's Army, Mexican Civilians, and Guerrilla War

Scott's campaign was intended to force the Mexican government to be willing to give up massive amounts of territory in a settlement. Historian Timothy Johnson points out that Scott approached this goal with a mind-set derived from the eighteenth-century Western military tradition of limited warfare.[75] However, Scott's decisions were also shaped by more recent trends in warfare. The wars that had shaken Europe for more than two decades between the French Revolution and the 1815 Battle of Waterloo had been intimately interwoven with the increasingly popular notion that governments represented nations, peoples tied by a common territory, history, and destiny, and that therefore wars between states necessarily involved conflict between peoples. Although the French revolutionary state had been the first to promote this vision of warfare, it was also the French state that showed how badly the equation of states with peoples could hamper an invading army. Thousands of French soldiers died at the hands of Spanish guerrillas. Scott, like most military leaders of his era, studied the Napoleonic Wars avidly, and he understood that a campaign into the densely populated center of Mexico could be seriously hampered and possibly even destroyed by a mobilized populace. A guerrilla war could be sustained for a very long time and could be the death knell for not only many American soldiers but also American dreams of acquiring title to Mexican territory.[76] Scott was also well aware of the crimes that American volunteers had committed in the north, and how those crimes had enraged the populace against the American army there. He believed that the best way to avoid civilian mobilization against his army was to prevent similar acts. Thus, from the beginning Scott worked to keep his troops from committing crimes against Mexican civilians. He also insisted that his army would pay for any supplies it acquired from Mexican civilians. Neither of these measures was particularly popular with Scott's troops, especially the volunteers.[77]

Many volunteers were also unhappy with Scott's very public effort to convince Mexicans in general, and influential clergymen in particular, that Catholicism had little to fear from the invasion. Here he was following the policy of the Polk administration, which wanted to avoid the notion that this was an anti-Catholic war in order to woo immigrant voters for the Democratic Party and reduce the fervor of Mexican resistance. Scott took this policy much further than Democratic politicians did, probably because he understood how the actions of anti-Catholic volunteers in the north had inflamed Mexican resistance there and perhaps due to his understanding of why the French army had inspired such hatred in Spain. Rather than simply keeping troops from looting churches and carrying out other sacrilegious acts, Scott and his officers went on a charm offensive. Scott himself attended Mass soon after the capture of Veracruz, actually carrying a candle in one of the processions that many anti-Catholic volunteers viewed as superstitious mumbo jumbo. Many regular army officers in Scott's force followed his lead. He ordered both officers and men to show due respect to Catholic rituals.[78]

In May 1847 Colonel Thomas Childs, a regular officer commanding in Xalapa, took Scott's orders to show respect for Catholicism so seriously that he sparked far-flung controversy by marching in a procession in which priests and civic leaders accompanied the Holy Eucharist through the streets. Childs and several other regular officers went hatless and carried candles. Moreover, Childs had earlier ordered the commander of the American troops on guard in the public square to have those troops doff their own hats and kneel when the procession passed. The troops on duty included regulars, who complied without question, and Pennsylvania volunteers, who flatly refused. Volunteer Thomas Barclay explained their point of view, pointing out that many of the volunteers were pious Protestants and "a man's religious principles should be respected and held sacred and the forcing men of Puritan principles to kneel to a procession of this kind is about as just as it would be to force Catholics to trample upon the holy cross. Protestants consider such ceremonies as idolatrous." He added that many volunteers said they would prefer being punished to following such orders. The Pennsylvania volunteers seethed, and news of the incident soon found its way into nativist, anti-Catholic newspapers in the United States, where Childs was severely criticized as a kind of proxy for the apparent coddling of Mexican Catholics.[79]

How successful were Scott's efforts to maintain relatively cordial relationships with the civilian population? He and his officers repeatedly proclaimed that his army would respect Mexican lives, property, and religion, but Mexicans understood the difference between policy and belief. Although they might appreciate the apparent respect of American officers at religious ceremonies, they knew this was a conscious tool of conquest and that those officers who were not Catholic were simply going through the motions.[80] Besides, claiming that American troops would behave and making it happen were not quite the same thing. Anti-Catholicism was rife in the many volunteer units assigned to Scott's campaign, and they committed many mocking or larcenous attacks on religious objects or ceremonies. Volunteers in Scott's army also stole from and sometimes murdered Mexicans, and they got away with those crimes for the same reasons volunteers in Taylor's forces had: volunteers refused to testify against each other, and Mexican witnesses rarely came forward for fear of reprisals. Still, it seems that American soldiers in Scott's army committed fewer crimes against civilians than American soldiers in Taylor's army did, lessening the toll of war on civilians for much of the campaign.[81]

Mexican civilians may have benefited from Scott's efforts, but those efforts did not prevent guerrilla resistance. By the summer of 1847 many guerrillas were operating along the road between Puebla and Veracruz, making life difficult for Scott's army. The guerrilla war in eastern and central Mexico began after the Battle of Cerro Gordo and continued until the end of the war. In the northern zones occupied by Taylor's army, guerrilla war arose without much planning as Mexicans reacted to the depredations of American volunteers using the same tactics they had used in conflicts with Native Americans. The American response to the guerrillas there was similarly organic, employing both tactics and cultural references from the long history of warfare between informal American units and Native Americans and from the Jacksonian penchant for vigilantism. Undoubtedly, American crimes against Mexican civilians inspired some people in central and eastern Mexico to resist the occupation, but the origins of the guerrilla war there were mostly different. In these regions the fighting during the Mexican War of Independence had been fierce, involving not only guerrilla tactics but also intense political processes through which many inhabitants came to see themselves as distinct from foreigners.[82] These were the most populated areas of the country, where dense networks of government institutions and written communications had helped spread a sense of national identity in the decades between independence and 1846. Once the war started, those very same networks were used to encourage people of all social groups to contribute to the war effort and resist Scott. This, in other words, was an area primed for conflict. Moreover, many people believed that the successful separation of Mexico from Spain and the defeat of Napoleon's armies in Spain were both proof of the efficacy of guerrilla tactics.[83]

Still, not all Mexican politicians embraced guerrilla warfare against the Americans. Attitudes about it divided along party and class lines. Many conservative and wealthy Mexicans remembered the insurgency of the War of Independence not as a heroic triumph of national identity but instead as a period of anarchy and social unrest in which they had been the targets of popular ire. These men believed a mobilized and armed populace might turn on them.[84] Moreover, they knew that guerrilla war and the counterinsurgency efforts used against it had exacted a severe toll on even civilians of humble means. Peasants had often been forced to support the guerrillas with supplies and then punished for this by royalist forces. Attitudes on the other side of the political spectrum were very different. For many radical federalists the success of guerrillas during the Mexican War of Independence was crucial in making the nation, and they took it as a given that guerrilla tactics would negate the organizational and technological advantages of the Americans. These radical federalists, including Governors Melchor Ocampo of Michoacán and Adame of San Luis Potosí, as well as former insurgent leader Juan Alvarez, believed in guerrilla warfare in part because they believed that even relatively poor Mexicans could understand the importance of nationalism and participate in the politics of a national state.[85]

Some Mexican regular officers had fought as guerrillas on the insurgent side during the War of Independence, and most of these men were aligned politically with radical federalists. Not surprisingly, many advocated guerrilla tactics against the Americans. However, most regular officers were more comfortable with the eighteenth-century tradition of professional armies. Guerrilla tactics clashed with their own cultural conceptions of limited warfare. The veterans of the War of Independence had fought on the royalist side until near the end of the war, often in counterinsurgency campaigns. They grudgingly respected how difficult it was for a conventional army to defeat guerrillas, but they also understood how the guerrilla campaign in 1810–1821 had devastated civilians and severely damaged Mexico's economy. Moreover, although these officers knew that the long guerrilla struggle had helped make independence possible, they also knew a guerrilla campaign alone was not enough: Spanish authority in Mexico was not defeated until much of the royalist army had switched sides and begun conventional military operations against the remaining loyalists. These regular army officers also knew that the successful Spanish resistance to Napoleon had relied on both guerrillas and conventional armies. Most Mexican officers believed that guerrillas could be useful in conjunction with regular operations, but they saw radical federalists as too enthusiastic about them.[86] In the north, Santa Anna did not promote guerrilla warfare until he was ready to advance toward San Luis Potosí. He then sent General José Urrea with some regular cavalry to help the guerrillas there harass the Americans and cut their supply lines. With the extra manpower provided by the regular cavalry, these forces were able to defeat, capture, and destroy several American wagon trains of supplies. Guerrilla activities increased all over Tamaulipas and Nuevo León.[87] Something similar happened in the east and center of the country. Although a few guerrillas were beginning to form before Cerro Gordo, the regular military did not encourage them until after the defeat there. They were seen as a useful adjunct, harassing the Americans and forcing them to dedicate some of their limited troops to protecting their supply line. The army's interest in guerrillas increased dramatically as the Americans made their final push toward Mexico City, the subject of Chapter 6. Although most guerrilla units were raised by civilians, Santa Anna placed Alvarez in a coordinating role with some regular cavalry to give more teeth to guerrilla attacks. The guerrillas around the Valley of Mexico were supposed to gather intelligence, hamper American movements, and, hopefully, harry the retreating American army after it failed to penetrate the defenses manned by conventional forces.[88]

In the spring of 1847 the American victory at Veracruz increased politicians' interest in guerrilla warfare. In many regions politicians encouraged influential people to organize guerrilla units, and they eagerly complied. After Cerro Gordo, substitute president Pedro María Anaya called on concerned citizens with means and influence in their regions to establish "light sections of the National Guard." This decree provided a national administrative framework, but there were clearly already many units in formation. As historian Irving Levinson points out, the decree shows that the moderate federalists then in charge of the government believed that guerrilla units should be commanded by men with the prestige and wealth needed to recruit, arm, and feed groups of fifty or more men. Wealth was needed because, even though the government promised to reimburse their expenses, such reimbursement was likely to be slow and uncertain. Putting guerrillas under the direct control of local elites would also reduce the chance that they would target the wealthy instead of the Americans.[89] Here practical considerations dovetailed with social concerns. Rural people of wealth had the economic resources needed and they could recruit their own employees or tenants. They could even use their economic power to encourage men to join these risky endeavors: in San Luis Potosí, for instance, Paulo Antonio Verástegui invited men to join a guerrilla unit, offering to help feed their families, pay for their equipment, and pay pensions for any man crippled or killed. He also stated that when renting out his land, he would give preference for those who served as guerrillas, and he offered prizes to those who distinguished themselves. Men of wealth could increase their local political influence by this kind of generosity, but this does not mean that guerrilla leaders and their men did not also act out of some form of national sentiment. After all, how different were the actions of Verástegui from those of American politicians who recruited volunteer units and plied the men with alcohol to win elections, or those of Mexican urban politicians who organized National Guard units? In all of these cases, people were integrating their political and social goals with the idea of the nation.[90]

The wealthy and influential were not the only men who sought to do this. However, the nature of the records makes it difficult to understand the social origins and motivations of the many common people who joined or supported the guerrillas. In Veracruz some guerrilla leaders had fought for the insurgents in the War of Independence, suggesting not only patriotism but also an orientation toward poor rural people. We also know that some guerrillas were peasants. Probably some had been members of militia units before 1846 or had other experience in Mexico's tumultuous postindependence political life. They were also no doubt exposed to the arguments seen in the written propaganda about independence, the need to protect Mexican women and family honor, and the threat that the Americans posed to Catholicism. Participation in guerrilla units organized by local politicians and other influential men brought the possibility of personal benefits alongside the honor that came from participating in the nation. Rural people were sometimes very supportive of guerrillas: Juan Climaco de Rebolledo, leader of the guerrillas in Veracruz, reported in late July 1847 that he was able to pull together eight hundred men for a major attack due to the "extreme enthusiasm" of rural inhabitants. Yet, only a couple of weeks later, National Guardsmen from Misantla, Veracruz, balked at joining guerrilla attacks because their participation would require them to leave their families.[91]

Not every guerrilla or even every guerrilla leader was Mexican. Deserters from the American army sometimes fought as guerrillas on the Mexican side. Scotchman Santiago Humphrey, who had been a surgeon in the Mexican army, asked to be allowed to raise a guerrilla unit that would include foreign residents of Mexico.[92] The most famous guerrilla leader in the war was a Spanish priest named Celedonio de Jarauta. Jarauta had recently immigrated to Mexico after participating on the conservative side in Spanish civil wars. He was appointed chaplain of a Mexican regiment in Veracruz. After the fall of the port, he led guerrilla forces first in Veracruz and then elsewhere in eastern and central Mexico. His fame spread, leading to poems about his prowess and American charges that he was not really even a priest. For Americans, Jarauta became a hated symbol both of guerrillas and of priests encouraging resistance. Although for months many Mexicans celebrated Jarauta's intransigence and efficacy, eventually his desire to continue the war after the fall of Mexico City separated him from Mexico's political elite. He helped lead a conservative rebellion and was executed.[93]

In the summer and fall of 1847, Mexican guerrillas were extremely active along the route from Veracruz to the central highlands. They captured or killed many Americans who had straggled behind their marching units or spread out in small groups to steal or buy food. Very soon the Americans realized that any men, money, or supplies they needed to bring up from Veracruz could only move in convoys escorted by hundreds or even thousands of soldiers. Even these convoys often lost many men and wagons of supplies. For example, in early June guerrillas made multiple attacks on a large wagon train escorted by over eight hundred American soldiers. The escort could not keep the guerrillas from capturing wagons, mules, and cash. An American officer described a scene of terror, saying that "the firing was very heavy and produced the utmost confusion among the teams, overturning and breaking the wagons and ambulances and the greatest consternation among the teamsters." A little later another attack occurred, "causing infinite panic and confusion: the teamsters leaving their teams and fleeing to the bush, the teams wheeling from the direct road, disengaging themselves, overturning and breaking the tongues of the wagons." The train was forced to take a defensive position and wait for five hundred more American soldiers to bring cannon to disperse the guerrillas.[94] American soldiers came to respect and fear the guerrillas. Describing a clash on the road to Veracruz, Jacob Oswandel wrote that the guerrillas "fought like so many tigers." Later he said that he and his fellow volunteers would rather face ten regular Mexican soldiers than one guerrilla. Guerrilla actions were often tactical successes, and tactical success had largely eluded Mexico's conventional army.[95]

Scott's army stayed in Puebla from June to August. American sources indicate that Scott paused to allow for negotiations, and that he needed to await reinforcements because his volunteer soldiers had not reenlisted. However, the guerrillas were making everything the Americans did difficult, and this contributed to the delay. For instance, when volunteer units arrived in Veracruz, they could not immediately march for the interior to escape the risk of yellow fever. American officers instead needed to wait for sufficient troops to accumulate in Veracruz to have a chance of defending themselves against determined guerrilla attacks. Unable to control the route to Veracruz, Scott economized on men by pulling them into just a couple of groups, each large enough to defend itself. Scott kept a force at Puebla to protect his wounded and sick and provide a fallback position, and marched the rest of his army to the Valley of Mexico, abandoning the towns between Puebla and Veracruz. Even the Puebla garrison was not large enough to be totally safe from guerrillas. They attacked American outposts and chased American patrols into the very center of the city, supported by many Pueblans.[96]

Many Mexicans were thrilled to hear about the widely reported exploits of the guerrillas, both as evidence that the war might be winnable and as signs that many Mexicans were willing to fight for their country. Politician and landowner Mariano Riva Palacio wrote proudly that "the bodies found in different places, sometimes wounded, sometimes rotting, hidden in ravines or wells, demonstrate the public spirit of the inhabitants."[97] However, not all Mexicans loved guerrilla warfare. Some agreed with the Americans that the line between guerrillas and bandits was thin indeed. Guerrillas needed both motivation and resources. The rules allowed guerrilla bands to share wealth plundered from the enemy, and because trading with the enemy was illegal, capturing from the enemy and confiscating illegal trade goods were close to the same thing. Merchants often came to hate guerrillas. Guerrillas also needed food, horses, and shelter, and when armed men sought these things from civilians, there was little the civilians could do but give them up and complain to the authorities later. The image of the guerrillas was not helped by their sometimes imperious manner, or the fact that some had been thieves before the war.[98]

The toll guerrilla warfare took on civilians was magnified by the American response. They increasingly made civilians responsible for the activities of guerrillas. At first this responsibility was limited to local political authorities. Soon after the battle of Cerro Gordo, Scott decreed that he would fine authorities who failed to find and turn over guerrillas, whom Scott described as "murderers and robbers."[99] This order was ineffective, and, as we will see in more detail later, American military commanders eventually employed the same kinds of reprisals against civilians that had developed informally in the north.[100]

Would it have made a difference if the Mexican state had put more resources into guerrilla warfare and less into the conventional armies that it raised time and time again? Certainly some Mexicans thought so.[101] As Levinson says, guerrilla warfare wore away at the Americans, causing hundreds and perhaps thousands of losses. The possibility that it might continue indefinitely made American soldiers and civilians eager to get out of Mexico sooner than might otherwise have been the case. It made some Americans understand that annexing the whole country would lead to endless war. Guerrilla warfare also may have decreased the territorial demands of the Polk administration.[102] Still, it was extremely costly for Mexican civilians, and it alone would not be enough to defeat the American army as long as that army could provision itself by buying food in Mexico. The guerrilla campaign against Scott provides evidence that many Mexicans were willing to fight for their country, but it also shows that their struggle could not be effective as long as they faced such a wealthy opponent.

CHAPTER 6

The Yankees Died Like Ants

Winfield Scott's pause at Puebla lasted a solid ten weeks. It was length-ened both by the slow recruiting of new troops in the United States and by the strength of Mexican guerrillas, which meant that American troops could only march from Veracruz in large contingents. On August 7, 1847, Scott's army of around ten thousand men finally departed, leaving only a small garrison of mostly ill soldiers in Puebla. In the next five weeks Scott's army would fight several bloody battles before finally capturing Mexico City. These weeks were the crescendo of the war. Although fighting continued elsewhere, the fall of Mexico City finally convinced the Mexican govern-ment that it needed to concede territory to end the war. The Mexico City campaign was an important triumph for the U.S. Army and the national state it represented, although it came at great cost. For Mexico, though, these five weeks were more ambivalent. Twice the politicization of its professional officer corps contributed to defeats, and throughout the campaign Mexican military efforts were hampered by the lack of financial resources. However, this was also a period in which the Mexican national state showed a great capacity to mobilize resources, and above all to convince people of many dif-ferent social groups to fight on its behalf. Given the weakness of the Mexican economy, the fractious nature of Mexican politics, and the army's failure to defeat its American counterpart in any of the previous six major battles, the fact that the Mexicans were able to muster a tenacious defense of the capital is nothing short of remarkable.

Scott's long pause in Puebla had allowed the Mexican government weeks to stitch together some of the political wounds opened by the polkos rebellion and convince the inhabitants of central Mexico that sacrifice was now impera-tive. Government missives stressed the idea that in the approaching crisis it would be necessary for all inhabitants, regardless of their political beliefs or social status, to pull together in the face of an invasion that threatened core values like family and religion.[1] Once again the mercurial Antonio López de Santa Anna was at the center of the effort. Politically, he sought to convince moderates and radicals that they had to work together, and the church that it had to be willing to do more. Militarily, Santa Anna, though never a tactical genius, was unparalleled as an organizer. In some sense his military skills were actually political ones: he could convince Mexico's many different kinds of political brokers to focus on raising, arming, and provisioning military forces. He was without peer in this ability, and he had already exercised it twice during this war, first to build the army he took from San Luis Potosí to La Angostura, and then to pull together the forces that had blocked the American way to the highlands at Cerro Gordo.[2] Now he did it once again.

Preparations for Defending the City

The army that Santa Anna put together with the help of Mexicans from just about every social group and political faction in Mexico was the most diverse force that Mexico fielded in the war. It included many regular army units, including some that had fought in the northern battles, and even a small unit of foreign soldiers. The men gathered also included thousands of part-time soldiers organized in National Guard units of diverse social origins and political inclinations. Strikingly, some had traveled from distant locations in Oaxaca, Michoacán, and present-day Guerrero. The Oaxaca and Guerrero men were poor rural people, many of whom were indigenous peasants who did not even speak Spanish. The Michoacán unit was from the city of Morelia and consisted mostly of urban, middle-class mestizos. Other National Guard units had been organized much closer at hand: most villages of the valley fielded contingents, and Mexico City itself contributed many men organized into battalions with either moderate or radical leanings that had been shooting at each other just a few months before. In August and September 1847 they put their political disagreements aside. The very diversity of this army bolstered the government's argument that these battles were the affair of all Mexicans, regardless of social class or politics.[3] This diversity is also worth exploring to help us understand how the national state was able to continue organizing resistance to the Americans and how the social character of different units affected events on the various battlefields.

Many of the soldiers Santa Anna gathered to face the Americans in the Valley of Mexico were from the regular army. As we have seen, most regulars had been conscripted from Mexico's lower classes, often because they were considered less useful to local society than their peers, but once they were in the army, fierce discipline, intensive training, the bonds of comradeship, and strong unit identities forged them into effective instruments of Napoleonic-age warfare whose intricate tactics were shaped by the inaccuracy and low rate of fire of muzzle-loading, smoothbore firearms. In this Mexican regular army, soldiers were very like their peers in the U.S. Army. However, in a crucial way they were different: Mexican soldiers were paid irregularly and often went hungry, and this led many to desert if they were not closely supervised.

Some regular units available for the campaign had participated in the Battle of Cerro Gordo. Although these units had dissolved in the precipitous retreat there, most of the dispersed soldiers had been gathered again into their units. As the Americans assembled their forces in Puebla, the Mexican government transferred the balance of the regular army units that still maintained a northern front in San Luis Potosí to the center of the country. Many of these soldiers were veterans of La Angostura, and some had fought in all of the northern battles. Most had been recruited in states north of Mexico City, including Querétaro, Aguascalientes, Guanajuato, and, especially, San Luis Potosí. Units decimated by desertion during the deadly retreat from La Angostura had been rebuilt in the following months by the voluntary and involuntary reintegration of the very same deserters, and filled out by new recruits.[4] One of the striking features of the social history of Mexico's regular army is how the civil and military authorities were able to bring many deserters back into the army during the war. The government repeatedly gave communities new recruitment quotas, and these communities preferred to fill them with men who had been conscripted, deserted, and returned. This made it very difficult for deserters to live in their original communities, but living in a new place was also hard. Demand for labor in Mexico's rickety economy was low, and earning enough money to have a satisfying life or even just survive was difficult without the family and social networks provided by living in one's community of birth. The government periodically offered to let deserters rejoin the army without punishment. For instance, a July 1847 decree threatened deserters with harsh punishment but offered amnesty to any who returned and even allowed them to serve in the units of their choice.[5] Many deserters returned to the ranks, even as the army recruited new men in preparation for the fight to come.[6]

Many men who gathered to confront the American army in the Valley of Mexico were part-time soldiers organized into National Guard units. As we have seen, National Guard recruits, unlike the ne'er-do-wells conscripted into the regular army, were typically men who responsibly fulfilled family obligations. That makes it all the more remarkable that so many National Guardsmen who fought in the Valley of Mexico were from other regions. These men were not only exposing themselves to physical harm, they were exposing their families to hunger by neglecting their crops and other economic pursuits. One contingent came from what Mexicans called "the South," an area that now forms the state of Guerrero but in 1847 was split among various states, while another contingent came from part of Oaxaca called the Mixteca Baja. Both groups were composed of peasants, especially indigenous peasants, who had been drawn into political alliances that extended beyond their regions in an effort to pursue their aspirations. Despite this similarity, the Guerrero units leaned politically to the left, while their Oaxacan counterparts leaned in the opposite direction.

General Juan Alvarez, one of the era's more controversial political figures, led the Guerrero peasants. A very young Alvarez had entered Mexican politics in 1810, fighting in a regional proindependence coalition of coastal mulatto sharecroppers and landowning families opposed to the mostly Spanish merchants who monopolized the cotton trade and disdained the mulattos. In the first few decades after independence, these men and their descendants developed an egalitarian and nationalist form of federalist politics that associated foreigners with centralist, tyrannical government and economic exploitation.[7] Some of the National Guardsmen who marched with Alvarez to the Valley of Mexico were from this social group. Many of the Guerrero National Guardsmen had been drawn into national politics more recently. Most inhabitants of Guerrero's mountains were indigenous villagers. Right after independence Mexico's federalist system had allowed them some local autonomy, but in the mid-1830s centralism placed local political authority firmly in the hands of relatively wealthy mestizos who lived in market towns and sometimes owned small haciendas. In the early 1840s this local elite tried to expand its landholdings at the expense of some indigenous villages, leading to a peasant rebellion. This unrest spread to many other villages when the centralist state imposed a head tax. Alvarez encouraged these peasants to develop a version of popular federalism that stressed low taxation and local autonomy, as well as, following the lead of earlier popular federalists, opposition to exploitative foreigners. Both the coastal mulatto and the mountain indigenous federalists participated in the movement that overthrew Mariano Paredes y Arrillaga and restored federalism in 1846. Their affiliation with federalism had both ideological and practical dimensions: indigenous peasants retained all of the disputed land, no longer paid the head tax, and gained more political autonomy.[8] They had been drawn into national politics and to some degree adopted an identity as Mexicans, something they made explicit in their proclamations. In 1847 they were joined in the Valley of Mexico by some National Guardsmen from market towns who had opposed the Indian rebels.[9] All of these National Guardsmen were mobilized for the war through some combination of ideological commitment, peer pressure, and political alliance. Families sent their men and also pulled together food and animals to send with them on the journey. Juan de Dios Ovando, the administrator of one mountain district, praised the sacrifices its inhabitants had made, and boasted that if the rest of the country were willing to sacrifice as much, not even Napoleon would have survived invading Mexico.[10] However, these men worried about the economic damage their absence was doing to their families, and Alvarez insisted that only his presence could prevent their desertion.[11] Does this make them prepolitical country bumpkins with no sense of national identity? If that is the case, we could probably say the same about the thousands of Americans who did not join the army during the war.

Some of the National Guardsmen from the Mixteca Baja in Oaxaca were also Indians, but the pattern of political mobilization that eventually brought them to the Valley of Mexico was different. In Oaxaca the state's elite had deliberately allowed indigenous villages a great deal of de facto autonomy even under centralism, and local elites generally did not try to strip indigenous peasants of agrarian resources. The head tax that was so unpopular in Guerrero was generally accepted in Oaxaca. Moreover, in the Mixteca Baja the Catholic Church had a strong institutional presence, and local elites cooperated as indigenous forms of Catholic worship flourished. Indigenous peasants and local elites together forged a social peace that combined indigenous autonomy with popular religiosity, a relatively conservative discourse, and support for centralists on the national level. In the 1840s, when peasant rebels from neighboring Guerrero began to affect the area, they were seen as outsiders disturbing the social peace, and many peasants of the Mixteca Baja were mobilized into part-time military units to combat them. These forces were eventually regularized as National Guard units. Antonio de León, a regional political leader who had been a royalist officer during the War of Independence and brokered various political alliances as a moderate centralist in the intervening decades, brought these units to the struggle for Mexico City. Rural villages also contributed supplies and money to support the troops. In sum, many people from the Mixteca Baja, including indigenous peasants who did not speak Spanish, had also come to understand themselves as having a stake in Mexico, although the Mexico they imagined was not quite the same one that most Guerrero peasants did.[12] Like their counterparts from Guerrero, people from the Mixteca Baja who served in the Valley of Mexico risked their lives and left their loved ones in difficult economic circumstances to participate in the war.

The same can be said of the urban National Guardsmen of Morelia in the state of Michoacán. This unit had been organized relatively recently, after the city heard of the fall of Veracruz. On Easter Sunday, April 2, more than 1,500 men met to establish the city's National Guard, and 800 of them were organized into the Matamoros Battalion, named after a hero of the War of Independence. They trained for two months and set out for Mexico City after receiving their unit flag in a ceremony at which both the openly anticlerical state governor Melchor Ocampo and a Catholic priest spoke. The battalion was composed of artisans, family men, and young men from distinguished families. Like their counterparts from Guerrero and Oaxaca, they left suffering families behind. During the long wait for Scott to leave Puebla, the battalion commander, Gabino Ortiz, complained that the men had not been paid, adding that they were "hardworking and honest artisans that have abandoned their houses and families, because they believed that they would be here only a month at most before the question was decided.

But when they see that combat is postponed and their families suffer the consequences of misery and they themselves lack resources they will be able to do nothing except abandon the cause that they embraced with such good faith." He worried that they might return home without permission, and asked that the whole battalion be allowed to return to Morelia until it was needed. Nevertheless, the battalion stayed and played an important part in the coming battles.[13]

Other National Guard units included the small companies from the valley's villages and the much larger battalions from the city itself. These units had originally been organized during the political effervescence of the fall of 1846. Radical federalists had orchestrated well-attended meetings in which urban politicians and relatively poor artisans pledged resistance to the Americans; criticized centralism; argued that everyone, including the wealthy, should make sacrifices for the war effort; and organized National Guard battalions of artisans. The moderate federalists had responded by warning about class warfare and setting up their own battalions. These National Guard units of different political persuasions came to blows when the polkos rebellion started in February 1847. Weeks of skirmishing between the groups paralyzed the capital but caused few casualties. Santa Anna decided the question in favor of the moderates and sent some of the radical units to Veracruz, where they fought well at Cerro Gordo. In the Valley of Mexico, both radical and moderate units fought, and when they passed through the city, they often drew admiring crowds. One anonymous observer noted that their units included the rich and the poor, "men of every opinion, of all the parties, of all ages, all classes of society, united by a fraternal bond, that of Mexicans."[14]

Santa Anna had under his command around twenty thousand men organized into formal military units, as well as an unknown number of guerrillas prepared to report American movements and pick off stragglers. His numbers gave him the possibility of mounting a successful defense, but many other factors worked against him. The biggest problem, as always, was financial. How could the government feed this many men, much less equip them? Throughout the war many Mexican soldiers received money for food erratically, and that problem tended to worsen over time. The American blockade had destroyed customs revenues; the uncertainty of war slowed business, reducing the revenue from internal taxes on commerce; and new direct taxes yielded little.[15] The army also needed weapons. Santa Anna and his officers worked tirelessly to purchase any available muskets, they sent the police to search for ones in civilian hands, and they put artisans to work repairing them, since they were all worn-out veterans of the Napoleonic Wars. They transferred cannon from other states and refurbished older cannon. They confiscated mules for transport. Church bells were melted to make cannon and musket balls, and women made uniforms. Officers and sergeants worked hard to train the men to use their firearms and to maneuver. However, in general, the quality of this army was lower than that of the armies Santa Anna had commanded at La Angostura or even Cerro Gordo. Although morale was surprisingly high, most units did not have sufficient training and equipment to take the offensive against the Americans, and in any event the advantage presented by American light artillery made formal battle in the open field very unattractive. Santa Anna's campaign would have to be defensive. Although twenty thousand men may sound like a large amount, Mexico City was one of the largest cities in the world, and it was impossible to cover every possible approach with so few men. Later, when American officers described the battles in the valley, they invariably overestimated the number of Mexicans engaged, enhancing their own glory. In fact, in all of these battles, Scott's men, with their ability to maneuver, concentrated against small parts of Santa Anna's army, achieving what military leaders call local superiority.[16]

The quality of the Mexican troops and the sheer size of the city hampered its defense, but we also should keep in mind that early modern cities were notoriously difficult to defend. Both physically and socially, cities were complicated and fragile environments that war could turn into lethal traps. Most foods except grain were continuously produced in the countryside and brought into the city. A siege could cut off these supplies, and a large city like Mexico City would quickly exhaust even stored supplies of grains, leading to famine. As we saw with Veracruz, buildings offered no protection from artillery bombardment, and the death toll for civilians could be tragic. Wealthy residents also worried about the kind of massive property damage that had occurred at Veracruz. Moreover, they were acutely aware of their precarious perch atop a population that was mostly living hand to mouth and that the elite both feared and disdained due to its mixed-race makeup. Fear of this "rabble" had partially inspired the polkos rebellion, and the end of that revolt did little to allay those fears. Finally, Western military culture assumed that if soldiers stormed a defended city, their fear and blood lust would be so overwhelming that their officers would not be able to keep them from robbing, killing, and raping civilians. This idea was very pervasive in military culture, one of the things that every soldier seemed to know. It could also be used to intimidate the enemy into surrender, and even before the Americans left Puebla, their diplomatic representative Nicholas Trist explicitly told the Mexican government through a go-between that American officers feared that their troops would loot, rape, and kill if they were forced to assault the city and fight street to street.[17] The city council in effect represented the city's elite, and according to established Hispanic political tradition, it was specifically charged with protecting the city's population during famines, epidemics, wars, and other disasters. In early June, after some internal debate, it tried to dissuade Santa Anna from exposing the population to famine, bombardment, social unrest, and looting. He saw this as evidence of an alarming lack of patriotism, but he also took the occasion to explain that he planned to stop the American army outside the populated area.[18]

Santa Anna's defense plan hinged on the particular geography of the Valley of Mexico, which is actually a volcanic plateau that is made into something of a bowl by the surrounding mountains and other higher ground. When the Spanish arrived in 1519, much of the valley floor was covered by lakes, and Tenochtitlán, the capital of the Aztec Empire, was an island. Massive colonial public works projects had drained much of this water, but some lakes persisted, and the land around them was often soggy, especially in the rainy season that began each June. The major roads were thus raised and in many places were effectively causeways. Mexican military engineers decided to enhance this natural defense by destroying the dikes that kept water out of the fields and pastures. This measure would dramatically restrict the approaches available to the Americans, and especially to American artillery.[19] They also planned fortifications that dominated the roads the Americans would have to use, especially the most direct road from Puebla, which wound past lakes until it approached a rocky ridge called El Peñon that Mexican engineers fortified as the major defense of the city. Santa Anna's government put much of its effort into these engineering projects. Both required massive amounts of labor, and many residents of the Valley of Mexico helped.

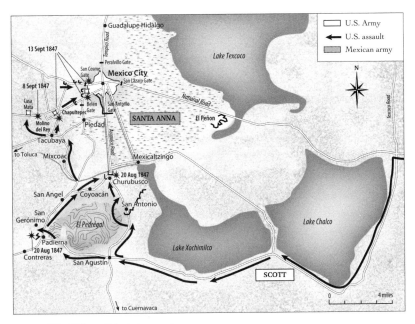

MAP 11 The Valley of Mexico campaign

The problem was how to pay for all of this work. The city government was ordered to contribute all of its public works laborers and their tools, and some National Guardsmen were put to work on the fortifications.[20] However, these two groups were not nearly enough. The government turned to local authorities in outlying villages to recruit workers. Military and city authorities also conscripted men to work on the fortifications.[21] In theory these workers, whether National Guardsmen, men impressed from the streets of the city, or indigenous peasants sent by their village authorities, were paid at least enough to eat, but the urgency of the task, the poverty of the government, and the fact that they had been coerced into the work in the first place all led to considerable hardship. Food and pay were intermittent, and those in charge of completing the fortifications sometimes used corporal punishment to spur workers on. Moreover, these men were not providing income to their families, which then suffered because they had neither savings nor a social safety net to rely on. Efforts to get men released from duty so that they could provide food for their families testify to the desperation these families faced.[22] This forced labor and mistreatment did not go without protest: the leaders of the village of Iztapalapa, for instance, complained that their men were being treated like slaves, subjected to beatings and forced to work in water up to their necks and without the necessary tools, while at the same time their own crops were lost to the deliberate flooding.[23]

Santa Anna hoped that the flooded terrain of the Valley of Mexico would force the Americans to attack his fixed defenses, which included not only the formidable fortifications at El Peñon but also various secondary defense lines and strongpoints. These fixed positions would be held by National Guardsmen and some of the less experienced regular regiments, while his most experienced regulars, the Army of the North which had recently arrived from San Luis Potosí, would serve as a mobile reserve, ready to reinforce as needed or attack any American force disorganized by failed attacks on the fixed defenses. Santa Anna also fielded a cavalry force to collect information, harass the Americans, and attack such disorganized American forces.[24] Finally, he counted on guerrillas to harass and spy on the Americans. The Mexicans knew that the American army was small and that a retreat to Puebla through a hostile populace could well be disastrous for it. This plan was a hopeful one, but its hope was not unreasonable. Santa Anna knew that at Monterrey and Cerro Gordo Mexican units had successfully held off American assaults, and the defenses at El Peñon were extremely strong. The Americans would have to advance many yards on a narrow causeway dominated by numerous Mexican cannon even to get close enough to charge the fortifications, and there would be very little room to deploy American artillery to support them.[25]

The First Battles in the Valley of Mexico

As the American army entered the valley, Scott gathered information and considered possibilities. Engineers reported the strength of the defenses at El Peñon, and Scott realized that even a successful attack there would leave the Americans far short of the city, separated from it by formidable secondary defenses. Scott considered taking a less direct route through Mexicalzingo, but an attack there would have the same problem. Finally he settled on a much more circuitous approach. A little-used and poorly maintained road passed from east to west far south of the city, crossing muddy ravines all the way to the hills on the west side of the valley. At first Scott heard that this road was unsuitable for transporting his army and especially its artillery, but more optimistic reports that American engineers could improve the road enough to make it feasible convinced him that this was the best option. He began moving his forces along this road, which was upgraded with help of American soldiers and the forced labor of indigenous peasants.[26] If Scott could move his army far enough west, he would come to two roads that ran north to the city. Once again, Scott was trying to outflank the Mexican army, his favorite tactic. This time Santa Anna was much more ready. Although undoubtedly he was disappointed that the Americans did not fall into the trap prepared for them at El Peñon, he still was in an interior position. Santa Anna began redeploying his troops to cover the roads Scott would have to take north to the city. He took many of the troops under his direct command to the village of San Antonio to block one of them, and he sent the Army of the North under General Gabriel Valencia to block the other at the village of San Angel.[27]

Santa Anna and Scott were engaged in an elaborate chess game, but the pieces of this game were men, drawn from different social groups in Mexico and the United States and brought to participate in the campaign by complicated equations of poverty, peer pressure, ambition, coercion, and patriotism. The moves of the chess game, very different from the quick placement of inert pieces on a pristine, flat surface, were executed by heavily laden and anxious men marching for days on muddy roads and jagged volcanic rocks. The first actual armed clash the game led to was the Battle of Padierna, which was notable not only as a tactical disaster for the Mexicans but also as the greatest moment of failure for Mexico's officer corps in the war. More than twenty years of coups and rebellions led by ambitious military politicians with different political ideologies and followed by promotions for the winners had created many personal rivalries among Mexican officers. These rivalries were evident at many moments during the war, but until Padierna they had relatively little impact on the outcomes of various battles. At Padierna they proved disastrous because they destroyed Santa Anna's efforts to present a coordinated defense of the southern approaches to Mexico City.

Once Santa Anna knew that Scott was trying to outflank his fixed defenses, he sent Valencia and his troops to San Angel, a village on the west side of the valley connected to Mexico City by a road. Valencia was a political rival of Santa Anna's, and he was one of the few Mexican generals who this late in the war had not yet faced the Americans in battle. Valencia decided that San Angel was not defensible, and he disobeyed his orders by moving his men a few miles south to Padierna. There the road the Americans had to follow passed between the gentle ridge where Valencia arrayed his approximately 4,800 men and a large, fractured jumble of volcanic rock called the Pedregal, which Valencia believed was impassible. Santa Anna had entrenched his own forces farther east and placed more forces in between at Coyoacán. Becoming wise to the ways of Scott, he soon understood that Scott was once more going around the strength of the Mexican defenses, and he decided to pull back to a secondary defense line closer to the city, where even American forces approaching on the west side of the valley would be forced to use the few roads raised above the soggy fields. This would shorten his lines and make things more difficult for the Americans. The problem, though, was that the retreat had to be orderly: to continue the defense of the city, he had to move his troops, their artillery, and their ammunition up the same narrow roads while keeping the Americans at bay. As a first step in this delicate process, he ordered Valencia to move east from San Angel to Coyoacán, pulling the Mexican forces into a stronger concentration. However, Valencia's army was not where it was supposed to be, and Valencia flatly refused to obey the order to pull back. He argued that moving his force from Padierna would leave the road to Mexico City through San Angel uncovered, and the Americans would be able to march all the way to the city. He also believed that his position in Padierna was strong, and that if he resisted an attack there and the Mexicans at San Antonio attacked the American rear, a great victory was possible. What becomes clear in their exchange of messages, and the way that both described it afterward, is that Valencia simply did not accept the authority of Santa Anna. This incensed Santa Anna, but a council of officers convinced him to try to salvage the situation more or less diplomatically, telling Valencia that he was responsible for his own decisions.

Meanwhile, Scott prepared to attack north toward Santa Anna's location at San Antonio, but he also sent Gideon Pillow's troops west through the Pedregal along a mule path that they widened to allow the passage of cannon and wagons. Scott ordered Pillow to prepare this road but not to engage the

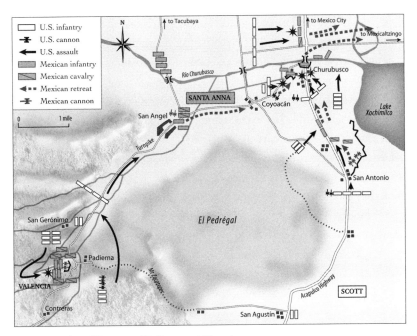

MAP 12   Battles of Contreras/Padierna and Churubusco

Mexicans. Pillow, however, soon violated those orders, becoming embroiled in a confrontation with Valencia's force. Valencia was very surprised when the Americans managed to get some artillery pieces through the Pedregal to fire on his troops, but Valencia's more numerous cannon took a heavy toll on their crews, and an American infantry attack on Valencia's position failed with heavy casualties. At this point Valencia believed that the Mexicans were winning. However, Pillow sent some men to work their way north through the pathless jumble of rocks, trying to outflank Valencia and get troops between him and any possible support. Surprisingly, such support was on its way. Santa Anna, although frustrated by Valencia's disobedience, realized that his force was in danger of being cut off, and he marched with a substantial force to San Angel and then south toward Padierna. However, when he arrived in the late afternoon, American forces were in position to block any approach to Valencia's location. The noose around the Army of the North was tightening.

That night a downpour made life miserable for the troops of both sides. Although Santa Anna understood the vise that Valencia was in, he was very conscious of the need to pull back to his secondary defense line in an orderly fashion. He brought the bulk of his forces back toward Coyoacán and ordered Valencia to abandon his cannon and bring his men and other weapons out of the trap using any available paths. Valencia again refused, and Santa Anna decided to make another effort to unite in the morning. However, the Americans were also not idle. In the drenching rains and dark of night, they found a path that would bring them south behind Valencia's forces, and they planned a dawn attack to take place while other American forces staged a diversionary attack on the front of the Mexicans. After a few hours' rest in the pouring rain, they stumbled off into the pitch black along a path scouted by American engineers. Although Valencia caught wind of this possibility and sent some troops to protect his rear, those units did not place sentries in the ravines through which the Americans might approach, probably because Mexican regulars placed on such duty were considered likely to desert. When the Americans attacked at dawn, they surprised the exhausted and soaked Mexican troops. They still put up a fierce resistance, but disorder and panic spread among the Mexican regulars, and soon units began to dissolve as individual soldiers realized that victory was not possible and salvation seemed to require headlong flight. Once again soldiers were most vulnerable when retreating, and many Mexicans fell. Santa Anna encountered this mass of fleeing men and realized that it was now imperative to try to save as much of his army as he could to defend the next line.[28]

Valencia's repeated refusal to follow orders had led to the dissolution of Mexico's most experienced and disciplined regiments and exposed the rest of the army to the same possibility. The strangest thing about this story is that Valencia, in his published justification of his actions, repeatedly confirmed his refusal to follow orders and insisted that Santa Anna should have followed his lead by sending forces to attack the Americans who confronted Valencia's forces at Padierna, while Santa Anna, in his own account, criticized Valencia but also described how he repeatedly tried to support him despite the latter's insubordination. The American victory, however, should not tempt us to totally overlook that Valencia was not the only general who disobeyed orders. The battle took place because Pillow did not carry out Scott's orders. Scott, like Santa Anna, arrived on the field to try to salvage a battle that he had not wanted to fight. The Americans succeeded because they once again were able to move men and even cannon through terrain that Mexican officers considered impassible. Here the social history of the two armies comes into play: it is likely that one reason that Mexican officers tended to overestimate the challenge of moving through difficult terrain is that when Mexican regular army units were unable march in tight formations, their officers could not prevent significant numbers of men from leaving behind the hunger of army life. They did not understand that the well-fed American troops were less likely to desert in such circumstances. The same desertion problem also prevented Mexican officers from posting soldiers in outlying locations to warn of enemy attacks, and, together with the American penchant for flanking strong positions, it made Mexican forces vulnerable to attacks from unexpected directions.

On the morning of August 20, after the defeat of Valencia's force, the Mexicans and the Americans faced different challenges. The Americans needed to pursue and destroy the Mexican army, or at the very least keep it from setting up on a new defense line. Those Mexican soldiers fleeing in disorder were a temptation no American officer could resist. Despite Valencia's earlier fears, the Americans did not move north from San Angel toward the city but instead followed the retreating Mexicans eastward toward Coyoacán. However, many American soldiers were exhausted and hungry, and their very success led to disorganization as the soldiers of different units mixed with each other in their eagerness to follow up on their victory. The Mexican challenge was simple: they had to save what they could and establish a defense closer to the city. Santa Anna and his officers worked desperately to get various units in San Angel, Coyoacán, and San Antonio on the march with their precious cannon and ammunition. Their efforts were hampered by panic and chaos: afraid of the Americans, civilians also took to the narrow and muddy roads with their possessions, impeding the retreat.[29] Santa Anna, knowing he could lose the city that day, needed time. Fortunately he knew what to do.

The roads the Mexicans near Padierna were using ran from San Angel to Coyoacán and then met the road that retreating Mexican forces from San Antonio were using before crossing a bridge at Churubusco, near the monastery of San Mateo Churubusco. As the Mexican forces converged there, this became a chaotic scene, but it also represented a chokepoint for the American pursuit, and in the previous days, as Santa Anna pondered Scott's moves and wrangled with Valencia, he had clearly thought about how to protect a possible retreat. He had already posted forces in an earthwork fortification at the bridge and at the stonewalled monastery. Now that the crisis was upon them, Santa Anna augmented them with fresh troops and artillery. Their task was simple: to hold off the Americans while the Mexican army retreated. It was a task they accomplished much better than Santa Anna could have dared to hope. As the disorganized Americans followed the road, they collided with this strongpoint in a shockingly violent battle.

The troops defending the small fort by the bridge, mostly regulars, held their position for hours, using cannon and muskets to beat back American assaults through the cornfields and causing them hundreds of casualties. American regular C. M. Reeves described how he sought to pull a wounded soldier out of a muddy ditch only to see the man struck and killed by another bullet before his eyes. The action just to the east at the monastery followed the same pattern. The Mexican troops had a slight advantage of position and enough determination to hold it. In the words of one Mexican, "The Yankees died like ants." The pursuit had been stopped by obstinate resistance. American commanders kept pushing more men into the fight, and Scott sent others to cross another bridge and try to cut the road to the city farther north. This force made its way to the road at the hacienda of Portales only to be confronted by units that Santa Anna had placed there precisely to stop this kind of flanking attack. Here the American commander on the spot was ashamed to see his volunteer troops take cover and refuse to advance under fire. Meanwhile, as precious minutes became an hour, and then that hour stretched into three hours, the rest of the Mexican army was making its way up the road toward Mexico City, taking with it many of its cannon and much of its precious ammunition.

Eventually the Mexican firing slackened as their muskets broke or they simply ran out of ammunition. American forces were able to approach first the bridge and then the convent. As they did so, some of their opponents retreated up the road, while others stayed to fire their last shots or resist with bayonets and swords. American soldiers finally broke into the convent, but hand-to-hand fighting continued inside until American captain James Smith began waving a white flag to stop his men from continuing to slaughter the penned-up enemy. The Americans had won, but at enormous cost. Almost

140 were killed, and nearly 900 were wounded. For once the Americans had attacked without careful scouting and analysis, and this had led them to collide with a heavily defended position. The Mexicans also paid heavily, with perhaps twice as many killed and also many wounded. Almost 2,000 Mexicans were captured. However, the battle's most important result was the preservation of the Mexican army. The resistance at the bridge, the convent, and the hacienda of Portales had prevented the Americans from destroying the retreating army and marching directly into Mexico City. Scott was able to send a few mounted men up the road, and some even reached the next defense line, but they were quickly repelled and did not represent a significant threat to the city.[30]

The rear guard that fought so well at the bridge and convent of Churubusco actually was a microcosm of the kinds of forces Santa Anna had gathered to defend Mexico City. It is not clear how Santa Anna chose whom to post there: it is possible that he simply picked units that were nearby and still relatively organized, although some suspect that he chose units that he was willing to sacrifice.[31] The bridge and the river near it were defended by a brigade of Mexican regulars, who, as we have seen, were mostly conscripts, men chosen to serve because they were not responsible patriarchs. These were men that even other poor Mexicans looked down on, but the training and discipline imposed by their officers and sergeants, combined with their feelings for each other, made them potent foes on the battlefield. Notably, relatively few of these men were captured at Churubusco. Most who were not killed or wounded joined the Mexican army in its successful retreat. Perhaps the relatively experienced regular officers knew how to judge when they had bought their comrades enough time to retreat, how to estimate when their ammunition would run out, and how to extricate their soldiers from the fight at the last minute. The defenders of the convent were different. One group deployed there were National Guardsmen from what is now Guerrero.[32] Most of the men, however, came from two more famous groups. The first were the moderate federalist National Guardsmen of the Bravos and Independencia Battalions. These battalions were actually composed of artisans, so they were not as wealthy as some moderate units, but they had participated in the rebellion against Valentín Gómez Farías out of fear of his radical politics and loyalty to the church. Now they had been called on to fight the Americans, and they had done so with great courage if not ter-rific skill. At one point in the fight, the National Guardsmen posted on the roof of the monastery were aiming their muskets so badly that they were killing comrades stationed outside. When the latter complained, command-ers removed all troops from the roof. Still, these battalions caused terrible casualties among the Americans, and they fought until they were completely out of ammunition and even beyond.[33]

The other unit defending the convent contained only around two hundred men, roughly 1 percent of the force that Santa Anna had gathered to defend Mexico City, but it was the most famous group to fight in this war. It was called the Saint Patrick's Battalion or *san patricios,* and most of its members were men who had formerly been in the American army.[34] This was not the first battle in which such men faced their former comrades: small units of san patricios had fought at Monterrey and La Angostura in the north, mostly as artillerymen. Here, however, a larger group was deployed, mostly as infantry. They fought desperately, partially because they knew that capture would bring execution. Moreover, they resisted to the end, and they were the last to have ammunition because the only resupply the defenders received during the battle did not fit the muskets of the Bravos and Independencia Battalions but did fit those of the san patricios. When Mexican National Guardsmen, having run out of ammunition, tried to raise a white flag, some san patricios stopped them. Although some san patricios escaped when the convent fell, more than 60 percent were either killed or captured there. American soldiers there that day claimed that the san patricios took particular aim at American officers, who had earned their hatred with the harsh discipline these soldiers had experienced in the American army.[35] The story of these couple of hundred men is so striking that it has been interpreted by scholarly books, popular histories, novels, a feature film, and a musical album by American roots musi-cian Ry Cooder and Irish folk popularizers the Chieftains.[36]

The San Patricios

The motivations of the san patricios are very difficult to ascertain with any certainty, partially because most were illiterate; partially because when some of them spoke directly about their motivations, they were on trial for their lives or in other settings in which they clearly shaped their words to appeal to specific audiences; and partially because so many different kinds of people have tried to understand the san patricios and use their story to make their own arguments about national identity. Nevertheless, what we can ascertain about them from reading the available documents in the context of European, American, and Mexican social history tells us much about this war, the experience of nineteenth-century impoverished people, and efforts to form national states in both Mexico and the United States.

How did men who had once been in the American army come to fight for the Mexicans? We must begin with how they departed the American army. All the san patricios we can identify as former soldiers in the American army had served in the regular army, not the volunteer regiments. We can presume that, like most regular army enlisted men, they enlisted for economic reasons. As we have seen, the peacetime regular army experienced much desertion, and this pattern continued during the war. In March 1846, when Zachary Taylor's army reached the Rio Grande opposite Matamoros, so many regular soldiers began deserting and swimming across the river that Taylor felt compelled to order sentries to kill anyone making the attempt. Regular army soldiers continued to desert in substantial numbers throughout the war, leaving both Taylor's forces in the north and Scott's forces in the center of the country. Many men who deserted were not native-born Americans: roughly 40 percent of regular army men were foreigners, typically Irish or German immigrants who had enlisted in eastern cities.[37]

Why did these men desert? American nativism was undoubtedly part of the story. Many Americans despised immigrants, especially Catholic immigrants. The mostly Protestant officers of the regular army sometimes pressured immigrant soldiers to attend Protestant services, and they sometimes subjected immigrants to more than their share of the physically harsh and sometimes arbitrary punishments that were a routine part of regular army life.[38] Reeves, a regular army enlisted man, wrote of Matamoros that "a great many men Deserted from the army at this place, it was caused in great degree by certain inducements held out, by the Mexicans, and those men that were easy gulled, and that doubtless had been ill used by their officers in some instances."[39] Here we notice another development that helps us make sense of the san patricios: Mexican authorities were very aware of the discontent in the American regular army, and they sought to take advantage of it by increasing the incentives to desert.[40] Throughout the conflict they worked to encourage regular army soldiers to leave the American ranks. Some of this encouragement was oral: the Mexican authorities reached out to regular soldiers through both Mexican and foreign civilians in territories occupied by the Americans. However, the Mexicans also composed many documents that they distributed surreptitiously in the American ranks.

Some of these documents only encouraged desertion, but others offered additional benefits to men who also agreed to join the Mexican army. These documents are by no means direct evidence of the motivations of deserters. However, they were not produced in a vacuum: Mexican authorities interrogated deserters about their own motives and the beliefs of other soldiers, and they used the information obtained to craft messages encouraging desertion. They knew, for instance, that many of those likely to desert were foreigners. Almost immediately after the arrival of Taylor on the Rio Grande, General Pedro de Ampudia sent an English-language handbill across the river addressing the foreigners in Taylor's army and offering deserters good treatment and economic support.[41] Ampudia's handbill did not mention the possibility that deserters might enlist in the Mexican army but stated that they would be sent south to Mexico City. Ampudia's successor as commander at Matamoros, Mariano Arista, followed with a second leaflet. He wrote that the foreigners had enlisted in the American army in peacetime and now were being required to fight in an unjust war against a powerful nation that would surely defeat them. The leaflet offered them land and the opportunity to become Mexican citizens if they deserted, but again there was no mention of enlistment in the Mexican army.[42] Only later, in September 1846, as the Americans approached Monterrey, did the Mexicans publicly address the possibility that foreign soldiers might want to fight for the Mexican army by offering to let them keep whatever rank they held for the Americans.[43] Later, rumors surfaced that men who agreed to fight for Mexico would also receive bonuses and promotions.[44] Still, more consistently Mexican authorities offered a chance to make a living as civilians in Mexico. After Cerro Gordo, Santa Anna offered deserters who wanted to serve in the Mexican army the chance to do so, but he also offered all deserters cash bonuses and land. In June 1847 Alvarez wrote an appeal that was translated into German and distributed in Puebla. He also offered economic support for deserters and said that those who wanted to stay in Mexico would be given enough land to make a decent living.[45]

Mexican authorities sometimes made more ideological appeals. These arguments were probably also informed by conversations with deserters. Handbills pointed out that the Americans were engaged in an aggressive land grab that sought to enslave Mexico. The vision of justice presented in such handbills was explicitly related to religion. The aggressive war was criticized on religious grounds, and the writers specifically directed the appeals to Catholic soldiers. In June 1847 Juan Soto, governor of Veracruz, stated that Catholic Irish, French, and German soldiers in the American army should not kill Catholic Mexicans and vice versa. He ended his appeal with the slogan "Long Live Our Holy Religion!" John Riley, the leader of the san patricios, wrote to potential deserters that Irishmen loved liberty and that Mexicans were fighting for the same holy religion loved by the Irish. In April 1847 Santa Anna himself also explicitly appealed to the Irish, stating that "our religion is the strongest of bonds" and criticizing both the nativist burning of Catholic churches in the United States and the crimes American volunteers committed against Catholic churches in Mexico.[46]

Public appeals were accompanied by the clandestine work of shopkeepers, priests, and German or Irish residents in the territories occupied by the Americans. These efforts irked American officers. Several men were tried in American military courts for soliciting desertion and distributing the handbills to soldiers. Soldiers in the American army were alert to the possibility, and some tried to curry favor with their superiors by reporting these efforts, sometimes with comical results.[47] Efforts to prevent desertion were motivated by the problem's persistence in the face of repeated American victories. Throughout the war, a steady stream of soldiers from the U.S. regular army left their units and turned themselves in to Mexican authorities. They continued to do so in the north, and they also deserted from Scott's army as it slowly made its way from Veracruz to the Valley of Mexico. Others deserted from the U.S. Navy landing forces that attacked ports, or its ships as they sailed near the shore. It is impossible to determine exactly how many men passed into Mexican-held territory this way, but clearly hundreds took this step. When Mexican officials asked them why they deserted, some spoke of their desire not to fight against Catholics, others of the financial incentives offered by the Mexicans, and others of not being paid regularly. Most also mentioned the harsh discipline imposed in American service.[48] As early as November 1845, with Taylor still at Corpus Christi, Mexican authorities anticipated this desertion. They ordered civilians and guerrillas to treat deserters well and forward them to the nearest unoccupied town. There local officials fed them, gave them safe-conduct passes, and sent them on, typically in groups with Mexican escorts to show them the way and prevent friction with Mexican civilians. Many deserters passed all the way from the Rio Grande to Mexico City, and then sometimes on to other destinations in Mexico.[49] At any moment in the war, there were probably dozens of deserters making these pilgrimages across the Mexican landscape. What did they see as their goal, and how did some of them end up at Churubusco?

Some joined the Mexican army soon after leaving their American units. The Mexican regular army, like its American counterpart, had a long tradition of welcoming foreigners into its ranks. In fact, this was typical of many early modern professional armies: military service was not culturally associated with citizenship but instead with employment. Even in peacetime soldiers often deserted the American army, especially when they felt that the explicit or implicit promises made when they were recruited were violated. They had a sort of contractual view of military service. Thus, if a soldier left the American army and was offered better pay or conditions in its Mexican counterpart, it made sense to accept. When we add this to the religious and ideological factors cited previously, we should not be surprised that some of the men who were being passed from village to village in Mexico sought to join the Mexican army.[50] Although there is no evidence that deserters from the American army fought with the Mexicans at Palo Alto or Resaca de Palma, the documents indicate that a substantial number served with the Mexicans at Monterrey, especially as artillerymen. When the Mexican army retreated from Monterrey, American witnesses saw several of these men march with them.[51] The army that Santa Anna built up in San Luis Potosí in the fall of 1846 included an artillery unit composed of more than one hundred deserters. They crossed the desert to La Angostura and caused significant American casualties. Twenty-two members of the unit were wounded and six killed at that battle, and the Mexican army decorated them for their bravery and effectiveness. At this point the deserters were in a defined unit, with a green unit flag sewn by the nuns of San Luis Potosí.[52] After the battle Taylor's forces captured at least three of them. Samuel Chamberlain reports that Taylor decided that the worst possible punishment was to send them back to the Mexican army, while Isaac Smith says that they were imprisoned. Military court records indicate that Isaac Maxfield was first sentenced to death but then instead dishonorably discharged, while John Gomery was whipped and imprisoned for the remainder of his enlistment.[53]

Chamberlain's colorful comment points to one of the problems that shaped the experience of the san patricios, along with that of all men of the Mexican army: the government lacked the financial resources needed to adequately pay, feed, and clothe the men. William Carpenter, after seeing the group march past him as they left Monterrey, pointed out that in the American army they had been well paid and fed, but in the Mexican army they were "ragged and dirty, not half paid, and still worse fed."[54] Conditions were particularly bad on the retreat from La Angostura, and some of the men who served there decided they were done with armies. This option was not open to their Mexican or even American colleagues, but apparently when they had signed up, the foreigners made a verbal agreement that only obligated three months' service. However, Mexico had a desperate need for manpower, and undoubtedly the agreement was so out of line with standard practice that army bureaucrats were reluctant to honor it. Sixty of the men turned to John Davis, the British consul in San Luis Potosí. They believed that as Irishmen they were British subjects entitled to his help, and when he told them that by serving in the American army they had given up that right, they replied bitterly that "a poor Irishman cannot get bread in his own country, or protection in a foreign." After consulting his superiors, Davis intervened with Mexican authorities, who released the men from service in June 1847.[55]

What alternatives were available for deserters who either never joined the Mexican army or only served in it temporarily? Oddly, at least ten of the Irishmen who had left the Mexican army after La Angostura joined a Mexican guerrilla force in northern Mexico. Apparently, serving in a guerrilla force was a more attractive option than serving in the Mexican regular army, with its scanty food and pay. This force, however, extorted goods and money from Mexicans whom it claimed traded illegally with the Americans, and it was disbanded after a few weeks.[56] A few men also served in a special force that protected commercial traffic near Mexico City from bandits.[57] However, most of the men released from Mexican service and most of the hundreds of other deserters who did not immediately join the Mexican army sought to work as civilians in Mexico. George Cook and Henry McLean, for instance, told authorities that "they were artisans and they only wanted to work at their trades."[58] These men left impoverished areas of Europe for the United States to try to better their economic situation. They had found the economic opportunities in the eastern United States to be very limited, and thus had heeded the call of American army recruiters. The steady pay, decent clothing, regular food, and shelter offered by recruiters were attractive by themselves, but many of these men undoubtedly knew that it was common for men to join the army in the East and then desert after they were transported to the frontier, where a laboring man might make a decent living. We cannot be sure that they believed that life in Mexico also offered that kind of opportunity, but we do know that Mexican authorities deliberately sought to convince potential deserters of this.

Mexican authorities also tried to help make it happen. The system through which they passed the men from village to village funneled them toward places where they might find employment, especially San Luis Potosí, Mexico City, or the state of Hidalgo. In the last, English investors had bought several mines and imported English mineworkers to help run them, and in fact there were so many Englishmen at Mineral del Monte, Hidalgo, that American officer Daniel Harvey Hill described it as "an English town with English houses, English manners and customs." This also seems to be where Davis sent the men he helped leave the Mexican army.[59] Many deserters worked at least for a while at various trades in San Luis Potosí, Mexico City, or Hidalgo, and Herman Schmidt even opened a school in Guadalajara.[60] However, there was a large problem with any trajectory that took an impoverished man from Ireland or Germany to the eastern United States, to the American army, and then to Mexico. The last place was the one with the least productive economy and the lowest wages. Even working-class foreigners were not accustomed to living in such poverty, and the deserters were at a huge disadvantage without the extended families that poor Mexicans relied on as a social safety net and source of the information and favors that allowed a decent living. Carpenter, an escaped prisoner of war who traveled through Mexico posing as a deserter, trying various ways of making a living, explained that "work could not be had at prices that would keep soul and body together."[61]

By June 1847 there were many deserters from the American army in Mexico City. The Mexican authorities had funneled them in from Matamoros, Monterrey, Saltillo, and Tampico in the north, and from Veracruz and Puebla in the east. As the American army prepared to march to Mexico City, these men knew that if they were captured, they faced severe punishment. Some former American soldiers in the city saw themselves more as prisoners of war than deserters. They had been picked up by Mexican authorities after they wandered from their units, typically on drinking sprees, and also funneled to Mexico City. Yet they, too, feared American military justice. Men missing for a few hours or even days typically would have been punished lightly, but weeks of absence in enemy hands was a more serious matter. Moreover, as the American army neared, the common people of Mexico City were inclined to see these foreigners less as curiosities and more as hated enemies. This made it harder for them to move about the city. Mexican military authorities had housed the men and provided money for food, but continuing fiscal problems and the new crisis that approached led the government to devote all funds to building an army to defend the city. Months earlier the government had stopped paying civilian government employees, and now it could no longer afford to support the deserters. Finally, the deserters themselves also represented a potential source of manpower for that army. Both deserters and American prisoners of war were often offered a chance to serve in the Mexican army. Now those in Mexico City were told that the government would only feed them if they joined.[62]

The pressure to join the Mexican army increased when the existing unit of san patricios arrived in June 1847. Although some sources indicate that they were at Cerro Gordo, these reports seem to confuse them with a separate group of Irish civilians who marched with Santa Anna to Veracruz to help the wounded. The san patricios stayed in San Luis Potosí until June 1847 and marched with Valencia's Army of the North to the Valley of Mexico. At this point there were only fifty or so left, the men who did not want to leave the Mexican army after La Angostura.[63] This small group soon grew again, and eventually it was officially reconstituted as an infantry unit called the

Foreign Legion or the Companies of Saint Patrick.[64] Although an English-speaking Mexican officer named Francisco Moreno remained in command, the san patricios are most often associated with his second, the Irishman Riley. Riley and Moreno repeatedly visited the former American soldiers in Mexico City and tried to persuade them to join the san patricios. They undoubtedly spoke about the justice of the Mexican cause, but when the men later testified to American military authorities, they stressed the less positive sides of the pitch. They told the men that, regardless of how they came to be there, the Americans would execute them all as deserters, that food was only available to men in the Mexican army, and that putting on Mexican uniforms would allow them to pass through the streets of the city unmolested by the crowds. Some of the men also complained that Riley and Moreno beat them to get them to agree to serve. Notably, Riley was the officer who had tried to keep many san patricios in the unit in San Luis Potosí. As despicable as this coercion might seem to us, we have to keep it in context: it was very common for early modern armies to conscript men into their ranks, and that was how most men came to be in the Mexican regular army. Although Mexican authorities continued to extol the san patricios as an example of men who had chosen to fight for the just cause of Mexico, they also seem to have turned a blind eye to the efforts of Moreno and Riley to pressure men to join.[65]

Riley spelled his name various ways, and he was one of those larger-than-life characters whom contemporaries loved to talk about, often with scant information. We know that he was born in Ireland and, like many impoverished Irishmen, served in the British army, possibly in Canada. Later he immigrated to Michigan, and after working on Mackinac Island for a time, he enlisted in the U.S. Army's First Infantry there. This unit was soon sent to Texas, and it marched with Taylor to the Rio Grande opposite Matamoros. There, Riley, who had been an efficient and trusted soldier during his few months in the American army, deserted and became a lieutenant in the Mexican army.[66] At his trial he claimed that he was captured while attending Mass and joined the Mexican army because Mexican officers threatened to execute him.[67] This seems unlikely, and the Mexicans were not in the habit of using conscripted men as officers. Once in the Mexican ranks, Riley showed himself to be a skilled artillerist and an effective leader of former American soldiers, with whom he fought at Monterrey and later La Angostura. He also helped compose several of the handbills distributed to encourage desertion. He rose steadily to the rank of major, far higher than he could have risen in the American army. In a letter he wrote to his former employer in Michigan, Riley claimed to be a fighter for Irish freedom, boasting that the san patricios had fought under flag of "the glorious Emblem of native rights, that being the banner that should have floated over our native Soil many years ago, it was St. Patrick, the Harp of Erin, the Shamrock upon a green field."[68] In the rough-and-tumble, often hungry world of the floating, international proletariat that men like Riley belonged to, a man who aspired to higher status and pursued a lofty ideal like Irish independence could also easily be a man who used physical force to impose his will on others. He also might spin different tales to manipulate different audiences, something Riley did constantly.

When the captured san patricios were tried in American military courts, few admitted to willingly joining the Mexican army. Most said that they had been captured while temporarily absent from their units on drinking sprees, a very common occurrence for regular army soldiers, as we have seen.[69] Others said they had been out stealing Mexican livestock or hunting when they were captured. Some told simply of being compelled to join the san patricios. Others specified that they were beaten until they gave in, or explained that they were told they would only be released from prison if they agreed to fight for Mexico.[70] However, one of the most common motives mentioned, either alone or in conjunction with these other issues, was hunger. Many ran out of economic options after the Mexican government decided it could no longer devote any of its scarce resources to feeding these men unless they were willing to defend it. Some who were Irish and therefore British subjects sought help from the British consul, and for a while he was able to support them, but eventually his funds ran out. He was unable to give them money to leave for the mining districts or even Belize, which some considered to be a possible refuge. With these options off the table, service in the Mexican army seemed imperative. As James Doyle testified, he "was compelled by actual starvation to join."[71] In Mexico's impoverished economy, it would have been difficult for these men to find work even if the blockade and the invasion had not further slowed economic activity, but they also faced a more deadly challenge. In June Alexander McGrotty and William Dwire wrote to the British consul that they were "hourly subject to insults and in danger of assassination by the lower orders of the people."[72] John Welden, an Englishman who had served in the san patricios but had never been in the American army, was required to testify for the prosecution at the trials. He stated that former American soldiers who were in Mexico City "were generally maltreated and abused when they went into the streets. In fact, that was the reason why I myself joined." San patricio Roger Hogan testified that the men "could not go out into the streets for fear of being pelted and beaten, and in risk of being killed, if they went out in American clothing."[73] Several men tried to escape the deadly trap they were in by leaving the city, but the crowds beat them and they returned.[74] These international men, compelled by hunger to emigrate and later join the U.S. Army, were now compelled by hunger to join the Mexican army, with the particular irony that the growing national consciousness of some Mexicans helped make impossible any assimilation into the Mexican working class.

The problem is how to interpret the trial records. Even if these men had more ideological motives for fighting for Mexico, they knew that voicing them in these trials would have meant certain death. Of course they claimed that they never intended to desert and were compelled to fight against the Americans. Some likely opposed American nativism and anti-Catholicism or believed that service in the Mexican army would afford them what service in the U.S. Army would not: respect and the chance to eventually become honorable citizens. Thomas O'Connor, who was wounded at Churubusco but escaped capture, insisted that he had fought for Mexico because its cause was just in a letter asking Mexico's city council for funds to help him rejoin the Mexican army.[75] Others might have deserted the U.S. Army to escape its harsh discipline or seek better economic fortunes in Mexico, but they only joined the Mexican army when there seemed to be no other way to survive.[76] In the end the tales they told to the American military courts did not affect their fates. The vast majority were sentenced to hang after hasty trials. A handful escaped death because Scott commuted the sentence or, more often, on the technicality that they had deserted before the declaration of war. Ironically, Riley, the most notorious san patricio, was one of these. Those who escaped death were instead tortured and imprisoned. These harsh punishments were no doubt partially motivated by the American officers' hatred for the prisoners, but above all they were utilitarian. Scott's army was still bleeding men to desertion, and he wanted to reduce that hemorrhage by making an example of the san patricios.[77] Sixteen were executed in a mass hanging at San Angel on September 10 and twenty-nine were executed in another mass hanging in the nearby village of Mixcoac on September 13. This draconian example did not halt desertion from Scott's army. Men continued to desert, and some even joined the Mexican army, which reconstituted the unit of foreigners. This search for better options continued until the end of the war and beyond.[78]

From the first evidence of the san patricios' existence at the September 1846 Battle of Monterrey to their punishment almost a year later, soldiers from both the regular and the volunteer units commented often about them. Volunteers tended to view them particularly harshly, and they were also more likely to see them as traitors to their country than as traitors to their comrades. Kentucky volunteer William H. Daniel wrote that "they ought to be shot for any men that would desert and fight against their country death is too good for them." Carpenter, another Kentucky volunteer, called a san patricio he met "a disgrace to himself and his country." The volunteers who stormed Churubusco wanted to kill the san patricios on the spot. Jacob Oswandel reports that volunteers from his Pennsylvania unit disinterred the bodies of some executed san patricios, planning to sell their skulls in the United States.[79] Some regulars were equally harsh. Reeves reports vividly that a wounded san patricio was summarily killed after his former comrades found him on the battlefield, and Irish soldiers in the regular army are said to have particularly hated the san patricios because their disloyalty tainted all of the Irish in the army.[80] Yet some regulars acknowledged that both religion and harsh treatment may have motivated the san patricios to desert and fight for the Mexicans.[81]

Mexicans saw the san patricios very differently. Mexican officers and politicians were very aware that many foreigners in the American regular army had immigrated to the United States seeking economic opportunity and joined the peacetime army because it was difficult to make a living. They believed that these men, unlike volunteer soldiers, were not making war on Mexico willingly.[82] To a degree, the extensive efforts to convince Mexican civilians to help deserters were an effort to give these men an out. However,

Mexican propagandists never mentioned that hunger might also drive some deserters into the Mexican army or that, like other Mexican regulars, some might have even been compelled to serve. Mexican authors instead saw the service of the san patricios in a different light, writing that these men had joined the Mexican forces to defend Catholicism or because they believed that the Mexican cause was just. In fact, the san patricios were played up in Mexican propaganda precisely to highlight the justice of the Mexican cause and the importance of defending Catholicism.[83] How much did common Mexicans believe this? The best evidence about popular attitudes toward the san patricios is provided by Carpenter, an escaped American prisoner of war who often pretended to be an Irish san patricio. Although he occasionally ran into some resentment, generally common people and local authorities went out of their way to help him when he was posing as a san patricio, because, in his words, they believed that the san patricios "had fought in defense of their country and religion."[84] This version of their motivations became even more well known after the war, and it drives the commemorations that still take place annually in Mexico and Ireland. It also drove the strenuous efforts that Mexican authorities and civilians made to aid the san patricios after their capture. Efforts to prevent the executions failed, but Mexicans, and particularly Mexican women, still sought to help the san patricios who escaped execution, especially by bringing them food, something they did not do for the prisoners of war from the Mexican regular army who were held along with them. When asked about this care for the san patricios, one of these ladies told Hill that "they had fought for her country and now they were prisoners in a strange land." One of these san patricios even escaped, disguised as one of the women who had come to give the group succor.[85] Whether or not they were ideologically motivated, the surviving san patricios benefited from being seen as people who had voluntarily fought for Mexico's cause.

They had varied fates after Churubusco. Those who had been captured but not executed were whipped, branded on their faces with the letter D for "deserter," forced to perform hard labor, and made to wear iron collars with protruding spikes that would not allow them to lie down to sleep comfortably for the nine months that the war continued. After their June 1848 release, some, including Riley, returned to the Mexican army, while others left Mexico for parts unknown. Continued service in the Mexican army, however, kept them in a force that reverted to its more politicized ways of the past. Soon they were suspected of involvement in an attempted coup, and after some of their officers were arrested, many of the men mutinied and disbanded. Riley retired from the Mexican army in 1850 and was awarded a pension. At that point he faded from the records. Various san patricios and foreigners claiming to have been san patricios stayed in Mexico for at least a year or two after the war, working or relying on the kindness of Mexicans who still felt a debt of gratitude.[86]

The san patricios have been interpreted many ways in recent years, and there is general agreement that no single motivation drove their actions.[87] Still, what the case brings out more than anything are the extremely limited choices faced by laboring people in Europe, the United States, and Mexico. This lack of choices forced people to move from country to country, region to region, and even job to job. In this way the san patricios were more than anything soldiers of the noncitizen variety common in the early modern world and represented in this war by both the Mexican and the American regular armies.[88] However, neither American nor Mexican intellectuals were comfortable with the fact that many of the men who spilled blood in this struggle between nascent nation-states were not motivated by national identity. This led many Americans to call the san patricios traitors to the nation and many Mexicans to see them as heroes of a just cause. It is this uncomfortable fit between how the san patricios and other regular soldiers came to be in armies and the perception that this was a war between nation-states that drives fascination with them even today.[89]

CHAPTER 7

The People of the Town
Were Firing

The Americans had mixed feelings about the Battles of Padierna and Churubusco. Padierna had clearly been a victory for the Americans and a disaster for the Mexicans. Some American officers wanted to see Churubusco in similarly positive terms, but the fact that the Mexican army had escaped prevented them from doing that. In describing both battles, the Americans dramatically exaggerated the number of Mexican troops actually engaged, and they often failed to mention that they were only able to overcome the Mexicans at Churubusco because the defenders ran out of ammunition. They also praised the courage of Mexican rank-and-file soldiers at both battles.[1] A cynic might suggest that American officers did these things in order to emphasize their own prowess and courage. In any event, Winfield Scott did not immediately attempt to follow up on what his troops had achieved. It is hard to see how he could have: his men had taken severe casualties, they were exhausted and disorganized, they had little food immediately available, and Antonio López de Santa Anna had successfully pulled back to his secondary defense line, which cleverly used the lakes and flooded fields to force the Americans to take on fortified and garrisoned strongpoints. Scott might quickly face another Churubusco if he pressed on, and his small army could not continue to take those kinds of casualties.

At this point Scott and Santa Anna were both amenable to a pause in operations, and they quickly formalized this pause with an explicit armistice. As historian Timothy Johnson argues, Scott's goal in this campaign was to bring the Mexicans to negotiate a peace that granted the James K. Polk administration what it wanted. An armistice would allow negotiations. Santa Anna was also interested in one. Although he had pulled back most of his soldiers to his secondary defense line, he had lost almost half of his cannon, as well as many men. Moreover, his secondary line had not yet been fortified much because Mexican officers had put most of their effort into fortifying the approach through El Peñon that Scott had avoided. Time was a precious commodity, and the armistice bought it. Santa Anna may also have believed that the Americans might actually offer peace terms that were politically acceptable.[2]

Polk had sent Nicholas Trist to negotiate an end to the war. During the armistice Trist met several times with Mexican representatives. In their discussions, representatives for both sides presented compromises that exceeded the instructions given by their governments, but they still remained far apart. The Mexican commissioners were willing to recognize American sovereignty over Texas but would not concede that the strip of land between the Nueces and Rio Grande was part of Texas. Trist agreed to submit the question to Polk, but that alone would have been enough to kill the agreement: Polk had to insist that this territory was part of Texas because his strongest justification for the war was that American blood shed there had been shed on American soil. Surprisingly, Mexican representatives were willing to grant the Americans most of New Mexico and California in exchange for an indemnity and guarantees for Mexican residents there. However, when this compromise was presented to the Mexican cabinet, its members rejected it, and after a stormy cabinet meeting they convinced Santa Anna to continue the war instead. Mexican politicians who opposed ceding territory were still too powerful, something that made some Americans believe that Santa Anna had only used the negotiations to play for time, making the Americans his dupes once again.[3]

Both Santa Anna and Scott used the armistice to strengthen the position of their forces. Santa Anna continued to fortify his secondary defense line, while Scott's army brought units up to strength and studied those new defenses. Scott's efforts to improve his situation led to an incident that if anything strengthened Santa Anna's determination to keep fighting. The terms of the armistice allowed the American army to buy food in the city, so American quartermasters sent a train of over one hundred wagons to pick this food up. The wagons were driven by civilian teamsters who worked for the U.S. Army. Many were former volunteer soldiers who had been hired after completing their military service. Others were immigrants who had been hired in port cities in the United States. Generally the teamsters were a rowdy lot, and they sometimes committed crimes against Mexicans. Scott warned Mexican officials that the teamsters might misbehave once they were among the civilians of the city.[4]

The teamsters drove their wagons right into the center of the city, where Mexicans of various social classes frequented open-air markets. Although the armistice gave them the right to do this, no Mexican official was notified on the day the Americans decided to pick up the supplies, and the inhabitants who suddenly saw this group roll into the city were astounded. Some began to shout that these teamsters were the vanguard of the American army, and that Santa Anna had betrayed the city by allowing the Americans to enter. Crowds gathered and violence broke out. Some said the violence started when the teamsters did not show proper respect to a religious procession carrying the Holy Eucharist. First boys and then women began to stone the teamsters. A woman who had a lost a son in a recent battle threw a stone and wounded a teamster. When the police grabbed her, she screamed that she was trying to kill him, and that she "would kill them all, because it was their fault that she had lost her poor son, and now instead of taking revenge, we are supposed to let them come and get food, this is very unjust." Up to thirty thousand people, more than 10 percent of the city's population, surrounded the teamsters, throwing stones and jeering. Two teamsters were killed. Fortunately for the teamsters, the commercial area where this took place was adjacent to the city hall and the national palace. First municipal police and then Mexican troops intervened to try to save the teamsters. General José Maria Tornel, the appointed governor of the city and, ironically, one of the fiercest advocates for fighting the Americans, tried to calm the crowds without effect. Their furor did not begin to die out until former president José Joaquín de Herrera waded into the crowd, shouting that they should be brave in battle but humane toward defenseless men like the teamsters. Although he was a moderate federalist and hardly a rabble-rouser, Herrera succeeded in saving most of the teamsters by appealing to the honor and humanity of these poor Mexicans. Note, however, that he implied that these Mexican civilians would later have their day of battle.[5]

By September 6 Scott believed that the armistice no longer served the interests of the American army. He wrote to Santa Anna that the Mexicans had violated it by impeding his army's acquisition of food and continuing to fortify the city. Santa Anna in turn accused the Americans of violating the armistice by not allowing mills in areas they controlled to send flour to the city and by completing fortifications themselves. He added that reports indicated that American soldiers were robbing churches, committing sacrilege, and raping women.[6] It seems likely that by September 6 both generals had gotten all they could hope for out of the pause. The American troops were now well rested and fed, and Scott had developed some ideas about how to defeat Santa Anna's new defense line. Mexican officers had reorganized their forces, they had been reassured that their defense still had popular support, and they had established a solid line of defense. Ulysses S. Grant described these defenses as very strong. The Americans would have to approach the city along causeways bordered by flooded fields and fortified at various points.[7] Flanking attacks were impossible, and frontal attacks would be costly.

After considering a frontal attack using the Niño Perdido and San Antonio roads from the south, Scott became nervous about the increasing strength of the defenses on these causeways and decided to try something else. Farther west the ground was drier, and Scott had heard that a flour mill there had been turned into a cannon foundry. Dismissing the qualms of officers who believed that his information was badly outdated, Scott ordered a frontal attack on the Molino del Rey and the Casa Mata, a nearby stone building. More than 3,500 American troops moved forward in the early morning hours of September 8. Their supporting cannon fired a few rounds, but when no one shot back the Americans advanced, thinking that the buildings were undefended. They could not have been more incorrect. Santa Anna had considered the possibility that Scott would try to flank the watery southern approaches of the city, and he had posted a number of cannon and thousands of infantrymen to block this move. The Mexicans included Antonio de León's Oaxacan peasant National Guardsmen, Mexico City National Guardsmen from both radical and moderate units, and regulars. These men stayed under cover and held their fire until the Americans were in killing range. The attacking Americans were decimated by cannon fire and musketry. When they faltered and retreated, Mexican infantry counterattacked, pressing the American retreat and in some cases finishing off American wounded. More American troops were sent forward, and at great cost they were able to push the Mexican infantry back to their defenses. As the battle raged, the Mexican muskets began to break down or become too fouled with gunpowder residue to be fired, and ammunition ran short. The Americans broke into the complex of buildings but still had to fight room by room to clear them. C. M. Reeves, who survived this close-quarter fighting, stated that the Mexicans "stood to their mark manfully, the fact is the Mexicans at this battle fought most desperately." After several hours of harsh fighting, the Americans took the buildings, which they found were not being used to make cannon and were actually a military liability that could not be adequately garrisoned by Scott's ever-shrinking army.[8]

To the degree to which the Battle of Molino del Rey was an American victory, it was a Pyrrhic one. One hundred and sixteen Americans, including many officers, had been killed and more than six hundred had been wounded in a pointless battle. Scott had acted on incorrect intelligence over the objections of some of his officers, the Americans had not ascertained the strength of the Mexican defenses before committing themselves, and they had attacked an entrenched Mexican force without any significant use of artillery to soften up the defense. The result was a demoralizing disaster for the Americans. However, the skill and courage shown by Mexican officers and men were not enough to make this battle a Mexican victory. They lost all the cannon they had on the scene, their infantry took severe casualties, and they were also demoralized after the battle. The Mexican commander, León, and various other National Guard officers were killed. Moreover, if Molino del Rey showed a dysfunctional American command structure, its Mexican army counterpart probably performed worse. In fact, at Molino del Rey the Mexican army lost an opportunity to follow up on its initial success and break the retreating American soldiers. The story of how this happened can tell us much about both the Mexican military and Mexican society.

Cavalry was the most expensive branch of early modern armies because horses were both costly and fragile, and they had to be fed constantly. Most armies considered it to be the most prestigious arm, and cavalry officers were often both well born and well heeled, but cavalrymen were of limited utility on the gunpowder-age battlefield. They were useful for scouting and pursuing

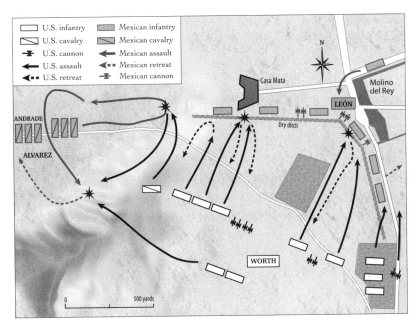

Legend:
- U.S. infantry
- U.S. cavalry
- U.S. cannon
- U.S. assault
- U.S. retreat
- Mexican infantry
- Mexican cavalry
- Mexican assault
- Mexican retreat
- Mexican cannon

ANDRADE
ALVAREZ
Casa Mata
Dry ditch
LEÓN
Molino del Rey
WORTH
N
0   500 yards

MAP 13 Battle of Molino del Rey

defeated and disorganized enemies, but disciplined and organized infantry nearly always could defeat cavalry because horses were large enough to be extremely vulnerable to even inaccurate smoothbore muskets. Moreover, horses tended to sensibly see any cohesive mass of men holding bayonet-tipped muskets as a dangerous obstacle that they should not charge into. In military doctrine cavalry units were only supposed to attack when opposing infantry were too disorganized to present a solid front, typically when they were retreating in disorder after a clash with another unit. Santa Anna had pulled together most of the cavalry in the regular army, and in the initial campaigning he had used them to observe American movements. Perhaps because this role required cooperation with guerrillas, he had put the cavalry under the command of Juan Alvarez, a former independence leader from present-day Guerrero. Alvarez was a radical federalist who had been particularly successful in bringing mulatto and indigenous peasants into federalism by offering both tangible benefits and ways to see their cultural and social desires as compatible with a more democratic and egalitarian Mexico.

Alvarez, however, was not a cavalryman, although wounds from the independence war prevented him from walking without crutches and therefore he spent more time on horseback than many officers.

When Santa Anna came to believe that the Americans would attack the western approaches of the city, he stationed several divisions of Mexican cavalry at a hacienda a short distance away, with orders to take advantage of any opportunity for an effective cavalry attack. Both the hacienda and fields through which the Americans attacked were mostly dry and free of obstacles and thus relatively good terrain for cavalry, but the two locations were separated by a deep ravine and there was only one spot where its slopes were gentle enough to allow horses to cross it. To make an attack, the Mexican troopers would have to pass through this narrow space in columns and then re-form on the Molino del Rey side. During their transit they would be very vulnerable to American cannon. As the Americans retreated after their initial assault, Alvarez seized the moment and ordered his three divisions to deploy. Two did so, but one, commanded by cavalry general Manuel Andrade, did not move despite repeated orders. As the golden moment in which a cavalry attack would have been devastating for the retreating Americans passed by, the Americans realized the danger and redirected their cannon to fire on the Mexican cavalrymen who awaited the order to charge. Soon it was too late. A frustrated Alvarez relieved Andrade of his command.

Why did Andrade not follow orders? Some believed that he was simply a coward, while some regular army officers believed that Alvarez had failed because he did not understand how to handle cavalry. There is significant evidence, however, that something deeper was at play. Alvarez had hinted in earlier correspondence that Andrade was inept and did not work to keep his men well fed enough to prevent desertion. Moreover, the day before the battle, Andrade had refused another order from Alvarez, saying that he did not recognize Alvarez's right to give him orders, in a manner that made Alvarez understand that Andrade considered him a social inferior. Alvarez was not poor, but he was racially mixed and widely reputed among Mexico's elite to be a mulatto in an era in which elite Mexicans considered people with African blood to be stupid and savage. When Andrade was later forced to defend his behavior in military court, he ridiculed Alvarez, calling him stupid and incompetent. It is hard to say whether Alvarez bore some responsibility for missing the moment. However, Santa Anna definitely blamed Andrade, which is striking because Santa Anna had long been identified with the regular army officer corps and Alvarez was a political enemy who had helped remove Santa Anna from the presidency just a few years before. When Andrade reported to him after the battle, Santa Anna stripped off the insignia of Andrade's rank and slapped him across the face with them. Moreover, a little more than a month later, the officers of Andrade's own regiment accused him of seeking a safe place where the regiment could avoid the Americans but still draw its pay. These officers stated that Andrade had shown himself a coward several times during the war.[9] Clearly Andrade had not won the respect of many of his regular army peers.

Oddly, after the Battle of Molino del Rey, both armies were less well off. The Americans had taken severe casualties and had not opened any approach around the defended causeways that worried Scott. The Mexicans had also taken severe casualties, and their morale was weakening. The Mexican army, with its diverse origins and social groupings, its inferior weaponry, and its poverty, had survived defeat after defeat, but now it was just barely hanging on. The units shattered at Molino del Rey could not be quickly reconstituted, and Santa Anna had a limited number of effective units to cover the various approaches the Americans might take. He could only try to ascertain where Scott would attack next, and move troops through the streets of the city to meet the threat. Meanwhile, American officers scouted and discussed different possibilities. The southern approaches were more direct, but Santa Anna had stationed many troops there and hundreds of laborers continued to build fortifications for them. Two other causeways entered the city from the west, but they were dominated by Chapultepec, a short hill topped by a large stone mansion that housed Mexico's military academy. To use the western approaches, the Americans would first have to take Chapultepec and then fight the Mexican troops defending the causeways. Scott still found this approach more attractive, partly because the ground was drier, making it easier to position cannon to soften up Mexican defenses and support an attack. Eventually he decided to try there.[10]

Attacking Chapultepec would seem to hold the same dangers that had led to so many American casualties at Molino del Rey, Churubusco, Cerro Gordo, and Monterrey. Mexican troops had repeatedly shown themselves to be tenacious and effective when defending fortified positions. Even a little cover seemed to give them confidence, and even relatively weak walls or shallow trenches gave them protection against the light artillery the Americans had used to break the coherence of Mexican units in the open field at Palo Alto and La Angostura. More cynically, one suspects that junior officers and sergeants found it easier to prevent desertion when their men were in enclosed positions, and that it was more difficult for fleeing men to elude the eyes of their comrades in these situations. In any event, Scott and his officers decided to approach Chapultepec very differently. They constructed positions for their heaviest guns, the ones used to break down fortified positions. They then used those guns to batter the hill, the building, and their defenders for a whole day before attempting an assault. Scott also sent a portion of his troops to feign an attack on the southern causeways.

These preparations were effective. Santa Anna, without enough troops to effectively defend both Chapultepec and the southern causeways, spent most of the crucial hours just before and during the American attack on Chapultepec convinced that it was a feint and that the real American effort would be in the south. By the time he sought to reinforce the troops defending the hill, it was too late. Moreover, Chapultepec, despite the imposing sight of the stone building perched on a steep hill, was not that strong a position. Although both Americans and Mexicans referred to it as a castle, it was a stone mansion built in the eighteenth century as a residence. Stone, as we have seen before, was easy for nineteenth-century heavy artillery to break. The Mexicans had made sporadic efforts to make it defensible by digging trenches and throwing up earthen or sandbagged strongpoints, but these efforts had been deemed less important than fortifying the southern causeways. Above all, there was no safe place for Mexican troops to shelter during the daylong bombardment. Nicolás Bravo, the elderly commanding general, did not have enough troops to defend it, especially since the hill was easily approachable from the south through woods that its few cannon could not effectively cover. When the American bombardment began on the morning of September 12, Bravo had around nine hundred men actually on the hill, divided into small groups from different regular units and, poignantly, several dozen young cadets from the academy who had volunteered to help defend it. However, the situation required these troops to do one of the most difficult things they could be required to do. Although Mexican artillerymen were able to fire some shots in reply, the hundreds of Mexican infantry had to sit still all day while American artillerymen they could not hurt killed them and demolished their physical environment, including the stone walls, piles of sand bags, and trenches that they were relying on to provide some protection during the impending infantry assault. For many of the Mexican soldiers this was too much: men began to slip away, first singly or in small groups, but then by the dozens. Meanwhile Santa Anna came to understand that this massive and prolonged bombardment meant that the American effort would be at Chapultepec, and he brought his reserve of about two thousand men to the low ground nearby. There, however, they were even more exposed than the men on the hill, and rather than watch them die uselessly, Santa Anna pulled them back, planning to rush them forward again when the bombardment ended and the assault began. That night Bravo and Santa Anna conferred. Bravo explained that the bombardment had demoralized his men and asked for new troops. Santa Anna replied that the reserve troops had also been demoralized, and sending any of them onto the hill before the bombardment ended would simply be sending them to useless deaths. He promised to bring more men forward as soon as the Americans began their infantry attack. The degree of desperation in this conversation is striking.[11]

The American artillery paused during the night, but in the predawn darkness of September 13, it opened fire again as the Americans marshaled their assault troops. One group, led by General Gideon Pillow, would approach the hill from the west, sending some men around the north side to cut off Mexican reinforcements, some men up the gentle slopes on the western side, and some to try to break into the Mexican defenses from the south. Another force, led by General John Quitman, would move along the Tacubaya road and then attack from the south. These troops included both regulars and volunteers, as well as a few U.S. Marines. The Americans found that, despite their careful preparation and the mounting problems of the Mexicans, Chapultepec would not be easy to take. Those Mexican defenders who had stayed on the hill fought desperately with both muskets and cannon. Moreover, the Michoacán National Guardsmen occupying a strongpoint on the Tacubaya road completely stopped Quitman's force, which took cover in the ditches. They were essentially out of the fight until Quitman redirected them to angle away from the National Guardsmen and approach the hill another way. The Americans benefited when the muskets of the National Guardsmen began to break or become clogged, and soon the Americans were closing in on the summit from several directions. Many Americans were killed and wounded, but step by step American numbers simply overwhelmed the small clumps of Mexican soldiers who made stands at different points on the slopes or on the road leading to the mansion. Soon the remaining Mexican defenders were forced onto the patio and into the mansion itself, and for most there was no exit. American soldiers, overcome by the stressful assault they had experienced or seeking revenge for the American wounded who had been killed at Molino del Rey, did what early modern soldiers typically did when they assaulted a defended fortification: they kept killing Mexican soldiers even as the latter tried to flee or surrender. Officers, distinguished by their insignia and swords, were taken into custody, as were most of the young cadets. The six cadets who died in this battle were immortalized as the Niños Héroes, or Boy Heroes, and later in the nineteenth century people began to say that some took the Mexican flag and leaped to their deaths rather than surrender, but no contemporary account includes such an act.[12]

The reserves Santa Anna sent forward were too late, and with the Americans now on the commanding hill, Santa Anna had no choice but to pull them and the surviving defenders back out of range of the American artillery. They retreated to the city along the San Cosme and Belén causeways. Like all of the causeways, these roads actually entered the city through masonry gates where in normal times goods were taxed. These gates had been turned into temporary fortifications that on most of the causeways commanded the raised roads for a good distance, which made attacking them a daunting proposition. The San Cosme and Belén gates, however, were more vulnerable than the others. San Cosme, on the west side of the city, was too far from the other gates to receive reinforcements or supporting fire from their defenders. Moreover, stone aqueducts ran along both the San Cosme and Belén causeways, giving significant cover to attackers. Scott wanted to make his main push along the San Cosme causeway because it was the most isolated from support, and he sent General William Worth's brigade to do it. Slowed by small forces of Mexicans posted to delay them, the men sprinted from arch to arch under fire until they neared the gate. There they found a more formidable Mexican force that included cannon and infantry in buildings that flanked the gate, giving them an angle that made the aqueduct less useful as cover. Mexican artillerymen and infantry swept the causeway with fire, checking the Americans. The Americans brought up their own artillery, including a mountain howitzer that a young lieutenant named Ulysses S. Grant managed to place on the roof of a nearby church. American infantry broke into the buildings on either side of the main defense and burrowed through the walls, driving the Mexican troops out of room after room and then firing on the defenders of the gate from the flat roofs. There were simply not enough Mexican defenders to prevent this, and in the late afternoon the Americans were able to rush the gate from the front, forcing the surviving defenders to retreat into the city. Santa Anna arrived at the scene and shepherded as many men as he could to his headquarters, but undoubtedly some melted away seeking safety, rest, and food.[13]

Even as Worth's men worked their way to the San Cosme gate, Quitman led a similar force down the Belén causeway. Here, too, the aqueduct provided cover for the attackers, and here, too, they were slowed by Mexican troops fighting rearguard actions. Quitman's force had a much shorter distance to go, though, and soon they were within range of the gate. The Mexican forces there were commanded by General Andrés Terrés, a Spaniard who had entered the Spanish army in 1790 and fought in many Europe battles before being sent to Mexico in 1812 to fight against independence. In 1821 he had joined the compromise movement that brought Mexican independence. He continued in the Mexican army, gradually rising in rank and distinguishing himself at La Angostura. At the Belén gate Terrés had only a couple of hundred men drawn from various units and some light cannon, with other units not under his command posted to protect his flanks. The fortifications were incomplete, and worse yet, the breastwork sheltering his cannon was actually under the arch of the gate, so that American cannonballs hitting the arch showered his artillerymen with falling stones that killed and wounded many. The Mexican units that streamed back along the causeway past his position were demoralized and out of ammunition, and there was no reserve. Yet somehow Terrés and his handful of men held for hours, making American attempts to advance extremely costly. After one o'clock in the afternoon, Terrés realized that the forces protecting his flanks had entirely melted away and that there was no more ammunition for his cannon. He pulled his cannon and eighty remaining men back a couple of blocks to the Ciudadela, a former cigar factory that was now the Mexican army headquarters. There an enraged Santa Anna screamed at Terrés for abandoning his post and ordered his execution. In the chaos the order was not carried out. Everyone was too busy shooting at the Americans, who found that although now technically they were within the city, Mexican resistance remained fierce. Night fell without them advancing another step.[14]

That night the Americans set up heavy artillery near the San Cosme gate and sent a few shells toward the city center.[15] The message was implicit but it was understood by all: the Americans were now close enough to the densely populated city to do what they had done at Veracruz: force a capitulation by bombarding civilians. Santa Anna and his senior commanders realized that they had ammunition for at most one more day of combat, and they had no food for their soldiers. American heavy artillery could destroy their headquarters easily, and any effort to fight street by street would cause heavy civilian casualties. They concluded that the Mexican army should retreat to preserve both civilian lives and its own existence, allowing Mexico to continue the war.[16] The evacuation would have to be clandestine to protect it from an American attack, and this caused further problems. Some wounded officers had gone to their homes for medical treatment, and others had gone to check on their families. Many of these men did not hear that the army was leaving until it was too late. National Guardsmen from the city were reluctant to abandon their families, who had no means to subsist without them. Recognizing this, the army disbanded their units. Some of the men took their weapons with them when they went home.[17] Once the army cleared the city, Santa Anna divided it in two. The infantry, who would be of little use in harassing the Americans, were sent to Querétaro, the new seat of the Mexican national government. Santa Anna believed that there was a chance they could be fed there, in one of the wealthiest regions of the country. The cavalry he kept close at hand, looking for some chance to strike at the Americans. As the infantry left for Querétaro, a few looted houses, and once they were out of the city, hungry men began to desert. Over the next hours and days, as they moved further from the possibility of fighting, starving in the ranks seems to have struck more and more men as pointless, and many deserted.

The army diminished drastically in size, and the deserters begged or extorted food from peasants or haciendas.[18]

Civilians Resist the Americans

The city council had collaborated somewhat reluctantly with efforts to fortify the city because it believed it had a duty to preserve the lives and property of its inhabitants. It did not want Mexico City to be bombarded like Veracruz. Even more vividly, it worried that a victorious American army might rampage through the city, looting, killing, and raping, which, as we have seen, early modern military culture considered inevitable if a city was defended to the ultimate instance.[19] The city councilmen were very anxious about this possibility, and when they heard that the army was pulling out, they resolved to ask Scott to guarantee the behavior of his troops in exchange for a formal submission to his authority. The committee they sent also asked him to safeguard the churches and allow the functioning of city government. Scott responded that he would try to control his troops but was not sure he could due to the intense fights they had just survived.[20]

Neither Scott nor the city council knew that the bloodletting was not yet over. Early in the morning of September 14, American troops entered the city, marching cautiously through silent streets toward the city center. These exhausted survivors of weeks of combat were wary because only a few hours earlier the Mexican army's fierce resistance had rebuffed their first effort to advance past the gates. Most did not know that the Mexican troops had left. Some marveled at the size and style of the stone buildings, which seemed to increase with every step toward the center. For many, this was the largest city they had ever seen. As the Americans moved toward the center, wariness and wonder no doubt began to be replaced by relief and a sense of accomplishment. Emotions also ran high among the civilian inhabitants. The previous day's fighting had been very close and audible, so the idea that the Americans would attack was not a surprise. What was a surprise was that they could enter so silently: most civilians did not know that the Mexican army had left either, so the ghostlike presence of the American columns astonished the few people out that early. However, soon more and more people gathered and murmured, and as the first American troops approached the central plaza, a shot wounded an American officer. Soon it was followed by others. A shower of stones rained from the flat rooftops of the city, and crowds confronted the Americans. As the Americans entered the plaza, the crowds shouted, "Death to the Americans" and "Death to Santa Anna." After the Americans reached the National Palace, Scott came out on a balcony to congratulate his troops. Several women interrupted the notably corpulent Scott, yelling, "Shut up, fattie!" and more fighting ensued.[21] It was not a day for victory speeches.

Fighting raged for all of September 14 and much of September 15. Mexicans fired muskets and pistols from doorways or rooftops, and they continued to throw stones from rooftops. Groups confronted the Americans in the streets with knives and clubs. Some civilians deliberately exposed themselves to draw Americans into ambushes. American private F. Brough reported that some Mexicans "were firing from the buildings and others were firing in the streets. Our troops came around them from different sides, then the Mexicans ran. . . . They were dressed in different ways. Some had soldiers' coats, some were dressed in white, some had cartridge boxes, others had bags. Some were armed with muskets and escopettes, others with clubs and stones, like a regular mob." Mexican colonel Nicomedes de Callejo had missed his army's departure because he had been given permission to go home with a colleague to eat and rest. In the chaos he saw Bernadino Belazco, the neighborhood justice of the peace, gathering a group of neighbors to oppose the Americans. Up until that moment Callejo had planned to catch up with the army, but Belazco invited the officers to join the civilians. Callejo testified that "as we were uniformed and armed, we would have been ashamed to not accept his invitation, so we contributed to the shots they took at the Americans." Callejo's friend Lieutenant Colonel Manuel Andonagui testified that Belazco had gathered many civilians and dispersed soldiers and invited the officers to take charge because "many enemy were coming and people were firing at them from different points. We did so, causing many casualties."[22] Callejo and Andonagui were protagonists and eyewitnesses to only a small part of a struggle that sprawled over many blocks. American general Persifor Smith wrote that "the people of the town were firing in all directions from the houses on our troops and particularly from the stores at the corners, and were only driven away after a severe contest of nearly two days."[23] The Americans, who a few minutes before thought they had captured one of the world's largest cities, were instead embroiled in vicious urban combat.

Official American reports downplayed this struggle in ways we will discuss later, and there is no official accounting of American casualties. Officers on the spot reported in their diaries or memoirs that those casualties were severe. John Henshaw wrote that in the street fighting the Americans lost more men than they had lost in the fighting at Chapultepec and the city gates the previous day, while Daniel Harvey Hill estimated that almost two hundred Americans were killed or wounded. Other estimates go up to three hundred.[24] Some American corpses were mutilated. The fighting subsided at nightfall on September 14 but began again the next morning and continued with varying intensity throughout that day. Only on September 16 did those who had disputed American control of the streets move from open resistance to clandestine activities, picking off isolated Americans at night. It was several months before these nocturnal assassinations ebbed and Americans began to feel relatively safe in the city.[25]

The American response indicates the severity of the resistance. The Americans quickly deployed artillery to destroy the houses from which Mexicans fired weapons or threw stones. They also turned cannon on the crowds, using grape and canister, the kinds of ammunition that during battle were used to attack exposed infantry. American soldiers were told to break into and loot any building from which they were fired on, killing or capturing the inhabitants. Understanding this, soldiers sometimes claimed to have heard firing from mansions and then looted them. Mexicans who were captured fighting the Americans were immediately killed, and in some cases their bodies were displayed as warnings. Even unarmed Mexicans were executed. Ethan Allen Hitchcock wrote in his diary on September 14 that "many Mexicans have been put to death. . . . I saw an unarmed Mexican deliberately shot a few moments since, and I thought it horrible." In the words of Hill, it was "a day of bloodshed and brutality such as I trust never to see again."[26] Scott also sent emissaries to the archbishop and city council, telling them that he would order his soldiers to loot all churches and houses if the resistance continued.[27] He clearly saw the resistance as a major problem requiring every weapon at his disposal.

Why did thousands of Mexicans take to the streets and fight the Americans? What can their actions tell us about Mexico and particularly Mexico City in 1847? One thing that stands out is that many inhabitants felt threatened by the approach of the American troops. All summer authorities had grappled with the dangers posed by the American invasion, and their fears were clearly shared by significant sectors of the city's population. The possibility of mass rape was taken so seriously that in June the city council suggested that the city's hundreds of virginal nuns be evacuated, and on September 6 officials authorized the evacuation of all women, although no mass exodus ensued.[28] The authorities also worried about hunger, always a threat for the urban poor because they relied on whatever they earned any given day for food for that very night. These people were finding it harder and harder to feed themselves as the city's economy suffered the uncertainty of having an enemy on its very doorstep.[29] The Americans who entered the city on September 14 were coming into contact with a population raised to a feverish pitch of anxiety.

Contrary to the views of some historians, that population was able to comprehend the war as a conflict between nations.[30] There is ample evidence that even the mostly illiterate poor of the city had developed a sense of themselves as Mexicans confronted by foreigners defined as Americans. We have seen the violence meted out to American deserters and to the teamsters during the armistice. Foreign civilians who spoke English were sometimes turned in to the authorities as possible American spies. During the Battle of Molino del Rey, groups of poor Mexicans had run through the streets, shouting, "Long live Mexico" and "Death to the Yankees."[31] The approach of American troops stoked the fires of nationalism in the city, but to understand the heights it reached on September 14 and 15, we also have to realize that Mexico City was the center of the country's political life. For more than two decades Mexico's political leaders had worked to convince its inhabitants that they were Mexicans through public civic rituals like oaths to constitutions and independence day celebrations, both of which were typically accompanied by religious services, speeches, music, and fireworks in the very streets American troops now trespassed on. Different political leaders had also sought to involve the residents of the city in partisan politics, seeking their support in elections and for coups. Even before the war, with its torrents of propaganda, an entire generation had been told that they were Mexicans.

Moreover, the ideas expressed in written political propaganda reached the ears of the illiterate through the long tradition of reading aloud and discussing political documents and newspapers in public spaces. Thus it should not surprise us that only a few months after the war began, Austrian traveler Karl Heller reported that the urban poor in Mexico City were already displaying a virulent popular nationalism.[32]

Authorities and intellectuals made greater efforts to encourage popular nationalism after Veracruz fell in March 1847. As we have seen, calls for resistance focused on the need to defend Mexican independence, Mexican access to eternal life through the Catholic Church, and the honor and bodies of Mexican women. The latter two themes made the conflict with the United States far from abstract, and they focused popular attention directly on the behavior of American troops in occupied areas, no doubt contributing to the fever pitch of anxiety the city reached in September 1847.[33] One of the most telling efforts to promote popular resistance came on September 7, when the national government sent the archbishop a letter explaining that, due to the sacrilege that American troops had committed, Mexican priests should encourage the people to "die if necessary, defending their country and religion." It went on to say that greedy American troops might try to steal the sacred image of the Virgin of Guadalupe, and ordered the archbishop to arrange for its protection. This letter was addressed to the archbishop, but its intended audience was much broader: three hundred copies were printed and posted on every street corner. The Virgin of Guadalupe was well on the way to becoming a symbol of national identity throughout the country, and she was certainly the most popular religious figure in the city.[34]

Until the American invasion of Veracruz, most war propaganda in the center of the country sought to convince Mexicans to contribute money or time to the war effort. The explicit aims changed as the Americans approached the city. Propagandists increasingly exhorted Mexicans to physically resist the invaders. In August the national government ordered local authorities to convince Mexicans to "rise up together with whatever weapons each individual has, large or small, firearm or edged weapon, long or short, even if there is nothing other than a stick and stones to attack by any means possible." This document pointed out that when the British had invaded Buenos Aires in 1807, its civilians had successfully defended the city and some

British soldiers had even been killed when women threw furniture or boiling water at them.[35] When the governor of the Federal District passed this on to the city council, he ordered that the paving stones of the city be carried up to the flat roofs so that they could be thrown at the Americans. This order was carried out, and one witness reported that some women asked that the medium-size stones be piled separately for their use when the moment came.[36] After the armistice ended, priests were asked to preach resistance in the streets. The new governor of the Federal District, José Maria Tornel, was one of the fiercest advocates of resisting the Americans, and he had witnessed the riot against the American teamsters. He now sought to lay the groundwork for resistance within the city. In theory, every neighborhood already had a justice of the peace and every block a block captain to keep order. Many of these posts had fallen vacant, but the remaining officials were ordered to gather residents and prepare them to take on the Americans. Some clearly took these orders very seriously. When the preparations are examined closely, it is clear that Tornel, a military officer, believed that the civilian defenders would come into play after the Americans pushed through organized military resistance at the city's edge. As Mexican troops fell back into the streets, the civilians would aid them by defending each block in turn. This scenario would probably have been even more lethal for American troops than what actually transpired. On September 14, the organized Mexican units had left the city, so the civilians were surprised by the silence of the American approach and were largely on their own.[37]

Who were the people who so desperately confronted the American army? Brough's account stressed the variety of people involved. He points out that some wore white, probably the white cotton clothing that most Mexican poor typically wore. Luis Fernando Granados, author of an excellent book on the street fighting, explains that many eyewitness accounts of the fighting show that resistance was strongest and most prolonged in the poorest neighborhoods. He identifies slaughterhouse workers, carpenters, tailors, and lottery vendors as part of the crowds. Most witnesses specifically cited "lepers," a slang term used to describe the ragged urban poor.[38] Henshaw, for instance, says the protagonists of the uprising against the Americans were the lepers, adding that they were "the same people who attacked our wagon train when it came in for provisions during the armistice."[39] The eyewitness accounts leave little doubt that many of the people who fought and died confronting the Americans were among the poorest of urban people.

They were not alone. As has been mentioned, when the Mexican army pulled out of the city, National Guardsmen from Mexico City were allowed to go home to their families. Many took their weapons with them, and more than a few had no intention of simply standing by as the Americans attacked their families. Thus, many descriptions of the fighting point out that National Guardsmen, alone or in small groups, fired from the buildings or led civilians in the streets.[40] They were joined by some regular officers surprised by the sudden departure of the army and unwilling to let the civilians fight on without them.[41] The National Guardsmen and regular officers were undoubtedly useful due to their knowledge of firearms and tactics, and civilians sometimes asked them to take leading roles. However, at least one regular officer trying to survive in the contested streets of the city that day reported later that some plebeians insulted and beat him, perhaps because they were disappointed that the army had abandoned the city. This fits with the reports that as the Americans entered the main plaza, the crowds had shouted not only "Death to the Americans" but also "Death to Santa Anna."[42]

Other social groups were also involved. The owners of the many small retail shops presided over places where neighbors congregated for news and discussion, and not surprisingly these men participated in the resistance. One exclaimed to the people gathered that the honor of the neighborhood was at stake and gave them food and ammunition.[43] Many priests and monks preached resistance and even took to the streets with weapons to lead the crowds against the Americans. The city council wrote that "a monk from the Convent of the Merced is going around on horseback brandishing a lance, exhorting the people to rise up against the American army that is already occupying this Capital. Other clerics are doing more or less the same . . . they keep urging the people to defend themselves and exhorting them to make war." Some brandished standards with the image of the Virgin of Guadalupe on them.[44] Women threw stones from rooftops, brandished knives and clubs in the crowds, taunted the Americans, and treated the Mexican wounded.[45]

Thousands fought the American army in the streets, but they were still a minority of the city's population of more than 150,000. Undoubtedly many people from a variety of social groups hunkered down, avoiding contact with the Americans and minimizing the risk to their persons, families, and property. Many wealthy Mexicans and foreigners frowned on the resistance. They understood that American soldiers could use the fighting to justify looting, killing, and raping.[46] Some tried to protect their properties by flying the flags of neutral nations, especially Spain, which many elite families still felt a strong cultural attachment to. American general Persifor Smith stated that more than a hundred houses that did not actually harbor Spanish citizens flew the Spanish flag during the fighting.[47] However, the specter of thousands of poor Mexicans in the streets armed with whatever weapons they could improvise tapped an older and more deeply rooted fear in elites as well. Early modern urban elites lived cheek to jowl with the urban poor, sharing the same streets and, in Mexico City, even the same buildings with them. They disdained and feared the ragged poor, whom they saw as desperate, conniving, violent, and irrational, prone to drunkenness and petty crime. The elite feared mass violence of the poor against their betters and believed that in any breakdown of order, crowds of ragged men and women would loot their residences and businesses. Many members of the elite saw the street fighting as this kind of urban riot, and undoubtedly their prejudices were reinforced when poor Mexicans sometimes also entered the houses that American soldiers had broken into, stealing items that the Americans had disdained or overlooked.[48]

Elite suspicion of the true motives of the poor very much shaped the role of the city council. Scott responded to the resistance not only by ordering his troops to repress it but also by telling the city council that his troops would sack the entire city if resistance continued. The city council, led by acting mayor Manuel Reyes Veramendi, wrote back immediately, very consciously adopting the role of representing not all inhabitants but instead only the wealthy and respectable, the "various families that form the sensible and judicious part of society," which it called "victim of the imprudence of an urban poor that works without a determined goal or end."[49] A few hours later it told Scott that "the shooting was neither started nor sustained by the respectable people of this capital but instead by a few from the lower people without noble sentiments."[50] Authorities soon marginalized the resisters even further. The justice of the peace and block captains of one of the wealthier neighborhoods asked the city council to tell Scott that in their neighborhood those resisting were not the residents but instead "many criminals who have left the jails, and their aims are none other than robbing and exterminating the honorable families, since none of them love their country or order." The city council immediately sent this to Scott, adding that "the disorder that has happened in this capital has not had any other origin except the depravity of a few criminals, of a handful of men who know no other patria, honor or morality than robbery and crime."[51] Many Americans would later insist that the combatants were criminals whom the national authorities had released from prison as they evacuated the city. This version came to American hands directly from the city council itself.

The city council immediately wrote to the neighborhood officials who had earlier been ordered to organize resistance, telling them of Scott's threats and ordering them to discourage fighting. It also posted a printed broadside on street corners explaining that Scott would not guarantee the security of the city's inhabitants while resistance continued and that he had ordered his troops to destroy any house used by resisters and kill its inhabitants. The broadside asked everyone to stop fighting the Americans. This missive was not well received by the angry crowds so deeply involved in the bloody street-by-street struggle. They tore down many of the broadsides or covered them in excrement.[52] The city council also reached out directly to a group of resisters organizing at the Santo Domingo monastery, just a couple of blocks from city hall, writing that "perhaps this behavior deserves to be considered the most patriotic thing to do," but the resisters should desist because their actions gave the American soldiers license to sack the city and kill noncombatants.[53]

Santa Anna was still on the northern outskirts with the Mexican cavalry and a few National Guard infantry when messengers from the resisters reached him. They stressed their successes against the Americans and asked him to send troops. He halted the retreat to gather information, consulting at length with Alvarez, who, though one of Santa Anna's fiercest political enemies, had in the context of the war become one of his closest collaborators. Santa Anna and Alvarez were moved by what they had heard, and they immediately turned back toward the city center with the available troops. Santa Anna and Alvarez rode ahead into the northern part of the city's central district. By the time they arrived there, the fighting on September 14 was dying down, and they were disappointed. However, they stationed some

National Guardsmen on the edge of the central district and sent some regular cavalry into the streets. The next morning, when the fighting started up, Santa Anna again sent cavalry detachments into the city, but the fighting was not as severe and the resistance movement was clearly now waning. Santa Anna lost hope of turning the tide in the streets of the city, and he decided to take the cavalry to Puebla.[54]

Before Santa Anna left, someone brought him one of the broadsides that the city council had posted, and he became incensed. He wrote to Reyes Veramendi, criticizing him for trying to stop the people from resisting "the barbarous enemy that sacks the town and churches, and rapes the women." Santa Anna said that if Reyes Veramendi and the town council persisted, they would be treated as traitors. Reyes Veramendi replied that he only sought to protect the population, and his conscience was clear. He also wrote that he did not believe that the fighting in the streets was really the result of patriotism or a people trying to defend itself from looters and rapists, but instead stemmed from the poor taking advantage of the situation to steal. This exchange only further confirms that Reyes Veramendi, a moderate federalist with their typical concern about class tensions in the city, saw the crowds as a bigger threat than the Americans.[55]

American soldiers and officers had quite a lot to say about the nature of the resistance. Their responses were shaped by their own prejudices about Mexicans and what the city council had communicated to Scott about the people in the streets. Generally they believed that Mexicans were capable of violence but not of patriotism, and this led many to delegitimize the resistance or even to oddly efface it from their accounts. The contradictions within even individual accounts are striking. Lieutenant Hill wrote that almost two hundred Americans and many Mexicans were killed or wounded on the first day of street fighting alone and played up the violence employed by the Americans, but a mere two pages later he stated that the city was occupied by the Americans "almost without a struggle."[56] Reeves, an American regular, also emphasized the severity of the fighting and the American casualties, but he disparaged the Mexicans' motives. He had been present when the Americans had taken Puebla a few months before. The Mexicans had not been able to defend the city, and crowds had watched the Americans march into it. Reeves wrote that the "big strapping fellows" in the streets of Puebla "did not come out manfully and fight for their country." Things were clearly different in Mexico City, but Reeves still could not admit the possibility that the Mexicans in the street were fighting for their country. Instead he wrote that they were "scoundrels" who fought "more for the purpose of plunder than feelings of patriotism."[57] George Ballentine, another rank-and-file regular, seems even more confused when he writes of resistance by "patriots" who were "mostly criminals."[58] Scott may have written the most incoherent interpretation of all. His official report states that the Americans were attacked by "some two thousand convicts, liberated the night before, by the flying government—joined by perhaps as many Mexican soldiers, who had disbanded themselves and thrown off their uniforms." Scott added that their objective was to "gratify national hatred, and, in the general alarm and confusion, to plunder the wealthy inhabitants." Let us take a second to think about this statement. If there were Mexicans who opposed the Americans, it was "to gratify national hatred." And exactly why were the American troops there? They were not exactly tourists. Scott, following the lead of the city council, also stated that many of the combatants were criminals who really wanted to steal the possessions of the wealthy.[59] How could he believe that people who really only wanted to steal would risk their lives by firing on the American troops, throwing stones at them from rooftops, or gathering in crowds to fight them hand to hand? Undoubtedly both some Mexicans and many American troops took advantage of the disorder to steal, but that does not explain the resistance. Some American officers took their dele-gitimization of the street fighting to ridiculous extremes. On September 16 they court-martialed a Mexican officer named Enrique García for violat-ing the laws of war by "threatening and attempting the lives of the United States troops after the Mexican troops had been withdrawn from the City, the capitulation having been made by the proper authorities." García was acquitted, but at his trial Lieutenant G. W. Lay, Scott's secretary, stated that the fighting in the street could not be called resistance and that "what was going on I considered assassination."[60] The logical twists and turns Americans used to deny legitimacy to the urban resistance were extreme.

That resistance did not continue indefinitely. The city government was soon joined in its efforts to convince people to stop resisting by religious authorities who feared the specific threat that Scott had made to churches.

Nevertheless, the end of the fighting seems to have been mostly a result of American repression and the growing realization that the Mexican army would not return. In other words, people lost hope. By the end of the second day, open resistance was essentially over, aside from the clandestine threats American soldiers faced at night. For several weeks the Americans worried that another general uprising might take place, so they ordered that the stones be brought down from the rooftops, many soldiers were assigned guard duty, and all were told to keep their weapons at hand. Both Americans and the city council were kept on edge by repeated rumors of planned uprisings. The first Sunday of the occupation, American officers noted a strange silence when they expected to hear church bells announcing Mass. They immediately suspected that the priests had decided to cancel Mass to provoke another uprising. Once more the American officers threatened to let their soldiers loot the churches, and soon masses were being held on schedule.[61]

A little more than five months after landing in Veracruz in March 1847, the American army had succeeded in capturing Mexico's capital and largest city. Some military historians attribute this success to Scott's intelligence and professionalism, as well as the high quality of his army, and there is some truth to this.[62] Scott certainly made some costly blunders, but he was definitely a better tactician than Santa Anna. In more general accounts of the war, the campaign is sometimes upheld as proof of the more effective organization of the American government, and again there is significant validity to this view. Mexican accounts stress the personal failures of Mexican leaders, especially Santa Anna, and they often suggest that most Mexicans simply lacked a firm attachment to the nation-state. Santa Anna made tactical errors, and other military leaders sometimes failed to effectively cooperate. In general, accounts of the war surround Scott's success with a certain of aura of inevitability.

Nevertheless, the fighting in the Valley of Mexico was not easy for the Americans. Henshaw called the cost "terrible" and stated that more than 2,700 of Scott's soldiers were killed or wounded in the fighting.[63] This grim toll invites us to consider what happened there in another way. The Mexican state was certainly less effective than its American counterpart. Ideological and social divisions hampered the war effort. More importantly, perched on top of a weak economy, the Mexican state had never developed a fiscal system adequate for even routine expenses, and the war dramatically worsened its situation by increasing expenses and removing the customs revenue that was its most important source of funds. Scott's principal advantage throughout the campaign was that he could always pay and feed his soldiers, something his Mexican counterparts could only dream of. When we consider this handicap, the story of the loss of Mexico City looks very different. Somehow the Mexican government, headed by the often shady figure of Santa Anna but aided by many other politicians and officers from every ideological group, managed to mount a serious, organized, and tenacious defense. It was able to recruit men, arm them, organize them into effective military units, and sometimes even feed them. Its officer corps, though justly much maligned for its internal politicking, led these men with surprising effectiveness. Moreover, the men themselves, whether conscripts or volunteers, fought very hard.

Those who fought, worked, or made financial sacrifices to defend the capital did so for many reasons. Some were successfully coerced into action by the Mexican state, which suggests that it was not quite as ineffective as it is sometimes portrayed. Yet, once in the ranks, even coerced soldiers often came to love each other and take pride in their regular army units, making them effective. Others who helped the defense were motivated by fear for their lives and those of loved ones, by peer pressure, or by the hope that participating would bring them later social or political advantages. When we look at units of citizen-soldiers, it seems clear that their service was at least partially motivated by the idea that they were fighting for Mexico, even if it was a Mexico that different groups imagined in different ways. The same can be said for less organized groups like the civilians who confronted the American teamsters during the armistice or those who took to the streets on September 14 and 15, armed not only with improvised weapons but also with ideas about who they were and how they were different from the invaders. They were insisting that they were Mexicans, and that insistence cost many of them dearly.

CHAPTER 8

Ashamed of My Country

W$_{\text{HEN}}$ M$_{\text{EXICO}}$ C$_{\text{ITY}}$ $_{\text{FELL}}$, Antonio López de Santa Anna had sent most Mexican soldiers who had survived its defense to Querétaro, believing that at the interim national capital in this relatively wealthy region they were more likely to find sustenance. He resigned the presidency but kept around a thousand regular army cavalrymen and a few hundred National Guardsmen from Guerrero, led by Juan Alvarez. Santa Anna had lost every battle with Scott's forces, but he knew that Scott had left a small force of mostly ill soldiers in Puebla and that Puebla's state government had gathered more than two thousand National Guardsmen. Together with roughly five hundred guerrillas led by Joaquín Rea, these troops had the American garrison cut off. Santa Anna took his troops there, hoping to overwhelm the garrison with the support of Puebla's civilians, whom he had heard were eager to throw out the Americans. He was welcomed to Puebla by applause and music that must have been audible to the American soldiers hunkered down in their fortified positions. Around four hundred American defenders were completely fit for duty, but they were supplemented by nearly two thousand convalescing from wounds or illnesses, many of whom helped defend the few buildings the Americans held. Over the next three weeks guerrillas, National Guardsmen, and regular cavalrymen kept the Americans hemmed in and under fire, working themselves ever closer to the Americans.[1]

Santa Anna hoped that a victory there would leave the American army isolated in central Mexico. However, even as the siege continued, three thousand new American troops began to march from Veracruz. This force, led by Brigadier General Joseph Lane, was able to relieve Puebla primarily due to the same problem that had hampered the Mexicans throughout the war. Santa Anna took some regulars and National Guardsmen out to stop

Lane's march, but he had no resources to keep these men fed. First National Guardsmen and then even regulars started to desert. After a few days Santa Anna realized that he no longer had enough men to block Lane, although he still hoped to harass the Americans. Lane, eager for glory, heard that Santa Anna was at Huamantla and rushed his force there, accidentally avoiding the ambush Santa Anna had prepared a few miles away. Lane's advance guard of cavalry drove away the few Mexicans at Huamantla and then dispersed to loot. Unfortunately for them, Santa Anna realized Lane's mistake, hurried back to Huamantla, and defeated the American cavalry. However, the Mexicans were pushed out of town in turn by the belated arrival of Lane's more numerous infantry, who then sacked the town before moving on to Puebla. Alvarez ordered the few Mexican troops still in Puebla to leave rather than try to fight a superior force in the streets of the city. Some refused, saying that they would rather be executed for disobeying orders than retreat. They stayed and fired on Lane's troops but eventually left.[2]

The bottom line was clear. Even when the Mexicans could pull together enough troops to achieve local numeric superiority, the odds were stacked against them. Santa Anna and his commanders had identified a vulnerable American force, they had concentrated various Mexican units against it, and they had enlisted the enthusiastic cooperation of local civilians. However, to succeed they had to keep their troops together, and they simply did not have the financial resources needed to feed them. The federal government had no money to send, and the state government could not even feed the National Guard troops, much less the regulars. What might have been a successful military operation was undermined and eventually defeated by hunger, as starving Mexican troops made the only choice open to them: they dispersed to look for food. Under these conditions the Mexican army was effectively out of the war.

Recriminations

The same could be said of Santa Anna. Dismayed that neither the national nor state governments had been able to support his effort to turn the tide, he began moving south toward Oaxaca, only to find that the governor of that state, bitter political enemy and future president Benito Juárez, did not want him there. American troops almost caught Santa Anna in Tehuacán, where he escaped capture but lost most of his remaining personal property. Relieved of military command, he hid until the Americans allowed him to go into exile in March 1848. Before he left, though, he began a sustained public relations campaign, giving his version of the defense of Mexico's capital, carefully explaining not only his decisions but also how various subordinates had frustrated his plans by not following orders: Gabriel Valencia had single-handedly undermined the defense by not following orders at Padierna; Manuel Andrade had refused Alvarez's orders at Molino del Rey; Andrés Terrés had retreated from the Belén gate. Santa Anna also criticized Nicolás Bravo for losing Chapultepec. Bickering among Mexican leaders continued in both published pamphlets and the Mexican military court system for many months after the war ended. The unseemly charges and countercharges were all topped by Congressman Ramón Gamboa's formal accusation that Santa Anna had repeatedly betrayed Mexico during his campaigns, deliberately losing the war. This charge has resonated with some Mexicans down to the present day, and in the early twentieth century the famed Mexican muralist Diego Rivera even painted into one of his historical panoramas the figure of Santa Anna handing Winfield Scott the keys to Mexico City. This dramatic indictment of Santa Anna simply does not hold up when we look at what he actually did during the war. He was not a great tactician, and he had many faults as politician, but only his extraordinary political and organizational talents and commitment to fighting the war allowed Mexico to repeatedly field conventional armies after October 1846.[3] In other words, if Santa Anna had really wanted to lose the war, he had done so in the least effective way possible.

It seems obvious that the military officers and politicians who preside over a losing cause would bicker about who was responsible, especially in a political system that was very fractious even before the war began. What might seem more surprising is that the Mexican bickering was perhaps surpassed by American bickering. Mexicans tended to argue about responsibility for military defeats, while American officers tended to clash over credit for victories, but the vehemence was surprisingly similar. The conflicts between American officers began even before the war. As Zachary Taylor gathered his army together at Corpus Christi, officers who in the frontier army would have been separated by hundreds of miles found themselves required to cooperate, raising the question of who outranked whom. David Twiggs had been a colonel longer than William Worth, but Worth also had the temporary rank of brigadier general. Both men campaigned publicly for precedence, and the thorny question was kicked all the way upstairs to President James K. Polk. When he decided in Twiggs's favor, Worth resigned in a huff and sat out the first few months of the war. He returned to service only after his conscience reminded him of his duty to his country or he realized that the war with Mexico was a crucial chance to gain prestige and promotion.[4] The struggles among American officers only escalated when the recruitment of volunteer regiments whose officers generally owed their positions to the partisan politics of the day more than doubled the size of the American army. Regular officers who had survived the strenuous curriculum of West Point and then served many years without promotions in the prewar period found themselves outranked by inexperienced men, some of whom had even flunked out of West Point. Campfire grumbling sometimes even escalated into conflict on the battlefield. Regular lieutenant Daniel Harvey Hill refused an order from volunteer general Gideon Pillow, calling him an "ignorant puppy" and shaking his sword at the general.[5] Regulars and volunteers bickered about who was responsible for the victories at Monterrey, Cerro Gordo, Churubusco, and other battles.[6] Not surprisingly, the greatest conflict arose after the Mexico City campaign. Even Polk's choice of Scott to command the campaign was driven mostly by the desire to prevent Whig and potential presidential candidate Taylor from gathering even more laurels. Scott was very competent, but he was also a proud man who enjoyed the prestige of command, and he was central to the most sordid bickering of the war. Scott, at first gently, tried to check the efforts of Pillow, Polk's old Tennessee friend and former law partner, to claim undue credit for several victories in the Valley of Mexico. Scott became incensed when an anonymous account in American newspapers placed Pillow at the center of the campaign, repeatedly crediting him with decisions actually made by Scott, and another anonymous account attributed some of Scott's decisions to Worth. Scott reminded the army that it was illegal for officers to publish such anonymous accounts, and soon both Pillow and Worth asked Polk to intervene. Hearing this, Scott arrested both, but Polk relieved Scott and placed him under court-martial. This temporarily derailed

Scott's career and angered him deeply. In sum, even the most accomplished general the United States had seen in the years between the American Revolution and the Civil War was dragged down by backbiting and pettiness.[7]

Ironically, the extreme nature of the bickering by both Mexican and American leaders suggests that a key value united them all: masculine honor, which many of these men believed was their most precious possession. Historians of both countries have written extensively about how this honor was valued so highly that it was often defended with physical violence. The most extreme form was that of formal duels, which were uncommon in Mexico but still frequent in the United States: even Andrew Jackson had killed a man in a duel. Honor was reputational: it was crucial to these men because it was crucial to how society saw them, and their standing as men of honor whose word had to be taken as valuable was central to their social position. Thus, despite the romance of dueling, most battles over honor took place in courtrooms or in print, venues where the means used to protect one's reputation were sometimes almost as violent.[8] Moreover, the careers of military officers and politicians depended on their reputations: a man denied due credit for his achievements by the distortions of others might just as well have stayed at home by the fire. Thus every military encounter was described in scrupulously weighed and documented reports, and those reports were dissected under the social and cultural equivalent of microscopes. Both blame and credit for military decisions and courage or its lack had to be apportioned correctly. Discrepancies of memory and differences of perspective, common in the confusion and stress of battle, could rapidly lead to contention because so much was at stake. Conflict on the battlefield was thus ironically followed by even more bloodletting in courtrooms and print, although these battles were thankfully less physically lethal.

Guerrilla Warfare and Atrocities

As the generals bickered about credit and blame for the results of conventional battles, more lethal kinds of fighting continued. Guerrilla successes had forced Scott to stop trying to maintain a continuous line of communication to Veracruz, and they continued even after the fall of Mexico City. Guerrillas caused significant casualties to even large units of Americans, and any American soldiers who lagged behind on the march were quickly killed or captured. Guerrilla activities showed Americans that their conquest of Mexico City had not ended the war. For most Americans Father Celedonio de Jarauta became the face of the guerrillas. The Americans seemed to see him anywhere guerrillas operated, and they were intrigued that a man of the cloth could also be a military leader. They called him a "rascally priest" and "the Prince of the Bandits," and they worked intensively to find this elusive prey.[9]

The Americans' attitude toward the guerrillas was influenced by guerrilla behavior. Those who began to operate in the north in 1846 in response to American crimes against the civilian population treated American volunteers as they had Indian raiders: they conducted a war of ambush driven by a cultural logic of revenge and very demonstrative violence, torturing Americans and displaying their mutilated bodies to convey their anger and inspire fear. Guerrilla operations in central Mexico originated more in official political decisions and probably stemmed more from a conventional sense of national identity, but these guerrillas also sometimes mutilated bodies and left them in locations where they were sure to be seen by American troops.[10] Americans saw guerrilla warfare not as proof of Mexican nationalism but instead as proof that many Mexicans were violent and treacherous racial inferiors. American volunteers in central Mexico responded to guerrilla attacks much as they had in the north: they went out in informal groups to attack the lives and property of nearby Mexican civilians. Describing one such revenge attack, volunteer Thomas Barclay of Pennsylvania wrote that Americans "killed all greasers that were seen, some no doubt innocently. One Mexican, I understand, was killed while plowing. However, that is the only way to deal with such men."[11]

The question of how "to deal with such men" was also on the minds of high-ranking American officers. Scott was, like many regular officers, genuinely appalled by the crimes that volunteers had committed against Mexican civilians in the north, and he believed that preventing such crimes during his central Mexico campaign would help prevent guerrilla warfare. Yet guerrilla warfare happened anyway, hampering his operations and costing hundreds of American lives. How did he respond? Some of his responses were official and therefore well documented, but some were deliberately unofficial, and discerning these requires more work. On the official plane, Scott had always believed that it might be necessary to make the civilian population pay the price for guerrilla warfare. After capturing Veracruz in April 1847, he proclaimed that his army would make war not on the Mexican people but instead on the Mexican government, and he stated that he would punish American soldiers who committed crimes against civilians. However, he added that guerrilla attacks, which he called "contrary to the laws of war," would be punished, and if Mexican authorities did not turn in guerrillas, that punishment would "fall upon entire cities, towns, or neighborhoods." Mexicans understood this order to threaten the wholesale destruction of civilian property. Later Scott also stated that civilian authorities who did not turn guerrillas in would be heavily fined.[12] Despite these threats, American officers did not explicitly authorize many reprisals against civilians before September 1847. They instead simply called guerrilla warfare illegitimate and turned a blind eye when soldiers conducted revenge attacks. Later, officers became more involved, and in December Scott ordered that captured guerrillas be shot. In his memoirs he made a point of justifying this order by saying that guerrillas routinely killed all American soldiers they captured, even the sick and wounded.[13]

Scott's order to kill helpless prisoners was not the most important act the American command performed against guerrillas and their civilian supporters. Scott's earlier statement that guerrilla tactics were against the laws of war had sent a powerful signal to American soldiers, and many captured guerrillas had already been killed. However, the most important and, in the end, most bloody move the American high command made against the guerrillas was to task particularly violent American units with pursuing them. Scott does not mention this in his memoirs, and no document produced by Scott or his superiors explicitly explains it. We need to reconstruct this development from more fragmentary bits of evidence. Most units tasked with counterinsurgency operations were of a particular category. The American army included regular units whose men signed for five years' service. It also came to include volunteer units recruited for temporary service. As we have seen, volunteers were typically convinced that Mexicans were racial and religious inferiors, and they were inclined to prey on Mexican civilians. In February 1847 Congress authorized the recruitment of ten new regiments that did not entirely fit in either category, forming instead a kind of hybrid. These regiments were administratively part of the regular army, but the men only signed for the duration of the war, each unit was usually recruited in a specific geographic location, and their officers were political appointees. The units were assigned numbers as regular army regiments, but informally many units used the names of the states where they were recruited. As historian Richard Bruce Winders points out, these were essentially volunteer units raised by the national government rather than the states.[14] Many of their officers and men had served in volunteer regiments that had fought in the north until their enlistments expired. The new regiments from Texas included many men who had already served with Texas volunteer units notorious for stealing from Mexican civilians and conducting revenge attacks on civilians after guerrilla activity. On June 16, 1847, Taylor, commanding in the north, wrote to his Washington superiors complaining that Texans recently enlisted in these new regiments had often committed atrocities, and requesting that he be sent no more troops from Texas. On July 17, probably a few days after receiving Taylor's letter, Secretary of War William Marcy ordered one of the new Texas regiments to proceed to Veracruz "for the purpose of dispersing the guerillas which infest the line between that place and the interior of Mexico." Assigning these men to counterinsurgency duty implicitly authorized them to use the same methods that had made them notorious in the north against civilians in central Mexico. Soon after reaching Veracruz, these men were sent to chase guerrillas, and they began burning villages, ranchos, and haciendas, citing dubious evidence that guerrillas had sheltered there. They also simply executed any guerrillas they captured. Other new regiments did the same.[15]

Further evidence that the American military hierarchy was complicit in the increasing number of attacks on Mexican civilians lies in the officers it chose for counterinsurgency duty. Colonel Jack Hays of the Texas regiment mentioned previously had been one of the most effective leaders in the ethnic cleansing campaigns that the Republic of Texas unleashed on its Native Americans in the early 1840s. During these campaigns, when any Native Americans attacked settlers, Texans killed whatever Native Americans could be found, including women and children from peaceful groups. The men engaged in these activities were called the Texas Rangers.[16] Texas Ranger Samuel Walker was famous for his fierce hatred of Mexicans. Walker, originally from Maryland, had immigrated to Texas while it was independent and participated as a Ranger in campaigns against both Native Americans and Mexicans. Captured during a Texan incursion into Mexico, Walker eventually escaped and returned to Texas. In 1847 American soldiers often said Walker hated Mexicans because they had executed his father and brother after some Texan prisoners tried to escape, but Walker's own account of the incident does not mention any relatives. In 1847 Walker and his men often executed captured Mexican guerrillas and punished Mexican civilians for guerrilla attacks.[17] Even some American soldiers who hated the guerrillas were appalled by Walker and his men. George Ballentine wrote that Walker, eager to revenge the deaths of his family, had returned to Mexico to "pour out the vials of his wrath on the wretched peasantry," while Barclay wrote in his diary that Walker "has an inveterate hatred against the Mexicans and when he has the power he carries on the war according to his own peculiar feelings. I do not think it is a very good policy to permit the gallant captain to thus exasperate the whole people."[18] Walker met a particularly ironic end. He led the mounted soldiers who had rushed into Huamantla on October 9. After driving off the few Mexican soldiers present, Walker's men dispersed to loot. They were surprised by a counterattack and Walker was killed. More American troops arrived and the Americans, including Walker's men, looted and killed many Mexican civilians. In the next few months Walker's company repeatedly avenged Walker by executing every Mexican male who fell into their hands.[19]

At Huamantla Walker was under the command of another officer famous for counterinsurgency operations. Lane, an Indiana merchant and politician, had been elected colonel of an Indiana volunteer regiment and then promoted to brigadier general. He earned praise for fighting well at La Angostura. He was later sent to Veracruz, and he commanded the force that attacked Huamantla and relieved the siege of Puebla.[20] He often led troops on expeditions seeking famous Mexican officers like Santa Anna, whom he almost trapped once, or Mexican guerrillas, especially Jarauta. He tried to surprise elusive enemies by rapidly covering long distances, often at night, and for this reason some began calling Lane the "Frances Marion of Mexico," after a Revolutionary War leader famous for similar tactics. Ironically, Marion earned his fame leading proindependence guerrillas, while Lane led invaders intent on defeating guerrillas.[21] Lane's forces were also famous for killing guerrilla prisoners, burning villages and ranches, and looting every place they entered. They ravaged Huamantla after Walker's death, and they looted Puebla after relieving the besieged American garrison. A failed attempt to catch Jarauta in Tulancingo ended in looting and mass rape.[22] In each case Lane's officers explained their troops' behavior by saying that they had lost control of their men during chaotic fighting, but the repetition suggests that the officers actually condoned their actions. Lieutenant William D. Wilkins, an officer in one of the new hybrid regiments, informed his father that Lane actually ordered his men to sack Huamantla to avenge Walker's death. Wilkins wrote that "well and fearfully was his mandate obeyed. Grog shops were broken open first, and them maddened with liquor every species of outrage was committed. Old women and girls were stripped of their clothing—and many suffered still greater outrages. Men were shot by dozens while concealing their property, churches, stores, and dwelling houses ransacked. . . . Such a scene I never hope to see again. It gave me a lamentable view of human nature, stripped of all disguise and free from all restraint, and made [me] for the first time, ashamed of my country."[23] Mexican guerrillas were very aware of the systematic reprisals of Lane's force. Rea reported on November 12, 1847, that some guerrillas were reluctant to serve because they were afraid that the Americans would attack their villages in revenge, "destroying and robbing even the sacred vessels as happened in Tlaxcala also raping the unfortunate women whose names are buried under the clay of silence to protect their honor."[24]

Lane's force committed one of the war's worst atrocities just before the armistice ended the fighting. In February 1848 Lane led a force that included Colonel Hays and Colonel William H. Polk, brother of President Polk. The force consisted of units like those described previously, nominally regular army but actually volunteers led by politically appointed officers. It also included some Mexican bandits working for the Americans, the famed contraguerrillas. Lane and his men were hunting guerillas, especially Jarauta, and their hunt took them to Teotihuacán and Tulancingo. Finding no guerrillas, they looted both towns. On February 25 they finally caught up with Jarauta and about two hundred Mexican guerrillas in Zacualtipán. Their dawn attack surprised the guerrillas and killed some, although Jarauta himself once again escaped. At that point the horror began. The soldiers mutilated and burned the corpse of one guerrilla leader. They looted the town, stealing anything they could from wealthy and poor alike. The Americans set fire to many houses and killed many Mexican civilians. In the parish church they stole the sacred vessels used in ceremonies, as well as the priest's vestments, and defecated in the sacristy. The Americans later brought a number of Mexican women to the church and raped them there.[25] The official reports of Lane, Hays, and Polk all extolled their cleverness and bravery in surprising and defeating the guerrillas, but only Lane mentioned any damage to civilian lives and property, claiming that a fire started accidentally during the battle destroyed part of the town.[26] Other American accounts were more forthcoming. Major Roswell Ripley wrote that "various excesses were committed by the troops in the confusion." Lieutenant Hill, who saw Lane's troops right after Zacualtipán, reported that they were overloaded with plunder, and that "all sorts of atrocities were committed by the troops of Lane, an indiscriminate slaughter was made of the inhabitants, women were forced, etc."[27] There is no direct evidence that Lane, Hays, or Polk ordered their troops to attack civilians or even gave them explicit permission to do so, but the prevalence of similar incidents under their command suggests that punishing civilians was for all intents and purposes a policy. And, of course, the presence of the president's brother at this particular scene is jarring.

Guerrilla warfare cost the Americans dearly, and guerrillas often achieved the kind of tactical victories that had eluded Mexico's conventional military forces. From the start of the war, American officers familiar with the problems faced by Napoleon's armies in Spain had feared guerrilla warfare. Scott first tried to prevent it by reining in his troops, yet in the end it is clear that a second strategy won out: American officers sought to separate guerrillas from their civilian base of support by terrorizing the latter. Thus, the guerrillas cost the Americans dearly, but indirectly they cost Mexican civilians more. Moreover, the massive financial advantages enjoyed by the American army negated some of the successes gained by the guerrillas. Guerrillas typically hamper conventional armies by interrupting the flow of supplies, but the Americans did not have to transport food, the most constant need of armies, because they could buy it from Mexicans. Thus the guerrillas alone could not defeat the Americans.[28]

The Debate over Continued Resistance

Even as the guerrilla war raged, Mexican politicians faced difficult decisions. Could Mexico continue to resist, and what might be gained by such resistance? At first glance these were questions for the national government, now located in the provincial city of Querétaro, but the ability to resist actually rested more with the politicians of each state. Resistance seemed to require conventional military forces, and these forces were melting away. Certainly the demoralization that inevitably follows defeats was a factor, but by far the bigger problem was hunger. After lifting the siege of Puebla, Alvarez took his remaining troops to the Cuernavaca area. In October 1847 he complained bitterly of having to appeal to local landowners "like a beggar" to get food and money for his troops, who he was sure would simply go home if they could not be fed. His superiors told him to send his National Guard units home to rest and reorganize, but he also had several regiments of regular cavalry. Alvarez pointed out that even the veterans among this latter group were starting to desert, and that without them to serve as cadre, the units would essentially cease to exist.[29] In November Alvarez went to Guerrero to reorganize National Guard units and recruit more men, relying again on the area's indigenous peasants. He wrote that he had convinced some of these peasants that fighting the Americans was the only way to recover their lands from landowners who had stolen them, and that "we Mexicans should have no other principles except unity, because only that will save us from the enemies that are invading our patria." Alvarez also collected food from peasants to feed the men, but he said he could only take them to the field if the government could provide cash from its revenues.[30]

Any cash would have to be raised by state governments, and some state politicians concluded that whatever might be gained by prolonging the war was not worth the material cost and human suffering. Politicians in Puebla State essentially gave up on the war after the failed attempt to recapture the city of Puebla. In late October Rea, commander of the military forces there, complained to his superiors that he was simply going to have to leave because the state government refused to support his troops. In early November he wrote again, warning that Governor Rafael Ynsunza was going to tell the government that the state had no more money. Rea insisted that it could support three thousand men, enough to tie up ten thousand Americans.[31] In his November letter Rea said that Alvarez, "an old and respectable patriot," could back up his claims, which is telling since before the war Alvarez and Rea were bitter political enemies and Rea had even accused Alvarez of plotting to have him assassinated.[32] Yet Alvarez and Rea both passionately believed that the war should be continued. In Alvarez's case this put him at loggerheads with state of Mexico governor Francisco Modesto de Olaguibel, a friend and fellow radical federalist. Until the fall of Mexico City, Olaguibel had balanced a very strong commitment to his state's autonomy with a fierce ideological commitment to the war, and he had even personally led National Guard troops during the defense of Mexico City. However, after Mexico City fell, public opinion in the state capital of Toluca swung so firmly against continuing the war that Mexican officers felt unwelcome there.[33] Olaguibel now opposed continuing sacrifices in a losing cause. He asked that Mexican soldiers not be sent to Toluca, saying they would draw the Americans' attention but would be unable to defend the city. In the southern part of the state, Alvarez and his remaining troops found state officials unwilling to support their material needs. Alvarez appealed to Olaguibel, who replied that the state had no money for the troops, but that he would ensure that state officials paid Alvarez's own salary. Alvarez, incensed, replied that he did not want to be paid while Mexican troops starved and the very offer was an insult to their friendship. Alvarez sent armed men to take money from state revenue offices, and Olaguibel publicly accused him of robbery. The dispute escalated until Alvarez engineered a mini-coup that removed Olaguibel from the governorship. One imagines that the dispute also definitely ended the men's friendship.[34]

As news of the battles around Mexico City spread across Mexico, some regional politicians became less willing to pour more scarce money and even more valuable blood into a lost cause.[35] Unlike Olaguibel, however, most radical federalists pushed to continue the fight. Between the annexation of Texas and the fall of Mexico City, support for the war had united the various political parties, but now it became a partisan question. The moderate federalists broke both with the radicals and with conservatives who saw the Americans as a threat to Catholicism. The congressional elections of August to October 1847 were only held in territories not occupied by American troops. The moderates won and they prepared to open negotiations with the United

States. The radicals controlled several state governments, and they now wore their defiance of the Americans as part of their partisan clothing, something that differentiated them from their opponents, whom they bitterly accused of betraying Mexico during the polkos rebellion.[36] Thus some politicians actually increased their rhetorical support for the war after many Mexicans deemed it already lost. One of the most famous radicals was Melchor Ocampo, governor of the state of Michoacán. In January 1848 he passionately declared that "the war should be waged because otherwise, if it does not continue, our enemies will return to take from us whatever they today believe they are letting us keep out of their goodness. The war should be waged if we do not want our nationality to be only a vain imitation in the future." The war was for him a test of the very question of whether Mexico was a nation.[37]

In San Luis Potosí the question of whether to continue the war became central to a fierce and long-running conflict in regional politics. Even before Mexico City fell, the radicals who controlled the state government had declared that they would refuse to recognize any Mexican government that signed a treaty ceding Mexican territory, and Governor Ramón Adame fiercely advocated continuing the war.[38] After the Americans took Monterrey and Saltillo in the fall of 1846, many inhabitants of San Luis Potosí saw themselves as being effectively on the front lines. San Luis Potosí had been central to the war effort as the place where armies headed north were organized. For months after La Angostura, both military and civilian leaders feared that Taylor would march American forces south to the city.[39] The stance of the San Luis Potosí radicals on the war was also tightly tied to their views about what kind of country Mexico should be. The radicals wanted a more egalitarian and democratic Mexico, and they were very willing to levy heavy taxes and forced loans on the wealthy to fund the war effort. These two questions were inseparable, and some of the most radical rhetoric about the war also stressed the problem of divisions of wealth. When radical Ponciano Arriaga heard of the August armistice between Santa Anna and Scott, he proposed new local military units and advocated exile for those who opposed the war. He also criticized merchants who did not let their employees attend National Guard training and suggested that private wealth be confiscated to support the war. Moderates believed Arriaga was using the struggle with the United States to incite class warfare, and they spread rumors that the poor were planning to rise up and loot the businesses of the wealthy. Arriaga responded that he did not see those he criticized as a class but instead as parasites, as "all the selfish people, all those who are able to take up arms but do not want to despite the dangers of the patria, all those who have abundant resources but claim they are scarce and hide them while our brave men are in misery."[40] None of this lowered political temperatures. When the San Luis Potosí radicals knew that the moderate national government was likely to negotiate a peace treaty with the United States, they began a revolt against the national government. Their local enemies quickly stepped in and removed them from office.[41]

Ironically, the stance of Mexican radicals was mirrored by some at the opposite end of the political spectrum. Priests led small rebellions in favor of continuing the war, but the largest one combined the efforts of centralist general Mariano Paredes y Arrillaga and Father Jarauta.[42] Paredes had sat out most of the war in exile, but after Mexico City fell he returned to try to grab a place on the political scene. Jarauta led guerrillas who continued their operations while the treaty that ended the war was negotiated and ratified, much to the discomfort of the Mexican government. In June 1848, after the ratification of the treaty, Paredes and Jarauta initiated a rebellion against the moderate government. They argued that the treaty that ended the war uncon-stitutionally ceded territory to the United States and that the government had sold out the Mexicans in the ceded territories. Ironically, their rhetoric essentially mirrored that of radical federalists like Valentín Gómez Farías, who had insisted that the constitution did not allow the government to cede territory and that the moderates were preparing to sell the residents of ceded territory "like a bunch of sheep or a group of slaves." Paredes and Jarauta were able to pull together substantial regular and National Guard military forces in the important city of Guanajuato, but they were defeated by government forces in July. Jarauta was executed immediately after he was captured, while Paredes was again allowed to go into exile, apparently because he had better political connections.[43]

California in the War

Mexican politicians eventually agreed to terms that were acceptable to Polk and the U.S. Senate. Why did they do so? Obviously the Mexican government lacked the financial resources needed to field new conventional armies, and the military consensus was that guerrilla resistance alone was not enough to defeat an invading conventional army. However, the most important reason that Mexico was willing to cede the territories that Polk wanted was that Mexican politicians came to understand that those territories were already irrevocably lost. All the blood and treasure that Mexicans had spent, from the prairie of Palo Alto to the streets of Mexico City, had not contributed one bit to the defense of New Mexico and California. They were simply too far away from the most populous and wealthy parts of Mexico and too close to the expanding population and economy of the United States. Here it is helpful to think not in terms of miles but instead about how people in the middle of the 1840s could travel and move objects. Railroads had not yet become common in the Western Hemisphere, and the internal combustion engine, needed not only to make highway travel efficient but also to construct thousands of miles of smooth, hard-surface roads through all kinds of terrain, had not yet been invented. That meant that navigable water in the form of rivers, seas, and canals was by far the best medium for transportation. Such bodies of water brought both New Mexico and California close to American economic and military power, and the absence of such water distanced the territory from Mexican economic and military power. The Mexican government could not effectively send significant numbers of troops to New Mexico or California. The comparatively few Mexicans who lived in these places had to face American aggression on their own. They resisted more than many people believe, but they were overwhelmed.

Let us consider the problem of California first, because it seems a little counterintuitive. After all, if one looks at a map, the Pacific Ocean clearly connects California to Mexico. However, in the middle of the nineteenth century, Mexico's Pacific coast was far from the Central Plateau, where the country's population and wealth were concentrated. The port of Acapulco was a small village separated from that plateau by several hundred miles of mountainous terrain without even a road fit for wagons. Although by the 1840s there was some trade through the port, it hardly generated enough revenue to keep a customhouse open. The port of San Blas, farther north, was even more isolated and impoverished. Californian ports did much more business with American ports on the Eastern Seaboard because their large populations and nascent industries provided markets for California's products. With cheap transportation in the form of sailing ships, products from California could be exported to the Eastern Seaboard much more profitably than they could ever have been sent to the cities of Mexico's Central Plateau. When we think about the projection of military power, the imbalance is even greater. By the middle of the 1840s the growing commercial activities and political power of American merchants and shipowners had led to the development of a U.S. Navy much larger than its Mexican equivalent, and California was within easy reach of its warships. Even before the war, the U.S. Navy had a Pacific squadron to safeguard American commercial interests and the Pacific whaling fleet. Certainly it took patience to bring both merchant ships and warships from the eastern United States around Cape Horn to California and back, but the technology was well tried, and it was very cheap. Moreover, the dominance of the American navy meant that even if the Mexican government could have quickly mobilized military forces and gotten them to the Mexican Pacific coast, any ships transporting them would have been intercepted before they could reinforce California.

New Mexico was also effectively closer to the eastern United States than it was to Mexico City. Water transport on navigable rivers, even more efficient since the recent massive introduction of steamboats, made Saint Louis and Independence, Missouri, eminently reachable from the eastern United States either through New Orleans or through the Ohio River to the Mississippi. Although Saint Louis was separated from Santa Fe by more than a thousand miles of land, the Santa Fe Trail that crossed it was relatively flat most of the way and both water and forage for animals were usually available along it. The Camino Real stretching from New Mexico to Mexico City was longer, and much more of its route passed through mountains or deserts, making the movement of goods or military forces difficult and expensive. Although through great fortitude and expense the Mexicans managed to move some forces to the Texas border near Matamoros during the buildup to the war, they made no similar effort to reinforce New Mexico. The same factors that facilitated commercial travel between Saint Louis and New Mexico made the travel of the American forces that eventually conquered New Mexico relatively easy.

The harsh realities of geography made it impossible to send troops from the densely populated regions of central Mexico to effectively defend

California and New Mexico, and this allowed relatively small American military forces to eventually establish military control of both vast regions. The battles in these regions, although fierce, involved relatively small numbers of people. However, there are several reasons to explore the struggles for California and New Mexico in this social history of the war. Most obviously, acquiring these regions was the principal goal of the Polk administration's Mexico policy. Although most of the fighting occurred elsewhere, these places were the object of the war. Moreover, they also provide a compelling window on the problems of national identity that both Mexico and the United States were wrestling with in the middle of the nineteenth century. Identities in both places were multifaceted and shifting, and although some people in Mexico's far north felt relatively detached from central authority and attracted to the opportunities posed by the burgeoning U.S. economy, many resisted American political and military control.

California and New Mexico were very different societies, and their differences were reflected in their histories during the war. The Mexican presence in California was both newer and much smaller than that in New Mexico. In the second half of the eighteenth century, Spanish friars began building missions in California to evangelize its Native American population. They were accompanied by Spanish-speaking migrants from northern Mexico who served as soldiers protecting the missions and also farmed to support themselves. Later these soldiers and their descendants also began to employ partially acculturated Indians to raise crops and livestock. Yet, before the 1820s, this settler group was peripheral to the missionary effort. The whole region of California, moreover, was at the very periphery of Mexico: because hostile natives controlled the land route, migration to California required arduous travel to Mexico's Pacific coast and then a sea voyage, both expensive propositions that seemed to be losing bets given the relatively low cost of land much closer to Mexican markets. In 1821 the Spanish-speaking population of California was less than 3,500.[44] Probably the only development that could have lured large numbers of Mexicans to migrate to California would have been the discovery of precious metals, and ironically that discovery did not occur until 1848, right after Mexico had lost control of the territory.

The possibilities for prosperity shifted significantly in the 1820s. Mexico became independent from the Spanish Empire, and its government legalized trade with foreigners. Better yet, this political change came just as American merchants and shipowners from ports on the East Coast were pushing into the Pacific in search of new products and markets. They found both in California. Far from that sunny and warm region, people in the rapidly industrializing eastern United States needed shoes in which to trudge to the factories, candles to light indoor work spaces on those gloomy New England winter days, and soap for urban people who no longer butchered their own animals. Soon California was exporting hides for shoe factories and tallow for candle and soap factories. The availability of vast amounts of cattle for this trade was not a simple result of California's benign climate. It was facilitated by political and social change. The sellers of hides and tallow needed labor to herd and butcher cattle, and to a large degree that labor was made available by the political decision to secularize Californian missions in the 1830s. Acculturated Indians who had before grown crops and raised cattle under the supervision of friars to support mission communities were now available to work for Mexican ranchers, and they were willing to work to ensure a steady food supply and access to manufactured goods. Those same acculturated Indians often helped ranchers protect the herds from independent Native American groups in a sort of low-level endemic warfare. Ranchers also needed land, and here political change helped as well. While Spanish officials had seen the area as one where settlement existed to support evangelization, Mexican officials saw settlement and economic growth as a way to protect California from encroachment by foreign powers. Generally land grants became easier to get, and they were often also used to reward political allies.[45]

American merchants immigrated to California in the 1820s and early 1830s to sell consumer goods imported from the East Coast of the United States and buy hides and tallow to send back East. These merchants often found that marrying Mexican women and becoming Mexican citizens further facilitated access to trade and even land grants. Many merchant immigrants also became acculturated into Mexican society, something that was more psychologically possible for them than it would be for later immigrants to California. They had left an American society in which religious fervor and diversity were flourishing, but prejudice against Catholics had not yet reached the fever pitch it would in the 1840s. It was also an American society in which anti-Mexican prejudice had not yet advanced to the point at which Mexicans were no longer considered white. These merchants were certainly bicultural, but there is no reason to believe that their religious conversions, integration into extended families of Mexicans, and adoption of Mexican customs of dress and behavior were insincere. Lower-class Americans who had worked in the notoriously racially diverse crews of merchant or whaling ships also settled in California, married, and acculturated into local society.[46] In the 1820s and early 1830s it was still possible to be both American and Mexican, evidence of the fluidity and flexibility of national identity.

Californian society in the 1820s and 1830s was no utopia. Although Americans had not established racial domination over Mexicans, American immigrants and Mexicans together dominated both the acculturated Native Americans who labored on ranches and those who lived in independent groups. This society was also politically unstable, as the elites of Northern and Southern California competed for supremacy and increasing economic opportunities made it more desirable to control local governments that could grant land and settle disputes. California was a very long way from the political debates of central Mexico, but those debates had ramifications because successive Mexican governments sent constitutions, laws, and administrators that could be utilized in local political disputes, some of which were decided by violence or at least shows of force. It became clear over time that the central government could not really exercise control in California. The only time it sent a large number of troops to the area, its effort fell prey to the same lack of revenue that crippled Mexico's government in so many ways. The conscripts could not be fed or paid, and soon local Mexicans tired of the fact that the soldiers stole food to survive. Local Mexicans forced out the governor who had brought them and established de facto independence from central political control. Many Mexicans in California were convinced that orders and administrators sent by the national government in Mexico City were at best irrelevant and sometimes pernicious.[47] Yet that does not necessarily mean that they were ready to join another country, much less accept a new place beneath Americans in a racially hierarchical society, the place Jacksonian democracy would eventually force them into. In many ways Californian Mexicans were fiercely attached to Mexican culture, with its language, its Catholicism, its emphasis on family relations and family honor, and even the way that racial social prejudice coexisted with legal racial equality and the recognition that individuals could shift their racial identity through their actions.

The socioeconomic model under which a Mexican California prospered by exporting products to the burgeoning economy of the United States was soon haunted by the specter of what had happened in Texas. Increasing American contact with California via the sea route brought more Americans, and by the early 1840s those who wrote about California increasingly stressed not only its commercial potential but also its fertile lands and relative lack of population. Like Texas before it, California came to be seen as a place of great agricultural opportunity for American settlers. Some of these writers also peddled anti-Mexican stereotypes that implied that an industrious American population would prosper there. If, as Richard Henry Dana wrote, Californians were "an idle, thriftless people," would not American settlers make this region prosper? Writers who were clearly aware of what had happened in Texas and saw Mexicans as racial others too lazy or improvident to hold their northern territories worked to convince Americans that California was ripe for American settlement.[48] At first American settlers were deterred by the mountain ranges that separated California from the Mississippi and Missouri valleys, with their easy water transportation, and few agricultural immigrants set out directly from the East Coast for any frontier. Generally, the Americans who arrived in California via the relatively easy sea route were merchants, and those who stayed were happy enough to settle into Californian society more or less as it was.

Eventually trappers pioneered land routes from the Missouri valley into Northern California. Originally they moved through the mountains seeking new beaver populations after they had decimated populations farther east. Yet demand for beaver hats was also declining, and soon trappers moved into another business entirely. They put their hard-earned knowledge about feasible mountain passes and where travelers might find water, grass for their animals, and other necessities to work by guiding the settler groups egged on by immigration promoters who sung of California's fertile lands. The land routes were so long and difficult that immigrants arrived in the autumn with little food and worn-out animals, and Mexican officials were reluctant to force them to turn back to near-certain death in the mountain snows. They also believed the immigrants could help the local economy, so they even legalized their presence by granting permits. The problem was that these new immigrants were not like the American merchants who had earlier integrated into the local community. The new immigrants arrived with a sense of their racial superiority and the belief that sooner or later American immigration to California would separate California from Mexico. They were classic Jacksonian Democrats, convinced of the superiority of white men to anyone they might encounter and already thoroughly exposed both to the racial stereotypes about Mexicans that became commonplace in the United States after the Texas Revolution and the renewed anti-Catholicism sparked by Catholic immigration to the United States. There was no chance that these newcomers would follow the lead of previous merchant immigrants, converting to Catholicism and marrying into Mexican families. They settled in separate locations, began farming without land titles, and made little or no attempt to become even nominally Mexicans. Moreover, the Texas Revolution did not just spark anti-Mexican prejudice: it provided these immigrants a blueprint for action, the idea that if enough Americans arrived, they could establish political independence from the Mexican government and reward themselves with land grants.[49]

Meanwhile the American government also had its eye on California. It offered an excellent natural harbor on the Pacific, an area of great interest to American merchants. It also offered agricultural land, the commodity dearest to the heart of the Jacksonian Democratic Party. By 1846 American naval commanders, whose ships were nominally in the Pacific to protect American merchant and whaling ships, had orders to seize Californian ports if they heard that war with Mexico had begun. Oddly these orders called on them to repeat an act one commander, Thomas ap Catesby Jones, had committed in error in 1842. Jones, acting on an outdated rumor that war had begun between the two countries, seized Monterrey, California, only to apologize the next day when American consul Thomas Larkin convinced him that his information was incorrect. In 1846, as Polk increased pressure on the Mexican government along the Texas border, he also prepared for a naval invasion of California. Polk appears to have gone even further in his contingency plans. American military officer John C. Fremont, who already had explored in the West and even visited California, was sent with a large exploring expedition in June 1845 even as Taylor's army was being assembled in Texas. Fremont and some sixty well-armed men reached California in late 1845. This alarmed Mexican authorities, but rather than force his group back into the snowy mountains, they agreed to let Fremont winter over as long as he stayed clear of Mexican settlements. He did not fulfill this condition, and Mexicans gathered militia troops to eject his group. In March 1846 Fremont defiantly established a defensive position and raised the American flag, but a few days later he backed down and marched away. This move only postponed the clash. In May Fremont and his men egged on a revolt by American settlers, who, following the Texas model, declared themselves to be a free republic. We do not know if Polk's official instructions called on Fremont to spark a settler revolt, because we do not know what those instructions were. Fremont, however, was extremely well connected to expansionist interests.[50]

The story of this so-called Bear Flag Republic links the unsanctioned behavior of classic Jacksonian adventurers to the more organized and centrally controlled aggression of the 1846–1848 war. In truth the line between the two had been blurred for decades. Jackson himself had illegally invaded Spanish Florida in 1818, and Polk had even praised Jones after his faux pas of 1842. Fremont's brief standoff with Mexican authorities in California and later dealings with the Bear Flaggers fit this pattern. These recent American arrivals in California were confident in their racial superiority and convinced that the hardships they had suffered in their overland journey entitled them to settle. They were also afraid. As Mexican authorities came to realize how different these new settlers were from the Americans who had previously integrated themselves into Californian society, some began to discuss the possibility of ejecting the new, illegal immigrants. When these rumors reached the recent arrivals, they were made more potent by the idea that government authorities might encourage Native Americans to attack settlers or burn their crops. The Americans who had traveled over the mountain ranges were inclined to believe this particular rumor because they had especially rocky relationships with Native Americans. Immigrant parties had treated all Native Americans with suspicion and sometimes launched unprovoked attacks on groups they encountered during their journeys. Even in California they had difficulty distinguishing between friendly and unfriendly Native Americans. The idea that the Mexicans would use Native Americans against them made perfect sense to the new arrivals. Independent Native American groups stayed on the sidelines, however, not helping either side during the Bear Flag Revolt and the subsequent official American invasion of California. Still, fueled by a potent mix of fear, ambition, and racial prejudice, the American settlers declared their intention to found an independent republic. They began confiscating livestock from Mexican authorities and captured some prominent Mexicans, all before they heard of the fighting that had taken place thousands of miles away near Matamoros and the official beginning of the war.[51]

In July 1846 American warships brought news of that official beginning and their sailors and marines began capturing coastal towns. Fremont and the American settlers quickly fell in line behind this effort, becoming nominally if not in discipline American soldiers. The problem faced by Mexican authorities was dire. There were only 7,300 Mexicans, of all ages and sexes, in the vast region, and, as was typical of cattle-raising societies, they were very spread out, so only a few men could be gathered in any one place to oppose the Americans. Thanks to the importance of the livestock industry, many were fine horsemen, but they had very few firearms. The American frontiersmen of the north were well armed, and the navy's several hundred disciplined sailors and their cannon were also relatively formidable even on land. The Mexicans were also divided by previous political conflicts, and some were at first ambivalent about the possibility of American conquest. Many had personal experience with the American merchants who had facilitated the export economy, and those Americans had integrated themselves into local culture and families. More than a few Mexicans knew Americans they considered friends or part of their extended families. Seeing Americans as alien invaders who threatened their way of life did not come naturally to these Mexicans. These military and political advantages allowed the Americans to quickly establish control of the most populated areas of the state.[52]

Yet the conquest of California would not prove to be quick and easy. Securing California was only one of the duties assigned to America's Pacific warships, as naval commanders also had orders to blockade Mexico's Pacific coast. As soon as things in California seemed quiet, ships and the disciplined men who had been taken from their crews to garrison towns withdrew and sailed south. This changed both the numeric balance of power and the character of the occupation, as sailors and marines were mostly replaced by the frontier adventurers of Fremont's ex–Bear Flaggers. These men despised Mexicans. They were much more like the American volunteers whose depredations sparked Mexican guerrilla resistance in Mexico's north, and in California the actions of the ex–Bear Flaggers had similar results. One prominent Mexican called these frontiersmen "white Indians," and they soon gained a reputation for stealing and treating Mexicans with great disrespect. In Los Angeles American commander Archibald Gillepsie made matters worse by imposing draconian punishments on Mexicans who committed petty offenses. In September 1846 he was rudely awakened to how the balance of power had changed with the withdrawal of most of the navy. Locals revolted and forced him to agree to withdraw his men to the coast to await evacuation. Instead he stalled there, waiting for navy reinforcements, but even when the navy arrived, the Americans could not retake the area. The resistance spread to other places, especially in Southern California. In December a Mexican force bloodily defeated the few American regulars that Stephen Kearny had led overland from New Mexico.[53] Even in the absence of effective political ties to Mexico or the hope of military help from the Mexican government, many Mexicans in Southern California were not willing to accept American conquest.

Violent resistance to American rule continued for months, but it labored under huge disadvantages. The population was spread out, and men who gathered to oppose the Americans could not support their families economically. The inhabitants had few firearms and those weapons were poor in quality. Northern California remained relatively quiet, and that allowed Fremont to pull together a large force of his frontiersmen and begin a slow march south. The survivors of Kearny's defeat were able to link up with naval forces, which were vastly reinforced when the bulk of America's Pacific naval squadron returned, bringing artillery and hundreds of disciplined sailors and marines. In the end the Americans simply could deploy too many men and too much firepower. More importantly, the resisters remained completely isolated from central Mexico, and they could not expect reinforcements. In January 1847 the Americans retook Los Angeles, and a few days later the Mexican leaders decided that further resistance was useless. The arrival of a new order in which American whites dominated both Mexican and Native American Californians was further driven home when gold was discovered in Northern California. The Gold Rush brought thousands of Americans to the region and increased the pace at which both groups were dispossessed of their lands through violence and the courts. For some Mexicans this process proved much more wrenching than the fighting of 1846–1847.[54]

New Mexico in the War

Most of the rest of the area transferred to the United States was part of the Mexican territory called New Mexico, which had long been settled by Spanish speakers. Colonial Spaniards had found it much more attractive than most of the far North. Its river valleys could support agriculture, and more importantly, they were already populated by sedentary Pueblo Indians whom the Spaniards had conquered and converted. Over the course of the colonial period, the Pueblo Indian population had declined substantially, but villages of Catholic Pueblos were still an important part of society. Hispanic settlers occupied increasing amounts of the arable valley land and raised sheep in the mountains. The people of New Mexico exported agricultural, animal, and textile products south toward Chihuahua and bought manufactured goods that had made the long journey from central Mexico. The potential for economic growth was limited by the inhabitants' distance from suppliers and markets. There were not enough economic opportunities to lure more Mexicans, and, as was the case with California, perhaps the only thing that could have changed that would have been the discovery of precious metals. After all, mineral bonanzas had earlier motivated the establishment of large Mexican populations in other dry northern regions, leading to great silver cities like Zacatecas and San Luis Potosí.[55] Ironically, though, the mineral strikes that would later dot New Mexico and Arizona with mining towns did not occur until after they were transferred to the United States, again much like California.

Before 1846 economic activities were also circumscribed by relations with several groups of independent Native Americans. These relations had existed for many decades, although the politics among different Native American groups were always shifting. At different moments any given group might raid Hispanic or Pueblo settlements and far-flung flocks to acquire livestock or peacefully visit to offer goods in trade. During the late colonial period the government had achieved a measure of peace by brokering agreements and offering gifts to Native American groups. After independence the Mexican government's fiscal problems undermined these policies and also reduced the amount of military force the government could provide to protect far northern settlements. Raiding became more common. Hispanic inhabitants and their Pueblo allies often pursued raiders and fought fiercely to avenge their dead and recover livestock or captives. Yet the very nature of the area's geography and economy limited the force they could deploy. Pasturing sheep or horses in the dry mountain climate meant that shepherds were often exposed far from help, and even the valleys where farming took place tended to be so narrow that settlements were necessarily small and far apart. American expansion into the western half of the Mississippi watershed worsened the situation by squeezing different Native American groups into a smaller area, forcing them to compete for resources. The growing American economy also provided a new market for raided goods. American traders were quite willing to provide weapons and other prized goods in exchange for stolen livestock or even New Mexican captives. Generally, the relative power of these independent Native American groups was rising and the growth of the Hispanic agricultural economy seemed stalled.[56]

New Mexico was tied to Mexico much more thoroughly than California was, thanks to the economic connection to Chihuahua, religious connections to Durango, and political connections to the colonial government in Mexico City. The territory's larger population allowed it to support a denser web of institutions and authorities. As Mexico became independent from Spain and developed its new political system, authorities tried to inculcate in New Mexicans a new national identity through education, oaths, and ceremonies like those being deployed in much more densely populated locations in central Mexico. They also sought to convince the Pueblos that they owed loyalty to the new national state. Politically active New Mexicans soon found themselves drawn into the debates about federalism and centralism that characterized politics in independent Mexico. These questions about where government power would lie were extremely pertinent to New Mexicans' efforts to carve out satisfying lives on the frontier, which required access to markets, the adjudication of local disputes, and help maintaining an acceptable relationship with independent Indians. As in other parts of Mexico, political disputes sometimes sparked violence, and one of the most important revolts against centralist rule took place in New Mexico in 1837.[57]

Mexico's independence was nearly simultaneous with another development of great importance to New Mexico. As Americans populated the Mississippi watershed, New Mexicans became connected to the American economy as consumers and producers. Mexican independence allowed entrepreneurs in New Mexico and Saint Louis to reach out to each other across the Great Plains, and soon the Santa Fe Trail became a famous commercial route. In the two decades between the opening of trade and 1843, commerce along the trail increased more than thirtyfold. New Mexico now had access to manufactured goods, especially clothing and tools, at much lower prices because they could be moved cheaply via water transportation all the way from their places of manufacture to Missouri and then carried on the Santa Fe Trail, much of which was relatively level and had good pasturage for draft animals. Goods shipped from central Mexico were more difficult and expensive to transport. New Mexicans mostly paid for goods shipped from the United States with cash that they obtained by sending sheep, woolen textiles, and agricultural products south to Chihuahua and nearby regions. They also sent mules, beaver pelts, and buffalo hides to eastern U.S. markets through Missouri. Within a few years American consumers, producers, and merchants became essential to the economic livelihood of New Mexico.[58]

The Santa Fe trade changed New Mexico's economic possibilities, but it also remade the region's social landscape, especially for wealthy New Mexicans. New Mexican merchants participated in this trade, often in partnership with American colleagues. The American merchants who made the journey to New Mexico were ambitious and adventurous. They were also the product of a social culture in which family networks were crucial to commerce. In the nineteenth-century world, marriage alliances were probably as common for merchants as they were for royal and noble families. Historian Anne Hyde points out how formal and informal marriages underpinned the trading networks that connected people of many different ethnic backgrounds in what is now the western United States.[59] In New Mexico, some American merchants married into the wealthiest Hispanic families. This strategy opened doors to more trade and to political favors, including land grants. Partial cultural and even religious assimilation into Hispanic society was a small price to pay for these advantages. Ironically, even as the propaganda sparked by the Texas Revolution made many Americans see Mexicans as racial and religious others, some Americans deliberately Mexicanized themselves. This did not require them to give up other forms of identity, and they kept a foot in American culture even as they joined Mexican extended families, converted to Catholicism, and learned Spanish. Charles Bent, for instance, married into a wealthy New Mexican family and established himself in Taos, developing many friendships among Mexicans. Yet in other ways he was a classic Jacksonian, inclined toward using violence to punish acts or words he saw as offenses to his honor. These merchants also kept an interested eye on the rapid expansion of American settlement in the West. American immigration helped bring New Mexico's population to about 65,000 by 1846. Yet, via the Santa Fe Trail, it was only a short distance from Missouri, which went from having 140,000 people in 1830 to more than 380,000 in 1840.[60]

The Santa Fe Trail and the tight connections among New Mexico's Hispanic elite, the American economy, and American merchants were crucial to the American conquest of New Mexico. The Polk administration prepared detailed contingency plans for invading New Mexico more than nine months before its Texas provocation initiated the war. Once Polk had his declaration of war, Colonel Kearny organized a mixed force of Missouri volunteers and regulars near Saint Louis and led them on the march of more than one thousand miles to New Mexico. Although they suffered hardships on the way, the soldiers were traveling a well-known route that over the previous two decades had been traversed by thousands of wagons carrying merchandise.[61] When the soldiers arrived in New Mexico, they found out that commerce had blazed not only their physical trail but also their political trail. American traders had multiple business and familial relationships with the region's wealthiest families, and the territorial governor, Manuel Armijo, participated fully in this newly integrated elite. American merchants made a major effort to convince their social peers, business partners, and in-laws that New Mexicans, and especially wealthy New Mexicans, would be better off under American rule. Armijo was one of the principal targets of their lobbying, and they met with him multiple times. This lobbying campaign was paralleled by Kearny's public proclamations that the Americans would respect Catholicism and that his mission was to bring New Mexicans American citizenship, good government, and protection from independent Indians.[62] Even so, many Hispanic New Mexicans saw the Americans as greedy heretics who sought to impose themselves as conquerors. Armijo felt great social pressure to mobilize some kind of resistance. The governor collected a large force of militia, but when the Americans were only a few miles away, he mysteriously ordered the militia to go home and retreated with his few regulars. Kearny occupied Santa Fe, proclaimed that the New Mexicans were now American citizens, and proceeded to set up an American administration with Bent as governor.[63]

Soon Kearny felt that American possession of New Mexico was secure enough that he could send some troops to invade Chihuahua and lead others toward California, leaving a relatively small occupying force of Missouri volunteers in New Mexico. Like those used elsewhere in the war, these volunteers held Jacksonian ideas about the proper places of white males and racial others, including Mexicans, and the volunteers' drunken brawling and boasting contradicted the conciliatory tone Kearny had tried to set. The Americans also requisitioned supplies from New Mexicans, and Bent himself displayed contempt toward those New Mexicans who did not actively help the Americans.[64] The Americans' alignment with many of the wealthiest families in the region did not bring with it the allegiance of all New Mexicans. New Mexico was divided by political and class tensions. Even within the territory's elite there were families who understood that American rule would undermine their privileged access to military and political posts, as well as people who genuinely believed that any weakening of the Catholic Church's exclusive access to New Mexican hearts and minds would expose people to the danger of eternal damnation. Priests and other prominent people were soon conspiring against the Americans.

This opposition was not confined to a faction of the region's elite. Many less wealthy Hispanic New Mexicans shared their commitment to Catholicism and their fear of social displacement. Pueblo Indians opposed the Americans for religious reasons, and some believed that their lands were threatened by land grants that Armijo had made before the invasion to prominent Americans, including Bent. Both the Pueblos and Hispanic Mexicans believed that American merchants had actually encouraged the violent raids of independent Native American groups by buying stolen livestock and even people. Some were also embittered by violence that Texans had inflicted on New Mexican settlements during the period of Texas's independence. British adventurer George Ruxton, who traveled through New Mexico in December 1846 and January 1847, wrote that "the most bitter feeling and most determined hostility existed against the Americans, who certainly in Santa Fe and elsewhere have not been very anxious to conciliate the people, but by their bullying and overbearing demeanor toward them, have in a great measure been the cause of this hatred." New Mexicans who believed Ruxton was an American harassed him and called him a donkey, and when he stopped at one isolated ranch, his New Mexican hostess proclaimed that she was glad Ruxton was English and therefore Christian, unlike the Americans.[65]

In December the Americans discovered a plot against their rule. They arrested some plotters, but in Santa Fe a crowd of over one hundred New Mexicans refused to allow the Americans to arrest one conspirator. In January 1847 an open revolt broke out in Taos, where people from the Pueblo community and Hispanics killed dozens of Americans and collaborationist Hispanics. Bent was there visiting his Mexican family, and the rebels first wounded, then scalped, and finally killed him. The degree of violence suggests that the Americans were now seen as representing the kind of threat posed by independent Native Americans, as New Mexicans and Native Americans had long communicated their anger and grief to each other through such exemplary violence. The Americans were not ignorant about this kind of communication. When they heard about the revolt, a group of American trappers and merchants moved into New Mexico, vowing to scalp any Mexican they found. Another force of Missouri volunteers and American merchants marched into northern New Mexico from Santa Fe. They used cannon to break up efforts to oppose them and eventually laid siege to the Pueblo community of Taos, where many rebels had holed up. The Americans took the village after a bloody attack in which many defenders were killed in the church. The Americans also burned another village that had opposed them, and wherever they went they meted out extreme repression. Some rebel leaders were executed after hasty trials in which jurors and other court personnel included Americans whose relatives had been killed by the rebels. Young American merchant Lewis Garrard participated in the efforts to put down the revolt, but as he observed the trials he was appalled. He wrote that "it certainly did appear to be a great assumption on the part of the Americans to conquer a country, and then arraign the revolting inhabitants for treason." Guerrilla resistance continued for several months, and Mexican propagandists in central Mexico urged people to follow New Mexicans' example.[66]

Fluid Identities

In both California and New Mexico the willingness of American merchants to marry Mexican women, convert to Catholicism, and become Mexican citizens speaks to the earlier fluidity of identities in what later became the western United States. Their assimilation was not definitive, and in both places many of these recent immigrants eventually facilitated the American conquest, but the relative ease with which they integrated into Mexican society before the war is noteworthy. Ironically, the nature of their presence before the war undoubtedly influenced some Mexicans to not oppose the Americans wholeheartedly. Some Mexicans might easily have imagined a postconquest era in which they were valued partners rather than racialized others near the bottom of the social hierarchy.

There were other groups whose position and actions also provide evidence of the fluidity of identities in the West before the war. The most obvious were independent Native American groups. Although in 1846 the Americans touted their ability to control these groups, in fact the Americans would not triumph over them for several decades. A much less obvious set of people also demonstrate the fluidity of these identities. In 1846 those planning the American invasion of New Mexico and its hoped-for continuation to Southern California needed troops, and American settlement was not particularly dense yet in Missouri, Kansas, and Iowa. The volunteer units recruited in Missouri did not seem sufficient, so the Polk administration turned to Mormon migrants to staff a new unit. The Mormons were one of the most controversial groups arising from the religious fervor of the Second Great Awakening. They first tried to settle together in Missouri and later in Illinois. Each time they faced extreme violence, and the group's founder, Joseph Smith, was killed in 1844 in Illinois. Now the Mormons were in the midst of seeking a place in the West where they could settle as a group and practice their religion. When the U.S. government began trying to recruit them, many men were reluctant to sign up. They were bitter about the violence that had been inflicted on them and they did not feel any particular political allegiance to an American society that had persecuted them. Some Mormons believed that God might make the United States lose the war to punish Americans for mistreating them. Mormon leaders, however, knew that continued movement into the West would require money, and such money could be earned by men serving in the American military. The Mormons also needed federal permission to temporarily live on lands belonging to Native Americans before continuing their trek to Utah. Government recruiters also promised the Mormons that their unit would continue on from New Mexico to California, where some might settle. More radically, the men were to be allowed to bring their families with them, an extraordinary exception to American military practice. Mormon leaders convinced hundreds of their followers to join up, and the group began its long journey to New Mexico. The Mormon battalion did not arrive in New Mexico until after both the initial conquest and the revolt had ended, but they later continued to California, building a wagon road as they went. They were embittered when American commanders did not allow the men with families to bring them from New Mexico to California. The Mormon recruits were almost totally motivated by the desire that their faith and families survive, and in this sense they differed from both regular army recruits and the men of all the other volunteer regiments.[67] Ironically, decades later the desire to freely practice controversial aspects of their faith would lead many Mormons to leave the United States and settle in northern Mexico.

CHAPTER 9

The Law of the Strongest

The James K. Polk administration had conquered New Mexico and California, gaining de facto possession of the territories Polk had originally hoped to obtain through sheer intimidation or perhaps a brief war. However, the war was far from brief. Mexicans from many different political factions and social backgrounds were committed to opposing the United States, and under these circumstances no Mexican government was willing to officially cede the conquered territories to the United States. Mere possession of them was not enough: Polk needed official recognition that they were now part of the United States, and this could only happen through negotiations. Fortunately for Polk, during the fall of 1847 the political balance in Mexico shifted. Although both radical federalists on the left and some conservatives on the right remained committed to further resistance, the moderates dominating the national government had come to believe that the war must be ended. Guerrillas alone could not succeed without conventional forces, and it was impossible to maintain conventional forces because the American blockade and occupation of ports starved the government of revenue. Moreover, even if resistance in the center of the country was able to continue, reconquering New Mexico and California was a sheer impossibility. By November 1847 the moderates believed that Mexico's future required the sacrifice of its northern possessions.

Some Americans, intoxicated by news of American military victories and the rhetoric of Manifest Destiny, believed that the United States should absorb more than just those northern possessions. Various Democrats advocated the complete absorption of Mexico into the United States or the establishment of a protectorate. Why should American expansionism not take full advantage of a defeated and racially inferior foe? Others were a bit less ambitious, lobbying for the acquisition of some territories that are now in northern Mexico. These people had differing visions of American possession of Mexico. Some believed that the superior American race would eventually bring Mexicans up to its level, while others assumed that Mexico would always be governed by an American elite, essentially as a colonial possession.[1] The movement to retain control of all of Mexico faced significant opposition. Annexing the entire country might seriously disrupt the sectional balance that was so shakily maintained in the United States. Some Southerners believed that under American rule, Mexico would be open to slavery, while others feared that Mexicans' abhorrence of slavery would mean that its territory would be divided into free states where slavery was not allowed. Northerners who opposed the expansion of slavery thought that incorporating Mexico would favor the South.[2] Yet, the effort to annex more or all of Mexico was stymied less by sectional issues that it was by concern about the racial inferiority of Mexicans. If American success in the world really rested on the superiority of Anglo-Saxon, Protestant, white people, what good could come of making millions of dark-skinned Catholics American citizens? And if these new residents were to be colonial subjects rather than citizens, was that not a threat to American democracy? Given these problems, it seemed to make sense to incorporate only regions that were thinly populated by Mexicans, in other words, New Mexico and California. Ironically, many of the most racist and anti-Catholic statements made in the U.S. Congress during the war were made not to justify unlimited American expansion but instead to advocate limiting it.[3]

The fact that some American politicians believed that the United States had enough military power to annex the entire country does not make it true. Even after the fall of Mexico City, many Mexicans on both the right and the left were willing to spend their treasure and spill their blood in continued resistance. They were convinced that their country had a core set of values and beliefs, and that the Americans threatened those in ways that were demonstrated both in relatively abstract racist and anti-Catholic rhetoric and in how American soldiers had often behaved in Mexico. Would these people ever have acquiesced to becoming part of the United States? Winfield Scott did not believe so. On December 25, 1847, he reported to his superiors that some Mexicans favored annexation but that it would mean the more or less permanent military occupation of Mexico. As he put it, "Annexation and military occupation would be, if we maintain the annexation, one and the same thing, as to the amount of force to be employed by us; for if, after the formal act, by treaty or otherwise, we should withdraw our troops, it cannot be doubted that Mexico, or rather the active part thereof, would again relapse into a permanent state of revolution, beginning with one *against* annexation."[4] Scott framed this statement with the ideas, so often expressed by Americans, that few Mexicans participated politically and that Mexicans were incapable of peaceful self-government, but he was also conceding that American possession of Mexico would have to rest on force. Scott's racial disdain cannot be separated from the fact of continued resistance.

By the end of 1847, after more than a year and a half of war, the moderates and Nicholas Trist, the American diplomat Polk had sent to negotiate with Mexico, were ready to reach a mutually acceptable agreement. It probably helped that the difficulty of communications mostly isolated Trist from American debates about the wisdom of annexing more Mexican territory, and that Trist himself was firmly convinced that annexing all of Mexico would damage the United States. Months earlier the Polk administration had given him firm instructions about the minimum it wanted in a treaty. Trist did not know that as the war wore on, an irritated Polk had begun to favor demanding even more territory to punish Mexico for its resistance. Polk became even more irritated when, during the August 1847 armistice, Trist deviated from his original instructions by suggesting that the American government might accept the Nueces River as the boundary of Texas, something that would have totally undercut Polk's original case for a declaration of war and left him with more than a little political egg on his face. Thus, on October 6, 1847, Polk's secretary of state, James Buchanan, sent a letter recalling Trist. It reached Trist on November 16, just as he thought the Mexican government was ready to give the United States an agreement matching or even slightly surpassing Polk's original desires. Trist believed that the Polk administration was acting on erroneous and outdated information and that obeying it would delay the treaty for months. He decided to stay and negotiate. This act might seem incomprehensible in our age of instantaneous communications. Yet, before the world was so tightly laced together, military officers and diplomats operating far from the centers of power were often given wide latitude with the understanding that they would be judged on success or failure rather than strict adherence to detailed instructions. Eventually Trist paid a price for his defiance: his career of public service was derailed.[5]

The moderates delayed for a few weeks, hoping that the British might be convinced to limit American demands or guarantee that the United States would not violate any agreement reached, but in January 1848 negotiations commenced. The Mexican government still sought the Nueces River boundary, but it was willing to cede New Mexico and California in exchange for a large sum and guarantees that the inhabitants of the ceded land could keep their property and practice Catholicism unmolested. The Mexican negotiators gave way on the Nueces issue and various details were worked out grudgingly. Ironically, negotiations were probably quickened by the precarious situation of Trist, who insisted that the Mexicans cede quickly on various points because any day he might receive a new letter from Polk ordering that he end negotiations.[6]

The Treaty of Guadalupe Hidalgo was named for the Mexico City suburb where it was signed on February 2, 1848, and thus it ironically combined the names of the religious patron of Mexico and the man who initiated the country's war of independence. American possession of Texas was officially recognized, as was the Rio Grande boundary. The United States also received all of the territory that currently forms the states of California, Arizona, Nevada, Utah, and New Mexico, as well as parts of Colorado, Wyoming, and Oklahoma. In compensation, the United States gave Mexico $15 million and agreed to pay the claims of American citizens for property damaged during Mexico's internal conflicts. These provisions, especially the transfer of territory, are what most knowledgeable Americans and Mexicans remember about the treaty, and generally it is known as a landmark of American expansionism and evidence of the strength of the expansionist desires embodied above all by Polk.

However, the treaty also indicates what and whom a Mexican government at the nadir of its power was still willing to fight for, if only through diplomacy. It sent its negotiators to the bargaining table with explicit instructions, and they achieved many of their aims. As historian Brian DeLay points out, one of the key provisions of the treaty was Article XI, which committed the United States to stopping Native American tribes in the newly transferred territories from raiding in Mexico. More practically, it made it illegal for American residents to buy Mexicans captured during such raids, as well as any livestock or property stolen. The U.S. government would also try to rescue any Mexican captives Native Americans held on U.S. territory. Native American raiding had devastated the residents of northern Mexico before and during the war, causing much human suffering and loss of property. American expansionists were convinced that such raids had made Mexican habitation of even the transferred territories nearly impossible, and this notion that Mexicans could not control Native Americans or defend themselves from them assuaged the conscience of expansionists, convincing them that the Mexicans were actually losing little with the territorial transfer. Ironically, intensified Native American raiding was in part a response to the market that the American economy provided for raided livestock and other goods produced by Mexicans the Comanche enslaved. At the negotiating table Mexican representatives worked to protect the inhabitants of northern Mexico by eliminating that market.[7]

However, the Mexican negotiators did not try to protect only Mexicans who lived in areas that would still belong to Mexico after the war. They also had instructions to work to protect the inhabitants of the territories that the treaty transferred. The Mexican commissioners knew that American expansionism was not simply about transferring sovereignty over territory from one government to another; it was about transferring the rights to use land from racial others to white Americans. They did not want the Mexicans in California and New Mexico to be treated the way that Native Americans repeatedly had been treated in the United States. The commissioners got Trist to agree to Article XVIII, which bound the United States to respect the property of Mexicans in California and New Mexico. The same article granted these Mexicans the right to continue living in those territories. They could choose to remain Mexican citizens, but if they did not declare their intention to keep their Mexican citizenship, they would automatically become American citizens. This provision might seem simply logical to us, but in the Jacksonian United States, the extension of citizenship to those considered racial others was a significant concession. Article X provided Mexicans in the ceded territories with even more explicit guarantees that lands granted to them by the Mexican government would be respected. The negotiators were also supremely conscious of the strength of anti-Catholic prejudice in the United States, and they got Trist to agree to specific protections for Catholic worship in the newly transferred territories. Article IX guaranteed that Catholic priests would be able to work unhindered in the transferred territories, that the properties of Catholic institutions would be protected, and that Mexican bishops would be allowed to freely communicate with their flocks in the transferred areas. Mexico's negotiators, in other words, worked on behalf of compatriots who would no longer be under the protection of the Mexican government. In the long run their efforts would not all be successful.

One reason was that the treaty had to be ratified by both governments. The first question was whether Polk would approve a treaty that did not give him all the territory he now wanted and that was negotiated by a representative he had already recalled. The answer to that question was a somewhat surprising yes. He simply came to believe that it was the best treaty he could get, and that if he rejected it the growing antiwar faction in Congress might begin to cut back on support for the army in Mexico. Polk objected to Article X, arguing that it might complicate land rights in Texas, but after noting that objection, he sent the treaty on to the Senate. The Senate removed Article X, but its deliberations and modifications did not stop there. Some American expansionists were upset that the United States had not acquired more territory, and some Whigs took the opposite tack, using the debates to criticize the war and the acquisition of territory. Yet the most controversial article was Article IX. Anti-Catholicism was extremely strong in the United States, and many senators were simply unwilling to approve a treaty that granted explicit rights for Catholics. In three days of fierce debate about specific wording, the senators gradually changed the article until it simply said that the inhabitants of the ceded territories would have religious freedom until they became American citizens, at which point they would have the same religious freedom conferred by that status.[8] On March 10, 1848, the Senate approved the amended treaty, but now the Mexican Congress had to also ratify it. Mexican and American representatives signed a memorandum stating that the amendment of Article IX did not really diminish the rights of Mexicans in the ceded territory. Proponents of ratification pointed out that enshrining the rights of Mexicans in the treaty meant that domestic laws could not override them. Mexican foreign minister Luis de la Rosa argued to Congress that continuing the war was impossible. There was not enough money for organized military forces, and state governments were no longer cooperating. Moreover, Mexicans faced the threat of rebellions by Mexico's indigenous peasants, rebellions that he said some former American soldiers were promoting for their own purposes. This fear of social conflict probably weighed heavily in the treaty's eventual ratification. Unfortunately, the rights granted to Mexicans under even the amended treaty were often trampled on in subsequent decades. Mexicans struggled to protect their rights and even their lives in a western United States dominated by the strident racialization of social conflict and intensive struggle over increasingly valuable agricultural and mineral resources.[9]

Occupation and Stark Choices

Nothing more potently signifies a defeat than a capital city occupied by an invading army, and the fall of 1847 was a bitter season in Mexico City. Peace negotiations had not begun, and the sight of thousands of American soldiers constantly reminded people of what had been already lost and what else might be lost in the future. Every November 2 Mexicans commemorate deceased loved ones on All Souls' Day, commonly known as the Day of the Dead. They visit burial places, decorate the graves, celebrate the lives of the fallen, and mourn. A Mexico City paper editorialized in 1847 that the American presence gave the occasion a different flavor. The anonymous author wrote,

> The families missing a father, son, husband, etc. moan within sight of their murderers, because the loved ones mourned were sacrificed at Churubusco, Molino del Rey, and other points, and on the very day in which the loyal dead are remembered, the Americans show off their weapons and insult us with their martial music, they come to our central plaza to drill, as if to say to our women: we have left you widows or orphans without support, well, we are still here learning how to use our weapons to continue filling your cities with mourning if you do not acquiesce to our ideas. Your men are weaker than us and your territory belongs to us by inheritance. The law of the strongest makes us the arbitrators of your future and present destiny.[10]

As if to prove the author's point, the American military authorities quickly threatened to shut the newspaper down if it published similar things in the future.

Residents of occupied Mexico City faced a grim situation, but the dilemmas faced by one particular group can help us understand how the war forced many people to make agonizing choices. Mexicans greatly valued their families, and the welfare of those families was the guiding principle of many decisions. The value placed on families sometimes inspired Mexicans to fight: it is no accident that propaganda efforts often mentioned the likelihood that Americans would kill, enslave, or rape the families of Mexican men. Other times the value placed on families had a more ambiguous effect on the war effort. As we have seen, forced recruitment into Mexico's regular army was designed to protect families as much as possible by focusing on men who did not support wives, children, aged parents, or younger siblings. Many Mexican men were willing to join National Guard units, but local political authorities usually wanted to keep those units close to home so that the men could support their families. When both regular soldiers and National Guardsmen were asked why they left their units without permission, they often cited the need to feed their families. The sustenance of most families depended on the paid and unpaid labor of all members. There was no social safety net to take up the slack left by absent members. When the landowner Paulo Antonio Verástegui was recruiting guerrillas in May 1847, he tried to solve this problem by offering to support the guerrillas' families. The same problem came into play when men were put to work fortifying Mexico City. People struggled to balance their perceived duties to Mexico with their duties to their families.[11] The government itself often signaled that duty to family was as important as duty to the nation. One of the wryest examples of this thinking was voiced by Congressman Ramón Gamboa. In August 1847 Gamboa formally accused Antonio López de Santa Anna of treason, and he repeated the accusation several times during the next two years. Gamboa's arguments interpreted each of Santa Anna's many failures to achieve victory as a conscious effort to help the Americans. More to the point here, when one of Santa Anna's defenders asked Gamboa why he did not take up arms himself, he stated that "since I was the only one who was supporting my family and had no one to trust its custody and sustenance to, it was impossible for me to leave it alone and abandoned to its good or bad luck."[12]

As mentioned in Chapter 7, when the Mexican army left Mexico City, its commanders let National Guardsmen from the city stay to support their families. Regular army officers with family in the city faced a grimmer set of choices. Mexico's regular army had a very large officer corps, partially because the frequent coups forced both civilian politicians and military leaders to reward their political allies with promotions and appointments. Some of these officers were worse than useless during the war with the Americans, but others were both competent and courageous. In September 1847 hundreds of officers were actually in Mexico City because the army was concentrated there and many officers without active postings resided there. In a situation in which there were more officers than posts, showing one's face often at headquarters to request a post or at least some back pay was an economic and social necessity. Officers recuperating from wounds or illnesses also congregated in Mexico City because that was the best chance they had to receive some of their pay. Other officers were employed in administrative tasks. There were so many officers there in August and September that most units had extra officers attached and some unattached officers organized an infantry company composed entirely of officers.

These men joined the regular army as officers for various reasons. Service was simultaneously a route to power, a way to help one's country, and an honorable and respectable means of supporting a family. The last was difficult. Postings often separated them from their families, a common problem for military personnel that was more dire for these Mexicans because there was no way for the government to give part of an officer's pay directly to relatives. Men instead saved or borrowed money to leave with their families.[13] Worse yet, officers' pay was typically months in arrears. This problem worsened as the war proceeded.[14] Service as a Mexican regular officer was a precarious base for a family's subsistence.

Nevertheless, whether they lacked options or prized their social identities, in the fall of 1847 many regular army officers desperately wanted to retain their commissions. Those left behind in Mexico City found themselves in a vise. The Americans decreed that any Mexican officer in occupied territory had to be paroled, giving his word of honor not to take further part in the war unless he was exchanged for an American prisoner of equivalent rank. Both sides often granted parole to prisoners of war.[15] Although it seems quaint to us, the custom of parole was highly valued in early modern military culture. It allowed prisoners to be freed quickly from confinement, which typically subjected them to food scarcity and an increased threat of disease. It also freed captors of the burden of feeding and guarding prisoners. Parole was taken very seriously, and officers who violated it were executed because violations threatened one of the few customs that alleviated the inhumanity of war.[16] The Americans knew that Mexican officers desperate for manpower had actually reincorporated into their army some Mexican enlisted men paroled after Cerro Gordo, and they were quite bitter about it.[17] Yet Mexican generals held officers to a different standard of honor and insisted that they not violate their oaths.[18] Mexican officers in occupied Mexico City did not want to be paroled, partially because they wanted to be free to fight again but also because the Mexican army did not pay paroled officers unless it could find them duties that would not require them to fight the Americans. The stranded officers soon heard that the Americans were offering rewards to anyone who helped find them, perhaps out of fear that the officers might lead a new uprising against the occupation.[19]

The Mexican government saw military officers who stayed in occupied territory as deserters who would lose their commissions unless they were cleared by court-martial. This rule placed the officers in Mexico City in an even more difficult position, but it also led to court cases in which Mexican officers seeking reinstatement testified about events in the city, the struggles they faced, and the decisions they made. The resulting documents give us a window on how these officers saw their lives and choices. Many testified that they could not immediately leave because they were ill and unable to travel. Others said that after months of little or no pay, they simply did not have the cash needed to do so.[20] Many others, however, cited their duty to their families. What could a family man do under the circumstances? Captain Marcelino Argumendo explained that he felt a particular responsibility to care for his elderly mother and demented father. The latter, a retired captain himself, had been in mortal danger during the street riot on September 14 until Argumendo found him and dragged him to temporary safety. Afterward Argumendo realized that both parents might starve if he left, so he stayed. Some officers similarly testified that they could not leave wounded or ill family members behind.[21] Others struggled to take their families with them, setting out with their wives and young children on long and dangerous journeys on foot or trying to find safe passage for them through the fighting.[22]

One of the most poignant cases was that of Lorenzo Pérez Castro, who had served for more than thirty years and fought at Monterrey and La Angostura. In the latter battle he had taken command of his regiment after his superior was wounded. Praised for his behavior there, he was still passed over for promotion in favor of a less experienced officer with better political connections. Pérez Castro had fought in the rearguard action at Churubusco and successfully extricated two cannon from the fight, leading the men who, lacking horses, pulled the cannon several miles by hand until they reached the new defense line. When he and fellow officers without positions heard the firing at Molino del Rey on September 8, they quickly formed an infantry company and fought as rank-and-file soldiers to defend the city. Pérez Castro's brother was killed at Chapultepec on September 13, and one of his sons was a cadet taken prisoner. That evening Pérez Castro went to his house to see to his family, since, in his words, "he could not look with calm eyes on the misfortunes of persons with whom he was so tightly tied." There he tried to comfort his wife and sister-in-law in their anxiety and grief. In the morning he heard that the army had evacuated the city, but as he prepared to follow, eight American soldiers looted his house, stealing all his money and all of the family's clothing. At this point he dedicated himself to "the most necessary for a father: feeding a numerous family which had just been condemned to great misery." He received help from family friends for two months and then, having lost hope that the Mexican government could continue the war, he looked for "any occupation, however humble, that was honorable" to fulfill "the obligations of husband and family after having completely fulfilled those of a military officer and citizen." He added that earlier he had ordered his wife to place his two sons in the army. He also pointed out that during the previous year he had received no more than three months' salary. Still, Pérez Castro insisted that if he had felt the government was actually willing or able to continue the war, he would have found a way to fight on and avenge his brother's death.[23] Pérez Castro, like most officers who sought to redeem their honor and positions through these trials, was absolved.

Masculine duties to provide for loved ones were probably equally important for American men, but they loomed less heavily in their war experiences. Most enlisted men who joined the regular army simply had not yet had the steady employment needed to form families. A handful brought wives into the army as laundresses, but most probably expected to remain single for the duration of their army hitch if not beyond. In the first wave of recruitment in 1846, most rank-and-file volunteers were young, single men. Their enlistment postponed courtship and marriage, which made both the soldiers and people back home anxious but definitely freed them from having to choose between fighting and feeding their families.[24] More married men signed up in the second wave of recruiting. They lobbied unsuccessfully to be given some pay before leaving for Mexico, and failure left some bitter.[25] Volunteer Albert Lombard wrote,

> If it is cruel to *drag* black men from their homes, how much more cruel it is to drag white men from their homes under *false* inducements, and compelling them to leave their wives and children, without leaving a *cent* or any protection, in the coldest season of the year, to die in a foreign and sickly climate! "But," says the reader, "why did they enlist, and leave their families in distress?" The answer is, many enlisted for the *sake* of their families, having no employment, and having been offered "three month's advance," and were promised that they could leave part of their pay for their families to draw in their absence. They, poor duped men, but with patriotic and noble feelings toward their wives and children, sacrificed everything for the *sole* purpose of their support.[26]

Notably, the tone here comes closest to that of the Mexican documents. During the recruitment of both the first and second waves of volunteers, community leaders sometimes offered to support families left behind, but there is no evidence that this promise was fulfilled. Volunteer officers were typically older and often left wives and children behind, but they also were wealthier, and although some agonized about separation, they rarely mentioned economic hardship. Many regular army officers were married. For them military service was a career, and postponing marriage until after service made little sense. However, they were paid regularly enough to keep their families fed, and they seem to have found ways to get these funds to them. Even so, separation was a hardship. Generally, the vastly more productive economy of the United States and the particular circumstances under which they served prevented the men of the American army from having to choose between the two obligations.

Life in occupied Mexico City was complicated and tense for all parties involved. The wealthy continued to live in luxury, the middle class, which had largely relied on employment with the national government, suffered economically, and the poor seethed, striking back at the Americans under the cover of the night.[27] The city council remained above all concerned with order. After the open resistance died down, it worried about criminal behavior by the poor, by American soldiers, and by Mexican contraguerrillas the Americans employed. It quickly asked the Americans to let its police force patrol, but many of the neighborhood justices of the peace and block captains it relied on for basic police functions resigned because they had to work harder to keep their families afloat. The fact that the Americans were using the principal jail to house prisoners of war also hampered anticrime efforts.[28] More than anything, though, the American volunteers acted like conquerors. They burglarized houses, took food from street vendors and refused to pay for it, and coerced the owners of drinking establishments into opening after hours. Americans abused the night watchmen and garbage collectors the city council relied on to keep the city livable, and they often provoked brawls with Mexicans in the streets. Many Mexicans believed that the Americans arbitrarily killed Mexicans for simply walking by the buildings used to house American troops.[29] We do not need to rely on Mexican sources for all of this: Americans also reported that their troops committed robberies and murders.[30]

The city's inhabitants did not simply accept this occupation. As C. M. Reeves put it, "The Mexican people were not inclined to peace." Throughout the fall, the streets of the city remained a war zone, especially at night. Americans who wandered alone or in small groups were knifed, poisoned, or beaten to death. Not all the violence was surreptitious. In drinking establishments and on the streets, poor Mexicans were more than ready to brawl openly with Americans. Mexicans sometimes stoned American soldiers, who retaliated by beating or whipping any Mexicans they could catch. Juan de la Granja wrote sarcastically of the "grand welcome" with which the plebeians of the city were bleeding the American army. Scott ordered American soldiers to stick together and carry their weapons, and some feigned drunkenness to trap potential assailants or simply attacked Mexicans they suspected of plotting violence. Daniel Harvey Hill reported that during the first two months of the occupation, nearly one hundred American soldiers were killed. Although during most of the war American regulars tended to get along well with Mexican civilians, they also found themselves warring with the people of Mexico City. Regular Frederick Zeh reports that "hardly a night passed, after we first occupied Mexico's capital, without five or six drunken soldiers falling victim to the Mexicans' bloodthirsty treachery. They resorted to poison and dagger with equal success to thin the ranks of their hated foe. Our soldiers, however, knew how to exact thorough revenge, inasmuch as they organized regular nightly raids on these furtive bands of murderers and thus tried to render them harmless." Perhaps the fierce discipline of the regular army was relaxed after the taking of the capital, or the people of Mexico City were not interested in the distinction between volunteers and regulars. It was rumored that during the occupation a Mexican killed the first soldier to raise an American flag over Mexico's National Palace.[31]

Scott ordered his soldiers to respect Catholic services, but this order was clearly not one the conquerors of Mexico City were all willing to follow. Hill called American troops "dirty blackguards" who entered churches without removing their hats or showing any other sign of respect. The Americans housed in the Santo Domingo monastery interrupted Mass by throwing cannonballs into the church, making a tremendous noise. Zeh believed that religion inspired the ire that Mexicans directed against the Americans. Although he was Protestant, in Mexico City he carried a rosary because it "provided more reliable protection against murder than my saber." When Mexican priests took the consecrated Eucharist to comfort the ill or dying, they did so in ceremonial procession. Passersby showed their deep respect for Christ by doffing their hats and kneeling when it passed them. The city council worried that Americans' failure to show this respect would lead to open fighting between them and city residents. Unable to influence the

Americans' behavior, it suggested that the archbishop order the priests to transport the Eucharist surreptitiously. The archbishop agreed to have priests carry it under their clothes.[32] Modifying the public religious practices that demonstrated their collective respect for God was another bitter pill for Mexico City residents to swallow.

American commanders and the city council both feared mass resistance against the occupation. The Americans vividly remembered the fighting that had engulfed the city during their first days there, and they knew that a new uprising would cause many American casualties.[33] The city council knew many Mexicans would also lose their lives in an uprising, and it feared that during the disorder both American soldiers and the Mexican poor would loot the houses of the wealthy. On different occasions in September, October, and November, the city council discussed rumors of imminent uprisings, and the Americans suspected both priests and National Guard officers of preparing to renew open resistance. They were particularly concerned when satirical verses suggesting mass violence were surreptitiously posted in prominent places.[34] Probably the closest the city came to a new explosion began on November 9. Mexican laws forbade corporal punishment for civilians, and many Mexicans, especially the poor, saw this as a symbol of their status as citizens. On November 9 the Americans prepared to flog a Mexican publicly in the central plaza for attempting to murder an American officer. The crowd that gathered began to stone the American guards, and soon American cavalry charged the crowd, beating Mexicans with the flats of their swords and arresting the supposed ringleaders. Relations between soldiers and Mexican civilians hit a low point. The city council immediately explained to American authorities that further floggings might spark an uprising, and asked that they at least not be held in public. American military governor John Quitman responded that if American soldiers were flogged for their crimes, it was only fair to apply the same penalty to Mexican criminals, adding that he would deploy enough soldiers to put down any possible attempt to interrupt a flogging. The next flogging was protected by 1,500 American soldiers.[35] For months occupied Mexico City was a powder keg, although in the end no spark set it off.

Wealthier Mexicans did not commit violence against the Americans, but they did find their presence both strange and galling. They derided American soldiers for not keeping themselves clean; marveled at the diversity of their funeral rites, which varied according to the religion of the soldiers; and found their culinary habits odd. Americans soon began patronizing even the more refined amusements of the wealthy, especially the theater, where they attended plays in both English and Spanish. Wealthy Mexicans immediately stopped attending, put off not only by the war but also by the boisterous yells of the appreciative American audience. Respectable Mexican women at first avoided the efforts of American officers to call on them, not only because they were national enemies but also because these Americans were Protestant and therefore unmarriageable. Later they softened their stance, especially after peace negotiations began.[36]

Economic transactions were very important to life during the occupation. The Americans had copious quantities of something that was in short supply in the rickety Mexican economy: money. The relative wealth of the American government had allowed the army to accomplish all it had during the long campaign, and the pay that now flowed regularly to American soldiers allowed them to purchase many things. In addition to theater tickets, they also bought books, tobacco, clothing, and, as we will see later, sexual companionship. They patronized not only drinking establishments but also hotels, restaurants, and cafés. The Americans employed seamstresses to make clothes, and in general they reactivated an urban economy that had not been particularly productive before the war and had been battered by the blockade and the fighting. Mexicans of all kinds soon become familiar with American coins in their various denominations. The Americans sometimes even handed out bread to the poor. A bitter Guillermo Prieto wrote that "it seems like money and corn are for these savages the means to seduce our poor, and they obtain much with them." Yet even the wealthy speculated in the many articles needed by these thousands of men, and, grudgingly or not, many residents took advantage of these new economic opportunities.[37] Was this evidence that they lacked loyalty to Mexico, or simply that providing a living for themselves and their families was essential? Individuals refusing to sell to the Americans would have had no significant impact on the Americans' ability to maintain the occupation, and even if some group had attempted an organized boycott, it would hurt the capital's people more than it would the

American war effort: after all, the Americans had already shown a willingness to take what they could not buy.

The limits of loyalty to the national state were much more explicit in the politics of city government during the occupation. As the Americans had neared the capital, the moderate federalist city council, led by Manuel Reyes Veramendi, had fretted about the consequences of the war for all of the city's inhabitants. During the street fighting, the moderates had quickly shifted to what for them was a more natural political stance, the idea that they needed to protect the wealthier, more respectable inhabitants not only from the Americans but also from the city's poor. Yet once the Americans were established as occupiers, the city council did not find them very easy to work with. Despite assurances that the American high command was trying to control the troops, they continued to commit abuses, and Americans and residents often seemed on the brink of open warfare. This was not a very comfortable situation for the city council, and its grudging cooperation with the Americans gradually deteriorated. More and more municipal police reports of American crimes found their way into the newspapers, and the Americans were increasingly irritated with the city council. The city council also realized that its stance during the resistance had undermined its chances in the municipal election scheduled for December 1847. At first it seemed that the local moderates would be saved by moderates' control of the national government, which banned elections in occupied territories. However, the American military insisted that elections be held. The radicals proceeded to hold and win elections boycotted by the moderates. American military governor Persifor Smith dismissed the moderate city council before its term ended, alleging that it was not cooperating enough in finding barracks for American troops.[38]

A new city council, led by radical Francisco Suárez Iriarte, took office. On the national level, the radicals argued for continuing the war indefinitely, but Suárez Iriarte and his colleagues tried to ease tensions with the Americans, arguing that their true duty was to protect the city's civilian population. The Americans made concessions such as no longer sentencing Mexican civilians to flogging. The city council offered to return American deserters to their units. They even convinced Scott to have some engineer officers conduct a topographical survey of the lakes to improve flood control. Even as the city council tried to smooth over relations between the occupiers and the population, its members participated in debates about Mexico's future. They sought to make Mexico City's government more autonomous from the federal government so that it could be more like a state in the federalist vision. A few Mexico City radicals even conversed informally with American officers about the possibility of establishing an American protectorate over Mexico. These conversations, in which it appears that Suárez Iriarte did not participate, quickly became ammunition in the bitter political conflict between moderates and radicals. When the radicals invited Scott and the officers who had surveyed the lakes to a banquet of thanks, their critics saw it as a sign of subservience and claimed that the diners had actually toasted the annexation of Mexico to the United States. Ironically, even as they criticized the radicals for cozying up to the Americans, the moderates arranged for the Americans to dissolve the radical city council in exchange for agreeing to an official armistice while the Treaty of Guadalupe Hidalgo was sent to the United States for ratification. The moderate city council of 1847 was reinstalled and it, too, cooperated closely with the Americans during the last few months of the occupation. Suárez Iriarte was later indicted for treason, but he died before a trial could be held. In reality, both parties had found that responsible local government in a large city occupied by an invading force required cooperation, even though cooperation had high political costs.[39]

Political tensions between radicals and moderates, and moderates' fear of lower-class Mexicans, generated anxieties as American troops prepared to leave the city after the treaty was ratified. By May 1848 news had begun to spread about indigenous peasant rebellions in the Sierra Gorda of north central Mexico, in the Yucatán, and even in the state of Mexico near the capital city. Wealthy Mexicans never viewed peasant rebellions as motivated by indigenous peasants' desires to advance their interests but instead saw them as "caste wars," attempts to exterminate white and mestizo Mexicans. The moderate city council heard that nearby indigenous peasants had asked the American army for weapons to support a rebellion that, in the words of Councilman Juan Ycaza, "tends toward the extermination of all the races of the Mexican nation, that are not of the aborigines."[40] Yet the city council was even more afraid that the radicals, who had long organized electorally among the poor of the city and had helped lead the September 1847 resistance to the Americans, might take advantage of the exit of the American army. Rumors circulated that the radicals planned a mass uprising to gain control of the city as the Americans left. Combining their disdain for the lower-class supporters of the radicals with their visceral belief that crime and social unrest were linked, the councilmen fretted that the poor would be aided by criminals released from jail, and that together they would use weapons hidden in the city after the withdrawal of the Mexican army. The city government recruited new armed units under its control, appointed block captains to spy on potential opponents, and asked the Americans to give ample warning before pulling out. The government arranged to suspend alcohol sales on the day of the Americans' departure. Anxieties rose to such a fever pitch that the council considered asking the Americans to leave the city without holding the ceremony in which the American flag would be lowered and the Mexican flag raised in its place, fearing that it might be used as the signal to initiate violence.[41]

Eventually, cooler heads prevailed. Token forces from both armies saluted each other, and official control of the city passed to the Mexicans. However, in the run-up to the ceremony, it was not clear that all American soldiers would actually leave. There were still many deserters in the city, and the city council pointedly refused when it was asked to publicize that the Americans would pay the princely sum of thirty dollars to any Mexican bringing in an American deserter.[42] What was behind this sudden rebuff a mere two days before the American flag was lowered? In fact the city council was a bit miffed at the American commanders. Influential Mexicans and Americans had been discussing the possibility that some Americans might stay to help keep order as employees of the Mexican government. This was yet more evidence that the moderates distrusted the masses. The principal American advocating this idea was John Peoples, editor of an English-language newspaper published in Mexico City during the occupation. He believed that up to five thousand American troops could be convinced to remain. Peoples discussed this with José Maria Flores, governor of the Federal District, telling him that such troops would be Irish and Germans, implying that they were Catholics and regulars. Flores received permission from the Mexican government to raise such a force. The Mexicans saw them as a version of the san patricios, following the early modern tradition of laboring men seeking employment in foreign armies. The American commander, William Butler, at first agreed that this might be acceptable, a necessary step since he would have to discharge these men in Mexico rather than waiting until they were transported to the United States. However, here we see the rub: Peoples implied that he was recruiting regulars, but the regulars were bound to multiyear contracts and were not due to be discharged at the end of the war. The men interested in working for the Mexican government were instead volunteers, like Daniel Runyon of Kentucky, who wrote home on May 20 saying that he would join this force if he was offered a post as an officer. This letter must have alarmed his family, but fortunately for them Butler received orders from Washington that discharges could only be granted once the troops reached the United States. This scuttled the plan for Mexico City, but Peoples, undaunted, sought to raise a similar force to help combat the peasant insurrection in the Yucatán. In effect, some American veterans were flirting with the idea of becoming filibusters, soldiers of fortune who pursued Manifest Destiny without the sanction of the American government. In the summer of 1848 several hundred American soldiers discharged in Alabama agreed to fight in the Yucatán for eight dollars a month and a land grant. They proved no match for the peasant rebels, and apparently the survivors left.[43]

In Love and War?

The departure of the American army from the Valley of Mexico brought a startling sight that opens the door to some uncomfortable truths about the war. Rank-and-file American regular Reeves wrote that when his unit left,

> there were many of the girls and women that followed some distance. These had become attached to some of our men who in many instances had promised that when the army left they would remain. Many of our men had taken up with and kept Mexican women and had promised to marry them. There were also young women that had become attached to some favorite amongst the men. Some numbers of very pretty girls who had doubtless their eye upon some handsome soldier and had expected him to marry them. These came out to see us start. No doubt there were very sorrowful hearts amongst those maidens, reaching after their

Dashing soldier boy, and when we finally left the outskirts of the town, there were many *wet eyes* among poor creatures.

He added that some women followed the unit all the way to Veracruz, hoping that their men could desert and stay behind, but "the majority of *the trusting girls* were doomed to disappointment."[44] Other American accounts also indicate that women who had formed lasting arrangements with American soldiers lamented their departure and tried to follow them, and similar scenes seem to have played out in other locations where American men had been stationed for a long time.[45]

There is a strong temptation to see these stories as the embellishments of American soldiers boasting that they had conquered Mexico in more than one way, and that is probably true of the accounts of some, such as Samuel Chamberlain, whose picaresque chronicle of the war includes several such scenes.[46] Yet Mexicans also believed that some Mexican women had formed lasting attachments with American soldiers. They called these women *margaritas* and sang satirical songs about them.[47] Some American rhetoric about the war stridently exclaimed that Mexican women would find masculine American men irresistible, and that annexation would take place on a personal as well as a territorial level. At least some Americans expected their soldiers to marry Mexican women, and American soldiers thus often wrote about the women they saw with this possibility in mind.[48] They believed that Mexican women found them very attractive, and they were convinced that any attention Mexican women gave them was further proof of their martial handsomeness.[49] Their interpretation has to be taken with a grain of salt: women's mere curiosity or sometimes even pity could spark the Americans to think of romance. Certainly sometimes Mexican women, perhaps accustomed to the hard lot that Mexican soldiers faced marching with limited food and water, helped American soldiers in similar circumstances. Notably, in each case they helped regulars, not the hated volunteers.[50]

Mexican women also socialized with American soldiers. Mexicans from various social classes and distinct regions had vibrant social lives and traditions of hospitality. The hardworking people of northern Mexico were willing to travel miles to attend dances or *fandangos,* and after the Americans arrived, they too began to attend. Despite the language barrier and strange appearance of the newcomers, often they were more or less welcome as long as they behaved well. American men also came from a culture where social dancing was common, and they were happy enough to dance with Mexican women. Often whoever hosted the dance sold food and drink to finance the party, and American men found that they were expected to buy refreshments for the women they danced with. They noted that in the rural north, people of all social classes attended the same dances. Dances were also common in cities, although there was more class segregation. Wealthy urban families also had social customs that revolved around visiting and conversation. At first respectable families shut the Americans out of this world. Before Mexico City fell, Juan de la Granja wrote to a friend in an occupied part of the Valley of Mexico that her family should never lose sight of the fact that "those new people" were "enemies of the patria. I say this because here people are already criticizing the fact that they often visit your house, and various people have told me that Pepita is going to one of the officers, who takes her out for walks holding her arm." After peace negotiations began, American officers were sometimes invited into this kind of social circle. In Mexico City, after peace seemed in the offing, Mexicans also began to attend the same plays, although Americans noted that wealthier Mexicans were more willing to socialize with them than poor Mexicans were.[51]

In addition to sometimes participating in these Mexican forms of social life, American soldiers created a very different kind of social life in the way young, well-paid men far from home often do. This was particularly evident in Mexico City, where many Mexicans were scandalized by the racy behavior centered on an establishment known as the Hotel Bella Unión, or Beautiful Union Hotel. At this establishment and others like it, Americans could socialize, gamble, and buy food, drink, and female companionship. Even some Americans found it infamous, while many others enjoyed its pleasures without detailing them in their memoirs.[52] Mexicans saw the Bella Unión as a disgraceful place where money induced Mexican women to engage in orgies. In his memoirs Guillermo Prieto reproduces a letter from an anonymous friend who wrote of the Bella Unión, "Everything in that place was raucous, intense, fevered. Its excited men disheveled, with their coats and jackets unbuttoned, women almost nude, everything that was most repugnant: drunkenness, the most disgusting women uncovered, the most repellant scream and guffaw of

FIG. 9.1 A fandango in northern Mexico. Drawing by Samuel Chamberlain.

orgy, there was seen a combination of degradation that would have made a savage and a beast smile, and I leave in shadow much of this picture, because although this is a private letter, that is what decency demands."[53] The Bella Unión, and the Americans' use of prostitutes in other places of Mexico, set in place a binary in the minds of many Mexicans, especially men. Women who had sexual relations with Americans were prostitutes who dishonored themselves for money. Mexicans sang sarcastic songs about the avarice and treason of these women.[54]

Yet even some Mexican writers acknowledged that some women slept with Americans not because they were dishonorable prostitutes but because they needed food for their children.[55] Economic insecurity was probably also a factor for women who had more lasting relationships with American soldiers. Mexico's economy was unproductive, and many families struggled to survive. People not in domestic partnerships generally found making a living even more difficult, Mexico City's residents included more females than males, and undoubtedly the disruptions of the war, with its forced military recruitment and high mortality rate for men, put even more women in a bad spot. Under these circumstances sexual attention from a gentle and kindly American soldier might be tolerated or even welcomed.[56] This kind of seduction might lead to longer arrangements in which women thanked men for their economic support not only through companionship but also by cooking and washing clothes. Such lasting arrangements became fairly common and sometimes led to formal marriage.[57] Probably more commonly, they led to informal but enduring relationships in which American soldiers and lower-class women formed couples. After all, there was a long tradition of this kind of arrangement between Mexican women and Mexican soldiers. Becoming a soldadera was an attractive economic option because even Mexican soldiers probably had more abundant and frequent food and income than these women might otherwise have been able to obtain. An extreme version of this arrangement seems to have taken place after the Battle of La Angostura in the winter of 1847. Thousands of soldaderas accompanied Santa Anna's army on its harrowing march through the desert to the battlefield. As the army started its even more desperate retreat through the same desert, it left many wounded behind at a hacienda. Hearing of their plight, the Americans sent wagons of supplies escorted by cavalry. These men found more than four hundred soldaderas nursing men with grievous wounds while a small detachment of half-starved Mexican soldiers struggled to bury those who had recently died. The Americans tried to treat the wounded and distributed food to the women. When the Americans left, many women went with them rather than face the probably fatal road back to San Luis Potosí.[58] Although Mexicans might see domestic, romantic, or simply sexual relationships between Mexican women and American men as dishonor or even treason, these relationships were, like the relationships between Mexican soldiers and soldaderas, often at least partly a survival strategy. The imperative of survival does not rule out bonds of romance or affection between the soldiers of both armies and their temporary mates.

During and after the Mexican Revolution that began in 1910, soldaderas became for many Mexicans almost a national icon, a symbol of the resilience of poor Mexican women and their role in the great events of history. Yet the soldaderas who had formed relationships with American men in 1846–1848 were not understood that way at all. It is possible that many American soldiers

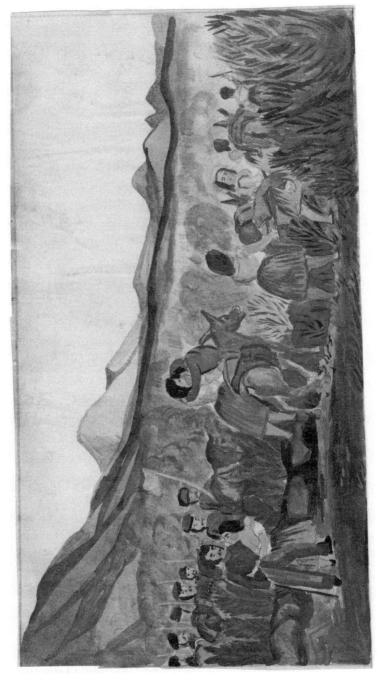

FIG. 9.2 Soldaderas carrying Mexican wounded. Drawing by Samuel Chamberlain.

had promised to marry these women. Lower-class Mexicans often began sexual relations or even cohabitation before they could afford to marry, and the promises made in these situations were taken seriously enough that deceived women could successfully sue for compensation.[59] Even if Americans had made such promises in good faith, the American army was not willing to grant discharges in Mexico and it made no arrangements for Mexican women to accompany the soldiers as they departed. These women were essentially widowed, something that one sarcastic Mexican song cruelly emphasized, calling them "little widows" and threatening them with violence.[60] Sadly, the threats were not empty. Some women who had relationships with American soldiers were singled out for horrific punishment. Their heads were shorn, they were branded, or their ears were cut off, physical assaults that deliberately added lingering public shame. Crowds stoned or beat the women. Some were raped, and others were killed.[61] These were acts of mob violence in which no authorities participated, but neither did they stop them. A degree of cultural toleration of violence toward women seen as dishonorable, combined with pent-up frustration about the war, seems to have brought stomach-churning results.[62] Some of the least powerful people in Mexico became scapegoats for losing the war.

Whether or not they left Mexican women behind, thousands of American soldiers began withdrawing from Mexican territory in June 1848. Undoubtedly they had scarred Mexico, but just as undoubtedly, their experiences there had scarred many of them. Whether regulars or volunteers, most followed the routes used previously by volunteers who returned home after shorter enlistments. These routes tended to funnel men to New Orleans, where they could get ships to the East Coast and steamboats to many parts of the great Mississippi watershed. During these journeys many reflected on the friends they left behind, victims of violence and disease. Some even brought the preserved corpses with them. It was not uncommon for illnesses contracted during their army service to kill men on the way home or even in their hometowns.[63] In the aftermath of the war, the fates of regulars and volunteers diverged sharply. Regulars were in for five-year terms, and few of these enlistments happened to expire at the end of the war. For them peace meant not freedom but instead a new posting, often at a frontier or coastal fort. The U.S. Army quickly shed its volunteer units and became again a force of working-class noncitizen-soldiers commanded by middle-class professionals. It would not again expand until the cataclysm of the U.S. Civil War, whose manpower demands immediately made both the North and South return to the citizen-soldier model of military service.

In 1848, though, the citizen-soldiers of American volunteer and quasi-volunteer regiments manned by men whose enlistments also ended with the war went home. Many were discharged as soon as they reached American soil, typically in New Orleans. Still, the regiments traveled together to their home states, saluted by the people of the river towns they passed and then thoroughly feted in their places of origin. Before this happened, though, most were given what at first seemed an important bit of wealth. As previously mentioned, in February 1847 Congress decreed that each new enlistee who completed twelve months' service would receive 160 acres of public land in the West. The men were being offered, in a sense, a personal piece of America's Manifest Destiny. War veterans were given certificates for this land when they were discharged in New Orleans, and they were immediately approached by speculators who claimed that converting the documents into actual land required arcane knowledge and political pull. In the words of Indiana soldier Isaac Smith, the "land speculators were eloquent in their descriptions of the great difficulties in procuring land warrants, as though the legal process was only exceeded by the mathematical calculations of the number of square inches on the moon, or the aggregate weight of the flying fish in the gulf. But these land sharks were so *patriotic* and so *benevolent* that they would, for the sake of our accommodation, pay us $65 for each claim to 160 acres of land and run the risk of figuring out the complicated questions before the world should come to an end."[64] Some men were offered as little as $35 for certificates that their officers believed to be worth as much as $200. The business proceeded at a frantic pace since the speculators understood that most men due land would pass through New Orleans and scatter to their regions of origin by mid-July.[65] In the raucous market economy of the United States, even, or perhaps especially, a bit of Manifest Destiny bought with blood, sweat, and tears was just another commodity.

Conclusion

WAR WILL BREAK YOUR HEART. On August 7, 1847, Francisco de Garay, commander of Mexican military forces in an isolated region known as the Huasteca, wrote to his superiors from the town of Huejutla. He reported the death of James Taneyhill, a grievously wounded American lieutenant who spent the last few weeks of his life as a prisoner of war. The Mexicans did what they could for him, but a musket ball had shattered his thigh, and the wound was so high up that they could not prevent gangrene from setting in. It seems that even before his death Taneyhill's body was literally rotting away, as Garay reported that the decay was too advanced to allow the body to be interred in the local church, a common Mexican custom. He was instead buried outside town, accompanied by a funeral party that included all the Mexican officers in the town, its civil and religious authorities and most prominent citizens, and an honor guard of twenty Mexican soldiers. Most likely Taneyhill and the Mexicans knew even before he was brought to Huejutla that the wound was mortal. The American comrades who abandoned him during a retreat believed he would only live a few more hours. Instead he lasted three weeks, and Garay himself spent a considerable amount of time with the dying man. Garay reports that Taneyhill asked to be baptized before he died, and that at Taneyhill's request Garay served as the godfather. Very clearly the two officers, one American and one Mexican, had formed a significant emotional bond. Probably they communicated in Spanish, as Taneyhill had been in Mexico over a year, serving first in a Maryland regiment of volunteers and then in one of the new regiments of temporary regulars established late in the war.[1]

Taneyhill's death was unusually senseless. The battle in which he fell was based on a misunderstanding. One hundred and eighty American prisoners of war had been moved to Huejutla to facilitate a possible prisoner exchange. During several months in Mexican custody, these men had been marched from the desert near Saltillo all the way south to Mexico City and then up to Huejutla, which was probably selected as a place to await the exchange because, although it was near the American garrison in Tampico, little fighting was going on nearby. The Americans had not stirred from Tampico for months, and the Mexicans had done little to harass them, as both sides were devoting all their efforts to the battles in central Mexico. Unfortunately, the government budget in Huejutla was very thin, and the prisoners were fed miserably. William Gates, the American commander in Tampico, heard about their plight, and he believed incorrectly that Mexican and American authorities in central Mexico had already agreed to the exchange. Gates wrote to Garay asking that the prisoners be released. Garay replied that, to his knowledge, no agreement had yet been made, but he would inquire with his superiors. The Mexican government confirmed that there was not yet an agreement, but by then the Americans, believing Garay was simply stalling, were on the move. Around 120 men with a small cannon marched from Tampico, determined to recover the prisoners by force. Garay quickly gathered together what military force he could in this quiet and rugged corner of Mexico. They amounted to about 180 men, mostly untrained National Guardsmen from nearby areas. On July 12 they ambushed the American force as it crossed a river near Huejutla, driving the Americans back in panic. One Mexican was wounded, and of the Americans, eleven were killed, five wounded, and fifteen captured. Taneyhill was abandoned because the fleeing Americans could no longer carry him. This was described to the American public as a gallant fighting retreat against terrible odds, as usual vastly exaggerating the number of Mexicans they faced, but it was undoubtedly one of the least successful engagements the Americans fought in this war. It was probably also one of the least necessary. The prisoners in Huejutla were never exchanged, but a few weeks later the Mexicans released them after they promised not to participate further in the war. The prisoners probably found this easy to promise since they were volunteers whose one-year term of service had already expired, something the Mexicans may or may not have understood.[2] Taneyhill, in short, was mortally wounded trying to rescue prisoners of war the Mexicans were eager to release.

The 1846–1848 war caused thousands of deaths, so many that often the lives of these people and the way they ended fade into a numbing litany of numbers. Only rarely do the documents available yield up the kind of detail about a single death found for Taneyhill, and even rarer are the cases where both Americans and Mexicans comment on that single death. As we contemplate wars, we often think about why they began; about why people were willing to kill, to die, and to make other sacrifices; about the successes and failures of military leaders; and, more generally, about why one side won and another lost. These are all vital questions, but none of them should overshadow the tragedy of war. It is often lethal for soldiers, for whom going to war is, in the words of Carlos Maria de Bustamante, not "going to a dance, nor a banquet, it is going to search for death and gamble with one's life."[3] Of course, that tragedy seemed greater for Mexico: more Mexicans than Americans died, even if we consider only soldiers. The ratio is much more disproportionate if we include civilians, such as those who fell victim to American volunteers avenging guerrilla attacks or the American artillerymen who bombarded Veracruz so that Winfield Scott's army could escape yellow fever territory before the dread disease entered its killing season. These civilian deaths, whose numbers are amorphous already, could easily be expanded to include the impoverished Mexican women, children, and elders who slipped over the line between dire poverty and lethal malnutrition when the Mexican government conscripted the men whose labor supported them. Some might add that dying in a losing cause is more tragic than dying in a winning cause, and there is no doubt that in the end Mexico's was a losing cause.

War and Mexican National Identity

As has been discussed, historians often argue that Mexico lost the war because it was not yet a nation. In their view, Mexico was too divided, and many of its people did not see themselves as Mexicans. These historians hold that most inhabitants did not believe they had important things in common with other Mexicans who lived different lives far away, and they were not willing to commit their resources or their blood to fight for a Mexican government that was at best alien and often worked against their interests. The statements made to this effect are often quite stark, and some trends in historical research during the last half century have made them more common. As historians have delved into Mexico's very diverse regions and the kinds of lives people lived in them, they have been more likely to emphasize difference than commitment to any common values. Mexico's national government did little for people in its far-flung regions, so why would they rally to its defense? The same has been true as historians have turned more attention to Mexico's common people, the mostly impoverished men and women of its countryside, towns, and cities. Understanding how exploited many Mexicans were and how wealthy Mexicans despised the less fortunate has often made us believe that the poor had little stake in the system. This has been doubly true for indigenous people who often did not even speak Spanish. Many very good historians have thus written that most Mexicans had little sense of national identity, and that this was the most important factor in the country's defeat.[4]

Many people who lived during the war, including both Mexicans and Americans, made similar statements. American soldiers loved to compare their patriotism to that of the Mexicans, and they were not exactly unbiased observers. Some were sympathetic, arguing that Mexicans lacked patriotism because for them their government was only a source of oppression. Volunteer Franklin Smith wrote, for instance, that many people had no "patriotism or love for their government. Why should they strike for a government which they have only known by its oppressions?"[5] Contemporary Mexican statements also often bemoan some Mexicans' lack of commitment to the nation. Mexico's weak economy and political instability made many Mexican politicians and intellectuals quite pessimistic about the success of the national state and the country's future prospects, and the war produced many statements that decried Mexico's political divisions or the lack of attachment that one or another group had to the *patria*. Often Mexicans aimed these accusations at their political enemies. Other times they singled out a social group, and the group most often singled out as having little interest in national politics or the war was the indigenous peasantry. Some even took seriously unsubstantiated rumors that Indian rebels had contacted the Americans looking for support.[6] The most famous statement blaming Mexico's defeat on a lack of nationalism is from an anonymous pamphlet that people often assume was written by the politician Mariano Otero. The pamphlet states baldly that "in Mexico there is not nor has there been able to be that which is called national spirit, because there is not a nation."[7]

Yet detailed, grounded evidence that Mexican commitment to opposing the United States was weak is hard to find, even though both Mexicans and Americans looked very hard for it. As discussed in Chapter 4, some Mexicans criticized the inhabitants of Puebla, one of its largest cities and the capital of the state of the same name, for letting their city be occupied without a fight following the disastrous Mexican defeat at Cerro Gordo. However, this lack of resistance did not necessarily reflect the desires of most residents. Most of the state government's firearms had been lost at Cerro Gordo, where Puebla's National Guard troops had fought fiercely until they were surrounded without food and water. Preparations for the same battle had emptied the state government's coffers. Under these circumstances the city government agreed to the American occupation to prevent the American troops from sacking the city. Most poor Pueblans seem to have opposed this choice. American soldiers who walked the streets of the occupied city at night were often attacked and, a few months later, when the Mexican military tried to recapture the city, many Pueblans worked hard to oust the Americans.[8] Puebla's reputation for disloyalty undoubtedly owed something to a very small group of Pueblans that many Mexicans found particularly obnoxious: several dozen men hired by the Americans to collect intelligence, hunt guerrillas, and carry messages through guerrilla-infested territory. Most were hired directly from Puebla's jail, and they served the Americans right up to the departure of the American army about a year later.[9] They were more than willing to loot Mexican villages and towns alongside American antiguerrilla forces. Mexicans held these extremely well-paid men in contempt. Mexican captain Rafael Bernardo de la Colina called them "the infamous Pueblans who, forgetting what they owe the patria, have degraded themselves to the extreme that they serve the enemies of the nation."[10] Americans also despised them as mercenary robbers. Ironically, American contempt for their Mexican auxiliaries was sometimes used to bolster their more general contempt for Mexicans. Albert Brackett, who worked closely with the auxiliaries, said they were all criminals and that "a worse body of men could not have been collected together." He later added that "Mexican treachery is proverbial, and these contra-guerillas were a complete embodiment of it."[11]

Americans despised the disloyalty of their Mexican auxiliaries, but they greatly appreciated Mexicans who somehow made them feel welcome in

Mexico. Some Mexicans were willing to converse with Americans or help them in difficulties. American troops were surprised to find that some residents of Parras, Coahuila, had been educated in Bardstown, Kentucky, the center of Catholicism in what was then the American West, and when these residents were friendly, the Americans construed their behavior as approval of the invasion.[12] The tendency of Americans to view any friendliness as approval of American culture or even American territorial ambitions seems to have been wishful thinking. Mexicans often pitied American prisoners of war, possibly because as strangers in a strange land they had no recourse to family and friends, who in Mexico were typically expected to provide food for prisoners. Some Mexicans were friendly to American occupation troops due to curiosity, but this tended to happen only when armed resistance was impossible. Many Mexicans sold food, drink, transportation, or even souvenirs to the Americans. Both Americans and Mexicans sometimes interpreted willingness to do business as evidence of a lack of patriotism. C. M. Reeves, for instance, stated of Mexicans who transported goods for the Americans that their "love of money overruled their patriotism," while Colonel José Antonio del Castillo complained that some men in rural San Luis Potosí failed to report for National Guard service "because they are more interested in doing business with them [the Americans] than in defending the independence of their *patria.*"[13] However, the notion that those who sold goods to the American army were disloyal seems simplistic. It could be difficult not to sell things the Americans desired. The Americans sometimes took what they wanted by force and then paid for it. S. Compton Smith explained that in one northern Mexican village, when American soldiers were told that no food was available for sale, they choked a local leader until he agreed to make the villagers sell them food.[14] Mostly, though, the willingness of Mexicans to sell goods to the Americans is evidence of a lack of economic alternatives, not a lack of national loyalty. The general weakness of Mexico's economy combined with the disruption of the invasion to cause serious hardship that Mexicans could alleviate by tapping the market the Americans represented. In fact, the Americans believed that some people who came to their camps to sell food or firewood were also simultaneously spying on them, and the generally accurate information Mexican authorities had about American troop numbers and movements seems to confirm their suspicions.

The widespread view that Mexico lost the war because it was not a nation and therefore many people were not willing to defend it does not withstand sustained scrutiny. Resistance to the American invasion of Mexico was fierce and sustained. Many people from different social groups sacrificed their wealth and their lives for something they called Mexico. José María Roa Bárcena, who was a young man in 1846–1848 and later wrote one of Mexico's best histories of the war, stressed this in implicit response to the pessimistic views expressed by so many contemporaries. He also noted that Otero made essentially the same point, writing that in less than a year, forty thousand Mexicans from all social groups had gone to the battlefields and many had died there.[15] When we carefully consider the war's social and cultural history along with the nineteenth-century logistics, weapons, and tactics that shaped the behavior of soldiers, it is impossible to sustain the idea that it was an easy victory for the Americans or that many Mexicans did not fiercely oppose them. Time and time again, Mexicans reacted to battlefield defeats by renewing their efforts, working to build new armies and continue the fight.[16] James K. Polk was denied his short war.

Certainly, many soldiers of Mexico's regular army were conscripts, but discipline and comradeship often motivated these men to perform on the battlefield in ways that earned the admiration of their adversaries. Thousands of Mexicans took up arms voluntarily as National Guardsmen or guerrillas, and they were often deeply committed fighters. Many who did not actually engage in battle gave up their wealth and labor to oppose the Americans. As we have seen, women from Mexico's middle and upper classes led fund drives and made clothing or bandages, while thousands of lower-class women shared the dangers and discomforts of army life as soldaderas or provided food for passing troops. Upper- and middle-class families donated money and goods, and poor families did likewise, in addition to providing labor for military needs such as moving weapons or building fortifications. The people who made all of these sacrifices had a variety of motives. Some soldaderas no doubt were compelled by emotional bonds to soldiers or by their own struggle for survival, motivations that were not mutually exclusive. Families sometimes sacrificed wealth or time to build or retain social status in their communities, and similar peer pressure encouraged volunteer service in the National Guard or the work of guerrillas. These more self-serving motives, though, do not preclude patriotism, and Mexican officials, in describing the sacrifices made, often pointed out that people said they were making them for Mexico.

Mexican archives contain thousands of documents in which people expressed nationalism. Perhaps an example from Puebla would be fitting, since so many people called the patriotism of its population into question. In August 1847, during the American occupation, Mexican guerrillas attacked a group of Americans who had ventured out of the city and then pursued the fleeing Americans into downtown Puebla. When one guerrilla fell from his horse and was too badly injured to remount, many poor Pueblans rushed to his aid, carrying him to his horse and placing him on it so he could make his escape. The commander reporting this added that the population's enthusiasm for opposing the Americans was great, and all one heard in the streets of the city were cries of "Long live Mexico" and "Death to the Yankees."[17]

The argument that Mexico lost the war because it was not really a nation is a powerful one. However, it is based on an unsophisticated and unrealistic vision of what nationalism was. Often people assume that nationalism is an abstract value, one that is somehow separate from other forms of identity. Some also believe that as modern nation-states came into being, shaping the political world we live in now, nationalism superseded other forms of identity. Yet many historians and other social scientists have come to understand that often people's ideas of what the nation was and why loyalty to it was important were actually based on other kinds of identity, some of which predated the formation of national states. The nation was always intertwined with other values important to people. Moreover, it was not the same for everyone. People of different social groups, regions, ethnicities, and political inclinations all tried to use the relatively new idea that governments now represented some group of people of a single nationality to make sense of their lives and engage in politics. At any given moment there were many different versions of every nation, including Mexico.

One way to think about how many different versions of Mexico were in play during the war is to consider accusations of disloyalty. Radical federalists accused moderate federalists of disloyalty, especially during the polkos rebellion, while during the American occupation, moderates returned the favor, claiming that the radicals desired an American protectorate. In both cases evidence of an actual desire that the Americans triumph is weak, and the accusations show more than anything how much these political groups' visions of Mexico's preferred future differed. The same can be said for political strife during the war more generally. In 1845 Mariano Paredes y Arrillaga marched his army south toward the capital and not north toward a possible confrontation with the United States because he had convinced himself that he had to save Mexico by protecting traditional order and hierarchy against a looming threat of egalitarianism and social revolution. When the radicals and moderates fought in Mexico City even as Scott invaded Veracruz, they were engaged in a struggle about what Mexico was to be. Neither side actually wanted to help the United States. All of the participants in these domestic conflicts believed in the importance of their Mexican identity and the existence of a Mexican national state.

The relatively wealthy and literate Mexicans who held political office were not the only ones who tried to bring to fruition different versions of what Mexico should be. After the War of Independence, the idea that there was a Mexico and that it should be the primary focus of political loyalties became the most prominent feature of all kinds of Mexican political conversations. The importance of the nation was stressed not only in print media but also in civic ceremonies and the justifications of judicial decisions. Even impoverished Mexicans who lived in relatively isolated areas were exposed to these ideas and began to use them during social conflicts. Some also sought allies among politicians and explicitly tried to connect their concerns to the rhetoric of different political groups. Thus, at least some of the people who many elite Mexicans feared had no stake in or even knowledge of the nation were actually fashioning versions of what it meant to be Mexican. In these cases poor Mexicans engaged in mental operations like those that occupied wealthier Mexicans. They thought about the values that were important to them, how their material interests could be justly defended, and how they were an important part of that vague collectivity known as Mexico. Thus, some rural people in places like present-day Guerrero, Oaxaca, and Veracruz constructed visions of what Mexico was and why it was worth defending, visions that fueled their participation in the fight against the Americans.[18] The same could be said for the urban poor of Mexico City who fought the Americans in those dark days of September 1847 or those of Puebla who lifted that fallen guerrilla onto his horse and shouted, "Viva México!" There was nothing abstract about these commitments to nationalism. Defending the nation was defending the land they needed for subsistence, their access to eternal life, their loved ones, their self-respect, and the sacrifices their forebears had made, in other words, a number of overlapping values.[19]

American National Identity

The argument that Mexico lost the war because it was not a nation is actually a comparative argument. Before the Texas Rebellion intensified tensions with the United States, many Mexican intellectuals had been impressed by its prosperity, demographic growth, and relative political stability, and some saw it as a potential model for Mexico. Mexicans came to see it differently as they became more aware of American territorial ambitions and views of Mexican inferiority, but many still viewed it as stronger if not more moral than their own country. Their critiques of their own country were always at least implicitly comparative.[20] The same could be said for American critiques of Mexico, which typically boldly asserted the superiority of all things American, including American patriotism. Americans who joined the army to fight Mexico were very inclined to stress American unity, as we can see in the words of Illinois volunteer Thomas Tennery, who looked on American regiments from different states encamped together and wrote, "Let those who are vain or ignorant enough, to talk of a disunion in the United States, be silent forever, when they consider the ties of kindred and the feelings existing from Maine to the Rio Grande, and from Florida to Oregon."[21] Few American historians of our own era have doubted that the United States was more unified, and that Americans were more committed to their country than Mexicans.[22]

How true was this? Can we make this comparison more careful and explicit? One way to approach the problem is by thinking about the two major American wars that preceded and followed the war with Mexico. In 1812 the United States went to war with the British Empire, which had one of the most powerful governments in the world but was preoccupied with its long struggle with Napoleonic France. The decision to go to war was justified by disputes over shipping and the freedom of sailors, but the driving force behind the conflict was the desire to conquer Canada to acquire new territory and weaken Native American tribes resisting the expansion of American settlement.[23] The last goal was certainly achieved: large-scale, organized resistance by Native American tribes east of the Mississippi was almost completely snuffed out, and this was very important to both the soon-to-be displaced tribes and American society.[24] Yet the military confrontation with a British Empire distracted by its struggle against Napoleon's European empire was in most ways a defeat for the United States. American land forces were almost never able to effectively go on the offensive. Repeated efforts to invade Canada failed miserably, and a handful of Canadians, British, and Native Americans even temporarily drove the Americans from parts of the Midwest. Many states kept what men and money they devoted to the war close to home to defend their own people from British or Native American attacks. Despite tactical victories, the war at sea was a strategic defeat for the United States, as the more powerful British navy successfully strangled American commerce. The war was so unpopular in New England that there was an open movement toward secession. Perhaps the low point came when a small force of British troops captured and burned the American national capital. The Battle of New Orleans, the greatest American victory of the war, took place after the peace treaty was signed and therefore did not affect its content. This treaty simply restored the status quo of 1812, making no concessions on trade or the freedom of sailors and leaving Canada in British hands.[25] Ironically, the propaganda used, mostly unsuccessfully, to try to mobilize support during the war and even more strenuous efforts afterward to portray it as a glorious victory gave a huge impulse to American nationalism.[26] Yet, as Mexican historians Marcela Terrazas y Basante and Gerardo Gurza Lavalle argue, the War of 1812 shows that the national state and national unity were weak about twenty years after American independence. The 1846–1848 war was likewise roughly twenty years after Mexican independence, and Mexican historian Josefina Zoraida Vázquez points out that Mexico's military performance in 1846–1848 was not much worse than America's performance in 1812–1815.[27]

The second war that might help us sharpen the comparison between Mexico and the United States is the American Civil War, which began in 1861. When relating this war to the Mexican-American War, we usually focus on how the vast territories acquired from Mexico through the Treaty of Guadalupe Hidalgo put the United States on a fast track to civil war. Although the story is complicated, the possibilities so much new land offered for expanding America and its economy underlined the existence of multiple and mutually incompatible versions of American society, some based on slave labor and others on free labor. Many Northerners were unwilling to allow slavery to expand into much of the new territory, and this made many Southerners fear the eventual extinction of their slave-based society even where it existed. Thus, sectional tensions grew practically from the moment the treaty was signed, and the American victory over Mexico led directly to the Civil War. Ulysses S. Grant, a Mexican-American War veteran who believed that war unjust and also knew a thing or two about the Civil War, stated the connection very strongly when he wrote of the Mexican-American War that "nations, like individuals, are punished for their transgressions. We got our punishment in the most sanguinary and expensive war of modern times."[28]

However, there is another way to consider the Civil War in relation to the Mexican-American War, one that is more useful for our purposes here. The Civil War presents overwhelming evidence that the United States was not a consolidated nation in which most people believed that what they had in common with other Americans outweighed other concerns, and even more overwhelming evidence that many Americans were not loyal to the national government that supposedly represented them. West Point was probably the first educational institution in the United States that drew together young men from every region of the country, and after their education was completed, officers were rotated from post to post throughout the United States. Many of these men even served against Mexico in 1846–1848. They were much more likely to be committed to the idea that the United States should be the focus of their loyalties than most people, who had little to do with the national government and lived in tightly woven webs of local identities. When the sectional conflict approached a crisis after the 1860 presidential election, however, these officers faced agonizing choices. Most from the Southern states resigned their U.S. Army commissions to fight for the Confederates, and those who did not were often ostracized by their families. Robert E. Lee, like Grant a Mexican-American War veteran, was offered a generalship in the U.S. Army, but he turned it down and resigned his commission as a colonel. A few days later he agreed to command Virginia's troops, writing that "trusting to Almighty God, an approving conscience, and the aid of my fellow citizens, I will devote myself to the defense and service of my native state, in whose behalf alone would I have ever drawn my sword."[29] Regional identity trumped all. The specter of so many men who had shown their talents in 1846–1848 making this kind of choice sometimes seems to befuddle American historians of the Mexican-American War. The editors of Daniel Harvey Hill's Mexican War diary call Hill "a patriotic American to the core of his being," even though Hill, like his more famous brother A. P. Hill, joined the Confederate army.[30] Ever since the Civil War occurred, some have tried to see it as not challenging the idea of a fundamentally unified country. However, the vast scale of death and destruction that characterized it makes this argument difficult to sustain. If in the United States of today a war killed the same proportion of Americans killed in the Civil War, more than seven million would die.[31] Moreover, the war did not end because the people fighting suddenly realized that their common values outweighed their differences. It was a lengthy and fierce war of attrition that ended when the South simply could no longer resist.

Perhaps the drastic divisions that led to so much death during the Civil War do not accurately reflect the United States as it was in 1846, and the country that confronted Mexico then was actually politically stable, united, and institutionally strong. The evidence does not support this view, either. Although the question of slavery had not reached the fever pitch it would rise to after the Mexican-American War, the United States of 1846 was roiling with tensions and controversy. The market revolution had increased class divisions, regionalism was very strong, immigration sparked intense nativism, religious intensity and diversity were increasing, Indian removal was controversial, and party conflict was fierce.[32] These conflicts were sometimes managed through institutions in a more or less peaceful manner, but violence was extraordinarily common in American life. Though Americans of the period tended to believe that Mexico was an extremely violent place where death was meted out casually, they might better have looked in the mirror. As discussed in the introduction, in the United States, individuals, including prominent politicians, often used violence to defend their interests and, especially, their status or honor.[33] The United States was also riven by collective violence. Mob attacks on religious groups like the Mormons, members of opposing political parties, immigrants, free blacks, and abolitionists were common. Some of the most lethal attacks were vigilante lynchings, and the selection of lynching victims was in many ways a reflection of social divisions. These acts of collective violence were justified as the exercise of direct democracy, but they were also evidence that government institutions were simply not very strong.[34]

The American men who participated in the war against Mexico in 1846–1848 were typically very attached to their localities and very aware of the ways in which social systems, customs, and even regional differences divided them from other Americans in the same army. Brawls between the men of different regions were common, as were comments about how different other regions were.[35] The fragile unity embodied in a national state that was still quite weak might unravel, and politics was an intense balancing act on a high wire that people learned in 1861 was not strung over a safety net. The federal government had at most a symbolic presence in the lives of most people, and state governments were not much stronger.[36] The United States was not a unified national state in 1846. The war with Mexico faced fierce opposition right from the beginning, and, as we have seen, Polk had to hide crucial information and engage in intense partisan maneuvering to start the war. Opposition increased during the war, but Polk was able to hold his political coalition together just long enough to pursue it to a conclusion. When we see the United States of 1846 in comparison to Mexico, it seems fair to say that both nations were still in the process of constituting themselves.

Wars themselves influence nation formation. The sacrifices governments ask of their constituents in times of war have to be justified. Thus governments, intellectuals, and artists work intensely to convince people not only about the justice of their cause but also about the importance of the fundamental values that unite them. These campaigns also seek to define the enemy in negative ways. The process is particularly important in wars that are fought between national states, polities that at least in theory are supposed to represent the will, and the character, of particular groups of people called nations. This was not the first national war for either Mexico or the United States. The Mexican War of Independence, a Spanish effort to reconquer Mexico in 1829, and a French expedition that had tried to occupy part of

Mexico's territory in 1838 all sparked efforts to mobilize Mexicans to fight for their new country by defining what it meant to be Mexican and contrasting those values with those of a nefarious foreign enemy.[37] Similar processes took place in the United States during the American Revolution and the War of 1812.[38] In both countries the 1846–1848 war eventually led to civil wars, but in the short term it stimulated nationalism. An enormous outpouring of speeches, newspaper articles, novels, and memoirs encouraged American civilians to participate vicariously in this war and see themselves as Americans.[39] Mexico was a less literate society, but the ideas from a similar outpouring of propaganda were transmitted even to illiterate Mexicans. Moreover, in many ways the actual experience of the war was more intense for Mexican civilians. It was fought on their territory, bringing them into contact with American soldiers whose behavior greatly helped Mexican propagandists. Moreover, the poverty of the Mexican government meant that it needed the voluntary contributions of Mexicans, allowing them to continuously experience the vibrant connection to the war that some Americans only felt briefly during the sendoffs of volunteer units. Thus, while the war did not demand much of average American citizens, the intensity of the Mexican experience of it, and the impassioned efforts to inspire loyalty that it stimulated, helped many Mexicans become more deeply attached to the idea that they were Mexicans. This process continued throughout the war, and volunteer Franklin Smith commented in his diary that "the longer the war lasts the more national it will become."[40]

Why Mexico Lost

The idea that Mexico lost the war primarily because it was not yet a nation captures the view of many contemporaries, but it is less than satisfying as an explanation. Many Mexicans were willing to make sacrifices for their country during the war, and the U.S. nation-state was hardly more unified and stable than Mexico. The war promoted nationalism in both countries. In the end there are simply more satisfying explanations of the outcome. One that contemporaries in both countries often mentioned was political conflict within Mexico. There was also such conflict in the United States, but there it remained confined to institutional channels and, more importantly, its effect on the American war effort was minimized by most Whigs' unwillingness to withdraw support for American soldiers already in the field.

It seems very likely that the constant stream of Mexican political clashes encouraged Polk in his ambitions by making Mexico seem even weaker than it was. Harsh political divisions made it much harder to raise money to support Mexico's armies, as different plans to finance the war tended to run aground on the reefs of party politics. Moreover, many military officers had actively participated in Mexican politics through repeated coups and revolutions. The support of armed forces had become crucial because Mexico had not developed a pluralistic political culture and most of the time politics operated in crisis mode. Civilian politicians wooed Mexican officers and encouraged their ambitions, and shifting alliances within the officer corps backed various political actions. Officers also had different political ideologies. When the time came to confront the United States, it was sometimes difficult for generals of differing political opinions to cooperate. This caused military disaster at Padierna in August 1847 when Gabriel Valencia refused to follow the orders of his political enemy, Antonio López de Santa Anna.[41] However, political rivalries among officers were not always so important. For instance, before the war Santa Anna had also clashed repeatedly with Juan Alvarez, but during the war they set aside their differences and cooperated closely.

Mexican political conflicts were probably most crucial when they prevented Mexico from taking advantage of two moments in which the American war effort was particularly vulnerable. The first was in late 1845, after Polk had begun his saber rattling and moved Zachary Taylor's army into Texas. Paredes believed that Polk was bluffing, and he wanted to save Mexico from excessive egalitarianism by placing himself in the presidency. He took the thousands of troops that he was supposed to move to within supporting distance of Mexico's frontier and instead marched on Mexico City. The troops Paredes commanded might have made all the difference when Taylor reached the Rio Grande, preventing the early American victories of Palo Alto and Resaca de Palma. The second time Mexican political conflict prevented the Mexicans from taking advantage of American vulnerability was in February and March 1847. Moderate federalists with Catholic Church backing tried to overthrow the Valentín Gómez Farías government in Mexico City, both to protect the principle that church wealth was not subject to government control and to prevent the radical federalists, with their egalitarian ideology, from continuing to dominate politics. Few Mexicans were killed in this internal fighting, but it prevented any reinforcements from being sent to confront Scott's invasion of Veracruz. Reinforcements might have stalled Scott enough to keep his army in the low country during yellow fever season, drastically hampering the campaign that eventually won the war for the United States.[42]

Contemporaries often attributed American victories to the superior knowledge and skill of American officers, including the younger officers educated at West Point. The fact that so many of these young men later became generals during the Civil War is one of the staple stories of traditional American military history. Scott, an avid student of Napoleonic tactics not trained at West Point, was the most effective general in this war and possibly one of the most effective American generals in any war. However, he still lost control of the rapidly changing situation that led to the Battle of Churubusco and ordered an unnecessary and badly organized attack at Molino del Rey, causing massive American casualties on each occasion. The Mexican officer corps was certainly more politicized, but many Mexican officers studied the military science of the day just as avidly as their American counterparts. As a group they were probably about average for nineteenth-century officers in the Western world, and they usually made reasonable tactical choices. At the very least they made no blunders quite as impressive as the tragicomic errors that just a few years later led British troops to take horrific casualties in the famous Charge of the Light Brigade during the Crimean War.

Average military acumen was simply not good enough to allow Mexican officers to win this war. Every single battle was shaped by, and every single Mexican tactical mistake was exacerbated by, the greatest problem that Mexico faced in this war: the disparity between the resources the two countries could mobilize to finance the war was huge. The U.S. national government was weak, but it was perched atop an extraordinarily wealthy society, and taxes that were quite modest were sufficient to support a navy large enough to totally blockade Mexican ports and a well-equipped army with enough cash to feed itself for months on Mexican territory. The Mexican economy was much weaker. Per capita income was perhaps one-third that of the United States, and it was highly concentrated. Moreover, most national government revenue came from foreign trade.[43] Revenue had not been sufficient before the war, and the blockade devastated it. As we have seen, throughout the war, Mexico was able to find men to fill the ranks of army unit after army unit, but every unit was poorly equipped and, more importantly, poorly paid and fed. Men who were not fed could be kept in the ranks for a while by their patriotism, discipline, and love of their comrades, but eventually they tended to leave the army to seek sustenance. This story was repeated again and again throughout the war, and it shaped the tactical and strategic choices of every Mexican military officer. The desperate need for more financial resources shows up incessantly in the documents, from the first efforts to gather men near the Texas border to the arguments that the government made to justify accepting the terms of the Treaty of Guadalupe Hidalgo.[44] In short, Mexico lost the war because it was poor, not because it was not a nation.

Today the economic disparity between Mexico and the United States still dominates the relationship, both uniting and dividing them by driving cross-border flows of capital, products, and people. Lower wages in Mexico have encouraged many corporations to build factories there to service the U.S. market, and these wages have also facilitated the export of Mexican agricultural products to the United States. Mexico is also a crucial market for American farmers and industrial enterprises. Every day astonishing amounts of commerce travel between the two countries on thousands of trucks. This commerce certainly has its critics in both countries, but their governments have steadfastly defended it for decades. People also cross the border. American tourists and retirees are drawn south not only by Mexico's natural and cultural charms but also by how affordable Mexico's low wages make life there for them. These wage levels have prompted many Mexicans to seek work north of the border, usually in occupations that many Americans avoid due to their low rates of compensation. Yet American politicians, most of whom accept economists' arguments that the United States benefits from Mexicans working for low wages south of the border, refuse to accept the argument that the United States also benefits when they work north of the border. Mexicans who want to work in the United States are often demonized as an invading force of racial and cultural others. Pandering to this fearful mind-set, the American government has spent huge amounts of money fortifying and militarizing the border, ostensibly trying to impede the flow of Mexican workers to the United States. This effort has deterred few border crossers and, ironically, it has increased the number of Mexicans who settle in the United States. Mexican men who before worked in the United States and returned to Mexico periodically to visit their wives and children no longer could easily reenter the United States, and many responded by transferring their families to the United States and settling permanently.[45]

The fortification of the border has pushed many Mexicans who simply want to work in the United States away from the paved, multilane border crossings used by semitrailers full of merchandise or American tourists seeking affordable vacations, sending them instead on dangerous foot journeys through the desert sustained only by what food and water they can carry.[46] In recent decades thousands of Mexican men and women have faced deprivation and many have died. Their journeys have been, startlingly, very much like those experienced by Mexican soldiers sent to defend northern Mexico in the 1840s, journeys also stalked by hunger, thirst, and exposure. When they reached their destinations, those soldiers often fought against Irish and German immigrants in the American regular army whom many Americans demonized as alien and even racially distinct, just as many contemporary Americans demonize Mexican immigrants today. Regular army soldiers were later joined by American volunteers who accepted the premise of American racial superiority and inflicted great harm on Mexican civilians even as they themselves also suffered grievously during the war. Recent Mexican immigrants, like the Mexican soldiers, Mexican civilians, immigrant regular soldiers, and American volunteers of the 1840s, have been victims of a politics in which demagogic, nationalist appeals to fear and racial solidarity continue to be wielded as the ultimate trump card. Similar tragedies will continue until we all insist that what unites us is more important than what divides us, and that our hope is more powerful than our fear.

Abbreviations

ADN	Archivo de Defensa Nacional, Mexico City, Mexico
AGA	Archivo General de la Administración, Alcalá de Henares, Spain
AGEG	Archivo General del Estado de Guanajuato, Guanajuato, Mexico
AGEO	Archivo General del Estado de Oaxaca, Oaxaca, Mexico
AGN	Archivo General de la Nación, Mexico City, Mexico
AHDF	Archivo Histórico del Distrito Federal, Mexico City, Mexico
AHESLP	Archivo Histórico del Estado de San Luis Potosí, San Luis Potosí, Mexico
CHSL	Cincinnati Historical Society Library, Cincinnati, Ohio
exp.	expediente
FHS	Filson Historical Society, Louisville, Kentucky
fol.	folio
ISHS	Indiana State Historical Society, Indianapolis, Indiana
leg.	legajo
LEPOSLP	*La Época Periódico Oficial de San Luis Potosí*
NA	National Archives, Washington, DC
RG	Record Group
SGG	Secretaria General del Gobierno
STJ	Supremo Tribunal de Justicia

Notes

Introduction

1. Isaac Smith, *Reminiscences of a Campaign in Mexico: An Account of the Operations of the Indiana Brigade on the Line of the Rio Grande and Sierra Madre, and a Vindication of the Volunteers against the Aspirations of Officials and Unofficials,* 2nd ed. (Indianapolis: Chapman and Spann, 1848), 7. For the prevalence of this mournful music, see also Richard Coulter, *Volunteers: The Mexican War Journals of Private Richard Coulter and Sergeant Thomas Barclay,* ed. Allan Peskin (Kent, OH: Kent State University Press, 1991), 89, 114; Henry S. Lane, "The Mexican War Journal of Henry S. Lane," ed. Graham Barringer, *Indiana Magazine of History* 53, no. 4 (December 1957): 400; and Frederick Zeh, *An Immigrant Soldier in the Mexican War* (College Station: Texas A&M University Press, 1995), 80.

2. Richard Bruce Winders, *Mr. Polk's Army: The American Military Experience in the Mexican War* (College Station: Texas A&M University Press, 1997), 139; Daniel Walker Howe, *What Hath God Wrought: The Transformation of America, 1815–1848* (New York: Oxford University Press, 2007), 752; Irving Levinson, *Wars within War: Mexican Guerrillas, Domestic Elites and the United States of America, 1846–1848* (Fort Worth: Texas Christian University Press, 2005), 123–124; Amy Greenberg, *A Wicked War: Polk, Clay, Lincoln and the 1846 U.S. Invasion of Mexico* (New York: Knopf, 2012), xvii.

3. J. David Hacker, "A Census-Based Count of the Civil War Dead," *Civil War History* 57, no. 4 (December 2011): 311.

4. Fred Anderson and Andrew Cayton, *The Dominion of War: Empire and Liberty in North America, 1500–2000* (New York: Penguin, 2004), xiii–xxi.

5. Ibid., x–xiii; Josefina Zoraida Vázquez, *Mexicanos y norteamericanos ante la guerra del 47* (Mexico City: SepSetentas, 1972), 10; Josefina Zoraida Vázquez, "¿Dos guerras contra Estados Unidos?," in *De la rebelión de Texas a la Guerra del 47,* ed. Josefina Zoraida Vázquez (Mexico City: Nueva Imagen, 1994), 11–12; Michael Van Wagenen, *Remembering the Forgotten War: The Enduring Legacies of the U.S.-Mexican War* (Amherst: University of Massachusetts Press, 2012), 5–6, 242–243; Greenberg, *Wicked War,* 274, 278.

6. Vázquez, *Mexicanos y norteamericanos,* 10; Vázquez, "Dos guerras," 11–12; Van Wagenen, *Remembering,* 242–243.

7. Robert Citino, "Military Histories Old and New: A Reintroduction," *American Historical Review* 112, no. 4 (October 2007): 1071; Maria Isabel Monroy, "San Luis Potosí 1836–1849," in *Catálogo de fuentes documentales, hemerográficas y bibliográficas de la Guerra entre México y Estados Unidos 1845–48,* ed. Martha Rodríguez García (Brownsville, TX: Centro de Estudios Sociales y Humanísticos / National Park Service, Palo Alto Battlefield National Historic Site, 2002), 3.

8. The study of Mexico's fiscal struggles after independence was in many ways opened by Barbara Tenenbaum, *The Politics of Penury: Debt and Taxes in Mexico, 1821–1856* (Albuquerque: University of New Mexico Press, 1986). For a more recent overview, see Carlos Marichal, "Una difícil transición fiscal: Del regimen colonial al México independiente, 1750–1860," in *De colonia a nación: Impuestos y política en México, 1750–1860,* ed. Carlos Marichal and Daniel Marino (Mexico City: El Colegio de México, 2001), 19–58. On fiscal problems in Mexico in the decades before the war, see Jesús Hernández Jaimes, *La formación de la hacienda pública mexicana y las tensiones centro-periferia, 1821–1835* (Mexico City: El Colegio de México / Instituto Mora / Universidad Nacional Autónoma de México, 2013), and Javier Torres Medina, *Centralismo y reorganización: La hacienda pública y la administración durante la primera república central de México, 1835–1842* (Mexico City: Instituto Mora, 2013). On Mexico's foreign debt, see Carlos Marichal, *A Century of Debt Crises in Latin America* (Princeton, NJ: Princeton University Press, 1989), 61–64, and especially Richard Salvucci, *Politics, Markets, and Mexico's "London Debt," 1823–1887* (New York: Cambridge University Press, 2009). Despite all of this excellent work on Mexico's fiscal problems, few have emphasized the way in which the small size of Mexico's economy helped drive them. Even a very efficient tax system would have had great difficulty generating enough revenue to govern such a vast territory.

9. On the importance of comparison, see Alan Knight, preface to *Las relaciones México-Estados Unidos, 1756–2010,* vol. 1, *Imperios, repúblicas y pueblos en pugna por el territorio, 1756–1867,* by Marcela Terrazas y Basante and Gerardo Gurza Lavalle (Mexico City: Universidad Nacional Autónoma de México / Secretaría de Relaciones Exteriores, 2012), 13.

10. Jutta Bolt and Jan Luiten Van Zanden, "The Maddison Project: Collaborative Research on Historical National Accounts," *Economic History Review* 67, no. 3 (2014): 627–651. See also John Coatsworth, "Obstacles to Economic Growth in Nineteenth-Century Mexico," *American Historical Review* 83, no. 1 (February 1978): 81, and John Coatsworth, "Notes on the Comparative Economic History of Latin America and the United States," in *Development and Underdevelopment in America: Contrasts of Economic Growth in North and Latin America in Historical Perspective,* ed. W. L. Bernecker and H. W. Tobler (Berlin: De Gruyter, 1993), 11.

11. Terrazas y Basante and Gurza Lavalle, *Las relaciones México-Estados Unidos,* 1:108–109.

12. David Pletcher, *The Diplomacy of Annexation: Texas, Oregon, and the Mexican War* (Columbia: University of Missouri Press, 1973), 32; Timothy J. Henderson, *A Glorious Defeat: Mexico and Its War with the United States* (New York: Hill and Wang, 2007), 11; Coatsworth, "Obstacles," 91; John Coatsworth, "Inequality, Institutions, and Economic Growth in Latin America," *Journal of Latin American Studies* 40, no. 3 (August 2008): 556; Terrazas y Basante and Gurza Lavalle, *Las relaciones México-Estados Unidos,* 1:106–108.

13. Coatsworth, "Obstacles," 92–94; Coatsworth, "Notes," 18; Coatsworth, "Inequality," 558–559.

14. Coatsworth, "Notes," 20; Josefina Zoraida Vázquez, "La guerra que puso en peligro la unidad nacional," in *Symposium La Angostura en la Intervención Norteamericana, 1846–1848* (Saltillo, Mexico: Secretaría de Educación Pública de Coahuila, 1998), 10–11; Terrazas y Basante and Gurza Lavalle, *Las relaciones México-Estados Unidos,* 1:87.

15. Terrazas y Basante and Gurza Lavalle, *Las relaciones México-Estados Unidos,* 1:106.

16. Ibid.

17. Henderson, *Glorious Defeat,* 4–5; Terrazas y Basante and Gurza Lavalle, *Las relaciones México-Estados Unidos,* 59–60, 108–109.

18. Terrazas y Basante and Gurza Lavalle, *Las relaciones México-Estados Unidos,* 1:61, 109.

19. Reynaldo Sordo Cedeño, "El faccionalismo en la Guerra con los Estados Unidos 1846–1848," in *Symposium,* 23–24; Peter Guardino, *The Time of Liberty: Popular Political Culture in Oaxaca, 1750–1850* (Durham, NC: Duke University Press, 2005), 277.

20. Terrazas y Basante and Gurza Lavalle, *Las relaciones México-Estados Unidos,* 1:57–58.

21. See Knight, preface, 24–25.

22. Harry Watson, *Liberty and Power: The Politics of Jacksonian America,* updated ed. (New York: Hill and Wang, 2006), 47.

23. Michael Feldberg, *The Turbulent Era: Riot and Discord in Jacksonian America* (New York: Oxford University Press, 1980), 55–61.

24. David Grimsted, *American Mobbing: Toward Civil War* (New York: Oxford University Press, 1998); Feldberg, *Turbulent Era.*

25. Grimsted, *American Mobbing,* viii.

26. Feldberg, *Turbulent Era,* 90–91, 96–97, quote from 7.

27. Abraham Lincoln, *Selected Speeches, Messages, and Letters,* ed. T. Harry Williams (New York: Holt, Rinehart and Winston, 1962), 6–7.

28. Michael J. Pfeifer, *The Roots of Rough Justice: Origins of American Lynching* (Urbana: University of Illinois Press, 2011), 2, 4, 11–12.

29. Grimsted, *American Mobbing*, 19–22, 26, 35–38, 46–49, 58–64.

30. John Grenier, *The First Way of War: American War Making on the Frontier, 1607–1814* (New York: Cambridge University Press, 2005); Peter Silver, *Our Savage Neighbors: How Indian War Transformed Early America* (New York: W. W. Norton, 2008); Bruce Vandervort, *Indian Wars of Mexico, Canada, and the United States, 1812–1900* (New York: Routledge, 2006).

31. Grimsted, *American Mobbing*, 89–92.

32. Thomas R. Hietala, *Manifest Design: Anxious Aggrandizement in Late Jacksonian America* (Ithaca, NY: Cornell University Press, 1985), 191.

33. David Bushnell and Neill MaCauley, *The Emergence of Latin America in the Nineteenth Century* (New York: Oxford University Press, 1988), 30.

34. This is a somewhat newer take on the phenomenon of the caudillo. Its strongest and most explicit expression to date is probably Will Fowler, *Santa Anna of Mexico* (Lincoln: University of Nebraska Press, 2007), although it fits many of the arguments about nineteenth-century Latin American politics made by other historians recently.

35. Knight, preface, 13.

36. Feldberg, *Turbulent Era*, 96.

37. Anderson and Cayton, *Dominion*, 237–244.

38. Reginald Horsman, *Race and Manifest Destiny: The Origins of American Racial Anglo-Saxonism* (Cambridge, MA: Harvard University Press, 1981), 82–83.

39. Anderson and Cayton, *Dominion*, 246; Hietala, *Manifest Design*, 6, 10, 23–24, 33–34, 97, 262; Amy Kaplan, *The Anarchy of Empire in the Making of US Culture* (Cambridge, MA: Harvard University Press, 2002), 27.

40. Howe, *What Hath*, 42, 142; Pletcher, *Diplomacy*, 14; Jesús Velasco Márquez, "Regionalismo, partidismo y expansionismo: La política interna de Estados Unidos durante la guerra contra México," *Historia Mexicana* 47, no. 2 (October–December 1997): 319.

41. Bruce Dorsey, *Reforming Men and Women: Gender in the Antebellum City* (Ithaca, NY: Cornell University Press, 2002), 8.

42. Michael Pierson, *Free Hearts and Free Homes: Gender and American Antislavery Politics* (Chapel Hill: University of North Carolina Press, 2007), 6; Howe, *What Hath*, 851.

43. Amy Greenberg, *Manifest Manhood and the Antebellum American Empire* (New York: Cambridge University Press, 2005), 20.

44. Ibid., 10–14. For a somewhat different analysis of gender and expansionism, see Lynea Magnuson, "In the Service of Columbia: Gendered Politics and Manifest Destiny Expansion" (PhD diss., University of Illinois, 2001).

45. Greenberg, *Manifest Manhood,* 55.

46. Howe, *What Hath,* 704–705. For a statement that Manifest Destiny was largely secular by the 1840s, see Henderson, *Glorious Defeat,* 31.

47. Anders Stephanson, *Manifest Destiny: American Expansion and the Empire of the Right* (New York: Hill and Wang, 1995), 5; Robert Johannsen, *To the Halls of Montezuma: The Mexican War in the American Imagination* (New York: Oxford University Press, 1985), 49–50. See, for example, Corydon Donnavan, *Adventures in Mexico: Experienced during a Captivity of Seven Months in the Interior* (Cincinnati: Robinson and Jones, 1847), 109.

48. Watson, *Liberty,* 245; Stephanson, *Manifest Destiny,* 32; Howe, *What Hath,* 705.

49. Howe, *What Hath,* 583, 687, 706; John Pinheiro, *Missionaries of Republicanism: A Religious History of the Mexican-American War* (Oxford: Oxford University Press, 2014), 89; Andrea Tinnemeyer, "Embodying the West: Lyrics from the U.S.-Mexican War," *American Studies* 56, no. 1 (2005): 71–72.

50. Pinheiro, *Missionaries,* 89; Velasco Márquez, "Regionalismo," 317–318; Watson, *Liberty,* 245.

51. Hietala, *Manifest Design,* 5–6; Howe, *What Hath,* 493, 510, 582–584, 686–687, 701, 705; Velasco Márquez, "Regionalismo," 317; Kevin Phillips, *The Cousins' Wars: Religion, Politics, and the Triumph of Anglo-America* (New York: Basic Books, 1999), 339, 350, 391; Hietala, *Manifest Design,* 6, 256, 263; Watson, *Liberty,* 241, 245; Noel Ignatiev, *How the Irish Became White* (New York: Routledge, 2009), 79; Alexander Saxton, *The Rise and Fall of the White Republic: Class Politics and Mass Culture in Nineteenth Century America* (London: Verso, 1990), 145; David Roediger, *The Wages of Whiteness: Race and the Making of the American Working Class* (London: Verso, 2007), 22; Carlos Bosch Garcia, "La política diplomática de la expansión de Estados Unidos," in Vázquez, *De la rebelión de Texas,* 108.

52. Horsman, *Race,* 157, 159.

53. Watson, *Liberty,* 5, 13, 42–43; Lori Ginzberg, *Women and the Work of Benevolence: Morality, Politics, and Class in the Nineteenth-Century United States* (New Haven, CT: Yale University Press, 1992), 70.

54. The quote is from Watson, *Liberty,* 53. See also ibid., 19, 51–52; Greenberg, *Manifest Manhood,* 46; Howe, *What Hath,* 586; Gregory Knouff, "White Men in Arms: Concepts of Citizenship and Masculinity in Revolutionary America," in *Representing Masculinity: Male Citizenship in Modern Western Culture,* ed. Stefan Dudink, Karen Hagemann, and Anna Clark (New York: Palgrave Macmillan, 2007), 25; Saxton, *Rise and Fall,* 127, 142–144, 200.

55. Howe, *What Hath,* 497, 851; Greenberg, *Wicked War,* 185; Ignatiev, *How the Irish,* 89–90; Roediger, *Wages of Whiteness,* 57, 59; Amrita Myers, *Forging Freedom: Black Women*

and the Pursuit of Liberty in Antebellum Charleston (Chapel Hill: University of North Carolina Press, 2011), 120–122.

56. Anthony F. C. Wallace, The Long, Bitter Trail: Andrew Jackson and the Indians (New York: Hill and Wang, 1993); Theda Perdue and Michael Green, The Cherokee Nation and the Trail of Tears (New York: Penguin, 2007); Hietala, Manifest Design, 261–262; Howe, What Hath, 386.

57. Johannsen, To the Halls, 293; Horsman, Race, 165–167, 211–212; Hietala, Manifest Design, 152–158.

58. Johannsen, To the Halls, 291–292.

59. Horsman, Race, 208–215; Brian DeLay, "Independent Indians and the U.S. Mexican War," American Historical Review 112, no. 1 (February 2007): 36, 49–53; Brian DeLay, War of a Thousand Deserts: Indian Raids and the Mexican-American War (New Haven, CT: Yale University Press, 2009), xvii, 227–229, 233, 245–247, 299; George Wilkins Kendall, Dispatches from the Mexican War (Norman: University of Oklahoma Press, 1999), 86.

60. The most complete account of the racialization of Mexicans before and during the war is Horsman, Race, 208–248. See also Johannsen, To the Halls, 290–293, and DeLay, War, 243–247.

61. Horsman, Race, 210; Howe, What Hath, 703.

62. Horsman, Race, 182, 231; Shelley Streeby, American Sensations: Class, Empire and the Production of American Culture (Berkeley: University of California Press, 2002), 167–171.

63. Paul Foos, A Short, Offhand Killing Affair: Soldiers and Social Conflict during the Mexican-American War (Chapel Hill: University of North Carolina Press, 2002), 98, 145; Greenberg, Wicked War, 142, 183; Felice Flannery Lewis, Trailing Clouds of Glory: Zachary Taylor's Mexican War Campaign and His Emerging Civil War Leaders (Tuscaloosa: University of Alabama Press, 2010), 56; Tom Reilly, War with Mexico! America's Reporters Cover the Battlefront (Lawrence: University of Kansas Press, 2010), 76; Encarnacion Prisoners: Comprising an Account of the March of the Kentucky Cavalry from Louisville to the Rio Grande . . . (Louisville, KY: Prentice and Weissanger, 1848), 50–51. The quote is from Encarnacion, 51. On the relative weakness of racial prejudice in the lower classes, see Guardino, Time of Liberty, 23–24.

64. Margaret Chowning, "Elite Families and Popular Politics in Early Nineteenth-Century Michoacán: The Strange Case of Juan José Codallos and the Censored Genealogy," Americas 55, no. 1 (July 1988): 35–61; Guardino, Time of Liberty, 194.

65. Peter Guardino, Peasants, Politics, and the Formation of Mexico's National State: Guerrero, 1800–1857 (Stanford, CA: Stanford University Press, 1996), 168.

66. Carmen McEvoy, "De la mano de Dios: El nacionalismo católico chileno y la Guerra del Pacífico, 1879–1881," *Histórica* 28, no. 2 (2004): 84; Pinheiro, *Missionaries,* 1; Gene Brack, *Mexico Views Manifest Destiny* (Albuquerque: University of New Mexico Press, 1975), 170.

67. Howe, *What Hath,* 104–195, 285–286, 854; Brack, *Mexico,* 2.

68. Pinheiro, *Missionaries,* 27, 46; John Pinheiro, "'Religion without Restriction': Anti-Catholicism, All Mexico, and the Treaty of Guadalupe Hidalgo," *Journal of the Early Republic* 23, no. 1 (2003): 74; John Pinheiro, "Crusade and Conquest: Anti-Catholicism, Manifest Destiny, and the U.S.-Mexican War of 1846–48" (PhD diss., University of Tennessee, Knoxville, 2001), 50.

69. Michael Hogan, *The Irish Soldiers of Mexico* (Guadalajara, Mexico: Fondo Editorial Universitario, 1997), 128–132; Jennie Franchot, *Roads to Rome: The Antebellum Protestant Encounter with Catholicism* (Berkeley: University of California Press, 1994), xix–xx, 137–138; Pinheiro, *Missionaries,* 6, 18–20.

70. Pinheiro, "Crusade," 2, 51; Pinheiro, "'Religion without Restriction,'" 74; Streeby, *American Sensations,* 50–51; Greenberg, *Manifest Manhood,* 21.

71. Howe, *What Hath,* 704–705; Pinheiro, *Missionaries,* 14, 37–39; Pinheiro, "Crusade," 2–3, 92, 95–97.

72. Pinheiro, *Missionaries,* 4, 17; Pinheiro, "'Religion without Restriction,'" 72, 77, 81, 87; John Pinheiro, "'Extending the Light and Blessings of Our Purer Faith': Anti-Catholic Sentiment among American Soldiers in the Mexican War," *Journal of Popular Culture* 35, no. 2 (2001): 129; Pinheiro, "Crusade," 3, 26–32, 36–45.

73. Peter Guardino, "In the Name of Civilization and with a Bible in Their Hands: Religion and the 1846–48 Mexican American War," *Mexican Studies / Estudios Mexicanos* 30, no. 2 (Summer 2014): 353; Brian Connaughton, "Conjuring the Body Politic from the Corpus Mysticum: The Post-independent Pursuit of Public Opinion in Mexico, 1821–1854," *Americas* 55, no. 3 (January 1999): 462–463; Osvaldo Pardo, *The Origins of Mexican Catholicism* (Ann Arbor: University of Michigan Press, 2004); Moisés Guzmán Pérez, *Las relaciones clero-gobierno en Michoacán: La gestión episcopal de Juan Cayetano Gómez de Portugal* (Mexico City: LIX Legislatura Cámara de Diputados, 2005), 180; Carlos Maria de Bustamante, *El nuevo Bernal Díaz del Castillo* (Mexico City: Instituto Nacional de Estudios Históricos de la Revolución Mexicana-Gobierno del Estado de Puebla, 1994), 2:7.

74. Gobernación, sin sección, vol. 291, exp. 15, AGN; James Sanders, *The Vanguard of the Atlantic World: Creating Modernity, Nation, and Democracy in Nineteenth-Century Latin America* (Durham, NC: Duke University Press, 2014), 6; exp. 2493, fol. 40, ADN.

75. Terrazas y Basante and Gurza Lavalle, *Las relaciones México-Estados Unidos*, 1:182.

76. Brack, *Mexico*, 96, 128.

77. DeLay, "Independent," 56–58; DeLay, *War*, 212, 220, 224.

78. Horsman, *Race*, 232.

79. Terrazas y Basante and Gurza Lavalle, *Las relaciones México-Estados Unidos*, 1:128–129, 134.

CHAPTER 1 · The Men Most Damaging to the Population

1. Justin Smith, *The War with Mexico* (Gloucester, MA: Peter Smith, 1963), 1:143; Abner Doubleday, *My Life in the Old Army* (Fort Worth: Texas Christian University Press, 1998), 42–43; Peter Stevens, *The Rogue's March: John Riley and the St. Patrick's Battalion, 1846–1848* (Washington, DC: Brassey's, 1999), 45; Ethan Allen Hitchcock, *Fifty Years in Camp and Field: Diary of Major General Ethan Allen Hitchcock, USA* (New York: G. P. Putnam's Sons, 1909), 198–199, 215; George W. Smith and Charles Judah, *The Chronicles of the Gringos: The US Army in the Mexican War, 1846–48: Accounts of Eyewitnesses and Combatants* (Albuquerque: University of New Mexico Press, 1968), 275–276; Felice Flannery Lewis, *Trailing Clouds of Glory: Zachary Taylor's Mexican War Campaign and His Emerging Civil War Leaders* (Tuscaloosa: University of Alabama Press, 2010), 44.

2. Jesús Velasco Márquez, "La separación y la anexión de Texas en la Historia de México y los Estados Unidos," in *De la rebelión de Texas a la Guerra del 47*, ed. Josefina Zoraida Vázquez (Mexico City: Nueva Imagen, 1994), 142; Daniel Walker Howe, *What Hath God Wrought: The Transformation of America, 1815–1848* (New York: Oxford University Press, 2007), 659; David Pletcher, *The Diplomacy of Annexation: Texas, Oregon, and the Mexican War* (Columbia: University of Missouri Press, 1973), 70.

3. Andrés Reséndez, *Changing National Identities at the Frontier: Texas and New Mexico, 1800–1850* (New York: Cambridge University Press, 2004), 161–163; Marcela Terrazas y Basante and Gerardo Gurza Lavalle, *Las relaciones México-Estados Unidos, 1756–2010*, vol. 1, *Imperios, repúblicas y pueblos en pugna por el territorio, 1756–1867* (Mexico City: Universidad Nacional Autónoma de México / Secretaría de Relaciones Exteriores, 2012), 145, 149.

4. Reséndez, *Changing National Identities*, 149–164.

5. Ibid., 164–170; Howe, *What Hath*, 662; Robert E. May, *Manifest Destiny's Underworld: Filibustering in Antebellum America* (Chapel Hill: University of North Carolina Press, 2002), 9; Terrazas y Basante and Gurza Lavalle, *Las relaciones México-Estados Unidos*, 1:193–194.

6. The best account of this transition remains Reginald Horsman, *Race and Manifest Destiny: The Origins of American Racial Anglo-Saxonism* (Cambridge, MA: Harvard

University Press, 1981). See also Brian DeLay, *War of a Thousand Deserts: Indian Raids and the Mexican-American War* (New Haven, CT: Yale University Press, 2009), 226–249.

7. Howe, *What Hath,* 680, 698; Pletcher, *Diplomacy,* 148–149; Amy Greenberg, *A Wicked War: Polk, Clay, Lincoln and the 1846 U.S. Invasion of Mexico* (New York: Knopf, 2012), 61.

8. Hitchcock, *Fifty Years,* 198; José María Roa Bárcena, *Recuerdos de la invasión norteamericana (1846–1849)* (Xalapa, Mexico: Universidad Veracruzana, 1986), 3. See also Hitchcock, *Fifty Years,* 200, 212, 224; DeLay, *War,* 73; Greenberg, *Wicked War,* 99; and Douglas Murphy, *Two Armies on the Rio Grande: The First Campaign of the U.S. Mexican War* (College Station: Texas A&M University Press, 2015), 15–16, 97. General William Worth also saw through the fiction but he refused to condemn it, writing from Corpus Christi on November 1, 1845, "Have not our Anglo-Saxon race been land stealers from time immemorial and why shouldn't they?" George Smith and Charles Judah, *Chronicles,* 57–58.

9. Greenberg, *Wicked War,* 76, 78, 95–96; Horsman, *Race,* 232; Josefina Zoraida Vázquez, "¿Dos guerras contra Estados Unidos?," in Vázquez, *De la rebelión de Texas,* 26. There is some evidence that Alejandro Atocha, a Mexican exile who claimed ties to important Mexican politicians, encouraged Polk in his belief that Mexico could be intimidated into the concessions he sought, but any influence Atocha may have had on events is undoubtedly less important than Polk's own suppositions about the Mexicans. A. Brooke Caruso, *The Mexican Spy Company: United States Covert Operations in Mexico* (Jefferson, NC: McFarland, 1991), 63–64.

10. Howe, *What Hath,* 735; Josefina Zoraida Vázquez, "El origen de la guerra con Estados Unidos," *Historia Mexicana* 47, no. 2 (October–December 1997): 291–292, 299; Greenberg, *Wicked War,* 78; Vázquez, "Dos guerras," 25; Josefina Zoraida Vázquez, "A ciento cincuenta años de una guerra costosa," *Historia Mexicana* 47, no. 2 (October–December 1997): 35; George Meade, *The Life and Letters of George Gordon Meade, Major General United States Army* (New York: Charles Scribner's Sons, 1913), 64; Terrazas y Basante and Gurza Lavalle, *Las relaciones México-Estados Unidos,* 1:213. Terrazas and Gurza see the problem of Slidell's credentials more as the result of an error of communication than as a deliberate provocation.

11. Justin Smith, *War,* 1:145; Greenberg, *Wicked War,* 100–101; Pletcher, *Diplomacy,* 256; Murphy, *Two Armies,* 24.

12. Frederick Zeh, *An Immigrant Soldier in the Mexican War* (College Station: Texas A&M University Press, 1995), 4; George Ballentine, *Autobiography of an English Soldier in the United States Army* (Chicago: Lakeside, 1986), 3–11; fol. 299, Foreign Office 203-93 British Public Record Office, London; *El Liberal Católico,* March 21, 1847. See also Edward Coffman, *The Old Army: A Portrait of the American Army in Peacetime, 1784–1898* (New York: Oxford University Press, 1986), 16, 137, 145–146, 210; Francis Prucha, *Broadax and*

Bayonet: The Role of the United States Army in the Development of the Northwest, 1815–1860 (Madison: State Historical Society of Wisconsin, 1953), 56; Francis Prucha, *The Sword of the Republic: The United States Army on the Frontier, 1783–1846* (1969; repr., Lincoln: University of Nebraska Press, 1986), 323–324; Corydon Donnavan, *Adventures in Mexico: Experienced during a Captivity of Seven Months in the Interior* (Cincinnati: Robinson and Jones, 1847), 19; C. M. Reeves, "Five Years Experience in the Regular Army, including the War with Mexico," manuscript, MS qr332f RMV, chsl (hereafter cited as Reeves Manuscript), 1, 17, 26–27, 31–32.

13. Greenberg, *Wicked War,* 130. For the literacy rate for whites, see James Machor, *Reading Fiction in Antebellum America: Informed Response and Reception Histories, 1820–1865* (Baltimore: Johns Hopkins University Press, 2011), 21.

14. Bruce Dorsey, *Reforming Men and Women: Gender in the Antebellum City* (Ithaca, NY: Cornell University Press, 2002), 7, 60; Amy Greenberg, *Manifest Manhood and the Antebellum American Empire* (New York: Cambridge University Press, 2005), 109; Howe, *What Hath,* 504–505, 538, 539; May, *Manifest Destiny's Underworld,* 93–96, 99–100, 110; Seth Rockman, *Scraping By: Wage Labor, Slavery and Survival in Early Baltimore* (Baltimore: Johns Hopkins University Press, 2009), 3, 14, 29, 43; Harry Watson, *Liberty and Power: The Politics of Jacksonian America,* updated ed. (New York: Hill and Wang, 2006), 19, 17–41, 150; Sean Wilentz, *Chants Democratic: New York City and the Rise of the American Working Class, 1788–1850* (New York: Oxford University Press, 1984), 299–300.

15. Paul Foos, *A Short, Offhand Killing Affair: Soldiers and Social Conflict during the Mexican-American War* (Chapel Hill: University of North Carolina Press, 2002), 4, 14, 130; David Roediger, *The Wages of Whiteness: Race and the Making of the American Working Class* (London: Verso, 2007), 227; Alonzo D. Sampson, *Three Times around the World: Life and Adventures of Alonzo D. Sampson* (Buffalo, NY: Express, 1867), 8. On their international military experience see Ballentine, *Autobiography,* xx–xvii, 191; Samuel Chamberlain, *My Confession: Recollections of a Rogue* (Austin: Texas State Historical Association, 1996), 107–108; Stevens, *Rogue's March,* 45; Zeh, *Immigrant Soldier,* 50; Foos, *Short,* 23, 104.

16. Dorsey, *Reforming,* 61; Foos, *Short,* 14; Rockman, *Scraping By,* 26, 75–76, 86, 93, 160–165; Roediger, *Wages of Whiteness,* 153; Peter Way, *Common Labour: Workers and the Digging of North American Canals, 1780–1860* (New York: Cambridge University Press, 1993), 6, 90, 100, 146; Peter Way, "Evil Humors and Ardent Spirits: The Rough Culture of Canal Construction Laborers," *Journal of American History* 79, no. 4 (1993): 1398, 1400, 1406; May, *Manifest Destiny's Underworld,* 94–95, 100.

17. Way, "Evil Humors," 1410.

18. Noel Ignatiev, *How the Irish Became White* (New York: Routledge, 2009), 102; Roediger, *Wages of Whiteness,* 141.

19. Dorsey, *Reforming*, 58–63, 75; Rockman, *Scraping By*, 53, 75–76, 159, 191; Wilentz, *Chants Democratic*, 283.

20. Jorge Belarmino, *Cuestión de sangre* (Mexico City: Planeta, 2008), 11–12; Coffman, *Old Army*, 141; Foos, *Short*, 23; Prucha, *Broadax*, 36; Stevens, *Rogue's March*, xi, 33, 36; Ballentine, *Autobiography*, 25, 40; Ignatiev, *How the Irish*, 19; May, *Manifest Destiny's Underworld*, 97, 99; Watson, *Liberty*, 194; Dorsey, *Reforming*, 197.

21. Dorsey, *Reforming*, 122, 195–196, 231; Horsman, *Race*, 225; Matthew Frye Jacobsen, *Whiteness of a Different Color: European Immigrants and the Alchemy of Race* (Cambridge, MA: Harvard University Press, 1998), 72; Stevens, *Rogue's March*, 20–25; Watson, *Liberty*, 194.

22. Ballentine, *Autobiography*, 39; Zeh, *Immigrant Soldier*, 4–5; Timothy D. Johnson, *A Gallant Little Army: The Mexico City Campaign* (Lawrence: University of Kansas Press, 2007), 136; Stevens, *Rogue's March*, 43, 204; Richard Bruce Winders, *Mr. Polk's Army: The American Military Experience in the Mexican War* (College Station: Texas A&M University Press, 1997), 60; Reeves Manuscript, 3, 19, 426–427; George McClellan, *The Mexican War Diary and Correspondence of George B. McClellan*, ed. Thomas Cutrer (Baton Rouge: Louisiana State University Press, 2009), 17.

23. Dorsey, *Reforming*, 195, 201, 237; Jennie Franchot, *Roads to Rome: The Antebellum Protestant Encounter with Catholicism* (Berkeley: University of California Press, 1994), xx; Ignatiev, *How the Irish*, 170–175; Jacobsen, *Whiteness*, 70; John Pinheiro, "Crusade and Conquest: Anti-Catholicism, Manifest Destiny, and the U.S.-Mexican War of 1846–48" (PhD diss., University of Tennessee, Knoxville, 2001), 2–3, 14–24; John Pinheiro, *Missionaries of Republicanism: A Religious History of the Mexican-American War* (Oxford: Oxford University Press, 2014), 18–19; Stevens, *Rogue's March*, 19; Watson, *Liberty*, 55.

24. Way, "Evil Humors," 1403; Dorsey, *Reforming*, 122, 199, 219; Michael Hogan, *The Irish Soldiers of Mexico*, (Guadalajara, Mexico: Fondo Editorial Universitario, 1997), 97–98; Ignatiev, *How the Irish*, 49, 89, 129, 130; Jacobsen, *Whiteness*, 48; Roediger, *Wages of Whiteness*, 133, 146; Shelley Streeby, *American Sensations: Class, Empire and the Production of American Culture* (Berkeley: University of California Press, 2002), 15–16.

25. Ballentine, *Autobiography*, 42–44; Coffman, *Old Army*, 179; Foos, *Short*, 26; Pinheiro, "Crusade," 182; Pinheiro, *Missionaries*, 85; Michael Tate, *The Frontier Army in the Settlement of the West* (Norman: University of Oklahoma Press, 1999), 197.

26. Achilles Murat, *America and the Americans* (New York: W. H. Graham, 1849), 161–162; James E. Alexander, *Transatlantic Sketches, Comprising Visits to the Most Interesting Scenes in North and South America and the West Indies, with Notes on Negro Slavery and Canadian Emigration* (London: Richard Bentley, 1833), 281.

27. Ballentine, *Autobiography,* 34–35; Reeves Manuscript, 26; Ulysses S. Grant, *Personal Memoirs* (Westminster, MD: Random House, 1999), 18.

28. Reeves Manuscript, 13; Coffman, *Old Army,* 137; Foos, *Short,* 13; Greenberg, *Wicked War,* 130; Prucha, *Broadax,* 38; Winders, *Mr. Polk's,* 64; Guillaume Tell Poussin, *The United States: Its Power and Progress* (Philadelphia: Lippincott, Grambo, 1849), 393; Murat, *America and the Americans,* 161–162; Dorsey, *Reforming,* 7, 19, 35, 75; Roediger, *Wages of Whiteness,* 29, 55.

29. Ballentine, *Autobiography,* 332–333.

30. Reeves Manuscript, 402–409.

31. Doubleday, *My Life,* 20; Thomas Tennery, *The Mexican War Diary of Thomas D. Tennery* (Norman: University of Oklahoma Press, 1970), 88; Reeves Manuscript, 403. See also Foos, *Short,* 16–17, and Myra Glenn, *Campaigns against Corporal Punishment: Prisoners, Sailors, Women, and Children in Antebellum America* (Albany: State University of New York Press, 1984).

32. Winders, *Mr. Polk's,* 62–36; Ballentine, *Autobiography,* 285–286, 332; Doubleday, *My Life,* 31; Stevens, *Rogue's March,* 47–48, 51, 172, 260; C. M. Reeves, "Five Years an American Soldier, Comprising Adventures at Palo Alto, Resaca de la Palma, Monterrey, Vera Cruz, Cerro Gordo, and in the Battles in the Valley of Mexico, Interspersed with Anecdotes of Military Life, in Peace and War," in *Adventures and Achievements of Americans, a Series of Narratives Illustrating Their Heroism, Self-Reliance, Genius and Enterprise,* ed. Henry Howe (Cincinnati: Henry Howe; New York: Geo. F. Tuttle, 1860), 478–479.

33. Ballentine, *Autobiography,* 272.

34. EE527, RG 153, NA.

35. Tate, *Frontier Army,* x, 306–308; Prucha, *Broadax,* ix, 35, 104–105, 129–148. The Taylor comment is from Prucha, *Broadax,* 104.

36. Zeh, *Immigrant Soldier,* 40–41. For other protests, see EE523, RG 153, NA; Stevens, *Rogue's March,* 57; McClellan, *Mexican War Diary,* 162–163.

37. Ballentine, *Autobiography,* 28; Coffman, *Old Army,* 23; EE530, RG 153, NA.

38. Coffman, *Old Army,* 193–196.

39. EE542, EE507, EE530, EE535, RG 153, NA.

40. Foos, *Short,* 25; Prucha, *Sword,* 328.

41. Stevens, *Rogue's March,* 2–3.

42. EE522, EE528, EE544, EE582, RG 153, NA.

43. Dorsey, *Reforming Men,* 92–98, 223–225; Amy Greenberg, *Cause for Alarm: The Volunteer Fire Department in the Nineteenth Century City* (Princeton, NJ: Princeton University Press, 1998), 68; Howe, *What Hath,* 528; Paul E. Johnson, *Sam Patch: The Famous Jumper* (New York: Hill and Wang, 2003), 127–160; Way, *Common Labour,* 14, 143, 165, 167; Way, "Evil Humors," 1408; Wilentz, *Chants Democratic,* 308; Franklin Smith, *The Mexican War Journal of Captain Franklin Smith* (Jackson: University Press of Mississippi, 1991), 57–59.

44. Coffman, *Old Army,* 198.

45. Reeves Manuscript, 20–24; Coffman, *Old Army,* 198; Doubleday, *My Life,* 14; Ballentine, *Autobiography,* 55–65; EE512, EE527, EE530, EE535, EE536, EE541, EE545, EE555, RG 153, NA.

46. Reeves Manuscript, 7, 44–45, 93–98, 271; Coffman, *Old Army,* 25, 112–116; Howe, *What Hath,* 247; Robert Johannsen, *To the Halls of Montezuma: The Mexican War in the American Imagination* (New York: Oxford University Press, 1985), 139; Winders, *Mr. Polk's,* 22. See Way, *Common Labour,* 171–172, for women in construction camps.

47. Coffman, *Old Army,* 202–203; Prucha, *Sword,* 323–324. For references to these promotions and the hope for them, see Reeves Manuscript, 356–357, 424; and Archivo de Guerra, leg. 921, no exp., no fol., AGN.

48. Reeves Manuscript, 51, 195–196; Ballentine, *Autobiography,* 14, 182–185; Stevens, *Rogue's March,* 142.

49. Reeves Manuscript, 134.

50. Ibid., 51. See also 366, 412.

51. Coffman, *Old Army,* 207; Winders, *Mr. Polk's,* 17; Alexander, *Transatlantic,* 282.

52. Jay Luvas, ed. and trans., *Frederick the Great on the Art of War* (New York: Free Press, 1966), 78.

53. Ibid., 78; Reeves Manuscript, 133–134; Coffman, *Old Army,* 211; Justin Smith, *War,* 2:144. For similar bonds of comradeship among seamen of the period, see Marcus Rediker, *The Slave Ship: A Human History* (New York: Viking, 2007), 230.

54. Ballentine, *Autobiography,* 269–270.

55. Leg. 17, 1845, SGG, AHESLP; LEPOSLP, August 9, 1845.

56. *Campaña contra los americanos del norte; Primera parte: Relación histórica de los cuarenta días que mandó en Gefe el Ejército del norte El E. Sr. General de División Don Mariano Arista* (Mexico City: Ignacio Cumplido, 1846), 31; Gobernación, sin sección, vol. 291, exp. 15, AGN; leg. 17, exp. 8, 1846, SGG, AHESLP; Actas de Cabildo Ordinarios, vol. 168-A, October 6, 1846, AHDF.

57. Robert Scheina, *Latin America's Wars,* vol. 1, *The Age of the Caudillo, 1791–1899* (Washington: Brassey, 2003), 159; Maria Isabel Monroy and Tomás Calvillo Unna, *Breve historia de San Luis Potosí* (Mexico City: El Colegio de México / Fideicomiso Historia de las Américas / Fondo de Cultura Económica, 1997), 166; Manuel Muro Rocha, *Historia de San Luis Potosí* (Mexico City: Sociedad Potosina de Estudios Históricos, 1973), 2:116–118, 136–147; Primo Feliciano Velázquez, *Historia General de San Luis Potosí* (San Luis Potosí, Mexico: El Colegio de San Luis, A. C. y la Universidad Autónoma de San Luis Potosí, 2007), 534, 543–544; Rosa Helis Villa de Mebius, *San Luis Potosí: Una historia compartida* (Mexico City: Instituto de Investigaciones Dr. José María Luis Mora, 1988), 96; Manuel Balbontín, *La invasión norteamericana, 1846 a 1849: Apuntes del subteniente de artillería* (Mexico City: Tip de B. A. Esteva, 1883), 20–21. Officers disliked posting to the far north because scant government revenues in the region meant that they would not be paid regularly. Archivo de Guerra, leg. 406, no exp., no fol., AGN; LEPOSLP, July 20, 1844.

58. For the August 1845 incident, see LEPOSLP, September 3, 1845; and Archivo de Guerra, leg. 417, no exp., fols. 1–30, AGN. For the possible political connection, see Carlos Maria de Bustamante, *El nuevo Bernal Díaz del Castillo* (Mexico City: Instituto Nacional de Estudios Históricos de la Revolución Mexicana-Gobierno del Estado de Puebla, 1994), 1:61; Pedro Santoni, *Mexicans at Arms: Puro Federalists and the Politics of War, 1845–1848* (Fort Worth: Texas Christian University Press, 1996), 54–55; *Apuntes para la historia de la guerra entre México y los Estados Unidos* (Mexico City: Consejo Nacional para la Cultura y las Artes, 1991), 69; and Velázquez, *Historia General,* 565. For the second incident, in March 1846, see leg. 7, exp. 16, 1846, SGG, AHESLP; Gobernación, vol. 323, exp. 3, AGN; LEPOSLP, March 14, 1846, February 9, 1847; leg. 9, exp. 5, 1846, SGG, AHESLP; leg. 6, exp. 48, 1846, SGG, AHESLP; leg. 6, exp. 51, 1846, SGG, AHESLP; leg. 13, exp. 14, 1846, SGG, AHESLP; Alonso García Chávez, "Las Memorias del General Andrés Terrés y Masaguera (1784–1850): Edición crítica y paleografía" (tesina de licenciatura, Universidad Nacional Autónoma de México, Facultad de Filosofía y Letras, 1997), 86–87; and Miguel Soto, *La conspiración monárquica en México, 1845–1846* (Mexico City: EOSA, 1988), 184. For the August 1846 incident, see Bustamante, *El nuevo,* 2:76; Muro Rocha, *Historia,* 2:387–388; and Velázquez, *Historia General,* 568–569.

59. Leg. 12, 1845, SGG, AHESLP.

60. Josefina Zoraida Vázquez, "In Search of Power: The Pronunciamientos of General Mariano Paredes y Arrillaga," in *Malcontents, Rebels, and Pronunciados: The Politics of Insurrection in Nineteenth-Century Mexico,* ed. Will Fowler (Lincoln: University of Nebraska Press, 2012), 193, 195–196; Soto, *La conspiración,* 57.

61. *Contestaciones habidas entre los exmos: Señores Generales de División D. Mariano Paredes y Arrillaga, D. Mariano Arista y el Supremo Gobierno* (San Luis Potosí, Mexico: Imprenta del Gobierno, 1845).

62. Soto, *La conspiración*, 53.

63. García Chávez, "Las Memorias del General Andrés Terrés," 85; Manuel Balbontín, *Memorias del Coronel Manuel Balbontín* (San Luis Potosí, Mexico: Tip. de la Escuela I. Militar, 1896), 7–9.

64. For the first claim, see LEPOSLP, January 17, 1846; and leg. 35, 1845, SGG, AHESLP. For the second, see leg. 35, 1845, SGG, AHESLP; LEPOSLP, December 17, 1845, January 3, 1846, January 8, 1846; leg. 34, 1845, SGG, AHESLP; and Santoni, *Mexicans at Arms*, 106.

65. Vázquez, "In Search of Power"; Soto, *La conspiración*.

66. Impresos, December 12, 1845, SGG, AHESLP; leg. 35, 1845, SGG, AHESLP; Alicia Tecuanhuey Sandoval, "Puebla durante la Invasión Norteamericana," in *México al tiempo de su guerra con los Estados Unidos (1846–1848),* ed. Josefina Zoraida Vázquez (Mexico City: Secretaría de Relaciones Exteriores, El Colegio de México, Fondo de Cultura Económica, 1997), 388–389; Mercedes de la Vega, "Puros y moderados: Un obstáculo para la defensa nacional, Zacatecas: 1846–1848," in Vázquez, *México al tiempo de su guerra con los Estados Unidos,* 619.

67. See *Memoria del Secretaría de Estado y del Despacho de Guerra y Marina, leída en la Cámara de Senadores el día 10 y la de Diputados el día 11 de marzo de 1845* (Mexico City: Vicente García Torres, 1845; hereafter cited as *Memoria de Guerra 1845),* 25; and Esteban Sánchez de Tagle, "La ciudad y los ejércitos," in *Ciudad de México: Ensayo de construcción de una historia,* ed. Alejandra Moreno Toscazo (Mexico City: Instituto Nacional de Antropología e Historia, 1978), 145. The Batallón de Morelia, originally from Michoacán, for instance, was stationed at the border at the beginning of the war. Moisés Guzmán Pérez, *Las relaciones clero-gobierno en Michoacán: La gestión episcopal de Juan Cayetano Gómez de Portugal* (Mexico City: LIX Legislatura Cámara de Diputados, 2005), 174.

68. For a general sense of the officer corps and the origins of its members, see Plana mayor general del ejército, *Escalafón general que comprende a los exmos. sres. generales de división a los de brigada efectivos y graduados* (Mexico City: Imprenta de la Calle de Medinas núm. 6, 1849); Alberto Carreño, *Jefes del ejército mexicano en 1847: Biografías de generales de division y de brigada y de coroneles del ejército mexicano por fines del año de 1847* (Mexico City: Secretaría de Fomento, 1914); Maria Gayón Córdova, *La ocupación yanqui de la ciudad de México, 1847–1848* (Mexico City: Consejo Nacional para la Cultura y las Artes, 1997), 190.

69. For the military academy, see *Memoria de Guerra 1845,* 31–32; William A. De Paulo Jr., *The Mexican National Army, 1822–1852* (College Station: Texas A&M University Press, 1997), 73, 89, 123; and Archivo de Guerra, leg. 153, fols. 383–447, AGN.

70. See, for instance, exp. 2390, fol. 3, ADN; exp. 2427, fol. 1, ADN; exp. 2428, fol. 1, ADN; exp. 2444, no fol., ADN; Archivo de Guerra, leg. 406, no exp., no fol., AGN; Archivo de Guerra, leg. 619, no exp., no fol., AGN; Archivo de Guerra, leg. 715, no exp., no fol., AGN.

71. Balbontín, *Memorias,* 1.

72. See, for instance, exp. 2396, no fol., ADN; and Archivo de Guerra, leg. 273, fol. 293, AGN. Americans often criticized the tactical skill of Mexican officers. Pletcher, *Diplomacy,* 440; Grant, *Personal Memoirs,* 84.

73. For examples, see Archivo de Guerra, leg. 406, no exp., no fol., AGN; Archivo de Guerra, leg. 422, fols. 106–336, AGN; Archivo de Guerra, leg. 139, fols. 184–254, AGN; Archivo de Guerra, leg. 209, fol. 490, AGN; Archivo de Guerra, leg. 525, no exp., no fol., AGN; and Archivo de Guerra, leg. 715, no exp., no fol., AGN.

74. Belarmino, *Cuestión,* 85; Gobernación, leg. 184, caja 1, exp. 3, AGN; exp. 2431, no fol., ADN; leg. 1, 1848, SGG, AHESLP.

75. Archivo de Guerra, leg. 921, no exp., no fol., AGN. See also Stevens, *Rogue's March,* 99–100.

76. Manuel Esparza, "El difícil camino de sentirse nación: Oaxaca y la guerra contra Estados Unidos," in *México en Guerra (1846–1848): Perspectivas regionales,* ed. Laura Herrera Serna (Mexico City: Conaculta, Museo Nacional de las Intervenciones, 1997), 504; Juan Ortiz Escamilla, "Michoacán: Federalismo e Intervención Norteamericana," in Vázquez, *México al tiempo de su guerra con los Estados Unidos,* 320.

77. See leg. 30, 1845, SGG, AHESLP, for an example of a volunteer. Omar Valerio-Jiménez says sometimes indebted workers joined the army to escape their employers. Omar Valerio-Jiménez, *River of Hope: Forging Identity and Nation in the Rio Grande Borderlands* (Durham, NC: Duke University Press, 2013), 119. For the six-year term, see leg. 23, 1844, SGG, AHESLP; and leg. 24, 1845, SGG, AHESLP. Some documents indicate that men were at least sometimes kept beyond their six-year term. This may even have been a common practice. See leg. 21, leg. 1, 1847, SGG, AHESLP; Gobernación, vol. 331, exp. 1, AGN; and Lino Alcorta, *Proyecto de arreglo del ejército, presentado por el gefe de la plana mayor, en cumplimiento de la orden de 24 de octubre de 1847* (Querétaro, Mexico: Imprenta de J. M. Lara, 1847), 53.

78. José Antonio Serrano Ortega, *El contingente de sangre: Los gobiernos estatales y departamentales y los métodos de reclutamiento del ejército permanente mexicano, 1824–1844* (Mexico City: Instituto Nacional de Antropología e Historia, 1993), esp. 43–48. This book is the best study of the recruiting system.

79. LEPOSLP, January 13, 1844, August 3, 1844, September 26, 1846; Impresos, August 23, 1844, SGG, AHESLP; leg. 12, 1844, SGG, AHESLP.

80. Leg. 12, leg. 13, leg. 16, 1844, SGG, AHESLP; leg. 7, 1845, SGG, AHESLP.

81. Impresos, November 5, 1845; leg. 11, leg. 12, leg. 19, 1844, SGG, AHESLP; leg. 19, 1845, SGG, AHESLP; leg. 1, exp. 30, 1846, SGG, AHESLP.

82. Leg. 7, leg. 14, 1844, SGG, AHESLP; leg. 18, 1845, SGG, AHESLP; Serrano Ortega, *El contingente,* 107–110; Cecilia Sheridan Prieto, "Coahuila y la invasión norteamericana," in Vázquez, *México al tiempo de su guerra con los Estados Unidos,* 166. Even the national government lamented the effect of the draft on the labor supply. See *Memoria de la primera Secretaría del Estado y del Despacho de Relaciones Interiores y Exteriores de los Estados Unidos Mexicanos leída al Soberano Congreso Constituyente en los días 14, 15, y 16 de diciembre de 1846 por el Ministro del Ramo, José Maria Lafragua* (Mexico City: Imprenta de Vicente García Torres, 1847), 69.

83. *LEPOSLP,* August 10, 1844; leg. 1, exp. 53, 1846, SGG, AHESLP; leg. 15, 1844, SGG, AHESLP.

84. *LEPOSLP,* January 26, 1847; *Memoria sobre el estado que guarda la administración pública de Michoacán leída al Honorable Congreso por el Secretario del Despacho en 22 de enero de 1848* (Morelia, Mexico: I. Arango, 1848), 27.

85. Gobernación, leg. 183, caja 1, exp. 2, AGN.

86. Leg. 33, leg. 34, 1845, SGG, AHESLP; leg. 1, exp. 71, 1846, SGG, AHESLP; leg. 24, exp. 22, 1846, SGG, AHESLP; leg. 24, exp. 39, 1846, SGG, AHESLP.

87. Sonia Pérez Toledo, *Trabajadores, espacio urbano y sociabilidad en la Ciudad de México, 1790–1867* (Mexico City: Universidad Autónoma Metropolitana / Miguel Angel Porrua, 2011), 178–179; leg. 21, 1845, SGG, AHESLP.

88. Leg. 5, leg. 6, leg. 8, leg. 21, 1844, SGG, AHESLP; leg. 9, 1845, SGG, AHESLP; leg. 6, exp. 47, 1846, SGG, AHESLP; Periodo Independiente, vol. 51, exp. 3, February 16, 1846, AGEO; Gobernación, vol. 304, exp. 20, AGN; August 1, 1846, exp. 32, STJ, AHESLP.

89. For examples, see leg. 16 and leg. 18, 1844, SGG, AHESLP.

90. Quote from leg. 4, exp. 16, 1846, SGG, AHESLP. See also Maria Isabel Monroy, "San Luis Potosí 1836–1849," in *Catálogo de fuentes documentales, hemerográficas y bibliográficas de la Guerra entre México y Estados Unidos 1845–48,* ed. Martha Rodríguez García (Brownsville, TX: Centro de Estudios Sociales y Humanísticos / National Park Service, Palo Alto Battlefield National Historic Site, 2002), 3; Manuel Chust, "Milicia, milicias y milicianos nacionales y cívicos en la formación del estado-nación mexicano, 1812–1835," in *Fuerzas militares en Iberoamérica, siglos XVIII y XIX,* ed. Juan Ortiz Escamilla (Mexico City: El Colegio de México, El Colegio de Michoacán y la Universidad Veracruzana, 2005), 184; Romana Falcón, "Indígenas y justicia durante la era juarista: El costo social de la 'contrbución de sangre' en el Estado de México," in *Los pueblos indios en los tiempos e Benito Juárez (1847–1872),* ed. Antonio Escobar (Mexico City: Universidad Autónoma Benito Juárez de Oaxaca / Universidad Autónoma Metropolitana, 2007), 131; and Serrano Ortega, *El contingente,* 15–16, 79–80. Timo Schaefer provides a penetrating analysis of how military recruitment gave local government a key role in the formation of the national state and led to increased crime in Mexico in "Citizen-Breadwinners and

Vagabond-Soldiers: Military Recruitment in Early Republican Southern Mexico," *Journal of Social History* 46, no. 4 (Summer 2013): 953–970.

91. Leg. 13, 1844, SGG, AHESLP; Falcón, "Indígenas y justicia," 132. Of course, they could also protect political allies from the draft. See Pérez Toledo, *Trabajadores,* 162.

92. Donnavan, *Adventures,* 38; LEPOSLP, April 13, April 6, 1844; leg. 10, leg. 2, leg. 5, leg. 7, leg. 9, leg. 20, 1844, SGG, AHESLP; leg. 4, leg. 7, leg. 21, leg. 2, 1845, SGG, AHESLP; leg. 1, exp. 8, 1846, SGG, AHESLP; leg. 1, exp. 29, 1846, SGG, AHESLP; leg. 1, exp. 31, 1846, SGG, AHESLP; leg. 1, exp. 77, 1846, SGG, AHESLP.

93. The quotes are from leg. 6, 1846, SGG, AHESLP. For Durango, see Gobernación, leg. 183, caja 1, exp. 3, AGN. For San Luis Potosí, see leg. 2, leg. 7, leg. 12, and leg. 21, 1844, SGG, AHESLP. More generally, see Serrano Ortega, *El contingente,* 46.

94. Leg. 11, 1844, SGG, AHESLP.

95. Leg. 4, 1844, SGG, AHESLP.

96. Leg. 4, 1845, SGG, AHESLP. See also leg. 14, leg. 1, leg. 23, 1844, SGG, AHESLP; leg. 6, exp. 6, 1846, SGG, AHESLP; leg. 13, exp. 3, 1846, SGG, AHESLP; and leg. 13, exp. 31, 1846, SGG, AHESLP.

97. Leg. 17, exp. 1, 1846, SGG, AHESLP; leg. 6, exp. 19, 1846, SGG, AHESLP; leg. 8, leg. 16, 1844, SGG, AHESLP.

98. Leg. 18, 1844, SGG, AHESLP; leg. 13, leg. 30, 1845, SGG, AHESLP; leg. 6, exp. 6, 1846, SGG, AHESLP.

99. The quotes are from leg. 35 and leg. 24, 1845, SGG, AHESLP. See also leg. 1, leg. 16, 1844 SGG, AHESLP; leg. 1, 1845, SGG, AHESLP; leg. 15, 1847, SGG, AHESLP; leg. 14, 1844, SGG, AHESLP. On repeated behavior, see leg. 34, 1845, and leg. 6, exp. 19, 1846, SGG, AHESLP. Some of these illicit affairs were more damaging than others. One man was drafted for sleeping with his godmother, and another for sleeping with his mother-in-law. Leg. 2, leg. 11, 1844, SGG, AHESLP.

100. Laura Shelton discusses these mores in *For Tranquility and Order: Family and Community on Mexico's Northern Frontier, 1800–1850* (Tucson: University of Arizona Press, 2010), 50. See also Valerio-Jiménez, *River of Hope,* 78, 81. For men drafted simply for having long-term sexual relationships without marrying, see leg. 14 and leg. 16, 1844, SGG, AHESLP. Coronado Gallardo was accused of having serial long-term relationships but never actually marrying any of the women. Leg. 8, 1844, SGG, AHESLP. For violations of the promise of marriage, see leg. 11, 1844, SGG, AHESLP.

101. For mores surrounding elopement, see Shelton, *For Tranquility and Order,* 53, and Valerio-Jiménez, *River of Hope,* 80. For cases where men were drafted for elopement,

see leg. 16, leg. 18, 1844, SGG, AHESLP; leg. 10, 1845, SGG, AHESLP; and leg. 17, exp. 18, 1846, SGG, AHESLP.

102. Leg. 10, exp. 33, and leg. 13, exp. 31, 1846, SGG, AHESLP.

103. Leg. 14, leg. 15, leg. 18, 1844, SGG, AHESLP; leg. 1, leg. 23, 1845, SGG, AHESLP; leg. 9, exp. 7, 1846; leg. 24, 1847, SGG, AHESLP.

104. Sonya Lipsett-Rivera, *Gender and the Negotiation of Daily Life in Mexico, 1750–1850* (Lincoln: University of Nebraska Press, 2012), 177, 180–181, 214–215; Valerio-Jiménez, *River of Hope*, 86–87; leg. 14, leg. 16, leg. 20, 1844, SGG, AHESLP; leg. 15, 1847, SGG, AHESLP.

105. Leg. 14, leg. 15, leg. 16, leg. 20, SGG, AHESLP; leg. 9, leg. 21, leg. 24, leg. 34, leg. 35, 1845, SGG, AHESLP; leg. 10, exp. 21, 1846, SGG, AHESLP; leg. 10, exp. 33, 1846, SGG, AHESLP; Peter Guardino, *The Time of Liberty: Popular Political Culture in Oaxaca, 1750–1850* (Durham, NC: Duke University Press, 2005), 247. Sonia Pérez Toledo believes that women sometimes used the threat of conscription to moderate the behavior of their husbands. Pérez Toledo, *Trabajadores*, 169.

106. Deborah Kanter, *Hijos del pueblo: Gender, Family and Community in Rural Mexico, 1730–1850* (Austin: University of Texas Press, 2008), 58–59.

107. Quotes from leg. 30 and leg. 25, 1845, SGG, AHESLP. See also leg. 4, 1844, SGG, AHESLP; leg. 9, exp. 16, 1846, SGG, AHESLP; leg. 10, exp. 21, 1846, SGG, AHESLP; leg. 19, 1847, SGG, AHESLP; and leg. 13, exp. 11, 1846, SGG, AHESLP.

108. Quotes from leg. 14, 1844, SGG, AHESLP, and leg. 1, exp. 23, 1846, SGG, AHESLP. See also leg. 11, 1844, SGG, AHESLP; leg. 4, 1845, SGG, AHESLP; and leg. 6, exp. 1, 1846, SGG, AHESLP.

109. Leg. 10, leg. 18, 1844, SGG, AHESLP.

110. Will Fowler, *Santa Anna of Mexico* (Lincoln: University of Nebraska Press, 2007), 17. Fanny Calderón de la Barca points out that Mexican's passion for gambling spanned classes and sometimes brought the wealthy and poor together in friendly competition. Fanny Calderón de la Barca, *Life in Mexico during a Residence of Two Years in That Country* (Berkeley: University of California Press, 1982), 215. John Henshaw reports that after a battle even severely wounded Mexican troops gambled while they awaited aid. John Corey Henshaw, *Recollections of the War with Mexico* (Columbia: University of Missouri Press, 2008), 68.

111. Leg. 9, exp. 16, 1846, SGG, AHESLP; leg. 11, leg. 23, 1844, SGG, AHESLP.

112. Quote from leg. 15, 1847, SGG, AHESLP. See also leg. 13, exp. 31, 1846, SGG, AHESLP; leg. 21, leg. 23, 1844, SGG, AHESLP; and leg. 25, 1845, SGG, AHESLP.

113. On wanderers, see leg. 16, 1844, SGG, AHESLP, and leg. 25, 1845, SGG, AHESLP. On *vagos* more generally, see Shelton, *For Tranquility and Order*, 141; leg. 6, exp. 6, 1846, SGG,

AHESLP; leg. 34, 1845, SGG, AHESLP; and leg. 2, leg. 14, 1844, SGG, AHESLP. Leg. 18, 1844, SGG, AHESLP, makes the connection to gender very explicit.

114. Leg. 18, 1844, SGG, AHESLP. For an official warning to a father, see leg. 24, 1845, SGG, AHESLP.

115. These actions were taken after verbal investigations and recorded in what were called "verbal trial books." See leg. 3, exp. 18, 1846, SGG, AHESLP, and leg. 2, 1844, SGG, AHESLP.

116. Serrano Ortega, *El contingente,* 15–16, 51; leg. 7, leg. 17, 1844, SGG, AHESLP; *Memoria de Guerra 1845,* 19; leg. 6, exp. 9, 1846, SGG, AHESLP; Alcorta, *Proyecto,* 36. For the law, see Manuel Dublán and José Maria Lozano, *Legislación mexicana; ó, Colección completa de las disposiciones legislativas expedidas desde la independencia de la República* (Mexico City: Imprenta del Comercio, 1876), 4:582–589.

117. Municipalidades, Guadalupe Hidalgo, caja 186, AHDF; leg. 11, 1844, SGG, AHESLP; exp. 2107, fols. 7–8, ADN; Serrano Ortega, *El contingente,* 15–16, 53–59, 77–81; Mario Alberto García Suárez, "El puerto de Veracruz, espacio de la guerra franco-mexicana (1838–1839)" (tesis de licenciatura, Universidad Veracruzana, 2014), 57–58.

118. Pérez Toledo, *Trabajadores,* 159, 172; Sonia Pérez Toledo, "Movilización social y poder político en la Ciudad de México en la década de 1830," in *Prácticas Populares, Cultura Política y Poder en México, Siglo XIX,* ed. Brian Connaughton (Mexico City: Universidad Autónoma Metropolitana-Iztapalapa / Juan Pablos, 2008), 352; Lipsett-Rivera, *Gender,* 7, 12–14.

119. Quote from leg. 12, 1844, SGG, AHESLP. See also leg. 13, 1845, SGG, AHESLP, and leg. 4, exp. 16, 1846, SGG, AHESLP.

120. This idea runs through thousands of documents. See, for example, the dozens of references to honor in Municipalidades, Guadalupe Hidalgo, caja 186, AHDF.

121. Archivo de Guerra, leg. 375, fols. 22–33, AGN. For the conditions described, see Archivo de Guerra, leg. 375, fols. 384–517, AGN; Schaefer, "Citizen-Breadwinners and Vagabond-Soldiers," 957; Franklin Smith, *Mexican War Journal,* 136; Monroy Castillo, "San Luis Potosí 1836–1849," 4; Monroy and Calvillo Unna, *Breve historia,* 172–173; Ortiz Escamilla, "Michoacán," 321; Donnavan, *Adventures,* 62; and leg. 2, leg. 25, leg. 12, leg. 15, 1844, SGG, AHESLP. Carlos Mara de Bustamante reports that in Oaxaca twenty-five recruits drowned when the boat they were on overturned in a river. Carlos Maria de Bustamante, entry for October 6, 1846, in *Diario histórico de México 1822–1848,* ed. Josefina Zoraida Vázquez and Héctor Cuauhtémoc Hernández Silva (Mexico City: El Colegio de México / Centro de Investigaciones y Estudios Superiores en Antropología Social, 2003).

122. Leg. 18, 1844, SGG, AHESLP. See also leg. 13, leg. 14, leg. 18, and leg. 21, 1844, SGG, AHESLP.

123. Bustamante, entry for September 18, 1847, in *Diario*. Army officers themselves understood this. See Gobernación, leg. 183, caja 1, exp. 3, AGN.

124. For just a few examples of successful appeals, see leg. 2, leg. 7, leg. 14, leg. 15, leg. 16, and leg. 18, 1844, SGG, AHESLP.

125. Leg. 8, leg. 13, leg. 14, leg. 15, leg. 18, leg. 21, leg. 23, 1844, SGG, AHESLP; leg. 1, exp. 53, 1846, SGG, AHESLP; leg. 11, exp. 9, 1846, SGG, AHESLP. See Peter Beattie, *The Tribute of Blood: Army, Honor, Race and Nation in Brazil, 1864–1945* (Durham, NC: Duke University Press, 2001), 34–35, for landowners protecting their employees from the draft in Brazil.

126. Leg. 11, leg. 23, leg. 16, leg. 18, leg. 21, 1844, SGG, AHESLP; leg. 9, exp. 9, 1846, SGG, AHESLP.

127. Quotes from leg. 14, 1844, SGG, AHESLP. For references to recruits as *hombres de bien,* see leg. 14 and leg. 15, 1845, SGG, AHESLP.

128. Leg. 15, leg. 14, leg. 21, 1844, SGG, AHESLP; leg. 1, exp. 10, 1846, SGG, AHESLP; leg. 10, exp. 3, 1846, SGG, AHESLP; leg. 9, exp. 25, 1846, SGG, AHESLP; leg. 12, exp. 12, 1846, SGG, AHESLP.

129. LEPOSLP, February 1, 1845, May 18, 1846. Soldiers crippled in battle were likely to live out their days as beggars. See Ballentine, *Autobiography,* 322.

130. Doubleday, *My Life,* 99.

131. The numerous references to soldaderas in memoirs testify to the curiosity. See Streeby, *American Sensations,* 83; Zeh, *Immigrant Soldier,* 21–22; Chamberlain, *My Confession,* 100; Richard Coulter, *Volunteers: The Mexican War Journals of Private Richard Coulter and Sergeant Thomas Barclay,* ed. Allan Peskin (Kent, OH: Kent State University Press, 1991), 61; J. Jacob Oswandel, *Notes on the Mexican War, 1846–1848* (Knoxville: University of Tennessee Press, 2010), 51; and William W. Carpenter, *Travels and Adventures in Mexico: In the Course of Journeys of Upward of 2500 Miles, Performed on Foot, Giving an Account of the Manners and Customs of the People, and the Agricultural and Mineral Resources of That Country* (New York: Harper Brothers, 1851), 52. For pity elicited by these women's hard lots and even the way their husbands treated them, see Coulter, *Volunteers,* 82, For contempt, see William H. Daniel Military Diary, 62, MS A D184, FHS, and *Encarnacion Prisoners: Comprising an Account of the March of the Kentucky Cavalry from Louisville to the Rio Grande . . .* (Louisville, KY: Prentice and Weissanger, 1848), 44. For the idea that soldaderas were there to rob the dead, see Justin Smith, *War,* 1:380, and Lewis, *Trailing,* 83. Keep in mind that it was common for soldiers in all armies to steal from corpses found on the battlefield. See, for instance, Ballentine, *Autobiography,* 198.

132. On women fighting and being killed or wounded, see Johannsen, *To the Halls,* 137, and Coulter, *Volunteers,* 83. On soldaderas, food, and marching see Belarmino, *Cuestión,* 61;

Carlos Sánchez Navarro, *La guerra de Téjas: Memorias de un soldado* (Mexico City: Editorial Jus, 1960), 47; Tom Reilly, *War with Mexico! America's Reporters Cover the Battlefront* (Lawrence: University of Kansas Press, 2010), 234; S. Compton Smith, *Chile con Carne; or, The Camp and the Field* (New York: Miller and Curtis, 1857), 258; and *Campaña contra los americanos*, 34. On treating wounded soldiers, see Ballentine, *Autobiography*, 208; Johnson, *Gallant*, 100; and Antonio García Cubas, *El libro de mis recuerdos: Narraciones históricas, anecdóticas y de costumbres mexicanas, anteriores al actual estado social, ilustrada con más de trescientos fotograbados* (Mexico City: Imprenta de Arturo García Cubas, 1904), 427.

133. Sonia Pérez Toledo points out that in the 1842 census more than half of the rank-and-file soldiers stationed in Mexico City were married. Pérez Toledo, *Trabajadores*, 178. On women forming new partnerships with soldiers in Mexico City, see, for instance, Indiferente de Guerra, leg. 74A, no exp., no fol., AGN. Sometimes domestic servants in northern Mexico also formed these relationships with soldiers. Valerio-Jiménez, *River of Hope*, 71.

134. Belarmino, *Cuestión*, 60; Muro Rocha, *Historia*, 2:201; leg. 33, 1845, SGG, AHESLP; leg. 13, exp. 23, 1846, SGG, AHESLP; leg. 16, 1844, SGG, AHESLP; leg. 17, 1845, SGG, AHESLP; leg. 24, 1847, SGG, AHESLP; Serrano Ortega, *El contingente*, 111; leg. 1, exp. 73, 1846, SGG, AHESLP.

135. See the comments of Oaxacan governor Benito Juárez in Brian Hamnett, "El Estado de Oaxaca durante la Guerra contra los Estados Unidos; 1846–1848," in Vázquez, *México al tiempo de su guerra con los Estados Unidos*, 30–31. Guardino, *Time of Liberty*, 253; Schaefer, "Citizen-Breadwinners and Vagabond-Soldiers," 958. For Indians feigning monolingualism, see Mercedes de la Vega and Maria Cecilia Zuleta, *Testimonios de una guerra: México, 1846–1848* (Mexico City: Secretaría de Relaciones Exteriores, 2001), 2:201; leg. 10, leg. 30, 1845, SGG, AHESLP; leg. 1, exp. 30, 1846, SGG, AHESLP.

136. For a few cases, see Impresos, December 13, 1844, SGG, AHESLP; leg. 14, leg. 16, 1844, SGG, AHESLP; leg. 21, 1845; and leg. 1, exp. 72, 1846, SGG, AHESLP.

137. Impresos, August 23, 1844, SGG, AHESLP; leg. 1, exp. 5, 1846, SGG, AHESLP; Serrano Ortega, *El contingente*, 113; Barbara Corbett, "Race, Class and Nation in Wartime San Luis Potosí" (paper presented at the meeting of the Latin American Studies Association, Guadalajara, April 17, 1997), 6; Monroy and Calvillo Unna, *Breve historia*, 172–173; Carmen Reyna, "Ciudad de México: Crisis políticas y sus manifestaciones callejeras," in *Ciudad de México: Ensayo de construcción de una historia*, ed. Alejandra Moreno Toscano (Mexico City: Instituto Nacional de Antropología e Historia, 1978), 156; leg. 20, exp. 36, 1846, SGG, AHESLP; leg. 8, 1847, SGG, AHESLP. For the Santa Anna case, see leg. 22, 1844, SGG, AHESLP. For resistance to conscription in Veracruz, see Michael Ducey, "El Reto del orden liberal: Ciudadanos indígenas y prácticas populares en el México independiente: La política cotidiana en el Cantón de Misantla, Veracuz," in *Los efectos del liberalismo en México siglo XIX*, ed. Antonio Escobar Ohmstede, José Marcos Medina Bustos, and

Zulema Trejo Contreras (Mexico City: El Colegio de Sonora / Centro de Investigaciones y Estudios Superiores en Antropología Social, 2015), 258–259, and Roberto Reyes Landa, "Resistencia campesina en Misantla, Veracruz: Los totonacos contra el servicio militar y la individualización de las tierras en el siglo XIX," *Ulúa: Revista de historia, sociedad y cultura* 14 (July–December 2009): 83–88.

138. The Hernandez quote is in leg. 16, 1844, SGG, AHESLP. See also, for example, leg. 14, 1844, SGG, AHESLP.

139. Valerio-Jiménez, *River of Hope,* 119. For the theft of food, see leg. 31, 1845, SGG, AHESLP. For gambling, see leg. 15, 1847, SGG, AHESLP. For looting the dead, see Roa Bárcena, *Recuerdos,* 436. For looting Mexican civilians after defeats, see Carmen Blázquez Domínguez, "Veracruz: Restablecimiento del federalismo e intervención norteamericana," in Vázquez, *México al tiempo de su guerra con los Estados Unidos,* 574; Miguel González Quiroga, "Nuevo León ante la invasión norteamericana, 1846–1849," in Herrera Serna, *México en Guerra,* 441.

140. Leg. 31, 1845, SGG, AHESLP; Ayuntamiento, Policía en General, vol. 3631, exp. 325, fol. 18, AHDF; Ayuntamiento, Policía Seguridad, vol. 3690, exp. 61, AHDF; Municipalidades, San Angel, Milicia Civica, caja 166, exp. 48, AHDF.

141. For fear, see Karl Heller, *Alone in Mexico: The Astonishing Travels of Karl Heller, 1845–1848,* ed. and trans. Terry Rugeley (Tuscaloosa: University of Alabama Press, 2007), 106, and leg. 30, 1847, SGG, AHESLP. For brawling, see leg. 24, 1844, SGG, AHESLP, and LEPOSLP, December 20, 1845.

142. For praise of their skill, see Oswandel, *Notes,* 46, 51, 179. See also Pedro de Ampudia, *Conciudadanos: Siendo para mí una mácsima incontrovertible que todo hombre público cuanto mayor sea categoría tiene en los paises donde imperan las leyes y la libertad, la obligacion precisa de dar cuenta de su conducta* (San Luis Potosí, Mexico, 1846), 12; Oswandel, *Notes,* 50; Roa Bárcena, *Recuerdos,* 45, 118, 378, 409; Tennery, *Diary,* 81; Christopher Dishman, *A Perfect Gibraltar: The Battle of Monterrey, Mexico, 1846* (Norman: University of Oklahoma Press, 2010), xviii, 146, 192–193; James M. McCaffrey, *Army of Manifest Destiny: The American Soldier in the Mexican War, 1846–1848* (New York: New York University Press, 1992), 10; LEPOSLP, October 17, 1846; Reilly, *War!,* 74, 170, 180; Muro Rocha, *Historia,* 2:453; and Reeves Manuscript, 141, 150, 185, 347, 366.

143. Johannsen, *To the Halls,* 23; Michael Van Wagenen, *Remembering the Forgotten War: The Enduring Legacies of the U.S.-Mexican War* (Amherst: University of Massachusetts Press, 2012), 14. Justin Smith, the first professional American historian of the war, writing in an early twentieth century marked by its own severe racism, attributed every virtue of Mexican soldiers to their Indian race, including their courage, which to him stemmed from "animal courage, racial apathy or indifference about their miserable

lives." Justin Smith, *War,* 1:10. Notably, American sources that denigrated the courage of Mexican troops tended to originate from people who had not participated in the war. For examples, see Greenberg, *Manifest Manhood,* 106, and Horsman, *Race,* 254. See also Theodore Laidley, *Surrounded by Dangers of All Kinds: The Mexican War Letters of Lieutenant Theodore Laidley* (Denton: University of North Texas Press, 1997), 57–58, 135, 155. These criticisms tended to be after Mexican troops retreated in disorder. McCaffrey, *Army,* 173.

144. Grant, *Personal Memoirs,* 84.

145. Muro Rocha, *Historia,* 2:453; Belarmino, *Cuestión,* 61, 162; Pletcher, *Diplomacy,* 440; Justin Smith, *War,* 1:10, 2:311; Stevens, *Rogue's March,* 128; LEPOSLP, May 23, 1846; leg. 13, 1847, SGG, AHESLP.

146. Archivo de Guerra, leg. 439, fol. 126, AGN; Archivo de Guerra, leg. 941, no exp., no fol., AGN; Archivo de Guerra, leg. 1004, no exp., no fol., AGN; Indiferente de Guerra, leg. 74A, no exp., no fol., AGN; leg. 30, 1845, SGG, AHESLP; *Encarnacion,* 49.

147. Leg. 10, 1847, SGG, AHESLP; Bustamante, entry for September 18, 1847, in *Diario;* Gayón Córdova, *La ocupación,* 189; Stevens, *Rogue's March,* 100; Archivo de Guerra, leg. 401, fol. 19, AGN; May 1, 1848, exp. 17, STJ, AHESLP; Carpenter, *Travels,* 57, 66–67, 75, 80; *Encarnacion,* 52.

148. This is based on an analysis of the personnel records of the Batalión Fijo de México for 1846–1847. See Indiferente de Guerra, leg. 64, no exp., no fol., AGN.

149. Ayuntumiento, 1846–1847, leg. 1, exp. 1, AHESLP.

150. December 1, 1846, exp. 15, STJ, AHESLP; Archivo de Guerra, leg. 921, no exp., no fol., AGN. For other documents that stress comradeship, see Archivo de Guerra, leg. 941, no exp., no fol., AGN, and December 1, 1846, exp. 3, STJ, AHESLP.

151. Archivo de Guerra, leg. 374, exp. 3813, fols. 220–225, AGN.

152. Laidley, *Surrounded,* 3. See also Gene Brack, *Mexico Views Manifest Destiny* (Albuquerque: University of New Mexico Press, 1975), 79; Josiah Gregg, *Diary and Letters of Josiah Gregg,* ed. Maurice Garland Fulton (Norman: University of Oklahoma Press, 1944), 2:56; and Valerio-Jiménez, *River of Hope,* 119.

153. Gayón Córdova, *La ocupación,* 189; Sánchez Navarro, *La guerra,* 67–68.

154. Gayón Córdova, *La ocupación,* 190; Sánchez Navarro, *La guerra,* 48; Belarmino, *Cuestión,* 93–94; Archivo de Guerra, leg. 406, no fol., no exp., AGN.

155. Alcorta, *Proyecto,* 36; Gobernación, 331, exp. 1, AGN; Gobernación, leg. 183, caja 1, exp. 6, AGN; exp. 2673, fols. 7–8, 18, 23, 29, ADN; Gobernación, leg. 183, caja 1, exp. 4, AGN.

156. Indiferente de Guerra, leg. 74, no exp., no fol., AGN.

157. Archivo de Guerra, leg. 275, exp. 2698, fols. 55–76, AGN; leg. 13, leg. 28, leg. 33, 1847, SGG, AHESLP; exp. 2173, fols. 46, 48, ADN; Sánchez Navarro, *La guerra,* 74; Ampudia, *Conciudadanos,* 19; *Campaña contra los americanos,* 30 and anexos; Lewis, *Trailing,* 80; McCaffrey, *Army,* 10.

158. Indiferente de Guerra, leg. 64, no exp., no fol., AGN.

159. *LEPOSLP,* January 19, 1847; leg. 13, 1847, SGG, AHESLP; exp. 2319, fol. 21, ADN; exp. 2567, fol. 19, ADN. For Quiñonez's statement, see leg. 13, 1845, SGG, AHESLP, and Bustamante, entry for February 11, 1847, in *Diario.*

160. Leg. 4, 1845, SGG, AHESLP. See also leg. 1, exp. 10, 1846, SGG, AHESLP.

161. Garay's quote is in exp. 2487, fol. 13, ADN. See also exp. 2062, ADN; exp. 2673, fols. 7–8, 18, ADN; Sánchez Navarro, *La guerra,* 74; Brack, *Mexico,* 154; and Municipalidades, San Angel, Milicia Cívica, caja 166, exp. 52, AHDF. For the personnel records, see, for example, Indiferente de Guerra, leg. 76, no exp., no fol., AGN.

162. Leg. 11, 1847, SGG, AHESLP; leg. 19, leg. 28, 1845, SGG, AHESLP; *Memoria, Michoacán, 1848,* anexo 22.

163. Impresos, January 7, 1845, SGG, AHESLP; Impresos, 1847, exp. 34, SGG, AHESLP; Ayuntamiento, 1846–1847, leg. 1, exp. 1, SGG, AHESLP; leg. 4, leg. 17, 1844, SGG, AHESLP; José Arturo Salazar y García, "Guanajuato durante la guerra de 1846–1848," in Herrera Serna, *México en Guerra,* 309–310.

164. Schaefer, "Citizen-Breadwinners and Vagabond-Soldiers," 964; Sánchez de Tagle, "La ciudad y los ejércitos," 147.

165. Leg. 9, 1845, SGG, AHESLP; leg. 23, exp. 45, 1846, SGG, AHESLP. For estate owners hiding deserters in order to exploit their labor, see exp. 2179, fol. 58, ADN. For military suspicions of civilian authorities, see leg. 19, leg. 22, 1845, SGG, AHESLP; leg. 19, exp. 10, 1846, SGG, AHESLP; leg. 21, exp. 54, 1846; and leg. 12, 1848, SGG, AHESLP.

166. Balbontín, *La invasión,* 68–69.

167. Richard Holmes, *Redcoat: The British Soldier in the Age of Horse and Musket* (New York: W. W. Norton, 2002), 16, 32–33, 138, 215, 268; Wayne E. Lee, *Barbarians and Brothers: Anglo-American Warfare, 1500–1865* (New York: Oxford University Press, 2011), 178–179, 190–192; Hoffman Nickerson, *The Armed Horde, 1893–1939: A Study of the Rise, Survival and Decline of the Mass Army* (New York: G. P. Putnam's Sons, 1942), 40–42; Steven Hoch, *Serfdom and Social Control in Russia: Petrovskoe, a Village in Tambov* (Chicago: University of Chicago Press, 1986), 134, 136, 151–152, 155; Eugen Weber, *Peasants into Frenchmen: The Modernization of Rural France, 1870–1914* (Stanford, CA: Stanford University Press, 1976), 295, 297. Charles Haecker and Geoffrey G. Mauck, *On the Prairie of Palo Alto: Historical Archeology of the U.S.-Mexican Battlefield* (College Station: Texas

A&M University Press, 1997), 97–103, is an excellent introduction to the set of tactics both armies were trained to use.

168. David Bell, *The First Total War: Napoleon's Europe and the Birth of Warfare as We Know It* (Boston: Houghton Mifflin, 2007), 29, 36; Geoffrey Best, *War and Society in Revolutionary Europe, 1770–1870* (Buffalo, NY: McGill-Queen's University Press, 1998), 30, 225, 246; Hoch, *Serfdom,* 136, 157; Lee, *Barbarians and Brothers,* 205; Ricardo Salvatore, *Wandering Paysanos: State Order and Subaltern Experience in the Rosas Era* (Durham, NC: Duke University Press, 2003), 264–265; Luvas, *Frederick the Great,* 72.

169. Best, *War,* 20, 27–28, 31, 255; Karen Hagemann, "Of 'Manly Valor' and 'German Honor': Nation, War and Masculinity in the Age of the Prussian Uprising against Napoleon," *Central European History* 31, no. 2 (1997): 194; Holmes, *Redcoat,* 48, 55; Nickerson, *Armed Horde,* 61, 68.

CHAPTER 2 · We're the Boys for Mexico

1. Brian DeLay, *War of a Thousand Deserts: Indian Raids and the Mexican-American War* (New Haven, CT: Yale University Press, 2009), 86–109; Pekka Hämäläinen, *The Comanche Empire* (New Haven, CT: Yale University Press, 2008), 182, 292, 350–351, 358; Cuauhtémoc Velasco Avila, "Sociedad, identidad y guerra entre los comanches, 1825–1835," in *La reindianización de América, siglo xix,* ed. Leticia Reina (Mexico City: Siglo Veintiuno / Centro de Investigaciones y Estudios Superiores en Antropología Social, 1997); Carlos Maria de Bustamante, *El nuevo Bernal Díaz del Castillo* (Mexico City: Instituto Nacional de Estudios Históricos de la Revolución Mexicana-Gobierno del Estado de Puebla, 1994), 1:64; David Weber, *The Mexican Frontier, 1821–1846: The American Southwest under Mexico* (Albuquerque: University of New Mexico Press, 1982), 95, 97; Douglas Murphy, *Two Armies on the Rio Grande: The First Campaign of the U.S. Mexican War* (College Station: Texas A&M University Press, 2015), 78–79.

2. David Weber, *Mexican Frontier,* 122–123; Andrés Reséndez, *Changing National Identities at the Frontier: Texas and New Mexico, 1800–1850* (New York: Cambridge University Press, 2004), 4, 6, 266, 268; Omar Valerio-Jiménez, *River of Hope: Forging Identity and Nation in the Rio Grande Borderlands* (Durham, NC: Duke University Press, 2013), 111. See the comments of General Francisco Mejía in exp. 2179, fols. 4–5, ADN.

3. Anders Stephanson, *Manifest Destiny: American Expansion and the Empire of the Right* (New York, Hill and Wang, 1995), 36; Josefina Zoraida Vázquez, "¿Dos guerras contra Estados Unidos?," in *De la rebelión de Texas a la Guerra del 47,* ed. Josefina Zoraida Vázquez (Mexico City: Nueva Imagen, 1994), 27; David Pletcher, *The Diplomacy of Annexation: Texas, Oregon, and the Mexican War* (Columbia: University of Missouri Press, 1973), 454–455; Daniel Walker Howe, *What Hath God Wrought:*

The Transformation of America, 1815–1848 (New York: Oxford University Press, 2007), 748–749.

4. The argument here coincides with that in Marcela Terrazas y Basante and Gerardo Gurza Lavalle, *Las relaciones México-Estados Unidos, 1756–2010,* vol. 1, *Imperios, repúblicas y pueblos en pugna por el territorio, 1756–1867* (Mexico City: Universidad Nacional Autónoma de México / Secretaría de Relaciones Exteriores, 2012), 128–129.

5. Vázquez, "Dos guerras," 22; Timothy J. Henderson, *A Glorious Defeat: Mexico and Its War with the United States* (New York: Hill and Wang, 2007), 189; Gene Brack, *Mexico Views Manifest Destiny* (Albuquerque: University of New Mexico Press, 1975), 56, 58, 85, 88–89; Terrazas y Basante and Gurza Lavalle, *Las relaciones México-Estados Unidos,* 1:211.

6. Pletcher, *Diplomacy,* 367; Pedro Santoni, *Mexicans at Arms: Puro Federalists and the Politics of War, 1845–1848* (Fort Worth: Texas Christian University Press, 1996), 2–4, 9; Miguel Soto, *La conspiración monárquica en México, 1845–1846* (Mexico City: EOSA, 1988), 186; *La verdad desnuda sobre la guerra de Tejas o sea contestación al folleto titulado la guerra de Tejas sin máscara* (Mexico City: n.p., 1845).

7. Josefina Zoraida Vázquez, "La guerra que puso en peligro la unidad nacional," in *Symposium La Angostura en la Intervención Norteamericana, 1846–1848* (Saltillo, Mexico: Secretaría de Educación Pública de Coahuila, 1998), 13; *Memoria del Ministro de Relaciones Exteriores y Gobernación, leída en el Senado el 11 y en la Cámara de Diputados el 12 de Marzo de 1845* (Mexico City: Ignacio Cumplido, 1845); *La guerra de Tejas sin máscara* (Mexico City: Imprenta de V. G. Torres, 1845).

8. This is the view of Timothy Henderson. Henderson, *Glorious Defeat,* 188.

9. Vázquez, "La guerra que puso en peligro," 14; Soto, *La conspiración,* 188.

10. Brack, *Mexico,* 58, 82–83.

11. Ibid., 117; Felice Flannery Lewis, *Trailing Clouds of Glory: Zachary Taylor's Mexican War Campaign and His Emerging Civil War Leaders* (Tuscaloosa: University of Alabama Press, 2010), 60–61; Pletcher, *Diplomacy,* 375; Jack Bauer, *Surfboats and Horse Marines: U.S. Naval Operations in the Mexican War, 1846–48* (Annapolis, MD: Naval Institute, 1969), 9, 13; George W. Smith and Charles Judah, *The Chronicles of the Gringos: The US Army in the Mexican War, 1846–48: Accounts of Eyewitnesses and Combatants* (Albuquerque: University of New Mexico Press, 1968), 60; exp. 2174, fols. 167–168, ADN.

12. George McClellan, *The Mexican War Diary and Correspondence of George B. McClellan,* ed. Thomas Cutrer (Baton Rouge: Louisiana State University Press, 2009), 17; exp. 2176, fols. 83–88, ADN; Pedro de Ampudia, *Conciudadanos: Siendo para mí una mácsima incontrovertible que todo hombre público cuanto mayor sea categoría tiene en los paises donde imperan las leyes y la libertad, la obligacion precisa de dar cuenta de su conducta* (San Luis Potosí, Mexico,

1846), 7; Moisés Guzmán Pérez, *Las relaciones clero-gobierno en Michoacán: La gestión episcopal de Juan Cayetano Gómez de Portugal* (Mexico City: LIX Legislatura Cámara de Diputados, 2005), 167.

13. Richard Bruce Winders, *Mr. Polk's Army: The American Military Experience in the Mexican War* (College Station: Texas A&M University Press, 1997), 24, 89; *Memoria del Secretaría de Estado y del Despacho de Guerra y Marina, leída en la Cámara de Senadores el día 10 y la de Diputados el día 11 de marzo de 1845* (Mexico City: Vicente García Torres, 1845), 21; George Meade, *The Life and Letters of George Gordon Meade, Major General United States Army* (New York: Charles Scribner's Sons, 1913), 77; Murphy, *Two Armies,* 45, 151, 196–200. The best descriptions of the contrast between the effectiveness of the two armies' cannon are Charles Haecker and Geoffrey G. Mauck, *On the Prairie of Palo Alto: Historical Archeology of the U.S.-Mexican Battlefield* (College Station: Texas A&M University Press, 1997), 75–87, and Murphy, *Two Armies,* 197–199.

14. Ulysses S. Grant, *Personal Memoirs* (Westminster, MD: Random House, 1999), 44; C. M. Reeves, "Five Years an American Soldier, Comprising Adventures at Palo Alto, Resaca de la Palma, Monterrey, Vera Cruz, Cerro Gordo, and in the Battles in the Valley of Mexico, Interspersed with Anecdotes of Military Life, in Peace and War," in *Adventures and Achievements of Americans, a Series of Narratives Illustrating Their Heroism, Self-Reliance, Genius and Enterprise,* ed. Henry Howe (Cincinnati: Henry Howe; New York: Geo. F. Tuttle, 1860), 443.

15. C. M. Reeves, "Five Years Experience in the Regular Army, including the War with Mexico," manuscript, MS qr332f RMV, CHSL (hereafter cited as Reeves Manuscript), 146.

16. Ibid., 141.

17. José María Roa Bárcena, *Recuerdos de la invasión norteamericana (1846–1849)* (Xalapa, Mexico: Universidad Veracruzana, 1986), 85; *Campaña contra los americanos del norte; Primera parte: Relación histórica de los cuarenta días que mandó en Gefe el Ejército del norte El E. Sr. General de División Don Mariano Arista* (Mexico City: Ignacio Cumplido, 1846), 10; Ampudia, *Conciudadanos,* 12.

18. Ampudia, *Conciudadanos,* 9–10, 18, 22; exp. 2174, fols. 2–4, 56, ADN; *Campaña contra los americanos,* 13; José López Uraga, *Sumaria mandada formar a pedimento del Sr. Coronel del 4 Regimento de infantería* (Mexico City: Navarro, 1846), 14–16, 18.

19. James M. McCaffrey, *Army of Manifest Destiny: The American Soldier in the Mexican War, 1846–1848* (New York: New York University Press, 1992), 10; Lewis, *Trailing,* 80.

20. An excellent detailed account of the battle is found in Haecker and Mauck, *On the Prairie of Palo Alto,* 29–48.

21. Exp. 2174, fol. 5, ADN; Justin Smith, *The War with Mexico* (Gloucester, MA: Peter Smith, 1963), 1:170–171.

22. Justin Smith, *War,* 1:172; *Campaña contra los americanos,* 14–15. Douglas Murphy believes that Arista's political opponents in the Mexican forces, especially Ampudia, encouraged rumors of Arista's treason. Murphy, *Two Armies,* 39, 155.

23. Justin Smith, *War,* 1:171; *Campaña contra los americanos,* 19; exp. 2174, fols. 53, 56, 99–100, ADN; Reeves Manuscript, 150; Murphy, *Two Armies,* 223.

24. McCaffrey, *Army,* 13; *Campaña contra los americanos,* anexo 2; Murphy, *Two Armies,* 234.

25. Roa Bárcena, *Recuerdos,* 48; *Campaña contra los americanos,* 22, 30–33; exp. 2178, fol. 66, ADN; Peter Stevens, *The Rogue's March: John Riley and the St. Patrick's Battalion, 1846–1848* (Washington, DC: Brassey's, 1999), 128; Murphy, *Two Armies,* 238, 258–260.

26. Howe, *What Hath,* 741; Amy Greenberg, *A Wicked War: Polk, Clay, Lincoln and the 1846 U.S. Invasion of Mexico* (New York: Knopf, 2012), 101–105; Pletcher, *Diplomacy,* 384–390. Polk's message is found in *A Compilation of the Messages and Papers of the Presidents Prepared under the Direction of the Joint Committee on Printing of the House and Senate* (New York: Bureau of National Literature, 1908), 2287–2292. The quote is from 2292.

27. Murphy, *Two Armies,* 262.

28. Maria Cristina González Ortiz, "La rivalidad regional y partidista en los debates del Congreso de Estados Unidos durante la guerra con México," in *Historia y nación II: Política y diplomacia en el siglo xix mexicano,* ed. Luis Jáuregui and José Antonio Serrano Ortega (Mexico City: El Colegio de México, 1998), 382; Thomas R. Hietala, *Manifest Design: Anxious Aggrandizement in Late Jacksonian America* (Ithaca, NY: Cornell University Press, 1985), Howe, *What Hath,* 741–742; David Clary, *Eagles and Empire: The United States, Mexico, and the Struggle for a Continent* (New York: Bantam Books, 2009), 100–101; Greenberg, *Wicked War,* 103–108; Winders, *Mr. Polk's,* 11; Pletcher, *Diplomacy,* 384–390, quote from 392.

29. Greenberg, *Wicked War,* 115; Joseph W. Pearson, "The Dilemma of Dissent: Kentucky's Whigs and the Mexican War," *Ohio Valley History* 12, no. 2 (Summer 2012): 26–27, 30, 34; Robert Johannsen, *To the Halls of Montezuma: The Mexican War in the American Imagination* (New York: Oxford University Press, 1985), 10–12.

30. Soto, *La conspiración;* Michael Costeloe, *The Central Republic in Mexico: Hombres de Bien in the Age of Santa Anna* (New York: Cambridge University Press, 1993), 284–297.

31. Barbara Corbett, "La política potosina y la Guerra con Estados Unidos," in *México al tiempo de su guerra con los Estados Unidos (1846–1848),* ed. Josefina Zoraida Vázquez (Mexico City: Secretaría de Relaciones Exteriores, El Colegio de México, Fondo de Cultura Económica, 1997), 457–458; Will Fowler, *Mexico in the Age of Proposals, 1821–1853*

(Westport, CT: Greenwood, 1998), 129–161; José Antonio Serrano Ortega, *Jerarquía territorial y transición política: Guanajuato, 1790–1836* (Zamora, Mexico: El Colegio de Michoacán / Instituto Mora, 2001), 295–301.

32. Peter Guardino, *Peasants, Politics, and the Formation of Mexico's National State: Guerrero, 1800–1857* (Stanford, CA: Stanford University Press, 1996), 81–177; Michael Ducey, *A Nation of Villages: Riot and Rebellion in the Mexican Huasteca, 1750–1850* (Tucson: University of Arizona Press, 2004), 120–141. This version of federalism was probably more common than people realize. See, for instance, Gobernación, sin sección, leg. 323, exp. 3, AGN; Gobernación, sin sección, leg. 324, exp. 1, AGN; and Gobernación, leg. 244, caja 2, exp. 2, AGN.

33. Richard Warren, *Vagrants and Citizens: Politics and the Masses in Mexico City from Colony to Republic* (Wilmington, DE: SR Books, 2001); Pedro Santoni, *Mexicans at Arms: Puro Federalists and the Politics of War, 1845–1848* (Fort Worth: Texas Christian University Press, 1996); Rosalina Rios Zúñiga, "Popular Uprising and Political Culture in Zacatecas: The Sombrerete Uprisings (1829)," *Hispanic American Historical Review* 87, no. 3 (August 2007): 499–536; Peter Guardino, *The Time of Liberty: Popular Political Culture in Oaxaca, 1750–1850* (Durham, NC: Duke University Press, 2005), 156–222; Peter Guardino, "La identidad nacional y los afromexicanos en el siglo XIX," in *Prácticas Populares, Cultura Política y Poder en México, Siglo XIX,* ed. Brian Connaughton (Mexico City: Universidad Autónoma Metropolitana-Iztapalapa / Juan Pablos, 2008); José Fernando Ramírez, *México durante la guerra con Estados Unidos* (Mexico City: Librería de la Viuda de Ch. Bouret, 1905), 132.

34. Rios Zúñiga, "Popular Uprising"; Peter Guardino, "Identity and Nationalism in Mexico: Guerrero, 1780–1840," *Journal of Historical Sociology* 7, no. 3 (September 1994): 314–342; Guardino, *Time of Liberty,* 156–222.

35. By far the best analysis of Santa Anna's career and political choices is Will Fowler, *Santa Anna of Mexico* (Lincoln: University of Nebraska Press, 2007).

36. Guardino, *Peasants,* 168–169; Josefina Zoraida Vázquez, "México y la Guerra con los Estados Unidos," in Vázquez, *México al tiempo de su guerra con los Estados Unidos,* 42; Justin Smith, *War,* 2:312; Santoni, *Mexicans at Arms,* 74–76.

37. Costeloe, *Central,* 293–294.

38. Fowler, *Santa Anna,* 251–255; A. Brooke Caruso, *The Mexican Spy Company: United States Covert Operations in Mexico* (Jefferson, NC: McFarland, 1991), 62–78; Bauer, *Surfboats,* 27.

39. Costeloe, *Central,* 296–297.

40. Vázquez, "México y la Guerra," 41; Antonio Escobar Ohmstede, "La Guerra entre México y los Estados Unidos en 1848 y sus consecuencias en las Huastecas," in Vázquez,

México al tiempo de su guerra con los Estados Unidos, 267; José Antonio Serrano Ortega, "Hacienda y guerra, élites políticas y gobierno nacional: Guanajuato, 1835–1847," in Vázquez, *México al tiempo de su guerra con los Estados Unidos,* 244; Maria del Carmen Salinas Sandoval, "El Estado de México durante la Guerra México-Estados Unidos, 1846–1848," in Vázquez, *México al tiempo de su guerra con los Estados Unidos,* 217–223; Maria del Carmen Salinas Sandoval, *Política interna e invasión norteamericana en el Estado de México, 1846–1848* (Zinacantepec, Mexico: El Colegio Mexiquense, 2000), 119–121, 125–126; Jesús Gómez Serrano, "El otro frente de la guerra," in *México en Guerra (1846–1848): Perspectivas regionales,* ed. Laura Herrera Serna (Mexico City: Conaculta, Museo Nacional de las Intervenciones, 1997), 107; El Cronista Mexicano, *La feliz aparición del 19 de mayo del corriente año* (Mexico City: Imprenta de Mariano Arévalo, 1847); Roa Bárcena, *Recuerdos,* 79; Mercedes de la Vega, "Puros y moderados: Un obstáculo para la defensa nacional, Zacatecas: 1846–1848," in Vázquez, *México al tiempo de su guerra con los Estados Unidos,* 617, 619, 621, 626–628.

41. Leg. 14, exp. 22, 1846, SGG, AHESLP; Gobernación, leg. 220, caja 1, exp. 1, AGN; Carlos Rodríguez Venegas, "Las finanzas públicas y la Guerra contra los Estados Unidos, 1846–1848," in Vázquez, *México al tiempo de su guerra con los Estados Unidos,* 127; Manuel Muro Rocha, *Historia de San Luis Potosí* (Mexico City: Sociedad Potosina de Estudios Históricos, 1973), 2:559–563; Mercedes de la Vega, "Zacatecas: Entre la guerra y el federalismo radical," in Herrera Serna, *México en Guerra,* 702; Terrazas y Basante and Gurza Lavalle, *Las relaciones México-Estados Unidos,* 1:229.

42. Government of Guanajuato, *Exposición y expediente que el Gobierno de Guanajuato dirige a Honorable Congreso del mismo, con motivo de las contestaciones ocurridas entre el Ministerio de la Guerra, General en Gefe del Ejército del Norte y el propio gobierno, sobre varios puntos del mayor interés para la administración pública del Estado* (Guanajuato, Mexico: Tipografía de Oñate, 1847); Serrano Ortega, "Hacienda y guerra," 261; Mercedes de la Vega and Maria Cecilia Zuleta, *Testimonios de una guerra: México, 1846–1848* (Mexico City: Secretaría de Relaciones Exteriores, 2001), 2:526–528.

43. Michael Ducey has pointed this out to me in a personal communication. See, for example, *Constitución política del Estado de México* (Mexico City: Imprenta de Vicente G. Torres, 1846), 3–4.

44. Guardino, *Peasants,* 169; Santoni, *Mexicans at Arms,* 2–3; Reynaldo Sordo Cedeño, "El faccionalismo en la Guerra con los Estados Unidos 1846–1848," in *Symposium,* 27. The quote is from a letter cited in Bustamante, *El nuevo,* 2:138.

45. Several authors have pointed to this contradictory effect. Maria del Pilar Iracheta Cenecorta, "Federalismo e invasión norteamericana en el Estado de México (1846–1848)," in Herrera Serna, *México en Guerra,* 298.

46. Winders, *Mr. Polk's*, 9, 59; Paul Foos, *A Short, Offhand Killing Affair: Soldiers and Social Conflict during the Mexican-American War* (Chapel Hill: University of North Carolina Press, 2002), 84.

47. David Bell, *The First Total War: Napoleon's Europe and the Birth of Warfare as We Know It* (Boston: Houghton Mifflin, 2007), 81; Geoffrey Best, *War and Society in Revolutionary Europe, 1770–1870* (Buffalo, NY: McGill-Queen's University Press, 1998), 78; Anna Clark "The Rhetoric of Masculine Citizenship: Concepts and Representations in Modern Western Culture," in *Representing Masculinity: Male Citizenship in Modern Western Culture*, ed. Stefan Dudink, Karen Hagemann, and Anna Clark (New York: Palgrave Macmillan, 2007), 5; Karen Hagemann, "Of 'Manly Valor' and 'German Honor': Nation, War and Masculinity in the Age of the Prussian Uprising against Napoleon," *Central European History* 31, no. 2 (1997): 205; Luis Fernando Granados, "Crust and Crumb of the U.S.-Mexican War: Soldiers Citizens, and the Course of Liberalism in North America" (unpublished manuscript, n.d.), 2.

48. Clark, "Rhetoric," 11; Bell, *Total War,* 28; Best, *War,* 77; Romana Falcón, "Indígenas y justicia durante la era juarista: El costo social de la 'contrbución de sangre' en el Estado de México," in *Los pueblos indios en los tiempos e Benito Juárez (1847–1872),* ed. Antonio Escobar (Mexico City: Universidad Autónoma Benito Juárez de Oaxaca / Universidad Autónoma Metropolitana, 2007), 132–133; Eugen Weber, *Peasants into Frenchmen: The Modernization of Rural France, 1870–1914* (Stanford, CA: Stanford University Press, 1976), 298–302.

49. Clark, "Rhetoric," 5; Hagemann, "Of 'Manly Valor,'" 214, 219; Karen Hagemann, "A Valorous Folk Family: The Nation, the Military, and the Gender Order in Prussia in the Time of the Anti-Napoleonic Wars, 1806–1815," in *Gendered Nations: Nationalisms and Gender Order in the Long Nineteenth Century,* ed. Ida Blom, Karen Hagemann, and Catherine Hall (Oxford: Berg, 2000), 189; Gregory Knouff, "White Men in Arms: Concepts of Citizenship and Masculinity in Revolutionary America," in Dudink, Hagemann, and Clark, *Representing Masculinity,* 38; Genevieve Lloyd, "Selfhood, War, and Masculinity," in *Feminist Challenges: Social and Political Theory,* ed. Carol Pateman and E. Gross (Boston: Northeastern University Press, 1987), 64, 75; Robert Nye, "Western Masculinities in War and Peace," *American Historical Review* 112, no. 2 (April 2007): 417–418.

50. Matthew Brown, "Adventurers, Foreign Women and Masculinity in the Colombian Wars of Independence," *Feminist Review* 79 (2005): 40.

51. Bell, *Total War,* esp. 9, 126, 251; Hoffman Nickerson, *The Armed Horde, 1893–1939: A Study of the Rise, Survival and Decline of the Mass Army* (New York: G. P. Putnam's Sons, 1942), 92.

52. Laura Jensen, *Patriots, Settlers, and the Origins of American Social Policy* (New York: Cambridge University Press, 2003), 53; Johannsen, *To the Halls,* 39; Foos, *Short,* 33–34; Fred Anderson and Andrew Cayton, *The Dominion of War: Empire and Liberty in North America, 1500–2000* (New York: Penguin, 2004), 178.

53. Knouff, "White," 26, 38.

54. Granados, "Crust," 24, 25; Anderson and Cayton, *Dominion,* 213, 217, 289; Alexander Saxton, *The Rise and Fall of the White Republic: Class Politics and Mass Culture in Nineteenth Century America* (London: Verso, 1990), 145.

55. Winders, *Mr. Polk's,* 68, 195; Hietala, *Manifest Design,* 207. In fact many of the men whom Jackson led at the Battle of New Orleans were not white citizen-soldier militia-men. His army included free blacks, Gulf pirates, Native Americans, and even some slaves. Yet the Tennessee and Kentucky militiamen were those glorified by supporters of Jackson. Howe, *What Hath,* 8–9, 17–18.

56. Richard Coulter, *Volunteers: The Mexican War Journals of Private Richard Coulter and Sergeant Thomas Barclay,* ed. Allan Peskin (Kent, OH: Kent State University Press, 1991), 2–4; R. C. Buley, "Indiana in the Mexican War: The Indiana Volunteers," *Indiana Magazine of History* 15, no. 3 (September 1919): 263; Johannsen, *To the Halls,* 27; Wind-ers, *Mr. Polk's,* 25; Benjamin Franklin Scribner, *Camp Life of a Volunteer: A Campaign in Mexico; or, A Glimpse at Life in Camp by "One Who Has Seen the Elephant"* (Austin: Jenkins, 1975), 16.

57. Winders, *Mr. Polk's,* 68.

58. Theodore Laidley, *Surrounded by Dangers of All Kinds: The Mexican War Letters of Lieutenant Theodore Laidley* (Denton: University of North Texas Press, 1997), 13; Foos, *Short,* 8; Howe, *What Hath,* 749; Kim Gruenwald, *River of Enterprise: The Commercial Origins of Regional Identity in the Ohio Valley, 1790–1850* (Bloomington: Indiana University Press, 2002), xi.

59. Foos, *Short,* 49; Howe, *What Hath,* 137–139; Lynea Magnuson, "In the Service of Columbia: Gendered Politics and Manifest Destiny Expansion" (PhD diss., University of Illinois, 2001), 208–211; Julie Mujic, "A Border Community's Unfulfilled Appeals: The Rise and Fall of the 1840s Anti-abolitionist Movement in Cincinnati," *Ohio Valley History* 7, no. 2 (Summer 2007): 53–58; Kevin Phillips, *The Cousins' Wars: Religion, Politics, and the Triumph of Anglo-America* (New York: Basic Books, 1999), 345, 375, 419–420; Malcolm Rohrbough, *The Trans-Appalachian Frontier: Peoples, Societies, Institutions,* 3rd ed. (Bloom-ington: Indiana University Press, 2008), 230; James Simeone, *Democracy and Slavery in Frontier Illinois: The Bottomland Republic* (DeKalb: Northern Illinois University Press, 2000), 4–6; Roger A. Van Bolt, "Hoosiers and the Western Program, 1844–1848," *Indiana Magazine of History* 58, no. 3 (1952): 169; Gruenwald, *River of Enterprise,* 49, 121, 141.

60. Rohrbough, *Trans-Appalachian Frontier,* 575–576; Howe, *What Hath,* 86; Theda Perdue and Michael Green, *The Cherokee Nation and the Trail of Tears* (New York: Penguin, 2007), 48–49; Justin Smith, *War,* 1:124–125.

61. William Hugh Robarts, *Mexican War Veterans: A Complete Roster of the Regular and Volunteer Troops in the War between the United States and Mexico, from 1846 to 1848* (Washington, DC: Brentano's, 1887).

62. Ted C. Hinckley, "American Anti-Catholicism during the Mexican War," *Pacific Historical Review* 31 (May 1962): 130; Johannsen, *To the Halls,* 26; Winders, *Mr. Polk's,* 71; Pearson, "Dilemma," 26–34; Greenberg, *Wicked War,* 113–118; George Smith and Charles Judah, *Chronicles,* 6; *Encarnacion Prisoners: Comprising an Account of the March of the Kentucky Cavalry from Louisville to the Rio Grande . . .* (Louisville, KY: Prentice and Weissanger, 1848), 3. The quote is from May 1, 1846, MS qB918RM, Robert Buchanan Letters, CHSL.

63. Johannsen, *To the Halls,* 25, 27; Winders, *Mr. Polk's,* 71–73; McCaffrey, *Army,* 18–19; Foos, *Short,* 47; Miguel González Quiroga, "Nuevo León ante la invasión norteamericana, 1846–1849," in Herrera Serna, *México en Guerra,* 436.

64. Albert G. Brackett, *General Lane's Brigade in Central Mexico* (Cincinnati: H. W. Derby, 1854), 261; A. C. Pickett, *A. C. Pickett's Private Journal of the U.S.-Mexican War,* ed. Jo Blatti (Little Rock, AR: Butler Center Books, 2011), 45; S. Compton Smith, *Chile con Carne; or, The Camp and the Field,* (New York: Miller and Curtis, 1857), 66; Entry 111, Book Records of Volunteer Organizations: Mexican War, 1846–1848, Capt. Duncan's Independent Co., Mounted Volunteers, RG 94, NA; Coulter, *Volunteers,* appendix; Adolphus Engelman, "The Second Illinois in the Mexican War: The Mexican War Letters of Adolphus Engelman, 1846–1847," *Journal of the Illinois State Historical Society* 26 (January 1934): 393; Henry S. Lane, "The Mexican War Journal of Henry S. Lane," ed. Graham Barringer, *Indiana Magazine of History* 53, no. 4 (December 1957): 403, 410; George Smith and Charles Judah, *Chronicles,* 42–43.

65. Johannsen, *To the Halls,* 66–67; Pearson, "Dilemma," 32, 37; Isaac Smith, *Reminiscences of a Campaign in Mexico: An Account of the Operations of the Indiana Brigade on the Line of the Rio Grande and Sierra Madre, and a Vindication of the Volunteers against the Aspirations of Officials and Unofficials,* 2nd ed. (Indianapolis: Chapman and Spann, 1848), 6; Oran Perry, comp., *Indiana in the Mexican War* (Indianapolis: W. B. Burford, 1908), 32–47; Henry Clay Duncan, "Monroe County in the Mexican War," *Indiana Magazine of History* 12, no. 4 (1916): 291. For a man who enlisted away from home, see J. Jacob Oswandel, *Notes on the Mexican War, 1846–1848* (Knoxville: University of Tennessee Press, 2010), 7.

66. William H. Daniel Military Diary, 98, 100, MS A D184, FHS.

67. Oswandel, *Notes,* 8, 65, 220; Coulter, *Volunteers,* 80, 142; Isaac Smith, *Reminiscences,* 31–33; Pearson, "Dilemma," 31–32; Foos, *Short,* 94; Johannsen, *To the Halls,* 52, 64; McCaffrey, *Army,* 136.

68. Franklin Smith, *The Mexican War Journal of Captain Franklin Smith* (Jackson: University Press of Mississippi, 1991), 85.

69. September 13, 1846, MS A 585, Levi White Papers, FHS.

70. William H. Daniel Military Diary, 63.

71. Oswandel, *Notes,* 30, 232; Coulter, *Volunteers,* 170, 175; *Volunteers! Men of the Granite State!* (Portsmouth, NH: n.p., February 2, 1847); Perry, *Indiana,* 52, 229, 298.

72. Pickett, *A. C. Pickett's Private Journal,* 86, 92.

73. Jorge Belarmino, *Cuestión de sangre* (Mexico City: Planeta, 2008), 106; Christopher Dishman, *A Perfect Gibraltar: The Battle of Monterrey, Mexico, 1846* (Norman: University of Oklahoma Press, 2010), 50–51; Lewis, *Trailing,* 125; McCaffrey, *Army,* 117–118; Winders, *Mr. Polk's,* 87; Coulter, *Volunteers,* 241, 259; July 28, 1846, MS C S, Thomas T. Summers, FHS; Henry Edwards, Diary during Mexican War Service, 1846–1846, 24, ISHS.

74. Foos, *Short,* 116. See also Johannsen, *To the Halls,* 63, and Winders, *Mr. Polk's,* 200.

75. Foos, *Short,* 32; Joshua S. Goldstein, *War and Gender: How Gender Shapes the War System and Vice Versa* (Cambridge: Cambridge University Press, 2001), 169; Coulter, *Volunteers,* 121–122; EE382, RG 153, NA.

76. Coulter, *Volunteers,* 203, 216, 226, 295–296; Oswandel, *Notes,* 88. Nineteenth-century American men slept together for warmth and their doing so did not imply erotic behavior. James Broomall, "'We Are a Band of Brothers': Manhood and Community in Confederate Camps and Beyond," *Civil War History* 60, no. 3 (2014): 293.

77. Winders, *Mr. Polk's,* 125–127; Perry, *Indiana,* 193; Scribner, *Camp,* 23, 39; Timothy D. Johnson, *A Gallant Little Army: The Mexico City Campaign* (Lawrence: University of Kansas Press, 2007), 133; Coulter, *Volunteers,* 125–127; Broomall, "'We Are a Band of Brothers,'" 294, 298.

78. April 21, 1848, MS A R943 2, Runyon Family Papers, FHS; Lane, "Mexican," 406; Thomas Tennery, *The Mexican War Diary of Thomas D. Tennery* (Norman: University of Oklahoma Press, 1970), 15.

79. Foos, *Short,* 51; Perry, *Indiana,* 193.

80. McCaffrey, *Army,* 25–26; Perry, *Indiana,* 65. The supposed memoir is Eliza Allen Billings, *The Female Volunteer; or, The Life and Adventures of Miss Eliza Allen, a Young Lady of Eastport, Maine* (n.p.: 1851).

81. Foos, *Short,* 51; Steven Aron, *How the West Was Lost: The Transformation of Kentucky from Daniel Boone to Henry Clay* (Baltimore: Johns Hopkins University Press, 1996), 24.

82. Oswandel, *Notes,* 9. See also ibid., 8–13; Buley, "Indiana in the Mexican War: The Indiana Volunteers," 267; Johannsen, *To the Halls,* 27; Samuel Curtis, *Mexico under Fire: Being the Diary of Samuel Ryan Curtis, 3rd Ohio Volunteer Regiment, during the American Military Occupation of Northern Mexico, 1846–1847* (Fort Worth: Texas Christian University Press, 1994), 5; Lane, "Mexican," 387; and Scribner, *Camp,* 11.

83. Pearson, "Dilemma," 35; Perry, *Indiana,* 31, 52; Buley, "Indiana in the Mexican War: The Indiana Volunteers," 267; McCaffrey, *Army,* 21–22; Winders, *Mr. Polk's,* 71.

84. Duncan, "Monroe County," 290; McCaffrey, *Army,* 21–22; Winders, *Mr. Polk's,* 71; Buley, "Indiana in the Mexican War: The Indiana Volunteers," 267; Perry, *Indiana,* 39, 41–42, 48, 54, 56, 205. For the Louisville flag, see Abner Doubleday, *My Life in the Old Army* (Fort Worth: Texas Christian University Press, 1998), 103, and for the Columbus flag, see Perry, *Indiana,* 173.

85. Rohrbough, *Trans-Appalachian Frontier,* 11.

86. Oswandel, *Notes,* 247; Tennery, *Diary,* 66. See also January 18, 1847, Carr Family Papers, ISHS; October 9, 1847, April 21, 1848, MS A R943 2, Runyon Family Papers, FHS; Robert H. Milroy, Samuel I. Milroy, E. M. H. Beck, and William E. Pearsons, "Mexican War Letters," *Indiana Magazine of History* 25, no. 2 (1929): 166, 168; and Perry, *Indiana,* 49–50.

87. September 10, October 24, 1846, folder 2, and November 12, November 21, 1846, January 3, January 13, 1847, folder 3, all in Benjamin Franklin Scribner Papers, ISHS; Thomas Ware Gibson, "The Mexican War, Some Personal Correspondence," *Indiana Magazine of History* 65, no. 2 (1969): 138.

88. November 4, November 3, 1846, MS A C877 1, Cox Family Papers, FHS. See also January 10, 1847, August 1, 1846, MS A C877 1, Cox Family Papers, FHS; December 31, December 17, 1847, Smith-Holliday Family Papers, ISHS; McCaffrey, *Army,* 87.

89. Amy Greenberg, *Manifest Manhood and the Antebellum American Empire* (New York: Cambridge University Press, 2005), 55, 88–91. For anxiety expressed about this, see March 16, 1848, Smith-Holliday Family Papers, ISHS.

90. March 1, 1847, MS A C877 1, Cox Family Papers, FHS; n.d., folder 3, Benjamin Franklin Scribner Papers, ISHS.

91. Johannsen, *To the Halls,* 26; Franklin Smith, *Mexican War Journal,* 171.

92. November 4, 1846, MS A C877 1, Cox Family Papers, FHS.

93. Perry, *Indiana,* 70, 92, 126–127; Buley, "Indiana in the Mexican War: The Indiana Volunteers," 275–276; Johannsen, *To the Halls,* 261; Pearson, "Dilemma," 35.

94. Foos, *Short,* 68; Albert Lombard, *"The High Private" with a Full and Exciting History of the New York Volunteers, and the "Mysteries and Miseries" of the Mexican War, in Three Parts—Part First* (New York: Printed for the Publisher, 1848), 7–10, 19, 25, 47.

95. Duncan, "Monroe County," 291–292; Franklin Smith, *Mexican War Journal,* 26, 67, 102, 141–142, 158, 169, 209; May 28, July 1, 1846, MS A B628 3, Blackburn Family Papers, FHS.

96. Reeves Manuscript, 221–222.

97. Johannsen, *To the Halls,* 142; Michael Van Wagenen, *Remembering the Forgotten War: The Enduring Legacies of the U.S.-Mexican War* (Amherst: University of Massachusetts Press, 2012), 28–29; July 28, 1848, MS A T636 1, Todd Family Papers, FHS; Isaac Smith, *Reminiscences,* 90; Duncan, "Monroe County," 292; August 23, 1846, MS A B628 3, Blackburn Family Papers, FHS; Perry, *Indiana,* 172–173, 297, 321–322; Oswandel, *Notes,* 329–333, 339.

98. McCaffrey, *Army,* 210; Greenberg, *Wicked War,* 130; Alonzo D. Sampson, *Three Times around the World: Life and Adventures of Alonzo D. Sampson* (Buffalo, NY: Express, 1867), 7.

99. Greenberg, *Manifest Manhood,* 8–14, 139–140, 178–180. See also, for instance, Michael Pierson, *Free Hearts and Free Homes: Gender and American Antislavery Politics* (Chapel Hill: University of North Carolina Press, 2007), 8, and Bruce Dorsey, *Reforming Men and Women: Gender in the Antebellum City* (Ithaca, NY: Cornell University Press, 2002), 146.

100. Aron, *How the West Was Lost,* 86, 114–115; Howe, *What Hath,* 127, 330, 435, 528, 707, 771; Nicole Etcheson, *The Emerging Midwest: Upland Southerners and the Political Culture of the Old Northwest, 1787–1861* (Bloomington: Indiana University Press, 1996), 28–31; Knouff, "White," 28; Rohrbough, *Trans-Appalachian Frontier,* 126; Bertram Wyatt-Brown, *Southern Honor: Ethics and Behavior in the Old South,* 25th anniversary ed. (New York: Oxford University Press, 2007), 168–169, 353, 366–370; Curtis, *Mexico,* 73; Franklin Smith, *Mexican War Journal,* 26–27, 40–41; May 28, 1848, MS C W, FHS.

101. Peter Guardino, "Gender, Soldiering, and Citizenship in the Mexican-American War of 1846–1848," *American Historical Review* 119, no. 1 (February 2014): 42–43; Howe, *What Hath,* 771.

102. Coulter, *Volunteers,* 14; Isaac Smith, *Reminiscences,* 6; Perry, *Indiana,* 16, 66, 76; Winders, *Mr. Polk's,* 12, 78, 83; Buley, "Indiana in the Mexican War: The Indiana Volunteers," 269–271; *Arkansas State Gazette,* February 6, 1847.

103. Oswandel, *Notes,* 10. See also Rohrbough, *Trans-Appalachian Frontier,* 551; Howe, *What Hath,* 491, 497; Samuel Chamberlain, *My Confession: Recollections of a Rogue* (Austin: Texas State Historical Association, 1996), 50; and George Smith and Charles Judah, *Chronicles,* 38, 47.

104. Engelman, "Second Illinois," 366, 374, 378–379; Milroy et al., "Mexican," 168; Winders, *Mr. Polk's,* 77.

105. Daniel Harvey Hill, *A Fighter from Way Back: The Mexican War Diary of Lt. Daniel Harvey Hill, 4th Artillery, USA,* ed. Nathaniel Cheairs Hughes Jr. and Timothy D. Johnson (Kent, OH: Kent State University Press, 2002), 174; Foos, *Short,* 13, 32; Winders, *Mr. Polk's,* 13, 81; Tennery, *Diary,* 94; Engelman, "Second Illinois," 426; Scribner, *Camp,* 11.

106. Oswandel, *Notes,* 57. See also ibid., 136, and Lombard, *"The High Private,"* 23.

107. Jonathan W. Buhoup, *Narrative of the Central Division, or Army of Chihuahua, Commanded by Brigadier General Wool* . . . (Pittsburgh: M. P. Morse, 1847), 67–72; EE371, RG 153, NA.

108. EE303, RG 153, NA.

109. EE374, RG 153, NA.

110. Timothy Johnson, *Gallant,* 109–110; Winders, *Mr. Polk's,* 85; Coulter, *Volunteers,* 98, 243, 250, 258.

111. Coulter, *Volunteers,* 37, 226. On the uniforms, see Brackett, *General,* 34–35; Foos, *Short,* 101; Winders, *Mr. Polk's,* 112.

112. June 22, 1846, box 2 249, MS qJ72RM, Col. John Johnston Letters, CHSL; Josiah Gregg, *Diary and Letters of Josiah Gregg,* ed. Maurice Garland Fulton (Norman: University of Oklahoma Press, 1944), 2:34; George McClellan, *The Mexican War Diary of George B. McClellan* (Princeton: Princeton University Press, 1917), 43; Tom Reilly, *War with Mexico! America's Reporters Cover the Battlefront* (Lawrence: University of Kansas Press, 2010), 15, 40; Winders, *Mr. Polk's,* 84.

113. EE329, RG 153, NA; Winders, *Mr. Polk's,* 82; Coulter, *Volunteers,* 267; Franklin Smith, *Mexican War Journal,* 85. The Lowe quote is from George Smith and Charles Judah, *Chronicles,* 44.

114. Franklin Smith, *Mexican War Journal,* 147–148.

115. Buhoup, *Narrative,* 39; Curtis, *Mexico,* 174; Zachary Taylor, *Letters of Zachary Taylor from the Battle-Fields of the Mexican War* (Rochester, NY: Genesee, 1908), 22; González Quiroga, "Nuevo León," 451.

116. *Arkansas State Gazette,* February 6, 1847; September 2, 1846, MS C Ra, Rogers Family, FHS; Buhoup, *Narrative,* 25; Chamberlain, *My Confession,* 50; Lane, "Mexican," 406, 418; McClellan, *Mexican War Diary and Correspondence,* 39; Justin Smith, *War,* 2:319.

117. McCaffrey, *Army,* 42–44; Buhoup, *Narrative,* 14–15. For accidents, see Doubleday, *My Life,* 67; Engelman, "Second Illinois," 377; Perry, *Indiana,* 65; Foos, *Short,* 90; Buhoup, *Narrative,* 23, 33; and EE312, EE405, RG 153, NA.

118. Buhoup, *Narrative,* 15, 20, 22; Oswandel, *Notes,* 97, 268, 329; *Coulter, Volunteers,* 104, 226; Isaac Smith, *Reminiscences,* 39.

119. EE553, EE554, RG 153, NA.

120. EE382, RG 153, NA; Oswandel, *Notes,* 220–221.

121. For large groups of soldiers verbally defying officers, see Pickett, *A. C. Pickett's Private Journal,* 108, and Oswandel, *Notes,* 222. For the use of rotten eggs, see Coulter, *Volunteers,* 257, 281, and Oswandel, *Notes,* 307.

122. For cases that ended in compromises, see Edwards, Diary during Mexican War Service, 22–23, 32–33; Chamberlain, *My Confession,* 50–52; and Buhoup, *Narrative,* 67–72.

123. Winders, *Mr. Polk's,* 190–191; Reilly, *War!,* 156; EE554, RG 153, NA; George Smith and Charles Judah, *Chronicles,* 424–429.

124. McCaffrey, *Army,* 91–92; EE554, RG 153, NA; Chamberlain, *My Confession,* 167.

125. Hill, *Fighter,* 45; Perry, *Indiana,* 96; Franklin Smith, *Mexican War Journal,* 90–91; Chamberlain, *My Confession,* 103–107; Oswandel, *Notes,* 222.

126. Chamberlain, *My Confession,* 143. For other similar incidents, see Reilly, *War!,* 156, and McClellan, *Mexican War Diary of George B. McClellan,* 35.

127. For instance, 80 percent of the men who deserted from one Indiana regiment did so before it reached the Rio Grande, and almost all the rest did so before it proceeded farther into Mexico. Perry, *Indiana,* 273. One company of the Fourth Ohio lost all of its deserters either in Ohio or in Louisiana. Entry 111, Book Records of Volunteer Organizations: Mexican War, 1846–1848, Ohio 4th Infantry, Descriptive Book, RG 94, NA. See also Foos, *Short,* 47, 56, 77, 100–102; Duncan, "Monroe County," 291–292; McCaffrey, *Army,* 21, 45; June 6, 1846, MS A L729 5, Lillard Family Papers, FHS; Edwards, Diary during Mexican War Service, 9; Thomas Bailey, "Diary of the Mexican War," *Indiana Magazine of History* 14, no. 2 (1918): 135; Coulter, *Volunteers,* 22; Oswandel, *Notes,* 22–23; and EE497, RG 153, NA. For temporary separations in Mexico, see August 6, 1846, MS A L729 5, Lillard Family Papers, FHS; Buhoup, *Narrative,* 15; and EE318, RG 153, NA. For the public humiliation, see June 5, 1846, MS C S, Thomas T. Summers, FHS. The statistics on regular and volunteer desertion are from John Pinheiro, "Crusade and Conquest: Anti-Catholicism, Manifest Destiny, and the U.S.-Mexican War of 1846–48" (PhD diss., University of Tennessee, Knoxville, 2001), 177.

128. Buhoup, *Narrative,* 34; Chamberlain, *My Confession,* 50, 55, 103; Coulter, *Volunteers,* 21–22; Hill, *Fighter,* 2; Pickett, *A. C. Pickett's Private Journal,* 116; Franklin Smith, *Mexican War Journal,* 12, 83–84; Lewis, *Trailing,* 162; McCaffrey, *Army,* 99; Entry 111, Book Records of Volunteer Organizations: Mexican War, 1846–1848, Ohio 2nd Infantry Irwin Morning Reports Co. D, RG 94, NA; EE303, EE312, EE318, EE373, EE382, EE516, RG 153, NA.

129. October 9, 1847, April 21, 1848, MS A R943 2, Runyon Family Papers, FHS; Winders, *Mr. Polk's,* 137.

130. *Encarnacion,* 7; Edwards, Diary during Mexican War Service, 8, 13–15; Oswandel, *Notes,* 18–21; Coulter, *Volunteers,* 21–23; Foos, *Short,* 58; Brackett, *General,* 14; George Smith and Charles Judah, *Chronicles,* 37.

131. Coulter, *Volunteers,* 317, 321; Hill, *Fighter,* 63.

132. Oswandel, *Notes,* 25, 208–210; Reeves Manuscript, 225; Hill, *Fighter,* 83; Timothy Johnson, *Gallant,* 36.

133. Foos, *Short,* 113. On the patterns of warfare against Native Americans, see John Grenier, *The First Way of War: American War Making on the Frontier, 1607–1814* (New York: Cambridge University Press, 2005).

134. Quoted in Mark E. Neely Jr., *The Civil War and the Limits of Destruction* (Cambridge, MA: Harvard University Press, 2007), 9, and Charles Winslow Elliot, *Winfield Scott: The Soldier and the Man* (New York: Macmillan, 1937), 448. See also Johannsen, *To the Halls,* 35.

135. Oswandel, *Notes,* 100.

136. William W. Carpenter, *Travels and Adventures in Mexico: In the Course of Journeys of Upward of 2500 Miles, Performed on Foot, Giving an Account of the Manners and Customs of the People, and the Agricultural and Mineral Resources of That Country* (New York: Harper Brothers, 1851), 33; Oswandel, *Notes,* 76, 80, 82, 177, 196, 210, 216–219, 266; Coulter, *Volunteers,* 49, 60, 83–84, 88–89, 99–100, 108, 150, 187, 191, 193, 214, 223–224, 240, 263, 281, 298, 302, 309, 314, 323; Curtis, *Mexico,* 90; S. Compton Smith, *Chile,* 190; John Corey Henshaw, *Recollections of the War with Mexico* (Columbia: University of Missouri Press, 2008), 70–71, 79, 88; Pickett, *A. C. Pickett's Private Journal,* 105; Tennery, *Diary,* 41, 73–74; *Encarnacion,* 20; Brackett, *General,* 62, 70–71, 74–75, 81–83; Buhoup, *Narrative,* 26, 37–38, 40–41, 43, 46, 50, 52, 55; Sampson, *Three Times,* 5; Franklin Smith, *Mexican War Journal,* 34, 109, 120–121, 156; Hill, *Fighter,* 2, 90; LEPOSLP, October 17, 1846, June 3, 1847; Laidley, *Surrounded,* 109; Journal of Surgeon and Brevet Brigadier General Madison Mills, 2, 4–6, 13, MS A M657, FHS; Edwards, Diary during Mexican War Service, 29, 32–35; Timothy Johnson, *Gallant,* 36–37, 55, 74–75; Neely, *Civil War,* 14; EE541, EE497, RG 153, NA.

137. Edwards, Diary during Mexican War Service, 39; Lane, "Mexican," 406; September 26, 1846, MS C, Richard M. Creagh, FHS; Coulter, *Volunteers,* 249.

138. EE318, EE405, RG 153, NA; Maria del Pilar Iracheta Cenecorta, *La ocupación estadounidense de la Ciudad de Toluca* (Toluca, Mexico: Ayuntamiento de Toluca, 2006), 30–31.

139. Hill does this very often. Hill, *Fighter,* 2, 58–59, 61, 110–111.

140. For instance, see Hill, *Fighter,* 3, 8, 28, 47, 61.

141. Engelman, "Second Illinois," 424; Curtis, *Mexico,* 94; Franklin Smith, *Mexican War Journal,* 188–189.

142. McClellan, *Mexican War Diary of George B. McClellan,* 18; Hill, *Fighter,* 3, 28, 47, 61; Brackett, *General,* 30; Chamberlain, *My Confession,* 206; Franklin Smith, *Mexican War Journal,* 80, 110; Samuel C. Reid, *The Scouting Expeditions of McCulloch's Texas Rangers; or, The Summer and Fall Campaign of the Army of the United States in Mexico—1846* (Philadelphia: G. B. Zieber, 1848), 53; EE534, RG 153, NA; Foos, *Short,* 116; Vega and Zuleta, *Testimonios de una guerra,* 1:494; LEPOSLP, June 26, 1847.

143. Hill, *Fighter,* 47.

144. Laidley, *Surrounded,* 120; exp. 2194, fol. 28, ADN.

145. Chamberlain, *My Confession,* 137; González Quiroga, "Nuevo León," 450–451.

146. For Native Americans, see Mark Grimsley "'Rebels' and 'Redskins': U.S. Military Conduct toward White Southerners and Native Americans in Comparative Perspective," in *Civilians in the Path of War,* ed. Mark Grimsley and Clifford J. Rogers (Lincoln: University of Nebraska Press, 2002), 151.

147. Hill, *Fighter,* 3, 28, 61; Reilly, *War!,* 48, 160; Chamberlain, *My Confession,* 176, 178; Greenberg, *Wicked War,* 132; McCaffrey, *Army,* 123; LEPOSLP, October 22, 1846, July 27, 1846, July 28, 1847; exp. 2703, fol. 5, ADN; Henshaw, *Recollections,* 70–71.

148. Scribner, *Camp;* July 21, 1846, MS A B937a 4, Bullitt-Chenoweth Family Papers, FHS; Brackett, *General,* 314; Johannsen, *To the Halls,* 29. For use of the term more generally, see Corydon Donnavan, *Adventures in Mexico: Experienced during a Captivity of Seven Months in the Interior* (Cincinnati: Robinson and Jones, 1847), 99; Howe, *What Hath,* 819; James M. McPherson, *For Cause and Comrades: Why Men Fought in the Civil War* (New York: Oxford University Press, 1997), 30.

149. Foos, *Short,* 51, 54, 88; Jensen, *Patriots,* 10–12, 131, 155, 180, 186, 189.

150. Greenberg, *Wicked War,* 115; Lombard, *"The High Private."*

151. Johannsen, *To the Halls,* 45–46, 54, 58–59, 62; Pearson, "Dilemma," 30; Oswandel, *Notes,* 8; Coulter, *Volunteers,* 119.

152. For the Revolutionary War, see Johannsen, *To the Halls,* 57–58, and Shelley Streeby, *American Sensations: Class, Empire and the Production of American Culture* (Berkeley: University of California Press, 2002), 56. On the War of 1812 and the Battle of New Orleans, see Nicole Eustace, *1812: War and the Passions of Patriotism* (Philadelphia: University of Pennsylvania Press, 2012), xiii, 221; Howe, *What Hath,* 71; July 7, 1846, MS A C877 1, Cox Family Papers, FHS; July 23, 1846, MS A L729 5, Lillard Family Papers, FHS; Brackett, *General,* 226; Coulter, *Volunteers,* 19; Lane, "Mexican," 388; Johannsen, *To the Halls,* 56; Pearson, "Dilemma," 34; Winders, *Mr. Polk's,* 115; and Scribner, *Camp,* 13.

153. Johannsen, *To the Halls,* 68. See also Johannsen, *To the Halls,* 11, 71, 155, 180, 182; S. Compton Smith, *Chile,* 4; and Foos, *Short,* 4.

154. Oswandel, *Notes,* 41, 50; McClellan, *Mexican War Diary of George B. McClellan,* 69, 80; Franklin Smith, *Mexican War Journal,* 28, 139–140; Scribner, *Camp,* 11, 24–26.

155. Foos, *Short,* 89; Timothy Johnson, *Gallant,* 32; McCaffrey, *Army,* 120; Buhoup, *Narrative,* 59; Franklin Smith, *Mexican War Journal,* 40–41; EE386, RG 153, NA.

156. Oswandel, *Notes,* 90.

157. *Daily National Intelligencer,* March 23, 1847.

158. Chamberlain, *My Confession,* 152.

159. Horsman has written an excellent book on this: Reginald Horsman, *Race and Manifest Destiny: The Origins of American Racial Anglo-Saxonism* (Cambridge, MA: Harvard University Press, 1981).

160. Ibid., 210–213; *Encarnacion,* 29.

161. Greenberg, *Manifest Manhood,* 55, 96; Horsman, *Race,* 233–234; Winders, *Mr. Polk's,* 175. For a dissenter, see September 26, 1846, MS C, Richard M. Creagh, FHS.

162. Coulter, *Volunteers,* 125; Carpenter, *Travels,* 17. See also Buhoup, *Narrative,* 63; Isaac Smith, *Reminiscences,* 35; and Tennery, *Diary,* 37.

163. November 5, 1846, MS C L, Henry Smith Lane 1811–1881, FHS.

164. Pickett, *A. C. Pickett's Private Journal,* 91; Matthew Frye Jacobsen, *Whiteness of a Different Color: European Immigrants and the Alchemy of Race* (Cambridge, MA: Harvard University Press, 1998), 21; Scribner, *Camp,* 49.

165. September 21, 1846, MS A L729 5, Lillard Family Papers, FHS; Brackett, *General,* 111, 242; Greenberg, *Manifest Manhood,* 101.

166. Franklin Smith, *Mexican War Journal,* 89, 108.

167. Milroy et al., "Mexican," 172.

168. Greenberg, *Manifest Manhood,* 23. See also ibid., 22, 92, 101; Coulter, *Volunteers,* 229; and Streeby, *American Sensations,* 82–83.

169. Greenberg, *Manifest Manhood,* 19, 26, 55, 88–90; Streeby, *American Sensations,* 64–65, 112–134; Amy Kaplan, *The Anarchy of Empire in the Making of US Culture* (Cambridge, MA: Harvard University Press, 2002), 27; Horsman, *Race,* 233–234, 244; Pletcher, *Diplomacy,* 551, 555; McCaffrey, *Army,* 200.

170. Oswandel, *Notes,* 76; Carpenter, *Travels,* 236; Chamberlain, *My Confession,* 119; Lane, "Mexican," 408; Coulter, *Volunteers,* 86; Scribner, *Camp,* 29.

171. On the kindness of Mexican women, see Carpenter, *Travels,* 234.

172. For the idea that Mexican women were not chaste, see Chamberlain, *My Confession,* 123; Carpenter, *Travels,* 234; Franklin Smith, *Mexican War Journal,* 89; and September 21, 1846, MS A L729 5, Lillard Family Papers, FHS. For the idea that they were, see Curtis, *Mexico,* 65. On clothing styles in Mexico, see Sonya Lipsett-Rivera, *Gender and the Negotiation of Daily Life in Mexico, 1750–1850* (Lincoln: University of Nebraska Press, 2012), 165–166. For volunteers' comments on them, see Lane, "Mexican," 422.

173. April 21, 1848, MS A R943 2, Runyon Family Papers, FHS; March 16, April 11, 1848, Smith-Holliday Family Papers, ISHS; November 13, 1846, MS C S, Thomas T. Summers, FHS.

174. Carlos Recio Dávila reports that four Arkansas volunteers married Mexican women in or near Saltillo. Carlos Recio Dávila, *Saltillo durante la guerra México-Estados Unidos: 1846–1848* (Saltillo, Mexico: Museo de la Batalla de la Angostura, 2002), 126–127. Samuel Chamberlain took particular delight in recounting such adventures. Chamberlain, *My Confession,* 119–121. Oswandel notes that some of his comrades tried to seduce plantation slaves during an overnight stop on their journey to Mexico. Oswandel, *Notes,* 14. The only references I can find to a volunteer actually marrying a Mexican bride are in Winders, *Mr. Polk's,* 175, and *Mexican Treacheries and Cruelties: Incidents and Sufferings in the Mexican War: With Accounts of Hardship Endured; Treacheries of the Mexicans; Battles Fought, and Success of Americans Arms* . . . (Boston: n.p., 1847), n.p., and the latter seems apocryphal.

175. Chamberlain, *My Confession,* 119–121; Buhoup, *Narrative,* 141–142. For a more general reference, see Oswandel, *Notes,* 202.

176. For "greaserita," see Brackett, *General,* 200. For the use of the word "greaser," see Gibson, "Mexican War," 135; Coulter, *Volunteers,* 88, 213, 221, 233–234; Chamberlain, *My Confession,* 123; and Brackett, *General,* 7.

177. October 5, 1846, MS A 585, Levi White Papers, FHS. See also Engelman, "Second Illinois," 399; Foos, *Short,* 59; July 2, 1846, MS A S751 3, Sperry-Gathright Family Papers, FHS; Tennery, *Diary,* 25, 37; McCaffrey, *Army,* 74.

178. Engelman, "Second Illinois," 373.

179. Brackett, *General,* 44.

180. Streeby, *American Sensations,* 96.

181. John Pinheiro has written an excellent book on anti-Catholicism and the war. John Pinheiro, *Missionaries of Republicanism: A Religious History of the Mexican-American War* (Oxford: Oxford University Press, 2014), esp. 2, 17, 190. On its roots in older English clashes over religion, see John Dichtl, *Frontiers of Faith: Bringing Catholicism to the West*

in the Early Republic (Lexington: University of Kentucky Press, 2008), 15; Wayne E. Lee, *Barbarians and Brothers: Anglo-American Warfare, 1500–1865* (New York: Oxford University Press, 2011), 102; and Pinheiro, *Missionaries*, 26. On its revival before the war, see, in addition to Pinheiro, Dichtl, *Frontiers of Faith*, 170–171, 182, and Jennie Franchot, *Roads to Rome: The Antebellum Protestant Encounter with Catholicism* (Berkeley: University of California Press, 1994), xix.

182. Lane, "Mexican," 415; Carpenter, *Travels*, 83; Pickett, *A. C. Pickett's Private Journal*, 94; Tennery, *Diary*, 28; Pinheiro, *Missionaries*, 118.

183. William H. Daniel Military Diary, 16–18; Buhoup, *Narrative*, 158; Scribner, *Camp*, 74.

184. November 5, 1846, MS C L, Henry Lane Smith 1811–1881, FHS; Oswandel, *Notes*, 120, 325; Coulter, *Volunteers*, 100, 195; Horsman, *Race*, 238; June 11, 1846, MS A B628 3 Blackburn Family Papers, FHS. For the use of the word "mummery," see Curtis, *Mexico*, 164; Coulter, *Volunteers*, 125, 275; and Pinheiro, *Missionaries*, 36, 117.

185. For references to the rich churches, see Oswandel, *Notes*, 269; Carpenter, *Travels*, 40, 82; Chamberlain, *My Confession*, 123; Coulter, *Volunteers*, 64, 124; and Scribner, *Camp*, 52, 56. For the same attitude displayed toward Catholic churches in the United States, see Dichtl, *Frontiers of Faith*, 87–91. For the church exploiting Mexicans, see Curtis, *Mexico*, 197, and Coulter, *Volunteers*, 195–196. The quote is from Coulter, *Volunteers*, 181.

186. Dichtl, *Frontiers of Faith*, 182; Howe, *What Hath*, 288, 320; Winders, *Mr. Polk's*, 183; Oswandel, *Notes*, 150, 213, 229–230, 280; Lane, "Mexican," 410, 426.

187. Franchot, *Roads to Rome*, 154–160; Dichtl, *Frontiers of Faith*, 71–72; Oswandel, *Notes*, 239; Pinheiro, *Missionaries*, 37, 48, 119.

188. Greenberg, *Manifest Manhood*, 98; Pinheiro, "Crusade," 145.

189. Pinheiro, *Missionaries*, 114–115.

190. Exp. 2605, fol. 59, ADN; Justicia y Negocios Eclesiásticos, vol. 154, fol. 264, AGN; Justicia y Negocios Eclesiásticos, vol. 155, fol. 211, AGN; Carpenter, *Travels*, 83; Foos, *Short*, 131; Pinheiro, *Missionaries*, 121; Recio Dávila, *Saltillo*, 68.

191. The song is found in Pinheiro, *Missionaries*, 73. For references to golden Jesuses made during the recruitment of volunteers, see Chamberlain, *My Confession*, 50, 201; Streeby, *American Sensations*, 175; Tyler V. Johnson, *Devotion to the Adopted Country: U.S. Immigrant Volunteers in the Mexican War* (Columbia: University of Missouri Press, 2012), 103–104; and Clary, *Eagles and Empire*, 145. See also Pinheiro, "Crusade," 135–141; John Pinheiro, "'Extending the Light and Blessings of Our Purer Faith': Anti-Catholic Sentiment among American Soldiers in the Mexican War," *Journal of Popular Culture* 35, no. 2 (2001): 128–151; Pinheiro, *Missionaries*, 71–77, 124; and Carlos Maria de Busta-mante, entries for August 9, August 24, 1847, in *Diario histórico de México, 1822–1848*, ed.

Josefina Zoraida Vázquez and Héctor Cuauhtémoc Hernández Silva (Mexico City: El Colegio de México / Centro de Investigaciones y Estudios Superiores en Antropología Social, 2003). The story of the sweetheart is in February 3, 1847, MS A L729 5, Lillard Family Papers, FHS.

192. Exp. 2703, fol. 5, ADN; Mariano Riva Palacio, "Breve diario de don Mariano Riva Palacio (agosto de 1847)," ed. Josefina Vázquez, *Historia Mexicana* 47, no. 2 (October–December 1997): 450; Foos, *Short,* 128; Tyler Johnson, *Devotion,* 37; Salinas Sandoval, *Política interna,* 188; Bustamante, entries for August 23, September 5, 1847, in *Diario.*

193. Brackett, *General,* 151; Coulter, *Volunteers,* 242; Lombard, *"The High Private,"* 12; Franklin Smith, *Mexican War Journal,* 20, 135.

194. Tyler V. Johnson writes about this extensively in Johnson, *Devotion.* See also Dorsey, *Reforming,* 227, 230; Foos, *Short,* 42–43, 47; Streeby, *American Sensations,* 16, 98, 103–105; Harry Watson, *Liberty and Power: The Politics of Jacksonian America,* updated ed. (New York: Hill and Wang, 2006), 242, 245; Engelman, "Second Illinois," 357–452; George Smith and Charles Judah, *Chronicles,* 34–36; and Noel Ignatiev, *How the Irish Became White* (New York: Routledge, 2009), 185–186.

195. In addition to Tyler Johnson, *Devotion,* and Tyler V. Johnson, "Punishing the Lies on the Rio Grande: Catholic and Immigrant Volunteers in Zachary Taylor's Army and the Fight against Nativism," *Journal of the Early Republic* 30, no. 1 (Spring 2010): 63–84, see Lombard, *"The High Private,"* 12, 14; Tennery, *Diary,* 18–20, 108; and Foos, *Short,* 96.

196. Lane, "Mexican," 390. See also ibid., 394, 405, and Franklin Smith, *Mexican War Journal,* 66. Eustace points out that camp life was seen as having a similar effect in the War of 1812. Eustace, *1812,* 59–60.

197. Franklin Smith, *Mexican War Journal,* 10, 110–111; Reilly, *War!,* 48.

198. Laidley, *Surrounded,* 150. See also McCaffrey, *Army,* 122; Justin Smith, *War,* 2:211; Winders, *Mr. Polk's,* 85; Greenberg, *Wicked War,* 191–192, 238; and Scribner, *Camp,* 24.

199. N.d., folder 3, Benjamin Franklin Scribner Papers, ISHS. See also January 26, 1848, Smith-Holliday Family Papers, ISHS.

200. McCaffrey, *Army,* 52–53; Winders, *Mr. Polk's,* 140; Duncan, "Monroe County," 294–296.

201. For disease beginning right when units were organized, see Tennery, *Diary,* 7. For illness in New Orleans, see June 6, June 30, 1846, MS A L729 5, Lillard Family Papers, FHS. For illness in the northern campaign, see Tennery, *Diary,* 33–36, 65, and González Quiroga, "Nuevo León," 434. For the toll taken during Scott's campaign in central

Mexico, see Oswandel, *Notes,* 95–96, 101, 103, 112, 117, 249; Coulter, *Volunteers,* 89, 90, 131, 307; Tennery, *Diary,* 92; and Laidley, *Surrounded,* 114–115. For deaths on the way home, see Oswandel, *Notes,* 331, and Perry, *Indiana,* 102, 197. Vincent Cirillo provides an excellent overview in Vincent Cirillo, "'More Fatal than Powder and Shot': Dysentery in the U.S. Army during the Mexican War, 1846–48," *Perspectives in Biology and Medicine* 52, no. 3 (2009): 400–413.

202. Buley, "Indiana in the Mexican War: The Indiana Volunteers," 285; September 7, September 15, 1846, MS A L729 5, Lillard Family Papers, FHS; September 21, 1846, MS C, Richard M. Creagh, FHS; Curtis, *Mexico,* 10, 13, 24–25, 31–35, 61; Milroy et al., "Mexican," 168–169; Isaac Smith, *Reminiscences,* 8–9, 25–26; Tennery, *Diary,* 15–22, 25. Lane's accounting is from November 5, 1846, MS C L, Henry Lane Smith 1811–1881, FHS. The quotes are from Lane, "Mexican," 388, 399.

203. The quote is from Isaac Smith, *Reminiscences,* 7. See also ibid., 26; McCaffrey, *Army,* 53; Lane, "Mexican," 400; and Cirillo, "More Fatal," 404.

204. Curtis, *Mexico,* 98; Tennery, *Diary,* 28; Engelman, "Second Illinois," 376; Cirillo, "More Fatal," 408–409.

205. Engelman, "Second Illinois," 426; Lane, "Mexican," 390, 396.

206. Nicholas Marshall, "The Great Exaggeration: Death and the Civil War," *Journal of the Civil War Era* 4, no. 1 (March 2014): 14; McCaffrey, *Army,* 61–62; Greenberg, *Wicked War,* 129; Cirillo, "More Fatal," 403.

207. Laidley, *Surrounded,* 62; McClellan, *Mexican War Diary and Correspondence,* 49; Timothy Johnson, *Gallant,* 108, 137; Dishman, *Perfect,* 64; Cirillo, "More Fatal," 403.

CHAPTER 3 · Like Civilized Nations

1. Irving Levinson, *Wars within War: Mexican Guerrillas, Domestic Elites and the United States of America, 1846–1848* (Fort Worth: Texas Christian University Press, 2005), 16; Carlos Maria de Bustamante, *El nuevo Bernal Díaz del Castillo* (Mexico City: Instituto Nacional de Estudios Históricos de la Revolución Mexicana-Gobierno del Estado de Puebla, 1994), 2:176; *Apuntes para la historia de la guerra entre México y los Estados Unidos* (Mexico City: Consejo Nacional para la Cultura y las Artes, 1991), 439.

2. Exp. 2319, fols. 2, 5, ADN; Octavio Herrera Pérez, "Tamaulipas ante la guerra de la Invasión Norteamericana," in *México al tiempo de su guerra con los Estados Unidos (1846–1848),* ed. Josefina Zoraida Vázquez (Mexico City: Secretaría de Relaciones Exteriores, El Colegio de México, Fondo de Cultura Económica, 1997), 545; Manuel Muro Rocha, *Historia de San Luis Potosí* (Mexico City: Sociedad Potosina de Estudios Históricos, 1973), 2:478–482.

3. Omar Valerio-Jiménez, *River of Hope: Forging Identity and Nation in the Rio Grande Borderlands* (Durham, NC: Duke University Press, 2013), 41–44, 94; Pekka Hämäläinen, *The Comanche Empire* (New Haven, CT: Yale University Press, 2008), 226, 251, 280; Cuauhtémoc Velasco Avila, "Sociedad, identidad y guerra entre los comanches, 1825–1835," in *La reindianización de América, siglo xix,* ed. Leticia Reina (Mexico City: Siglo Veintiuno / Centro de Investigaciones y Estudios Superiores en Antropología Social, 1997), 327–328. Brian DeLay extensively discusses revenge as a motive for Comanche violence against Mexicans. Brian DeLay, *War of a Thousand Deserts: Indian Raids and the Mexican-American War* (New Haven, CT: Yale University Press, 2009), 129–138.

4. Journal of Surgeon and Brevet Brigadier General Madison Mills, 21, MS A M657, FHS.

5. Valerio-Jiménez, *River of Hope,* 124–135; exp. 2179, fols. 4–5, ADN; DeLay, *War,* 262–264.

6. Valerio-Jiménez, *River of Hope,* 135–137; Amy Greenberg, *A Wicked War: Polk, Clay, Lincoln and the 1846 U.S. Invasion of Mexico* (New York: Knopf, 2012), 132; Eliud Santiago Aparicio, "Las atrocidades en la guerra entre México y Estados Unidos (1846–1848)" (tesis de licenciatura en historia, Universidad Autónoma Metropolitana, 2013), 125–126, 128, 206; Paul Foos, *A Short, Offhand Killing Affair: Soldiers and Social Conflict during the Mexican-American War* (Chapel Hill: University of North Carolina Press, 2002), 121; Walter Prescott Webb, *The Texas Rangers in the Mexican War* (Austin: Jenkins Garrett, 1975), 42; Samuel Curtis, *Mexico under Fire: Being the Diary of Samuel Ryan Curtis, 3rd Ohio Volunteer Regiment, during the American Military Occupation of Northern Mexico, 1846–1847* (Fort Worth: Texas Christian University Press, 1994), 22–23, 36; Daniel Harvey Hill, *A Fighter from Way Back: The Mexican War Diary of Lt. Daniel Harvey Hill, 4th Artillery, USA,* ed. Nathaniel Cheairs Hughes Jr. and Timothy D. Johnson (Kent, OH: Kent State University Press, 2002), 19–20; Samuel C. Reid, *The Scouting Expeditions of McCulloch's Texas Rangers; or, The Summer and Fall Campaign of the Army of the United States in Mexico—1846* (Philadelphia: G. B. Zieber, 1848), 154; S. Compton Smith, *Chile con Carne; or, The Camp and the Field* (New York: Miller and Curtis, 1857), 51–52; George W. Smith and Charles Judah, *The Chronicles of the Gringos: The US Army in the Mexican War, 1846–48: Accounts of Eyewitnesses and Combatants* (Albuquerque: University of New Mexico Press, 1968), 286–287; "Mexican War Correspondence," 30th Congress, 1st Session, 1847, House Executive Document 60, 1178; Carlos Maria de Bustamante, entries for July 29, July 15, 1846, in *Diario histórico de México, 1822–1848,* ed. Josefina Zoraida Vázquez and Héctor Cuauhtémoc Hernández Silva (Mexico City: El Colegio de México / Centro de Investigaciones y Estudios Superiores en Antropología Social, 2003).

7. George Meade, *The Life and Letters of George Gordon Meade, Major General United States Army* (New York: Charles Scribner's Sons, 1913), 109. The other quotes are from Hill, *Fighter,* 16, and John Corey Henshaw, *Recollections of the War with Mexico* (Columbia: University of Missouri Press, 2008), 89. See also Meade, *Life,* 108–109. On another

occasion Meade says the volunteers were like Goths or Vandals, laying waste to the country and terrorizing innocent Mexicans. Meade, *Life*, 162.

8. Quote from Hill, *Fighter*, 60. See also DeLay, *War*, 281, and Santiago Aparicio, "Las atrocidades," 57–58.

9. Valerio-Jiménez, *River of Hope*, 137–138; Santiago Aparicio, "Las atrocidades," 114, 123; William H. Daniel Military Diary, 39, MS A D184, FHS; William W. Carpenter, *Travels and Adventures in Mexico: In the Course of Journeys of Upward of 2500 Miles, Performed on Foot, Giving an Account of the Manners and Customs of the People, and the Agricultural and Mineral Resources of That Country* (New York: Harper Brothers, 1851), 112; Samuel Chamberlain, *My Confession: Recollections of a Rogue* (Austin: Texas State Historical Association, 1996), 116, 201, 203. The same fate sometimes befell the civilian teamsters who drove American supply wagons, although in fact many such teamsters were volunteers who had completed their terms of service before taking up this lucrative work. S. Compton Smith, *Chile*, 161–162.

10. See exp. 2178, fol. 40, ADN, for how Mexican officers disapproved of the atrocities committed by the guerrillas, and exp. 2194, fol. 8, ADN, for the report on Taylor's attitude.

11. "Mexican War Correspondence," 1178; Hill, *Fighter*, 62.

12. Foos, *Short*, 121; Santiago Aparicio, "Las atrocidades," 115, 125; González Quiroga, "Nuevo León," 450, 454, 456; Greenberg, *Wicked War*, 133; Tom Reilly, *War with Mexico! America's Reporters Cover the Battlefront* (Lawrence: University of Kansas Press, 2010), 81; Curtis, *Mexico*, 172–174; *Mexican Treacheries and Cruelties: Incidents and Sufferings in the Mexican War: With Accounts of Hardship Endured; Treacheries of the Mexicans; Battles Fought, and Success of Americans Arms . . .* (Boston: n.p., 1847); Justin Smith, *The War with Mexico* (Gloucester, MA: Peter Smith, 1963), 2:169–170; *Daily Picayune*, May 13, 1847; S. Compton Smith, *Chile*, 315–316, 318; Chamberlain, *My Confession*, 201; Mercedes de la Vega and Maria Cecilia Zuleta, *Testimonios de una guerra: México, 1846–1848* (Mexico City: Secretaría de Relaciones Exteriores, 2001), 1:497; George McClellan, *The Mexican War Diary of George B. McClellan* (Princeton, NJ: Princeton University Press, 1917), 20.

13. David Bell, *The First Total War: Napoleon's Europe and the Birth of Warfare as We Know It* (Boston: Houghton Mifflin, 2007), 289–290; Reginald Horsman, *Race and Manifest Destiny: The Origins of American Racial Anglo-Saxonism* (Cambridge, MA: Harvard University Press, 1981), 235–236; Wayne E. Lee, *Barbarians and Brothers: Anglo-American Warfare, 1500–1865* (New York: Oxford University Press, 2011), esp. 138, 229; Mark Grimsley " 'Rebels' and 'Redskins': U.S. Military Conduct toward White Southerners and Native Americans in Comparative Perspective," in *Civilians in the Path of War*, ed. Mark Grimsley and Clifford J. Rogers (Lincoln: University of Nebraska Press, 2002), 138–140; James M. McCaffrey, *Army of Manifest Destiny: The American Soldier in the*

Mexican War, 1846–1848 (New York: New York University Press, 1992), 127–128; Santiago Aparicio, "Las atrocidades," 127.

14. William H. Daniel Military Diary, 12. See also Samuel I. Milroy, E. M. H. Beck, and William E. Pearsons, "Mexican War Letters," *Indiana Magazine of History* 25, no. 2 (1929): 172.

15. Timothy D. Johnson, *A Gallant Little Army: The Mexico City Campaign* (Lawrence: University of Kansas Press, 2007), 134, 137; Albert G. Brackett, *General Lane's Brigade in Central Mexico* (Cincinnati: H. W. Derby, 1854), 253–254; J. Jacob Oswandel, *Notes on the Mexican War, 1846–1848* (Knoxville: University of Tennessee Press, 2010), 32, 40, 42, 53, 78–79, 112, 137, 198; George Wilkins Kendall, *Dispatches from the Mexican War* (Norman: University of Oklahoma Press, 1999), 87; Foos, *Short*, 136; Greenberg, *Wicked War*, 132. Union volunteers during the Civil War likewise did not see guerrilla tactics as legitimate, and their use led to reprisals against the property of Southern civilians. See Gerald Linderman, *Embattled Courage: The Experience of Combat in the American Civil War* (New York: Free Press, 1987), 197–198.

16. William H. Daniel Military Diary, 24. See also Thomas R. Hietala, *Manifest Design: Anxious Aggrandizement in Late Jacksonian America* (Ithaca, NY: Cornell University Press, 1985), 152–158, and Richard Coulter, *Volunteers: The Mexican War Journals of Private Richard Coulter and Sergeant Thomas Barclay*, ed. Allan Peskin (Kent, OH: Kent State University Press, 1991), 311. Even regulars saw guerrilla tactics as like Indian tactics. Meade, *Life*, 66.

17. John Grenier, *The First Way of War: American War Making on the Frontier, 1607–1814* (New York: Cambridge University Press, 2005), 1, 4, 5, 10–12, 19, 33–39, 170–171, 224–225. See also Gary Anderson, *The Conquest of Texas: Ethnic Cleansing in the Promised Land, 1820–1875* (Norman: University of Oklahoma Press, 2005), 53–54, 127–139; Grimsley, "'Rebels' and 'Redskins,'" 140–141, 150–153, 155; Hämäläinen, *Comanche*, 215, 309, 311; and Peter Silver, *Our Savage Neighbors: How Indian War Transformed Early America* (New York: W. W. Norton, 2008), 58–59, 161–162, 165, 203. Greenberg, *Wicked War*, 132, specifically points out the connection between Indian warfare and the volunteers' attacks on Mexican civilians.

18. Daniel Walker Howe, *What Hath God Wrought: The Transformation of America, 1815–1848* (New York: Oxford University Press, 2007), 430–434; Bertram Wyatt-Brown, *Southern Honor: Ethics and Behavior in the Old South*, 25th anniversary ed. (New York: Oxford University Press, 2007), 370; Malcolm Rohrbough, *The Trans-Appalachian Frontier: Peoples, Societies, Institutions*, 3rd ed. (Bloomington: Indiana University Press, 2008), 414; Michael J. Pfeifer, *The Roots of Rough Justice: Origins of American Lynching* (Urbana: University of Illinois Press 2011), 15, 32, 56–59; David Grimsted, *American Mobbing: Toward Civil War* (New York: Oxford University Press, 1998), 101–113; Michael

Feldberg, *The Turbulent Era: Riot and Discord in Jacksonian America* (New York: Oxford University Press, 1980), 73–75.

19. Pfeifer, *Roots*, 2, 4, 11–13.

20. For examples, see Carpenter, *Travels*, 29–30; Chamberlain, *My Confession*, 183.

21. Journal of Surgeon and Brevet Brigadier General Madison Mills, 46; Carpenter, *Travels*, 29; Meade, *Life*, 161–162. Quote from "Mexican War Correspondence," 1178.

22. Vega and Zuleta, *Testimonios de una guerra*, 1:505–506; González Quiroga, "Nuevo León," 457; Eduardo Enrique Terrazas, "La estancia del ejército de ocupación norteamericano en Saltillo, octubre de 1846–julio de 1848," in *México en Guerra (1846–1848): Perspectivas regionales*, ed. Laura Herrera Serna (Mexico City: Conaculta, Museo Nacional de las Intervenciones, 1997), 190–191; February 10, 1847, MS A L729 5, Lillard Family Papers, FHS; Chamberlain, *My Confession*, 203; Muro Rocha, *Historia*, 2:393.

23. The Arkansas account is Jonathan W. Buhoup, *Narrative of the Central Division, or Army of Chihuahua, Commanded by Brigadier General Wool . . .* (Pittsburgh: M. P. Morse, 1847), 106–109, 134, and the Illinois diary is Adolphus Engelman, "The Second Illinois in the Mexican War: The Mexican War Letters of Adolphus Engelman, 1846–1847," *Journal of the Illinois State Historical Society* 26 (January 1934): 439. Chamberlain, *My Confession*, 130–132, claims to have actually been present, but in this as in other parts of his memoir, Chamberlain seems to have embellished. He was stationed in the area with a regular army unit that no other account places at the massacre. Interestingly, though, Chamberlain had previously served in the Illinois unit that was present, and he may have based his account on what he heard from his former comrades. For other versions, see *Commercial Advertiser*, April 7, 1847; *Ottawa Free Trader*, April 2, 1847; William H. Daniel Military Diary, 58, 123; Josiah Gregg, *Diary and Letters of Josiah Gregg*, ed. Maurice Garland Fulton (Norman: University of Oklahoma Press, 1944), 2:36–40; Isaac Smith, *Reminiscences of a Campaign in Mexico: An Account of the Operations of the Indiana Brigade on the Line of the Rio Grande and Sierra Madre, and a Vindication of the Volunteers against the Aspirations of Officials and Unofficials*, 2nd ed. (Indianapolis: Chapman and Spann, 1848), 43; and Reilly, *War!*, 155, 157. For a Mexican account, see *LEPOSLP*, March 3, 1847.

24. Rohrbough, *Trans-Appalachian Frontier*, 405, 415; *Arkansas State Gazette*, February 6, 1847; Santiago Aparicio, "Las atrocidades," 125–126; Greenberg, *Wicked War*, 156; Chamberlain, *My Confession*, 115, 171; Clary, *Eagles and Empire*, 165, 223.

25. Taylor's letter is reproduced in *Arkansas Weekly Gazette*, March 27, 1847. See also William H. Daniel Military Diary, 123; Buhoup, *Narrative*, 135; Chamberlain, *My Confession*, 134; Isaac Smith, *Reminiscences*, 78–79; and Foos, *Short*, 124. Taylor also describes the Agua Nueva events and his inability to discover those responsible in a May 23, 1847,

letter to the War Department, reproduced in House Executive Document 56, 30th Congress, 1st Session, 1847, 328.

26. The exchange is duplicated in English in House Executive Document 56, 329–330. The Spanish version is in LEPOSLP, June 6, 1847, as well as Muro Rocha, *Historia*, 2:527–534. Anaya's order to Mora y Villamil and a copy of Taylor's reply to the latter's letter are in exp. 2560, fols. 1–3, ADN. For the Buhoup quote, see Buhoup, *Narrative*, 138.

27. Carpenter, *Travels*, 135; Henry S. Lane, "The Mexican War Journal of Henry S. Lane," ed. Graham Barringer, *Indiana Magazine of History* 53, no. 4 (December 1957): 423, 428; S. Compton Smith, *Chile*, 294–298.

28. Greenberg, *Wicked War*, 193–195.

29. DeLay, *War*, 283–284.

30. Miguel González Quiroga, "Nuevo León ante la invasión norteamericana, 1846–1849," in Herrera Serna, *México en Guerra*, 439–440; Felice Flannery Lewis, *Trailing Clouds of Glory: Zachary Taylor's Mexican War Campaign and His Emerging Civil War Leaders* (Tuscaloosa: University of Alabama Press, 2010), 125–128; C. M. Reeves, "Five Years Experience in the Regular Army, including the War with Mexico," manuscript, MS qR332f RMV, CHSL (hereafter cited as Reeves Manuscript), 176; Hill, *Fighter*, 16, 153; Reid, *Scouting Expeditions*, 29; Benjamin Franklin Scribner, *Camp Life of a Volunteer: A Campaign in Mexico; or, A Glimpse at Life in Camp by "One Who Has Seen the Elephant"* (Austin: Jenkins, 1975), 24.

31. Christopher Dishman, *A Perfect Gibraltar: The Battle of Monterrey, Mexico, 1846* (Norman: University of Oklahoma Press, 2010), 39; Justin Smith, *War*, 1:230–231.

32. Exp. 2179, fols. 58, 81, ADN; exp. 2191, fols. 197–199, ADN.

33. LEPOSLP, August 15, 1846; leg. 17, exp. 25, 1846, SGG, AHESLP; leg. 18, exp. 2, 1846, SGG, AHESLP; Manuel Balbontín, *La invasión norteamericana, 1846 a 1849: Apuntes del subteniente de artillería* (Mexico City: Tip de B. A. Esteva, 1883), 20–23.

34. Dishman, *Perfect*, 33; González Quiroga, "Nuevo León," 344–345; Pedro de Ampudia, *Manifiesto del General Ampudia a sus conciudadanos* (Mexico City: Ignacio Cumplido, 1847), 4.

35. Reeves Manuscript, 178–179; October 2, 1847, folder I 22, MS qG198PRM, Gano Family Papers, CHSL.

36. Generally, the summary of the Battle of Monterrey presented here is based on the detailed account in Dishman, *Perfect*. On the behavior of the volunteers, see George Smith and Charles Judah, *Chronicles*, 40, 80–81.

37. Again, I am relying mostly on Dishman's very detailed account. Dishman, *Perfect*. On the possibility of an explosion, see Justin Smith, *War*, 1:258–259.

38. Exp. 2241, fol. 2, ADN; Dishman, *Perfect,* 196.

39. George Smith and Charles Judah, *Chronicles,* 91; Justin Smith, *War,* 1:259–260.

40. Ampudia, *Manifiesto del General Ampudia,* 8.

41. Dishman, *Perfect,* 198.

42. The Santa Anna quote is from exp. 2252, fol. 7, ADN. See also exp. 2241, fol. 2, ADN; leg. 20, exp. 5, 1846, SGG, AHESLP; leg. 20, exp. 42, 1846, SGG, AHESLP; leg. 26, exp. 12, 1846, SGG, AHESLP; and Maria Isabel Monroy and Tomás Calvillo Unna, *Breve historia de San Luis Potosí* (Mexico City: El Colegio de México / Fideicomiso Historia de las Américas / Fondo de Cultura Económica, 1997), 173.

43. Will Fowler, *Santa Anna of Mexico* (Lincoln: University of Nebraska Press, 2007), 253–254; Tomás Calvillo Unna and Maria Isabel Monroy Castillo, "Entre regionalismo y federalismo: San Luis Potosí, 1846–1848," in *México al tiempo de su guerra con los Estados Unidos (1846–1848),* ed. Josefina Zoraida Vázquez (Mexico City: Secretaría de Relaciones Exteriores, El Colegio de México, Fondo de Cultura Económica, 1997), 432; Lewis, *Trailing,* 187–188; Hill, *Fighter,* 33; Carlos Recio Dávila, *Saltillo durante la guerra México-Estados Unidos: 1846–1848* (Saltillo, Mexico: Museo de la Batalla de la Angostura, 2002), 48; *Encarnacion,* 43.

44. José Daniel Ramírez Reyes, "Veracruz y las guerrillas del Camino Nacional durante la Invasión Norteamericana en 1847–1848" (unpublished manuscript, Universidad Autónoma Metropolitana, n.d.), 61; exp. 2409, ADN; leg. 22, exp. 31, 1846, SGG, AHESLP; *Apuntes para la historia de la guerra,* 118; leg. 20, exp. 29, 1846, SGG, AHESLP.

45. Muro Rocha, *Historia,* 2:403–404; Barbara Corbett, "La política potosina y la Guerra con Estados Unidos," in Vázquez, *México al tiempo de su guerra con los Estados Unidos,* 458–460; Primo Feliciano Velázquez, *Historia General de San Luis Potosí* (San Luis Potosí, Mexico: El Colegio de San Luis, A. C. y la Universidad Autónoma de San Luis Potosí, 2007), 571–572; *LEPOSLP,* December 17, December 22, December 26, 1846; leg. 22, exp. 40, 1846, SGG, AHESLP; leg. 26, exp. 20, 1846, SGG, AHESLP; Manuel Maria Giménez, *Memorias del Coronel Manuel María Giménez ayudante del campo del General Santa Anna, 1798–1878* (Mexico City, 1863), reprinted in *Documentos inéditos o muy raros para la historia de México,* ed. Genero García (Mexico City: Librería de la Vda. de Ch. Bouret, 1911), 34:96–97.

46. Leg. 20, exp. 31, 1846, SGG, AHESLP.

47. Leg. 21, exp. 6, 1846, SGG, AHESLP; leg. 22, exp. 39, 1846, SGG, AHESLP; *Apuntes para la historia de la guerra,* 114; leg. 25, exp. 4, 1846, SGG, AHESLP; *LEPOSLP,* October 6, November 10, 1846; Muro Rocha, *Historia,* 2:403; Velázquez, *Historia General,* 571.

48. Carlos Rodríguez Venegas, "Las finanzas públicas y la Guerra contra los Estados Unidos, 1846–1848," in Vázquez, *México al tiempo de su guerra con los Estados Unidos;*

LEPOSLP, December 26, 1846; leg. 1, leg. 2, 1847, SGG, AHESLP; Impresos, 1847, exp. 28, SGG, AHESLP; Muro Rocha, *Historia,* 2:433; Velázquez, *Historia General,* 572–573. The Santa Anna quote is from *LEPOSLP,* January 26, 1847.

49. R. S. Ripley, *War with Mexico* (New York: Harper and Brothers, 1849), 1:345; Theodore Laidley, *Surrounded by Dangers of All Kinds: The Mexican War Letters of Lieutenant Theodore Laidley* (Denton: University of North Texas Press, 1997), 29; Monroy and Calvillo Unna, *Breve historia,* 174. Santa Anna had already heard rumors that Taylor was not expecting to advance. Leg. 22, exp. 50, 1846, SGG, AHESLP.

50. Greenberg, *Wicked War,* 156; DeLay, *War,* 284; Muro Rocha, *Historia,* 2:427; Hill, *Fighter,* 42. The quote is from Hill, *Fighter,* 71.

51. *Apuntes para la historia de la guerra,* 119; Muro Rocha, *Historia,* 2:415; Balbontín, *La invasión,* 55, 61; McCaffrey, *Army,* 141; Dishman, *Perfect,* 193; Justin Smith, *War,* 1:377–378.

52. Fowler, *Santa Anna,* 260; *LEPOSLP,* January 30, 1847; Balbontín, *La invasión,* 58; Giménez, *Memorias del Coronel,* 98–100. The quote is found in Muro Rocha, *Historia,* 2:424.

53. Quote from Balbontín, *La invasión,* 70. On the conditions of the march, see Monroy and Calvillo Unna, *Breve historia,* 175; Muro Rocha, *Historia,* 2:428–429, 436; exp. 2358, fol. 6, ADN; Balbontín, *La invasión,* 65–70; *Apuntes para la historia de la guerra,* 142–146; and Alonso García Chávez, "Las Memorias del General Andrés Terrés y Masaguera (1784–1850): Edición crítica y paleografía" (tesina de licenciatura, Universidad Nacional Autónoma de México, Facultad de Filosofía y Letras, 1997), 88. On the drought, which limited supplies en route, see *LEPOSLP,* February 23, February 27, 1847. In the latter, the military commander of Catorce says that its inhabitants gave the army essentially all the available food, imperiling their own survival.

54. Justin Smith, *War,* 1:373; Muro Rocha, *Historia,* 2:435–437; Chamberlain, *My Confession,* 143, 147, 152; García Chávez, "Las Memorias del General Andrés Terrés," 89; *Apuntes para la historia de la guerra,* 146–147.

55. The quote is from García Chávez, "Las Memorias del General Andrés Terrés," 89. The best detailed account of the battle is David Sievert Lavender, *Climax at Buena Vista: The American Campaign in Northeastern Mexico, 1846–1847* (Philadelphia: J. B. Lippincott, 1966). For this first part of the battle, see 176–187.

56. This summary relies heavily on Lavender, *Climax,* 176–211. Another useful summary is Stephen A. Carney, *Desperate Stand: The Battle of Buena Vista* ([Washington, DC]: United States Army Center for Military History, 2008). See also García Chávez, "Las Memorias del General Andrés Terrés," 90; Balbontín, *La invasión,* 81–83; Chamberlain, *My Confession,* 157–165; Greenberg, *Wicked War,* 156–163; and David Heidler and Jeanne Heidler, *Henry Clay: The Essential American* (New York: Random House, 2010), 414. On the

Indiana troops, see Scribner, *Camp,* 21, 58–63; Gregg, *Diary,* 2:45, 48; Chamberlain, *My Confession,* 147, 159; Isaac Smith, *Reminiscences,* 50–53; April 23, 1847, Kimball Manuscripts, Lilly Library, Indiana University, Bloomington; Calvin Fletcher, *The Diary of Calvin Fletcher, including Letters to and from Calvin Fletcher, 1817–1866* (Indianapolis: Indiana Historical Society, 1972), 346, 355; R. C. Buley, "Indiana in the Mexican War: The Buena Vista Controversy," *Indiana Magazine of History* 16, no. 1 (March 1920): 53–59, 64–66; R. C. Buley, "Indiana in the Mexican War: The Buena Vista Campaign," *Indiana Magazine of History* 15, no. 4 (December 1919): 299; Oran Perry, comp., *Indiana in the Mexican War* (Indianapolis: W. B. Burford, 1908), 132–134, 186–191, 294–296; EE405, RG 153, NA; and Milroy et al., "Mexican," 171. Santa Anna's report is in LEPOSLP, March 18, March 20, 1847.

57. Abner Doubleday, *My Life in the Old Army* (Fort Worth: Texas Christian University Press, 1998), 111; Perry, *Indiana,* 148; LEPOSLP, February 27, 1847; Balbontín, *La invasión,* 89–90.

58. Recio Dávila, *Saltillo,* 129; March 21, 1847, MSA H196 43, Edmund T. Halsey Collection, FHS; Doubleday, *My Life,* 112–114; Gregg, *Diary,* 2:66; *Apuntes para la historia de la guerra,* 154; Buhoup, *Narrative,* 128; García Chávez, "Las Memorias del General Andrés Terrés," 90. For the casualty numbers, see Carney, *Desperate Stand,* 35.

59. Justin Smith, *War,* 1:398; *Apuntes para la historia de la guerra,* 155–157; LEPOSLP, March 2, March 18, April 10, 1847; Greenberg, *Wicked War,* 160. The interaction between the escort and the soldaderas is detailed in Chamberlain, *My Confession,* 171.

60. LEPOSLP, March 4, 1847; *Apuntes para la historia de la guerra,* 157–158; William H. Daniel Military Diary, 116; Chamberlain, *My Confession,* 174; Buhoup, *Narrative,* 132.

61. García Chávez, "Las Memorias del General Andrés Terrés," 91; *Apuntes para la historia de la guerra,* 159.

62. Jaime Olveda, "Jalisco frente a la invasión norteamericana de 1846–1848," in Vázquez, *México al tiempo de su guerra con los Estados Unidos,* 233; leg. 13, leg. 15, 1847, SGG, AHESLP; Indiferente de Guerra, vol. 64, AGN.

63. LEPOSLP, March 9, March 13, April 1, 1847; leg. 13, leg. 12, leg. 14, 1847, SGG, AHESLP; Muro Rocha, *Historia,* 2:431–432; Velázquez, *Historia General,* 581; García Chávez, "Las Memorias del General Andrés Terrés," 91; Calvillo Unna and Monroy Castillo, "Entre regionalismo y federalismo," 433; *Apuntes para la historia de la guerra,* 161.

64. Monroy and Calvillo Unna, *Breve historia,* 175; *Apuntes para la historia de la guerra,* 151, 165; leg. 12, 1847, SGG, AHESLP; Corydon Donnavan, *Adventures in Mexico: Experienced during a Captivity of Seven Months in the Interior* (Cincinnati: Robinson and Jones, 1847), 73; Juan de la Granja, *Epistolario: Con un estudio biográfico preliminar por Luis Castillo Ledón y notas de Neréo Rodríguez Barragán* (Mexico City: Talleres Gráficos del Museo Nacional

de Arqueología, Historia y Etnografía, 1937), 58; *leposlp*, March 11, 1847. The way the Angostura campaign was shaped by the Mexican army's need for sustenance partially parallels the experience of Lee's army in the Gettysburg campaign. See the incisive analysis in Mark Fiege, *The Republic of Nature: An Environmental History of the United States* (Seattle: University of Washington Press, 2012), 199–225.

65. McCaffrey, *Army,* 119; September 26, 1846, MS C, Richard M. Creagh, FHS; Robert Johannsen, *To the Halls of Montezuma: The Mexican War in the American Imagination* (New York: Oxford University Press, 1985), 40, 43; September 28, 1846, MS A L729 5, Lillard Family Papers, FHS; Coulter, *Volunteers,* 170, 226; Perry, *Indiana,* 122.

66. Hill, *Fighter,* 91, 107, 174–176; Ethan Allen Hitchcock, *Fifty Years in Camp and Field: Diary of Major General Ethan Allen Hitchcock, USA* (New York: G. P. Putnam's Sons, 1909), 346; McClellan, *Mexican War Diary of George B. McClellan,* 38, 83–84; George McClellan, *The Mexican War Diary and Correspondence of George B. McClellan,* ed. Thomas Cutrer (Baton Rouge: Louisiana State University Press, 2009), 18; Isaac Smith, *Reminiscences,* 21–25, 40–41; Dishman, *Perfect,* 16, 51, 72, 105; Greenberg, *Wicked War,* 131; Doubleday, *My Life,* 64.

67. William H. Daniel Military Diary, 124; Carpenter, *Travels,* 41; Scribner, *Camp,* 71. The Mary Gibson quote is from April 5, 1847, MS C G, Columbus Goodwin, FHS, and also can be found in Thomas Ware Gibson, "The Mexican War, Some Personal Correspondence," *Indiana Magazine of History* 65, no. 2 (1969): 139.

68. Buley, "Indiana in the Mexican War: The Buena Vista Controversy"; April 23, 1847, Kimball Manuscripts, Lilly Library; Isaac Smith, *Reminiscences,* 68, 73–5; Scribner, *Camp,* 60–71.

CHAPTER 4 · Even the Fathers of Families

1. Manuel Chust, "Milicia, milicias y milicianos nacionales y cívicos en la formación del estado-nación mexicano, 1812–1835," in *Fuerzas militares en Iberoamérica, siglos XVIII y XIX,* ed. Juan Ortiz Escamilla (Mexico City: El Colegio de México, El Colegio de Michoacán y la Universidad Veracruzana, 2005), 182–183, 189; Juan Ortiz Escamilla, "Los militares veracruzanos al servicio de la nación, 1821–1854," in Escamilla, *Fuerzas militares en Iberoamérica,* 255, 257; Timo Schaefer, "The Social Origins of Justice: Mexico in the Age of Utopian Failure, 1821–1870" (PhD diss., Indiana University, 2015), 102–114.

2. For the part-time police, see Schaefer, "Social Origins of Justice," 102–116; leg. 19, exp. 31, 1846, SGG, AHESLP; and leg. 19, exp. 35, 1846, SGG, AHESLP. On the 1845 law, see Ayuntamiento, Militares, Guardia Nacional, leg. 3276, exp. 3, AHDF; Impresos, June 7, 1845, SGG, AHESLP; leg. 12, 1845, SGG, AHESLP; and especially Pedro Santoni, *Mexicans*

at Arms: Puro Federalists and the Politics of War, 1845–1848 (Fort Worth: Texas Christian University Press, 1996), 62–67.

3. The quote is from LEPOSLP, August 3, 1847. For the Federal District, see Gobernación, leg. 244, caja 1, exp. 2, AGN; Gobernación, leg. 244, caja 1, exp. 4, AGN; Gobernación, leg. 244, caja 2, exp. 2, AGN; and Ayuntamiento, Militares, Guardia Nacional, leg. 3276, exp. 4, AHDF. For Xalapa, see Rafael Laloth Jiménez, "Xalapa durante la Intervención Norteamericana (1846–1848)" (tesis de licenciatura, Universidad Veracruzana, 2014), 28–31.

4. Leg. 21, exp. 27, 1846, SGG, AHESLP; Ayuntamiento, Militares, Guardia Nacional, leg. 3276, exp. 7, AHDF; Gobernación, leg. 220, caja 1, exp. 2, AGN; Gobernación, leg. 220, caja 1, exp. 3, AGN.

5. Isidro Alemán and Moisés Guzmán Pérez, *Apuntes para la historia del Batallón Matamoros de Morelia* (Morelia, Mexico: Universidad Michoacana de San Nicolás de Hidalgo, Instituto de Investigaciones Históricas, 1997), 13–15, 59, 61; Gerardo Sánchez Díaz, "Michoacán frente a la intervención norteamericana, 1847–1848," in *México en Guerra (1846–1848): Perspectivas regionales,* ed. Laura Herrera Serna (Mexico City: Conaculta, Museo Nacional de las Intervenciones, 1997), 404; Raúl Jiménez Lescas, "Los michoacanos ante la guerra de conquista," in Raúl Jiménez Lescas and James D. Cockroft, *Michoacanos e irlandeses en la Guerra Antiimperialista, 1846–1848* (Morelia, Mexico: Secretaría de Desarrollo Social / Escuela Nacional para Trabajadores, 2006), 50; Ronald Spores, Irene Huesca, and Manuel Esparza, comps., *Benito Juárez Gobernador de Oaxaca: Documentos de su mandato y servicio público* (Oaxaca, Mexico: Archivo General del Estado de Oaxaca, Serie Documentos del Archivo 8, 1987), 39; Pedro Santoni, "'Where Did the Other Heroes Go?' Exalting the 'Polko' National Guard Battalions in Nineteenth-Century Mexico," *Journal of Latin American Studies* 34, no. 4 (November 2002): 813.

6. LEPOSLP, August 3, 1847; Maria Gayón Córdova, *La ocupación yanqui de la ciudad de México, 1847–1848* (Mexico City: Consejo Nacional para la Cultura y las Artes, 1997), 59; Rubén Amador Zamora, "El manejo del fusil y la espada: Los intereses partidistas en la formación de la Guardia Nacional en la Ciudad de México: Agosto-octubre 1846" (tesina de licenciatura, Universidad Nacional Autónoma de México, Facultad de Filosofía y Letras, 1998), 32. The quotes are from *Reglamento para organizar, armar y disciplinar la Guardia Nacional en los Estados, Distrito y Territorios de la Federación* (San Luis Potosí, Mexico: Imprenta del Estado, 1846), 3, 10–11, and Impresos, September 21, 1846, SGG, AHESLP.

7. Chust, "Milicia," 189; Manuel Dublán and José Maria Lozano, *Legislación mexicana; ó, Colección completa de las disposiciones legislativas expedidas desde la independencia de la República* (Mexico City: Imprenta del Comercio, 1876), 5:165; Guillermo Prieto, *Memorias de mis*

tiempos (Mexico City: Editorial Porrua, 1996), 252; LEPOSLP, August 5, August 7, August 10, 1847; leg. 33, leg. 2, leg. 23, 1847, SGG, AHESLP; Gobernación, leg. 244, caja 1, exp. 3, AGN.

8. On Oaxaca, see Benjamin Smith, *The Roots of Conservatism in Mexico: Catholicism, Society and Politics in the Mixteca Baja, 1750–1962* (Albuquerque: University of New Mexico Press, 2012), 115–116, 140. On Morelos, see Florencia Mallon, "Peasants and State Formation in Nineteenth Century Mexico: Morelos, 1848–1858," *Political Power and Social Theory* 7 (1988): 1–54. On Veracruz, see Michael Ducey, *A Nation of Villages: Riot and Rebellion in the Mexican Huasteca, 1750–1850* (Tucson: University of Arizona Press, 2004), 110–170. On Guerrero, see Peter Guardino, *Peasants, Politics, and the Formation of Mexico's National State: Guerrero, 1800–1857* (Stanford, CA: Stanford University Press, 1996), 111–177, as well as exp. 2493, fols. 9, 41–42, 54, ADN. On the Federal District, see Amador Zamora, "El manejo del fusil," 19; Luis Fernando Granados, "Pequeños patricios, hermanos mayores: Francisco Prospero Pérez como emblema de los sans-culottes capitalinos hacia 1846–1847," *Historias* 54 (January–March 2003): 25, 28, 31; Luis Fernando Granados, "Diez tipos (a medias) reales en busca de uno ideal: Liberales plebeyos de la Ciudad de México en la primera mitad del siglo XIX," in *Disidencia y disidentes en la Historia de México,* ed. Felipe Castro and Marcela Terrazas (Mexico City: Universidad Nacional Autónoma de México, 2003), 196–197; and Santoni, *Mexicans at Arms,* 129–197.

9. Dublán and Lozano, *Legislación mexicana,* 5:162; Ayuntamiento, Militares, Guardia Nacional, leg. 3276, exp. 6, AHDF; *Apuntes para la historia de la guerra entre México y los Estados Unidos* (Mexico City: Consejo Nacional para la Cultura y las Artes, 1991), 261; Gayón Córdova, *La ocupación,* 107.

10. Prieto, *Memorias,* 260; Karl Heller, *Alone in Mexico: The Astonishing Travels of Karl Heller, 1845–1848,* ed. and trans. Terry Rugeley (Tuscaloosa: University of Alabama Press, 2007), 142; Impresos, 1847, leg. 4, exp. 45, SGG, AHESLP; *Apuntes para la historia de la guerra,* 169, 262, 272; Sánchez Díaz, "Michoacán frente a la intervención norteamericana," 404; Jiménez Lescas, "Los michoacanos," 19; LEPOSLP, February 11, August 17, 1847; Gobernación, leg. 220, caja 2, exp. 8, AGN; *Reglamento para organizar,* 13; leg. 9, 1847, SGG, AHESLP.

11. See, for example, the appeals in leg. 29, 1847, SGG, AHESLP, and especially the many petitions in August 1, 1846, exp. 32, STJ, AHESLP.

12. Leg. 22, exp. 12, 1846, SGG, AHESLP; leg. 25, 1847, SGG, AHESLP; leg. 22, exp. 27, 1846, SGG, AHESLP; Municipalidades, Guadalupe Hidalgo, caja 186, 1846, AHDF. These problems were so severe that, in an effort to encourage men to put their military duties ahead of their families, the government of San Luis Potosí published a letter from Mariano Martinez, owner of the hacienda of Bledos, in which he explained that the hacienda employees, despite their poverty and family occupations, were all enthusiastic about serving. LEPOSLP, November 26, 1846.

13. Leg. 33, 1847, SGG, AHESLP; Michael Ducey, "El Reto del orden liberal: Ciudadanos indígenas y prácticas populares en el México independiente: La política cotidiana en el Cantón de Misantla, Veracuz," in *Los efectos del liberalismo en México siglo XIX,* ed. Antonio Escobar Ohmstede, José Marcos Medina Bustos, and Zulema Trejo Contreras (Mexico City: El Colegio de Sonora / Centro de Investigciones y Estudios Superiores en Antropología Social, 2015), 260.

14. Leg. 33, leg. 29, leg. 9, 1847, SGG, AHESLP.

15. Gobernación, leg. 220, caja 2, exp. 2, AGN; exp. 6, 1848, SGG, AHESLP; Mercedes de la Vega and Maria Cecilia Zuleta, *Testimonios de una guerra: México 1846–1848* (Mexico City: Secretaría de Relaciones Exteriores, 2001), 2:526–528; exp. 10, 1848, SGG, AHESLP.

16. Brian DeLay, *War of a Thousand Deserts: Indian Raids and the Mexican-American War* (New Haven, CT: Yale University Press, 2009), 283–288.

17. Government of Guanajuato, *Exposición y expediente que el Gobierno de Guanajuato dirige a Honorable Congreso del mismo, con motivo de las contestaciones ocurridas entre el Ministerio de la Guerra, General en Gefe del Ejército del Norte y el propio gobierno, sobre varios puntos del mayor interés para la administración pública del Estado* (Guanajuato, Mexico: Tipografía de Oñate, 1847), 7; *Memoria sobre el estado que guarda la administración pública de Michoacán leída al Honorable Congreso por el Secretario del Despacho en 22 de enero de 1848,* (Morelia, Mexico: I. Arango, 1848; hereafter cited as *Memoria, Michoacán*), 27. The War Ministry itself recognized this. See leg. 19, 1847, SGG, AHESLP. See also Laloth Jiménez, "Xalapa durante la Intervención Norteamericana," 34.

18. Exp. 2547, fols. 26–28, ADN.

19. Heller, *Alone,* 142.

20. Leg. 23, exp. 21, 1846, SGG, AHESLP; leg. 30, 1847, SGG, AHESLP; Gobernación, leg. 220, caja 2, exp. 1, AGN; Gobernación, leg. 220, caja 2, exp. 4, AGN; Gobernación, leg. 220, caja 2, exp. 7, AGN; Archivo de Guerra, leg. 375, fols. 518–530, AGN; Alemán and Guzmán Pérez, *Apuntes para la historia,* 12, 48, 49; Prieto, *Memorias,* 257. The quote is from exp. 2565, fols. 53–54, ADN.

21. Leg. 6, 1848, SGG, AHESLP; Mercedes de la Vega, "Zacatecas: Entre la guerra y el federalismo radical," in Herrera Serna, *México en Guerra,* 702; LEPOSLP, October 19, 1847; *Memoria, Michoacán,* 6; Gobernación, leg. 330, exp. 4, AGN.

22. Dublán and Lozano, *Legislación mexicana,* 5:167; LEPOSLP, February 11, 1847; leg. 6, 1848, SGG, AHESLP. See leg. 10, 1847, SGG, AHESLP, for a similar comment from the organizer of a guerrilla force who sought someone to instruct his men in the use of military weapons who could do so without using corporal punishment, "because if they don't learn as quickly as one wants, it is because they don't understand, not because they are not trying."

23. Leg. 26, exp. 1, 1846, SGG, AHESLP; leg. 22, leg. 24, 1847, SGG, AHESLP.

24. Archivo de Guerra, leg. 139, fols. 184–254, AGN; Archivo de Guerra, leg. 153, fols. 452–454, AGN; Archivo de Guerra, leg. 375, fols. 518–530, AGN; Carlos Ruiz Abreu, coord., *Fortificaciones, guerra y defensa de la Ciudad de México (1844, 1847–1848): Documentos para su historia* (Mexico City: Gobierno del Distrito Federal, Secretaría de Cultura, Archivo Histórico del Distrito Federal, 2003), 84; leg. 25, leg. 33, 1847, SGG, AHESLP; Chust, "Milicia," 193; Secretaria de Gobierno, Municipios, caja 83, exp. 2, AGEG; *LEPOSLP,* January 12, 1847; Ayuntamiento, Militares, Guardia Nacional, leg. 3276, exp. 5, AHDF; Juan Ortiz Escamilla, "Michoacán: Federalismo e Intervención Norteamericana," in *México al tiempo de su guerra con los Estados Unidos (1846–1848),* ed. Josefina Zoraida Vázquez (Mexico City: Secretaría de Relaciones Exteriores, El Colegio de México, Fondo de Cultura Económica, 1997), 323.

25. *Apuntes para la historia de la guerra,* 169; Santoni, "'Where Did the Other Heroes Go?,'" 817; *Documentos históricos sobre la defensa de Chapultepec* (Mexico City: Archivo General de la Nación, 1999), 64.

26. Exp. 2602, fols. 70–71, ADN; exp. 2673, fol. 23, ADN; leg. 17, leg. 14, 1847, SGG, AHESLP.

27. The definitive work on these fiscal struggles is still Barbara Tenenbaum, *The Politics of Penury: Debt and Taxes in Mexico, 1821–1856* (Albuquerque: University of New Mexico Press, 1986). See also Daniel Walker Howe, *What Hath God Wrought: The Transformation of America, 1815–1848* (New York: Oxford University Press, 2007), 746; Josefina Zoraida Vázquez, "La guerra que puso en peligro la unidad nacional," in *Symposium La Angostura en la Intervención Norteamericana, 1846–1848* (Saltillo, Mexico: Secretaría de Educación Pública de Coahuila, 1998), 16; leg. 22, leg. 24, 1844, SGG, AHESLP.

28. Tenenbaum, *Politics of Penury,* xii, xiv, 28, 49, 76–82; leg. 18, exp. 2, 1846, SGG, AHESLP; Carlos Rodríguez Venegas, "Las finanzas públicas y la Guerra contra los Estados Unidos, 1846–1848," in Vázquez, *México al tiempo de su guerra con los Estados Unidos,* 107; *Memoria, Michoacán,* anexos; A. Brooke Caruso, *The Mexican Spy Company: United States Covert Operations in Mexico* (Jefferson, NC: McFarland, 1991), 55.

29. Jack Bauer, *Surfboats and Horse Marines: U.S. Naval Operations in the Mexican War, 1846–48* (Annapolis, MD: Naval Institute, 1969), 236; Barbara Corbett, "La política potosina y la Guerra con Estados Unidos," in Vázquez, *México al tiempo de su guerra con los Estados Unidos,* 460–462; Jaime Olveda, "Jalisco frente a la invasión norteamericana de 1846–1848," in Vázquez, *México al tiempo de su guerra con los Estados Unidos,* 287; Omar Valerio-Jiménez, *River of Hope: Forging Identity and Nation in the Rio Grande Borderlands* (Durham, NC: Duke University Press, 2013), 112; Rodríguez Venegas, "Las finanzas públicas," 105; Howe, *What Hath,* 797; Justin Smith, *The War with Mexico* (Gloucester, MA: Peter Smith, 1963), 2:253; Josefina Zoraida Vázquez, "Un desastre anunciado e

inevitable: La Guerra con Estados Unidos," in Josefina Zoraida Vázquez et al., *La guerra entre México y Estados Unidos, 1846–1848: Cuatro miradas* (San Luis Potosí, Mexico: El Colegio de San Luis, 1998), 11; David Weber, *The Mexican Frontier 1821–1846: The American Southwest under Mexico* (Albuquerque: University of New Mexico Press, 1982), 149; Marcela Terrazas y Basante and Gerardo Gurza Lavalle, *Las relaciones México-Estados Unidos, 1756–2010,* vol. 1, *Imperios, repúblicas y pueblos en pugna por el territorio, 1756–1867* (Mexico City: Universidad Nacional Autónoma de México / Secretaría de Relaciones Exteriores, 2012), 281.

30. José María Roa Bárcena, *Recuerdos de la invasión norteamericana (1846–1849)* (Xalapa, Mexico: Universidad Veracruzana, 1986), 40–41; leg. 26, exp. 36, 1846, SGG, AHESLP; leg. 22, 1847, SGG, AHESLP; Richard Coulter, *Volunteers: The Mexican War Journals of Private Richard Coulter and Sergeant Thomas Barclay,* ed. Allan Peskin (Kent, OH: Kent State University Press, 1991), 53; Mariano Riva Palacio, "Breve diario de don Mariano Riva Palacio (agosto de 1847)," ed. Josefina Vázquez, *Historia Mexicana* 47, no. 2 (October–December 1997): 447–449; José Fernando Ramírez, *México durante la guerra con Estados Unidos* (Mexico City: Librería de la Viuda de Ch. Bouret, 1905), 260; Laloth Jiménez, "Xalapa durante la Intervención Norteamericana," 78.

31. Exp. 2181, fols. 197–199, ADN; exp. 2252, fol. 22, ADN; Corydon Donnavan, *Adventures in Mexico: Experienced during a Captivity of Seven Months in the Interior* (Cincinnati: Robinson and Jones, 1847), 28; exp. 2319, fol. 21, ADN; exp. 2355, fol. 15, ADN; exp. 2358, fols. 4, 11, ADN; Justin Smith, *War,* 2:20, 31, 183; exp. 2493, fols. 41–42, 52, 54, 60–62, ADN; exp. 2487, fol. 13, ADN; exp. 2591, fol. 186, ADN; Mariano Riva Palacio, "Breve diario," 445; exp. 2545, fol. 14, ADN; Archivo de Guerra, leg. 619, AGN; Manuel Balbontín, *Memorias del Coronel Manuel Balbontín* (San Luis Potosí, Mexico: Tip. de la Escuela I. Militar, 1896), 12–14. For instances of confiscations, see leg. 6, 1847, SGG, AHESLP; exp. 2757, fols. 1–2, ADN; exp. 2545, fol. 3, ADN.

32. Exp. 2406, fol. 9, ADN; Archivo de Guerra, leg. 155, fols. 260–285, AGN; Archivo de Guerra, leg. 375, fols. 186–216, AGN.

33. Periodo Independiente, vol. 51, exp. 3, AGEO; George Ballentine, *Autobiography of an English Soldier in the United States Army* (Chicago: Lakeside, 1986), 207; Samuel Chamberlain, *My Confession: Recollections of a Rogue* (Austin: Texas State Historical Association, 1996), 115; Frederick Zeh, *An Immigrant Soldier in the Mexican War* (College Station: Texas A&M University Press, 1995), 36.

34. Examples of both a fundraising committee and a benefit event can be seen in leg. 11, exp. 24, 1846, SGG, AHESLP. On early nineteenth-century campaigns in Europe, see, for instance, Karen Hagemann, "Female Patriots: Women, War and Nation in the Period of the Prussian-German Anti-Napoleonic Wars," *Gender and History* 16, no. 2 (August 2004): 402. On those campaigns in Mexico, see, for instance, Peter Guardino,

The Time of Liberty: Popular Political Culture in Oaxaca, 1750–1850 (Durham: Duke University Press, 2005), 125–127.

35. Sergio Cañedo Gamboa, *Los festejos septembrinos en San Luis Potosí: Protocolo, discurso y transformaciones, 1824–1847* (San Luis Potosí, Mexico: El Colegio de San Luis, 2001), 120–123; leg. 28, 1845, SGG, AHESLP; *LEPOSLP,* September 8, 1845, May 16, June 6, June 25, 1846; leg. 5, leg. 14, 1847, SGG, AHESLP; leg. 11, exp. 25, 1846, SGG, AHESLP; leg. 22, exp. 15, 1846, SGG, AHESLP; leg. 9, leg. 13, leg. 15, 1847, SGG, AHESLP; Cañedo Gamboa, *Los festejos,* 139; Olveda, "Jalisco," 299–302.

36. Leg. 26, exp. 36, 1846, SGG, AHESLP; leg. 11, exp. 25, 1846, SGG, AHESLP; leg. 35, 1845, SGG, AHESLP; leg. 26, exp. 36, 1846, SGG, AHESLP; *LEPOSLP,* May 23, June 6, October 10, December 22, 1846; Maria Isabel Monroy and Tomás Calvillo Unna, *Breve historia de San Luis Potosí* (Mexico City: El Colegio de México / Fideicomiso Historia de las Américas / Fondo de Cultura Económica, 1997), 174; leg. 20, 1847, SGG, AHESLP; Valentín López González, "La intervención norteamericana en Cuernavaca," in Herrera Serna, *México en Guerra,* 411; Manuel Muro Rocha, *Historia de San Luis Potosí* (Mexico City: Sociedad Potosina de Estudios Históricos, 1973), 2:431–432, 490–491; leg. 14, leg. 20, 1847, SGG, AHESLP; Guardino, *Time of Liberty,* 253.

37. For committees and meetings, see, for instance, leg. 28, 1845, SGG, AHESLP, and *LEPOSLP,* November 14, 1846. On women, see leg. 11, exp. 24, 1846, SGG, AHESLP; leg. 12, exp. 30, 1846, SGG, AHESLP; *LEPOSLP,* June 3, June 6, June 25, September 26, 1846; and Cañedo Gamboa, *Los festejos,* 123–124. For a call for participation by all, see *LEPOSLP,* October 3, 1846.

38. The Mazatlán quote is in leg. 14, 1847, SGG, AHESLP. For donations from far-flung locales, see Guardino, *Time of Liberty,* 253; Cañedo Gamboa, *Los festejos,* 123–124; Impresos, June 6, 1846, SGG, AHESLP; Spores, Huesca, and Esparza, *Benito Juárez Gobernador,* 37; Vega and Zuleta, *Testimonios,* 1:524; Manuel Esparza, "El difícil camino de sentirse nación: Oaxaca y la guerra contra Estados Unidos," in Herrera Serna, *México en Guerra,* 508–509; Moisés Guzmán Pérez, *Las relaciones clero-gobierno en Michoacán: La gestión episcopal de Juan Cayetano Gómez de Portugal* (Mexico City: LIX Legislatura Cámara de Diputados, 2005), 167–168; and Olveda, "Jalisco," 299–302.

39. *LEPOSLP,* May 31, 1846. On previous resistance to the head tax, see José Antonio Serrano Ortega, "Hacienda y guerra, élites políticas y gobierno nacional: Guanajuato, 1835–1847," in Vázquez, *México al tiempo de su guerra con los Estados Unidos,* 247; Guardino, *Peasants,* 154–156; and Benjamin Smith, *Roots,* 111, 137–139.

40. Fol. 8, Foreign Office 203-92, British Public Record Office, London; Gobernación, sin sección, leg. 331, exp. 7, AGN; Serrano Ortega, "Hacienda y guerra"; Rodríguez Venegas, "Las finanzas públicas," 116–118.

41. Impresos, October 1, 1846, SGG, AHESLP; leg. 22, exp. 1, 1846, SGG, AHESLP; leg. 22, exp. 6, 1846, SGG, AHESLP; leg. 22, exp. 7, 1846, SGG, AHESLP; leg. 3, leg. 12, 1847, SGG, AHESLP; fol. 7, Foreign Office 203-92, British Public Record Office; leg. 26, exp. 29, 1846, SGG, AHESLP; leg. 26, exp. 17, 1846, SGG, AHESLP; Corbett, "La política," 463.

42. Leg. 16, leg. 20, leg. 22, 1847, SGG, AHESLP. For the Rio Verde incident, see leg. 15, 1847, SGG, AHESLP. The quote is from leg. 2, 1847, SGG, AHESLP.

43. Monroy and Calvillo Unna, *Breve historia,* 420–422; Barbara Corbett, "Las fibras del poder: La guerra contra Texas (1835–36) y la construcción de un estado fisco-militar en San Luis Potosí," in *Circuitos mercantiles y mercados en Latinoamérica, siglos XVIII-XIX,* comp. Jorge Silva Riquer, Juan Carlos Grosso, and Carmen Yuste (Mexico City: Instituto de Investigaciones Dr. José Ma. Luis Mora / Instituto de Investigaciones Históricas, Universidad Nacional Autónoma de México, 1995); Corbett, "La política," 463–466; Antonio Escobar Ohmstede, "La Guerra entre México y los Estados Unidos en 1848 y sus consecuencias en las Huastecas," in Vázquez, *México al tiempo de su guerra con los Estados Unidos,* 271–275; Edith Ortiz Díaz, "Sobreviviendo a la guerra México-Estados Unidos: La ruptura del contrato social ante la invasión norteamericana: El caso de la Ciudad de México," in *Culturas de pobreza y resistencia: Estudios de marginados, proscritos y descontentos, México, 1804–1910,* coord. Romana Falcón (Mexico City: Colegio de México / Universidad Autónoma de Querétaro, 2005), 141. For the political cartoons, see Helia Emma Bonilla Reyna, "El Calavera: La Caricatura en tiempos de Guerra," *Anales del Instituto de Investigaciones Estéticas* 23, no. 79 (Autumn 2001): 91–92.

44. See, for instance, Vicente Riva Palacio, *México a Través de los siglos* (Mexico City: Editorial Cumbre, 1989), 192, 197.

45. *LEPOSLP,* January 19, 1847; Impresos, 1847, exp. 28, SGG, AHESLP; leg. 1, leg. 2, leg. 3, 1847, SGG, AHESLP.

46. The law is in Dublán and Lozano, *Legislación mexicana,* 5:246–247. For the debates, see Reynaldo Sordo Cedeño, "El Congreso y la Guerra con los Estados Unidos," in Vázquez, *México al tiempo de su guerra con los Estados Unidos,* 60–65.

47. Will Fowler, "Valentín Gómez Farías: Perceptions of Radicalism in Independent Mexico, 1821–1847," *Bulletin of Latin American Research* 15, no. 1 (1996): 49. Alvarez certainly believed this. Jesús Guzmán Urióstegui, "El sur ante la presencia norteamericana (1846–1847): Juan Alvarez y la guerra," in Herrera Serna, *México en Guerra,* 349–350; Ramírez, *México,* 188.

48. Vicente Riva Palacio, *México a Través de los siglos,* 165.

49. For reports of church leaders who believed American assurances, see Ramírez, *México,* 238–239, and John Pinheiro, "Crusade and Conquest: Anti-Catholicism,

Manifest Destiny, and the U.S.-Mexican War of 1846–48" (PhD diss., University of Tennessee, Knoxville, 2001), 218–220.

50. Peter Guardino, "In the Name of Civilization and with a Bible in Their Hands: Religion and the 1846–48 Mexican American War," *Mexican Studies / Estudios Mexicanos* 30, no. 2 (Summer 2014): 355–356; Guzmán Pérez, *Las relaciones,* 169–170; Angélica Peregrina, "Visión de los jaliscenses en torno a la guerra de intervención norteamericana," in Herrera Serna, *México en Guerra,* 380; leg. 5, exp. 28, 1846, SGG, AHESLP; Justicia y Negocios Eclesiásticos, leg. 160, fols. 53, 55, 57, 58, 62, AGN.

51. Leg. 5, exp. 28, 1846, SGG, AHESLP. The quote is from leg. 20, exp. 44, 1846, SGG, AHESLP, where there are numerous similar documents. See also Esparza, "El difícil camino," 514–515; Peregrina, "Visión de los jaliscenses," 380.

52. Tenenbaum, *Politics of Penury,* 78, 82; Brian Connaughton, "Agio, clero y bancarrota fiscal, 1846–1847," *Mexican Studies / Estudios Mexicanos* 14, no. 2 (Summer 1998): 263–285; Ruiz Abreu, *Fortificaciones,* 95; Esparza, "El difícil camino," 509, 521; Guzmán Pérez, *Las relaciones,* 176, 182; Olveda, "Jalisco," 295–298; Vega and Zuleta, *Testimonios,* 1:416. For church bells, see Ayuntamiento, Guerra con los Estados Unidos, vol. 2264, exp. 8, AHDF; Ayuntamiento, Guerra con los Estados Unidos, vol. 2267, exp. 73, fols. 470–516, AHDF; leg. 20, 1847, SGG, AHESLP; Spores, Huesca, and Esparza, *Benito Juárez Gobernador,* 38; Ruiz Abreu, *Fortificaciones,* 148, 411; Cañedo Gamboa, *Los festejos,* 235; Guzmán Pérez, *Las relaciones,* 177.

53. Esparza, "El difícil camino," 517; Guzmán Pérez, *Las relaciones,* 186–187; Peregrina, "Visión de los jaliscenses," 381; César Navarro Gallegos, "Una 'Santa Alianza': El gobierno duranguense y la jerarquía eclesiástica durante la intervención norteamericana," in Herrera Serna, *México en Guerra,* 248; Vicente Riva Palacio, *México a Través de los siglos,* 167.

54. *Protesta hecha por los señores curas de las parroquias de esta capital al Sr. Vicario Capitular* (Mexico City: Imprenta de Vicente Garcia Torres, 1847); *Bienes de la Iglesia, ó sea Impugnacion al Discurso sobre bienes eclesiásticos inserto en el Diario del Gobierno* (Guadalajara, Mexico: Imprenta de Dionisio Rodriguez, 1847); Carlos Maria de Bustamante, entries for January 12, January 13, 1847, in *Diario histórico de México 1822–1848,* ed. Josefina Zoraida Vázquez and Héctor Cuauhtémoc Hernández Silva (Mexico City: El Colegio de México / Centro de Investigaciones y Estudios Superiores en Antropología Social, 2003); Guzmán Pérez, *Las relaciones,* 189–191; *Planes en la Nación Mexicana* (Mexico City: Cámara de Diputados, 1987), 4:372; Corbett, "La política," 464.

55. For the United States, see Nicholas Marshall, "The Great Exaggeration: Death and the Civil War," *Journal of the Civil War Era* 4, no. 1 (March 2014): 11.

56. Amador Zamora, "El manejo del fusil," 87–88.

57. See, for instance, the poem in *El Republicano,* November 19, 1846.

58. The history of these conflicts is fascinating, and, due to the inherent difficulties of studying largely illiterate groups, there is much still to be learned. See Richard Warren, *Vagrants and Citizens: Politics and the Masses in Mexico City from Colony to Republic* (Wilmington, DE: SR Books, 2001); Sylvia Arrom, "Popular Politics in Mexico City: The Parián Riot, 1828," *Hispanic American Historical Review* 68, no. 2 (1988): 245–268; Rosalina Rios Zúñiga, "Popular Uprising and Political Culture in Zacatecas: The Sombrerete Uprisings (1829)," *Hispanic American Historical Review* 87, no. 3 (August 2007): 499–536; Guardino, *Time of Liberty,* 156–222; and Santoni, *Mexicans at Arms,* esp. 16–17, 20–21, 128–162. See also Ramírez, *México,* 142–146, for a sense of the atmosphere that accompanied radical federalist meetings in Mexico City.

59. Santoni, *Mexicans at Arms,* 130, 147, 150, 161, 167; *El Monitor Republicano,* September 29, 1846; LEPOSLP, October 20, 1846; Carlos Maria de Bustamante, *El nuevo Bernal Díaz del Castillo* (Mexico City: Instituto Nacional de Estudios Históricos de la Revolución Mexicana-Gobierno del Estado de Puebla, 1994), 1:39; Roa Bárcena, *Recuerdos,* 79; and Bustamante, entries for August 9, September 8, September 11, September 13, September 22, September 27, October 3, October 4, October 7, 1846, in *Diario.* The quotes are from Bustamante, entries for September 8, September 13, 1846, in *Diario.*

60. Amador Zamora, "El manejo del fusil"; Prieto, *Memorias,* 252–253; Gobernación, leg. 220, caja 2, exp. 5, AGN; Gobernación, leg. 244, caja 1, exp. 2, AGN; Gobernación, leg. 244, caja 2, exp. 3, AGN; Impresos, 1845 [despite its mistaken archival classification this document is actually from the fall of 1846], SGG, AHESLP; *Apuntes para la historia de la guerra,* 117, 173, 265; Bustamante, *El nuevo,* 2:75; Bustamante, entry for April 2, 1847, in *Diario*; Granados, "Pequeños patricios," 31; Roa Bárcena, *Recuerdos,* 351–352. The dynamic of organization and counterorganization is captured very well by the discussion of the city council in Actas de Cabildo Ordinarios, vol. 168-A, October 12, 1846, and October 13, 1846, AHDF. The quote is from Bustamante, entry for January 10, 1846, in *Diario.*

61. Santoni, *Mexicans at Arms,* 191; Archivo de Guerra, leg. 507b, AGN; *Décimas al pronunciamiento de los niños polquitos* (n.p., n.d.); *Marcha que cantan los polcos en la musica de ponchada* (n.p., n.d.); José Bravo Ugarte, *Temas históricos diversos* (Mexico City: Editorial Jus, 1966), 134; Bustamante, entries for October 9, October 10, October 14, 1846, in *Diario.*

62. Santoni, *Mexicans at Arms,* 183–188; *Apuntes para la historia de la guerra,* 180.

63. Exp. 2342, fols. 3–4, ADN; Vicente Riva Palacio, *México a Través de los siglos,* 167–169; Actas de Cabildo Secretas, vol. 300-A, January 14, 1847, AHDF; Actas de Cabildo Ordinarios, vol. 169-A, January 14, 1847, AHDF; Vega and Zuleta, *Testimonios,* 2:65.

64. Guzmán Pérez, *Las relaciones,* 192–193; Vega and Zuleta, *Testimonios,* 1:582, 2:61–65; Angela Moyano Pahissa, *Querétaro en la Guerra con los Estados Unidos, 1846–1848*

(Querétaro, Mexico: Gobierno del Estado de Querétaro Oficilía Mayor, 1998), 38; Navarro Gallegos, "Una 'Santa Alianza,'" 244.

65. Santoni, *Mexicans at Arms,* 179–185.

66. Santoni, *Mexicans at Arms,* 185; *Apuntes para la historia de la guerra,* 178; Bravo Ugarte, *Temas históricos,* 134–135; Roa Bárcena, *Recuerdos,* 145; Ramírez, *México,* 199–200; Bustamante, entry for February 25, 1847, in *Diario.*

67. *Planes en la Nación Mexicana,* 4:372–373; LEPOSLP, March 4, 1847.

68. Michael Costeloe, "The Mexican Church and the Rebellion of the Polkos," *Hispanic American Historical Review* 46, no. 2 (1966): 175–178; Vicente Riva Palacio, *México a Través de los siglos,* 198; Prieto, *Memorias,* 255; Ramírez, *México,* 200.

69. Prieto, *Memorias,* 253; Ramírez, *México,* 201; Guzmán Pérez, *Las relaciones,* 195. This was also the way the rebellion was seen in the provinces. See, for instance, LEPOSLP, March 25, 1847, and William W. Carpenter, *Travels and Adventures in Mexico: In the Course of Journeys of Upward of 2500 Miles, Performed on Foot, Giving an Account of the Manners and Customs of the People, and the Agricultural and Mineral Resources of That Country* (New York: Harper Brothers, 1851), 113–114. For a sense of how this narrative took shape as the war continued, see José Maria Lafragua to Manuel de la Peña y Peña, Querétaro, November 25, 1847, and "La revolución llamada de los polkos," manuscript, both in Colección Lafragua, Fondo Reservado, Biblioteca Nacional, Mexico City.

70. Santoni, *Mexicans at Arms,* 186–192; LEPOSLP, March 3, March 16, 1847; Impresos, 1847, leg. 2, exp. 19, SGG, AHESLP; Impresos, 1847, leg. 2, exp. 24, SGG, AHESLP; Prieto, *Memorias,* 254; Ramírez, *México,* 203–204; Vicente Riva Palacio, *México a Través de los siglos,* 198.

71. Santoni, *Mexicans at Arms,* 190–197; Gobernación, leg. 244, caja 1, exp. 3, AGN; Gobernación, leg. 244, caja 1, exp. 1, AGN. The quote is from Gobernación, leg. 244, caja 1, exp. 3, AGN.

72. Caruso, *Mexican,* 142–143; Timothy D. Johnson, *A Gallant Little Army: The Mexico City Campaign* (Lawrence: University of Kansas Press, 2007), 61, 120; Tom Reilly, *War with Mexico! America's Reporters Cover the Battlefront* (Lawrence: University of Kansas Press, 2010), 117; Justin Smith, *War,* 2:12–13; Guzmán Pérez, *Las relaciones,* 178; Pinheiro, "Crusade," 69.

73. LEPOSLP, May 8, 1847; Impresos, 1847, leg. 3, exp. 28, SGG, AHESLP; Brian Connaughton, "Soberania y religiosidad: La disputa por la grey en el movimiento de la Reforma," in *Clérigos, políticos y política: Las relaciones Iglesia Estado en Puebla, siglos xix y xx,* ed. Alica Tecuanhuey Sandoval (Puebla, Mexico: Instituto de Ciencias Sociales y Humanidades, Benemérita Universidad Autónoma de Puebla, 2002), 120.

74. Amy Greenberg, *A Wicked War: Polk, Clay, Lincoln and the 1846 U.S. Invasion of Mexico* (New York: Knopf, 2012), 143–144; Bauer, *Surfboats,* 63–64, 69; Daniel Harvey Hill, *A Fighter from Way Back: The Mexican War Diary of Lt. Daniel Harvey Hill, 4th Artillery, USA,* ed. Nathaniel Cheairs Hughes Jr. and Timothy D. Johnson (Kent, OH: Kent State University Press, 2002), 62. On Scott and flanking maneuvers, see Johnson, *Gallant,* 77, 268.

75. Exp. 2355, fol. 15, ADN; Bauer, *Surfboats,* 85; Carmen Blázquez Domínguez, "Presencia norteamericana en Veracruz durante el conflicto de 1847," in Herrera Serna, *México en Guerra,* 664; Bustamante, entry for February 3, 1847, in *Diario*; Laloth Jiménez, "Xalapa durante la Intervención Norteamericana," 35. The quote is from Muro Rocha, *Historia,* 2:493–494.

76. Bauer, *Surfboats,* 88, 95; Johnson, *Gallant,* 44. The bombardment of fortified cities was not unprecedented, and Scott undoubtedly knew this. See David Bell, *The First Total War: Napoleon's Europe and the Birth of Warfare as We Know It* (Boston: Houghton Mifflin, 2007), 281–284, on the French bombardment of Saragossa.

77. Greenberg, *Wicked War,* 171; Irving Levinson, *Wars within War: Mexican Guerrillas, Domestic Elites and the United States of America, 1846–1848* (Fort Worth: Texas Christian University Press, 2005), 26; Theodore Laidley, *Surrounded by Dangers of All Kinds: the Mexican War Letters of Lieutenant Theodore Laidley* (Denton: University of North Texas Press, 1997), 48, 53; Juan de la Granja, *Epistolario: Con un estudio biográfico preliminar por Luis Castillo Ledón y notas de Neréo Rodríguez Barragán* (Mexico City: Talleres Gráficos del Museo Nacional de Arqueología, Historia y Etnografía, 1937), 64–65; Roa Bárcena, *Recuerdos,* 168–179; C. M. Reeves, "Five Years Experience in the Regular Army, including the War with Mexico," manuscript, MS QR332f RMV, CHSL (hereafter cited as Reeves Manuscript), 220; Zeh, *Immigrant Soldier,* 22; *Apuntes para la historia de la guerra,* 209–212; Laloth Jiménez, "Xalapa durante la Intervención Norteamericana," 42–43. The quote is from Winfield Scott, *Memoirs of Lieut.-General Scott, LL.D, Written by Himself* (New York: Sheldon, 1864), 2:427. Notably Scott's decision in this regard was exactly the opposite of that taken by the French admiral Charles Baudin when his forces had attacked the port less than ten years earlier during the so-called Pastry War. Baudin and his Mexican counterpart had worked to minimize the risk to the civilian population. Mario Alberto García Suárez, "El puerto de Veracruz, espacio de la guerra franco-mexicana (1838–1839)" (tesis de licenciatura, Universidad Veracruzana, 2014), 71, 105.

78. Muro Rocha, *Historia,* 2:500; *Apuntes para la historia de la guerra,* 212, 217; Roa Bárcena, *Recuerdos,* 177. For Morales's report, see exp. 2268, fol. 16, ADN. For the Oswandel quote, see Jacob Oswandel, *Notes on the Mexican War, 1846–1848* (Knoxville: University of Tennessee Press, 2010), 47, 50–51. The quote is from 51.

79. For casualty figures, see Muro Rocha, *Historia,* 2:503; Roa Bárcena, *Recuerdos,* 178; *Apuntes para la historia de la guerra,* 215. For Rode, see LEPOSLP, April 22, 1847, and for Alvarez, see exp. 2493 fols. 57–58, ADN.

80. Reilly, *War!,* 108, 119; George Wilkins Kendall, *Dispatches from the Mexican War* (Norman: University of Oklahoma Press, 1999), 177, 185–187; Actas de Cabildo Secretas, vol. 300-A, April 27, 1847, AHDF; Ruiz Abreu, *Fortificaciones,* 388; Muro Rocha, *Historia de San Luis Potosí,* 2:503; Impresos, 1847, exp. 2, SGG, AHESLP; LEPOSLP, April 8, April 13, April 15, July 3, 1847; Bustamante, entry for March 27, 1847, in *Diario*; George W. Smith and Charles Judah, *The Chronicles of the Gringos: The US Army in the Mexican War, 1846–48: Accounts of Eyewitnesses and Combatants,* (Albuquerque: University of New Mexico Press, 1968), 192–194; *Times of London,* May 10, 1847.

81. *Apuntes para la historia de la guerra,* 172; Coulter, *Volunteers,* 82; Ulysses S. Grant, *Personal Memoirs* (Westminster, MD: Random House, 1999), 65. Grant says it was almost a thousand miles using the route these men had to take, but I have been unable to find confirmation.

82. *Apuntes para la historia de la guerra,* 221; Roa Bárcena, *Recuerdos,* 231; Granados, "Diez tipos," 197; Laidley, *Surrounded,* 67; exp. 2496, fols. 2, 6, ADN.

83. Levinson, *Wars,* 16; exp. 2355, fols. 12, 34, ADN; exp. 2281, fol. 1, ADN; Ballentine, *Autobiography,* 159. Disease helped defeat the American effort to take control of Tabasco. See Maria Eugenia Arias Gómez, "La defensa en el territorio tabasqueño," in Herrera Serna, *México en Guerra,* 607.

84. Carmen Blázquez Domínguez, "Veracruz: Restablecimiento del federalismo e intervención norteamericana," in Vázquez, *México al tiempo de su guerra con los Estados Unidos,* 572; Roa Bárcena, *Recuerdos,* 229; Gobernación, leg. 184, caja 1, exp. 3, AGN; *Apuntes para la historia de la guerra,* 220; Bustamante, entry for March 28, 1847, in *Diario*; Will Fowler, *Santa Anna of Mexico* (Lincoln: University of Nebraska Press, 2007), 267–268; Justin Smith, *War,* 2:42–45. Since the colonial period, Cerro Gordo had in fact been considered a point at which an army could defend against an invasion, and it is possible that Santa Anna knew this. José Daniel Ramírez Reyes, "Veracruz y las guerrillas del Camino Nacional durante la Invasión Norteamericana en 1847–1848" (unpublished manuscript, Universidad Autónoma Metropolitana, n.d.), 30.

85. John Corey Henshaw, *Recollections of the War with Mexico* (Columbia: University of Missouri Press, 2008), 131; Reeves Manuscript, 232.

86. The account of the battle here is based mostly on the detailed descriptions in Johnson, *Gallant,* 66–100, and Roa Bárcena, *Recuerdos,* 194–230. On the killing of the wounded, see Henshaw, *Recollections,* 137.

87. James M. McCaffrey, *Army of Manifest Destiny: The American Soldier in the Mexican War, 1846–1848* (New York: New York University Press, 1992), 173.

88. For a description, see George Smith and Charles Judah, *Chronicles,* 207–209.

89. Justin Smith, *War,* 2:68–70.

90. Cristina Gómez Alvarez and Francisco Téllez Guerrero, "Las finanzas municipales y la Guerra: El impacto de la intervención estadunidense en la ciudad de Puebla," in Herrera Serna, *México en Guerra,* 531–534; Daniel Molina Alvarez, *La pasión de padre Jarauta* (Mexico City: Gobierno del Distrito Federal, 1999), 59–60; Alicia Tecuanhuey Sandoval, "Puebla durante la Invasión Norteamericana," in Vázquez, *México al tiempo de su guerra con los Estados Unidos,* 405–409; *Apuntes para la historia de la guerra,* 247. On the reputation of Pueblans as not inclined to oppose the Americans, see *Apuntes para la historia de la guerra,* 244–245; Johnson, *Gallant,* 123; and Vicente Quirarte, "Tiempo de canallas, héroes y artistas: El imaginario de la guerra entre México y Estados Unidos," in Herrera Serna, *México en Guerra,* 61.

91. Oswandel, *Notes,* 137–138, 141.

92. Henshaw, *Recollections,* 150; Johnson, *Gallant,* 125, 133; Justin Smith, *War,* 2:72; exp. 2504, fols. 15, 20, ADN; exp. 2550, fol. 2, ADN; Oswandel, *Notes,* 133–135.

93. Oswandel, *Notes,* 142, 193, 322; Coulter, *Volunteers,* 308.

CHAPTER 5 · Each Chapter We Write in Mexican Blood

1. David Pletcher, *The Diplomacy of Annexation: Texas, Oregon, and the Mexican War,* (Columbia: University of Missouri Press, 1973), 456–459; Daniel Walker Howe, *What Hath God Wrought: The Transformation of America, 1815–1848* (New York: Oxford University Press, 2007), 6.

2. On mono-cropping cotton and its consequences, see Walter Johnson, *Empire of Dark Dreams: Slavery and Empire in the Cotton Kingdom* (Cambridge, MA: Belknap Press of Harvard University Press, 2013), 156–157, 180–184. For abolitionist opposition to the war, see Robert Johannsen, *To the Halls of Montezuma: The Mexican War in the American Imagination* (New York: Oxford University Press, 1985), 214; Shelley Streeby, *American Sensations: Class, Empire and the Production of American Culture* (Berkeley: University of California Press, 2002), 20; and, especially, Amy Greenberg, *A Wicked War: Polk, Clay, Lincoln and the 1846 U.S. Invasion of Mexico* (New York: Knopf, 2012), 116, 196–198.

3. Amy Greenberg, *Manifest Manhood and the Antebellum American Empire* (New York: Cambridge University Press, 2005), esp. 25.

4. Reginald Horsman, *Race and Manifest Destiny: The Origins of American Racial Anglo-Saxonism* (Cambridge, MA: Harvard University Press, 1981), 250, 257–261.

5. Jesús Velasco Márquez, "Regionalismo, partidismo y expansionismo: La política interna de Estados Unidos durante la guerra contra México," *Historia Mexicana* 47, no. 2 (October–December 1997): 337; Howe, *What Hath,* 762–763, 811–812; Hal W. Bochin, "Caleb B. Smith's Opposition to the Mexican War," *Indiana Magazine of History* 69, no. 2 (1973): 98; Jorge Belarmino, *Cuestión de sangre* (Mexico City: Planeta, 2008), 184; Ted C. Hinckley, "American Anti-Catholicism during the Mexican War," *Pacific Historical Review* 31 (May 1962): 133; Greenberg, *Wicked War,* 101, 106.

6. Velasco Márquez, "Regionalismo," 338; Justin Smith, *The War with Mexico* (Gloucester, MA: Peter Smith, 1963), 1:347, 2:273; Greenberg, *Wicked War,* 129, 254; Bochin, "Caleb B. Smith's Opposition," 106; Johannsen, *To the Halls,* 276; Howe, *What Hath,* 770.

7. The standard-bearer for this view was South Carolina senator John C. Calhoun. Howe, *What Hath,* 764; Greenberg, *Wicked War,* 247–248.

8. Howe, *What Hath,* 767; Greenberg, *Wicked War,* 196–197.

9. Greenberg, *Wicked War,* 190–195.

10. Justin Smith, *War,* 2:269; Jesús Velasco Márquez, *La guerra del 47 y la opinión pública (1845–1848)* (Mexico City: Sepsetentas, 1975), 46; Greenberg, *Wicked War,* 196, 248–254; Howe, *What Hath,* 624, 762, 770, 797.

11. *Congressional Globe,* 29th Congress, 2nd Session, appendix, 211–218 (1847). The quotes are from 211, 214, 217.

12. Greenberg, *Wicked War,* 44–47, 55–60.

13. Ibid., 162–168.

14. Ibid., 229–238.

15. Ibid., 263; Justin Smith, *War,* 2:73.

16. Justin Smith, *War,* 2:280; *LEPOSLP,* June 20, October 5, 1844, January 1, January 25, 1848, November 19, December 5, 1846; Corydon Donnavan, *Adventures in Mexico: Experienced during a Captivity of Seven Months in the Interior* (Cincinnati: Robinson and Jones, 1847), 73; Carlos Maria de Bustamante, entries for December 18, 1846, February 11, 1847, in *Diario histórico de México, 1822–1848,* ed. Josefina Zoraida Vázquez and Héctor Cuauhtémoc Hernández Silva (Mexico City: El Colegio de México / Centro de Investigaciones y Estudios Superiores en Antropología Social, 2003).

17. Justin Smith, *War,* 1:351; *LEPOSLP,* June 15, July 15, July 24, August 10, 1847.

18. Paul Foos, *A Short, Offhand Killing Affair: Soldiers and Social Conflict during the Mexican-American War* (Chapel Hill: University of North Carolina Press, 2002), 5, 8, 64, 68, 80;

Greenberg, *Wicked War*, 190; Justin Smith, *War*, 1:537; Richard Bruce Winders, *Mr. Polk's Army: The American Military Experience in the Mexican War* (College Station: Texas A&M University Press, 1997), 81; Albert Lombard, *"The High Private" with a Full and Exciting History of the New York Volunteers, and the "Mysteries and Miseries" of the Mexican War, in Three Parts—Part First* (New York: Printed for the Publisher, 1848), 9; Streeby, *American Sensations*, 173; George W. Smith and Charles Judah, *The Chronicles of the Gringos: The US Army in the Mexican War, 1846–48: Accounts of Eyewitnesses and Combatants* (Albuquerque: University of New Mexico Press, 1968), 11–12; S. Compton Smith, *Chile con Carne; or, The Camp and the Field* (New York: Miller and Curtis, 1857), 299–310. The recruiting poster cited is displayed in the American Cemetery in Mexico City, and the Blackburn quote is from September 6, 1847, MS A B 628 3, Blackburn Family Papers, FHS.

19. Winders, *Mr. Polk's*, 57–59; Foos, *Short*, 156–158.

20. Greenberg, *Wicked War*, 205; Howe, *What Hath*, 784; Richard Coulter, *Volunteers: The Mexican War Journals of Private Richard Coulter and Sergeant Thomas Barclay*, ed. Allan Peskin (Kent, OH: Kent State University Press, 1991), 92.

21. July 29, 1846, MS A s751 3, Sperry-Gathright Family Papers, FHS; J. Jacob Oswandel, *Notes on the Mexican War, 1846–1848* (Knoxville: University of Tennessee Press, 2010), 285.

22. *Daily Picayune*, June 1, 1847; Zachary Taylor, *Letters of Zachary Taylor from the Battle-Fields of the Mexican War* (Rochester, NY: Genesee, 1908), 75.

23. Theodore Laidley, *Surrounded by Dangers of All Kinds: The Mexican War Letters of Lieutenant Theodore Laidley* (Denton: University of North Texas Press, 1997), 90–91; Greenberg, *Wicked War*, xvii, 151–152; Justin Smith, *War*, 2:63–64; Timothy D. Johnson, *A Gallant Little Army: The Mexico City Campaign* (Lawrence: University of Kansas Press, 2007), 136; Oswandel, *Notes*, 79, 81. Even volunteers already in for the duration were not pleased at the prospect of endless occupation duty. See Coulter, *Volunteers*, 216.

24. Carlos Maria de Bustamante, *El nuevo Bernal Díaz del Castillo* (Mexico City: Instituto Nacional de Estudios Históricos de la Revolución Mexicana-Gobierno del Estado de Puebla, 1994), 2:138–139; LEPOSLP, June 10, July 27, 1847; Mercedes de la Vega and Maria Cecilia Zuleta, *Testimonios de una guerra: México, 1846–1848* (Mexico City: Secretaría de Relaciones Exteriores, 2001), 2:430; Johannsen, *To the Halls*, 46.

25. Peter Guardino, *The Time of Liberty: Popular Political Culture in Oaxaca, 1750–1850* (Durham, NC: Duke University Press, 2005), 75–79, 164–166.

26. See, for instance, the work of Sergio Cañedo Gamboa on independence day celebrations. Sergio Cañedo Gamboa, *Los festejos septembrinos en San Luis Potosí: Protocolo, discurso y transformaciones, 1824–1847* (San Luis Potosí, Mexico: El Colegio de San Luis, 2001), esp. 126–132, 141–143, 148.

27. Vega and Zuleta, *Testimonios,* 1:39, 328, 2:201–202, 235, 242; Manuel Muro Rocha, *Historia de San Luis Potosí* (Mexico City: Sociedad Potosina de Estudios Históricos, 1973), 2:412; Andrés Delgadillo Sánchez, *San Luis de la Patria durante la Guerra contra Estados Unidos de Norteamérica: Identidad nacional, símbolos y héroes patrios, 1846–1848* (San Luis Potosí, Mexico: Editorial Ponciano Arriaga, 2012), 91–102, 177, 181; LEPOSLP, March 29, 1845, March 28, 1846; Impresos, 1847, leg. 3, exp. 7, SGG, AHESLP; Impresos, 1847, leg. 3, exp. 13, SGG, AHESLP; Impresos, 1847, exp. 2, SGG, AHESLP; Impresos, 1847, exp. 6, SGG, AHESLP.

28. Exp. 2493, fol. 40, ADN.

29. Gobernación, Legajo 184, caja 1, exp. 3, AGN; Vega and Zuleta, *Testimonios,* 2:429.

30. Brian Connaughton, "Conjuring the Body Politic from the Corpus Mysticum: the Post-independent Pursuit of Public Opinion in Mexico, 1821–1854," *Americas* 55, no. 3 (January 1999): 459–479.

31. Justicia y Negocios Eclesiásticos, leg. 159, fol. 287, AGN; Ignacio Sampallo, *Sermón político religioso de María Santísima Guadalupe, que predicó en la Santa Iglesia Parroquial de San Luis Potosí, en el día de acción de gracias de la conclusión del novenario llamado de las Flores* (San Luis Potosí, Mexico: M. Escontria, 1847); Gobernación, sin sección, leg. 327, exp. 5, AGN; *La Voz Popular,* August 25, 1847.

32. The San Luis Potosí quote is from LEPOSLP, June 3, 1846, and the Garza y Flores quote is in LEPOSLP, April 11, 1846. See also LEPOSLP, May 9, 1846, May 27, 1847; Impresos, 1847, exp. 1, SGG, AHESLP; Vega and Zuleta, *Testimonios,* 2:235.

33. For examples, see Justicia y Negocios Eclesiásticos, leg. 159, fol. 287, AGN; LEPOSLP, April 11, June 3, October 8, 1846, April 6, 1847; Impresos, 1847, leg. 3, exp. 18, SGG, AHESLP; Impresos, 1847, exp. 2, SGG, AHESLP; Vega and Zuleta, *Testimonios,* 1:361–362, 2:201–202; Manuel Esparza, "El difícil camino de sentirse nación: Oaxaca y la guerra contra Estados Unidos," in *México en Guerra (1846–1848): Perspectivas regionales,* ed. Laura Herrera Serna (Mexico City: Conaculta, Museo Nacional de las Intervenciones, 1997), 507–508; Daniel Molina Alvarez, *La pasión de padre Jarauta* (Mexico City: Gobierno del Distrito Federal, 1999), 143; Armando Quijada Hernández, "Impacto de la guerra de intervención angloamericana en Sonora, 1846–1848," in Herrera Serna, *México en Guerra,* 586; Jaime Sánchez Sánchez, "El territorio tlaxcalteca y la guerra contra Estados Unidos," in Herrera Serna, *México en Guerra,* 638; and Secretaría de Gobierno, Municipios, caja 172, exp. 20, AGEG. For Adame, see LEPOSLP, April 15, 1847, and for Olaguibel, see Vega and Zuleta, *Testimonios,* 1:340, and Maria del Carmen Salinas Sandoval, *Política interna e invasión norteamericana en el Estado de México 1846–1848,* (Zinacantepec, Mexico: El Colegio Mexiquense, 2000), 130.

34. The Ihary quote is from LEPOSLP, January 12, 1847, and the San Luis Potosí quote is from LEPOSLP, October 8, 1846. See also exp. 2474, ADN; exp. 2493, fol. 40, ADN; Gobernación, sin sección, leg. 327, exp. 5, AGN; LEPOSLP, October 8, October 13, November 11, 1846, April 13, May 4, 1847; Impresos, 1847, leg. 3, exp. 18, SGG, AHESLP; Impresos, 1847, leg. 5, SGG, AHESLP; Impresos, 1847, exp. 1, SGG, AHESLP; Impresos, 1847, exp. 2, SGG, AHESLP; Impresos, 1847, exp. 6, SGG, AHESLP; leg. 19, 1847, SGG, AHESLP; Vega and Zuleta, *Testimonios,* 1:328; and Muro Rocha, *Historia,* 2:411–412, 519.

35. LEPOSLP, May 4, 1847; Impresos, 1847, leg. 3, exp. 28, SGG, AHESLP; Impresos, 1847, exp. 1, SGG, AHESLP.

36. See, for instance, the case of Prussia in the Napoleonic wars in Karen Hagemann, "Of 'Manly Valor' and 'German Honor': Nation, War and Masculinity in the Age of the Prussian Uprising against Napoleon," *Central European History* 31, no. 2 (1997): 216.

37. Greenberg, *Manifest Manhood,* 55, 88–91.

38. For a mere sampling of the evidence, see Daniel Harvey Hill, *A Fighter from Way Back: The Mexican War Diary of Lt. Daniel Harvey Hill, 4th Artillery, USA,* ed. Nathaniel Cheairs Hughes Jr. and Timothy D. Johnson (Kent, OH: Kent State University Press, 2002), 3, 28, 61; Tom Reilly, *War with Mexico! America's Reporters Cover the Battlefront* (Lawrence: University of Kansas Press, 2010), 48, 160; Samuel Chamberlain, *My Confession: Recollections of a Rogue* (Austin: Texas State Historical Association, 1996), 176, 178; Greenberg, *Wicked War,* 132; James M. McCaffrey, *Army of Manifest Destiny: The American Soldier in the Mexican War, 1846–1848* (New York: New York University Press, 1992), 123; LEPOSLP, October 22, 1846, July 27, July 29, 1847; exp. 2703, fol. 5, ADN; and John Corey Henshaw, *Recollections of the War with Mexico* (Columbia: University of Missouri Press, 2008), 70–71.

39. The Zacatecas quote is in Impresos, 1847, leg. 3, exp. 18, SGG, AHESLP. See also LEPOSLP, October 13, 1846, April 17, 1847; leg. 22, exp. 15, 1846, SGG, AHESLP; Vega and Zuleta, *Testimonios,* 1:47, 2:235; Jesús Cosamalón Aguilar, "Léperos y yanquis: El control social en la Ciudad de México durante la ocupación norteamericana, 1847–1848," in *Culturas de pobreza y resistencia: Estudios de marginados, proscritos y descontentos, México, 1804–1910,* coord. Romana Falcón (Mexico City: Colegio de México / Universidad Autónoma de Querétaro, 2005), 118.

40. For Santa Anna, see Muro Rocha, *Historia,* 2:507; LEPOSLP, April 6, 1846; and Impresos, 1847, leg. 5, SGG, AHESLP. For more references to rapes, see Vega and Zuleta, *Testimonios,* 1:39; *Mexicanos* (Mexico City: Imprenta de la Calle de Medinas n. 6, September 10, 1847); Impresos, 1847, leg. 3, exp. 28, SGG, AHESLP; Muro Rocha, *Historia,* 2:412, 513; Sampallo, *Sermón político religioso;* Guzmán Urióstegui, "El sur," 349; Impresos, 1847, exp. 2, SGG, AHESLP; Impresos, 1847, exp. 6, SGG, AHESLP; LEPOSLP, November 14, 1846, January 5, April 13, April 29, July 8, 1847; and Delgadillo Sánchez, *San Luis,* 77, 85, 164, 178.

41. Ronald Spores, Irene Huesca, and Manuel Esparza, comps., *Benito Juárez Gobernador de Oaxaca: Documentos de su mandato y servicio público* (Oaxaca, Mexico: Archivo General del Estado de Oaxaca, Serie Documentos del Archivo 8, 1987), 24.

42. For virgins, see *La Voz Popular,* August 25, 1847; LEPOSLP, March 9, 1847; leg. 18, 1847, SGG, AHESLP; Jaime Olveda, "Jalisco frente a la invasión norteamericana de 1846–1848," in *México al tiempo de su guerra con los Estados Unidos (1846–1848),* ed. Josefina Zoraida Vázquez (Mexico City: Secretaría de Relaciones Exteriores, El Colegio de México, Fondo de Cultura Económica, 1997), 303; exp. 2493, fol. 40, ADN; and leg. 18, 1847, SGG, AHESLP. For nuns, see Impresos, 1847, exp. 1, SGG, AHESLP. For men forced to watch, see Vega and Zuleta, *Testimonios,* 1:47, and LEPOSLP, November 17, 1846, May 4, January 12, 1847. The quote is from Secretaría de Gobierno, Municipios, caja 83, exp. 8, AGEG.

43. LEPOSLP, October 8, 1846, July 8, 1847.

44. The quote is from LEPOSLP, May 8, 1847. For just a few more of the many examples, see Impresos, 1847, exp. 6, SGG, AHESLP; Vega and Zuleta, *Testimonios,* 1:39; Delgadillo Sánchez, *San Luis,* 73, 182; Muro Rocha, *Historia,* 2:412, 424.

45. LEPOSLP, April 5, 1845, August 1, 1846; Impresos, 1845, leg. 4, exp. 6, SGG, AHESLP.

46. The Zavala quote is from Vega and Zuleta, *Testimonios,* 1:39; the second quote is from LEPOSLP, October 28, 1847; and the satirical quote is from LEPOSLP, January 2, 1847. The bandit quote is from LEPOSLP, January 5, 1847. See also Muro Rocha, *Historia,* 2:496, and Carlos Ruiz Abreu, coord., *Fortificaciones, guerra y defensa de la Ciudad de México (1844, 1847–1848): Documentos para su historia* (Mexico City: Gobierno del Distrito Federal, Secretaría de Cultura, Archivo Histórico del Distrito Federal, 2003), 388–389.

47. LEPOSLP, May 4, 1847. For other classical references, see leg. 12, exp. 51, 1846, SGG, AHESLP, and Ignacio de Mora y Villamil's dialogue with Taylor from Chapter 3.

48. Ruiz Abreu, *Fortificaciones,* 388; Maria Gayón Córdova, *La ocupación yanqui de la ciudad de México, 1847–1848* (Mexico City: Consejo Nacional para la Cultura y las Artes, 1997), 314.

49. Johannsen, *To the Halls,* 292; Horsman, *Race,* 208–228; Tomás Pérez Vejo, *España en el debate público mexicano, 1836–1867: Aportaciones para una historia de la nación* (Mexico City: El Colegio de México, 2008), 162–163.

50. John Pinheiro, *Missionaries of Republicanism: A Religious History of the Mexican-American War* (Oxford: Oxford University Press, 2014), 65; Gene Brack, *Mexico Views Manifest Destiny* (Albuquerque: University of New Mexico Press, 1975), 122; Horsman, *Race,* 184.

51. Gobernación, leg. 220, caja 2, exp. 1, AGN; *LEPOSLP,* October 20, October 2, 1846, May 4, 1847; Maria del Carmen Salinas Sandoval, "El Estado de México durante la Guerra México-Estados Unidos, 1846–1848," in Vázquez, *México al tiempo de su guerra con los Estados Unidos,* 222. The quote is from Bustamante, *El nuevo,* 1:17.

52. Pedro de Ampudia, *Manifiesto del General Ampudia a sus conciudadanos* (Mexico City: Ignacio Cumplido, 1847), 12; *LEPOSLP,* September 28, 1847, October 13, 1846, July 8, 1847; Salinas Sandoval, *Política interna,* 124; Salinas Sandoval, "El Estado de México," 237.

53. *LEPOSLP,* April 11, June 4, November 24, 1846, January 2, April 24, May 15, 1847.

54. Pérez Vejo, *España en el debate público,* 154, 157, 161–162. For examples, see Pedro de Anaya, *El ciudadano Pedro María Anaya, a los gefes, oficiales y soldados del Ejército Permanente, y de la Guardia Nacional* ([Mexico]: Imprenta de la Calle de Santa Clara núm. 23, [1847]), and *LEPOSLP,* May 9, 1846. This view was supported by some people in Spain itself. See *LEPOSLP,* August 15, 1847.

55. It would take an extensive analysis to confirm this, though. Still, see Brack, *Mexico,* 109; Pérez Vejo, *España en el debate público,* 162–164; and Velasco Márquez, *La guerra del 47,* 76.

56. The quote is from *LEPOSLP,* April 11, 1846. See also *LEPOSLP,* April 29, 1847, October 26, 1846; Delgadillo Sánchez, *San Luis,* 69, 180.

57. *LEPOSLP,* May 15, 1847; exp. 2605, fol. 66, ADN; Barbara Corbett, "Race, Class and Nation in Wartime San Luis Potosí" (paper presented at the Latin American Studies Association, Guadalajara, April 17, 1997), 8–9.

58. Brack, *Mexico,* 181; Timothy J. Henderson, *A Glorious Defeat: Mexico and Its War with the United States* (New York: Hill and Wang, 2007), 144–145; *LEPOSLP,* November 11, 1847.

59. Brack, *Mexico,* 46.

60. For the United States, see Eric Foner, *The Story of American Freedom* (New York: W. W. Norton, 1998), 29–31, 47–94. For Mexico, see Peter Guardino, "La identidad nacional y los afromexicanos en el siglo XIX," in *Prácticas Populares, Cultura Política y Poder en México, Siglo XIX,* ed. Brian Connaughton (Mexico City: Universidad Autónoma Metropolitana-Iztapalapa / Juan Pablos, 2008), 267–269.

61. The quote is from Vega and Zuleta, *Testimonios,* 1:39. Bustamante, *El nuevo,* 2:51, 195; Bustamante, entry for May 14, 1847, in *Diario.* See also Brack, *Mexico,* 99, 131; *LEPOSLP,* May 15, June 1, September 29, 1847; Impresos, 1845, exp. 2, SGG, AHESLP; Impresos, 1847, leg. 3, exp. 17, SGG, AHESLP; Impresos, 1847, exp. 6, SGG, AHESLP; leg. 19, exp. 38, 1846, SGG, AHESLP; and James Sanders, *The Vanguard of the Atlantic World: Creating Modernity, Nation, and Democracy in Nineteenth-Century Latin America* (Durham, NC: Duke University Press, 2014), 71.

62. Secretaría de Justicia y Negocios Eclesiásticos, *Invitación dirigida por el Supremo Gobierno Mexicano, al Venerable Cabildo Metropolitano, para el auxilio de las más urgentes necesidades de la República* (Mexico City: Imprenta de Santiago Pérez, 1847), 9–12; Bustamante, *El nuevo,* 1:17; exp. 2605, fol. 66, ADN.

63. The quotes are from LEPOSLP, June 3, 1846, and Bustamante, *El nuevo,* 1:17.

64. LEPOSLP, May 22, 1847; Secretaría de Justicia y Negocios Eclesiásticos, *Invitación dirigida por el Supremo Gobierno Mexicano,* 7; Delgadillo Sánchez, *San Luis,* 83–84; Brack, *Mexico,* 62, 99, 122; Will Fowler, *Santa Anna of Mexico* (Lincoln: University of Nebraska Press, 2007), 273; Rosario Rodríguez Díaz, "Mexico's Vision of Manifest Destiny during the 1847 War," *Journal of Popular Culture* 35, no. 2 (Fall 2001): 46; Velasco Márquez, *La guerra del 47,* 78–79; Sanders, *Vanguard,* 69.

65. Moises González Navarro, "¿Honroso empate?," in *Symposium La Angostura en la Intervención Norteamericana 1846–1848* (Saltillo, Mexico: Secretaría de Educación Pública de Coahuila, 1998), 38; Bustamante, entry for March 3, 1847, in *Diario.*

66. Impresos, 1847, leg. 3, exp. 7, SGG, AHESLP; Delgadillo Sánchez, *San Luis,* 66; Impresos, 1847, exp. 2, SGG, AHESLP; Ayuntamiento, Guerra con los Estados Unidos, vol. 2265, exp. 27, fol. 3, AHDF.

67. References to the Spanish war against the French are nearly innumerable. See, for example, Impresos, 1847, exp. 2, SGG, AHESLP; exp. 2250, fol. 12, ADN; LEPOSLP, April 5, 1845, April 24, 1847.

68. Brian Hamnett, *Roots of Insurgency: Mexican Regions, 1750–1824* (New York: Cambridge University Press, 1986), 26–27, 32–33; Marco Antonio Landavazzo, *La máscara de Fernando VII: Discurso e imaginario monárquicos en una época de crisis, Nueva España, 1808–1822* (Mexico City: El Colegio de México / Universidad Michoacana de San Nicolás de Hidalgo / El Colegio de Michoacán, 2001), 141–152; Peter Guardino, *Peasants, Politics, and the Formation of Mexico's National State: Guerrero, 1800–1857* (Stanford, CA: Stanford University Press, 1996), 61–65.

69. Peter Guardino, "Identity and Nationalism in Mexico: Guerrero, 1780–1840," *Journal of Historical Sociology* 7, no. 3 (September 1994): 314–342; Rosalina Rios Zúñiga, "Popular Uprising and Political Culture in Zacatecas: The Sombrerete Uprisings (1829)," *Hispanic American Historical Review* 87, no. 3 (August 2007): 499–536; Sylvia Arrom, "Popular Politics in Mexico City: The Parián Riot, 1828," *Hispanic American Historical Review* 68, no. 2 (1988): 245–268.

70. Gobernación, sin sección, leg. 323, exp. 3, AGN; Gobernación, sin sección, leg. 324, exp. 1, AGN; Barbara Corbett, "La política potosina y la Guerra con Estados Unidos," in Vázquez, *México al tiempo de su guerra con los Estados Unidos,* 471; Corbett, "Race, Class and Nation," 6–7; leg. 19, exp. 28, 1846, SGG, AHESLP.

71. *LEPOSLP,* October 24, 1846; leg. 19, exp. 7, 1846, SGG, AHESLP; leg. 19, exp. 37, 1846, SGG, AHESLP; leg. 22, exp. 4, 1846, SGG, AHESLP; fols. 1, 5, Foreign Office 203-92, British Public Record Office, London. For William War Duck, see leg. 23, exp. 1, 1846, SGG, AHESLP. For a similar situation in Querétaro, see Archivo de Guerra, leg. 375, fol. 532, AGN.

72. Hill, *Fighter,* 42, 44.

73. William W. Carpenter, *Travels and Adventures in Mexico: In the Course of Journeys of Upward of 2500 Miles, Performed on Foot, Giving an Account of the Manners and Customs of the People, and the Agricultural and Mineral Resources of That Country* (New York: Harper Brothers, 1851), 57, 68, 89–90, 151–152, 173, 203–204. The quote is from 90. For the Querétaro incident, see Reilly, *War,* 238. See also *Encarnacion Prisoners: Comprising an Account of the March of the Kentucky Cavalry from Louisville to the Rio Grande . . .* (Louisville, KY: Prentice and Weissanger, 1848), 49, 53–54, 76, 85.

74. *Léperos* was a term used for the urban poor. Karl Heller, *Alone in Mexico: The Astonishing Travels of Karl Heller, 1845–1848,* ed. and trans. Terry Rugeley (Tuscaloosa: University of Alabama Press, 2007), 141; fol. 82, Foreign Office 203-92, British Public Record Office. See also Archivo de Guerra, leg. 375, fols. 531–536, AGN.

75. Timothy Johnson, *Gallant,* 16.

76. Irving Levinson, *Wars within War: Mexican Guerrillas, Domestic Elites and the United States of America, 1846–1848* (Fort Worth: Texas Christian University Press, 2005), 21, 41, 66–67; Laidley, *Surrounded,* 76; Henshaw, *Recollections,* 112.

77. Timothy Johnson, *Gallant,* 16–17; Pedro Santoni, "The Civilian Experience in Mexico during the War with the United States, 1846–1848," in *Civilians in Wartime Latin America: From the Wars of Independence to the Central American Civil Wars,* ed. Pedro Santoni (Westport, CT: Greenwood, 2008), 58–59; C. M. Reeves, "Five Years Experience in the Regular Army, including the War with Mexico," manuscript, MS qr332f RMV, CHSL (hereafter cited as Reeves Manuscript), 223; Oswandel, *Notes,* 53–56, 220; George Ballentine, *Autobiography of an English Soldier in the United States Army* (Chicago: Lakeside, 1986), 226–227. For cases in which military authorities punished American troops for crimes against civilians, see EE542, EE546, EE552, RG 153, NA; Timothy Johnson, *Gallant,* 109–110.

78. John Pinheiro, "Crusade and Conquest: Anti-Catholicism, Manifest Destiny, and the U.S.-Mexican War of 1846–48" (PhD diss., University of Tennessee, Knoxville, 2001), 53, 71–72, 145, 191–192; Pletcher, *Diplomacy,* 495; Timothy Johnson, *Gallant,* 59; Levinson, *Wars,* 70–71; *LEPOSLP,* June 3, 1847.

79. Pinheiro, "Crusade," 197–199; Pinheiro, *Missionaries,* 106; Ballentine, *Autobiography,* 227–229. The Barclay quote is from Coulter, *Volunteers,* 100.

80. José María Roa Bárcena, *Recuerdos de la invasión norteamericana (1846–1849)* (Xalapa, Mexico: Universidad Veracruzana, 1986), 240; Bustamante, *El nuevo,* 2:172; and the anonymous letter from Puebla in LEPOSLP, June 24, 1847. Justin Smith claimed that church leaders came to trust Scott, but his source for this is none other than the self-promoting and gullible Moses Beach. Justin Smith, *War,* 2:65.

81. Pinheiro, *Missionaries,* 120–121; Timothy Johnson, *Gallant,* 36–37, 255–256, 269; George Wilkins Kendall, *Dispatches from the Mexican War* (Norman: University of Oklahoma Press, 1999), 167. Soldiers claiming that Scott succeeded in protecting civilians tended to be regulars, which is not surprising because discipline in their units was much more strict. Reeves Manuscript, 223; Ballentine, *Autobiography,* 315.

82. For this war and these processes, see Michael Ducey, *A Nation of Villages: Riot and Rebellion in the Mexican Huasteca, 1750–1850* (Tucson: University of Arizona Press, 2004), 23–93, and Juan Ortiz Escamilla, "Los militares veracruzanos al servicio de la nación, 1821–1854," in *Fuerzas militares en Iberoamérica, siglos XVIII y XIX,* ed. Juan Ortiz Escamilla (Mexico City: El Colegio de México, El Colegio de Michoacán y la Universidad Veracruzana, 2005).

83. Conrado Hernández López, "Entre la guerra exterior y los conflictos internos: Las guerrillas en el camino México-Veracruz (1847–1848)," in *Discursos públicos, negociaciones y estrategias de lucha colectiva,* ed. José Alfredo Rangel Silva and Carlos Rubén Ruiz Medrano (San Luis Potosí, Mexico: Colegio de San Luis / Archivo Histórico del Estado de San Luis, 2006), 126; Marcela Terrazas y Basante and Gerardo Gurza Lavalle, *Las relaciones México-Estados Unidos, 1756–2010,* vol. 1, *Imperios, repúblicas y pueblos en pugna por el territorio, 1756–1867* (Mexico City: Universidad Nacional Autónoma de México / Secretaría de Relaciones Exteriores, 2012), 272.

84. Tomás Calvillo Unna and María Isabel Monroy Castillo, "San Luis Potosí: Entre el Ejército Nacional y la Guerrilla (1846–1848)," in Josefina Zoraida Vázquez et al., *La guerra entre México y Estados Unidos, 1846–1848: Cuatro miradas* (San Luis Potosí, Mexico: El Colegio de San Luis, 1998), 39–40; Hernández López, "Entre la guerra," 128–129, 146; Henderson, *Glorious Defeat,* 172.

85. Hernández López, "Entre la guerra," 127; Juan Ortiz Escamilla, "Michoacán: Federalismo e Intervención Norteamericana," in Vázquez, *México al tiempo de su guerra con los Estados Unidos,* 319; Gerardo Sánchez Díaz, "Michoacán frente a la intervención norteamericana, 1847–1848," in Herrera Serna, *México en Guerra,* 398; Donnavan, *Adventures,* 71–72; LEPOSLP, May 4, May 6, May 11, 1847; Hernández López, "Entre la guerra," 42–43; Impresos, 1847, leg. 3, exp. 17, SGG, AHESLP; Salinas Sandoval, "El Estado de México," 224; Salinas Sandoval, *Política interna,* 50.

86. Leg. 19, leg. 15, 1847, SGG, AHESLP.

87. Octavio Herrera Pérez, "Tamaulipas ante la guerra de la Invasión Norteamericana," in Vázquez, *México al tiempo de su guerra con los Estados Unidos,* 545; Muro Rocha, *Historia,* 2:478–482.

88. *Apuntes para la historia de la guerra entre México y los Estados Unidos* (Mexico City: Consejo Nacional para la Cultura y las Artes, 1991), 236; Ayuntamiento, Guerra con los Estados Unidos, vol. 2265, exp. 21, AHDF; exp. 2605, fol. 49, ADN.

89. Levinson, *Wars,* 34–36; Hernández López, "Entre la guerra," 132–133; Vega and Zuleta, *Testimonios,* 1:44–45, 47; Gobernación, leg. 333, exp. 3, AGN; exp. 2582, ADN.

90. *LEPOSLP,* May 25, 1847; Maria Isabel Monroy and Tomás Calvillo Unna, *Breve historia de San Luis Potosí* (Mexico City: El Colegio de México / Fideicomiso Historia de las Américas / Fondo de Cultura Económica, 1997), 176. For other examples of landowners organizing guerrillas, see leg. 10, 1847, SGG, AHESLP, and Ortiz Escamilla, "Los militares veracruzanos," 263.

91. The Rebolledo quote is from exp. 2581, fol. 151, ADN. See also exp. 2554, fols. 2–4, 21, ADN; Vega and Zuleta, *Testimonios,* 1:429; José Daniel Ramírez Reyes, "Veracruz y las guerrillas del Camino Nacional durante la Invasión Norteamericana en 1847–1848" (unpublished manuscript, Universidad Autónoma Metropolitana, n.d.), 3, 127; leg. 19, leg. 20, 1847, SGG, AHESLP.

92. For the deserters, see leg. 18, 1847, SGG, AHESLP. On Humphrey, see exp. 2582, fol. 57, ADN, and Levinson, *Wars,* 35–36.

93. See Justicia y Negocios Eclesiásticos, leg. 16, fol. 83, AGN; Muro Rocha, *Historia,* 2:540–541; Ramírez Reyes, "Veracruz y las guerrillas," 154; Levinson, *Wars,* 39, 69, 87; and, especially, Molina Alvarez, *La pasión.*

94. Timothy Johnson, *Gallant,* 116–118, 137–138, 140–141, 147; Ramírez Reyes, "Veracruz y las guerrillas," 114, 116–119, 130–131; Reilly, *War,* 140–141, 236; Journal of Surgeon and Brevet Brigadier General Madison Mills, 55–58, 60, MS A M657, FHS; exp. 2554, fol. 25, ADN; exp. 2581, fols. 138–139, 151, ADN. The quotes about the June 1847 attack are from EE518, RG 153, NA. See also *LEPOSLP,* June 26, 1846.

95. The quote is from Oswandel, *Notes,* 99. See also Oswandel, *Notes,* 113, and Muro Rocha, *Historia,* 2:590–592.

96. Ramírez Reyes, "Veracruz y las guerrillas," 4; Timothy Johnson, *Gallant,* 139–40, 147, 246; exp. 2550, fol. 2, ADN; August 10, 1847, Ross Wilkins Papers, Burton Historical Collection, Detroit Public Library.

97. Mariano Riva Palacio, "Breve diario de don Mariano Riva Palacio (agosto de 1847)," ed. Josefina Vázquez, *Historia Mexicana* 47, no. 2 (October–December 1997): 452. For reports of distant guerrilla victories, see *LEPOSLP,* June 22, August 5, September 14, 1847.

98. Carmen Blázquez Domínguez, "Veracruz: Restablecimiento del federalismo e intervención norteamericana," in Vázquez, *México al tiempo de su guerra con los Estados Unidos,* 574; Hernández López, "Entre la guerra," 135; exp. 2581, fols. 179–181, ADN; Timothy Johnson, *Gallant,* 134, 137, 251–252; Gobernación, leg. 355, exp. 5, AGN; leg. 19, leg. 18, leg. 23, 1847, SGG, AHESLP; exp. 2726, fols. 6–7, ADN; exp. 2627, fol. 2, ADN.

99. Exp. 2565, fol. 109, ADN.

100. Exp. 2581, fols. 138–139, ADN.

101. *Apuntes para la historia de la guerra,* 439; Bustamante, *El nuevo,* 2:176.

102. Levinson, *Wars,* 114–118, 123–124.

CHAPTER 6 · The Yankees Died Like Ants

1. Leg. 16, 1847, SGG, AHESLP; El Cronista Mexicano, *La feliz aparición* El Cronista Mexicano, *La feliz aparición del 19 de mayo del corriente año* (Mexico City: Imprenta de Mariano Arévalo, 1847); *Alcance al número 41 de la Nueva Era,* May 28, 1847.

2. *LEPOSLP,* January 1, 1848; Justin Smith, *The War with Mexico* (Gloucester, MA: Peter Smith 1963), 2:68.

3. See, for instance, *La Nueva Era Constitucional,* August 28, 1847.

4. *Apuntes para la historia de la guerra entre México y los Estados Unidos* (Mexico City: Consejo Nacional para la Cultura y las Artes, 1991), 261; exp. 2602, fol. 39, ADN; Alonso García Chávez, "Las Memorias del General Andrés Terrés y Masaguera (1784–1850): Edición crítica y paleografía" (tesina de licenciatura, Universidad Nacional Autónoma de México, Facultad de Filosofía y Letras, 1997), 92.

5. Ayuntamiento, Guerra con los Estados Unidos, vol. 2265, exp. 21, AHDF.

6. Gobernación, leg. 183, caja 1, exp. 4, AGN.

7. Peter Guardino, *Peasants, Politics, and the Formation of Mexico's National State: Guerrero, 1800–1857* (Stanford, CA: Stanford University Press, 1996), 110–146.

8. Ibid., 147–177.

9. For a list of the units with Alvarez, see exp. 2503, fol. 13, ADN. See also exp. 2505, fols. 18–19, 69, ADN.

10. Exp. 2547, fols. 16–28, ADN. Ovando's statement is on fol. 28.

11. Exp. 2602, fols. 70–71, ADN.

12. Benjamin Smith, *The Roots of Conservatism in Mexico: Catholicism, Society and Politics in the Mixteca Baja, 1750–1962* (Albuquerque: University of New Mexico Press, 2012), 75–141.

13. Raúl Jiménez Lescas, "Los michoacanos ante la guerra de conquista," in Raúl Jiménez Lescas and James D. Cockroft, *Michoacanos e irlandeses en la Guerra Anti-imperialista, 1846–1848,* (Morelia, Mexico: Secretaría de Desarrollo Social / Escuela Nacional para Trabajadores, 2006), 19, 63–64. The quote is from exp. 2591, fol. 186, ADN.

14. *Apuntes para la historia de la guerra,* 261. See in general ibid., 261–269.

15. Ayuntamiento, Guerra con los Estados Unidos, Vol. 2264, exp. 4, AHDF.

16. Ibid.; Antonio López de Santa Anna, *Detalle de las operaciones ocurridas en la defensa de la Capital de la República atacada por el ejército de los Estados Unidos del Norte en el año de 1847* (Mexico City: Imprenta de Ignacio Cumplido, 1848), 9–10; Gobernación, sin sección, leg. 330, exp. 22, AGN; Ayuntamiento, Policia Seguridad, vol. 3690, exp. 74, AHDF; Justin Smith, *War,* 2:87; Elecciones Federales, vol. 873, exp. 15, AHDF; José María Roa Bárcena, *Recuerdos de la invasión norteamericana (1846–1849)* (Xalapa, Mexico: Universidad Veracruzana, 1986), 514–515; Maria Gayón Córdova, *La ocupación yanqui de la ciudad de México, 1847–1848* (Mexico City: Consejo Nacional para la Cultura y las Artes, 1997), 62–63, 69; Mariano Riva Palacio, "Breve diario de don Mariano Riva Palacio (agosto de 1847)," ed. Josefina Vázquez, *Historia Mexicana* 47, no. 2 (October–December 1997): 451.

17. Trist made this point to British consular representative Edward Thornton, who was serving as a go-between in an effort to get formal negotiations started. See Reel 76, vol. 210, fol. 26, FO50 Foreign Office Mexico, 1822–1882, British Public Record Office, London. See George Ballentine, *Autobiography of an English Soldier in the United States Army* (Chicago: Lakeside, 1986), 138–140, for a rank-and-file soldier discussing this possibility. For elite fears of famine, bombardment, and social unrest, see Carlos Ruiz Abreu, coord., *Fortificaciones, guerra y defensa de la Ciudad de México (1844, 1847–1848): Documentos para su historia* (Mexico City: Gobierno del Distrito Federal, Secretaría de Cultura, Archivo Histórico del Distrito Federal, 2003), 130–131, 146–147, 408; Ayuntamiento, Guerra con los Estados Unidos, vol. 2265, exp. 24, AHDF; *LEPOSLP,* May 25, 1847; Esteban Sánchez de Tagle, "1847: Un protectorado americano para la ciudad de México," *Relaciones* 86, no. 22 (Spring 2001): 213; Actas de Cabildo Secretas, vol. 300-A, April 12, May 20, August 5, 1847, AHDF; Gayón Córdova, *La ocupación,* 62–63; Pedro Santoni, *Mexicans at Arms: Puro Federalists and the Politics of War, 1845–1848* (Fort Worth: Texas Christian University Press, 1996), 207; Justin Smith, *War,* 2:81.

18. Ruiz Abreu, *Fortificaciones,* 130–131, 146–147.

19. Ibid., 62, 130, 148, 408; *Apuntes para la historia de la guerra,* 258–259; Roa Bárcena, *Recuerdos,* 515.

20. Ruiz Abreu, *Fortificaciones,* 72; Ayuntamiento, Guerra con los Estados Unidos, vol. 2265, exp. 24, AHDF.

21. Ruiz Abreu, *Fortificaciones,* 6–7, 133, 190, 203.

22. Ibid., 6–7, 84, 100–101, 108, 112, 117, 124, 133, 135, 156, 164, 172, 175, 180, 190–191, 195, 203, 205, 228–229, 250, 264; Municipalidades, San Angel, Milicia Cívica, caja 167, exp. 19, AHDF.

23. Ruiz Abreu, *Fortificaciones,* 228–229.

24. Santa Anna, *Detalle,* 9–11.

25. Daniel Harvey Hill, *A Fighter from Way Back: The Mexican War Diary of Lt. Daniel Harvey Hill, 4th Artillery, USA,* ed. Nathaniel Cheairs Hughes Jr. and Timothy D. Johnson (Kent, OH: Kent State University Press, 2002), 173–174; John Corey Henshaw, *Recollections of the War* (Columbia: University of Missouri Press, 2008), 175; Roa Bárcena, *Recuerdos,* 316.

26. Timothy D. Johnson, *A Gallant Little Army: The Mexico City Campaign* (Lawrence: University of Kansas Press, 2007), 153–157; Roa Bárcena, *Recuerdos,* 319.

27. Santa Anna, *Detalle,* 11–12.

28. The account of the Battle of Padierna here is based on various sources, especially the very coherent and detailed account in Johnson, *Gallant,* 158–176, as well as the published accounts of Gabriel Valencia, *Detalle de las acciones de los días 19 y 20 en los campos de Padierna y otros pormenores recientemente comunicados por personas fidedignas* (Morelia, Mexico: Ignacio Arango, 1847), and Santa Anna, *Detalle,* 11–14. See also Frederick Zeh, *An Immigrant Soldier in the Mexican War* (College Station: Texas A&M University Press, 1995), 61–68; Henshaw, *Recollections,* 160–162.

29. Roa Bárcena, *Recuerdos,* 353.

30. For this description of Churubusco, Johnson, *Gallant,* 179–193, was again helpful, as was Roa Bárcena, *Recuerdos,* 346–374. The quote about Americans dying like ants is from Gayón Córdova, *La ocupación,* 85. See also Henshaw, *Recollections,* 163–164; C. M. Reeves, "Five Years Experience in the Regular Army, including the War with Mexico," manuscript, MS qR332f RMV, CHSL (hereafter cited as Reeves Manuscript), 304–305, 313; *Apuntes para la historia de la guerra,* 300–306; and Santa Anna, *Detalle,* 15.

31. Roa Bárcena, *Recuerdos,* 363; Jorge Belarmino, *Cuestión de sangre* (Mexico City: Planeta, 2008), 234.

32. Exp. 2505, fols. 18–19, ADN; exp. 2547, fols. 16–19, ADN; Roa Bárcena, *Recuerdos,* 363; *Apuntes para la historia de la guerra,* 306; Jesús Guzmán Urióstegui, "El sur ante la presencia norteamericana (1846–1847): Juan Alvarez y la guerra," in *México en Guerra (1846–1848): Perspectivas regionales,* ed. Laura Herrera Serna (Mexico City: Conaculta, Museo Nacional de las Intervenciones, 1997), 356.

33. Luis Fernando Granados, "Diez tipos (a medias) reales en busca de uno ideal: Liberales plebeyos de la Ciudad de México en la primera mitad del siglo XIX," in *Disidencia y disidentes en la Historia de México,* ed. Felipe Castro and Marcela Terrazas (Mexico City: Universidad Nacional Autónoma de México, 2003), 198; Roa Bárcena, *Recuerdos,* 363, 374; *Apuntes para la historia de la guerra,* 302; Vicente Quirarte, "Tiempo de canallas, héroes y artistas: El imaginario de la guerra entre México y Estados Unidos," in Herrera Serna, *México en Guerra,* 64, 71; Perfecto Falcón, "La gloriosa jornada de Churubusco relatada por un superviviente," in *Batalla de Churubusco: El 20 de agosto de 1847* (Mexico City: Departamento del Distrito Federal, 1983), 117–123.

34. Some san patricios were foreigners who had never served in the U.S. Army, and some were even Mexicans. Michael Hogan, *The Irish Soldiers of Mexico* (Guadalajara, Mexico: Fondo Editorial Universitario, 1997), 57–58; Robert Ryal Miller, *Shamrock and Sword: The Saint Patrick's Battalion in the U.S. Mexican War* (Norman: University of Oklahoma Press, 1989), 34.

35. Reeves Manuscript, 315; *Apuntes para la historia de la guerra,* 306; Laura Herrera Serna, "Ficción y realidad del Batallón de San Patricio," *Bicentenario* 1, no. 2 (September 2008): 22; Miller, *Shamrock,* 89; Ballentine, *Autobiography,* 285–286.

36. The novels are Patricia Cox, *Batallón de San Patricio* (Mexico City: San Jerónimo Editores, 1999), and James Alexander Thom, *St. Patrick's Battalion* (New York: Ballentine, 2006). The movie is *One Man's Hero* (1999), directed by Lance Hool, and the album is *San Patricio* (2010), which also includes the collaboration of Linda Ronstadt, Lila Downs, and Los Tigres del Norte. Books by academic historians include Miller, *Shamrock,* and Dennis J. Wynn, *The San Patricio Soldiers: Mexico's Foreign Legion* (El Paso: Texas Western, 1984). Popular histories of value and note include Peter Stevens, *The Rogue's March: John Riley and the St. Patrick's Battalion 1846–1848* (Washington, DC: Brassey's, 1999); Hogan, *Irish;* and Belarmino, *Cuestión.*

37. These patterns are discernible in the invaluable research that Robert Ryal Miller conducted on the san patricios. See Miller, *Shamrock,* especially the appendix. Also see Reeves Manuscript, 114; LEPOSLP, April 18, 1846; and Stevens, *Rogue's March,* 112, 130.

38. George McClellan, *The Mexican War Diary and Correspondence of George B. McClellan,* ed. Thomas Cutrer (Baton Rouge: Louisiana State University Press, 2009), 26; Hogan, *Irish,* 133, 137–138; Stevens, *Rogue's March,* 54, 64–65, 173; Johnson, *Gallant,* 136.

39. Reeves Manuscript, 114.

40. See, for instance, leg. 10, leg. 22, 1847, SGG, AHESLP; Miller, *Shamrock,* 67; exp. 2176, fols. 83–88, ADN; and *Apuntes para la historia de la guerra,* 251.

41. Miller, *Shamrock,* 17; Robert Ryal Miller, "Los San Patricios en la guerra de 1847," *Historia Mexicana* 47, no. 2 (1997): 346; Stevens, *Rogue's March,* 82.

42. Stevens, *Rogue's March,* 107.

43. See Pedro de Ampudia, broadside, September 15, 1846, exp. 2250, fol. 18, ADN; Miller, *Shamrock,* 46; Stevens, *Rogue's March,* 140–141, 147.

44. Journal of Surgeon and Brevet Brigadier General Madison Mills, November 28, 1846, MS A M657, FHS.

45. Miller, *Shamrock,* 66; exp. 2505, fol. 86, ADN; exp. 2508, fol. 24, ADN. I am indebted to Kerry MacDonald for the translation.

46. For Soto, see Paul Foos, *A Short, Offhand Killing Affair: Soldiers and Social Conflict during the Mexican-American War* (Chapel Hill: University of North Carolina Press, 2002), 106. For Riley, see Stevens, *Rogue's March,* 232–233. For Santa Anna, see Stevens, *Rogue's March,* 221–222.

47. Hogan, *Irish,* 144–145; Agustín Franco, *Alegato de defensa que ante un consejo de guerra de oficiales del ejército de los Estados-Unidos del Norte, pronunció el licenciado Agustín Franco el día 14 de febrero de 1848* (Toluca, Mexico: Reimpreso por Manuel R. Gallo, 1848); Johnson, *Gallant,* 136; Belarmino, *Cuestión,* 215–216; Stevens, *Rogue's March,* 223, 227; EE547, EE548, EE549, EE550, RG 153, NA.

48. Ballentine, *Autobiography,* 235; Johnson, *Gallant,* 135; Carlos Martínez Assad, "Los lagartos durante la intervención de los Estados Unidos en Tabasco," in *México al tiempo de su guerra con los Estados Unidos (1846–1848),* ed. Josefina Zoraida Vázquez (Mexico City: Secretaría de Relaciones Exteriores, El Colegio de México, Fondo de Cultura Económica, 1997), 518; exp. 2267, fols. 12–13, ADN; exp. 2281, fol. 18, ADN; exp. 2355, fols. 41–45, ADN; exp. 2456, fols. 1–33, ADN; exp. 2508, fols. 21–27, ADN; exp. 2545, fols. 16–18, ADN; exp. 2554, fol. 74, ADN; *El Liberal Católico,* March 21, 1847.

49. Leg. 32, 1845, SGG, AHESLP; leg. 13, exp. 1, 1846, SGG, AHESLP; leg.1, exp. 5, 1846, SGG, AHESLP; leg. 22, exp. 14, 1846, SGG, AHESLP; leg. 24, exp. 14, 1846, SGG, AHESLP; leg. 24, exp. 39, 1846, SGG, AHESLP; leg. 20, exp. 25, 1846, SGG, AHESLP; leg. 5, leg. 6, leg. 8, 1847, SGG, AHESLP; exp. 2176, fols. 12–22, ADN; exp. 2178, fols. 3–33, ADN; *LEPOSLP,* November 24, 1846; August 1, 1846, exp. 32, STJ, AHESLP; fol. 86, Foreign Office 203-93, British Public Record Office.

50. Exp. 2256, fol. 16, ADN; exp. 2300, fols. 3, 9, 27, ADN; exp. 2307, fols. 1, 6, 8, 11, 12, ADN; exp. 2358, fols. 1, 15, 17, ADN; Archivo de Guerra, leg. 1035, AGN; leg. 19, exp. 2, 1846, SGG, AHESLP; leg. 5, 1847, SGG, AHESLP; fols. 9–11, Foreign Office 203-92, British Public Record Office.

51. Stevens, *Rogue's March,* 40, 97, 156; Manuel Balbontín, *La invasión norteamericana, 1846 a 1849: Apuntes del subteniente de artillería* (Mexico City: Tip de B. A. Esteva, 1883), 23; Hogan, *Irish,* 43; William W. Carpenter, *Travels and Adventures in Mexico: In the Course of Journeys of Upward of 2500 Miles, Performed on Foot, Giving an Account of the Manners*

and Customs of the People, and the Agricultural and Mineral Resources of That Country (New York: Harper Brothers, 1851), 28.

52. Belarmino, *Cuestión,* 193; Herrera Serna, "Ficción y realidad," 20; Balbontín, *La invasión,* 60; Samuel Chamberlain, *My Confession: Recollections of a Rogue* (Austin: Texas State Historical Association, 1996), 161; *National Niles Register,* March 13, 1847; Stevens, *Rogue's March,* 164; Miller, "Los San Patricios," 357; exp. 2445, fol. 1, ADN; exp. 2445, fol. 23, ADN; Carlos Maria de Bustamante, entry for February 2, 1847, in *Diario histórico de México 1822–1848,* ed. Josefina Zoraida Vázquez and Héctor Cuauhtémoc Hernández Silva, (Mexico City: El Colegio de México / Centro de Investigaciones y Estudios Superiores en Antropología Social, 2003).

53. William H. Daniel Military Diary, 62, MS A D184, FHS; Chamberlain, *My Confession,* 171; Isaac Smith, *Reminiscences of a Campaign in Mexico: An Account of the Operations of the Indiana Brigade on the Line of the Rio Grande and Sierra Madre, and a Vindication of the Volunteers against the Aspirations of Officials and Unofficials,* 2nd ed. (Indianapolis: Chapman and Spann, 1848), 78; EE382, RG 153, NA.

54. Carpenter, *Travels,* 28. See also ibid., 100; Foos, *Short,* 107; Stevens, *Rogue's March,* 229; Franklin Smith, *The Mexican War Journal of Captain Franklin Smith* (Jackson: University Press of Mississippi, 1991), 136.

55. Exp. 2456, fol. 23, ADN; fols. 13–15, Foreign Office 203-92, British Public Record Office. The quote is from fol. 8, Foreign Office 203-92-3, British Public Record Office.

56. Leg. 3, leg. 9, leg. 18, leg. 21, leg. 24, 1847, SGG, AHESLP. Apparently there was another such force in Tamaulipas. See leg. 25, 1847, SGG, AHESLP.

57. Miller, *Shamrock,* 74; Archivo de Guerra, leg. 921, no fol, AGN.

58. The quote is from leg. 33, 1847, SGG, AHESLP. See also Miller, *Shamrock,* 24; Foos, *Short,* 6, 109; exp. 2176, fol. 12, ADN; exp. 2178, fol. 20, ADN; and exp. 2344, fol. 19, ADN.

59. The quote is from Hill, *Fighter,* 168. See also ibid., 157; exp. 2307, fol. 4, ADN; fols. 13–15, Foreign Office 203-92, British Public Record Office; fol. 66, Foreign Office 203-93, British Public Record Office.

60. EE531, pp. 106–108, 110–113, 116–118, RG 153, NA.

61. Carpenter, *Travels,* 92, 212–214, 265. The quote is from 213–214.

62. Ibid., 214; Corydon Donnavan, *Adventures in Mexico: Experienced during a Captivity of Seven Months in the Interior* (Cincinnati: Robinson and Jones, 1847), 63; Foos, *Short,* 105; Belarmino, *Cuestión,* 216–217; George Wilkins Kendall, *Dispatches from the Mexican War* (Norman: University of Oklahoma Press, 1999), 238.

63. Carpenter, *Travels,* 99, 100, 102; EE531, RG 153, NA.

64. *LEPOSLP,* July 27, August 24, 1847; Miller, *Shamrock,* 73; Stevens, *Rogue's March,* 230.

65. Fols. 13–15, Foreign Office 203-92, British Public Record Office; fol. 105, Foreign Office 203-93, British Public Record Office; Miller, *Shamrock,* 73–74; Miller, "Los San Patricios," 362; Stevens, *Rogue's March,* 217–218.

66. Miller, "Los San Patricios," 349; Miller, *Shamrock,* 26–29; Stevens, *Rogue's March,* 8–10, 15–17, 26, 32, 92–93.

67. EE531, pp. 145–150, RG 153, NA.

68. Stevens, *Rogue's March,* 284–285. Kendall describes this flag in Kendall, *Dispatches,* 350.

69. EE525, EE531, RG 153, NA.

70. EE525, EE531, RG 153, NA.

71. EE525, RG 153, NA. The quote is from EE531, p. 124, RG 153, NA. For their appeals to the British consul, see fols. 66, 105, 107, Foreign Office 203-93, British Public Record Office.

72. Fol. 105, Foreign Office 203-93, British Public Record Office. See also fol. 107.

73. EE525, pp. 130–131, 156, RG 153, NA.

74. EE525, pp. 177–179, 191, RG 153, NA; EE531, pp. 125–128, RG 153, NA.

75. Foos, *Short,* 104. For O'Connor's words, see Ayuntamiento, Guerra con los Estados Unidos, vol. 2268, exp. 81, fol. 327, AHDF.

76. Franklin Smith, *Mexican War Journal,* 136.

77. Some of the san patricios were apparently killed by American soldiers who refused to accept their surrender when Churubusco fell. James Sanders, *The Vanguard of the Atlantic World: Creating Modernity, Nation, and Democracy in Nineteenth-Century Latin America* (Durham, NC: Duke University Press, 2014), 65; José Fernando Ramírez, *México durante la guerra con Estados Unidos* (Mexico City: Librería de la Viuda de Ch. Bouret, 1905), 298. On the trials and sentences, in addition to the transcripts in EE525 and EE531, RG 153, NA, see Miller, *Shamrock,* 94, 180–181, and Stevens, *Rogue's March,* 247–262.

78. Stevens, *Rogue's March,* 286; Miller, *Shamrock,* 116, 125; Ayuntamiento, Guerra con los Estados Unidos, vol. 2265, exp. 30, fol. 1, AHDF; J. Jacob Oswandel, *Notes on the Mexican War, 1846–1848* (Knoxville: University of Tennessee Press, 2010), 166, 189, 251; Justin Smith, *War,* 2:236; exp. 2699, fols. 4–17, ADN; exp. 2810, fol. 1, ADN.

79. William H. Daniel Military Diary, 62; Carpenter, *Travels,* 262–263; Oswandel, *Notes,* 270, 315; Richard Coulter, *Volunteers: The Mexican War Journals of Private Richard Coulter and Sergeant Thomas Barclay,* ed. Allan Peskin (Kent, OH: Kent State University Press, 1991), 146–147.

80. Reeves Manuscript, 353; Kendall, *Dispatches,* 350.

81. Zeh, *Immigrant Soldier,* 55; Ballentine, *Autobiography,* 285–286, 332–333.

82. *LEPOSLP,* August 12, September 21, 1847, February 11, 1848; *Mexicanos,* (Mexico City: Imprenta de la Calle de Medinas n. 6, September 10, 1847).

83. Sanders, *Vanguard,* 66; *National Niles Register,* March 13, 1847; *Mexicanos;* Miller, "Los San Patricios," 355.

84. Carpenter, *Travels,* quote from 131. See also ibid., 139, 170, and Herrera Serna, "Ficción y realidad," 19–20.

85. Stevens, *Rogue's March,* 278; *Mexicanos; LEPOSLP,* November 16, 1847; Gayón Córdova, *La ocupación,* 193; Sanders, *Vanguard,* 67; Ayuntamiento, Guerra con los Estados Unidos, vol. 2265, exp. 31, fol. 1, AHDF; Ayuntamiento, Guerra con los Estados Unidos, vol. 2268, exp. 80, fols. 276–277, AHDF; Actas de Cabildo Ordinarios, vol. 170-A, May 2, 1848, AHDF. Quote from Hill, *Fighter,* 134. On the escape, see Miller, *Shamrock,* 120–121.

86. Miller, *Shamrock,* 140, 142; Stevens, *Rogue's March,* 289, 292, 293; Sanders, *Vanguard,* 67; Hogan, *Irish,* 205; Herrera Serna, "Ficción y realidad," 24–26; Miller, "Los San Patricios," 372–374; Carpenter, *Travels,* 136, 139. On the coup attempt and subsequent problems of the san patricios, see Miller, *Shamrock,* 132–133, 136–139; exp. 2837, fol. 11, ADN; exp. 2844, fol. 10, ADN; exp. 2848, fols. 1–25, ADN; exp. 2877, fols. 1–17, ADN; fols. 365, 367, 388, Foreign Office 203-93, British Public Record Office.

87. Sanders, *Vanguard,* 67; Stevens, *Rogue's March;* Belarmino, *Cuestión;* Herrera Serna, "Ficción y realidad."

88. Belarmino, *Cuestión,* 8, 48; Foos, *Short,* 108; Herrera Serna, "Ficción y realidad."

89. Peter Guardino, "Gender, Soldiering, and Citizenship in the Mexican-American War of 1846–1848," *American Historical Review* 119, no. 1 (February 2014): 45–46.

CHAPTER 7 · The People of the Town Were Firing

1. José María Roa Bárcena, *Recuerdos de la invasión norteamericana (1846–1849)* (Xalapa, Mexico: Universidad Veracruzana, 1986), 378. Even some very good American military historians have sometimes simply echoed American reports of the number of Mexicans engaged without checking the Mexican sources. See, for example, Timothy D. Johnson, *A Gallant Little Army: The Mexico City Campaign* (Lawrence: University of Kansas Press, 2007), 185, 189.

2. On varying motives for the armistice, see Antonio López de Santa Anna, *Detalle de las operaciones ocurridas en la defensa de la Capital de la República atacada por el ejército de los Estados Unidos del Norte en el año de 1847* (Mexico City: Imprenta de Ignacio Cumplido,

1848), 16; Johnson, *Gallant*, 195–199; Daniel Harvey Hill, *A Fighter from Way Back: The Mexican War Diary of Lt. Daniel Harvey Hill, 4th Artillery, USA*, ed. Nathaniel Cheairs Hughes Jr. and Timothy D. Johnson (Kent, OH: Kent State University Press, 2002), 115, 119; George Ballentine, *Autobiography of an English Soldier in the United States Army* (Chicago: Lakeside, 1986), 289.

3. Johnson, *Gallant*, 200. For a very clear account of the negotiations, see David Pletcher, *The Diplomacy of Annexation: Texas, Oregon, and the Mexican War* (Columbia: University of Missouri Press, 1973), 513–521. For a more detailed account, see Roa Bárcena, *Recuerdos*, 384–408.

4. Exp. 2594, fols. 61–62, ADN; John Corey Henshaw, *Recollections of the War with Mexico* (Columbia: University of Missouri Press, 2008), 166.

5. Exp. 2648, fols. 3–4, ADN. The quote is from *Apuntes para la historia de la guerra entre México y los Estados Unidos* (Mexico City: Consejo Nacional para la Cultura y las Artes, 1991), 322. See also Maria Gayón Córdova, *La ocupación yanqui de la ciudad de México, 1847–1848* (Mexico City: Consejo Nacional para la Cultura y las Artes, 1997), 118; Roa Bárcena, *Recuerdos*, 387; C. M. Reeves, "Five Years Experience in the Regular Army, including the War with Mexico," manuscript, MS QR332f RMV, CHSL (hereafter cited as Reeves Manuscript), 331; Johnson, *Gallant*, 198; Carlos Alberto Reyes Tosqui, "Violencia, oportunismo y resistencia en la Ciudad de México durante la ocupación norteamericana, 1847–1848" (tesis de licenciatura, Escuela Nacional de Antropología e Historia, 2006), 107–108; Esteban Sánchez de Tagle, "1847: Un protectorado americano para la ciudad de México," *Relaciones* 86, no. 22 (Spring 2001): 221; Ethan Allen Hitchcock, *Fifty Years in Camp and Field: Diary of Major General Ethan Allen Hitchcock, USA* (New York: G. P. Putnam's Sons, 1909), 288–289; and George Wilkins Kendall, *Dispatches from the Mexican War* (Norman: University of Oklahoma Press, 1999), 350–351, 356.

6. Johnson, *Gallant*, 201; Roa Bárcena, *Recuerdos*, 407; Actas de Cabildo Secretas, vol. 300-A, August 26, 1847, AHDF; exp. 2651, fols. 2–3, ADN.

7. Ulysses S. Grant, *Personal Memoirs* (Westminster, MD: Random House, 1999), 74.

8. The quote is from Reeves Manuscript, 347. See also ibid., 333–353; Johnson, *Gallant*, 202–209; Ayuntamiento, Militares, Guardia Nacional, vol. 3276, exp. 7, AHDF; Justin Smith, *The War with Mexico* (Gloucester, MA: Peter Smith, 1963), 2:145; Roa Bárcena, *Recuerdos*, 425–453; Henshaw, *Recollections*, 169; Santa Anna, *Detalle*, 23–25; exp. 2612, fol. 1, ADN; Luis Fernando Granados, "Diez tipos (a medias) reales en busca de uno ideal: Liberales plebeyos de la Ciudad de México en la primera mitad del siglo XIX," in *Disidencia y disidentes en la Historia de México*, ed. Felipe Castro and Marcela Terrazas (Mexico City: Universidad Nacional Autónoma de México, 2003), 198; and Hitchcock, *Fifty Years*, 296–298.

9. Accounts of the failure of the Mexican cavalry to act at Molino del Rey are myriad. Alvarez's version is published in Santa Anna, *Detalle,* 38–42, and both it and Andrade's defense can be found in Gobernación, sin sección, leg. 328, exp. 14, AGN. In the end Andrade was absolved on various technicalities. See exp. 2842, fols. 273–277, ADN. See also Carlos Maria de Bustamante, *El nuevo Bernal Díaz del Castillo* (Mexico City: Instituto Nacional de Estudios Históricos de la Revolución Mexicana-Gobierno del Estado de Puebla, 1994), 1:4; José Fernando Ramírez, *México durante la guerra con Estados Unidos* (Mexico City: Librería de la Viuda de Ch. Bouret, 1905), 305–306; Gayón Córdova, *La ocupación,* 146–147; *Apuntes para la historia de la guerra,* 348; and Henshaw, *Recollections,* 167. For the incident in which Andrade's fellow cavalry officers accused him of repeatedly acting as a coward, see Archivo de Guerra, leg. 272, fols. 225–375, AGN. Carlos Maria de Bustamante, who hated Alvarez, also reported as fact Andrade's cowardice and refusal to follow orders. Carlos Maria de Bustamante, entry for September 8, 1847, in *Diario histórico de México, 1822–1848,* ed. Josefina Zoraida Vázquez and Héctor Cuauhtémoc Hernández Silva (Mexico City: El Colegio de México / Centro de Investigaciones y Estudios Superiores en Antropología Social, 2003).

10. Johnson, *Gallant,* 210–214, gives an excellent account of the options and discussions.

11. *Documentos históricos sobre la defensa de Chapultepec* (Mexico City: Archivo General de la Nación, 1999), 28–62; Nicolás Bravo, *Parte del general Bravo al ministro de la guerra sobre los sucesos ocorridos los dias 12 y 13 del actual: En la accion de Chapultepec* (Mexico City: Imprenta de Vincente Garcia Torres, 1847); Santa Anna, *Detalle,* 26–27; Roa Bárcena, *Recuerdos,* 469, 471, 481; Justin Smith, *War,* 2:152.

12. Johnson, *Gallant,* 218–225, provides an excellent account synthesizing the American sources. For the other side, see Bravo, *Parte del general Bravo; Documentos históricos sobre la defensa de Chapultepec,* 48–52; Roa Bárcena, *Recuerdos,* 459–487; R. S. Ripley, *War with Mexico* (New York: Harper and Brothers, 1849), 2:423–424; and Richard Coulter, *Volunteers: The Mexican War Journals of Private Richard Coulter and Sergeant Thomas Barclay,* ed. Allan Peskin (Kent, OH: Kent State University Press, 1991), 168–172. On the Niños Héroes, see Michael Van Wagenen, *Remembering the Forgotten War: The Enduring Legacies of the U.S.-Mexican War* (Amherst: University of Massachusetts Press, 2012), 47–49, 87–88; Vicente Quirarte, "Tiempo de canallas, héroes y artistas: El imaginario de la guerra entre México y Estados Unidos," in *México en Guerra (1846–1848): Perspectivas regionales,* ed. Laura Herrera Serna (Mexico City: Conaculta, Museo Nacional de las Intervenciones, 1997), 59; William A. De Paulo Jr., *The Mexican National Army, 1822–1852* (College Station: Texas A&M University Press, 1997), 138; and Archivo de Guerra, leg. 155, fols. 260–285, AGN.

13. Roa Bárcena, *Recuerdos,* 496–502; Reeves Manuscript, 366–372; Ripley, *War,* 2:438–439; Grant, *Personal Memoirs,* 77; Santa Anna, *Detalle,* 31–32.

14. Later Terrés wrote his memoirs, which begin with his boyhood and describe his many years of adventures. The section on the defense of the Belén gate is Alonso García Chávez, "Las Memorias del General Andrés Terrés y Masaguera (1784–1850): Edición crítica y paleografía" (tesina de licenciatura, Universidad Nacional Autónoma de México, Facultad de Filosofía y Letras, 1997), 93–97. See also Gayón Córdova, *La ocupación,* 204; Roa Bárcena, *Recuerdos,* 491–495; Ripley, *War,* 2:434–436; Johnson, *Gallant,* 230–232; Justin Smith, *War,* 2:159–160; Gobernación, sin sección, leg. 342, exp. 3, AGN; Coulter, *Volunteers,* 173–174; Santa Anna, *Detalle,* 29–30; and Hill, *Fighter,* 126–128.

15. Henshaw, *Recollections,* 172; Reeves Manuscript, 375.

16. Raúl Jiménez Lescas, "Los michoacanos ante la guerra de conquista," in Raúl Jiménez Lescas and James D. Cockroft, *Michoacanos e irlandeses en la Guerra Antiimperialista, 1846–1848* (Morelia, Mexico: Secretaría de Desarrollo Social / Escuela Nacional para Trabajadores, 2006), 57; Santa Anna, *Detalle,* 32–33.

17. Archivo de Guerra, vol. 155, fols. 260–285, AGN; Gobernación, sin sección, leg. 342, exp. 2, AGN; Archivo de Guerra, leg. 154, fol. 111, AGN; *Apuntes para la historia de la guerra,* 375.

18. *Apuntes para la historia de la guerra,* 384, 388–390; Roa Bárcena, *Recuerdos,* 516–519; Archivo de Guerra, leg. 273, fol. 329, AGN.

19. The same was true of soldiers who had to storm a fort. For this feature of early modern political culture, see Ballentine, *Autobiography,* 138–140, 289; Henshaw, *Recollections,* 60; Geoffrey Best, *War and Society in Revolutionary Europe, 1770–1870* (Buffalo, NY: McGill-Queen's University Press, 1998), 100–102; Richard Holmes, *Redcoat: The British Soldier in the Age of Horse and Musket* (New York: W. W. Norton, 2002), 381, 390–391; Wayne E. Lee, *Barbarians and Brothers: Anglo-American Warfare, 1500–1865* (New York: Oxford University Press, 2011), 33; Embajada de España en Washington, caja 54 / 7918, leg. 543, AGA; Archivo de Guerra, leg. 921, no fol., AGN; and Winfield Scott, *Memoirs of Lieut.-General Scott, LL.D, Written by Himself* (New York: Sheldon, 1864), 2:424.

20. Ayuntamiento, Guerra con los Estados Unidos, vol. 2268, exp. 76, fol. 131, AHDF; Actas de Cabildo Secretas, vol. 300-A, September 13, 1847, AHDF.

21. *Apuntes para la historia de la guerra,* 375–376; Gayón Córdova, *La ocupación,* 258, 268; Antonio García Cubas, *El libro de mis recuerdos: Narraciones históricas, anecdóticas y de costumbres mexicanas, anteriores al actual estado social, ilustrada con más de trescientos fotograbados* (Mexico City: Imprenta de Arturo García Cubas, 1904), 435; Bustamante, entry for September 14, 1847, in *Diario;* Luis Fernando Granados, *Sueñan las piedras: Alzamiento ocurrido en la ciudad de México, 14, 15 y 16 de septiembre de 1847* (Mexico City: Ediciones Era / Consejo Nacional para la Cultura y las Artes / Instituto Nacional de Antropología e Historia, 2003), 47.

22. Brough's testimony is in EE517, RG 153, NA. The testimonies of Callejo and Andonagui are in Archivo de Guerra, leg. 274, fols. 323, 326, AGN. See also *Apuntes para la historia de*

la guerra, 377–378, and Guillermo Prieto, *Memorias de mis tiempos* (Mexico City: Editorial Porrua, 1996), 275.

23. Embajada de España en Washington, caja 54 / 7918, leg. 543, AGA.

24. Henshaw, *Recollections,* 174; Hill, *Fighter,* 128; Roa Bárcena, *Recuerdos,* 510; Granados, *Sueñan las piedras,* 87; Justin Smith, *War,* 2:168.

25. Gayón Córdova, *La ocupación,* 259; *Apuntes para la historia de la guerra,* 379–381; Roa Bárcena, *Recuerdos,* 510; Justin Smith, *War,* 2:168.

26. The Hitchcock quote is from Hitchcock, *Fifty Years,* 305. The Hill quote is from Hill, *Fighter,* 128. See also Hill, *Fighter,* 128; *Apuntes para la historia de la guerra,* 378; Henshaw, *Recollections,* 174; Gayón Córdova, *La ocupación,* 249, 253; Juan de la Granja, *Epistolario: Con un estudio biográfico preliminar por Luis Castillo Ledón y notas de Neréo Rodríguez Barragán,* (Mexico City: Talleres Gráficos del Museo Nacional de Arqueología, Historia y Etnografía, 1937), 175–176; George McClellan, *The Mexican War Diary and Correspondence of George B. McClellan,* ed. Thomas Cutrer (Baton Rouge: Louisiana State University Press, 2009), 111; Johnson, *Gallant,* 241; Ripley, *War,* 2:444; and Ayuntamiento, Guerra con los Estados Unidos, vol. 2268, exp. 77, fols. 153–154, 156, 158, 161, 184, 191, AHDF.

27. Gayón Córdova, *La ocupación,* 253–254; Hitchcock, *Fifty Years,* 306; Ayuntamiento, Guerra con los Estados Unidos, vol. 2265, exp. 28, fols. 21, 26–30, AHDF.

28. Sánchez de Tagle, "1847," 218; Mercedes de la Vega and Maria Cecilia Zuleta, *Testimonios de una guerra: México, 1846–1848* (Mexico City: Secretaría de Relaciones Exteriores, 2001), 1:265.

29. Ayuntamiento, Guerra con los Estados Unidos, vol. 2264, exp. 11, AHDF; Ayuntamiento, Guerra con los Estados Unidos, vol. 2265, exp. 21, AHDF; Ayuntamiento, Guerra con los Estados Unidos, vol. 2267, exp. 1, fol. 18, AHDF; Ayuntamiento, Guerra con los Estados Unidos, vol. 2268, exp. 70, fols. 1–3, 7, AHDF.

30. See, for example, Sánchez de Tagle, "1847," 221.

31. Ayuntamiento, Guerra con los Estados Unidos, vol. 2267, exp. 58, fol. 420, AHDF; Gayón Córdova, *La ocupación,* 153; García Cubas, *El libro,* 432.

32. Karl Heller, *Alone in Mexico: The Astonishing Travels of Karl Heller, 1845–1848,* ed. and trans. Terry Rugeley (Tuscaloosa: University of Alabama Press, 2007), 141.

33. Carlos Ruiz Abreu, coord., *Fortificaciones, guerra y defensa de la Ciudad de México (1844, 1847–1848): Documentos para su historia* (Mexico City: Gobierno del Distrito Federal, Secretaría de Cultura, Archivo Histórico del Distrito Federal, 2003), 388.

34. The broadside is in Ayuntamiento, Guerra con los Estados Unidos, vol. 2265, exp. 28, fol. 5, AHDF. The government argument that the Americans might steal the

image of Guadalupe actually repeated what Archbishop Juan Manuel Irizarri y Peralta had said in an earlier broadside from early August. Juan Manuel Irizarri y Peralta, *Pastoral del Illmo. Sr. arzobispo de Cesarea, sobre la guerra* ([Mexico City]: Imprenta de la calle de Medinas numero 6., [1847]). For other evidence of fears about what Americans might do with the image, see Justicia y Negocios Eclesiásticos, leg. 160, fols. 5–6, AGN, and *LEPOSLP,* August 17, 1847.

35. Ayuntamiento, Guerra con los Estados Unidos, vol. 2265, exp. 27, fol. 3, AHDF. This message may have been influenced by a very similar message that Prussian king Frederick Wilhelm had issued during the Napoleonic Wars. For that letter, see Best, *War,* 296.

36. For the request of the women, see exp. 2668, fol. 11, ADN. For the stones thrown at the teamsters, see Hitchcock, *Fifty Years,* 288.

37. Sánchez de Tagle, "1847," 222; Actas de Cabildo Secretas, vol. 300-A, August 9, 1847, AHDF; Ayuntamiento, Guerra con los Estados Unidos, vol. 2264, exp. 5, AHDF; Gayón Córdova, *La ocupación,* 105, 140; Prieto, *Memorias,* 275; Granados, *Sueñan las piedras,* 29; Ripley, *War,* 2:442; Ayuntamiento, Guerra con los Estados Unidos, vol. 2265, exp. 27, fols. 19–20, 23–24, 32, 36–43, AHDF; Ayuntamiento, Guerra con los Estados Unidos, vol. 2265, exp. 28, fol. 12, AHDF.

38. Granados, *Sueñan las piedras,* 19, 52, 88.

39. Henshaw, *Recollections,* 173. For other uses of the term by witnesses, see Archivo de Guerra, leg. 273, fol. 359, AGN; Gayón Córdova, *La ocupación,* 271; Prieto, *Memorias,* 275; and George W. Smith and Charles Judah, *The Chronicles of the Gringos: The US Army in the Mexican War, 1846–48: Accounts of Eyewitnesses and Combatants* (Albuquerque: University of New Mexico Press, 1968), 266.

40. Roa Bárcena, *Recuerdos,* 507; *Apuntes para la historia de la guerra,* 375–376; Gayón Córdova, *La ocupación,* 249, 275–276; García Cubas, *El libro,* 436; George Smith and Charles Judah, *Chronicles,* 266; Granados, *Sueñan las piedras,* 32.

41. Archivo de Guerra, leg. 274, fols. 224, 308–374, AGN.

42. Archivo de Guerra, leg. 273, fol. 359, AGN; Gayón Córdova, *La ocupación,* 258; Granados, *Sueñan las piedras,* 105.

43. Gayón Córdova, *La ocupación,* 274. See also Granados, *Sueñan las piedras,* 52.

44. Gayón Córdova, *La ocupación,* 250–251, 271, 277; Granados, *Sueñan las piedras,* 69; García Cubas, *El libro,* 437. The quote is from Ayuntamiento, Guerra con los Estados Unidos, vol. 2265, exp. 28, fol. 30, AHDF.

45. Gayón Córdova, *La ocupación,* 271, 279; Reyes Tosqui, "Violencia, oportunismo y resistencia," 110–112.

46. *Apuntes para la historia de la guerra,* 378; Gayón Córdova, *La ocupación,* 62–63; Jesús Cosamalón Aguilar, "Léperos y yanquis: El control social en la Ciudad de México durante la ocupación norteamericana, 1847–1848," in *Culturas de pobreza y resistencia: Estudios de marginados, proscritos y descontentos, México, 1804–1910,* coord. Romana Falcón (Mexico City: Colegio de México / Universidad Autónoma de Querétaro, 2005), 121.

47. Embajada de España en Washington, caja 54 / 7918, leg. 543, AGA. See also Bustamante, *El nuevo,* 1:54 .

48. Ayuntamiento, Guerra con los Estados Unidos, 2268, exp. 77, fols. 168, 181, 185, AHDF; Embajada de España en Washington, caja 54 / 7918, leg. 543, AGA.

49. Ayuntamiento, Guerra con los Estados Unidos, vol. 2265, exp. 25, fol. 1, AHDF.

50. Ibid., fol. 7.

51. Ibid., fol. 9; Sánchez de Tagle, "1847," 224. For more dialogue with the Americans, see Actas de Cabildo Secretas, vol. 300-A, September 15, 1847, AHDF. Rumors that prisoners were being let out of jail to participate in the defense of the city actually predated the riot. Bustamante claimed on September 8 that they were being released and given clubs and stones. Bustamante, entry for September 8, 1847, in *Diario.* No other document has been found to substantiate this rumor.

52. The broadside can be found in Ayuntamiento, Guerra con los Estados Unidos, vol. 2265, exp. 25, fol. 4, AHDF and Ruiz Abreu, *Fortificaciones,* 449. For the reaction, see Maria Gayón Córdova, "Los invasores yanquis en la ciudad de México," in Herrera Serna, *México en Guerra,* 201, and Granados, *Sueñan las piedras,* 66. Another broadside simply communicated Scott's threat. See Ayuntamiento, Guerra con los Estados Unidos, vol. 2268, exp. 76, AHDF.

53. Ayuntamiento, Guerra con los Estados Unidos, vol. 2265, exp. 25, fols. 5–6, AHDF.

54. Roa Bárcena, *Recuerdos,* 509; *Apuntes para la historia de la guerra,* 388; Santa Anna, *Detalle,* 33–34.

55. Ayuntamiento, Guerra con los Estados Unidos, vol. 2268, exp. 76, fol. 136, AHDF. This dialogue is also reproduced in Santa Anna, *Detalle,* 42–44. On the politics of Reyes Veramendi, see Granados, *Sueñan las piedras,* 132–133.

56. Hill, *Fighter,* 128–130, quote from 130.

57. Reeves Manuscript, quotes from 315 and 377.

58. Ballentine, *Autobiography,* 306.

59. Scott, *Memoirs of Lieut.-General Scott,* 2:528–529.

60. EE517, RG 153, NA. See also George Kendall's comments in George Smith and Charles Judah, *Chronicles,* 266.

61. Ayuntamiento, Guerra con los Estados Unidos, vol. 2265, exp. 25, fol. 12, AHDF; Reeves Manuscript, 382; Gayón Córdova, "Los invasores," 211; Actas de Cabildo Secretas, vol. 300-A, September 25, 1847, AHDF; Johnson, *Gallant*, 242–243; Gayón Córdova, *La ocupación*, 354, 362; Ruiz Abreu, *Fortificaciones*, 425, 429–430, 435.

62. This is the thesis of Johnson's very good military history of the campaign, Johnson, *Gallant*.

63. Henshaw, *Recollections*, 176.

CHAPTER 8 · Ashamed of My Country

1. Antonio López de Santa Anna, *Detalle de las operaciones ocurridas en la defensa de la Capital de la República atacada por el ejército de los Estados Unidos del Norte en el año de 1847* (Mexico City: Imprenta de Ignacio Cumplido, 1848), 35–36; *Apuntes para la historia de la guerra entre México y los Estados Unidos* (Mexico City: Consejo Nacional para la Cultura y las Artes, 1991), 394.

2. *Apuntes para la historia de la guerra*, 396; Alicia Tecuanhuey Sandoval, "Puebla durante la Invasión Norteamericana," in *México al tiempo de su guerra con los Estados Unidos (1846–1848)*, ed. Josefina Zoraida Vázquez (Mexico City: Secretaría de Relaciones Exteriores, El Colegio de México, Fondo de Cultura Económica, 1997), 413; Justin Smith, *The War with Mexico* (Gloucester, MA: Peter Smith, 1963), 2:176–178; exp. 2673, fol. 3, ADN; Timothy D. Johnson, *A Gallant Little Army: The Mexico City Campaign* (Lawrence: University of Kansas Press, 2007), 249–250.

3. Carlos Maria de Bustamante, entries for August 9, September 17, 1847, in *Diario histórico de México 1822–1848,* ed. Josefina Zoraida Vázquez and Héctor Cuauhtémoc Hernández Silva, (Mexico City: El Colegio de México / Centro de Investigaciones y Estudios Superiores en Antropología Social, 2003); Will Fowler, *Santa Anna of Mexico* (Lincoln: University of Nebraska Press, 2007), 279–280; Michael Van Wagenen, *Remembering the Forgotten War: The Enduring Legacies of the U.S.-Mexican War* (Amherst: University of Massachusetts Press, 2012), 42–43; Santa Anna, *Detalle;* many expedientes in Archivo de Guerra, AGN; Conrado Hernández López, "Entre la guerra exterior y los conflictos internos: Las guerrillas en el camino México-Veracruz (1847–1848)," in *Discursos públicos, negociaciones y estrategias de lucha colectiva,* ed. José Alfredo Rangel Silva and Carlos Rubén Ruiz Medrano (San Luis Potosí, Mexico: Colegio de San Luis / Archivo Histórico del Estado de San Luis, 2006), 124; José María Roa Bárcena, *Recuerdos de la invasión norteamericana (1846–1849)* (Xalapa, Mexico: Universidad Veracruzana, 1986), 418–419; George Wilkins Kendall, *Dispatches from the Mexican War* (Norman: University of Oklahoma Press, 1999), 222–223. The Rivera mural is in the Museo Mural Diego Rivera in downtown Mexico City.

4. John Corey Henshaw, *Recollections of the War with Mexico* (Columbia: University of Missouri Press, 2008), 46–47; Justin Smith, *War,* 1:144.

5. Daniel Harvey Hill, *A Fighter from Way Back: The Mexican War Diary of Lt. Daniel Harvey Hill, 4th Artillery, USA,* ed. Nathaniel Cheairs Hughes Jr. and Timothy D. Johnson (Kent, OH: Kent State University Press, 2002), 123; Johnson, *Gallant,* 211.

6. Johnson, *Gallant,* 111, 199; EE532, RG 153, NA.

7. Johnson, *Gallant,* 255–265.

8. Bertram Wyatt-Brown, *Southern Honor: Ethics and Behavior in the Old South,* 25th anniversary ed. (New York: Oxford University Press, 2007); Kenneth Greenberg, *Honor and Slavery: Lies, Duels, Noses, Masks, Dressing as a Woman, Gifts, Strangers, Humanitarianism, Death, Slave Rebellions, the Proslavery Argument, Baseball, Hunting and Gambling in the Old South* (Princeton, NJ: Princeton University Press, 1996), 7–8; Sonya Lipsett-Rivera, *Gender and the Negotiation of Daily Life in Mexico, 1750–1850* (Lincoln: University of Nebraska Press 2012), 7, 12–19.

9. The quotes are from February 1, 1848, MS C S, Dabney Howard Smith Papers, FHS, and *Daily American Star,* December 11, 1847. See also Johnson, *Gallant,* 246.

10. Jacob Oswandel, *Notes on the Mexican War, 1846–1848* (Knoxville: University of Tennessee Press, 2010), 113, 140–141, 311; Albert G. Brackett, *General Lane's Brigade in Central Mexico* (Cincinnati: H. W. Derby, 1854), 268–269.

11. Exp. 2726, fols. 2–3, ADN; exp. 2766, fol. 13, ADN; Oswandel, *Notes,* 79, 99, 140; Roa Bárcena, *Recuerdos,* 250; Kendall, *Dispatches,* 237. The quote is from Richard Coulter, *Volunteers: The Mexican War Journals of Private Richard Coulter and Sergeant Thomas Barclay,* ed. Allan Peskin (Kent, OH: Kent State University Press, 1991), 234.

12. Exp. 2565, fol. 109, ADN; Roa Bárcena, *Recuerdos,* 249; Hernández López, "Entre la guerra," 139. The quotes are from 30th Congress, 1st Session, 1848, House Executive Document 56, 127.

13. Johnson, *Gallant,* 251; Brackett, *General,* 220–222; Winfield Scott, *Memoirs of Lieut.-General Scott, LL.D, Written by Himself* (New York: Sheldon, 1864), 2:575.

14. Richard Bruce Winders, *Mr. Polk's Army: The American Military Experience in the Mexican War* (College Station: Texas A&M University Press, 1997), 10, 58–59, 192–193, 196. Lieutenant Hill refused to recognize them as part of the regular army, repeatedly calling them instead "raw levies." Hill, *Fighter,* 135, 175.

15. John S. Ford, *Rip Ford's Texas,* ed. Stephen B. Oates (Austin: University of Texas Press, 1963), 66–68; Oswandel, *Notes,* 225–226; Brackett, *General,* 203–206; George W. Smith and Charles Judah, *The Chronicles of the Gringos: The US Army in the Mexican War, 1846–48: Accounts of Eyewitnesses and Combatants* (Albuquerque: University of New Mexico Press,

1968), 40–43; Justin Smith, *War,* 2:172; 30th Congress, 1st Session, House Executive Document, 335; Walter Prescott Webb, *The Texas Rangers in the Mexican War* (Austin: Jenkins Garrett, 1975), 24, 69. Taylor's letter is in "Mexican War Correspondence," 30th Congress, 1st Session, 1848, House Executive Document 60, 1178. Quote from 30th Congress, 1st Session, House Executive Document, 385. American newspaper correspondent George Wilkins Kendall had actually suggested the use of Texans against the guerrillas in a dispatch published in New Orleans in May 1847. Kendall, *Dispatches,* 236.

16. Gary Anderson, *The Conquest of Texas: Ethnic Cleansing in the Promised Land, 1820–1875* (Norman: University of Oklahoma Press, 2005), 130, 134, 176, 190–191.

17. Johnson, *Gallant,* 140–141; Roa Bárcena, *Recuerdos,* 250, 253; Samuel H. Walker, *Samuel H. Walker's Account of the Mier Expedition,* ed. Marilyn McAdams Sibley (Austin: Texas State Historical Association, 1978); *Apuntes para la historia de la guerra,* 438; Henshaw, *Recollections,* 146.

18. George Ballentine, *Autobiography of an English Soldier in the United States Army* (Chicago: Lakeside, 1986), 244; Coulter, *Volunteers,* 110.

19. *Apuntes para la historia de la guerra,* 397–399; Roa Bárcena, *Recuerdos,* 520; Jaime Sánchez Sánchez, "El territorio tlaxcalteca y la guerra contra Estados Unidos," in *México en Guerra (1846–1848): Perspectivas regionales,* ed. Laura Herrera Serna (Mexico City: Conaculta, Museo Nacional de las Intervenciones, 1997), 651–652; Justin Smith, *War,* 2:177; Hill, *Fighter,* 140; Santa Anna, *Detalle,* 46–48; Embajada de España en Washington, caja 54 / 7918, leg. 543, AGA; Oswandel, *Notes,* 198, 202, 207–209.

20. Winders, *Mr. Polk's,* 40, 47.

21. Robert Johannsen, *To the Halls of Montezuma: The Mexican War in the American Imagination* (New York: Oxford University Press, 1985), 123.

22. Brackett, *General,* 203–206; Johnson, *Gallant,* 249–250; *Apuntes para la historia de la guerra,* 400; Hill, *Fighter,* 140, 152, 171, 179; Roa Bárcena, *Recuerdos,* 523; Daniel Molina Alvarez, *La pasión de padre Jarauta* (Mexico City: Gobierno del Distrito Federal, 1999), 130; Oswandel, *Notes,* 206.

23. Brackett, *General,* 210–216; Hill, *Fighter,* 162. The Wilkins quote is from October 22, 1847, Ross Wilkins Papers, Burton Historical Collection, Detroit Public Library. It is also reproduced in George Smith and Charles Judah, *Chronicles,* 271.

24. Exp. 2703, fol. 5, ADN.

25. The report of the parish priest is in Justicia y Negocios Eclesiásticos, leg. 154, fol. 264, AGN. The reports of Mexican civilian authorities on events in Teotihuacán, Tulancingo, and Zacualtipán are all in exp. 2783, fols. 4, 7, 35, 37–39, 42–44, ADN. See also Roa Bárcena, *Recuerdos,* 530–531; Molina Alvarez, *La pasión,* 128–130; Daniel Escorza Rodríguez, "La

ocupación norteamericana en Pachuca y Real del Monte en 1848," in Herrera Serna, *México en Guerra,* 370–371; and Michael Ducey, *A Nation of Villages: Riot and Rebellion in the Mexican Huasteca, 1750–1850* (Tucson: University of Arizona Press, 2004), 163.

26. These reports are printed in Message of the President of the United States to the Two Houses of Congress at the Commencement of the Second Session of the Thirtieth Congress, 1848, 85–103. Lane's report can also be found in Brackett, *General,* 262–266. See also the memoir of Texan John Ford. Ford, *Rip Ford's Texas,* 94–98.

27. R. S. Ripley, *War with Mexico* (New York: Harper and Brothers, 1849), 2:636; Hill, *Fighter,* 172.

28. Johnson, *Gallant,* 252; Manuel Muro Rocha, *Historia de San Luis Potosí* (Mexico City: Sociedad Potosina de Estudios Históricos, 1973), 2:589–590.

29. Roa Bárcena, *Recuerdos,* 568–569, 573; exp. 2673, fols. 7–8, 14, 23, 25, 29, ADN. The quote is from fol. 8.

30. Exp. 2682, fol. 409, ADN. The quote is from fol. 16.

31. Exp. 2636, fols. 2–4, ADN; exp. 2726, fols. 2–4, ADN. See also exp. 2700, fol. 1, ADN.

32. Peter Guardino, *Peasants, Politics, and the Formation of Mexico's National State: Guerrero, 1800–1857* (Stanford, CA: Stanford University Press, 1996), 156–158.

33. Maria del Carmen Salinas Sandoval, *Política interna e invasión norteamericana en el Estado de México 1846–1848* (Zinacantepec, Mexico: El Colegio Mexiquense, 2000), 119–121; Archivo de Guerra, leg. 272, fols. 180–204, AGN.

34. Gobernación, sin sección, leg. 334, exp. 14, AGN; exp. 2673, fols. 14, 18, ADN; exp. 2741, fols. 8–12, ADN; Maria del Pilar Iracheta Cenecorta, "Federalismo e invasión norteamericana en el Estado de México (1846–1848)," in Herrera Serna *México en Guerra,* 294–296.

35. For Tamaulipas, see leg. 25, 1847, SGG, AHESLP, and for Guanajuato, see Secretaría de Gobierno, Guerra, caja 83, exp. 9, AGEG.

36. Reynaldo Sordo Cedeño, "El faccionalismo en la Guerra con los Estados Unidos 1846–1848," in *Symposium La Angostura en la Intervención Norteamericana, 1846–1848* (Saltillo, Mexico: Secretaría de Educación Pública de Coahuila, 1998), 34–35; Archivo de Guerra, leg. 274, fol. 64, AGN; Pedro Santoni, *Mexicans at Arms: Puro Federalists and the Politics of War, 1845–1848* (Fort Worth: Texas Christian University Press, 1996), 218–220.

37. For Zacatecas, see Impresos, January 13, 1848, SGG, AHESLP. For Ocampo, see Moisés Guzmán Pérez, *Las relaciones clero-gobierno en Michoacán: La gestión episcopal de Juan Cayetano Gómez de Portugal* (Mexico City: LIX Legislatura Cámara de Diputados, 2005), 170–171; and Juan Ortiz Escamilla, "Michoacán: Federalismo e Intervención Norteamericana," in Vázquez, *México al tiempo de su guerra con los Estados Unidos,* 320, 325–326. The

quote is from *Memoria sobre el estado que guarda la administración pública de Michoacán leída al Honorable Congreso por el Secretario del Despacho en 22 de enero de 1848* (Morelia, Mexico: I. Arango, 1848; hereafter cited as *Memoria, Michoacán*), 30.

38. Tomás Calvillo Unna and Sergio Cañedo Gamboa, *El Congreso del estado de San Luis Potosí y la nación: Selección de documentos (1824–1923)* (San Luis Potosí, Mexico: El Colegio de San Luis, 1999), 76–77.

39. Leg. 8, leg. 9, leg. 11, leg. 17, leg. 19, leg. 20, leg. 22, leg. 24, leg. 25, 1847, SGG, AHESLP.

40. Barbara Corbett, "La política potosina y la Guerra con Estados Unidos," in Vázquez, *México al tiempo de su guerra con los Estados Unidos,* 466–467, 473–474; fols. 17–18, Foreign Office, 203-92, British Public Record Office, London; LEPOSLP, August 31, September 7, September 10, November 4, December 7, 1847. The quote is from LEPOSLP, September 18, 1847.

41. Muro Rocha, *Historia,* 2:578–587; Santoni, *Mexicans at Arms,* 223–224; fol. 61, Foreign Office, 203-92-7, British Public Record Office.

42. *Memoria, Michoacán,* 8; *Daily American Star,* December 11, 1847.

43. Molina Alvarez, *La pasión,* 135–178; *Planes en la Nación Mexicana* (Mexico City: Cámara de Diputados, 1987), 4:387. The quote is from *Planes en la Nación Mexicana,* 4:381.

44. David Weber, *The Mexican Frontier, 1821–1846: The American Southwest under Mexico* (Albuquerque: University of New Mexico Press, 1982), 187–188, 206.

45. Douglas Monroy, *Thrown among Strangers: The Making of Mexican Culture in Frontier California* (Berkeley: University of California Press, 1990), 100, 155; Angela Moyano Pahissa, *La resistencia de las Californias a la invasión norteamericana, 1846–1848* (Mexico City: Conaculta, 1992), 37; Douglas Monroy, "The Creation and Re-creation of Californio Society," in *Contested Eden: California before the Gold Rush,* ed. Ramón Guttiérrez and Richard Orsi (Berkeley: University of California Press, 1998), 177–190; Weber, *Mexican Frontier,* 60–68, 137–139, 196; David Weber, "Conflicts and Accommodations: Hispanic and Anglo-American Borders in Historical Perspective, 1670–1853," *Journal of the Southwest* 39, no. 2 (1997): 1–32; Marcela Terrazas y Basante and Gerardo Gurza Lavalle, *Las relaciones México-Estados Unidos, 1756–2010,* vol. 1, *Imperios, repúblicas y pueblos en pugna por el territorio, 1756–1867* (Mexico City: Universidad Nacional Autónoma de México / Secretaría de Relaciones Exteriores, 2012), 133, 154; Harlan Hague and David J. Langum, *Thomas O. Larkin: A Life of Patriotism and Profit in Old California* (Norman: University of Oklahoma Press, 1990), 7, 57–58.

46. Weber, "Conflicts and Accommodations," 18–20; Monroy, *Thrown among Strangers,* 157, 160–161; Doyce B. Nunis, "Alta California's Trojan Horse: Foreign Immigration," in Guttiérrez and Orsi, *Contested Eden,* 306–309; Hague and Langum, *Thomas O. Larkin,*

7–8; Stephen J. Hyslop, *Contest for California: From Spanish Colonization to the American Conquest*, vol. 2 of *Before Gold: California under Spain and Mexico* (Norman: University of Oklahoma Press, 2012), 219–220. The case of Benjamin Davis Wilson, detailed in Anne Hyde, *Empires, Nations, and Families: A History of the North American West, 1800–1860* (Lincoln: University of Nebraska Press, 2011), 75–78, is very instructive.

47. Monroy, "Creation and Re-creation," 180–181; Weber, *Mexican Frontier*, 196; Hyslop, *Contest for California*, 336–337; Hague and Langum, *Thomas O. Larkin*, 87; Gregorio Mora-Torres, ed., *California Voices: The Oral Memoirs of José Maria Amador and Lorenzo Asisara* (Denton: University of North Texas Press, 2005), 173–175; Alan Rosenus, *General M. G. Vallejo and the Advent of the Americans: A Biography* (Albuquerque: University of New Mexico Press, 1995), 3–80.

48. Richard Henry Dana, *Two Years before the Mast: A Personal Narrative of Life at Sea* (New York: Harper and Brothers, 1840), 94; Hague and Langum, *Thomas O. Larkin*, 109.

49. Nunis, "Alta California's Trojan Horse," 311–312, 321–322; Weber, *Mexican Frontier*, 179, 202–203; Monroy, *Thrown among Strangers*, 163–165; Hague and Langum, *Thomas O. Larkin*, 10; Hyslop, *Contest for California*, 215, 298; Lisbeth Haas, "War in California, 1846–1848," in Guttiérrez and Orsi, *Contested Eden*, 336–337.

50. Neal Harlow, *California Conquered: War and Peace on the Pacific, 1846–1850* (Berkeley: University of California Press, 1982), 67–114; Hyslop, *Contest for California*, 305–310; Haas, "War in California," 337–341; Hyde, *Empires, Nations, and Families*, 376.

51. Hyslop, *Contest for California*, 305–306, 249–251; Janin Hunt and Ursula Carson, *The California Campaigns of the U.S.-Mexican War, 1846–1848* (Jefferson, NC: McFarland, 2015), 15, 91.

52. Hyslop, *Contest for California*, 369–380.

53. Ibid., 371–372, 380–384; Mora-Torres, *California Voices*, 191; Haas, "War in California," 343–345; Harlow, *California Conquered*, 157–192; *Apuntes para la historia de la guerra*, 404.

54. Harlow, *California Conquered*, 193–243; Jeanne Farr McDonnell, *Juana Briones of 19th Century California* (Tucson: University of Arizona Press, 2008), 155, 164–178.

55. I owe this insight to Michael Ducey (personal communication).

56. Weber, *Mexican Frontier*, 95, 97, 118–120; Andrés Reséndez, *Changing National Identities at the Frontier: Texas and New Mexico, 1800–1850* (New York: Cambridge University Press, 2004), 105; Phillip St. George Cooke, *The Conquest of New Mexico and California: An Historical and Personal Narrative* (Albuquerque: Horn and Wallace, 1964), 19.

57. Reséndez, *Changing National Identities*, 83–91, 241–246; Weber, *Mexican Frontier*, 15–42, 261–265.

58. Reséndez, *Changing National Identities*, 4–6, 93–106; Weber, *Mexican Frontier*, 125–135; Ross Frank, *From Settler to Citizen: New Mexican Economic Development and the Creation of Vecino Society, 1750–1820* (Berkeley: University of California Press, 2000), 226; John O. Baxter, *Las Carneradas: Sheep Trade in New Mexico, 1700–1860* (Albuquerque: University of New Mexico Press, 1987), 89–95; Terrazas y Basante and Gurza Lavalle, *Las relaciones México-Estados Unidos*, 1:154.

59. Hyde, *Empires, Nations, and Families*.

60. Weber, "Conflicts and Accommodations," 18–20; Reséndez, *Changing National Identities*, 124–134. On Bent in Taos, see Stephen J. Hyslop, *Bound for Santa Fe: The Road to New Mexico and the American Conquest, 1806–1848* (Norman: University of Oklahoma Press, 2002), 298–302. The population figures for Missouri are from the U.S. Census.

61. James M. McCaffrey, *Army of Manifest Destiny: The American Soldier in the Mexican War, 1846–1848* (New York: New York University Press, 1992), 147–150; Justin Smith, *War*, 1:284–289. On the contingency plans, see George Smith and Charles Judah, *Chronicles*, 107.

62. Reséndez, *Changing National Identities*, 241–244, 249–252; Martín González de la Vara, "Los nuevomexicanos ante la invasión norteamericana, 1846–1848," in Herrera Serna, *México en Guerra*, 475; Hyslop, *Bound for Santa Fe*, 325, 335–337; Cooke, *Conquest of New Mexico and California*, 34–35.

63. González de la Vara, "Los nuevomexicanos," 477, 480; George Smith and Charles Judah, *Chronicles*, 113.

64. George Ruxton, *Adventures in Mexico and the Rocky Mountains* (New York: Harper and Brothers, 1848), 190; James Crutchfield, *Revolt at Taos: The New Mexican and Indian Insurrection of 1847* (Yardley, PA: Westhome, 2015), 66; Hyslop, *Bound for Santa Fe*, 360, 367, 407.

65. Reséndez, *Changing National Identities*, 247, 253–263; Hyde, *Empires, Nations, and Families*, 385–386; Weber, *Mexican Frontier*, 193; Hyslop, *Bound for Santa Fe*, 285–286, 292–294, 351–358, 385; González de la Vara, "Los nuevomexicanos," 485–489. The quote is from Ruxton, *Adventures in Mexico and the Rocky Mountains*, 197. See also 204–205.

66. The Garrard quote is from Lewis Hector Garrard, *Wah-To-Yah, and the Taos Trail; or, Prairie Travel and Scalp Dances, with a Look at Los Rancheros and the Rocky Mountain Camp Fire* (Cincinnati: H. W. Derby; New York: A. S. Barnes, 1850), 197–198. See also ibid., 138, 189–198; Rafael Chacón, *Legacy of Honor: The Life of Rafael Chacón, a Nineteenth-Century New Mexican*, ed. Jaqueline Dorgan Meketa (Albuquerque: University of New Mexico Press, 1986), 67; Crutchfield, *Revolt at Taos*, 68, 91, 96, 105–106, 117–119; Reséndez, *Changing National Identities*, 254; Laura E. Gómez, *Manifest Destinies: The Making of the Mexican American Race* (New York: New York University Press, 2007), 25–41; LEPOSLP, August 10, 1847; and Impresos, 1847, exp. 5, SGG, AHESLP.

67. Sherman L. Fleek, *History May Be Searched in Vain: A Military History of the Mormon Battalion* (Spokane, WA: Arthur H. Clark, 2006), 28–29, 54–59, 109–131, 136, 139, 200–201, 235; Cooke, *Conquest of New Mexico and California,* 91.

CHAPTER 9 · The Law of the Strongest

1. Reginald Horsman, *Race and Manifest Destiny: The Origins of American Racial Anglo-Saxonism* (Cambridge, MA: Harvard University Press, 1981), 230, 235.

2. Jesús Velasco Márquez, "La crisis del vencedor: Los Estados Unidos durante la guerra contra Mexico," in Josefina Zoraida Vázquez et al., *La guerra entre México y Estados Unidos, 1846–1848: Cuatro miradas* (San Luis Potosí, Mexico: El Colegio de San Luis, 1998), 27–28.

3. John Pinheiro, "'Religion without Restriction': Anti-Catholicism, All Mexico, and the Treaty of Guadalupe Hidalgo," *Journal of the Early Republic* 23, no. 1 (2003): 88; Horsman, *Race,* 231, 236–245.

4. Winfield Scott, *Memoirs of Lieut.-General Scott, LL.D, Written by Himself* (New York: Sheldon, 1864), 2:560–561.

5. Timothy D. Johnson, *A Gallant Little Army: The Mexico City Campaign* (Lawrence: University of Kansas Press, 2007), 267; Robert W. Drexler, *Guilty of Making a Peace: A Biography of Nicholas P. Trist* (Lanham, MD: University Press of America, 1991), 103–143; Wallace Ohrt, *Defiant Peacemaker: Nicholas Trist and the Mexican War* (College Station: Texas A&M University Press, 1997), 135–157; Alejandro Sobarzo, *Deber y conciencia: Nicolas Trist, el negociador norteamericano en la guerra del 47* (Mexico City: Diana, 1990), 213–234; Marcela Terrazas y Basante and Gerardo Gurza Lavalle, *Las relaciones México-Estados Unidos, 1756–2010,* vol. 1, *Imperios, repúblicas y pueblos en pugna por el territorio, 1756–1867* (Mexico City: Universidad Nacional Autónoma de México / Secretaría de Relaciones Exteriores, 2012), 263.

6. David Pletcher, *The Diplomacy of Annexation: Texas, Oregon, and the Mexican War* (Columbia: University of Missouri Press, 1973), 535–560.

7. Brian DeLay, *War of a Thousand Deserts: Indian Raids and the Mexican-American War* (New Haven, CT: Yale University Press, 2009), 288–296.

8. John Pinheiro, *Missionaries of Republicanism: A Religious History of the Mexican-American War* (Oxford: Oxford University Press, 2014), 157–160.

9. The memorandum is in LEPOSLP, June 8, 1848. De la Rosa's speech is printed in LEPOSLP, May 20, May 23, May 27, June 1, 1848. On the ratification and the subsequent erosion of Mexicans' rights, see Richard Griswold del Castillo, *The Treaty of*

Guadalupe Hidalgo: A Legacy of Conflict (Norman: University of Oklahoma Press, 1990), 44–107.

10. First published in Mexico City in *El Judio Errante,* it is reprinted in LEPOSLP, November 23, 1847.

11. Leg. 33, SGG, AHESLP, 1845; leg. 29, SGG, AHESLP, 1847; leg. 6, SGG, AHESLP, 1848; August 1, 1846, exp. 32, STJ, AHESLP; Carlos Alberto Reyes Tosqui, "Historia de los grupos populares de la ciudad de México durante la ocupación norteamericana, 1847–1848" (tesis de maestría, Universidad Autónoma Metropolitana Unidad Iztapalapa, 2009), 97, 99–100; Secretaría de Gobierno, Guerra, caja 83, exp. 7, AGEG.

12. José María Roa Bárcena, *Recuerdos de la invasión norteamericana (1846–1849)* (Xalapa, Mexico: Universidad Veracruzana, 1986), 418–419. The quote is from 419.

13. Archivo de Guerra, leg. 406, no fol., AGN.

14. Exp. 2444, no fol., ADN; exp. 2256, fol. 11, ADN; exp. 2602, fols. 16–17, ADN.

15. J. Jacob Oswandel, *Notes on the Mexican War, 1846–1848* (Knoxville: University of Tennessee Press, 2010), 72; EE529, RG 153, NA; exp. 2300, fol. 18, ADN; exp. 2668, fol. 2, ADN; Archivo de Guerra, leg. 922, no fol., AGN; Archivo de Guerra, leg. 1035, no fol., AGN; Scott, *Memoirs of Lieut.-General Scott,* 2:441.

16. See, for example, the case in Oswandel, *Notes,* 291, 221; Roa Bárcena, *Recuerdos,* 263; and Conrado Hernández López, "Entre la guerra exterior y los conflictos internos: Las guerrillas en el camino México-Veracruz (1847–1848)," in *Discursos públicos, negociaciones y estrategias de lucha colectiva,* ed. José Alfredo Rangel Silva and Carlos Rubén Ruiz Medrano (San Luis Potosí, Mexico: Colegio de San Luis / Archivo Histórico del Estado de San Luis, 2006), 141. On at least one occasion, Americans feared that one of their own captured officers would be executed for violating parole. See William W. Carpenter, *Travels and Adventures in Mexico: In the Course of Journeys of Upward of 2500 Miles, Performed on Foot, Giving an Account of the Manners and Customs of the People, and the Agricultural and Mineral Resources of That Country* (New York: Harper Brothers, 1851), 45.

17. LEPOSLP, November 25, 1847; *Apuntes para la historia de la guerra entre México y los Estados Unidos* (Mexico City: Consejo Nacional para la Cultura y las Artes, 1991), 219.

18. See, for instance, Archivo de Guerra, leg. 416, fols. 1–6, AGN; Archivo de Guerra, leg. 490, no fol., AGN

19. On the policy of not paying paroled officers, see Roa Bárcena, *Recuerdos,* 189–190; exp. 2490, fols. 5, 15, ADN; exp. 2489, fols. 1–4, ADN; and Ayuntamiento, Guerra con los Estados Unidos, vol. 2264, exp. 13, AHDF. On the hunt for hidden officers, see Archivo de Guerra, leg. 454, fol. 10, AGN.

20. Impresos, 1847, leg. 4, exp. 42, SGG; Archivo de Guerra, leg. 619, no fol., AGN.

21. Archivo de Guerra, leg. 153, fols. 452–454, AGN; Archivo de Guerra, leg. 273, fol. 329, AGN.

22. Archivo de Guerra, leg. 273, fols. 252–272, 359, AGN.

23. Archivo de Guerra, leg. 155, fols. 260–285, AGN. The quotes are from fol. 264.

24. Oswandel, *Notes,* 247; January 18, 1847, Carr Family Papers, ISHS; October 9, 1847, April 21, 1848, MS A R943 2, Runyon Family Papers, FHS; Oran Perry, comp., *Indiana in the Mexican War* (Indianapolis: W. B. Burford, 1908), 49–50.

25. Paul Foos, *A Short, Offhand Killing Affair: Soldiers and Social Conflict during the Mexican-American War* (Chapel Hill: University of North Carolina Press, 2002), 68.

26. Albert Lombard, *"The High Private" with a Full and Exciting History of the New York Volunteers, and the "Mysteries and Miseries" of the Mexican War, in Three Parts—Part First* (New York: Printed for the Publisher, 1848), 7–10, 19, 25, 47. The quote is from 25.

27. *Apuntes para la historia de la guerra,* 413–414.

28. Ayuntamiento, Policia Seguridad, vol. 3690, exp. 97, AHDF; Ayuntamiento, Policia Seguridad, vol. 3691, exp. 106, fols. 1–5, 11–20, AHDF; Justicia Alcaldes, vol. 2749, exp. 6, exp. 7, AHDF; Carlos Ruiz Abreu, coord., *Fortificaciones, guerra y defensa de la Ciudad de México (1844, 1847–1848): Documentos para su historia* (Mexico City: Gobierno del Distrito Federal, Secretaría de Cultura, Archivo Histórico del Distrito Federal, 2003), 430.

29. Ayuntamiento, Policia Seguridad, vol. 3690, exp. 98, AHDF; Ayuntamiento, Guerra con los Estados Unidos, vol. 2265 exp. 25, fol. 14, AHDF; Ayuntamiento, Guerra con los Estados Unidos, vol. 2268, exp. 84, fols. 375, 378, AHDF; Actas de Cabildo Secretas, vol. 300-A, September 29, 1847, AHDF; Actas de Cabildo Secretas, vol. 300-A, October 5, 1847, AHDF; LEPOSLP, November 20, 1847; Ruiz Abreu, *Fortificaciones,* 430, 433; Carlos Maria de Bustamante, entry for September 17, 1847, in *Diario histórico de México, 1822–1848,* ed. Josefina Zoraida Vázquez and Héctor Cuauhtémoc Hernández Silva (Mexico City: El Colegio de México / Centro de Investigaciones y Estudios Superiores en Antropología Social, 2003).

30. George Ballentine, *Autobiography of an English Soldier in the United States Army* (Chicago: Lakeside, 1986), 314; Daniel Harvey Hill, *A Fighter from Way Back: The Mexican War Diary of Lt. Daniel Harvey Hill, 4th Artillery, USA,* ed. Nathaniel Cheairs Hughes Jr. and Timothy D. Johnson (Kent, OH: Kent State University Press, 2002), 135, 169; Maria Gayón Córdova, *La ocupación yanqui de la ciudad de México, 1847–1848* (Mexico City: Consejo Nacional para la Cultura y las Artes, 1997), 311, 356–357.

31. LEPOSLP, November 20, 1847; Juan de la Granja, *Epistolario: Con un estudio biográfico preliminar por Luis Castillo Ledón y notas de Neréo Rodríguez Barragán* (Mexico City:

Talleres Gráficos del Museo Nacional de Arqueología, Historia y Etnografía, 1937), 210; Maria Gayón Córdova, "Los invasores yanquis en la ciudad de México," in *México en Guerra (1846–1848): Perspectivas regionales,* ed. Laura Herrera Serna (Mexico City: Conaculta, Museo Nacional de las Intervenciones, 1997), 211; Johnson *Gallant,* 254; Ballentine, *Autobiography,* 319–320; Roa Bárcena, *Recuerdos,* 542; *Apuntes para la historia de la guerra,* 416; Richard Coulter, *Volunteers: The Mexican War Journals of Private Richard Coulter and Sergeant Thomas Barclay,* ed. Allan Peskin (Kent, OH: Kent State University Press, 1991), 197, 221; Hill, *Fighter,* 134, 138, 142; Gayón Córdova, *La ocupación,* 348–361, 367; George Wilkins Kendall, *Dispatches from the Mexican War* (Norman: University of Oklahoma Press, 1999), 396, 413; Bustamante, entry for September 20, 1847, in *Diario.* The quotes are from C. M. Reeves, "Five Years Experience in the Regular Army, including the War with Mexico," manuscript, MS qR332f RMV, CHSL (hereafter cited as Reeves Manuscript), 382; Granja, *Epistolario,* 203; and Frederick Zeh, *An Immigrant Soldier in the Mexican War* (College Station: Texas A&M University Press, 1995), 48.

32. Gayón Córdova, *La ocupación,* 296, 313; Justicia y Negocios Eclesiásticos, leg. 155, fol. 211, AGN; Hill, *Fighter,* 135; Zeh, *Immigrant Soldier,* 82; Ruiz Abreu, *Fortificaciones,* 429; LEPOSLP, December 9, 1847.

33. Reeves Manuscript, 382.

34. Ruiz Abreu, *Fortificaciones,* 425, 435; Gayón Córdova, *La ocupación,* 354, 362; Actas de Cabildo Secretas, vol. 300-A, September 15, October 6, 1847, AHDF; Ayuntamiento, Policia Seguridad, vol. 3691, exp. 104, fol. 4, AHDF; Ayuntamiento, Policia Seguridad, vol. 3690, exp. 98, AHDF.

35. Ayuntamiento, Policia Seguridad, vol. 3690, exp. 95, AHDF; Coulter, *Volunteers,* 213–214; Gayón Córdova, "Los invasores," 213–214.

36. LEPOSLP, October 12, 1847; Coulter, *Volunteers,* 204; Gayón Córdova, "Los invasores," 207–208; Guillermo Prieto, *Memorias de mis tiempos* (Mexico City: Editorial Porrua, 1996), 276.

37. *Daily American Star,* December 11, 1847; Carlos Alberto Reyes Tosqui, "Violencia, oportunismo y resistencia en la Ciudad de México durante la ocupación norteamericana, 1847–1848" (tesis de licenciatura, Escuela Nacional de Antropología e Historia, 2006), 86–97; Gayón Córdova, "Los invasores," 204–205; Gayón Córdova, *La ocupación,* 22–23, 333. The quote is from Prieto, *Memorias,* 277.

38. Dennis Berge, "A Mexican Dilemma: The Mexico City Ayuntamiento and the Question of Loyalty, 1846–1848," *Hispanic American Historical Review* 50, no. 2 (May 1970): 240–246; Gayón Córdova, "Los invasores," 218–219; Reyes Tosqui, "Violencia, oportunismo y resistencia," 37–40; Elecciones, vol. 863, no fol., AHDF; Ruiz Abreu, *Fortificaciones,* 436–437, 446.

39. Berge, "Mexican Dilemma," 249–255; Elecciones, vol. 863, no fol., AHDF; Pedro Santoni, *Mexicans at Arms: Puro Federalists and the Politics of War, 1845–1848* (Fort Worth: Texas Christian University Press, 1996), 215–219; Gayón Córdova, "Los invasores," 221–223; Roa Bárcena, *Recuerdos*, 549–559.

40. Actas Secretas, vol. 301-A, May 10, 1848, AHDF.

41. Ayuntamiento, Guerra con los Estados Unidos, vol. 2268, exp. 88, fols. 480–481, AHDF; Ayuntamiento, Policia Seguridad, vol. 3691, exp. 113, AHDF; Actas Secretas, vol. 301-A, May 16, June 6, 1848, AHDF; Santoni, *Mexicans at Arms*, 229–230; exp. 2815, fol. 57, ADN.

42. Ayuntamiento, Guerra con los Estados Unidos, vol. 2265, exp. 30, fol. 1, AHDF.

43. Exp. 2815, fol. 57, ADN; Gobernación, sin sección, leg. 351, exp. 5, AGN; Tom Reilly, *War with Mexico! America's Reporters Cover the Battlefront* (Lawrence: University of Kansas Press, 2010), 240–241; Nelson Reed, *The Caste War of the Yucatán* (Stanford, CA: Stanford University Press, 1964), 110–112; May 20, May 27, 1848, MS A R943 2, Runyon Family Papers, FHS; Robert E. May, *Manifest Destiny's Underworld: Filibustering in Antebellum America* (Chapel Hill: University of North Carolina Press, 2002), 14.

44. Reeves Manuscript, 414–415.

45. Reilly, *War!*, 240; Oswandel, *Notes*, 104.

46. Samuel Chamberlain, *My Confession: Recollections of a Rogue* (Austin: Texas State Historical Association, 1996), 115, 277, 280, 284.

47. Gayón Córdova, "Los invasores," 209–210; Chamberlain, *My Confession*, 264; Gayón Córdova, *La ocupación*, 370; Johnson, *Gallant*, 255. Antonio García Cubas, who was a young man in the city during the occupation, says that the Americans themselves were the ones who began to call these women *margaritas*. Antonio García Cubas, *El libro de mis recuerdos: Narraciones históricas, anecdóticas y de costumbres mexicanas, anteriores al actual estado social, ilustrada con más de trescientos fotograbados* (Mexico City: Imprenta de Arturo García Cubas, 1904), 439.

48. Reeves Manuscript, 389; Oswandel, *Notes*, 76; June 11, 1846, MS A B628 3, Blackburn Family Papers, FHS.

49. Reeves Manuscript, 259, 264; Chamberlain, *My Confession*, 76; Oswandel, *Notes*, 251.

50. Reeves Manuscript, 255; Chamberlain, *My Confession*, 171; Zeh, *Immigrant Soldier*, 46.

51. Reeves Manuscript, 191, 389; Chamberlain, *My Confession*, 182, 209; Oswandel, *Notes*, 262; Gayón Córdova, *La ocupación*, 313; Reyes Tosqui, "Violencia, oportunismo y resistencia," 113–114. The quote is from Granja, *Epistolario*, 169. This may have been the

young woman who was criticized in the Mexico newspaper *El Monitor Republicana*, and act that led an American officer to beat the editor. Kendall, *Dispatches*, 421.

52. Albert G. Brackett, *General Lane's Brigade in Central Mexico* (Cincinnati: H. W. Derby, 1854), 283.

53. Roa Bárcena, *Recuerdos*, 544; Gayón Córdova, *La ocupación*, 309. The quote is from Prieto, *Memorias*, 277.

54. Carlos Maria de Bustamante, *El nuevo Bernal Díaz del Castillo* (Mexico City: Instituto Nacional de Estudios Históricos de la Revolución Mexicana-Gobierno del Estado de Puebla 1994), 2,:215.

55. *Apuntes para la historia de la guerra*, 312.

56. Reeves implies success in this area, although the fact that he wrote his memoir after returning to the United States and marrying an American girl kept him from making the point too explicitly. Reeves Manuscript, 251–253. See also James M. McCaffrey, *Army of Manifest Destiny: The American Soldier in the Mexican War, 1846–1848* (New York: New York University Press, 1992), 104. On the demographic prevalence of women in the city, see Sylvia Arrom, *The Women of Mexico City, 1790–1857* (Stanford, CA: Stanford University Press, 1985), 110.

57. Chamberlain, *My Confession*, 178; McCaffrey, *Army*, 200; William H. Daniel Military Diary, 30, MS A D184, FHS; Reyes Tosqui, "Violencia, oportunismo y resistencia," 124.

58. Gayón Córdova, *La ocupación*, 255; Coulter, *Volunteers*, 266; Chamberlain, *My Confession*, 174–176.

59. Laura Shelton, *For Tranquility and Order: Family and Community on Mexico's Northern Frontier, 1800–1850* (Tucson: University of Arizona Press, 2010), 50–54.

60. The quote is from Gayón Córdova, *La ocupación*, 469. See also 320–321, 467–470.

61. Chamberlain, *My Confession*, 231, 269, 273; Gayón Córdova, *La ocupación*, 466; McCaffrey, *Army*, 200; Reilly, *War!*, 239–240; Reyes Tosqui, "Violencia, oportunismo y resistencia," 122–123.

62. On the cultural toleration of violence toward women accused of transgressing norms, see in particular Sonya Lipsett-Rivera, *Gender and the Negotiation of Daily Life in Mexico, 1750–1850* (Lincoln: University of Nebraska Press, 2012), 128–135.

63. Perry, *Indiana*, 197, 201–202.

64. Quote from Isaac Smith, *Reminiscences of a Campaign in Mexico: An Account of the Operations of the Indiana Brigade on the Line of the Rio Grande and Sierra Madre, and a Vindication of the Volunteers against the Aspirations of Officials and Unofficials*, 2nd ed. (Indianapolis: Chapman and Spann, 1848), 88.

65. Perry, *Indiana*, 197–198; George W. Smith and Charles Judah, *The Chronicles of the Gringos: The US Army in the Mexican War, 1846–48: Accounts of Eyewitnesses and Combatants* (Albuquerque: University of New Mexico Press, 1968), 456–457; July 2, 1848, MS A B628 3, Blackburn Family Papers, FHS.

Conclusion

1. Exp. 2622, fols. 4–28, ADN; John R. Kenly, *Memoirs of a Maryland Volunteer: War with Mexico in the Years 1846–1848* (Philadelphia: J. B. Lippincott, 1873), 22, 274, 481–484.

2. Exp. 2465, fols. 1–7, ADN; Michael Ducey, *A Nation of Villages: Riot and Rebellion in the Mexican Huasteca, 1750–1850* (Tucson: University of Arizona Press, 2004), 163; Justin Smith, *The War with Mexico* (Gloucester, MA: Peter Smith, 1963), 2:418; *Apuntes para la historia de la guerra entre México y los Estados Unidos* (Mexico City: Consejo Nacional para la Cultura y las Artes, 1991), 433–435; *Niles National Register,* August 7, 1847; *Encarnacion Prisoners: Comprising an Account of the March of the Kentucky Cavalry from Louisville to the Rio Grande . . .* (Louisville, KY: Prentice and Weissanger, 1848), 70–71. Other prisoners were exchanged around this period. See exp. 2624, fol. 2, ADN; and exp. 2754, fol. 1, AND.

3. Carlos Maria de Bustamante, entry for September 3, 1846, *Diario histórico de México, 1822–1848,* ed. Josefina Zoraida Vázquez and Héctor Cuauhtémoc Hernández Silva, (Mexico City: El Colegio de México / Centro de Investigaciones y Estudios Superiores en Antropología Social, 2003).

4. Fernando Escalante Gonzalbo, *Ciudadanos imaginarios: Memorial de los afanes y desventuras de la virtud y apología del vicio triunfante en la República Mexicana: Tratado de moral pública* (Mexico City: El Colegio de México, 1993), 56; Luis Fernando Granados, *Sueñan las piedras: Alzamiento ocurrido en la ciudad de México, 14, 15 y 16 de septiembre de 1847* (Mexico City: Ediciones Era / Consejo Nacional para la Cultura y las Artes / Instituto Nacional de Antropología e Historia, 2003), 17; Timothy J. Henderson, *A Glorious Defeat: Mexico and Its War with the United States* (New York: Hill and Wang, 2007), xviii, xx, 11–12, 15, 158, 190; Cecilia Sheridan Prieto, "Coahuila y la invasión norteamericana," in *México al tiempo de su guerra con los Estados Unidos (1846–1848),* ed. Josefina Zoraida Vázquez (Mexico City: Secretaría de Relaciones Exteriores, El Colegio de México, Fondo de Cultura Económica, 1997), 172; Josefina Zoraida Vázquez, "Un desastre anunciado e inevitable: La Guerra con Estados Unidos," in Josefina Zoraida Vázquez et al., *La guerra entre México y Estados Unidos, 1846–1848: Cuatro miradas* (San Luis Potosí, Mexico: El Colegio de San Luis, 1998), 5.

5. Franklin Smith, *The Mexican War Journal of Captain Franklin Smith* (Jackson: University Press of Mississippi, 1991), 179.

6. See Escalante Gonzalbo, *Ciudadanos imaginarios,* 13–17, on the general pessimism of Mexican elites. For specific references to the indigenous peasantry, see Gobernación, sin sección, leg. 324, exp. 4, AGN, and Mariano Otero, *Obras,* compilation, selection, and introduction by Jesús Reyes Heroles (Mexico City: Editoria Porrua, 1967), 103. For the rumors of peasant rebels seeking help from the Americans, see José María Roa Bárcena, *Recuerdos de la invasión norteamericana (1846–1849)* (Xalapa, Mexico: Universidad Veracruzana, 1986), 575, and leg. 30, 1847, SGG, AHESLP. Ironically, these rebels actually expressed fierce opposition to the United States instead. Leticia Reina, "The Sierra Gorda Peasant Rebellion, 1847–50," in *Riot, Rebellion, and Revolution: Rural Social Conflict in Mexico,* ed. Friedrich Katz (Princeton, NJ: Princeton University Press, 1988), 279.

7. Otero, *Obras,* 127. Otero may have helped write the pamphlet, but it is unlikely that he was its sole author. Escalante Gonzalbo, *Ciudadanos imaginarios,* 55–56.

8. See LEPOSLP, May 27, 1847; *Apuntes para la historia de la guerra,* 244–245; Timothy D. Johnson, *A Gallant Little Army: The Mexico City Campaign* (Lawrence: University of Kansas Press, 2007), 123; and Bustamante, entry for May 14, 1847, in *Diario,* for statements that Puebla was not inclined to resist the Americans. On events there, see Justin Smith, *War,* 2:68–70; Alicia Tecuanhuey Sandoval, "Puebla durante la Invasión Norteamericana," in Vázquez, *México al tiempo de su guerra con los Estados Unidos,* 405–409; *Apuntes para la historia de la guerra,* 247; J. Jacob Oswandel, *Notes on the Mexican War, 1846–1848* (Knoxville: University of Tennessee Press, 2010), 133–135, 137–138, 141; Johnson, *Gallant,* 125, 133; Justin Smith, *War,* 2:72; exp. 2504, fols. 15–42, ADN; and exp. 2550, fol. 2, ADN.

9. Ethan Allen Hitchcock, *Fifty Years in Camp and Field: Diary of Major General Ethan Allen Hitchcock, USA* (New York: G. P. Putnam's Sons, 1909), 263–265.

10. Oswandel, *Notes,* 166; Archivo de Guerra, leg. 921, no fol., AGN; Ayuntamiento, Guerra con los Estados Unidos, vol. 2267, exp. 62, fol. 319, AHDF; Ayuntamiento, Guerra con los Estados Unidos, vol. 2268, exp. 88, fol. 476, AHDF; Ayuntamiento, Policia Seguridad, vol. 3691, exp. 106, fol. 21, AHDF; Actas de Cabildo Ordinarios, vol. 170-A, May 9, 1848, AHDF. The Colina quote is from exp. 2597, fol. 25, ADN.

11. Albert G. Brackett, *General Lane's Brigade in Central Mexico* (Cincinnati: H. W. Derby, 1854), 187. For another expression of American contempt, see Actas Secretas, vol. 301-A, May 10, 1848, AHDF.

12. *Encarnacion,* 86–87; William W. Carpenter, *Travels and Adventures in Mexico: In the Course of Journeys of Upward of 2500 Miles, Performed on Foot, Giving an Account of the Manners and Customs of the People, and the Agricultural and Mineral Resources of that Country* (New York: Harper Brothers, 1851), 39. On Parras, see Abner Doubleday, *My Life in the Old Army* (Fort Worth: Texas Christian University Press, 1998), 133; Sheridan Prieto, "Coahuila y la invasión," 173; and Eduardo Enrique Terrazas, "La estancia del ejército

de ocupación norteamericano en Saltillo, octubre de 1846–julio de 1848," in *México en Guerra (1846–1848): Perspectivas regionales,* ed. Laura Herrera Serna (Mexico City: Conaculta, Museo Nacional de las Intervenciones, 1997), 186. On Bardstown, see John Dichtl, *Frontiers of Faith: Bringing Catholicism to the West in the Early Republic* (Lexington: University of Kentucky Press, 2008), 99, 126, 150.

13. On souvenirs, see LEPOSLP, August 7, 1847. The Reeves quote is from C. M. Reeves, "Five Years Experience in the Regular Army, including the War with Mexico," manuscript, MS QR332f RMV, CHSL, 166. The del Castillo quote is from leg. 20, 1847, SGG, AHESLP. See also exp. 2570, fol. 21, ADN; and leg. 22, 1847, SGG, AHESLP. There were rumors that Santa Anna himself sold cattle to help feed the American army. See Johnson, *Gallant,* 64–65.

14. Samuel C. Reid, *The Scouting Expeditions of McCulloch's Texas Rangers; or, The Summer and Fall Campaign of the Army of the United States in Mexico—1846* (Philadelphia: G. B. Zieber, 1848), 120; Johnson, *Gallant,* 198; Mariano Riva Palacio, "Breve diario de don Mariano Riva Palacio (agosto de 1847)," ed. Josefina Vázquez, *Historia Mexicana* 47, no. 2 (October–December 1997): 443, 447; S. Compton Smith, *Chile con Carne; or, The Camp and the Field,* (New York: Miller and Curtis, 1857), 389–395.

15. Roa Bárcena, *Recuerdos,* 1, 312, 514; Mariano Otero, *Exposición que hace el ciudadano Mariano Otero, diputado por Xalisco al congreso nacional, al supremo gobierno del estado sobre la guerra que sostiene la república contra los Estados Unidos del Norte* (Mexico City: Vargas Rea, 1944), 53–54. The pamphlet Otero probably contributed to that was cited earlier actually made a similar point. Otero, *Obras,* 115.

16. Josefina Zoraida Vázquez, "La guerra que puso en peligro la unidad nacional," in *Symposium La Angostura en la Intervención Norteamericana, 1846–1848* (Saltillo, Mexico: Secretaría de Educación Pública de Coahuila, 1998), 16.

17. For just a few examples, see Gobernación, leg. 184, caja 1, exp. 3, AGN; leg. 18, 1847, SGG, AHESLP; leg. 26, exp. 34, 1846, SGG, AHESLP; leg. 26, exp. 36, 1846, SGG, AHESLP; leg. 17, exp. 50, 1846, SGG, AHESLP; LEPOSLP, January 2, January 9, 1847; Justicia y Negocios Eclesiásticos, leg. 150, fol. 271, AGN; Riva Palacio, "Breve diario," 452; and Sergio Cañedo Gamboa, *Los festejos septembrinos en San Luis Potosí: Protocolo, discurso y transformaciones, 1824–1847* (San Luis Potosí, Mexico: El Colegio de San Luis, 2001), 139. The Puebla incident is from exp. 2550, fol. 2, ADN.

18. On Guerrero, see Peter Guardino, *Peasants, Politics, and the Formation of Mexico's National State: Guerrero, 1800–1857* (Stanford, CA: Stanford University Press, 1996), 147–177, and exp. 2682, fol. 16, ADN. On Oaxaca, see Benjamin Smith, *The Roots of Conservatism in Mexico: Catholicism, Society and Politics in the Mixteca Baja, 1750–1962* (Albuquerque: University of New Mexico Press, 2012), 75–141. On Veracruz, see Ducey, *Nation,* 142–170.

19. Maria del Carmen Salinas Sandoval, *Política interna e invasión norteamericana en el Estado de México 1846–1848* (Zinacantepec: El Colegio Mexiquense, 2000), 149; José Arturo Salazar y García, "Guanajuato durante la guerra de 1846–1848," in Herrera Serna, *México en Guerra,* 353; and Roa Bárcena, *Recuerdos,* 278.

20. Escalante Gonzalbo, *Ciudadanos imaginarios,* 17–18. Carlos Maria de Bustamante acknowledged this acerbically when he wrote that Mexicans who worried that the fact that some Mexican troops had to be coerced to go on campaign indicated a lack of patriotism did not understand the French revolutionary armies were also coerced. Bustamante, entry for September 3, 1846, in *Diario.*

21. Thomas Tennery, *The Mexican War Diary of Thomas D. Tennery* (Norman: University of Oklahoma Press, 1970), 14.

22. See Henderson, *Glorious Defeat,* 15, for a bold statement that Americans were more nationalist than Mexicans. Jesús Velasco Márquez, "Regionalismo, partidismo y expansionismo. La política interna de Estados Unidos durante la guerra contra México," *Historia Mexicana* 47, no. 2 (October–December 1997): 312, points out that this view is quite general among American historians. See, for instance, Joseph W. Pearson, "The Dilemma of Dissent: Kentucky's Whigs and the Mexican War," *Ohio Valley History* 12, no. 2 (Summer 2012): 30.

23. Nicole Eustace, *1812: War and the Passions of Patriotism* (Philadelphia: University of Pennsylvania Press, 1012), xi; Fred Anderson and Andrew Cayton, *The Dominion of War: Empire and Liberty in North America, 1500–2000* (New York: Penguin, 2004), 223–227; Alan Taylor, *The Civil War of 1812: American Citizens, British Subjects, Irish Rebels, and Indian Allies* (New York: Vintage Books, 2010).

24. Daniel Walker Howe, *What Hath God Wrought: The Transformation of America, 1815–1848,* (New York: Oxford University Press, 2007), 72–76; Anderson and Cayton, *Dominion,* 229–234.

25. Eustace, *1812,* xi; Howe, *What Hath,* 63–69, 72–76; Marcela Terrazas y Basante and Gerardo Gurza Lavalle, *Las relaciones México-Estados Unidos, 1756–2010,* vol. 1, *Imperios, repúblicas y pueblos en pugna por el territorio, 1756–1867* (Mexico City: Universidad Nacional Autónoma de México / Secretaría de Relaciones Exteriores, 2012), 100; Jeremy Black, *The War of 1812 in the Age of Napoleon* (New York: Continuum, 2009), xiii, 4; Robert S. Quimby, *The U.S. Army in the War of 1812: An Operational and Command Study* (East Lansing: Michigan State University Press, 1997), 2:953; Jon Latimer, *1812: War with America* (Cambridge, MA: Belknap Press of Harvard University Press, 2007), 3–4.

26. Terrazas y Basante and Gurza Lavalle, *Las relaciones México-Estados Unidos,* 1:101; Howe, *What Hath,* 71; and esp. Eustace, *1812.*

27. Terrazas y Basante and Gurza Lavalle, *Las relaciones México-Estados Unidos,* 1:100; Josefina Zoraida Vázquez, *Mexicanos y norteamericanos ante la guerra del 47* (Mexico City: SepSetentas, 1972), 29.

28. Terrazas y Basante and Gurza Lavalle, *Las relaciones México-Estados Unidos,* 1:110, 112. The Grant quote is from Ulysses S. Grant, *Personal Memoirs* (Westminster, MD: Random House, 1999), 24.

29. The quote is from Robert E. Lee, *Recollections and Letters of General Robert E. Lee* (New York: Doubleday, Page, 1904), 28. On Lee's decision, see Elizabeth Brown Pryor, *Reading the Man: A Portrait of Robert E. Lee through his Private Letters* (New York: Viking, 2007), 276–297.

30. Daniel Harvey Hill, *A Fighter from Way Back: The Mexican War Diary of Lt. Daniel Harvey Hill, 4th Artillery, USA,* ed. Nathaniel Cheairs Hughes Jr. and Timothy D. Johnson (Kent, OH: Kent State University Press, 2002), xiv.

31. Nicholas Marshall, "The Great Exaggeration: Death and the Civil War," *Journal of the Civil War Era* 4, no. 1 (March 2014): 3. On the destructiveness of the Civil War see Mark E. Neely Jr., *The Civil War and the Limits of Destruction* (Cambridge, MA: Harvard University Press, 2007), 199.

32. Amy Greenberg, *A Wicked War: Polk, Clay, Lincoln and the 1846 U.S. Invasion of Mexico* (New York: Knopf, 2012), 35; Shelley Streeby, *American Sensations: Class, Empire and the Production of American Culture* (Berkeley: University of California Press, 2002), 39.

33. Michael Feldberg, *The Turbulent Era: Riot and Discord in Jacksonian America* (New York: Oxford University Press, 1980), 96; David Grimsted, *American Mobbing: Toward Civil War* (New York: Oxford University Press, 1998), 90–92; Howe, *What Hath,* 330, 411, 435; Bertram Wyatt-Brown, *Southern Honor: Ethics and Behavior in the Old South,* 25th anniversary ed. (New York: Oxford University Press, 2007), 168–169, 353, 366, 369.

34. Feldberg, *Turbulent Era,* 7, 55–61, 73–75, 90–91, 96–97; Grimsted, *American Mobbing,* viii, viii, 86, 89, 101–113; Howe, *What Hath,* 430–434; Wyatt-Brown, *Southern Honor,* 370.

35. Brackett, *General,* 13; Pearson, "Dilemma," 32.

36. Harry Watson, *Liberty and Power: The Politics of Jacksonian America,* updated ed. (New York: Hill and Wang, 2006), 88, 127; Velasco Márquez, "Regionalismo," 313–315; Melinda Lawson, *Patriot Fires: Forging a New American Nationalism in the Civil War North* (Lawrence: University Press of Kansas, 2002), 2, 5.

37. There is a vast literature on the War of Independence; for an example, see Marco Antonio Landavazzo, *La máscara de Fernando VII: Discurso e imaginario monárquicos en una época de crisis, Nueva España, 1808–1822* (Mexico City: El Colegio de México / Universidad

Michoacana de San Nicolás de Hidalgo / El Colegio de Michoacán, 2001). There is less for the Spanish and French incidents. See Cañedo Gamboa, *Los festejos,* 139, 150, and Peter Guardino, "Identity and Nationalism in Mexico: Guerrero, 1780–1840," *Journal of Historical Sociology* 7, no. 3 (September 1994): 314–342.

38. Again, the literature on independence is vast, but there is less for the War of 1812. For the latter, see Terrazas y Basante and Gurza Lavalle, *Las relaciones México-Estados Unidos,* 1:101, and, especially, Eustace, *1812.*

39. Streeby, *American Sensations,* 39, and, especially, Robert Johannsen, *To the Halls of Montezuma: The Mexican War in the American Imagination* (New York: Oxford University Press, 1985).

40. Alan Knight, preface to *Las relaciones México-Estados Unidos,* by Terrazas y Basante and Gurza Lavalle, 1:23–24; Vázquez, "La guerra que puso en peligro," 21; Lawson, *Patriot Fires,* 7. The Smith quote is from Franklin Smith, *Mexican War Journal,* 196. See also 31–32.

41. Douglas Murphy believes that political differences between Mariano Arista and Pedro de Ampudia also weakened the Mexicans at Palo Alto and Resaca de Palma. Douglas Murphy, *Two Armies on the Rio Grande: The First Campaign of the U.S. Mexican War* (College Station: Texas A&M University Press, 2015), 155.

42. José Maria Lafragua to Manuel de la Peña y Peña, Querétaro, November 25, 1847.

43. John Coatsworth, "Obstacles to Economic Growth in Nineteenth-Century Mexico," *American Historical Review* 83, no. 1 (February 1978): 81; John Coatsworth, "Notes on the Comparative Economic History of Latin America and the United States," in *Development and Underdevelopment in America: Contrasts of Economic Growth in North and Latin America in Historical Perspective,* ed. W. L. Bernecker and H. W. Tobler (Berlin: De Gruyter, 1993), 11; Barbara Tenenbaum, *The Politics of Penury: Debt and Taxes in Mexico, 1821–1856* (Albuquerque: University of New Mexico Press, 1986), xii, xiv, 28, 49, 76–82; Vázquez, "La guerra que puso en peligro," 16. Right before the fall of Mexico City, merchants in the city were giving American army agents cash in exchange for drafts on U.S. government funds so that American troops could be fed. Hill, *Fighter,* 119.

44. On the problem of the lack of funds for the troops on the frontier on the eve of Taylor's invasion, see Murphy, *Two Armies,* 21–22. For the importance of the financial problems in the government's argument for accepting the treaty, see Foreign Minister Luis de la Rosa's speech in *leposlp,* May 23, 1848.

45. Douglas S. Massey, Jorge Durand, and Nolan J. Malone, *Beyond Smoke and Mirrors: Mexican Immigration in an Age of Economic Integration* (New York: Russell Sage Foundation, 2002); Douglas S. Massey, "America's Immigration Policy Fiasco: Learning from Past Mistakes," *Daedalus* 142, no. 3 (Summer 2013): 5–15.

46. Massey, "America's Immigration Policy Fiasco," 8; Wayne A. Cornelius, "Death at the Border: Efficacy and Unintended Consequences of US Immigration Control Policy," *Population and Development Review* 27, no. 4 (December 2001): 661–685; Wayne A. Cornelius, "Introduction: Does Border Enforcement Deter Unauthorized Immigration?," in *Impacts of Border Enforcement on Mexican Migration: The View from Sending Communities,* ed. Wayne A. Cornelius (La Jolla: Center for Comparative Immigration Studies, University of California, San Diego, 2007), 1–15.

Illustration Credits

Maps by Isabelle Lewis

Acknowledgments

One of the most rewarding things about writing books is the way it connects you to the many people whose help you need along the way. This book has been unusually complicated to research and write, and thus I have relied on the help of an even larger group of people than usual. Some I have known for most of my professional life and others are new acquaintances, but all contributed in important ways.

Everywhere I went, archivists and librarians cheerfully brought out documents and helped me as much as they could, whether I worked with them for months or hours. The doorway to the past they provide is crucial. It is also widening as archivists and librarians digitize and place more documents online, greatly facilitating access even as they reduce the chance that users will be able to thank archivists and librarians in person. Thus I would like to thank both those archivists and librarians I met while doing the research and those I never met even though their work was crucial to the project.

Much of the Mexican research for this book was funded by a U.S. Department of Education Fulbright-Hays Faculty Research Abroad Fellowship. More research in both Mexico and the United States was made possible by various grants from Indiana University's College Arts and Humanities Institute. Indiana University's Department of History also provided timely aid to finance the production and acquisition of the book's images.

Institutions finance research, but they are also crucial because they provide opportunities for scholars to present preliminary arguments and findings. Many times I found myself refining my ideas in response to questions or comments posed when I presented aspects of this work. I find myself in debt to those who organized those opportunities and those who generously took the time to attend my presentations at the University of Maryland, Stanford University, the Universidad Nacional Autónoma de México, San Diego State

University, the Archivo Histórico del Estado de San Luis Potosí, the Colegio de San Luis, the Universidad Veracruzana, the Universidad Autónoma Metropolitiana, the Colegio Mexiquense, the University of Chicago, Vanderbilt University, Indiana University, Yale University, the University of Michigan, Macalester College, Hamline University, and the Instituto Mora.

I was affiliated with the Colegio de San Luis during the year in which I did the bulk of the Mexican research. The personnel were exceedingly generous with their institutional support, efforts to make my family comfortable in San Luis Potosí, suggestions for sources, and ideas about the project. I would like to particularly thank Maria Isabel Monroy Castillo, Sergio Cañedo Gamboa, and Ana Maria Gutiérrez. Other members of Mexico's academic community also made extremely helpful comments about my work and suggestions for sources. Several gave me copies of difficult-to-locate theses either they or their students had written. Thus I am greatly in debt to Brian Connaughton, Andrés Delgadillo Sánchez, Michael Ducey, Antonio Escobar Ohmstede, Romana Falcón, Luis Fernando Granados, Claudia Guarisco, Pilar Iracheta, Maria Teresa Jarquín, Eduardo Miranda Arrieta, Juan Ortiz Escamilla, Sonia Pérez Toledo, José Daniel Ramírez Reyes, Carlos Reyes Tosqui, Flor Salazar Mendoza, Carlos Sánchez Silva, José Antonio Serrano Ortega, Miguel Soto Strata, and Josefina Zoraida Vázquez. I greatly appreciate the information, ideas, and encouragement generously provided by these scholars. Several people went even further than academics usually do. Michael Ducey drove me to the battlefield of Cerro Gordo and hiked through rugged terrain for hours in the hot sun, and scholars Gabriela Román and Antonio Reyes, along with local resident José Salas, did the same at La Angostura. I cannot possibly thank the people in Mexico enough for the ways in which they helped make this book possible.

Academic communities are, of course, international, and many scholars outside Mexico also provided ideas, encouragement, and leads. They include Linda Arnold, Peter Beattie, Kate Bjork, Dain Borges, Deborah Cohen, Brian DeLay, Caitlin Fitz, Will Fowler, Reena Goldthree, Amy Greenberg, John Hart, Kristin Hoganson, Justin Jackson, Alan Knight, Emilio Kourí, Kerry MacDonald, Simeon Mann, Nick Marshall, Rachel Moore, Tom Passananti, Aldo Lauria Santiago, Elizabeth Shesko, Nancy Shoemaker, Mauricio Tenorio, Jonathan Truitt, Charles Walker, and the late David Weber.

Many scholars from my home institution, Indiana University, aided me with leads or ideas. The breadth of this project sent me outside areas where I already had some expertise, and I often called on my Indiana colleagues to guide me on these forays into the unknown. I am grateful to Judith Allen, Stephanie Bower, J. Peter Burkholder, Arlene Díaz, Kon Dierks, Wendy Gamber, Jeff Gould, Danny James, Jessie Kindig, Sarah Knott, Lara Kriegel, Jason McGraw, Natalia Milanesio, Colleen Moore, Michelle Moyd, Timo Schaefer, Cesar Seveso, Christina Snyder, Rebecca Spang, Steve Stowe, Joseph Varga, and Dror Wahrman.

Some people who made intellectual contributions to this book are not academics in the strictest sense of the word. James Alexander Thom, historical novelist extraordinaire, provided both useful comments and leads on sources from the extensive research he did for his wonderful novel on the san patricios. Michael Lotus, an old friend from college with whom I have sporadically been holding conversations about both history and war for thirty-five years, suggested sources and also helped me understand how a book like this is military history.

Several colleagues did me the terrific favor of reading the manuscript in its entirety, and each of them was crucial to improving it. For this I thank both Brian DeLay and another, anonymous, reviewer for Harvard University Press, as well as Michael Ducey, Wendy Gamber, Christina Snyder, and Charles Walker. Kathleen McDermott of Harvard University Press provided invaluable advice and guidance on how to improve the book. Ashley Moore's copyediting was very helpful, and Brian Ostrander oversaw the book's production.

I am grateful to various institutions and individuals for timely and professional help with the images. Isabelle Lewis used her expertise to give the geographies of the war visual form. Lorraine Goonan of the Image Works, Lisa Struthers of the San Jacinto Museum, and Marlana Cook of the West Point Museum helped me locate and obtain permissions for art, and Chet Gordon photographed the paintings from the West Point Museum.

The members of my immediate family had an unusually strong role in making this book. Their constant moral support and the sacrifices they made to uproot themselves so I could spend an entire year in Mexico were crucial, and they also read drafts of various sections. My wife, Jane Walter, and our children, Rose Guardino and Walter Guardino, are all passionate and knowledgeable about history and writing. Many of the book's arguments and ideas were thoroughly discussed and refined at the family dinner table. The book would not exist without those conversations, and this is but one of the many things I owe them.

Index

Page numbers in italics refer to illustrations.

disease, 1, 97, 120–122, 143, 156, 193, 208, 210, 348. *See also* dysentery; yellow fever

Doubleday, Abner, 40, 61, 158

Doyle, James, 259

drunkenness, 284; among American soldiers, 57, 64, 97, 106–107, 109, 124, 319, 336, 344

Duck, William Ward, 221

duels, 17, 102, 294

Dwire, William, 259–260

dysentery, 121, 155

Elections: in Mexico, 8, 12, 13, 90, 161–162, 181, 302, 339; in the U.S., 14–15, 24–25, 102, 207

Engelman, Adolphus, 116

Epperance, James, 103

Federal District, 160, 165, 182, 282, 341. *See also* Mexico City

Feldberg, Michael, 15, 17

Flores, José María, 341

Florida, 17–18, 32, 312

Foos, Paul, 96

Fredrick the Great, 45–46

Fremont, John C., 311–312, 313–314

Gambling, 57, 64, 106

Gamboa, Ramón, 292, 330–331

Garay, Francisco de, 68, 350, 351

García, Enrique, 287

García, Father Luis, 178

Garrard, Lewis, 320–321

Garza y Flores, Juan Martín de la, 213

Gates, William, 351

gender, 19–20, 23–24, 54–64, 115–116. *See also* masculinity

Gillespie, Archibald, 314

Glass, William, 103

Gomery, John, 255

Gómez Farías, Valentín, 88, 144, 176; rebellion against, 179, 183–185, 249, 365–366

Granados, Luis Fernando, 282

Grant, Ulysses S., 39, 65, 267, 275, 361

Great Britain, 37, 70, 75, 220, 281, 366; and American colonies, 9, 10–11, 12; in War of 1812, 17, 111, 112, 359–360; and Pacific Northwest territorial dispute, 35, 76, 85, 205; and Mexican-American War, 76, 170, 255, 259–260, 326

Greenberg, Amy, 19, 20, 101, 115

Grenier, John, 127

Grimsley, Mark, 126

Grimsted, David, 15

group pride, 46, 66, 161; in Mexican army, 289

Guanajuato (city), *11,* 304

Guanajuato (state), 183, 215; troops from, 142, 234

Guerrero, 162–163; not yet a state, 88; peasant rebellions in, 88, 236, 237; troops from, 162–163, 165, 233, 235, 249, 290, 301, 358

guerrillas, 123, 144, 202, 210, 223, 225–231, 294–300, 304; in earlier wars, 123, 126, 220, 223, 225–226, 228, 330; and American volunteer troops, 123, 125–128, 131–133, 150, 295, 297–299; official encouragement of, 123, 131, 226–228, 242, 269, 290, 330; partial effectiveness of, 123, 226, 232, 294–295, 300; differing Mexican attitudes toward, 133, 202, 216, 225–228, 357; Taylor's and Scott's policies toward, 216, 225, 231, 232, 294, 295–296, 300;

some American deserters as, 228–229, 255–256; in New Mexico, 320–321

Gurza Lavalle, Gerardo, 30, 360

Gutierrez, Maria Bonifacia, 60

Guzmán, Damasio, 51–52

Haiti, 27, 193, 217

Halsey, John, 154

Harney, William, *195,* 197, 198

Hays, Jack, 297, 299, 300

Heller, Karl, 166, 222, 281

Henshaw, John, 279, 282, 288

Herrera, José Joaquín, 35, 48, 75, 84, 266; overthrow of, in 1845 coup, 49, 75, 84, 86

Hidalgo, 256

Hidalgo, Father Miguel, 26–27, 212

Hill, Daniel Harvey, 256, 262, 362; observations by, on volunteer troops, 103, 109–110, 293, 300; on occupation of Mexico City, 279, 286, 336

Hitchcock, Ethan Allen, 34–35, 279

Hogan, Roger, 260

Horsman, Reginald, 126

Hotel Bella Unión (Beautiful Union Hotel), 344–345

Huamantla, *191,* 291, 298–299

Huejutla, 350–351

Humphrey, Santiago, 228–229

hunger (of Mexican troops), 6, 48, 52, 62, 67, 154, 194; as cause of desertion, 6, 68, 144, 154, 155, 167–168, 170, 234, 247, 276–277, 291, 301; and stealing of food, 64; as motive for enlisting, 77, 259, 260

Hyde, Anne, 317

Ihary, Alejandro, 213

illiteracy, 36, 250; in Mexico, 211, 280–281, 364. *See also* literacy

illnesses. *See* disease

immigrants, 37; and party politics, 21, 118, 119, 223; backlash against, 28, 37–38, 119; to Mexico, 29, 32, 113; in the military, 37, 38, 77, 119, 251, 261, 368; to California and New Mexico, 308–309, 310–312, 318; recent, from Mexico, 368

Independencia Battalion, 183, 249–250

Indians. *See* Native Americans; Native Americans (in Mexico)

Isdepski, Charles, 36

Iturbide, Agustin de, 27

Jackson, Andrew, 14, 17–18, 111–112, 207, 294, 313; in War of 1812, 17, 93, 111, 112, 405n55

Jacksonian democracy, 24–25, 311, 318; and race, 24–25, 93, 110, 116, 309, 311, 319; and volunteer troops, 93, 105, 110, 111–112, 127–128, 218, 225

Jarauta, Father Celedonio de, 229, 295

Johannsen, Robert, 112

Johnson, Timothy, 222, 264

Jones, Thomas ap Catesby, 311, 312

Jones, W. C., 103

Juárez, Benito, 215, 291–292

Kearny, Stephen, 314, 318–319

Kendall, George Wilkins, 192

Kennedy, John, 42

Knight, Alan, 17

Laidley, Theodore, 67, 110, 120

Landero, Juan, 190

Lane, Henry Smith, 109, 114, 120, 121–122

Lane, James, 105

Morelos, José Maria, 26–27

Moreno, Francisco, 258

Mormons, 28, 321–322, 363

Morse, Samuel F. B., 37

Murat, Achilles, 38

muskets, 45, 70, 104, 250, 269; limited range of, 45, 150; poor quality of, for Mexican troops, 145, 170, 199, 268, 274

Napoleonic Wars, 50–51, 81, 220, 223, 359, 360, 366; guerrilla tactics during, 123, 126, 220, 223, 225, 226, 330; weaponry in, 145, 234, 239

National Guard, 159–168, 188, 201, 235–238, 290–291, 351; as citizen-soldiers, 159–160, 161, 163, 166; differences of, from regular army, 161, 166–167; parallels of, with American volunteer units, 161–162, 165–166; and Mexican political conflicts, 162–163, 175–176, 181–182, 183–184, 185, 238; and family obligations, 163–165, 228, 235, 276, 283, 330; in Battle of Cerro Gordo, 165, 167–168, 193, 198, 238, 354; and Valley of Mexico campaign, 193, 198, 201, 233, 235–238, 241, 242, 249–250, 267, 268, 273–274, 283, 290–291; and guerrillas, 227, 228

national identity, 5, 263, 307, 309; American, 5, 20, 28, 96, 111, 359–364; Mexican, 5, 29–30, 210–222, 225, 236, 281, 295, 307, 316, 352–359

nationalism, 357; Mexican, 5, 75–76, 143, 181, 280–282, 295, 353, 357–359, 364; American, 10, 25, 85, 96, 159, 359–364. See also national identity

Native Americans, 12, 16–17; in Texas republic, 25, 297–298; raids by, 30, 165, 326–327 (see also Comanche raids); in

California, 307, 308, 312–313; in New Mexico, 315–316, 319–320. See also Native Americans (in Mexico); Native Americans (in the U.S.)

Native Americans (in Mexico), 12, 26–27, 219, 236–237; in Mexican ancestry, 12, 25, 116, 218; and military recruitment, 52, 63, 236–237

Native Americans (in the U.S.), 321–322; displacement of, 12, 16–17, 19, 25, 32, 107, 127, 316, 360, 362; likening of Mexicans to, 32, 110, 127, 218; biased views of, 25, 125

naval blockade, 82, 168–169, 259, 313, 338, 366; and Mexican fiscal crisis, 6, 144, 168–169, 178, 238, 323, 367; and food shortages for Mexican soldiers, 76, 82, 238, 367

New Mexico, 315–321, 322; Polk's desire to obtain, 29, 72, 265, 307; distance of, from central Mexico, 72, 305, 306–307; transfer of, to U.S., 265, 323, 324, 326, 327; growing connection of, to American economy, 306, 317–318; Native Americans in, 315–316, 319–320

Nickerson, Hoffman, 92

Niños Héroes, 274

Nueces River, 34–35, 46, 84, 205; as traditional limit of Texas, 34–35, 46, 71, 206; land between, and the Rio Grande, 34, 71, 72, 84, 205, 265; and peace negotiations, 265, 325, 326

Nuevo León, 136, 227. See also Monterrey

Oaxaca, 172, 183, 215, 236–237, 291–292, 358; National Guard units from, 162, 165, 201, 233, 235, 236, 237

Ocampo, Melchor, 226, 237, 303